**Fifth Edition**

# Efficient and Flexible Reading

## Kathleen T. McWhorter

*Niagara County Community College*

**LONGMAN**

An imprint of Addison Wesley Longman, Inc.

New York • Reading, Massachusetts • Menlo Park, California • Harlow, England
Don Mills, Ontario • Sydney • Mexico City • Madrid • Amsterdam

*writing*
*class participation*
*test + quiz mid term*
*final exams 3*
*Nelson Denny*
*NJeBSPT*
*writing sample*

Acquisitions Editor: Steven Rigolosi
Development Editor: Leslie Taggart
Marketing Manager: Ann Stypuloski
Project Coordination, Text Design, and Electronic Page Makeup: WestWords Inc.
Cover Design Manager: Nancy Danahy
Cover Designer: Kay Petronio
Full Service Production Manager: Eric Jorgensen
Senior Print Buyer: Hugh Crawford
Printer and Binder: RR Donnelley & Sons Company
Cover Printer: The Lehigh Press, Inc.

For permission to use copyrighted material, grateful acknowledgment is made to the copyright holders on pp. C1–C12, which are hereby made part of this copyright page.

***Library of Congress Cataloging-in-Publication Data***
McWhorter, Kathleen T.
  Efficient and flexible reading / Kathleen T. McWhorter. — 5th ed.
    p.  cm.
  Includes bibliographical references and index.
  ISBN 0-321-01244-5
  1. Developmental reading—Handbooks, manuals, etc.  2. Reading (Higher education)—Handbooks, manuals, etc.  I. Title.
LB1050.53.M38      1998
428'.43—dc21                                          98–19302
                                                        CIP

Copyright © 1999 by Kathleen T. McWhorter

All rights reserved. No part of this publication may be reproduced, stored in a retrieval system, or transmitted in any form or by any means, electronic, mechanical, photocopying, recording, or otherwise, without the prior permission of the publisher. Printed in the United States.

ISBN 0-321-01244-5

2 3 4 5 6 7 8 9 10—DOC—01009998

# Brief Contents

# Contents

# Disciplinary Readings*

*EFFICIENT AND FLEXIBLE READING, FIFTH EDITION* contains numerous and diverse academic readings, as well as 38 readings from popular press sources. The table below demonstrates this text's academic focus.

| Academic Discipline | Number of Readings | Sample Topic | Page |
|---|---|---|---|
| Anatomy & Physiology | 5 | Skin as a communicative organ | 28 |
| | | Types of muscles | 157 |
| | | Hair roots | 241 |
| Anthropology | 7 | Primate communication | 110 |
| | | Study of fossils | 112 |
| | | Evolution of plants | 120 |
| Archaeology | 2 | Archeological sites | 93 |
| | | Archeology as a social science | 334 |
| Art | 1 | Photo enlarger | 302 |
| Astronomy | 2 | Communication with other planets | 108 |
| | | Study of the planets | 118 |
| General Biology | 10 | Steroid use | 113 |
| | | Pesticide pollution | 117 |
| | | Viruses | 253 |
| Botany | 8 | Food chain | 172 |
| | | Darwin and Mendel | 160 |
| | | Cloves | 469 |
| Business | 7 | Mortgages | 104 |
| | | Ethnic relations at work | 116 |
| | | Business operation | 257 |
| Chemistry | 1 | Nucleic acids | 322 |
| Communication | 15 | Nonverbal communication | 37 |
| | | Visual aids in speeches | 122 |
| | | Graffiti | 504 |
| Computer Science | 1 | Computer technology | 151 |
| Economics | 2 | Taxes | 105 |
| | | Farmers vs. bureaucrats | 275 |
| Education | 3 | Using the Internet | 180 |
| | | Gender bias | 221 |

*Note: A complete list of readings organized by discipline appears in the Instructor's Manual.

| Academic Discipline | Number of Readings | Sample Topic | Page |
|---|---|---|---|
| Environmental Studies | 1 | Absolute zero | 454 |
| Geology | 1 | Seismic belts | 131 |
| Government | 4 | Americans with disabilities | 115 |
| | | Federal expenditures | 251 |
| | | Racial composition of US | 253 |
| Health | 5 | Obesity | 163 |
| | | Smoking | 319 |
| | | Protein | 333 |
| History | 4 | African American writers | 29 |
| | | Gerald Ford | 492 |
| Literature | 10 | Plath, "Mirror" | 363 |
| | | Frost, "The Silken Tent" | 375 |
| | | Hughes, "Dream Deferred" | 374 |
| Marketing | 5 | Buying motives | 108 |
| | | Food service industry | 124 |
| | | Prices in world capitals | 247 |
| Philosophy | 1 | Existentialism | 330 |
| Physics | 7 | Color blindness | 104 |
| | | Kinetic energy | 106 |
| | | Function and effects of music | 518 |
| Political Science | 7 | Segregation | 153 |
| | | News and public opinion | 311 |
| | | Party voting differences | 398 |
| Psychology | 21 | Stages of humor | 139 |
| | | Television viewing and school achievement | 238 |
| | | Effects of color on mood | 497 |
| Sociology | 32 | Gender stereotypes | 116 |
| | | Conformity to norms | 131 |
| | | Urbanization of Third World countries | 133 |
| Statistics | 1 | Variables in design | |
| Zoology | 3 | Zoos of the future | 142 |
| | | Migration of birds | 471 |

# Preface

The reading demands of college students are wide and diverse. Textbooks, the student's primary reading material, represent unique academic disciplines. Each differs in style, content, and conceptual complexity. Many students are also required to read literature, supplementary assignments, reference materials, periodicals, manuals, handbooks, and study guides. Many instructors also use film, video, and computerized tutorials and may require students to use e-mail and Internet sources.

Each of these materials is also unique, and more importantly, the student's purpose for reading each is different: a student may read to prepare for a class lecture, make notes for a discussion, review for an exam, or locate information for a paper. To handle these diverse reading situations effectively, a student must develop reading flexibility skills, adjusting strategies and techniques to suit each reading situation.

College students face rigorous course requirements and must cope with time restraints created by jobs, family, and social activities. Reading and study must be accomplished within a realistic time frame and result in effective learning. Reading efficiency, then, is also vitally important. *Efficient and Flexible Reading* is designed to enable students to become efficient and flexible readers capable of meeting the challenging demands of college.

## ■ GOALS AND THEMES

The primary goal of this text is to present techniques and guided practice that will enable the reader to accomplish reading tasks within an efficient and realistic framework. It will guide students in developing reading flexibility—adjusting both comprehension and rate to suit purpose, type and complexity of the material, and degree of familiarity. A second, more specific goal of the text is to encourage students to develop successful active academic reading strategies. The text focuses on the development of vocabulary, comprehension, study-reading, and critical analysis techniques to enable students to interact with the material and learn more efficiently. A third goal of the text is to encourage students to approach reading as a thinking process. Metacomprehension—the student's awareness of and control over the reading and learning process and its attendant thought processes—is a theme emphasized throughout.

## ■ CONTENT OVERVIEW

The text offers a blend of reading comprehension, retention, vocabulary development, critical reading, and rate building techniques that have proven essential for college students.

### ■ Unit One, "Developing a Basis for Reading and Learning"

Presents the organization and framework for the text, developing and explaining the concepts and principles of efficiency and flexibility and emphasizing reading as a thinking process. Strategies for active reading are presented, concentration and retention techniques are described, and basic vocabulary building techniques are presented.

### ■ Unit Two, "Using Text Structure to Improve Your Comprehension"

Presents methods for improving comprehension skills through knowledge and use of text structure. The location of main ideas, the structure of paragraphs, and the organization of ideas into thought patterns are described. Strategies for reading articles, essays, and scholarly journal articles are presented.

### ■ Unit Three, "Reading and Learning from College Texts"

Is concerned with reading and learning from college textbooks. Graphic, visual, and electronic literary skills are presented and techniques for learning and retaining course materials including specialized and technical vocabulary are emphasized. Topics include SQ3R, highlighting, paraphrasing, outlining, mapping, and summarizing.

### ■ Unit Four, "Reading Critically"

Focuses on critical reading skills. The language and structure of expressive writing, in both short stories and poetry, are discussed. Skills in making inferences, distinguishing fact and opinion, identifying the author's purpose, understanding tone, recognizing generalizations, and identifying bias are included. Techniques for evaluating arguments and persuasive writing are emphasized and include evaluating sources, recognizing types of evidence, identifying reasoning errors, and evaluating nonlogical appeals.

### ■ Unit Five, "Increasing Your Rate and Flexibility"

Details specific techniques for improving reading rate and flexibility, including skimming, scanning, and techniques for reading faster.

Each chapter is organized as follows:

- Chapter objectives
- Context and purpose for learning each skill
- Instruction and demonstration
- Guided practice using in-chapter exercises
- Critical thinking tip
- Interactive chapter summary
- Two reading selections with questions

The units are designed to be interchangeable, allowing the instructor to organize the course to suit his or her preferred skill sequence and to accommodate the particular needs of each class.

# ■ FEATURES

The following features enhance the text's effectiveness for both instructor and student:

## ■ Focus on Academic Reading Skills

The text provides the necessary instruction in literal and critical reading, vocabulary development, and study-reading skills to meet the demands of academic reading assignments.

## ■ Emphasis on Active Reading

The text encourages students to become active readers by enabling them to interact with the text by predicting, questioning, and evaluating ideas (Chapter 2).

## ■ Focus on Graphic, Visual, and Electronic Literacy

Because college students are increasingly required to learn from film, video, computerized tutorials, and CD-ROMs and are expected to use e-mail and Internet sources, strategies for approaching these newer learning sources are introduced (Chapter 7).

## ■ Metacomprehension

Metacomprehension is the reader's awareness of his or her own comprehension processes. Mature and proficient readers exert a great deal of cognitive control over their reading; they analyze reading tasks, select appropriate reading strategies, and evaluate the effectiveness of those strategies. The text guides students in developing these metacognitive strategies and includes a Learning Style Questionnaire that enables students to assess how they learn and process information (Chapter 2).

### ■ Academic Thought Patterns

The text describes six thought patterns—chronological order, definition, classification, comparison-contrast, cause-effect, and enumeration—which are used in various academic disciplines to organize and structure ideas. These patterns, presented as organizing schemata, are used to improve comprehension and recall of textbook material (Chapter 5).

### ■ Comprehensive Skill Coverage

The text addresses each of four major skill areas: vocabulary, literal and critical comprehension, study-reading, and rate and flexibility. Individual chapters offer instruction, demonstration, and guided practice. Reading selections provide skill interpretation and application.

### ■ High-Interest and Relevant Reading Selections

Each chapter concludes with two reading selections representative of the types of reading expected of college students. Included are numerous textbook excerpts, as well as articles and essays. These readings provide an opportunity for direct skill application as well as a means by which students can measure and evaluate their progress. The questions that follow each reading have been grouped into three levels: "Checking Your Comprehension," measuring literal and critical comprehension; "Thinking Critically," requiring interpretive reading skills; and "Questions for Discussion." Odd-numbered readings use a multiple-choice format; even-numbered readings are open-ended questions for writing or group activities. The Appendix contains 14 sets of multiple-choice questions for the 14 even-numbered reading selections. These are provided for instructors who prefer objective evaluation or for students working independently.

## ■ NEW TO THE FIFTH EDITION

The primary thrust of this revision was to update the text in response to new research and recent innovations in the academic community. Specific changes include the following:

### ■ Learning Style Assessment

A learning style assessment has been added to Chapter 2. The questionnaire enables students to assess their strengths as learners and to select and adjust reading and study strategies accordingly.

### ■ Seventy-five New Exercises

Seventy-five new exercises have been added to the text. Included among these are academic application exercises that require students to apply skills and techniques to their own textbooks and exercises that require students to use electronic sources. Chapter 4, "Main Ideas and Paragraph Structure," has been expanded to include additional practice exercises.

### ■ New Chapter, "Graphic, Visual, and Electronic Literacy"

This chapter teaches students to read graphics effectively, to integrate text and graphics, to use electronic and multimedia study aids, and to interpret and evaluate graphic, visual and electronic sources. The chapter discusses strategies for reading and interpreting tables, graphs, charts, and photographs as well as film, video, computerized tutorials, e-mail, and the Internet.

### ■ New Chapter, "Reading Articles and Essays"

Because students need practice reading longer reading selections, this new chapter has been developed. The chapter demonstrates how to read expository articles and essays, as well as the descriptive and narrative modes found in the fourth edition. It discusses how to read academic journal articles, essays, and popular press articles (both feature-length and news articles), all of which are often suggested by instructors as supplementary readings. A brief annotated scholarly journal article within the chapter demonstrates the reading strategies suggested, and a longer scholarly article at the chapter's end provides practice for students in reading them.

### ■ Expanded Chapter on "Language and Literature"

This chapter integrates expressive features of language, such as connotative meanings, euphenisms, and figurative language with literary works in which they are commonly used.

### ■ New Readings

Numerous new readings have been added: Topics include medical privacy, sports hunting, employment skills, cyberspace, and the future of zoos. Included are two longer readings, one a scholarly journal article, the other an excerpt from a non-fiction book.

### ■ Interactive Chapter Summaries

The end-of-chapter summaries have been revised into an interactive question-answer format that students can use to test their recall of chapter content.

### ■ Greater Emphasis on Academic Reading

The book's focus on academic reading has been strengthened by the addition of a section on reading scholarly journal articles, including an annotated sample article, and by additional practice exercises based on academic textbook excerpts.

## ■ THE TEACHING AND LEARNING PACKAGE

### ■ Instructor's Manual

The Instructor's Manual provides numerous suggestions for using the text, including how to structure and organize the course and how to approach each section of the text, and contains a set of transparency masters. 0–321–02672–1

### ■ Test Banks

Several testing packages are available.

**Book Test Bank.** A new supplement features two sets of chapter quizzes and a mastery test for each chapter. It is printed in an 8-1/2 x 11 format that allows for easy photocopying and distribution. 0–321–02758–2

**CLAST Test Package.** These two 40-item objective tests evaluate students' readiness for the CLAST exams. Strategies for teaching CLAST preparedness are included. Free with any Longman English title. Reproducible sheets: 0–321–01950–4 Computerized IBM version: 0–321–01982–2 Computerized Mac version: 0–321–01983–0

**TASP Test Package.** These 12 practice pre-tests and post-tests assess the same reading and writing skills covered in the TASP examination. Free with any Longman English title. Reproducible sheets: 0–321–01959–8 Computerized IBM version: 0–321–01985–7 Computerized Mac version: 0–321–01984–9

### ■ Longman Reading Journeys Multimedia Software

This innovative and exciting multimedia reading software, available on CD-ROM or via site license, takes students on a tour of the United States. Students visit 15 cities and landmarks throughout the country. Each of the 15 modules corresponds to a reading or study skill (for example, finding the main idea, understanding patterns of organization, and thinking critically). Each module includes a video tour and presentation, instruction and tutorial, exercises, interactive feedback, and mastery tests. Please contact your Addison Wesley Longman sales consultant to see a demonstration disk. Student version: 0–321–04432–0. Demonstration version: 0–321–04619–6

## ■ PowerPoint Presentations

A series of PowerPoint presentations for each chapter in this text is available free on the Longman Web site at **http://longman.awl.com/ basicskills/mcwhorter**. Presentations are available for every chapter in this book. Each presentation contains approximately 15 to 25 slides.

## ■ Longman Englishpages Web site

The Longman Englishpages Web site **(http://longman.awl.com/ englishpages)** contains more than 60 additional readings and exercises. All readings are coded by grade level, and many ask students to visit other locations on the Word Wide Web. This content-rich Web site is free to all instructors and students who use Longman texts.

## ■ Longman Basic Skills Electronic Newsletter

Twice a month during the spring and fall, instructors who have subscribed will receive a free copy of the Longman Basic Skills Electronic Newsletter in their e-mailbox. Written by experienced classroom instructors, the newsletter offers teaching tips, classroom activities, book reviews, and more. To subscribe, visit the Longman Basic Skills Web site at **http://longman.awl.com/basicskills**, or send an e-mail to **BasicSkills@awl.com**

## ■ For Additional Reading and Reference

**The Dictionary Deal.** Two dictionaries can be shrinkwrapped with any Longman Basic Skills title at a nominal fee. The *New American Webster Handy College Dictionary* (0–451–18166–2) is a paperback reference text with more than 100,000 entries. *Merriam Webster's Collegiate Dictionary*, tenth edition (0–87779–709–9), is a hardback reference with a citation file of more than 14.5 million examples of English words drawn from actual use.

**Penguin Quality Paperback Titles.** A series of Penguin paperbacks is available at a significant discount when shrinkwrapped with any Longman Basic Skills title. Some titles available are: Toni Morrison's *Beloved* (0–452–26446–4), Julia Alvarez's *How the Garcia Girls Lost Their Accents* (0–452–26806–0), Mark Twain's *Huckleberry Finn* (0–451–52650–3), *Narrative of the Life of Frederick Douglass* (0–451–52673–2), Harriet Beecher Stowe's *Uncle Tom's Cabin* (0–451–52302–4), Dr. Martin Luther King, Jr.'s *Why We Can't Wait* (0–451–62754–7), and plays by Shakespeare, Miller, and Albee. For more information, please contact your Addison Wesley Longman sales consultant.

*80 Readings.* This inexpensive volume contains 80 brief readings (1–3 pages each) on a variety of themes: writers on writing, nature, women and men, customs and habits, politics, rights and obligations, and coming of age. 0–321–01648–3

# ■ ACKNOWLEDGMENTS

I wish to acknowledge the contributions of my colleagues and reviewers who provided valuable advice and suggestions, both in this edition and in previous editions:

Robyn Browder, Tidewater Community College
Pat Cookis, College of DuPage
Bertilda Garnica Henderson, Broward Community College
Paula Gibson, Cardinal Stritch College
Janice Hill-Matula, Moraine Valley Community College
Deborah Hunt, State Technical Institute at Memphis
Almarie Jones, Gloucester County College
Maxine Keats, Framingham State College
Evelyn Koperwas, Broward Community College
Barbara Levy, Nassau Community College
Caroline Lewis, West Valley College
Helen Muller, Essex County College
Ann Perez, Miami-Dade Community College
Barbara Sherman, Liberty University
Margaret Triplett, Central Oregon Community College
Simon Grist, Atlanta Metro College
Elizabeth Ince, U.S. Military Academy
Diane Starke, El Paso Community College
Patricia Malinowski, Finger Lakes Community College
Beth Parks, Kishwaukee Community College
Jeanne Shay Schumm, University of Miami, Coral Gables
Carol Chesler, Kishwaukee Community College
Steve Matthews, Wayne State University
Catherine Harvey, Grossmont College
Thomas W. Lackman, Temple University
Pam Smith, Pellissippi State Technical College

The editorial staff of Addison Wesley Longman deserves a special recognition and thanks for the guidance, support, and direction they have provided. In particular I wish to thank Leslie Taggart, my development editor, for her valuable advice and assistance and Steven Rigolosi, Basic Skills Editor, for his creative ideas and enthusiastic support of the revision.

*Kathleen T. McWhorter*

# UNIT 1
# Developing a Basis for Reading and Learning

The purpose of this unit is to help you get started reading better and faster. Before you learn specific techniques to increase your reading rate and comprehension, it is important to learn a little about reading efficiency and flexibility. You need to know what is involved in each and how you can improve your skill levels.

Chapter 1 explains reading efficiency and flexibility and introduces the basic principles involved. It also describes the factors that affect how well and how fast you read. Chapter 2 focuses on strategies for reading and learning actively and introduces several techniques that will give you a good start in becoming a more efficient reader. Chapter 3 explores ways to expand your vocabulary and presents methods for arriving at the meanings of new words you encounter.

# CHAPTER 1
# Developing Your Efficiency and Flexibility

IN THIS CHAPTER YOU WILL LEARN:

1. To analyze your reading efficiency and flexibility.
2. To understand factors that affect rate and comprehension.
3. The basic principles that govern efficiency and flexibility.

You have heard about "fuel efficient" cars. They use fuel "efficiently" and conserve energy. An "efficient" worker is one who does his or her job well and on time. Efficiency, then, is the ability to perform with the minimum amount of effort, expense, or waste.

Efficiency involves the effective use of time or resources to accomplish a specific task. As you think more about the concept of efficiency, you may begin to realize that it is a major objective in our work- and time-oriented society. For example, a mechanic who takes an hour to change a tire, a short order cook who takes 25 minutes to prepare a cheeseburger, or a sales clerk who takes five minutes to package a purchase is not efficient.

## ■ ANALYZING YOUR READING EFFICIENCY

As a college student, many heavy demands are placed on your time. Your course work, which includes reading textbook chapters, completing assignments, studying for exams, and writing papers, competes with part-time jobs and social, recreational, and housekeeping tasks. Each demands your valuable time. At times college may seem like a balancing act in which you are trying to do many things at once and trying to do all of them well. You are probably wondering if you will be able to keep up and how to get everything done. One of the best ways to handle the demands and pressures of college life is to become more efficient—to get more done in less time.

Many students think that the only way to become more efficient is to read faster. They believe that slow reading is poor reading. This is not true. *How* you read is more important than *how fast* you read. If you read

3

a 12-page assignment in one hour but remember only 60 percent of what you read, you are not reading efficiently. Efficient reading involves adequate comprehension and recall within a reasonable time frame. Reading efficiency increases as you develop techniques that improve your comprehension and retention, which will enable you to use your time most economically.

The following Efficiency Questionnaire will help you assess whether you are an efficient reader. Answer *yes* or *no* to each question in the spaces provided. Be honest with yourself!

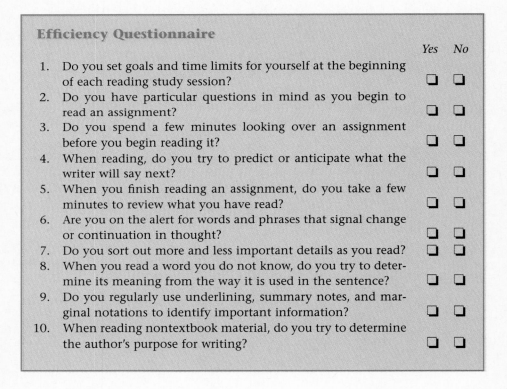

**Efficiency Questionnaire**

|  |  | Yes | No |
|---|---|---|---|
| 1. | Do you set goals and time limits for yourself at the beginning of each reading study session? | ❏ | ❏ |
| 2. | Do you have particular questions in mind as you begin to read an assignment? | ❏ | ❏ |
| 3. | Do you spend a few minutes looking over an assignment before you begin reading it? | ❏ | ❏ |
| 4. | When reading, do you try to predict or anticipate what the writer will say next? | ❏ | ❏ |
| 5. | When you finish reading an assignment, do you take a few minutes to review what you have read? | ❏ | ❏ |
| 6. | Are you on the alert for words and phrases that signal change or continuation in thought? | ❏ | ❏ |
| 7. | Do you sort out more and less important details as you read? | ❏ | ❏ |
| 8. | When you read a word you do not know, do you try to determine its meaning from the way it is used in the sentence? | ❏ | ❏ |
| 9. | Do you regularly use underlining, summary notes, and marginal notations to identify important information? | ❏ | ❏ |
| 10. | When reading nontextbook material, do you try to determine the author's purpose for writing? | ❏ | ❏ |

If you answered *yes* to all or most of these questions, you are well on your way to becoming an efficient reader. If you answered *no* to some or many of the questions, you need to improve your efficiency.

In this chapter we discuss how you can become a more efficient and flexible reader by varying your reading techniques to suit the material and your purpose for reading it. You will learn more specific approaches as you proceed through the rest of the text.

# ■ DEVELOPING READING FLEXIBILITY

Do you read the newspaper in the same way and at the same speed that you read a chemistry textbook? Do you read poetry in the same way and at the same speed that you read an article in *Time* magazine? Surprisingly, for many adults the answer to these questions is *yes*. Many adults, including college graduates, read everything in nearly the same way at the same rate.

Efficient and flexible readers, however, read the newspaper both *faster* and *differently* than the way they read a chemistry book because the newspaper is usually easier to read and because they have a different purpose for reading each. Flexible readers read poetry more slowly and in a different way than magazine articles. Your ability to adjust your reading rate and methods to suit the type of material you are reading and your purpose for reading is called *reading flexibility.*

To become a flexible reader, you make decisions about how you will read a given piece of material. *How* you read depends on *why* you are reading and *how much* you intend to remember. Rate and comprehension are the two most important factors. Think of them as weights on a balancing scale: as one increases, the other decreases. Your goal is to achieve a balance that suits the nature of the material and your purpose for reading. This chapter discusses how to achieve this balance.

## ■ Assessing Difficulty

The first step in determining how to read a given piece of writing is to assess its difficulty. Many features of the reading material itself influence how easily and how quickly you can read it. Here are a few important characteristics to consider:

1. **The format.** The physical arrangement of a page can influence how easily material can be read. For example, it is more difficult to read a page that is a solid block of print than it is to read a page on which the ideas are broken up by headings, spacing, and listing.

2. **Graphic and visual material.** The inclusion of maps, pictures, graphs, and charts also may influence your reading. Graphic elements present detailed information and require close, careful study.

3. **Typographical aids.** Features of print such as boldface, italics, colored type, and headings often make a page easier to read and understand. Headings announce the topic about to be discussed and together form an outline of ideas covered in the material. Words in italics, boldface, or colored type emphasize certain words and phrases.

4. **Language features.** Factors such as sentence length, paragraph length, and vocabulary level determine how difficult a piece of material is to read. Generally, the longer the sentences and paragraphs in a selection, the more difficult they are to read.

5. **Subject matter.** The type and number of ideas and concepts that an author presents influence difficulty. For instance, a passage that explains a complicated scientific theory or procedure requires close reading. Material that discusses everyday, newsworthy topics normally requires less careful attention. Also, a passage that explains one new idea is easier to read than a passage that presents three or four new, separate ideas in the same amount of space.

6. **Length.** Long chapters, articles, and essays are often more difficult to read than shorter ones. Lengthy materials demand sustained concentration and require you to relate larger numbers of ideas and to maintain a broader focus and perspective.

7. **Organization.** Some materials progress in an orderly, logical fashion from point to point. Others are more loosely organized, and the writer's pattern of thought is more difficult to identify. As a general rule, the less clearly organized written material is, the more difficult it is to read.

The easiest way to assess the difficulty of a selection is to preread it. Prereading (see Chapter 2) reveals how to determine how well organized the material is and will give you a feeling for the difficulty of the language and content. Once you have made a quick estimate of the material's difficulty, you can adjust your reading rate accordingly.

No rule tells you how much to slow down or speed up. You must use your judgment and adjust your reading to the conditions at hand. For example, you can slow down if you encounter a passage with long, complicated sentences or an article that presents complex ideas or uses technical vocabulary. You can speed up if you come across simple, straightforward ideas and everyday vocabulary. In addition to adjusting your rate, you should alter the manner in which you read the material, using different techniques to suit different types of material. A major portion of this book discusses techniques designed to increase your efficiency and flexibility.

## EXERCISE 1–1

*DIRECTIONS:* Use the seven characteristics described earlier to assess the difficulty of each reading selection that appears at the end of this chapter (pages 17–23). Then answer the following questions.

1. Which selection appears to be more difficult? List the features that make it appear difficult.

   _____

   _____

   _____

2. What features make the other selection seem easier to read?

   _____

   _____

   _____

## EXERCISE 1–2

*DIRECTIONS:* Use the seven characteristics listed earlier to assess the difficulty of each textbook you have been assigned this semester. Also consider your interest, skills, and background knowledge for each discipline. Rank your texts from most to least difficult:

Most difficult

1. _____

2. _____

3. _____

4. _____

### ■ Defining Your Purpose

Your purpose for reading a particular piece should influence *how* you read it. Different situations require different levels of comprehension and recall. For example, you may not need to recall every fact when leisurely reading an article in the newspaper, but you *do* need a high level of comprehension when reading a contract that you plan to sign. When reading course assignments, your purpose may also vary. You might read a psychology assignment very closely in preparation for an objective exam. You might read or reread a portion of a chemistry text only to learn how to solve a particular problem. Your comprehension can range from careful, close attention to a very brief, quick reading for only main ideas. Then, as your comprehension varies, so does your reading rate. If close, careful comprehension is not required, you can read faster. You will generally find that

**Table 1.1** The Relationship Among Purpose, Rate, and Comprehension

| Type of Material | Purpose in Reading | Desired Level of Comprehension | Approximate Range of Reading Rate |
|---|---|---|---|
| Poetry, legal documents, argumentative writing | Analyze, criticize, evaluate | Complete (100%) | Under 200 wpm |
| Textbooks, manuals, research documents | High comprehension recall for exams, writing research reports, following directions | High (90–100%) | 200–300 wpm |
| Novels, paperbacks, newspapers, magazines | Entertainment, enjoyment, general information | Moderate (60–90%) | 300–500 wpm |
| Reference materials, catalogs, magazines, nonfiction | Overview of material, locating specific facts, review of previously read material | Low (60% or below) | 600–800 wpm or above |

as your comprehension decreases, your reading rate increases. Table 1.1 illustrates this relationship.

## EXERCISE 1–3

*DIRECTIONS:* Each day you read a wide variety of materials, and your purpose is slightly different for each. Make a list of materials you have read this week and describe your purpose for reading each. (Don't forget such everyday items as labels, instructions, menus, etc.)

_____

_____

_____

_____

## EXERCISE 1–4

*DIRECTIONS:* For each of the following situations, define your purpose for reading and indicate the level of comprehension that seems appropriate. Refer to Table 1-1 if necessary.

1. You are reading a case study at the end of a chapter in your criminology textbook in preparation for an essay exam.

   Purpose: _____

   Level of Comprehension: _____

2.  You are reading sample problems in a chapter in your mathematics text that you feel confident you know how to solve.

    Purpose: _____

    Level of Comprehension: _____

3.  You are reading the end-of-chapter review questions in your economics text in preparation for an exam that is likely to contain similar questions.

    Purpose: _____

    Level of Comprehension: _____

4.  You are reading a section of a chapter in your economics textbook that refers to a series of graphs and illustrations in the chapter; you can understand the information in the graphs easily.

    Purpose: _____

    Level of Comprehension: _____

5.  You are reading a critical essay that discusses an e. e. cummings poem you are studying in a literature class in preparation for writing a paper on that poem.

    Purpose: _____

    Level of Comprehension: _____

## ■ Assessing Your Skills and Abilities

If you were a physics major, you would probably find a math or chemistry text easier to read than if you were a communications or art major. If you spent a long afternoon doing library research, you would likely have more difficulty completing a psychology reading assignment that evening than if you had spent the afternoon shopping. Thus you can see that the following characteristics and circumstances can affect your reading rate and comprehension:

### *Your Background Knowledge*

The amount of knowledge you have about a topic influences how easily and quickly you will be able to read about it. Suppose you were asked to read an excerpt from an organic chemistry text. If you have completed several chemistry courses, the excerpt would be fairly easy to understand. If you had never taken a chemistry course, even in high school, the excerpt would be extremely difficult to read, and you would probably understand very little.

### Your Physical and Mental State

How you feel, how much sleep you have had, whether or not you are recovering from a cold, and even whether or not you are happy or relaxed after enjoying dinner can all affect your ability to read and concentrate. Try to complete analytical or careful reading assignments when you are at your physical peak and can maintain a high level of concentration. (See Chapter 3 for suggestions about improving your concentration.)

### Your Interest Level

Most people have little difficulty understanding and remembering material if the subject is highly interesting. Interest can improve comprehension and rate; a lack of interest or motivation can have a negative effect.

### Your Reading Skills

Your ability to comprehend directly influences how well and how fast you are able to read a given page. Your vocabulary is also an important factor. If your vocabulary is limited you will encounter numerous unfamiliar words that will impair your comprehension and slow your reading down. On the other hand, an extensive, well-developed vocabulary will enable you to grasp meanings accurately and rapidly.

## ■ Varying Your Rate and Comprehension

Materials should not all be read in the same way or with the same level of comprehension. You should select a level of comprehension appropriate for what you are reading and why you are reading it. For example, if you are reading a textbook chapter to pass an objective exam based on that chapter, your purpose is to learn all the important facts and ideas, and you need a very high level of comprehension and recall.

Try the following techniques in order to find the appropriate level of comprehension and recall.

1. **Clearly define your purpose for reading the material.** Is it an assignment? Are you reading for general information, for details, for entertainment, or to keep up with current events?

2. **Analyze what, if anything, you will be required to do after you have read the material.** Will you have to pass an exam, participate in

a class discussion, or summarize the information in a short paper? To pass an exam, you need a very high level of comprehension. To prepare for a class discussion, a more moderate level of comprehension or retention is needed.

3. **Evaluate the relative difficulty of the material.** Assess your background knowledge and experience with the subject.

Once you have established your purpose for reading and have selected a desired level of comprehension, you must develop a reading strategy that suits your purpose. The remaining chapters in this text present a variety of techniques that allow you to choose a specific level of comprehension.

## EXERCISE 1–5

*DIRECTIONS:* For each of the following situations, identify the appropriate level of comprehension.

1. You are reading the classified ads to find an apartment to rent.

   _____

2. You are reading a friend's English composition to help him or her revise it.

   _____

3. You are reviewing an essay that you read last evening for a literature course.

   _____

4. You are reading your lab manual in preparation for a biology lab.

   _____

5. You are reading an article in *Newsweek* about trends in violent crime in America for a sociology class discussion.

   _____

## EXERCISE 1–6

*DIRECTIONS:* Make a list of reading assignments your instructors expect you to complete in the next two weeks. Indicate the level of comprehension that you should achieve for each assignment.

## ■ PRINCIPLES OF EFFICIENCY AND FLEXIBILITY

Each of the following statements expresses one of the major principles on which the techniques presented in this book are built. Are you surprised by any of them? Do any of the statements seem to contradict what you have been taught previously? Because each is a vital principle, a brief rationale for each follows:

1. **You do not always have to read everything.** In this text you will see that, depending on your purpose for reading, it may be perfectly acceptable and even advisable to skip portions of sentences, paragraphs, and articles.

2. **Not everything on a page is of equal importance.** Sentences, paragraphs, and longer selections each contain a mixture of important and less important information. You will learn to identify what is important and to see how the remaining parts of the sentence, paragraph, or article relate to it.

3. **Shortcuts can save valuable time and make reading or studying easier.** Reading is not simply a matter of opening a book and jumping in. There are specific techniques you can use before you begin reading, while you are reading, and after you have finished reading that will greatly increase your efficiency.

4. **You can increase your reading rate without losing comprehension.** Most students can increase their rate by applying techniques for improving their comprehension and retention. Of course, you cannot expect to double or triple your rate while maintaining a high level of comprehension, but a significant increase is usually noted.

5. **Not everything that appears in print is true.** An active reader must question and evaluate the source, authority, and evidence offered in support of statements that are not verifiable.

Throughout the rest of this book, each of these principles will be demonstrated and applied to a variety of reading situations.

## ■ EVALUATING YOUR RATE AND FLEXIBILITY

Now that you have read about rate and flexibility, you are probably wondering how fast and flexibly you read. Here is an easy method for estimating your reading rate for whatever material you are reading. (Use this method to complete Exercise 1-7.)

1. **After you have chosen a passage in a book or article, count the total number of words in any three lines.** Divide the total by three (3). Round off to the nearest whole number. This will give the average number of words per line.

2. **Count the number of lines in the article or book** (or on one page if it is longer than one page). Multiply the number of words per line by the total number of lines. This will give you a fairly accurate estimate of the total number of words.

3. **As you read, time yourself.** Record the hour, minute, and second of your starting time (for example, 4:20:18). Start reading when the second hand of the clock reaches 12. Record your finishing time. Subtract your starting time from your finishing time.

4. **Divide the total reading time into the total number of words.** To do this, round off the number of seconds to the nearest quarter of a minute and then divide. For example, if your total reading time was 3 minutes and 12 seconds, round it off to 3 ¼, or 3.25, minutes and then divide. Your answer will be your words per minute (WPM) score.

EXAMPLE:

Total number of words on 3 lines: 23

Divide by 3 and round off: $23/3 = 7⅔ = 8$

Total number of lines in article: 120

Multiply number of words per line by number of lines:

$8 \times 120 = 960$ (total words)

Subtract starting time from finishing time: $\begin{array}{r} 1{:}13{:}28 \\ -1{:}05 \\ \hline 8{:}28 \end{array}$

Round off to nearest quarter minute: 8.5 minutes

Divide time into total number of words:

$960/8.5 = 112 +$ a fraction (your WPM score)

## EXERCISE 1–7

*DIRECTIONS:* Measure how effectively you adjust your reading rate by reading each of the following materials for the purpose stated. Fill in your rate in the space provided, then compare your results with the rates given in Table 1.1.

1. Material: A portion of a legal document (insurance policy, financial aid statement, credit card agreement)

**Critical Thinking Tip #1**

**Developing Critical Thinking Skills**

An efficient and flexible reader is also a critical reader. Your college instructors expect you not only to understand and recall what you read, but also to interpret and evaluate it. They expect you to read and think critically. The word *critical,* when used in this context, does not mean being negative or finding fault. Instead, it means having a curious, questioning, and open mind. To get a better sense of what critical thinking involves, and to assess your current level of critical reading and thinking skills, complete the following mini-questionnaire.

| *When You Read Do You. . .* | *Always* | *Sometimes* | *Never* |
|---|---|---|---|
| 1. Question the author's motives? | ❑ | ❑ | ❑ |
| 2. Think about what the author *means* as well as what he or she *says*? | ❑ | ❑ | ❑ |
| 3. Ask questions such as Why? or How? as you read? | ❑ | ❑ | ❑ |
| 4. Pay attention to the author's choice of words and notice their impact on you? | ❑ | ❑ | ❑ |
| 5. Evaluate the evidence or reasons an author provides to support an idea? | ❑ | ❑ | ❑ |

If you answered *always* or *sometimes* to a number of the questions, you are well on your way to becoming a critical reader. If you answered *never,* you will learn more about these skills, as well as others, in the Critical Thinking boxes in each chapter.

    Purpose: Complete understanding

    Rate: _____

2. Material: A three-page assignment in one of your textbooks

    Purpose: High comprehension—recall for an objective exam

    Rate: _____

3. Material: An article in a favorite magazine

    Purpose: Moderate comprehension—entertainment

    Rate: _____

## EXERCISE 1–8

*DIRECTIONS:* Select one of the readings at the end of the chapter.

1. For the reading selected, choose a purpose for reading and a desired level of comprehension from Table 1.1 and record them here.

   Selection: _____

   Purpose:_____

   Desired Level of Comprehension: _____

2. Read the selection while keeping in mind the purpose you have chosen, then answer the questions that follow the reading.

3. Evaluate the difficulty of the reading and your approach to it by completing the checklist in Figure 1.1.

**Format**

❑ helpful
❑ difficult to follow

**Graphic/Visual Aids**

❑ yes
❑ no

**Typographical Aids**

❑ yes
❑ no

**Subject Matter**

❑ complex
❑ understandable
❑ familiar

**Length**

❑ short
❑ moderate
❑ long

**Organization**

❑ strong
❑ moderate
❑ weak

**Your Background Knowledge**

❑ strong
❑ moderate
❑ weak

**Your Physical/Mental State**

❑ alert
❑ moderately alert
❑ distractible

**Your Interest Level**

❑ high
❑ moderate
❑ low

**FIGURE 1.1**  A Checklist to Evaluate Difficulty

## SUMMARY

**1. What is meant by reading efficiency and reading flexibility?**

Reading efficiency and flexibility are vital concepts for college readers.
- Efficiency refers to the ability to accomplish tasks effectively within a reasonable period of time.
- Flexibility refers to the ability to adjust reading rates to the difficulty of the material, the purpose for reading, and the reader's skills and abilities.

**2. What are the features of a piece of writing that can affect its level of reading difficulty?**

Text features that affect difficulty include:
- Format
- Graphics
- Typographical aids
- Language features
- Subject matter
- Length
- Organization

**3. What characteristics or circumstances can affect your reading rate and comprehension?**

Reader characteristics that affect rate and comprehension are:
- Background knowledge
- Physical and mental state
- Interest
- Reading skills

**4. Why should you vary your reading rate and level of comprehension?**

Since reading materials differ widely and your purpose for reading them varies, you should adjust your rate and comprehension to form a strategy for each different reading situation.

**5. What are the five major principles behind the techniques presented in this book?**

- You do not always have to read everything.
- Not everything on a page is of equal importance.
- Shortcuts can save valuable reading time and make reading and studying easier.
- You can increase your reading rate without losing comprehension.
- Not everything that appears in print is true.

## READING SELECTION 1
### HOW TO BRAG ABOUT YOURSELF TO WIN AND HOLD A NEW JOB

James E. Challenger
From *the Buffalo News*

*Do you feel prepared for a job interview? Do you know how to sell yourself to a potential customer? This essay, written by the president of an international company that specializes in job placement, offers advice that will help you do well during a job interview.*

1   For most people, boasting about oneself does not come naturally. It is not easy or comfortable to tell someone all the wonderful things you have accomplished. But that is exactly what you need to do if you are seeking a new job, or trying to hold on to the one you have.

2   Of course, there is a fine line between self-confidence and arrogance, so to be successful in winning over the interviewer you must learn to maximize your accomplishments and attributes without antagonizing the interviewer.

3   The natural tendency for most job seekers is to behave modestly in a job interview. Although humility is usually an attractive trait, it will work against you when job hunting and moving up the corporate ladder. If you do not tell a prospective employer how good you are, who will?

4   More than half of the people interviewing for jobs fail to win an offer simply because they failed to sell their accomplishments. More than likely you have the qualifications for the jobs for which you are interviewing. That should give you the confidence to tell the interviewer why your accomplishments make you the best person for the position.

5   Give yourself a fighting chance at the interview. Your resume might have helped you get the interview, but its usefulness has ended there. It will not speak for itself. If it makes you feel more comfortable, take a step "outside yourself."

This means to view yourself as someone else may view you. Rather than thinking that you are talking about yourself, pretend you are giving a recommendation of a good friend.

6   To do the best job of selling yourself in an interview, you have to be prepared in advance. As part of your job-hunting check list, write down on a piece of paper your major job-related

*"If you do not tell a prospective employer how good you are, who will?"*

accomplishments. Commit them to memory. You will probably be pleasantly surprised to see in writing all that you have done.

7    By developing this list, you will have accomplished two things: the first is you will impress the interviewer by being able to talk confidently and succinctly about your accomplishments. You will not have to sit uncomfortably while you think of your successes. They will be at the tip of your tongue.

8    Secondly, rather than dwell on your own personality characteristics, such as how hardworking or creative you are, you can discuss hard facts, such as how you saved your employer money or an idea you developed that helped a customer make more money.

9    Let the interviewer know about the praise your accomplishments have won from your former supervisors. Make a point of mentioning any awards or honors you received in your work or a related field. If your job evaluations were consistently excellent, quote your supervisors' complimentary remarks.

10    When chronicling your accomplishments for the interviewer, take as much credit as you honestly can. If you were a key part behind a major group project, tell the interviewer. If you developed a specific idea without help from your supervisor, it is acceptable to say that. Remember, you are at that interview to sell yourself, not your former co-workers.

11    However, never criticize your former employer. Sharing your negative thoughts with the interviewer is an immediate turn-off and will only brand you as a complainer and gossip, whom no one likes or will hire.

12    Keep in mind that the most important part of a job interview is making the employer like you and presenting yourself as the person he or she wants you to be. Consciously or not most employers tend to hire people who reflect their own values and standards.

13    One important thing to keep in mind while you are discussing your accomplishments: Do not tell the employer how to run his or her business. Just discuss your qualifications and the good things you have done and let the interviewer decide how you might fill the company's needs.

14    Once you get the job you want, boasting about your accomplishments does not stop. Although you may think all your successes and achievements are highly visible, remember that you are only one of many people in a company. Lack of recognition is cited by a majority of discharged managers as the most frequent complaint against the former employer.

15    Do not let it happen to you. Make a point to tell your supervisor what you have done. Even if not asked, write down what you have accomplished on a regular basis and give it to your supervisor so he or she knows what you are doing. A written report can also be referred to during performance and salary reviews to document your achievements.

16    To help make yourself more visible in the company, volunteer for additional assignments—both job-related and non business related. These could include community relations or charitable activities in which your company is involved. These types of activities may enable you to have more time and access to top executives of the company to whom you may endear yourself. You might even have the opportunity to tell them what you are doing for the company, which can never hurt.

17    Remember, letting people know what you are doing and what you have accomplished is not a bad thing whether you are interviewing for a new job or working your way up the corporate hierarchy. Your worklife is a constant sales job. You must sell yourself like a product to win a job. Once you have a job, you must continually promote yourself and your accomplishments to hold on to your job and move successfully through the corporate ranks.

*James E. Challenger is president of Challenger, Gray & Christmas, Inc., an international outplacement consulting firm with 24 U.S. and foreign offices.*

## Comprehension Test 1

*Directions:   Circle the letter of the best answer.*

**Checking Your Comprehension**

1. This article is mostly about how to
   a. interview for a job.
   b. please your boss.
   c. get along with coworkers.
   d. get and keep a job.

2. Which of the following statements best expresses the central thought of this article?
   a. "More than likely you have the qualifications for the jobs for which you are interviewing."
   b. "Do not tell the employer how to run his or her business."
   c. "Make a point to tell your supervisor what you have done."
   d. "Your work life is a constant sales job."

3. According to the reading, more than half of the people who interview for jobs don't get offered one because they
   a. are not qualified.
   b. appear arrogant or too self confident.
   c. fail to sell their accomplishments.
   d. have no contacts within the company.

4. The author states that the one thing you should *never* do during an interview is
   a. criticize your former employer.
   b. promote your qualifications for the job.
   c. tell your potential boss about projects you've worked on.
   d. list your successes in previous jobs.

5. The author states that the most important part of a job interview is
   a. taking credit for your accomplishments and giving credit to your coworkers.
   b. showing your potential boss you have the initiative to do the job and will work hard.
   c. making your boss like you and appearing like the person he/she wants you to be.
   d. impressing your potential boss with your ideas for running his business.

6. In paragraph 2, the word "maximize" means to
   a. talk about.
   b. make the most of.
   c. be modest about.
   d. play down.

**Thinking Critically**

7. The author provides his views on winning and holding a new job by
   a. offering suggestions.
   b. presenting facts and statistics
   c. describing several situations.
   d. telling a story.

8. The author's primary purpose in writing the article is to
   a. criticize.
   b. inform.
   c. entertain.
   d. argue.

9. Based on the reading, which one of the following statements would the author think is best for you to make during a job interview for a sales position?
   a. "I'm the best person for the job because I am creative and hardworking."
   b. "You might want to hire me because of my background in sales and my ability to get along."
   c. "My present company increased sales by 25 percent this year as a result of an advertising campaign that I spearheaded."
   d. "I have played a part in helping the company to increase revenues over the last five years."

10. In light of his views on job interviews, the reader can conclude that the author is
    a. assertive.
    b. aggressive.
    c. humble.
    d. conceited.

**Questions for Discussion**

1. Some people worry that if they boast about themselves during a job interview, they'll appear to be conceited. Do you think this is true? Why or why not?

2. Do you agree that "your worklife is a constant sales job"? Justify your answer.

3. The author suggests that you should not tell the employer how to run his or her business. Do you agree or disagree? Why?

4. What other suggestions can you offer for success in getting and keeping a job?

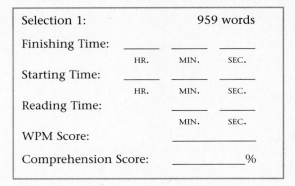

| Selection 1: | | 959 words | |
|---|---|---|---|
| Finishing Time: | _____ | _____ | _____ |
| | HR. | MIN. | SEC. |
| Starting Time: | _____ | _____ | _____ |
| | HR. | MIN. | SEC. |
| Reading Time: | | _____ | _____ |
| | | MIN. | SEC. |
| WPM Score: | | _____ | |
| Comprehension Score: | | _____% | |

## READING SELECTION 2
## HISPANIC, USA: THE CONVEYOR-BELT LADIES
Rose Del Castillo Guilbault
From *the San Francisco Chronicle*

*What types of relationships have you developed with coworkers? Have you ever been treated differently because you are a college student? This essay describes a college student's experience working with migrant women in a vegetable packing shed.*

1 The conveyor-belt ladies were the migrant women, mostly from Texas, I worked with during the summers of my teenage years. I call them .conveyor-belt ladies because our entire relationship took place while sorting tomatoes on a conveyor belt.

2 We were like a cast in a play where all the action occurs on one set. We'd return day after day to perform the same roles, only this stage was a vegetable-packing shed, and at the end of the season there was no applause. The players could look forward only to the same uninspiring parts on a string of grim real-life stages.

3 The women and their families arrived in May for the carrot season, spent the summer in the tomato sheds and stayed through October for the bean harvest. After that, they emptied the town, some returning to their homes in Texas (cities like McAllen, Douglas, Brownsville), while others continued on the migrant trail, picking cotton in the San Joaquin Valley or grapefruits and oranges in the Imperial Valley.

4 Most of these women had started in the fields. The vegetable packing sheds were a step up, easier than the back-breaking, grueling work the field demanded. The work was more tedious than strenuous, paid better, provided fairly steady hours and clean bathrooms. Best of all, you weren't subjected to the elements.

5 The summer I was 16, my mother got jobs for both of us as tomato sorters. That's how I came to be included in the seasonal sorority of the conveyor belt.

6 The work consisted of standing and picking flawed tomatoes off the conveyor belt before they rolled off into the shipping boxes at the end of the line. These boxes were immediately

loaded onto waiting delivery trucks, so it was crucial not to let imperfect tomatoes through.

7   The work could be slow or intense, depending on the quality of the tomatoes and how many there were. Work increased when the company's deliveries got backlogged or after rainy weather had delayed picking.

8   During those times, it was not unusual to work from 7 A.M. to midnight, playing catch-up. I never heard anyone complain about the overtime. Overtime meant desperately needed extra money.

9   I was not happy to be part of the agricultural work force. I would have preferred working in a dress shop or baby-sitting, like my friends. But I had a dream that would cost a lot of money— college. And the fact was, this was the highest-paying work I could do.

10   But it wasn't so much the work that bothered me. I was embarrassed because only Mexicans worked at packing sheds. I had heard my school-mates joke about the "ugly, fat Mexican women" at the sheds. They ridiculed the way they dressed and laughed at the "funny way" they talked. I feared working with them would irrevocably stigmatize me, setting me further apart from my Anglo classmates.

11   At 16 I was more American than Mexican and, with adolescent arrogance, felt superior to these "uneducated" women. I might be one of them, I reasoned, but I was not like them.

12   But it was difficult not to like the women. They were a gregarious, entertaining group, eas-ing the long, monotonous hours with bawdy humor, spicy gossip and inventive laments. They poked fun at all the male workers and did hys-terical impersonations of a dyspeptic Anglo supervisor. Although he didn't speak Spanish (other than *"Mujeres, trabajo, trabajo!"* Women, work, work!), he seemed to sense he was being laughed at. That would account for the sudden rages when he would stamp his foot and forbid us to talk until break time.

13   "I bet he understands Spanish and just pre-tends so he can hear what we say," I whispered to Rosa.

14   *"Ay, no, hija,* it's all the buzzing in his ears that alerts him that these *viejas* (old women) are bad-mouthing him!" Rosa giggled.

15   But it would have been easier to tie the women's tongues in a knot than to keep them quiet. Eventually the ladies had their way and their fun, and the men learned to ignore them.

16   We were often shifted around, another strate-gy to keep us quiet. This gave me ample oppor-tunity to get to know everyone, listen to their life stories and absorb the gossip.

17   Pretty Rosa described her romances and her impending wedding to a handsome field worker. Bertha, a heavy-set, dark-skinned woman, told me that Rosa's marriage would cause nothing but headaches because the man was younger and too handsome. Maria, large, moon-faced and placid, described the births of each of her nine children, warning me about the horrors of childbirth. Pragmatic Minnie, a tiny woman who always wore printed cotton dresses, scoffed at Maria's stupidity, telling me she wouldn't have so many kids if she had ignored that good-for-nothing priest and gotten her tubes tied!

18   In unexpected moments, they could turn melancholic: recounting the babies who died because their mothers couldn't afford medical care; the alcoholic, abusive husbands who were their "cross to bear"; the racism they experienced in Texas, where they were branded "dirty Mexicans" or "Mexican dogs" and not allowed in certain restaurants.

19   They spoke with the detached fatalism of peo-ple with limited choices and alternatives. Their lives were as raw and brutal as ghetto streets— something they accepted with an odd grace and resignation.

20   I was appalled and deeply affected by these confidences. The injustices they endured enraged me; their personal struggles overwhelmed me. I knew I could do little but sympathize.

21   My mother, no stranger to suffering, suggest-ed I was too impressionable when I emotionally told her the women's stories. "That's nothing," she'd say lightly. "If they were in Mexico, life

would be even harder. At least there's opportunities here, you can work."

22 My icy arrogance quickly thawed, that first summer, as my respect for the conveyor-belt ladies grew.

23 I worked in the packing sheds for several summers. The last season also turned out to be the last time I lived at home. It was the end of a chapter in my life, but I didn't know it then. I had just finished junior college and was transferring to the university. I was already over-educated for seasonal work, but if you counted the overtime, no other jobs came close to paying so well, so I went back one last time.

24 The ladies treated me with warmth and respect. I was a college student, deserving of special treatment.

25 Aguedita, the crew chief, moved me to softer and better-paying jobs within the plant. I went from the conveyor belt to shoving boxes down a chute and finally to weighing boxes of tomatoes on a scale—the highest-paying position for a woman.

26 When the union's dues collector showed up, the women hid me in the bathroom. They had decided it was unfair for me to have to join the union and pay dues, since I worked only during the summer.

27 "Where's the student?" the union rep would ask, opening the door to a barrage of complaints about the union's unfairness.

28 Maria (of the nine children) tried to feed me all summer, bringing extra tortillas, which were delicious. I accepted them guiltily, always wondering if I was taking food away from her children. Others would bring rental contracts or other documents for me to explain and translate.

29 The last day of work was splendidly beautiful, warm and sunny. If this had been a movie, these last scenes would have been shot in soft focus, with a crescendo of music in the background.

30 But real life is anti-climactic. As it was, nothing unusual happened. The conveyor belt's loud humming was turned off, silenced for the season. The women sighed as they removed their aprons. Some of them just walked off, calling *Hasta la próxima!* Until next time!

31 But most of the conveyor-belt ladies shook my hand, gave me a blessing or a big hug.

32 "Make us proud!" they said.

33 I hope I have.

---

## Comprehension Test 2*

### Checking Your Comprehension

1. Who were the "conveyor-belt ladies"? Where did they come from?

2. What was the primary job of those who worked on the conveyor belt?

3. Why was the author initially unhappy about working at the packing shed?

4. Why did the ladies hide the author when the union dues collector showed up?

### Thinking Critically

1. As a group, what were the "conveyor-belt ladies" really like in personality?

2. In what way did the author's attitude change toward her coworkers and why? Give a specific example.

3. Since the author herself was of Mexican-American descent, why did she initially feel superior to her Mexican-American coworkers?

---

*Multiple-choice questions are contained in Appendix B (page A6).

4. What effect did the stories the coworkers told about their lives have on the author?

**Questions for Discussion**

1. Working on a conveyor belt obviously has many disadvantages. What might be some advantages?

2. Have you ever experienced prejudice? Discuss how you did or would respond.

| Selection 2: | | 1320 words |
|---|---|---|
| Finishing Time: | | |
| | HR.    MIN. | SEC. |
| Starting Time: | | |
| | HR.    MIN. | SEC. |
| Reading Time: | | |
| | MIN. | SEC. |
| WPM Score: | | |
| Comprehension Score: | | _____% |

**Visit the Longman English Pages**

For additional readings and exercises, visit the Longman English Skills Web page at:

**http://longman.awl.com/englishpages**

For a username and password, please see your instructor.

# CHAPTER 2
# Active Reading and Learning

IN THIS CHAPTER YOU WILL LEARN:

1. To read actively.
2. To develop critical thinking skills.
3. To assess your learning style.
4. To preview and predict before reading.
5. To develop guide questions.
6. To monitor your comprehension.
7. To improve your ability to concentrate.

When reading and studying a textbook assignment, what could you do before reading to make the task easier? What could you do while you are reading to understand and remember more of the material? This chapter introduces numerous techniques that can make a noticeable difference in how well you read and how much you remember. These techniques— active reading and thinking, assessing your learning style, prereading and predicting, forming guide questions, monitoring your comprehension, and building your concentration—can make an immediate, significant improvement in your reading efficiency. Each technique demands that you become actively involved in reading—thinking, anticipating, connecting, and assessing your performance.

## ■ READING AND THINKING ACTIVELY

College instructors expect their students to read actively and think critically. This section offers strategies for improving these skills.

### ■ Reading Actively

Reading at first may appear to be a routine activity in which individual words are combined to produce meaning. Consequently, many college students approach reading as a single-step process. They open the book, read, and close the book. Research shows that effective reading is not a single-step process but a complex set of skills involving activities before, during, and after reading. Here is a partial list of some of those skills.

BEFORE READING

1. Determine the subject of the material
2. Determine how the material is organized
3. Decide what you need to remember from the material
4. Define your purpose for reading

DURING READING

1. Identify what is important
2. Determine how key ideas are supported
3. Identify patterns of thought
4. Draw connections between ideas
5. Anticipate what is to come next
6. Relate ideas to what you already know

DURING AND AFTER READING

1. Identify the author's purpose for writing
2. Analyze the writer's technique and language
3. Evaluate the writer's competence or authority
4. Ask critical questions
5. Evaluate the nature and type of supporting evidence

To better grasp the concept of active reading, consider a similar situation. Have you ever gone to a ball game and watched the fans? Most do not sit passively and watch the game. Instead they become actively involved; they direct players to make certain plays; they criticize calls, encourage players, and reprimand the coach. They feel and act as if it's *their* game, not just the players' game. Similarly, active readers get involved with the material they are reading. They think, question, challenge, and criticize the author's ideas. They try to make the material *their* material. Table 2.1 on page 26 lists examples of successful active reading strategies and contrasts them with passive (unsuccessful) approaches.

Throughout this chapter and the remainder of the text you will learn numerous techniques and strategies for becoming a more active reader.

**Table 2.1** Active Versus Passive Reading

| Active Readers... | Passive Readers... |
|---|---|
| Read each assignment differently | Read all assignments the same way |
| Analyze the purpose of an assignment | Read an assignment because it was assigned |
| Adjust their speed to suit their purpose | Read everything at the same speed |
| Question ideas | Accept whatever is in print as true |
| Compare and connect textbook readings with lecture content | Study each separately |
| Find out what an assignment is about before reading it | Check the length of an assignment before reading it |
| Keep track of their level of comprehension and concentration | Read until the assignment is completed |
| Read with pencil in hand, highlighting, jotting notes, and marking key vocabulary | Read |

## EXERCISE 2–1

*DIRECTIONS:* Consider each of the following reading assignments. Discuss ways to get actively involved in each assignment.

1. Reading two poems by Walt Whitman for an American literature class.
2. Reading the procedures for your next biology lab.
3. Reading an article in *Time* magazine assigned by your political science instructor in preparation for a class discussion.

## EXERCISE 2–2

*DIRECTIONS:* Compile a list of active reading strategies you already use. Discuss new strategies that could be used with your instructor or classmates. Add these to your list.

## ■ Thinking Critically

Active reading requires critical thinking. To be an active reader, you must think beyond a factual, literal level. Instructors expect you to understand ideas, but they also expect you to apply, analyze, synthesize, and evaluate information.

**Table 2.2** Levels of Thinking

| Level | Examples |
|---|---|
| **Knowledge:** Recalling information; repeating information with no changes | Recalling definitions; memorizing dates |
| **Comprehension:** Understanding ideas; using rules and following directions | Explaining a theory, recognizing what is important |
| **Application:** Applying knowledge to a new situation | Using knowledge of formulas to solve a new physics problem |
| **Analysis:** Seeing relationships; breaking information into parts; analyzing how things work | Comparing two essays by the same author |
| **Synthesis:** Putting ideas and information together in a unique way; creating something new | Designing a new computer program |
| **Evaluation:** Making judgments; assessing value or worth of information | Evaluating the effectiveness of an argument opposing the death penalty |

*Source:* Bloom, B., et al., eds, *Taxonomy of Educational Objectives.* New York: McKay, 1956.

Table 2.2 describes a progression of academic thinking skills ranging from basic to more complex.

When instructors assign papers, write exam questions, or conduct class discussions, they often ask you to function beyond the knowledge and comprehension levels. Table 2.3 gives a few sample exam questions from a course in interpersonal communication.

You don't need to identify the level of thinking that a particular assignment or test item requires. However, you should be able to think and work at each of these levels.

**Table 2.3** Test Items And Levels Of Thinking

| Test Item | Level of Thinking Required |
|---|---|
| Define nonverbal communication | Knowledge |
| Explain how nonverbal communication works | Comprehension |
| Describe three instances in which you have observed nonverbal communication | Application |
| Study the two pictures projected on the screen in the front of the classroom, and compare the nonverbal messages sent in each | Synthesis |
| Evaluate an essay whose major premise is: "Nonverbal communication skills should be taught formally as part of the educational process." | Evaluation |

The following passage is taken from a human biology textbook. Read the passage and study the list of questions that follow.

**COMMUNICATION AND THE SKIN**

We generally think of communication as a matter of voice and gesture, but the skin is an important communicative organ. Animals communicate their moods and sometimes make threats by fluffing their fur or causing it to rise on the backs of their neck and shoulders; humans cannot do that. However, the patterns of human hair distribution and color do signal sex and age. Fair-complexioned people can also—involuntarily—change blood flow to the skin and blush to indicate embarrassment, turn red with rage, and go pale with shock. In addition, we have considerable voluntary control over subcutaneous muscles in the face and neck, many of which attach to the skin to produce the stretchings and wrinklings of facial expressions.

An additional communicative role is served by the skin's apocrine sweat glands, particularly in adults. The substances they secrete have strong odors, especially after they have been worked on by the bacteria that dwell on the skin, and these glands are found in areas, such as the armpits, groin, and anal region, that have wicklike tufts of hair that can spread the odor into the air. Emotionally charged situations are likely to stimulate apocrine secretions, which may signal that a certain level of sexual readiness or fear or anxiety (emotional intensity) has been attained.

Rischer and Easton, *Focus on Human Biology.*

• • •

| | |
|---|---|
| Knowledge | What happens when fair-complexioned people blush? |
| Comprehension | Why is the skin an important vehicle for communication? |
| Application | Study two facial portraits and discuss how each person is using their skin to communicate. |
| Analysis | How does stretching of the skin produce communication? |
| Synthesis | Write a set of guidelines for determining what messages can be sent by skin movement. |
| Evaluation | Why is it important to know that skin can communicate? |

## EXERCISE 2–3

*DIRECTIONS:* For each of the following activities or situations, discuss which levels of thinking are primarily involved.

1. You are reading and comparing research from several sources to write a term paper for sociology.

2. You received a "C" grade on an essay you wrote for your freshman composition course. Your instructor will allow you to revise it to improve your grade.
3. You are translating an essay from Spanish to English.
4. You are dissecting a frog in your biology class.
5. You are bathing a patient as part of your clinical experience course in nursing.

## EXERCISE 2–4

*DIRECTIONS:* Read the following excerpt from a history textbook. Then study the questions that follow and identify the level of thinking that each requires.

### AFRICAN-AMERICAN WOMEN AS WRITERS

Phillis Wheatley was a young, African-American slave who belonged to landowner John Wheatley in Colonial America. She was also a poet and the first African-American ever to publish a book. Her *Poems on Various Subjects, Religious and Moral* was printed in Boston in 1773, three years before the penning of the Declaration of Independence.

Early slaves were generally denied education (it was deemed dangerous), but Wheatley was allowed by her owner to study poetry, Latin, and the Bible, and by the time she reached her late teens she had written enough poetry to put together a slender book of verse. Even so, publication was difficult. Proper Bostonians, fearful of a hoax, forced her to submit to a scholarly examination by a board of educated men, including the colonial governor and the same John Hancock who later copied out the Declaration of Independence and signed it with a flourish. The board of judges questioned Wheatley extensively and ruled that she was literate enough to have written the book. Only then was publication permitted.

Wheatley may have been the first, but she was not the only slave to write a book during the growing days of the republic. Unfortunately, most of the early popular African-American writers have been all but forgotten in modern times. Until now. A Cornell professor, Henry Louis Gates, recently started a research project, looking into 19th-century African-American fiction and poetry. In the process, he uncovered numerous lost works, almost half of which were written by African-American women. In varied literary styles, the newly resurfaced manuscripts offered a rich repository of African-American culture, recreating, among other things, the early days of slavery and the importance of religion to people under subjugation.

The literary finds were important. So important, in fact, that 30 of the lost books were republished in the late 1980s by Oxford University Press. The newly reclaimed writers range from poet Wheatley to novelist Frances Harper, essayist Ann Plato, and outspoken feminist Anna Julia Cooper. Perhaps this time they won't be lost.

Merrill, Lee and Friedlander, *Modern Mass Media.*

• • •

1. Who was the first African-American to publish a book?
2. Explain why Phillis Wheatley was forced to submit to a scholarly examination.
3. Name two writers that have been recently rediscovered.
4. Read two poems by Phillis Wheatley and compare them.
5. Why does the writer of this article hope the newly reclaimed work won't be lost?
6. Read a poem by Phillis Wheatley and explain what meaning it has to your life.
7. Critique one of Wheatley's poems; discuss its strengths and weaknesses.
8. Discuss the possible reasons Wheatley's owner allowed her to study.
9. Read five essays by Ann Plato, and develop a list of issues with which she is concerned.
10. Decide whether or not it was fair to ask Wheatley to submit to a scholarly examination.

## ■ LEARNING ACTIVELY

To get the most out of the time you spend studying, take action to ensure that you are concentrating on the task and that you are studying in the most effective way possible. This section of the chapter will show active strategies for building your concentration and adapting how you learn based on your learning style.

### ■ Assessing Your Learning Style

In addition to thinking critically, another aspect of reading and learning actively is choosing strategies that work best for you. Not everyone learns in the same way and not all reading and learning strategies are equally effective for everyone. Each person has his or her own unique way of learning, which is called *learning style*. Some students, for example, tend to be applied learners who prefer learning tasks that are practical, real-life situations. Other students may be conceptual learners who enjoy working with concepts and ideas; practical applications are not necessary for understanding. Here is another example. Some students tend to be spatial learners who work well with visual material—charts, diagrams, maps, and so forth. Others tend to be verbal learners who work well with language. The brief Learning Style Questionnaire in Appendix A, p. A1 at the end of the text, will help you discover the features of your learning style.

Once you have identified the features of your learning style, the next step is to use this information to become a more active and efficient learner.

**Table 2.4** Learning Styles And Reading/Learning Strategies

*If Your Learning Style Is . . . Then The Reading/Learning Strategies To Use Are . . .*

| | |
|---|---|
| **Auditory** | • Discuss/study with friends.<br>• Talk aloud when studying.<br>• Tape record self-testing questions and answers. |
| **Visual** | • Draw diagrams, charts, and/or tables.<br>• Try to visualize events.<br>• Use films and videos when available.<br>• Use computer assisted instruction when available. |
| **Applied** | • Think of practical situations to which learning applies.<br>• Associate ideas with their application.<br>• Use case studies, examples, and applications to cue your learning. |
| **Conceptual** | • Organize materials that lack order.<br>• Use outlining.<br>• Focus on organizational patterns. |
| **Spatial** | • Use mapping.<br>• Use outlining.<br>• Draw diagrams; make charts and sketches.<br>• Use visualization. |
| **Verbal** | • Translate diagrams and drawings into language.<br>• Record steps, processes, and procedures in words.<br>• Write summaries.<br>• Write your interpretation next to textbook drawings, maps, and graphics. |
| **Social** | • Form study groups.<br>• Find a study partner.<br>• Interact with the instructor.<br>• Work with a tutor. |
| **Independent** | • Use computer assisted instruction when available.<br>• Purchase review workbooks or study guides when available. |
| **Creative** | • Ask and answer questions.<br>• Record your own ideas in the margins of textbooks. |
| **Pragmatic** | • Study in an organized environment.<br>• Write lists of steps, procedures, and processes.<br>• Paraphrase difficult materials. |

Be prepared to change *how* you read and study. Be ready to experiment with new approaches, alter methods you have always used, and discard methods that no longer work.

If, however, you do disagree with any of the results of the Learning Style Questionnaire, be sure to follow your own instincts rather than the results indicated. Table 2.4 lists different aspects of learning styles and suggests how students who exhibit each style might learn most effectively from a reading assignment.

The Learning Style Questionnaire may also identify areas in which you are weak. Your learning style is not fixed or unchanging. It is possible to improve areas in which you scored lower. Even though you may be weak in conceptual learning, you will be required to read conceptual material. If you work on your approach to conceptual learning, you can learn to handle concepts and ideas effectively. Therefore make a conscious effort to improve areas of weakness as well as to take advantage of your strengths.

## EXERCISE 2–5

*DIRECTIONS:* The class should form two groups: concrete learners and abstract learners. Each group should discuss effective learning strategies that take into account this type of learning style.

## EXERCISE 2–6

*DIRECTIONS:* Write a brief description of yourself as a learner based on the results of the Learning Style Questionnaire. Describe your strengths and weaknesses. Include examples from your own experience as a student.

## ■ Improving Your Concentration

Do you have difficulty concentrating? If so, you are like many other college students who say that poor concentration is the main reason they cannot read or study effectively. Concentration is the ability to focus on the task at hand. Most students find that improving their concentration can reduce their reading time and improve their learning efficiency.

Take the quiz at the top of page 32 to assess your ability to concentrate. If your answer is *yes* to any of the questions, reading and studying this chapter will probably take you more time than it should. A *yes* answer indicates that you are not operating at your peak level of concentration.

Improving your concentration can best be achieved by controlling external distractions and increasing your attention span. Here are some suggestions for accomplishing these goals.

### Control External Distractions

A phone ringing, a dog barking, friends arguing, or parents reminding you about errands can break your concentration and cost you time. Each time you are interrupted, you have to find where you left off, and it takes you a minute or two to refocus your attention.

Although you cannot eliminate all distractions, you can control many of them through a wise choice of time and place for study. For a week or

**Concentration Quiz**

|  | Yes | No |
|---|---|---|
| 1. Are you sitting on a comfortable chair or lying on a comfortable bed? | ❑ | ❑ |
| 2. Is a television on nearby? | ❑ | ❑ |
| 3. Are friends or family who are not studying in the room with you? | ❑ | ❑ |
| 4. Do you wish you didn't have to read this chapter? | ❑ | ❑ |
| 5. Are you reading this chapter only because it was assigned by your instructor? | ❑ | ❑ |
| 6. Are you worried about anything or trying to make an important decision? | ❑ | ❑ |
| 7. Are you tired, either physically or mentally? | ❑ | ❑ |
| 8. Are you thinking about other things you have to do while you are reading? | ❑ | ❑ |

so, analyze where and when you study. Try to notice situations in which you accomplished a great deal as well as those in which you accomplished very little. At the end of the week, look for a pattern. Where and when did you find it was easy to concentrate? Where and when was it most difficult? Use the information from your analysis along with the following suggestions to choose a regular time and place for study.

1. **Choose a place to study that is relatively free from interruptions.** You may need to decide what types of distractions occur most frequently and then choose a place where you will be free of them. For instance, if your home, apartment, or dorm has many distractions such as phone calls, friends stopping by, or family members talking or watching TV, it may be necessary to find a different place to study. The campus or neighborhood library is often quiet and free of distractions.

2. **Choose a place free of distractions.** Although your living room, for example, may be quiet and free of interruptions, you may not be able to concentrate there. You may be distracted by noises from the street, the view from a window, the presence of a TV, or a project you are working on.

3. **Do not study where you are too comfortable.** If you study sitting in a lounge chair or lying across your bed, you may find it difficult to concentrate.

4. **Study in the same place.** Once you have located a good place to study, try to study in this place regularly. You will become familiar with the surroundings and begin to form associations between the place and the activity you perform there. Eventually, as soon as you enter the room or sit down at the desk, you will begin to feel as though you should study.

5. **Choose a time of day when you are mentally alert.** Give yourself the advantage of reading or studying when your mind is sharp and ready to pick up new information. Avoid studying when you are hungry or tired because it is most difficult to concentrate at these times.

6. **Establish a fixed time for reading or studying.** Studying at the same time each day will help you fall into the habit of studying more easily. For example, if you establish, as part of a schedule, that you will study right after dinner, soon it will become almost automatic.

### Increase Your Attention Span

Most people can keep their minds on one topic for only a limited period of time. This period of time represents their *attention span.* Your attention span varies from subject to subject, from book to book, and from speaker to speaker. It may also vary according to the time of day and place where you are studying. However, you can increase your attention span by using the following techniques:

1. **Set goals for yourself.** Before you begin to read or study, decide what you intend to accomplish during that session and about how much time it will take. You might write these goals on paper and keep the list in front of you. By having specific goals to meet, you may find that you feel more like working. For an evening of reading or studying, you might write goals like this:

   Complete math problems, page 72

   Revise English paper

   Review psychology notes for Chapters 7 and 8

2. **Read with a purpose.** If you are looking for specific information as you read, it will be easier to keep your attention focused on the material.

3. **Keep a distractions list.** As you are reading, often you will think of something you should remember to do. You might remember that you needed to call your sister or buy a Mother's Day card. An effective solution to this problem is to keep a "To Do" list. Keep a piece of paper nearby, and whenever something distracts you or you are reminded of something, jot it down on the paper. You will find that once you have written the item on paper it will no longer keep flashing through your mind. Your distractions list might look like this:

   Call Sam

   Buy lab manual for chemistry

   Get tire fixed

4. **Vary your reading.** It is easy to tire of reading about a particular subject if you spend too long on it. To overcome this problem, work on several assignments in an evening rather than finishing one assignment completely. The variety in subject matter will provide a needed change and maintain your interest.

5. **Combine physical and mental activities.** Reading is primarily a mental activity. Because the rest of your body is not involved in the reading process, it is easy to become restless or feel a need to *do* something. Activities such as highlighting, underlining, making marginal notes, or writing summary outlines provide an outlet for physical energy and supply useful study aids (see Chapter 9).

6. **Take frequent breaks.** Because your attention span is necessarily limited, take frequent breaks while you are reading. For instance, never decide to sit down and read for a solid three-hour block. After the first hour or so you will tire, begin to lose concentration, and accomplish less and less. For extremely difficult subjects such as foreign languages, take breaks more frequently and study for shorter periods.

7. **Approach your assignment positively.** If you think of a reading assignment as a waste of time, you will have difficulty concentrating. A negative mind-set almost guarantees poor comprehension and concentration. To overcome this, find some way to become interested in the subject. Question or challenge the authors as you read or try to develop questions about the material.

## EXERCISE 2–7

*DIRECTIONS:* Now that you are aware of the factors that influence your concentration, answer the following questions about where and how you are reading this chapter. Your answers will give you an idea of how well you are controlling the factors that influence concentration.

1. Are you reading in a place relatively free of distractions and interruptions?

   _____

2. Are you reading in the same place in which you usually read and study?

   _____

3. Notice what time of day it is. Is this a high or low concentration period? Is it the same time as you usually study?

   _____

4. What is your purpose for reading this chapter?

   _____

5. How long do you expect to spend reading this chapter?

_____

6. How many times has your mind wandered while you were doing this exercise?

_____

## ■ PREREADING AND PREDICTING

Before reading an assignment, it is useful to discover what it is about—prereading—and to anticipate what the material will cover—predicting. Prereading is an active way to approach any reading assignment.

### ■ Prereading

What is the first thing you do as you begin reading a text assignment? If you are like many students, you check to see how long it is and then begin to read. Many students do not realize that they can use a technique before they begin to read that will improve their comprehension and recall. This technique, called prereading, is a way to familiarize yourself quickly with the organization and content of the material. It is one of the easiest techniques to use and it makes a dramatic difference in your reading efficiency. Prereading involves getting a quick impression of what you are going to read before you read it. As a result, you will be able to read faster and follow the author's train of thought more easily. Prereading is similar to looking at a road map before you start out on a drive to an unfamiliar place. The road map, like prereading, gives you an idea of what lies ahead and how it is arranged.

#### How to Preread

When you preread you look only at those parts of the material that tell you what it is about or how it is organized. The portions to look at in reading a textbook chapter are listed here.

1. **Read the title.** Often the title functions as a label and tells you what the material is about. It identifies the overall topic or subject.

2. **Read the introduction or opening paragraphs.** The first few paragraphs of a piece of writing are usually introductory. The author may explain the subject, outline his or her ideas, or give some clues about his or her direction of thought. If the introduction is long, read only the first two or three paragraphs.

3. **Read each boldface heading.** Headings, like titles, serve as labels and identify the content of the material they head. Together, the headings form a mini-outline of the important ideas.

4. **Read the first sentence under each heading.** Although the heading often announces the topic that will be discussed, the first sentence following the heading frequently explains the heading and states the central thought of the passage. In the sample selection, notice that many of the first sentences further explain the heading.

5. **Notice any typographical aids.** The typographical aids include all features of the page that make facts or ideas outstanding or more understandable. These include italics (slanted print), boldface type, marginal notes, colored ink, capitalization, underlining, and enumeration (listing).

6. **Notice any graphs or pictures.** Graphs, charts, and pictures are used for two purposes. First, they emphasize important ideas. Second, they clarify or simplify information and relationships. Therefore they are always important to notice when you are prereading. The easiest way to quickly establish what important element of the text is being further explained by the graph or picture is to read the caption.

7. **Read the last paragraph or summary.** The last paragraph of a chapter often serves as a conclusion or summary. In some chapters, more than one paragraph may be used for this purpose. In some textbooks, these last few paragraphs may be labeled "Summary" or "Conclusion." By reading the summary before reading the chapter you will learn the general focus and content of the material.

Now preread the sample selection titled "Types of Nonverbal Cues." To illustrate how prereading is done, these pages have been specially marked. Everything that you should read has been shaded. After you have preread it, complete the quiz contained in Exercise 2–8.

## TYPES OF NONVERBAL CUES

Let's look more closely at these cues that tell others about us or that tell us about them. Our own self-awareness and empathic skills will increase as we become more sensitive to different kinds of nonverbal cues. The broader our base of understanding, the more likely we are to be able to interpret the cues we perceive. But we know that nonverbal communication can be ambiguous, and we must be careful not to overgeneralize from the behavior we observe. We may feel hurt by the listless "Hi" we receive from a good friend unless we remember that that listlessness could have been brought on by a headache, lack of sleep, preoccupation, or some other factor we don't know about. We would be unwise to assume we are being personally rejected if this friend doesn't smile and stop to talk with us every single morning.

We should always be alert to *all* cues and try to get as much information as possible on which to base our conclusions. One way to organize our thinking about nonverbal communication is to think in terms of spatial cues, visual cues, and vocal cues. In considering each of these, we should not overlook the fact that any communication occurs in a specific environmental setting. This setting influences much of the nonverbal interaction that takes place. The weather can affect how we behave just as much as the actual setting—cafeteria, classroom, car, park bench, or wherever.

## SPATIAL CUES

Spatial cues are the distances we choose to stand or sit from others. Each of us carries with us something called "informal space." We might think of this as a bubble; we occupy the center of the bubble. This bubble expands or contracts depending on varying conditions and circumstances such as the

Age and sex of those involved
Cultural and ethnic background of the participants
Topic or subject matter
Setting for the interaction
Physical characteristics of the participants (size or shape)
Attitudinal and emotional orientation of partners
Characteristics of the interpersonal relationship (like friendship)
Personality characteristics of those involved

In his book *The Silent Language,* Edward T. Hall, a cultural anthropologist, identifies the distances that we assume when we talk with others. He calls these distances intimate, personal, social, and public. In many cases, the adjustments that occur in these distances result from some of the factors listed above.

### Intimate Distance

At an *intimate distance* (0 to 18 inches), we often use a soft or barely audible whisper to share intimate or confidential information. Physical contact becomes easy at this distance. This is the distance we use for physical comforting, lovemaking, and physical fighting, among other things.

### Personal Distance

Hall identified the range of 18 inches to 4 feet as *personal distance.* When we disclose ourselves to someone, we are likely to do it within this distance. The topics we discuss at this range may be somewhat confidential, and usually are personal and mutually involving. At personal distance we are still able to touch each other if we want to. This is likely to be the distance between people conversing at a party, between classmates in a casual conversation, or within many work relationships. This distance assumes a well-established acquaintanceship. This is probably the most comfortable distance for free exchange of feedback.

### Social Distance

When we are talking at a normal level with another person, sharing concerns that are not of a personal nature, we usually use the *social distance* (4 to 12 feet). Many of our on-the-job conversations take place at this distance. Seating arrangements in living rooms may be based on "conversation groups" of chairs placed at a distance of 4 to 7 feet from each other. Hall calls 4 to 7 feet the close phase of social distance; from 7 to 12 feet is the far phase of social distance.

The greater the distance, the more formal the business or social discourse conducted is likely to be. Often, the desks of important people are broad enough to hold visitors at a distance of 7 to 12 feet. Eye contact at this distance becomes more important to the flow of communication; without visual contact one party is likely to feel shut out and the conversation may come to a halt.

### Public Distance

*Public distance* (12 feet and farther) is well outside the range for close involvement with another person. It is impractical for interpersonal communication. We are limited to what we can see and hear at that distance; topics for conversation are relatively impersonal and formal; and most of the communication that occurs is in the public-speaking style, with subjects planned in advance and limited opportunities for feedback. . . .

## VISUAL CUES

Greater visibility increases our potential for communicating because the more we see and the more we can be seen, the more information we can send and receive. Mehrabian found that the more we direct our face toward the person we're talking to, the more we convey a positive feeling to this person. Another researcher has confirmed something most of us discovered long ago, that looking directly at a person, smiling, and leaning toward him or her conveys a feeling of warmth.

### Facial Expression

The face is probably the most expressive part of the human body. It can reveal complex and often confusing kinds of information. It commands attention because it is visible and omnipresent. It can move from signs of ecstasy to signs of despair in less than a second. Research results suggest that there are ten basic classes of meaning that can be communicated facially: happiness, surprise, fear, anger, sadness, disgust, contempt, interest, bewilderment, and determination. Research has also shown that the face may communicate information other than the emotional state of the person—it may reveal the thought processes as well. In addition, it has been shown that we are capable of facially conveying not just a single emotional state but multiple emotions at the same time. . . .

### Eye Contact

A great deal can be conveyed through the eyes. If we seek feedback from another person, we usually maintain strong eye contact. We can open and close communication channels with our eyes as well. Think of a conversation involving more than two people. . .

### The Body

The body reinforces facial communication. But gestures, postures, and other body movements can also communicate attitudes. They can reveal differences in status, and they can also indicate the presence of deception. With respect to attitudes, as noted previously, body movements also reveal feelings of liking between people.

According to some investigators, a person who wants to be perceived as warm should shift his or her posture toward the other person, smile, maintain direct eye contact, and keep the hands still. People who are cold tend to look around, slump, drum their fingers, and, generally, refrain from smiling. . . .

### Personal Appearance

Even if we believe the cliché that beauty is only skin-deep, we must recognize that not only does our personal appearance have a profound effect on our self-image, but it also affects our behavior and the behavior of people around us. Our physical appearance provides a basis for first and sometimes long-lasting impressions. . . .

## EXERCISE 2–8

*DIRECTIONS:* Complete this exercise after you have preread the selection titled "Types of Nonverbal Cues." For each item, indicate whether the statement is true or false by marking "T" or "F" in the space provided.

_____ 1. Spatial cues refer to the manner and posture in which we sit or stand.

_____ 2. Nonverbal communication is sometimes ambiguous or unclear.

_____ 3. The social distance is used for nonpersonal conversations.

_____ 4. Voices are slightly louder and higher pitched in the intimate distance.

_____ 5. The distance in which people are farthest apart is the social distance.

_____ 6. Hands are the most expressive part of the body.

_____ 7. The author discusses four types of distance.

_____ 8. Personal distance can affect the behavior of other people.

_____ 9. Visual cues are provided by facial expression, eye contact, personal appearance, and body movement.

_____ 10. Gesture and posture provide important nonverbal cues.

Did you score 80 percent or higher on the exercise? You may have noticed that it did not test you on specific facts and details. Rather, the questions provided a fairly accurate measure of your recall of the *main ideas* of the selection. If you scored 80 percent or above, your prereading was successful because it acquainted you with most of the major ideas contained in the selection.

This exercise suggests that prereading provides you with a great deal of information about the overall content of the article before you read it. It allows you to become familiar with the main ideas and acquaints you with the basic structure of the material.

### Adapting Prereading to Various Types of Materials

If the key to becoming a flexible reader lies in adapting techniques to fit the material and your learning style, the key to successful prereading is the same. You must adjust the way you preread to the type of material you are working with. Here are a few suggestions to help you make these adjustments. These suggestions are summarized in Table 2.5.

**Table 2.5** How to Adjust Prereading to the Material

| Type of Material | Special Features to Consider |
| --- | --- |
| Textbooks | Title and subtitle<br>Preface<br>Table of contents<br>Appendix<br>Glossary |
| Textbook chapters | Summary<br>Vocabulary list<br>Review and discussion questions |
| Articles and essays | Title<br>Introductory paragraphs<br>Concluding paragraphs (see Chapter 6) |
| Articles without headings | First sentences of paragraphs |
| Tests and exams | Instructions and directions<br>Number of items<br>Types of questions<br>Point distribution |
| Internet Web site | Title<br>Features listed on home page<br>Links (see Chapter 7)<br>Sponsor |

### Why Prereading Is Effective

Prereading is effective because it

1. **Helps you become interested and involved with what you will read.**

2. **Gives you basic information about the organization and content of the article.**

3. **Focuses your attention on the content of the article.**

4. **Allows you to read somewhat faster because the material is familiar.**

5. **Provides you with a mental outline of the material.** You can anticipate the sequence of ideas, see relationships among topics, and follow the author's direction of thought. Also, reading becomes a process of completing or expanding the outline by identifying supporting details.

## EXERCISE 2–9

*DIRECTIONS:* Working with another student, choose three of the materials from the following list. Discuss how you would adapt your prereading technique to suit the material.

1. a front page newspaper article
2. a poem
3. a short story
4. a mathematics textbook
5. a newspaper editorial or letter to the editor
6. a new edition of your college catalog
7. a sales brochure from a local department store

## EXERCISE 2–10

*DIRECTIONS:* Select a chapter from one of your textbooks and preread it, using the guidelines included in this chapter. Then answer the following questions.

Textbook title: _____

Chapter title: _____

1. What general subject does the chapter discuss?

   _____

2. How does the textbook author approach or divide the subject?

   _____

3. What special features does the chapter contain to aid you in learning the content of the chapter?

_____

4. What are the major topics discussed in this chapter?

_____

## ■ Predicting

When you see a movie preview, you make a number of judgments and predictions. You decide what the film will be about, how it will achieve its cinematic goals, and whether or not you want to see it. To do this, you anticipate or make predictions based on the preview. For example, you may predict that the film will be violent and frightening or sentimental and romantic. You might also predict how the film will develop or how it will end. You use your life experience and your experience with other films to make those predictions.

Prereading is similar to watching a film preview. After prereading you should be able to make predictions about the content and organization of the material and make connections with what you already know about the topic.

### *Making Predictions*

Predictions are educated guesses about the material to be read. For example, you might predict an essay's focus, a chapter's method of development, or the key points to be presented within a chapter section. Table 2.6 presents examples of predictions that may be made.

You make predictions based on your experience with written language, your background knowledge, and your familiarity with the subject. As you work through remaining chapters in this text, you will become more familiar with the organization of written materials, and your ability to make predictions will improve.

To get started making predictions, keep the following questions in mind:

- What clues does the author give?

- What will this material be about?

- What logically would follow?

- How could this be organized?

**Table 2.6** Sample Predictions

| Title | Prediction |
|---|---|
| Highlights of Marketing Research History | An overview of the history of market research will be presented. |
| Why Do Hot Dogs Come in Packs of 10? | Packaging of products and profitability will be discussed. |
| A Sample Fast Food Promotional Plan | A fast food chain will be used as an example to show how fast food restaurants promote (sell) their products. |

| Opening Sentence | Prediction |
|---|---|
| Marketers have been the objects of criticism from several consumer groups as well as from governmental agencies. | The section will discuss consumer groups' objections first, then governmental objections. |
| The situations and problems consumers face directly influence their purchasing behavior. | The section will give examples of situations and problems and explain why or how purchasing behavior is affected. |
| The key to determining a product's demand is the estimation of the total market and its anticipated share. | The section will explain this process. |

## EXERCISE 2–11

*DIRECTIONS:* Predict the content or organization of each of the following textbook chapter headings taken from a sociology textbook.

1. Inequality in the United States

   _____

2. Nontraditional Marital and Family Lifestyles

   _____

3. The Development of Religious Movements

   _____

4. Education and Change in the 1980s

   _____

5. The Automobile, the Assembly Line, and Social Change

   _____

6. Health Care Systems in Other Countries

   _____

7. Computers in the Schools

   _____

8. Sociology and the Other Sciences

_____

9. The Consequences of Sexual Inequality

_____

10. What Is Religion?

_____

### *Making Connections*

Once you have preread an assignment and predicted its content and organization, an important next step is to call to mind what you already know about the subject. Do this by making connections between the material to be read and your background knowledge and experience.

There are several reasons for making such connections:

1. **Learning occurs more easily if you can relate new information to information already stored.**

2. **Tasks become more interesting and meaningful if you can connect them to your own experience or to a subject you have already learned.**

3. **Material is easier to learn if it is familiar and meaningful.** For example, it is easier to learn a list of real words (sat, tar, can) than a list of nonsense syllables (sar, taf, cag). Similarly, it is easier to learn basic laws of economics if you have examples from your experience with which to associate them.

Search your previous knowledge and experience for ideas or information that you can connect the new material to in an assignment. You might think of this process as tying a mental string between already stored information and new information. As you pull out or recall old information you will find that you also recall new information.

Here are a few examples of the kinds of connections students have made:

- "This chapter section is titled Stages of Adulthood—it should be interesting to see which one I'm in and which my parents are in."

- "I'll be reading about types of therapy for treating mental problems. I remember hearing about the group therapy sessions my aunt attended after her divorce. . . ."

- "This chapter is titled "Genetics"—I wonder if it will discuss chromosome mapping or sickle-cell anemia?"

To draw on your prior knowledge and experience for less familiar subjects, think about the subject using one of the following techniques:

1. **Ask as many questions as you can about the topic and attempt to answer them.**

2. **Divide the subject into as many features or subtopics as possible.**

3. **Free associate or write down anything that comes to mind related to the topic.**

Each of these techniques is demonstrated in Figure 2.1. Although the results differ, each technique forces you to think, draw from your experience, and focus your attention.

Which technique you use depends on the subject matter you are working with and on your learning style. Dividing a subject into subtopics may

## Topic: The Immune System

| Technique | Demonstration |
|---|---|
| Asking questions | How does the immune system work?<br>What does it do?<br>What happens when it does not work?<br>Are there other diseases, similar to AIDS, yet undiscovered?<br>Does stress affect the immune system?<br>Does diet affect the immune system? |
| Dividing into subtopics | Diseases of immune system<br>Operation<br>Functions<br>Effects<br>Limitations |
| Free association | The immune system protects the body from disease and infection.<br>It attacks body invaders and destroys them.<br>When illness occurs the immune system has failed. AIDS is a disease affecting the immune system.<br>Stress may affect the body's defenses. |

**FIGURE 2.1**  Techniques for activating your knowledge.

*not* work well for an essay in philosophy but may be effective for reading about television programming. Likewise, free association may work well for a creative learner, while dividing into subtopics may be more effective for a more pragmatic learner.

## EXERCISE 2–12

*DIRECTIONS:* Assume you have preread a chapter in a sociology text on domestic violence. Discover what you already know about domestic violence by writing a list of questions about the topic.

## EXERCISE 2–13

*DIRECTIONS:*
*STEP 1:* Preread one of the readings at the end of the chapter. Activate your previous knowledge and experience by

1. Dividing the subject into subtopics.
2. Writing a list of questions about the topic.
3. Writing for two minutes about the topic, recording whatever comes to mind.

*STEP 2:* Evaluate each of the techniques used in step 1 by answering the following questions:

1. Which technique seemed most effective? Why?
2. Might your choice of technique be influenced by the subject matter with which you are working?
3. Did you discover you knew more about the topic than you initially thought?

## EXERCISE 2–14

*DIRECTIONS:* Connect each of the following headings, taken from a psychology text, with your own knowledge or experience. Discuss or summarize what you already know about each subject.

1. Pain and Its Control
2. Television and Aggressive Behavior
3. Problems of Aging
4. Sources of Stress
5. Eating Disorders

Electronic Application

## EXERCISE 2–15

*DIRECTIONS:* Locate a Website for one of the following:

1. a college or university
2. a newspaper
3. a radio station or television network

Preview the site and write a list of what you think the site offers.

## ■ DEVELOPING GUIDE QUESTIONS

When you order a hamburger, go to the bank, or make a phone call, you have a specific purpose in mind. In fact, most of your daily activities are purposeful; you do things for specific reasons to accomplish some goal.

Reading should also be a purposeful activity. Before you begin reading any article, selection, or chapter, you should know what you want to accomplish by reading it. Your purpose should vary with the situation. You might read a magazine article on child abuse to learn more about the extent of the problem. You may read a sociology text chapter to locate facts and figures about the causes, effects, and extent of child abuse. Your purpose for reading should be as specific as possible. One of the best ways to develop specific purposes is to form guide questions.

### ■ How to Develop Guide Questions

Guide questions can be formed by turning the chapter or essay titles and headings into questions that you try to answer as you read. For instance, for a chapter from a sociology text titled "Methods of Studying Society," you could ask, "What are the methods of studying society?" As you read the chapter, look for the answer. Here are a few other titles or headings and questions that you might ask.

Title:       Our 10 Contributions to Civilization
Question:    What are our 10 contributions to civilization?

Title:       Bringing Science Under the Law
Questions:   How can science be brought under the law?
             Why should science be brought under the law?

Heading:     Unequal Distribution of Income
Question:    Why is income unequally distributed?

Heading:     The Life Cycle of Social Problems
Questions:   What are the stages in the life cycle of social problems?
             What social problems have a life cycle?

Heading:     The Development of the Women's Movement
Questions:   How did the women's movement develop?
             Why did it develop?

### ■ Asking the Right Guide Questions

To put guide questions to their best use, you must ask the right questions. Questions that begin with *what, why,* or *how* are useful because they usually require you to think or to consolidate information and ideas. Questions that begin with *who, when,* or *where* are less useful because they can often be answered in a word or two; they often refer to a specific fact or detail rather than to larger ideas or concepts. For a section titled "Treatment for Drug Abuse Conditions" you could ask, "Where does treatment take place?" or, "Who is treated for drug abuse?" Most likely these questions would not lead you to the main point of the section. However, a question such as "How is drug abuse treated?" would focus your attention on the main topic discussed.

## EXERCISE 2–16

*DIRECTIONS:* For each of the following titles or headings, write a guide question that would be useful in guiding your reading of the material.

1. We Ask the Wrong Questions About Crime

   _____

2. The Constitution: New Challenges

   _____

3. Political Party Functions

   _____

4. The Thinking of Men and Machines

   _____

5. Ghana and Zimbabwe—A Study in Contrasts

   _____

6. Magnetic Fields and Lines of Force

   _____

7. Comparing X-Rays and Visible Light

   _____

## EXERCISE 2–17

*DIRECTIONS:* Select a chapter from one of your textbooks that you are about to read. Write a guide question for each title and major heading. After you have used these questions to guide your reading, identify the weak questions and rephrase them in a way that would have been more useful to you.

## ■ MONITORING YOUR COMPREHENSION

Have you ever read an assignment only to realize later, perhaps much later during an exam, that you did not really understand it? Or have you ever spent your time supposedly reading several pages or more, only to discover later that you really understood very little? If so, you can develop a very important and useful skill to overcome these problems. It is known as *cognitive monitoring,* and it means keeping track or being aware of what is happening mentally as you read. In cognitive monitoring you stay aware of your level of understanding by picking up clues or signals that indicate whether you are understanding what you are reading.

Think for a moment about what occurs when you read material you can understand easily. Then compare this feeling with what happens when you read complicated material that is difficult for you to understand. When you read certain material, does it seem that everything "clicks"? Do ideas seem to fit together and make sense? At other times is that "click" noticeably absent?

Read each of the following paragraphs. As you read, be alert to your level of understanding of each.

### PARAGRAPH 1

The two most common drugs that are legal and do not require a prescription are caffeine and nicotine. *Caffeine* is the active ingredient in coffee, tea, and many cola drinks. It stimulates the central nervous system and heart and therefore is often used to stay awake. Heavy use—say, seven to ten cups of coffee per day—has toxic effects, acting like a mild poison. Prolonged heavy use appears to be addicting. *Nicotine* is the active ingredient in tobacco. One of the most addicting of all drugs and one of the most dangerous, at least when obtained by smoking, it has been implicated in lung cancer, emphysema, and heart disease.

Geiwitz, *Psychology: Looking at Ourselves.*

### PARAGRAPH 2

In the HOSC experiment, two variables were of sufficient importance to include as stratification (classification) variables prior to the random assignment of class sections to treatments. These two stratification variables were science subject (biology, chemistry, or physics) and teacher's understanding of science (high or low). Inclusion of these two variables in the HOSC design allowed the experimenter to make generalizations about the HOSC treatment in terms of science subject matter and the teacher's understanding of science. Even if the HOSC experiments had selected a completely random sample of American high school science teacher-class sections, generalizations regarding the effectiveness of the HOSC treatment would only be possible in terms of the factors included in the experimental design. . . .

Lohnes and Cooley, *Introduction to Statistical Procedures.*

● ● ●

Most likely, as you read Paragraph 1, everything seemed to fit together and make sense. Ideas led from one to another; you could easily follow the author's train of thought. While reading Paragraph 2 you may have experienced difficulty and confusion. You realized that ideas weren't making sense. Unfamiliar words were used and unfamiliar concepts were discussed; consequently, you could not see the flow of ideas.

## ■ Recognizing Comprehension Signals

The two examples were quite clear-cut: In one case understanding was easy; in the other it was difficult. In many situations, however, the distinction between understanding and the lack of it is not as clear. As you learned in Chapter 1, your comprehension depends on numerous factors; it may vary from high to low even with a single piece of material. In those cases, you have to pick up on more subtle clues or signals. Table 2.7 lists

**Table 2.7** Comprehension Signals

| *Positive Signals* | *Negative Signals* |
| --- | --- |
| Everything seems to fit and make sense; ideas flow logically from one to another | Some pieces do not seem to belong; the material seems disjointed |
| You are able to see where the author is leading | You feel as if you are struggling to stay with the author and are unable to think ahead |
| You are able to make connections and see patterns of thought developing | You are unable to detect relationships; the organization is not apparent |
| You read at a regular pace without slowing down or rereading | You need to reread frequently and you make frequent regressions (see Chapter 6) |
| You understand why the material was assigned | You do not know why the material was assigned and cannot explain why it is important |
| You feel comfortable and have some knowledge about the topic | The topic is unfamiliar, yet the author assumes you understand it |
| You recognize most words or can figure them out from context | Many words are unfamiliar |
| You can express the main ideas in your own words | You must reread and use the author's language to explain an idea |
| You read at a regular, comfortable pace | You often slow down or reread |
| You understand what is important | Nothing or everything seems important |

and compares some common signals that may assist you in monitoring your comprehension. Not all signals must appear at the same time, and not all signals work for everyone.

## EXERCISE 2–18

*DIRECTIONS:* Select a two- to three-page section from one of your textbooks or choose one of the readings at the end of the chapter. As you read it, monitor your level of understanding. After reading the material, answer the following questions.

1. In what sections was your comprehension strongest?

   _____

2. Did you feel at any time that you had lost, or were about to lose, comprehension? If so, go back to that section now. What made the section difficult to read?

   _____

3. Analyze any sections where you slowed down or reread. Why was this necessary?

   _____

4. How did you connect the content with your background knowledge and experience?

   _____

### ■ Correcting Incomplete Comprehension

Once you recognize clues that signal your level of understanding, you will find situations where you are not comprehending as well as you should. When this happens, try the following:

1. **Analyze the time and place in which you are reading.** If you've been reading or studying for several hours, mental fatigue may be the source of the problem. If you are reading in a place with numerous distractions or interruptions, lack of concentration may contribute to comprehension loss.

2. **Rephrase each paragraph in your own words.** For extremely complicated material, you might approach it sentence-by-sentence, expressing each in your own words.

**Critical Thinking Tip #2**

**Developing a Questioning Mind-Set**

Guide questions help you identify what is important to learn and remember, but they are not the only type of questions you should ask. It is also useful to ask critical questions—questions that will help you analyze and interpret what you read. Here are a few critical questions that will help you develop a critical mind-set.

1. What does the writer expect me to understand or believe after reading this?
2. What is the writer leading up to? (What ideas will come next?)
3. How much and what kind of evidence does the writer offer in support of his or her ideas?
4. Why is this idea important?
5. How does this information fit with other things I'm learning?
6. How can I use this information?

3. **Read aloud sentences or sections that are particularly difficult.** The auditory feedback signals that oral reading provides often aid comprehension.

4. **Write a brief outline of the major points of the article.** This will help you to see the overall organization and progression of ideas in the material. (Chapter 9 discusses outlining and summary notes in greater detail.)

5. **Do not hesitate to reread difficult or complicated sections.** In fact, at times several rereadings are appropriate and necessary.

6. **Highlight important ideas.** After you've read a section, go back and think about and **highlight** what is important. **Highlight** forces you to sort out what is important, and this sorting process facilitates overall comprehension and recall. (See Chapter 9 for suggestions about how to **highlight** effectively.)

7. **Slow down your reading rate if you feel you're beginning to lose comprehension.** On occasion simply reading more slowly will provide the needed boost in comprehension.

8. **Summarize.** Test your recall by summarizing each section after you have read it.

If none of these suggestions is effective, you may be lacking the necessary background knowledge that a particular writer assumes the reader has.

If you feel you are lacking background knowledge in a particular discipline or about a particular topic, take immediate steps to correct the problem. You might:

1. **Obtain a more basic text from the library that reviews basic principles and concepts.**

2. **Review several encyclopedia entries and other reference sources to obtain an overview of the subject.**

3. **Ask your instructor to suggest reference sources, guidebooks, or review books that will be helpful.**

## SUMMARY

**1. What is involved in reading and learning actively?**

Reading and learning actively means becoming engaged in the material you are reading and studying. It involves the activities of reading, thinking, predicting, connecting, focusing your concentration, knowing how you learn best, and assessing your performance.

**2. What does active reading mean?**

Active reading is a process of staying focused on the material you are reading before, during, and after the reading of it. It means participating consciously and directly in the reading process.

**3. What academic thinking skills do your instructors expect you to possess?**

Your instructors expect you to function at six different levels of thinking. They not only expect you to understand ideas that involve:
- Knowledge—recalling information or facts.
- Comprehension—grasping the meaning of facts.

They also expect:
- Application—using knowledge in new situations.
- Analysis—seeing relationships among ideas and how things work.
- Synthesis—putting ideas together to form something new.
- Evaluation—making judgments about ideas

**4. Why are prereading and predicting useful activities?**

Prereading allows you to become familiar with the organization and content of the material before reading it, providing you with a "road map" to guide you through the material. Predicting helps you to discover what you already know about a topic and to connect this with the material to be read.

**5. How are guide questions helpful?**

Guide questions enable you to establish purposes for reading. They focus your attention and improve your retention.

**6. What is the purpose of comprehension monitoring?**

Comprehension monitoring helps you keep track of your comprehension while reading. By recognizing positive and negative comprehension signals you will be aware of your level of comprehension and will be able to correct incomplete comprehension.

**7. What is involved in learning actively?**

Learning actively involves an awareness of your level of concentration and your particular learning style. You can improve your concentration by controlling external distractions and increasing your attention span. Assessing your learning style will not only help you see how you learn best but can help you build an action plan for more effective learning.

PSYCHOLOGY

## READING SELECTION 3
### PROBLEM SOLVING

Josh R. Gerow
From *Essentials of Psychology*

*This psychology textbook excerpt discusses problem-solving strategies. Activate your thinking by prereading and answering the following questions.*

*1. How would you define a problem? What are its characteristics?*

*2. What steps do you follow in working through a problem?*

1　　Sometimes our goals are obvious, our present situation is clear, and how to get from where we are to where we want to be is obvious. In these cases, we really don't have a problem, do we? Say you want to have a nice breakfast. You have butter, eggs, bacon, and bread. You also have the implements needed to prepare these foods, and you know how to use them. You know that, for you, a nice breakfast would be two eggs over easy, three strips of fried bacon, and a piece of buttered toast. With little hesitation, you can engage in the appropriate behaviors to reach your goal.

2   A problem exists when there is a discrepancy between one's present state and one's perceived goal, *and* there is no readily apparent way to get from one to the other. In situations where the path to goal attainment is not clear or obvious, you need to engage in problem-solving behaviors.

3   A problem situation has three major components: (1) an *initial state,* which is the situation as it is perceived to exist at the moment; (2) a *goal state,* which is the situation as the problem solver would like it to be; and (3) *routes or strategies* for getting from the initial state to the goal state.

*These students are faced with an ill-defined problem: "What should I choose as a college major?"*

4   In addition, psychologists make a distinction between well-defined and ill-defined problems. Well-defined problems are those in which both the initial state and the goal state are clearly defined. "What English word can be made from the letters *teralbay?*" We recognize this question as presenting a problem. We understand the question, have some ideas about how we might go about answering it, and surely we'll know when we have succeeded. "How do you get home from campus if you discover that your car won't start?" We know our initial state, we'll know when we have reached our goal (when we are at home), but we have to undertake a new or different way to get there.

5   Most of the problems that we face every day, though, are of the ill-defined variety. We don't have a clear idea of what we are starting with, nor are we able to identify a ready solution. "What should my college major be?" Many high school seniors (and some college seniors) do not even know what their options are. They have few ideas about how to find out about possible college majors. And once they have selected a major, they are not at all sure that their choice was the best one—which may be why so many college students change their majors so often.

6   Because ill-defined problems usually involve many variables that are difficult to define, much less control, psychologists tend to study problems that are at least reasonably well-defined.

## Problem Representation

7   Once we realize that we're faced with a problem, the first thing we need to do is to put it in a form that allows us to think about it in terms that we can work with. We need to come up with a way to *represent* the problem in our own minds, interpreting it so that the initial state and the goal state are clear to us. We also need to note if there are restrictions on how we can go about seeking solutions. In short, we need to understand the nature of the problem. We need to

make the problem meaningful, relating it to information we have available in our memories.

8 Finding the best way to represent a problem is not a simple task. Very often, problem representation is *the* stumbling block to finding a solution (Bourne, et al., 1983). Once you realize that you are faced with a problem, your first step should be to represent it in a variety of ways. Eliminate any inessential information. Relate the problem to other problems of a similar type that you have solved before. Having done so, if the solution is still not obvious, you may have to develop some strategy to find a solution. We now turn to how one might go about generating possible solutions.

## Problem-Solving Strategies

9 Once you have represented the initial state of a problem and have a clear idea of what an acceptable goal might be, you still have to figure out how to get to your goal. Even after you have adequately represented a problem, how to go about solving it may not be readily apparent. You might spend a few minutes guessing wildly at a solution, but soon you'll have to settle on some strategy. In this context, a strategy is a systematic plan for generating possible solutions that can be tested to see if they are correct. The main advantage of cognitive strategies appears to be that they permit the problem solver to exercise some degree of control over the task at hand. They allow individuals to choose the skills and knowledge that they will bring to bear on any particular problem (Gagné, 1984). There are several possible strategies that one might choose. In this section, we'll consider two different types of strategies—algorithms and heuristics.

10 An algorithm is a problem-solving strategy that guarantees that you will arrive at a solution. It will involve systematically exploring and evaluating all possible solutions until the correct one is found. It is sometimes referred to as a *generate-test* strategy because one generates hypotheses about potential solutions and then tests each one in

turn. Because of their speed of computation, most computer programs designed to solve problems use algorithmic strategies.

11 Simple anagram problems (letters of a word presented in a scrambled fashion) can be solved using an algorithm. "What English word has been scrambled to make *uleb*?" With sufficient patience, you systematically can rearrange these four letters until you hit on a correct solution: *leub, lueb, elub, uleb, buel, beul, blue!* There it is, *blue*. With only four letters to deal with, finding a solution generally doesn't take long—there are only 24 possible arrangements of four letters (4333231524).

12 On the other hand, consider the anagram composed of eight letters that we mentioned earlier: *teralbay*. There are 40,320 possible combinations of these eight letters—837363534333231540,320 (Reynolds & Flagg, 1983). Unless your system for moving letters around just happens to start in a good place, you could spend a lot of time before finding a combination that produces an English word. If we were dealing with a 10-letter word, there would be 3,628,800 possible combinations to check.

13 Imagine that you go to the supermarket to find just one item: a small jar of horseradish. You're sure the store has horseradish, but you have no idea where to find it. One plan would be to systematically go up and down every aisle of the store, checking first the top shelf, then the second, then the third, until you spied the horseradish. This strategy will work *if* the store really does carry horseradish *and if* you search carefully. There must be a better way to solve such problems. We could use some heuristic strategy.

14 A heuristic strategy is an informal, rule-of-thumb method for generating and testing problem solutions. Heuristics are more economical strategies than algorithms. When one uses a heuristic, there is no guarantee of success. On the other hand, heuristics are usually less time-consuming than algorithm strategies and lead toward goals in a logical, sensible way.

15 A heuristic strategy for finding horseradish in a supermarket might take you to different sections

in the store in the order you believed to be most reasonable. You might start with spices, and you'd be disappointed. You might look among the fresh vegetables. Then, upon recalling that horseradish needs to be refrigerated, you go to the dairy case, and there you'd find the horseradish. You would not have wasted your time searching the cereal aisle or the frozen food section—which you might have done if you tried an algorithmic search. Another, more reasonable, heuristic would be to ask an employee where the horseradish is kept.

16    If you have tried the *teralbay* anagram problem, you probably used a heuristic strategy. To do so, you rely on your knowledge of English.

You seriously consider only those letter combinations that you know occur frequently. You generate and test the most common combinations first. You just don't worry much about the possibility that the solution may contain a combination like *brty.* Nor do you search for a word with an *aae* string in it. You explore words that end in *able,* because you know these to be fairly common. But that doesn't work. What about *br* words? No, that doesn't work either. How about words with the combination *tray* in them? *Traybeal?* No. *Baletray?* No. "Oh! Now I see it: betrayal."

## Comprehension Test 3

*Directions:   Circle the letter of the best answer.*

**Checking Your Comprehension**

1. This reading is primarily concerned with
   a. types of problems
   b. the heuristics of problem solving
   c. the process of problem solving
   d. algorithms and heuristics

2. The main point of this reading is that problem solving
   a. depends largely on intuition
   b. is a random process
   c. is a systematic, logical process
   d. varies according to an individual's cognitive style

3. According to the reading, a problem can best be defined as
   a. being unable to make reasonable choices
   b. an unresolved or undefinable issue
   c. a conflict among strategies
   d. a discrepancy between present state and goal state

4. An algorithmic strategy is a process of
   a. brainstorming possible solutions
   b. generating and testing all possible solutions
   c. distinguishing initial state from goal state
   d. devising a systematic plan for problem solving

5. Ill-defined problems
   a. cannot be represented
   b. have no solutions
   c. are always solved in a similar way as well-defined problems
   d. usually involve many variables

6. As used in the reading, the word *generates* in paragraph 9 can best be defined as
   a. represents
   b. produces
   c. explores
   d. determines

**Thinking Critically**

7. A heuristic strategy differs from an algorithmic solution in that
   a. an algorithmic solution does not guarantee a solution
   b. a heuristic system explores fewer possible solutions
   c. a heuristic strategy is more systematic
   d. an algorithmic strategy is less time consuming

8. Searching for your lost car keys by checking places where you usually place them is an example of
   a. problem representation
   b. an ill-defined problem
   c. an algorithmic solution
   d. a heuristic solution

9. Which of the following words best describes the author's attitude toward his subject?
   a. casual
   b. respectful
   c. indifferent
   d. serious

10. The writer relies on which of the following to explain his ideas to the reader?
    a. examples
    b. comparisons
    c. statistics
    d. personal experiences

**Questions for Discussion**

1. Give an example of a well-defined problem faced by the government today. Explain a strategy that could be used to resolve it.

2. Discuss why a heuristic solution to a problem you currently have is more economical than an algorithmic solution.

3. Think about a problem you've had with transportation. How could it have been solved using an algorithmic strategy? How could it have been solved using a heuristic strategy?

| Selection 3: | 1514 words |
|---|---|
| Finishing Time: | _____ _____ _____ |
| | HR. MIN. SEC. |
| Starting Time: | _____ _____ _____ |
| | HR. MIN. SEC. |
| Reading Time: | _____ _____ |
| | MIN. SEC. |
| WPM Score: | _____ |
| Comprehension Score: | _____ % |

# READING SELECTION 4
## JUST WALK ON BY: A BLACK MAN PONDERS HIS POWER TO ALTER PUBLIC SPACE

Brent Staples
From *MS magazine*

*Brent Staples, a well-known black writer, describes how others respond to him in a variety of situations. Activate prereading and then read the essay to answer the following questions.*

*1. What stereotypes exist for black males?*
*2. How did Staples confront and overcome this stereotype?*

1   My first victim was a woman—white, well dressed, probably in her early twenties. I came upon her late one evening on a deserted street in Hyde Park, a relatively affluent neighborhood in an otherwise mean, impoverished section of Chicago. As I swung onto the avenue behind her, there seemed to be a discreet, uninflammatory distance between us. Not so. She cast back a worried glance. To her, the youngish black man—a broad six feet two inches with a beard and billowing hair, both hands shoved into the pockets of a bulky military jacket—seemed menacingly close. After a few more quick glimpses, she picked up her pace and was soon running in earnest. Within seconds she disappeared into a cross street.

2   That was more than a decade ago. I was twenty-two years old, a graduate student newly arrived at the University of Chicago. It was in the echo of that terrified woman's footfalls that I first began to know the unwieldy inheritance I'd come into—the ability to alter public space in ugly ways. It was clear that she thought herself the quarry of a mugger, a rapist, or worse. Suffering a bout of insomnia, however, I was stalking sleep, not defenseless wayfarers. As a softy who is scarcely able to take a knife to a raw chicken—let alone hold it to a person's throat—

I was surprised, embarrassed, and dismayed all at once. Her flight made me feel like an accomplice in tyranny. It also made it clear that I was indistinguishable from the muggers who occasionally seeped into the area from the surrounding ghetto. That first encounter, and those that followed, signified that a vast, unnerving gulf lay between nighttime pedestrians—particularly women—and me. And I soon gathered that being perceived as dangerous is a hazard in itself. I only needed to turn a corner into a dicey situation, or crowd some frightened, armed person in a foyer somewhere, or make an errant move after being pulled over by a policeman. Where fear and weapons meet—and they often do in urban America—there is always the possibility of death.

3   In that first year, my first away from my hometown, I was to become thoroughly familiar with the language of fear. At dark, shadowy intersections in Chicago, I could cross in front of a car stopped at a traffic light and elicit the *thunk, thunk, thunk, thunk* of the driver—black, white, male, or female—hammering down the door locks. On less traveled streets after dark, I grew accustomed to but never comfortable with people who crossed to the other side of the street rather than pass me. Then there were the standard unpleasantries with police, doormen, bouncers, cab drivers, and others whose business it is to screen out troublesome individuals *before* there is any nastiness.

4   I moved to New York nearly two years ago and I have remained an avid night walker. In central Manhattan, the near-constant crowd cover minimizes tense one-on-one street encounters. Elsewhere—visiting friends in SoHo, where sidewalks are narrow and tightly spaced buildings

shut out the sky—things can get very taut indeed.

5    Black men have a firm place in New York mugging literature. Norman Podhoretz in his famed (or infamous) 1963 essay, "My Negro Problem—And Ours," recalls growing up in terror of black males; they "were tougher than we were, more ruthless," he writes—and as an adult on the Upper West Side of Manhattan, he continues, he cannot constrain his nervousness when he meets black men on certain streets. Similarly, a decade later, the essayist and novelist Edward Hoagland extols a New York where once "Negro bitterness bore down mainly on other Negroes." Where some see mere panhandlers, Hoagland sees "a mugger who is clearly screwing up his nerve to do more than just *ask* for money." But Hoagland has "the New Yorker's quick-hunch posture for broken-field maneuvering," and the bad guy swerves away.

6    I often witness that "hunch posture," from women after dark on the warrenlike streets of Brooklyn where I live. They seem to set their faces on neutral and, with their purse straps strung across their chests bandolier style, they forge ahead as though bracing themselves against being tackled. I understand, of course, that the danger they perceive is not a hallucination. Women are particularly vulnerable to street violence, and young black males are drastically overrepresented among the perpetrators of that violence. Yet these truths are no solace against the kind of alienation that comes of being ever the suspect, against being set apart, a fearsome entity with whom pedestrians avoid making eye contact.

7    It is not altogether clear to me how I reached the ripe old age of twenty-two without being conscious of the lethality nighttime pedestrians attributed to me. Perhaps it was because in Chester, Pennsylvania, the small, angry industrial town where I came of age in the 1960s, I was scarcely noticeable against a backdrop of gang warfare, street knifings, and murders. I grew up one of the good boys, had perhaps a half-dozen fist fights. In retrospect, my shyness of combat has clear sources.

8    Many things go into the making of a young thug. One of those things is the consummation of the male romance with the power to intimidate. An infant discovers that random flailings send the baby bottle flying out of the crib and crashing to the floor. Delighted, the joyful babe repeats those motions again and again, seeking to duplicate the feat. Just so, I recall the points at which some of my boyhood friends were finally seduced by the perception of themselves as tough guys. When a mark cowered and surrendered his money without resistance, myth and reality merged—and paid off. It is, after all, only manly to embrace the power to frighten and intimidate. We, as men, are not supposed to give an inch of our lane on the highway; we are to seize the fighter's edge in work and in play and even in love; we are to be valiant in the face of hostile forces.

9    Unfortunately, poor and powerless young men seem to take all this nonsense literally. As a boy, I saw countless tough guys locked away; I have since buried several, too. They were babies, really—a teenage cousin, a brother of twenty-two, a childhood friend in his mid-twenties—all gone down in episodes of bravado played out in the streets. I came to doubt the virtues of intimidation early on. I chose, perhaps even unconsciously, to remain a shadow—timid, but a survivor.

10    The fearsomeness mistakenly attributed to me in public places often has a perilous flavor. The most frightening of these confusions occurred in the late 1970s and early 1980s when I worked as a journalist in Chicago. One day, rushing into the office of a magazine I was writing for with a deadline story in hand, I was mistaken for a burglar. The office manager called security and, with an ad hoc posse, pursued me through the labyrinthine halls, nearly to my editor's door. I had no way of proving who I was. I could only move briskly toward the company of someone who knew me.

11    Another time I was on assignment for a local paper and killing time before an interview. I entered a jewelry store on the city's affluent Near North Side. The proprietor excused herself and returned with an enormous red Doberman pinscher straining at the end of a leash. She stood, the dog extended toward me, silent to my questions, her eyes bulging nearly out of her head. I took a cursory look around, nodded, and bade her good night. Relatively speaking, however, I never fared as badly as another black male journalist. He went to nearby Waukegan, Illinois, a couple of summers ago to work on a story about a murderer who was born there. Mistaking the reporter for the killer, police hauled him from his car at gunpoint and but for his press credentials would probably have tried to book him. Such episodes are not uncommon. Black men trade tales like this all the time.

12    In "My Negro Problem—And Ours," Podhoretz writes that the hatred he feels for blacks makes itself known to him through a variety of avenues—one being his discomfort with that "special brand of paranoid touchiness" to which he says blacks are prone. No doubt he is speaking here of black men. In time, I learned to smother the rage I felt at so often being taken for a criminal. Not to do so would surely have led to madness—via that special "paranoid touchiness" that so annoyed Podhoretz at the time he wrote the essay.

13    I began to take precautions to make myself less threatening. I move about with care, particularly late in the evening. I give a wide berth to nervous people on subway platforms during the wee hours, particularly when I have exchanged business clothes for jeans. If I happen to be entering a building behind some people who appear skittish, I may walk by, letting them clear the lobby before I return, so as not to seem to be following them. I have been calm and extremely congenial on those rare occasions when I've been pulled over by the police.

14    And on late-evening constitutionals along streets less traveled by, I employ what has proved to be an excellent tension-reducing measure: I whistle melodies from Beethoven and Vivaldi and the more popular classical composers. Even steely New Yorkers hunching toward nighttime destinations seem to relax, and occasionally they even join in the tune. Virtually everybody seems to sense that a mugger wouldn't be warbling bright, sunny selections from Vivaldi's *Four Seasons*. It is my equivalent of the cowbell that hikers wear when they know they are in bear country.

---

## Comprehension Test 4*

### Checking Your Comprehension

1. Summarize the problem the author is describing.

2. Why was Staples unaware of this problem until the age of 22?

3. In what sense does Staples use the word *victim*? In what sense is Staples himself a "victim"?

4. How has Staples altered his behavior in public?

### Thinking Critically

1. Discuss the meaning of the title. How does Staples alter public space? How has it affected his life?

2. Discuss Staples' attitude toward his "victims." Does he perceive them as rational or irrational? Is he sympathetic? angry?

---

*Multiple-choice questions are contained in Appendix B (page A7).

**Questions for Discussion**

1. In what other situations can an individual alter public space?

2. What is your opinion of the behavior of Staples' "victims"?

3. Do you feel Staples should have altered his behavior in public? Would you do the same?

4. After reading only the first paragraph, what did you think was happening?

| Selection 4: | | | 1645 words |
|---|---|---|---|
| Finishing Time: | _____ | _____ | _____ |
| | HR. | MIN. | SEC. |
| Starting Time: | _____ | _____ | _____ |
| | HR. | MIN. | SEC. |
| Reading Time: | | _____ | _____ |
| | | MIN. | SEC. |
| WPM Score: | | | _____ |
| Comprehension Score: | | | _____% |

**Visit the Longman English Pages**

For additional readings and exercises, visit the Longman English Skills Web page at:

**http://longman.awl.com/englishpages**

For a username and password, please see your instructor.

# CHAPTER 3

# Strengthening Your Word Power

IN THIS CHAPTER YOU WILL LEARN:

1. To expand your vocabulary.
2. To determine a word's meaning from its context.
3. To use word parts to figure out meanings of new words.
4. How the index card system can expand your vocabulary.
5. How to select and use the best vocabulary reference sources.

Are you constantly looking for new words that can expand your vocabulary? To provoke your "word awareness" try the following quiz. Answer each item as either true or false.

_____ 1. There are 135 different meanings for the word *run*.

_____ 2. If you read an unfamiliar word in a textbook, the first thing you should do is look it up in the dictionary.

_____ 3. If *psycho* means mind and *-osis* means diseased or abonormal condition, then a psychosis is a disease of the mind.

_____ 4. Memorizing a list is the most effective way to learn new vocabulary.

_____ 5. An unabridged dictionary is more complete than a pocket dictionary.

_____ 6. If you were taking a psychology course and were having difficulty distinguishing between the terms *drive* and *motive,* the most detailed reference source to consult would be a collegiate dictionary.

Now, check your answers on p. 66.

These questions illustrate important topics covered in this chapter: expanding your vocabulary, using context to determine the meaning of unfamiliar words, using word parts to analyze word meanings, using reference sources, and systems for learning new vocabulary.

# ■ EXPANDING YOUR VOCABULARY

Your vocabulary can be one of your strongest assets or one of your greatest liabilities. It defines and describes you by revealing a great deal about your level of education and your experience. Your vocabulary contributes significantly to that all-important first impression people form when they meet you.

A strong vocabulary provides both immediate academic benefits as well as long-term career effects. This portion of the chapter offers numerous suggestions for directing and developing your vocabulary so that it becomes one of your most valuable assets.

## ■ Read Widely and Diversely

One of the best ways to improve your vocabulary is to read widely and diversely, sampling many subjects and styles of writing. Through reading you encounter new words as well as new uses for already familiar words. You may also notice words used in contexts in which you had never thought of them being used.

In addition to reading widely, being motivated to expand your vocabulary is critical to dramatically improving in it. You must be interested in expanding your vocabulary and willing to spend time and effort working at it. In other words, a powerful vocabulary doesn't just happen; you have to *make* it happen. In each of your courses, you encounter new words each day through reading text assignments and listening to lectures. Now is the ideal time to begin expanding your vocabulary.

## ■ Use Words To Remember Them

Regardless of how much time you spend recording and looking up words, most likely you will remember only those you use fairly soon after you learn them. Forgetting occurs rapidly after learning unless you take action to use and remember what you have learned.

## ■ Be Selective

An unabridged (most complete) dictionary lists approximately 600,000 words. But be realistic: you'll never learn them all—no one ever has. Your first task is to decide what to learn—to be selective. Some words are more useful to you than others, depending on a range of factors including your major, your career goals, and your social and recreational preferences. If you are a computer science major and plan to get a job in a major corporation,

**ANSWER KEY**

1. True. Yes! There are 135 meanings. One way you can expand your vocabulary is to learn additional meanings for already familiar words.
2. False. The first thing you should do is keep reading and try to figure out the word from the way it is used in the sentence (its context), as described in this chapter.
3. True. This item illustrates how knowledge of word parts can help you figure out unfamiliar words. Common word parts are discussed in this chapter.
4. False. List learning is ineffective; this chapter suggests a more effective index card system.
5. True. This chapter describes a variety of dictionaries, each designed for a different purpose.
6. False. A more detailed source is a subject area dictionary (see p. 90).

your effective working vocabulary should be different than if you are a biology major planning a career in genetic research.

## ■ Use What You Already Know

Most people think they have one vocabulary and that it is either weak or strong, good or bad. Actually, you have four different vocabulary levels—one for reading, writing, listening, and speaking. Although they share a common core of basic operational words, they range widely in both size and content. For example, you recognize and understand certain words as you read, but you never use them in your own writing. Similarly, you understand certain words while listening, but you don't use them as part of your speaking vocabulary. Most likely your listening and reading vocabularies are larger than your speaking and writing vocabularies. In other words, you already know a large number of words that you are not using. Read the following list of words. You may know or have heard each word, but you probably do not use them in your own speech or writing.

conform *fit*          congeal *Jello*
*Friendly—* congenial          contour *lines*
*From Birth* congenital          contrite *— Sorry*
contort          cosmopolitan *— city culture*
cosmic          cosmos *—*

You can begin to strengthen your vocabulary by experimenting with words you already know but do not use. Make a point of using one of these words each day, in both speaking and writing.

### ■ Work on Vaguely Familiar Words

One of the best groups of words to begin to learn are those that are vaguely familiar—those that you have heard or seen before but cannot precisely or accurately define. These are words that you see regularly but have never felt comfortable using. Such words might include:

polemic prodigy
pragmatism profuse
precept prototype

As you notice these words in your reading or hear them in class lectures, mark them or jot them down in the margin; later check their meanings in a dictionary.

### ■ Learn Multiple Word Meanings

When you took the word awareness quiz, were you surprised to learn that the word *run* has a total of 135 meanings? You probably thought of meanings such as to *run* fast, a home *run,* and a *run* in a stocking, but the word has so many meanings that the entry requires nearly an entire dictionary page. You certainly have heard the word used in the following ways: to *run* the store, *run* upstream, *run* a machine, *run* a fever. On the other hand, you may not have known that *run* is a term used in billiards meaning a series of uninterrupted strokes or that in golf, *run* means to cause the ball to roll.

Most words in the English language have more than one meaning. Just open any standard dictionary to any page and glance down one column of words. You will see that more than one meaning is given for most words. Also, you can see that there is considerable opportunity to expand your vocabulary by becoming aware of additional meanings of words you already know.

## EXERCISE 3–1

*DIRECTIONS:* Each of the following sentences uses a relatively uncommon meaning of the underlined word. After reading each sentence, write a synonym or brief definition of the underlined word. You may need to check a dictionary to locate a precise meaning.

1. Investors should keep at least a portion of their assets <u>fluid</u>.

   _____

2. The speech therapist noted that the child had difficulty with <u>glides</u>.

   _____

3. The prisoner held a <u>jaundiced</u> view of life.

_____

4. The two garden hoses could not be connected without a <u>male</u> fitting.

_____

5. The outcome of the debate was a <u>moral</u> certainty.

_____

## EXERCISE 3–2

*DIRECTIONS:* The Internet offers a variety of vocabulary improvement programs. Do a Web search to discover what online aids to vocabulary improvement are available. Share your findings with your classmates.

## ■ USING CONTEXTUAL AIDS

The following tests are intended to demonstrate an important principle of vocabulary development. Before continuing with this section, try these vocabulary tests. Complete *both* tests before checking your answers, which appear in the paragraph following test B. While working on the second test *do not* return to the first test to change any answers.

**Test A: Words Without Context**

*Directions:* *For each item choose the word that is closest in meaning to the first word. Write the letter of your answer in the space provided.*

_____ 1. verbatim
    a. word for word
    b. using verbs
    c. idea by idea
    d. using abbreviations
    e. using an outline

_____ 2. sedentary
    a. very routine
    b. dull and boring
    c. quiet
    d. exciting
    e. involves sitting

_____ 3. thwarted
    a. initiated
    b. blocked
    c. controlled
    d. disagreed
    e. imposed

_____ 4. renounced
    a. gave up
    b. kept
    c. transferred
    d. criticized
    e. applied for

_____ 5. audacity
   a. patience
   b. boldness
   c. good sense
   d. courtesy
   e. understanding

_____ 6. disparaging
   a. encouraging
   b. questioning
   c. sincere
   d. logical
   e. belittling

_____ 7. capricious
   a. changeable
   b. dependable
   c. rational
   d. unusual
   e. puzzling

_____ 8. periphery
   a. outside
   b. focus
   c. inside
   d. edge
   e. middle

_____ 9. indigenous
   a. natural
   b. fertile
   c. native
   d. adaptations
   e. mutations

_____ 10. abject
   a. cruel
   b. low and miserable
   c. frightening
   d. difficult to commit
   e. illogical

Number Correct: _____

## Test B: Words in Context

_Directions:  For each item choose the word that is closest in meaning to the underlined word. Write the letter of your answer in the space provided._

_____ 1. It is more efficient to take lecture notes in your own words than to try to record the lecture <u>verbatim</u>.
   a. word for word
   b. using verbs
   c. idea by idea
   d. using abbreviations
   e. using an outline

_____ 2. Office work is quite <u>sedentary</u>, while in factory work you are able to move around more.
   a. very routine
   b. dull and boring
   c. quiet
   d. exciting
   e. involves sitting

_____ 3. Joe's parents <u>thwarted</u> his efforts to get a student loan; they refused to cosign for him.
   a. initiated
   b. blocked
   c. controlled
   d. disagreed
   e. imposed

_____ 4. Despite his love of the country, he <u>renounced</u> his citizenship when the war broke out.
   a. gave up
   b. kept
   c. transferred
   d. criticized
   e. applied for

_____ 5. The woman had the <u>audacity</u> to return the dress to the store after wearing it several times.
   a. patience
   b. boldness
   c. good sense
   d. courtesy
   e. understanding

_____ 6. Despite her husband's <u>disparaging</u> remarks, the woman persisted in her efforts to find a full-time job.
   a. encouraging
   b. questioning
   c. sincere
   d. logical
   e. belittling

_____ 7. As evidence of his wife's <u>capricious</u> behavior, the husband described how frequently she shifted from one extreme to another.
   a. changeable
   b. dependable
   c. rational
   d. unusual
   e. puzzling

_____ 8. In certain societies, young children are always on the <u>periphery</u>, instead of in the center of family life.
   a. outside
   b. focus
   c. inside
   d. edge
   e. middle

_____ 9. Most types of pine trees are <u>indigenous</u> to North America, but many ornamental shrubs were brought here from other continents.
   a. natural
   b. fertile
   c. native
   d. adaptations
   e. mutations

_____ 10. Matricide, the killing of one's mother, is one of the most contemptible and <u>abject</u> crimes.
   a. cruel
   b. low and miserable
   c. frightening
   d. difficult to commit
   e. illogical

Number Correct: _____

Now score each test. The answers to both tests are the same. They are (1) a, (2) e, (3) b, (4) a, (5) b, (6) e, (7) a, (8) d, (9) c, (10) b. You most likely had more items correct on test B than on test A. Why did your scores differ when the words and choices were the same on both tests? The answer is that test B was easier because the words were presented *in context;* the words around the underlined word provide clues to its meaning. Test A, on the other hand, had no sentences in which the words were used, and it provided no meaningful clues at all.

The purpose of these tests, as you can see, is to demonstrate that you can often figure out the meaning of an unknown word by looking for clues in the sentence or paragraph in which it appears. In the rest of this section we show how to use the four most common clues that context can provide about the meaning of an unknown word.

## ■ Definition Clues

Many times a writer directly or indirectly defines a word immediately after its use. The writer usually does this when he or she suspects that some readers may be unfamiliar with the new term or concept. Sometimes a writer includes a formal definition like you might find in a dictionary. In these cases the meaning of the word will be stated directly. At other times a writer may informally restate the idea or offer a synonym, a word that means the same thing. Here are a few examples of each type of definition clue:

### FORMAL DEFINITIONS

1. **Horology** is the <u>science of measuring time</u>.

2. **Induction** refers to the <u>process of reasoning from the known to the unknown</u>.

3. **Metabolism** refers to the <u>rate at which the body's cells manufacture energy from food or produce new cells</u>.

Notice that in each example the boldface word is clearly and directly defined (by the underlined part of the sentence). In fact, each sentence was written for the sole purpose of defining a term.

### INDIRECT DEFINITIONS

1. **Hypochondria,** <u>excessive worry over one's health</u>, afflicts many Americans over forty.

2. There was a **consensus,** or <u>agreement</u>, among the faculty to require one term paper for each course.

3. <u>Referring to the ability to "see" without using the normal sensory organs</u>, **clairvoyance** is being studied at the Psychic Research Center.

4. **Middle age** (<u>35 years to 65 years</u>) is a time for strengthening and maintaining life goals.

In each of these examples, a meaning is also provided for the boldface term. A complete definition is not given, but sufficient information (underlined) is included to give you a general idea of the meaning so that you can continue reading without stopping to check a dictionary. These definitions are usually set apart from the main part of a sentence by commas or parentheses, or they are expressed in a phrase or clause that further explains the sentence's core parts.

## EXERCISE 3–3

*DIRECTIONS:* In each sentence underline the portion that gives a definition clue for the boldface term.

1. **Chemical reactivity**, the tendency of an element to participate in chemical reactions, is an important concept in combining elements.

2. The **effectiveness adjustment**, the process by which an organism meets the demands of its environment, depends on many factors.

3. **Deductive thinking** involves drawing a conclusion from a set of general principles.

4. **Interrogation**, or questioning, can be psychologically and emotionally draining.

5. The boy was **maimed,** or disfigured, as a result of the accident.

### ■ Example Clues

A second way to determine the meaning of an unknown word is to look for examples that explain or clarify it. Suppose you do not know the meaning of the word "trauma," and you find it used in the following sentence:

> Diane experienced many **traumas** during early childhood, including injury in an auto accident, the death of her grandmother, and the divorce of her parents.

This sentence gives three examples of **traumas**, and from the examples given you can conclude that "trauma" means a shocking or psychologically damaging experience. Here are a few other examples of sentences that contain example clues:

> **Toxic** materials, such as arsenic, asbestos, pesticides, and lead, can cause permanent bodily damage.
>
> **Unconditioned responses**, including heartbeat, blinking, and breathing, occur naturally in all humans.
>
> **Orthopterans** such as crickets, grasshoppers, and cockroaches thrive in damp conditions.

You may have noticed in these sentences that the examples are signaled by certain words or phrases. "Such as" and "including" are used here. Other common signals are "for example," "for instance," and "to illustrate."

## EXERCISE 3–4

*DIRECTIONS:* Read each sentence and write a definition or synonym for each boldface word or phrase. Use the example clue to help you determine the meaning of the word or phrase.

1. Because of their **metallic properties** such as thermal and electrical conductivity, luster, and ductility (ability to be shaped into thin pieces), copper and lead are used for electrical wiring.

   _____

2. Perceiving, learning, and thinking are examples of **cognitive** processes.

   _____

3. Many **debilities** of old age, including loss of hearing, poor eyesight, and diseases such as arthritis, can be treated medically.

   _____

4. **Phobias** such as fear of heights, fear of water, or fear of crowds can be eliminated through conditioning.

   _____

5. Humans have built-in **coping mechanisms**; we shout when we are angry, cry when we are sad, and tremble when we are nervous.

   _____

### ■ Contrast Clues

It is sometimes possible to determine the meaning of an unknown word from a word or phrase in the context that has an opposite meaning. In the following sentence, notice how a word opposite in meaning from the boldface word provides a clue to its meaning.

During the concert the audience was quiet, but afterward the crowd became **boisterous**.

Although you may not know the meaning of **boisterous**, you know that the audience was quiet during the concert and that afterward it acted differently. The word "but" suggests this. You know, then, that the crowd became the opposite of quiet (loud and noisy). Here are a few additional examples of sentences containing contrast clues:

I **loathe** cats even though most of my friends love them.

Although the cottage appeared **derelict**, we discovered that a family lived there on weekends.

Pete, through long hours of study, successfully passed the exam; on the other hand, Sam's efforts were **futile**.

In these examples, you may have noticed that each contains a word or phrase that indicates that an opposite or contrasting situation exists. The signal words used in the examples were "even though," "although," and "on the other hand." Other words that also signal a contrasting idea include "however," "despite," "rather," "while," "yet," and "nevertheless."

# EXERCISE 3–5

*DIRECTIONS:* Read each sentence and write a definition or synonym for each boldface word. Use the contrast clue to help you determine the meaning of the word.

1.  Al was always talkative, whereas Ed remained **taciturn**.

    _____

2.  The microwave oven is becoming **obsolete**; the newer microwave-convection oven offers the user more cooking options.

    _____

3.  My brother lives in the **remote** hills of Kentucky so he seldom has the opportunity to shop in big cities.

    _____

4.  One of the women shoppers **succumbed** to the temptation of buying a new dress, but the others resisted.

    _____

5.  Most members of Western society marry only one person at a time, but in other cultures **polygamy** is common and acceptable.

    _____

## ■ Inference Clues

Many times you can determine the meaning of a word you do not know by guessing or figuring it out. This process is called "drawing an inference." From the information that is given in the context you can infer the meaning of a word you are not familiar with. For instance, look at the following sentence:

My father is a **versatile** man; he is a successful businessman, sportsman, author, and sports car mechanic.

You can see that the father is successful at many types of activities, and you could reason that "versatile" means capable of doing many things competently. Similarly, in the following example the general sense of the context provides clues to the meaning of the word *robust:*

> At the age of 77, Mr. George was still playing a skillful game of tennis. He jogged four miles each day and seldom missed his daily swim. For a man of his age he was extremely **robust.**

From the facts presented about Mr. George, you can infer that "robust" means full of health and vigor.

Sometimes your knowledge and experience can help you figure out the meaning of an unknown word. Consider, for instance, the following sentence:

> After tasting and eating most of seven different desserts, my appetite was completely **satiated.**

Your own experience would suggest that if you ate seven desserts, you would no longer feel like eating. Thus you could reason that "satiated" means full or satisfied.

## EXERCISE 3–6

*DIRECTIONS:* Read each sentence and write a definition or synonym for each boldface word. Try to figure out the meaning of each word by using information provided in the context.

1. Although my grandfather is 82, he is far from **infirm;** he is active, ambitious, and healthy.

2. My **unscrupulous** uncle tried to sell as an antique a rocking chair he bought just last year.

3. My sister's lifestyle always angered and disappointed my mother; yet she **redeemed** herself by doing special favors for my mother's friends.

4. The wind howling around the corner of the house, the one rumored to have ghosts, made an **eerie** sound.

5. We burst out laughing at the **ludicrous** sight of the basketball team dressed up as cheerleaders.

## EXERCISE 3–7

*DIRECTIONS:* The meaning of the boldface word in each of the following sentences can be determined from the context. Underline the part of the sentence that contains the clue to the meaning of that word. Then write a definition or synonym for the boldface word.

1. Tremendous **variability** characterized the treatment of the mentally retarded during the Medieval Era, ranging from treatment as innocents, toleration as fools, and persecution as witches.

   _____

2. A citizen review panel **exonerated** the public official of any possible misconduct or involvement in the acceptance of bribes.

   _____

3. The **tenacious** residents living near the polluted landfill responded vehemently to the court's recommended settlement, while the chemical industry immediately agreed to the court settlement.

   _____

4. The economy was in continual **flux**; inflation increased one month and decreased the next.

   _____

5. The short story contained a series of **morbid** events: the death of the mother, the suicide of the grandmother, and the murder of a young child.

   _____

6. Certain societies practice the custom of **levirate**, the required remarriage of a widow to her deceased husband's brother.

   _____

7. Contrasted with the corporation, the risk and liability of a privately owned **proprietorship** are much higher.

   _____

8. Many cultural systems are **dynamic**; they change with environment, innovations, and contact with other groups.

   _____

9. Personality is the **configuration** of feelings and behaviors created in a person throughout the process of growing up.

   _____

10. A **cornucopia** of luxury and leisure-time goods, designed to meet the requirements of the upper–middle-class standard of living, has flooded the economic market.

## EXERCISE 3–8

*DIRECTIONS:* Select a chapter in one of your textbooks and identify at least five words whose meanings can be understood by using context clues. Write definitions for each of these words and list the types of context clues you used to arrive at their meanings.

## ■ ANALYZING WORD PARTS

Many words in the English language are made up of word parts called *prefixes, roots,* and *suffixes.* You might think of these as the beginning, middle, and ending of a word. These word parts have specific meanings and when added together can provide strong clues to the meanings of a particular word.

The prefixes, roots, and suffixes listed in the following tables (see Tables 3.1 to 3.3, pages 78–79) occur in thousands of words. For instance, suppose you do not know the meaning of the word *pseudonym.* However, if you know that *pseudo* means false and *nym* means name, you would be able to add the two parts together and realize that a pseudonym means a false name.

Before you begin to use these tables to figure out new words, you need to know a few things:

1. Words do not always have a prefix or suffix.

2. Roots may vary in spelling when they are combined with certain prefixes.

3. Some roots are commonly found at the beginnings of words, others at the end, and still others can be found in either position.

4. In certain situations, you may recognize a group of letters but find that it does not carry the meaning of prefix or root. For example, the word internal has nothing to do with the prefix *inter* meaning between.

5. Words can have more than one prefix, root, or suffix.

**Table 3.1** Common Prefixes

| Prefix | Meaning | Sample Word |
| --- | --- | --- |
| ad | to, at, for | adhere |
| anti | against | antiwar |
| circum | around | circumvent |
| com/col/con | with, together | compile |
| contra | against, opposite | contradict |
| de | away, from | deport |
| dis | apart, away, not | disagree |
| equi | equal | equidistant |
| ex/extra | from, out of, former | ex-wife |
| hyper | over, excessive | hyperactive |
| in/il/ir/im | in, into, not | illogical |
| inter | between | interpersonal |
| intro/intra | within, into, in | introduction |
| micro | small | microscope |
| mis | wrong | misleading |
| mono | one | monologue |
| multi | many | multipurpose |
| non | not | nonfiction |
| poly | many | polygon |
| post | after | posttest |
| pre | before | premarital |
| pseudo | false | pseudonym |
| re | back, again | repeat |
| retro | backward | retrospect |
| semi | half | semicircle |
| sub | under, below | submarine |
| super | above, extra, above average | supercharge |
| tele | far | telescope |
| trans | across, over | transcontinental |
| un | not | unskilled |

**Table 3.2** Common Roots

| Root | Meaning | Sample Word | Root | Meaning | Sample Word |
|---|---|---|---|---|---|
| aster/astro | star | astronaut | path | feeling | sympathy |
| aud/audit | hear | audible | phono | sound/voice | telephone |
| bio | life | biology | photo | light | photosensitive |
| cap | take, seize | captive | port | carry | transport |
| chron(o) | time | chronology | scop | seeing | microscope |
| corp | body | corpse | scrib/script | write | inscription |
| cred | believe | incredible | sen/sent | feel | insensitive |
| dict/dic | tell, say | predict | spec/spic | look, see | retrospect |
| duc/duct | lead | introduce | spect/spec | look at | spectacle |
| fact/fac | make, do | factory | terr/terre | land, earth | territory |
| geo | earth | geophysics | theo | god | theology |
| graph | write | telegraph | ven/vent | come | convention |
| log/logo/logy | study, thought | psychology | vert/vers | turn | invert |
| mit/miss | send | dismiss | vis/vid | see | invisible |
| mort/mor | die, death | immortal | voc | call | vocation |

**Table 3.3** Common Suffixes

| Suffix | Sample Word | Suffix | Sample Word |
|---|---|---|---|
| *Suffixes that refer to a state, condition, or quality* | | -ty | loyalty |
| -able | touchable | -y | creamy |
| -ance | assistance | *Suffixes that mean "one who"* | |
| -ation | confrontation | -ee | employee |
| -ence | reference | -eer | engineer |
| -ic | aerobic | -er | teacher |
| -ible | tangible | -ist | activist |
| -ion | discussion | -or | editor |
| -ity | superiority | *Suffixes that mean "pertaining to" or "referring to"* | |
| -ive | permissive | -al | autumnal |
| -ment | amazement | -ship | friendship |
| -ness | kindness | -hood | brotherhood |
| -ous | jealous | -ward | homeward |

## EXERCISE 3–9

*DIRECTIONS:* Use the list of common prefixes (Table 3.1) to determine the meaning of each of the following words. Write a brief definition or synonym for each. If you are unfamiliar with the root, you may need to check a dictionary.

1. misinformed _____
2. rephrase _____
3. interoffice _____
4. circumscribe _____
5. irreversible _____
6. substandard _____
7. supernatural _____
8. telecommunications _____
9. unqualified _____
10. subdivision _____
11. transcend _____
12. hypercritical *over action critical*
13. pseudointellectual _____
14. contraception _____
15. equivalence _____

## EXERCISE 3–10

*DIRECTIONS:* Use the list of common prefixes (Table 3.1), the list of common roots (Table 3.2), and the list of common suffixes (Table 3.3) to determine the meaning of each of the following words. Write a brief definition or synonym for each, checking a dictionary if necessary.

1. chronology _____
2. photocomposition _____
3. introspection _____
4. biology _____
5. subterranean _____

6. captivate _____

7. conversion _____

8. teleprompter _____

9. monotheism _____

10. exportation _____

## EXERCISE 3–11

*DIRECTIONS:* From a chapter of one of your textbooks, select at least five new words made up of two or more word parts. Identify those parts for each word, list the meaning of each part, and then write a brief definition of each new word.

## ■ A SYSTEM FOR LEARNING UNFAMILIAR WORDS

You are constantly exposed to new words in the normal course of your day. However, unless you make a deliberate effort to remember and use these words, many of them will fade from your memory. One of the most practical and easy to use systems for expanding your vocabulary is the index card system. It works like this:

1. **Whenever you hear or read a new word that you intend to learn, jot it down in the margin of your notes or mark it in some way in the material you are reading.**

2. **Later, write each new word on the front of an index card, then look up the meaning (or meanings) of the word and write it on the back.** You might also record the word's pronunciation or a sample sentence in which the word is used. Your cards should look like the ones shown in Figure 3.1 on page 82.

3. **Whenever you have a few spare minutes, go through your pack of index cards.** For each card, look at the word on the front and try to recall its meaning on the back. Then check the back of the card to see if you were unable to recall the meaning or if you confused it with another word, retest yourself. Shuffle the cards after each use.

4. **After you have gone through your pack of cards several times, sort the cards into two piles;** separate the words you know from those that

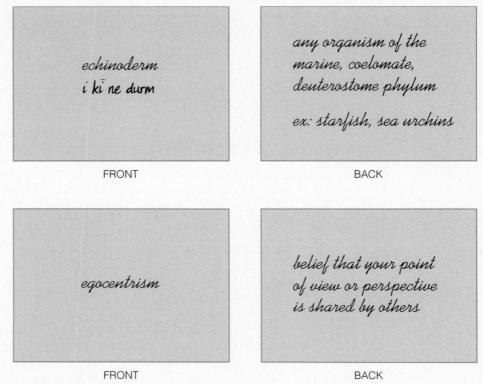

FRONT

BACK

FRONT

BACK

**FIGURE 3.1** Sample vocabulary cards.

you have not learned. Then, putting the "known words" aside, concentrate on the words still to be learned. Shuffle the cards to change their order.

5. **Once you have mastered the entire pack of cards, periodically review them to refresh your memory and to keep the words current in your mind.**

6. **If you tend to be a social learner (see Learning Style Questionnaire, p. A1 at the end of the text), arrange to work with a classmate.** Quiz each other and discuss ways to remember difficult or confusing terms.

This word card system of learning vocabulary is effective for several reasons.

- It can be accomplished in the spare moments that are often wasted waiting for a return phone call, waiting for a class to begin, or riding a bus.

- The system enables you to spend time learning what you do *not* know rather than wasting time studying what you already know.

- It prevents you from learning the material in a fixed order.

## EXERCISE 3–12

*DIRECTIONS:* Prepare a set of vocabulary cards for the new terminology in one chapter of one of your textbooks.

### ■ Using Newly Learned Words

A conscious effort is required to learn new words. You must *use* a word for it to remain a part of your vocabulary. The first time you use a new word you may be unsure if you are using it correctly. Don't let this element of risk discourage you from trying new words. The first place to use the new words is in course-related situations. Try to use new words when studying with a friend or participating in a class discussion.

Be conscious of your word choices as you write. Select words that most clearly and accurately convey the meaning you intend. As a general rule, it is best to record your ideas first without thinking about exact choices of words. Then, as you reread what you have written, try to think of words that express your ideas more accurately or that provide more complete information.

## ■ USING VOCABULARY REFERENCE SOURCES

To develop a strong vocabulary you need the basic tools with which to work. Just as an artist cannot begin to paint without having a canvas and brushes, you cannot begin to strengthen your vocabulary without owning the necessary reference sources—a dictionary and a thesaurus—and having access to a subject-area dictionary.

### ■ The Dictionary

#### *Which Dictionary To Buy?*

There are several types of dictionaries, each with its own purpose and use. A pocket or paperback dictionary is an inexpensive, easy-to-carry, shortened version of a standard desk dictionary. It is small enough to carry to classes and costs around $5.

A desk dictionary is a more complete and extensive dictionary. Although a pocket dictionary is convenient, it is also limited in use. A pocket edition lists about 50,000 to 60,000 words; a standard desk edition lists up to 150,000 words. Also, the desk edition provides much more complete information about each word. Desk dictionaries are usually hardbound and cost more than $20.

Several standard dictionaries are available in both desk and paperback editions. These include:

*Random House Dictionary of the English Language*
*Webster's New Collegiate Dictionary*
*The American Heritage Dictionary of the English Language*

Standard dictionaries are also available on CD-ROM and online; it may be convenient to access word meanings by using your computer. A third type is the unabridged dictionary. These are found in the reference section of the library. The unabridged edition provides the most complete information on each word in the English language.

Which dictionary should you buy? You should first purchase a pocket dictionary to carry with you regularly. If at all possible, you should also own a desk dictionary, either printed or electronic, preferably a collegiate edition. For most purposes, it is not necessary to have the newest, most current edition; a used dictionary works fine and costs considerably less.

### Using the Dictionary

The dictionary is a valuable reference source and an important tool in vocabulary development. Here are a few general principles to keep in mind when using a dictionary:

1. **Never spend time looking up long lists of words, even if you really want to learn each word on the list.** By the time you finish the list, you will have forgotten the first ones you looked up. Instead, look up a few words at a time.

2. **Do not interrupt your reading to check the meaning of a word in the dictionary unless the word is absolutely essential to the meaning of the sentence or paragraph.** Instead, mark unknown words and look them up later.

3. **Whenever you look up a word, be sure to read through all the meanings and choose the meaning that suits the context in which it is used.**

4. **Whenever you do look up a word, be sure to write down the word and its meaning.** (A later section of the chapter on organizational approaches suggests an effective way to do this.)

### Types of Information to Find in the Dictionary

Although the dictionary, of course, is a source for definitions of words, it also contains other types of useful information that can significantly expand your vocabulary. Here are some types of information a dictionary provides that we often overlook:

1. **Word pronunciation.** Have you even been unsure of how to pronounce a word? This situation most commonly arises when you attempt to use a word from your reading vocabulary in speech. Immediately after the word entry in a dictionary, you will find a pronunciation key. Suppose you are trying to figure out how to pronounce the word *deign*, meaning to agree in a condescending manner. After the word you would find the following: (dān). Here the word is spelled phonetically, the way it sounds, and the key at the bottom of the page explains how to interpret the phonetic symbols. For instance, the *American Heritage Desk Dictionary* lists the following key:

   ă pat   ā pay   â care   ä father   ĕ pet   ē be   hw which   ĭ pit   ī tie   î pier   ŏ pot   ō toe   ô paw, for   oi noise
   ŏŏ took   ōō boot   ou out   th thin   *th* this   ŭ cut   ü urge   zh vision   ə about, item, edible, gallop, circus

   From the key you learn that the "a" sound in "deign" rhymes with the word *pay*. An accent mark (´) is included for words with two or more syllables to indicate which part of the word should receive the greatest emphasis.

2. **Key to spelling.** The common complaint about using a dictionary as a spelling aid is: If I cannot spell the word, how can I locate it in the dictionary? Generally, however, most spelling errors do not occur at the beginnings of words (with the exception of words beginning with ph, mn, or ch/sh). Thus it is often possible to locate a particular word in a dictionary. In addition to the basic spelling of a word, the dictionary often shows how spellings change when the word becomes plural or when an "ing" ending is added.

3. **Useful tables and charts.** Many dictionaries contain numerous tables and charts that make the dictionary a handy general reference book rather than just an alphabetical list of words and meanings. Commonly included among a dictionary's tables and charts are tables of weights and measures with metric equivalents, lists of abbreviations, lists of various signs and symbols, a guide to punctuation, mechanics, and manuscript form (also called a style manual), a table of periodic elements used in chemistry, and lists of famous people (dead and alive) and what they are recognized for.

4. **Information on language history.** The dictionary also functions as a brief history of the English language. For each word entry, information is given about the origin of the word. This etymological information tells you the language or languages from which the word evolved. For example, in *Webster's New Collegiate Dictionary* you can see that the word *establish* is derived from Middle English (ME), Middle French (MF), and Latin (L).*

> **es•tab•lish** \is-'tab-lish\ *vt* [**ME** *establissen,* fr. **MF** *establiss-,* stem of *establir,* fr. **L** *stabilire,* fr. *stabilis* stable] (14c) **1** : to institute (as a law) permanently by enactment or agreement **2** *obsolete* : SETTLE 7 **3 a** : to make firm or stable **b** : to introduce and cause to grow and multiply [~ grass on pasturelands] **4 a** : to bring into existence FOUND [~ed a republic] **b** : BRING ABOUT, EFFECT [~ed friendly relations] **5 a** : to put on a firm basis: SET UP [~ his son in business] **b** : to put into a favorable position **c** : to gain full recognition or acceptance of [the role ~ed her as a star] **6** : to make (a church) a national or state institution **7** : to put beyond doubt: PROVE [~ed my innocence]
> — **es•tab•lish•able** \-shə-bəl\ *adjective*
> — **es•tab•lish•er** \-shər\ *noun*

5. **Foreign expressions used in English.** Certain expressions from other languages have become widely used in the English language. These phrases often more accurately express an idea or feeling than do the English translations. The French expression *faux pas,* translated to mean a social blunder, is a good example. Most dictionaries list foreign phrases alphabetically along with English words, although in some dictionaries you may find a separate list of foreign expressions. A few more examples of commonly used foreign expressions that are listed in most dictionaries are: *ad hoc, non sequitur, de facto, tête-à-tête,* and *bona fide.*

# EXERCISE 3–13

*DIRECTIONS:* Use a dictionary to answer each of the following items. Write your answer in the space provided.

1. What does the abbreviation *e.g.* stand for?

_____

2. How is the word *deleterious* pronounced? (Record its phonetic spelling.)

_____

3. From what language is the word *delicatessen* taken?

_____

*Definition of "establish" reprinted by permission. From *Merriam-Webster's Collegiate® Dictionary,* Tenth Edition. © 1996 by Merriam-Webster Incorporated.

4. How many feet are in a mile?

_____

5. What is the history of the word *mascot*?

_____

6. What is the plural spelling of "addendum"?

_____

7. What type of punctuation is a virgule?

_____

8. List a few words that contain the following sound: $\bar{\imath}$.

_____

9. Who or what is a Semite?

_____

10. Can the word *phrase* be used other than as a noun? If so, how?

_____

_____

### *Choosing the Appropriate Meaning*

The crucial part of looking a word up in the dictionary is finding the appropriate meaning to fit the context in which the word is used. A dictionary lists all the common meanings of a word, but you are looking for only one definition. For instance, suppose you were to read the following sentence and could not determine the meaning of *isometrics* from its context.

The executive found that doing isometrics helped him to relax between business meetings.

The dictionary entry (*American Heritage Desk Dictionary*) for *isometrics* is:

**i•so•met•ric** (ī s ə-mĕt´rĭk) or **i•so•met•ri[cal]** (-rī-k ə l) *adj.* **1.** Of or exhibiting equality in dimensions or measurements. **2.** Of or being a crystal system of three equal axes at right angles to one another. **3.** Of or involving muscle contractions in which the ends of the muscle are held in place so that there is an increase in tension rather than a shortening of the muscle: *isometric exercises.* —*n.* **1.** A line connecting isometric points. **2. isometrics** (*used with a sing. verb*). Isometric exercise. [From Greek *isometros,* of equal measure : *isos,* equal + *metron,* measure.]

Notice that the meanings are grouped and numbered consecutively according to parts of speech. The meanings of the word when used as an adjective are listed first, followed by two meanings for it as a noun. If you are able to identify the part of speech of the word you are looking up, you can skip over all parts of the entry that do not pertain to that part of speech.

For example, in the sample sentence, you can tell that *isometrics* is something the executive does; therefore it is a noun.

If you cannot identify the part of speech of a word you are looking up, begin with the first meaning listed. Generally, the most common meaning appears first, and more specialized meanings appear toward the end of the entry.

Choosing the right meaning is a process of substitution. When you find a meaning that could fit into the sentence you are working with, replace the word with its definition and then read the entire sentence. If the definition makes sense in the sentence, you can be fairly certain that you have selected the appropriate meaning.

## EXERCISE 3–14

*DIRECTIONS:* Write an appropriate meaning for the underlined word in each of the following sentences. Use the dictionary to help you find the meaning that makes sense in the sentence.

1. He affected a French accent.

   _____

2. The amphibian took us to our destination in less than an hour.

   _____

3. The plane stalled on the apron.

   _____

4. We circumvented the problem by calculating in metrics.

   _____

5. The rising inflation rate has embroiled many consumers.

   _____

## EXERCISE 3–15

*DIRECTIONS:* Explain the meaning of each of the following foreign expressions.

1. *non sequitur*


2. *coup d'état*

3. *kowtow*

4. *barrio*

5. *Zeitgeist*

## ■ The Thesaurus

A thesaurus is a dictionary of synonyms. It is available in hardback and paperback, as well as on CD-ROM and online using a computer. It is written for the specific purpose of grouping words with similar meanings. A thesaurus is particularly useful when you have a word on the "tip of your tongue," so to speak, but cannot think of the exact word. It is also useful for locating a precise, accurate, or descriptive phrase to fit a particular situation.

Suppose you want to find a more precise term for the expression "told us about" in the following sentence:

My instructor told us about an assignment that would be due next month.

*Roget's International Thesaurus* lists the following synonyms for the phrase:

.8 VERBS **Inform, tell, speak,** apprize, **advise, advertise,** advertise of, give word, mention to, **acquaint, enlighten,** familiarize, brief, verse, wise up [slang], give the facts, give an account of, give by the way of information; **Instruct** 562.11; possess *or* seize one of the facts; **let know, have one to know, give one to understand;** tell once and for all; notify, give notice *or* notification, serve notice; **communicate** 554.6,7; bring *or* send *or* leave word; **report** 558.11; **disclose** 556.4-7; put in a new light, shed new *or* fresh light upon.

.9 **post** *or* **keep one posted** [both informal]; fill one in, bring up to date, put one in the picture [Brit.]

.10 **hint, intimate, suggest, insinuate, imply, indicate,** adumbrate, lead *or* leave one to gather, justify one in a supposing, give *or* drop *or* throw out a hint, give an inkling of, **hint at; allude to,** make an allusion to, glance at [archaic]; **prompt,** give the cue; put in *or* into one's head.

Right away you can identify several words that are more descriptive than "told us about." Your next step is to choose a word from the list that most closely suggests the meaning you intend. The easiest way to do this is to test out or substitute various choices in your sentence to see which one is most appropriate. Be sure to choose only those words with which you are familiar and those whose shades of meaning you understand. Remember, a misused word is often worse than a wordy or imprecise expression.

The most widely used thesaurus was originally compiled by Peter Roget and is known today as *Roget's Thesaurus;* inexpensive paperback copies are readily available. When you first use a thesaurus you will have to learn how to use it. First, you have to look up the word in the back. Once you locate the number of the section in the main part of the thesaurus that lists its synonyms, turn to that section.

## EXERCISE 3–16

*DIRECTIONS:* Using a thesaurus, replace the underlined word or phrase with a more precise or descriptive word. You may rephrase the sentence if necessary.

1. The instructor <u>talked about</u> several economic theories.

2. My sisters, who had been apart for three years, were <u>happy</u> to be reunited at the wedding.

3. The professor announced a <u>big</u> test for the end of next week.

4. The student <u>watched</u> the elderly professor climb the stairs.

5. Although it was short, the movie was <u>good</u>.

## ■ Subject-Area Dictionaries

Many academic disciplines have specialized dictionaries that index important terminology used in that field. They list specialized meanings and indicate how and when the words are used. For instance, the field of music has *The New Grove Dictionary of Music and Musicians,* which lists and defines specialized vocabulary used in the field. Other subject-area dictionaries include:

*Taber's Cyclopedic Medical Dictionary*
*A Dictionary of Anthropology*
*A Dictionary of Economics*

**Critical Thinking Tip #3**
**Vague Versus Clear Meanings**

Word meaning can facilitate or interfere with communication. A word that is exact and specific can help communication. A word whose meaning is vague, relative, or unclear leads to misinterpretation and confusion. Here are a few sentences in which the meaning is unclear because the meaning of the underlined word is not specific.

The movie was <u>great</u>!
(What was good about it?)

All <u>drugs</u> should be tightly controlled.
(Which drugs? All drugs? Aspirin too?)

The candidate received a <u>large</u> sum of money.
(How large is large?)

The woman was <u>middle aged</u>.
(How old is middle aged?)

As a critical thinker, be alert for the use of undefined terms and unclear words. Writers may use them to avoid giving specific information ("substantial losses" instead of exact amounts) or to create a false impression.

Find out if there is a subject-area dictionary for your major. Most of these dictionaries are available only in hardbound editions and are likely to be expensive. Many students, however, find them to be worth the initial investment. Most libraries have copies of specialized dictionaries in their reference section.

## EXERCISE 3–17

*DIRECTIONS:* Visit your college library and discover which subject area dictionaries are available for the courses you are taking this semester. List the courses you are enrolled in and the subject-area dictionary or dictionaries that would be useful for each.

## SUMMARY

**1. How can you expand your vocabulary?**

You can expand your vocabulary and reap immediate benefits as well as long-term career advantages by:
- Reading widely.
- Deliberately using newly learned words.
- Being selective about words to learn.
- Using words you already know.
- Working on vaguely familiar words.
- Learning multiple word meanings.

**2. What are the four types of context clues?**

The four types of context clues are:
- Definition—a word's meaning is either stated directly or given indirectly.
- Example—the examples used explain or clarify a word's meaning.
- Contrast—a word or phrase opposite in meaning provides a clue to meaning.
- Inference—a word's meaning can be figured out by reasoning about contextual information.

**3. What are the three parts that many English words are formed from?**

Many words in our language are made up of:
- Prefixes—the beginnings of words
- Roots—the middles of words
- Suffixes—the endings of words

**4. Why is it useful to learn about word parts?**

When their meanings are added together they can provide strong clues to the meaning of a new word and can unlock the meanings of thousands of English words.

**5. What is the index card system?**

The index card system is a method for learning unfamiliar words. Write each new word on the front of an index card and its meaning on the back. Study by sorting the cards into two piles—known and unknown words. Review periodically to keep them fresh in your mind.

**6. What reference sources are useful in developing a strong vocabulary?**

Pocket dictionaries, standard desk dictionaries, and unabridged dictionaries along with thesauruses and subject-area dictionaries are all useful sources.

ARCHAEOLOGY

# READING SELECTION 5
## ARCHAEOLOGICAL SITES

Brian M. Fagan
From *World Prehistory: A Brief Introduction*

*What do you think might be left of your town or city in two or three thousand years? What evidence might be left of how you lived? This textbook excerpt describes different sites where archaeologists have discovered evidence of early human activity. Preread and then read the excerpt to discover the six types of sites archaeologists study.*

1    World prehistory is written from data recovered from thousands of *archaeological sites, places where traces of human activity are to be found.* Sites are normally identified through the presence of manufactured tools.

2    An archaeological site can consist of a single human burial, a huge rockshelter occupied over thousands of years, or a simple scatter of stone tools found on the surface of a plowed field in the Midwest. Sites can range in size from a huge prehistoric city like Teotihuacán in the Valley of Mexico to a small campsite occupied by hunter-gatherers 100,000 years ago. Sites available for study by archaeologists are limited in number and variety by preservation conditions and by the nature of the activities of the people who occupied them. Some, like Mesopotamian city mounds, were important settlements for hundreds, even thousands, of years. Some small sites were used only for a few hours, others for a generation or two.

3    Archaeological sites are most commonly classified by the activity that occurred there. *Habitation sites* are placed where people lived and carried out a wide range of different activities. Most prehistoric sites come under this category, but habitation sites can vary from a small open campsite, through rockshelters and caves, to large accumulations of shellfish remains (shell middens). Village habitation sites may consist of a small accumulation of occupation deposit and mud hut fragments, huge earthen mounds, or communes of stone buildings or entire buried cities. Each presents its own special excavation problems.

4    *Burial sites* provide a wealth of information on the prehistoric past. Grinning skeletons are very much part of popular archaeological legend, and human remains are common finds in the archaeological record. The earliest deliberate human burials are between fifty and seventy thousand years old. Individual burials are found in habitation sites, but often the inhabitants designated a special area for a cemetery. This cemetery could be a communal burial place where everyone was buried regardless of social status. Other burial sites, like the Shang royal cemeteries in China, were reserved for nobility alone. Parts of a cemetery were sometimes reserved for certain special individuals in society such as clan leaders or priests. The patterning of grave goods in a cemetery can provide information about intangible aspects of human society such as religious beliefs or social organization. So can the pattern of deposition of the burials, their orientation in their graves, even family groupings. Sometimes physical anthropologists can detect biological similarities between different skeletons that may reflect close family, or other, ties.

5    Burial sites, especially those of important individuals, are among the most spectacular of all archaeological discoveries. Tut-ankh-Amun's tomb, the royal graves of Sumerian and Semitic nobles of Ur-of-the-Chaldees, and the sepulchres of Chinese nobles are justly famous for their

remarkable wealth. People have buried their dead in cemeteries under stone pyramids in Egypt and Mexico, in great earthen mass burial mounds in the Midwest, in huge subterranean chambers in China, and in thousands of small, individual earthen mounds in western Europe. In each case, however, the features of the burials and their context in the sepulchre add valuable data to what the skeleton itself can tell us.

6 *Kill sites* consist of bones of slaughtered animals associated with hunting weapons. On the North American Great Plains, for example, the skeletons of eight-thousand-year-old bison are found along with stone spearpoints. The hunters camped by the carcasses while they butchered them, then moved elsewhere, leaving the carcasses, projectile heads and butchering tools where they lay for archaeologists to find thousands of years later.

7 *Quarry sites* are places where people mined prized raw materials such as obsidian (a volcanic glass used for fine knives and mirrors) or copper. Excavations at such sites yield roughed out blanks of stone, or metal ingots, as well as finished products ready for trading elsewhere.

Such objects were bartered widely in prehistoric times.

8 *Religious sites* include Stonehenge in southern England, Mesopotamian mudbrick temples, known as *ziggurats,* and the great ceremonial centers of the lowland Maya in Mesoamerica, such as Tikal, Copán, and Palenque. Religious sites may be small shrines or huge public temples. Some are localities where religious ceremonies were conducted, often to the exclusion of any habitation at all.

9 *Art sites* such as the cave of Altamira in northern Spain, or Lascaux in southwestern France, are commonplace in some areas of the world, noticeably southern Africa and parts of North America. Many are caves and rockshelters where prehistoric people painted or engraved game animals, scenes of daily life, or religious symbols. Some French art sites are at least fifteen thousand years old.

10 Each of these site types represents a particular form of human activity, one that is represented in the archaeological record by specific artifact patterns and surface indications found and recorded by the archaeologist.

# Comprehension Test 5

*Directions: Circle the letter of the best answer.*

**Checking Your Comprehension**

1. Archaeological sites are usually classified by
   a. the people who lived there
   b. the historical period during which they were occupied
   c. the type of activity for which they were used
   d. the degree of civilization of those who lived there

2. An archaeological site is defined as any place where
   a. some record of human activity is found
   b. humans bury beloved animals
   c. evidence of plant or animal life exits
   d. particular rock formations suggest the patterns of history

3. All of the following features of graves provide archaeologists with information about a particular society except
   a. the location of the grave
   b. the goods buried with the person
   c. the degree of preservation of the body
   d. the orientation of the body in the grave

4. Art sites often contain
   a. paintings showing scenes of daily life
   b. engravings of famous people
   c. paintings recording the location of burial sites
   d. tools and primitive devices used for engraving

5. Quarry sites are places where
   a. game was slaughtered
   b. prized animals were buried
   c. raw materials were dug from the earth
   d. raw materials for burial sites were located

6. A "sepulchre" (paragraph 5) is a
   a. prehistorical tool used for burial
   b. type of grave
   c. form of preserving animal carcasses
   d. religious ritual

## Thinking Critically

7. Which of the following items might you expect to find at a burial site?
   a. tools
   b. jewels
   c. bowls
   d. animal remains

8. The author suggests that different cultural groups
   a. have similar methods of mixing raw materials
   b. reserve hunting grounds for specific tribes
   c. have specific sites for celebrations
   d. have different burial patterns

9. The author feels that archaeologists
   a. learn a great deal about early history
   b. locate valuable jewels and art
   c. disturb natural history by excavating
   d. prove man's natural superiority

10. This article was written to
    a. explain the different types of archaeological sites
    b. discuss archaeological excavation techniques
    c. explain why archaeology is important
    d. describe how to identify a habitation site

## Questions for Discussion

1. Prehistoric people are often thought of as apes or monsters. After reading descriptions of their habitation, burial, religious, and art sites, how do you regard them? Were they human?

2. What do you think is the value in studying ancient peoples and their living habits?

3. What kinds of sites do you think future archaeologists might find when studying our civilization?

| Selection 5: | | 794 words |
|---|---|---|
| Finishing Time: | HR.    MIN. | SEC. |
| Starting Time: | HR.    MIN. | SEC. |
| Reading Time: | MIN. | SEC. |
| WPM Score: | | |
| Comprehension Score: | | _____ % |

PHYSICS

## READING SELECTION 6
### WHY THE SKY IS BLUE, SUNSETS ARE RED, AND CLOUDS ARE WHITE

Paul G. Hewitt
From *Conceptual Physics*

*We often tend to accept the physical world around us without questioning why it is as it is. This excerpt from a physics text asks questions about three common characteristics of our physical world. What other questions does this bring to mind?*

### Why the Sky is Blue

1     If a beam of a particular frequency of sound is directed to a tuning fork of similar frequency, the tuning fork will be set into vibration and will effectively redirect the beam in many directions. The tuning fork *scatters* the sound. A similar process occurs with the scattering of light from atoms and particles that are far apart from one another, as in the atmosphere.

2     We know that atoms behave like tiny optical tuning forks and re-emit light waves that shine on them. Very tiny particles do the same. The tinier the particle, the higher the frequency of light it will scatter. This is similar to the way small bells ring with higher notes than larger bells. The nitrogen and oxygen molecules and the tiny particles that make up the atmosphere are like tiny bells that "ring" with high frequencies when energized by sunlight. Like sound from the bells, the re-emitted light is sent in all directions. It is scattered (Figure 26.16).

3     Most of the ultraviolet light from the sun is absorbed by a thin protective layer of ozone gas in the upper atmosphere. The remaining ultraviolet sunlight that passes through the atmosphere is scattered by atmospheric particles and molecules. Of the visible frequencies, violet is scattered the most, followed by blue, green, yellow, orange, and red, in that order. Red is scattered only a tenth as much as violet. Although violet light is scattered more than blue, our eyes are not very sensitive to violet light. The lesser amount of blue predominates in our vision, so we see a blue sky!

4     The blue of the sky varies in different places under different conditions. A principal factor is the water-vapor content of the atmosphere. On clear dry days the sky is a much deeper blue than on clear days with high humidity. Places where the upper air is exceptionally dry, such as Italy and Greece, have beautifully blue skies that have inspired painters for centuries. Where there are a lot of particles of dust and other particles larger than oxygen and nitrogen molecules, the lower frequencies of light are scattered more. This makes the sky less blue, and it takes on a whitish appearance. After a heavy rainstorm when the particles have been washed away, the sky becomes a deeper blue.

5     The grayish haze in the skies of large cities is the result of particles emitted by internal com-

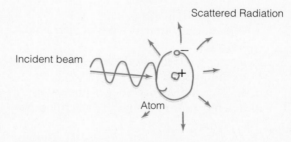

Scattered Radiation

Incident beam

Atom

**Figure 26.16** A beam of light falls on an atom and causes the electrons in the atom to vibrate. The vibrating electrons, in turn, re-emit light in various directions. Light is scattered.

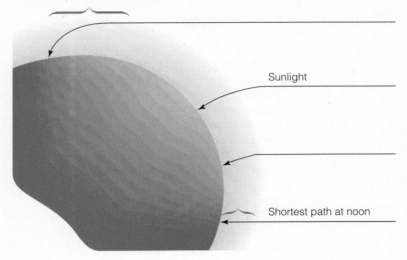

Greatest path of sunlight through atmosphere is at sunset (or sunrise)

Sunlight

Shortest path at noon

**Figure 26.18** A sunbeam must travel through more kilometers of atmosphere at sunset than at noon. As a result, more blue is scattered from the beam at sunset than at noon. By the time a beam of initially white light gets to the ground, only the lower frequencies survive to produce a red sunset.

bustion engines (cars, trucks, and industrial plants). Even when idling, a typical automobile engine emits more than 100 billion particles per second. Most are invisible and provide a framework to which other particles adhere. These are the primary scatterers of lower frequency light. For the larger of these particles, absorption rather than scattering takes place and a brownish haze is produced. Yuk!

## Why Sunsets Are Red

6    The lower frequencies of light are scattered the least by nitrogen and oxygen molecules, the primary components of our atmosphere. Therefore red, orange, and yellow light are transmitted through the atmosphere much more than violet and blue. Red, which is scattered the least, passes through more atmosphere than any other color. Therefore, when white light passes through a thick atmosphere, the higher frequencies are scattered most while the lower frequencies are transmitted with minimal scattering.

Such a thicker atmosphere is presented to sunlight at sunset.

7    At noon the sunlight travels through the least amount of atmosphere to reach the earth's surface. Only a small amount of high-frequency light is scattered from sunlight, enough to make the sun somewhat yellow. As the day progresses and the sun is lower in the sky (Figure 26.18), the path through the atmosphere is longer, and more blue is scattered from the sunlight. The removal of blue leaves the transmitted light more reddish in appearance. The sun becomes progressively redder, going from yellow to orange and finally to a red-orange at sunset.*

---

*Sunsets and sunrises would be unusually colorful if particles larger than atmospheric molecules were more abundant in the air. This was the case all over the world for three years following the eruption of the volcano Krakatoa in 1883, when micrometer-sized particles were spewed in abundance throughout the world's atmosphere. This occurred to a lesser extent following the 1991 eruption of Mount Pinatubo in the Philippines.

8 The colors of the sunset are consistent with our rules for color mixing. When blue is subtracted from white light, the complementary color that is left is yellow. When higher-frequency violet is subtracted, the result complementary color is orange. When medium-frequency green is subtracted, magenta is left. The combinations of resulting colors vary with atmospheric conditions, which change from day to day and give us a variety of sunsets.

9 Why do we see the scattered blue when the background is dark, but not when the background is bright? Because the scattered blue is faint. A faint color will show itself against a dark background, but not against a bright background. For example, when we look from the earth's surface at the atmosphere against the darkness of space, the atmosphere is sky blue. But astronauts above who look below through the same atmosphere to the bright surface of the earth do not see the same blueness.

### Why Clouds Are White

10 Clusters of water molecules in a variety of sizes make up clouds. The different-size clusters result in a variety of scattered frequencies: the tiniest, blue; slightly larger clusters, say, green; and still larger clusters, red. The overall result is a white cloud. Electrons close to one another in a cluster vibrate together and in step, which results in a greater intensity of scattered light than from the same number of electrons vibrating separately. Hence, clouds are bright!

11 Absorption occurs for larger droplets, and the scattered intensity is less. The clouds are darker. Further increase in the size of the drops causes them to fall to earth, and we have rain.

12 The next time you find yourself admiring a crisp blue sky, or delighting in the shapes of bright clouds, or watching a beautiful sunset, think about all those ultra-tiny optical tuning forks vibrating away—you'll appreciate these everyday wonders of nature even more!

## Comprehension Test 6*

### Checking Your Comprehension

1. Which of the visible colors is scattered the most? Which is scattered the least?

2. If violet light is scattered more than blue light, why isn't the sky violet?

3. What causes the sky to have a grayish hue in large cities?

4. What are the primary molecular components of our atmosphere?

### Thinking Critically

1. Why is the sky more blue in some countries than in others?

2. Why are red, orange, and yellow light more visible in the atmosphere than blue light?

3. What would make sunsets and sunrises even more colorful?

4. Why aren't all sunsets the same color? What causes them to have a variety of shades?

*Multiple-choice questions are contained in Appendix B (page A9).

**Questions for Discussion**

1. How can we solve the problem caused by automobiles emitting particles in the air?

2. Explain the process of rain, then discuss how seeding the clouds might affect this process.

3. Describe in nontechnical terms how clouds get to be white when they are made up of blue, green, and red particles.

4. Discuss the probable changes in the earth's atmosphere when the sky changes from one shade of blue to another.

| Selection 6: | | | 944 words |
|---|---|---|---|
| Finishing Time: | _____ | _____ | _____ |
| | HR. | MIN. | SEC. |
| Starting Time: | _____ | _____ | _____ |
| | HR. | MIN. | SEC. |
| Reading Time: | | _____ | _____ |
| | | MIN. | SEC. |
| WPM Score: | | _____ | |
| Comprehension Score: | | _____ % | |

**Visit the Longman English Pages**

For additional readings and exercises, visit the Longman English Skills Web page at:

**http://longman.awl.com/englishpages**

For a username and password, please see your instructor.

# Task Performance Assessment
# UNIT ONE

The following task is designed to assess your ability to use and apply the skills taught in this unit.

## THE SETTING

Assume you are taking an anthropology course this semester. On the first day of class your instructor accounced, "If you want to pass this course, you will need to learn to speak its language! You will also have to be able to think about language and its functions."

In class today your instructor returns your first exam; you got an "A," but your best friend got a "D." Your friend asks you what you did to earn such a high grade. When you reply that you heeded your instructor's first-day advice, your friend asks you to show her what you did, using tonight's reading assignment as an example.

## THE TASK

Assume you have been assigned Reading #5 (p. 93) as part of tonight's reading assignment. Complete each of the following tasks as if you were to use them as demonstrations for your friend.

1. Preread Reading Selection #5. Place brackets ([ ]) around everything you read as part of your prereading.
2. Write four guide questions that would be useful to focus your reading.
3. Prepare a set of vocabulary cards using the index card system. Include at least five words you will need to learn for the next exam.
4. Define each of the following words from context by using prefixes, roots, or suffixes.
   a. communal (para. 4)
   b. intangible (para. 4)
   c. subterranean (para.5)
   d. excavations (para. 7)
   e. obsidian (para. 7)
   f. *ziggurats* (para. 8)

# UNIT 2
# Using Text Structure to Improve Your Comprehension

Reading is a complex process. It involves much more than adding word meanings together and understanding ideas. A reader must also recognize the relationships and structures among ideas. To read efficiently you need to be able to grasp quickly each idea a writer expresses and then determine how it relates to the other ideas expressed in that piece of writing. To be able to grasp ideas and their relationships quickly, you must be familiar with the basic structure and organization of sentences, paragraphs, and longer selections. Once you understand how a particular piece of writing is organized, you can often follow the author's train of thought much more easily and more quickly.

The purpose of this unit is to acquaint you with the basic structure and organization of writing material. Chapter 4 is concerned with the essential elements of the paragraph and shows how understanding the elements of this structure can increase your efficiency. Chapter 5 presents five of the most common patterns used in organizing paragraphs and longer pieces of writing and shows how recognizing organizational patterns can increase your retention of content. Chapter 6 focuses on the structure of and strategies for reading articles and essays. Narrative, descriptive, and expository essays as well as scholarly journal articles are discussed.

# CHAPTER 4

# Main Idea and Paragraph Structure

IN THIS CHAPTER YOU WILL LEARN:

1. To identify the topic of a paragraph.
2. To identify the main idea and topic sentence of a paragraph.
3. To develop expectations about the writer's ideas.
4. To recognize supporting details and understand their relationship to the main idea.
5. To use transitions to see the connections between ideas.

When you shop you expect to find all types of cereal displayed on the same shelf and all size 34 pants hung together on a rack. All items of a similar type are grouped together for convenience. Ideas expressed in written form are also grouped together into paragraphs for the reader's convenience. Notice what happens when ideas are *not* grouped together, as in the following sentences:

Willow trees provide a great deal of shade, but it is difficult to mow the lawn underneath them. Outdoor barbecues or corn roasts are enjoyable ways to entertain during the summer. When beginning college, many students are worried about whether or not they will know someone in each of their classes. The income tax structure in our country has been changed so that it does not discriminate against married couples who are both employed. Most people do not realize that tea and cola drinks contain as much caffeine as coffee.

● ● ●

This so-called paragraph is confusing because the train of thought is impossible to follow. It is not clear which idea or ideas are important and which are not. You have no sense of whether or not the ideas are connected to each other and, if they are, how they are related.

To avoid the confusion demonstrated in the example paragraph and to express written ideas in a clear, understandable way, writers follow a general pattern in developing paragraphs. You need to recognize this structure in order to read paragraphs efficiently. You will then be able to follow the

**103**

author's train of thought more easily, anticipate ideas as they are about to be developed, and recall more of what you read.

A paragraph is structured around three essential elements: the topic, the main idea, and the supporting details that are often connected by transitional words or phrases. The function of each of these elements is discussed in this chapter.

## ■ IDENTIFYING THE TOPIC

A paragraph can be defined as a group of related ideas. The sentences relate to one another in the sense that each is about a common person, place, thing, or idea. This common subject or idea is called the *topic*. Simply defined, the topic is what the entire paragraph is about. As you read the following paragraph, notice that each sentence discusses mortgages.

> One of the largest components of debt is the mortgage, the debt owed on real estate. In speaking of the mortgage market it is important to distinguish between real estate mortgages and mortgages as a type of security for a debt obligation. In one sense, one mortgages a car to secure a car loan. Any time an asset is pledged to secure a loan, a mortgage is created. Since real estate loans are so typically secured by a pledge of real estate, such loans are themselves called mortgages. Mortgage borrowing exceeds the combined borrowing of corporations and municipalities by a wide margin.
>
> Kolb, *Investments.*

● ● ●

In this paragraph you can see that each sentence defines, explains, or provides examples of mortgages.

To identify the topic of a paragraph, ask yourself this question: "Who or what is the paragraph about?" Your answer to this question will be the topic of the paragraph. Now, try using this question as you read the following paragraph.

> People with normal vision need only the three additive primary colors to reproduce all the colors of the spectrum. People who are partially color blind need only two hues to reproduce all the colors they can see. The majority of partially color blind people can match all the hues they can see with combinations of only blue and yellow—they cannot distinguish between reds and greens, which take on a grayish appearance. (How many automobile accidents could have been avoided if traffic engineers had taken color blindness into account when stoplights were first designed?) A few people are yellow-blue blind, and all the colors they can see can be reproduced by combinations of red and green. The very few individuals who are totally color blind need but one color (any color at all—they all seem the same) to

reproduce all they can see. These few see no color at all—their world appears as one black-and-white movie.

Hewitt, *Conceptual Physics.*

• • •

In this paragraph, the question leads you directly to the topic—color blindness. Each sentence in the paragraph describes or defines color blindness. Now, try to identify the topic in the following paragraph.

Next time you fill up your tank, look at the price schedule on the pump. There you will see that several cents of each gallon's price is a federal tax. (In addition, most states—and some cities—charge a tax on gasoline.) Most of these federal tax collections flow into highway trust funds, on the assumption that motorists should pay for the construction and repair of the nation's highways. (If you own a boat, you still pay the tax for gasoline. But you can receive a rebate of the federal tax proceeds at the end of the year. The reason, of course, is that boats don't need highways.)

Chisholm and McCarty, *Principles of Economics.*

• • •

The topic of this paragraph is gasoline taxes. Each sentence discusses a type of or use for gasoline tax.

## EXERCISE 4–1

*DIRECTIONS:* Read each of the following paragraphs and then select the topic of the paragraph from the choices given.

1. Because conflict is inevitable, an essential relationship skill involves fighting fair. Winning at all costs, beating down the other person, getting one's own way, and the like have little use in a primary relationship or family. Instead, cooperation, compromise, and mutual understanding must be substituted. If we enter conflict with a person we love with the idea that we must win and the other must lose, the conflict has to hurt at least one partner, very often both. In these situations the loser gets hurt and frequently retaliates so that no one really wins in any meaningful sense. On the other hand, if we enter a conflict to achieve some kind of mutual understanding, neither party need be hurt. Both parties, in fact, may benefit from the clash of ideas or desires and from the airing of differences.

   DeVito, *Messages: Building Interpersonal Communication Skills.*

   a. relationships
   b. airing differences
   c. fighting fair
   d. conflicts

2. Both potential and kinetic energies can take many different forms. For example, a car battery has potential electrical energy. (We might also refer to it as chemical energy.) When the electrical energy is released to turn the starter, it becomes mechanical energy. As the parts of the starter move, friction causes some of the initial energy from the battery to be dissipated as heat energy. Thus, we see that not only can energy exist in different forms, it can also be converted from one form to another.

   Wallace, *Biology: The World of Life.*

   a. forms of energy
   b. energy in batteries
   c. potential and kinetic energy
   d. mechanical energy

3. Different species forage in different ways. Basically, animals can be described as either generalists or specialists. Generalists are those species with a broad range of acceptable food items. They are often opportunists and will take advantage of whatever is available, with certain preferences, depending on the situation. Crows are an example of feeding generalists; they will eat anything from corn to carrion. Specialists are those with narrow ranges of acceptable food items. Some species are extremely specialized, such as the Everglade kite, or snail kite, which feeds almost exclusively on freshwater snails. There is a wide range of intermediate types between the two extremes, and in some species an animal will switch from being one type to being another depending on conditions, such as food availability or the demands of offspring.

   Ferl, Wallace, and Sanders, *Biology: The Realm of Life.*

   a. species of animals
   b. generalists
   c. demands of offspring
   d. types of foragers

4. Much as we touch and are touched, we also avoid touch from certain people and in certain circumstances. Researchers in nonverbal communication have found some interesting relationships between touch avoidance and other significant communication variables. For example, touch avoidance is positively related to communication apprehension; those who fear oral communication also score high on touch avoidance. Touch avoidance is also high with those who self-disclose little. Both touch and self-disclosure are intimate forms of communication; thus, people who are reluctant to get close to another person by self-disclosing also seem reluctant to get close by touching.

   DeVito, *Messages: Building Interpersonal Communication Skills.*

    a.   nonverbal communication
    b.   self-disclosure
    c.   touch avoidance
    d.   communication apprehension

5.   The current high divorce rate in the United States does not mean, as common sense would suggest, that the institution of marriage is very unpopular. On the contrary, people seem to love marriage too much, as suggested by several pieces of evidence. First, our society has the highest rate of marriage in the industrial world despite having the highest rate of divorce. Second, within the United States, most of the southeastern, southwestern, and western states have higher divorce rates than the national average but also have higher marriage rates. And third, the majority of those who are divorced eventually remarry. Why don't they behave like Mark Twain's cat, who after having been burned by a hot stove would not go near any stove? Apparently, divorce in U.S. society does not represent a rejection of marriage but only a specific partner.

Thio, Sociology.

    a.   the marriage rate
    b.   popularity of marriage
    c.   high divorce rates
    d.   rejection of marriage

## EXERCISE 4–2

*DIRECTIONS:* Read each of the following paragraphs and identify the topic by writing it in the space provided.

1.   Coffee trees (actually they are more shrubs than trees) are relatively fast-growing, bearing fruits three to four years after planting. The fruits take another seven to nine months to mature. It is from these that the beverage used by at least a third of the world's people is produced. The mature fruits, or berries, are harvested by hand and are processed by one of two methods. The dry method is used in most of Brazil's coffee-producing regions: the fruits are spread out to dry in the sun for fifteen to twenty-five days and then hulled. The wet method calls for pulping the berries after picking to remove the outer layer and part of the fleshy inner layer of the fruit. The pulped fruit is them fermented in tanks, washed, and sun-dried for eight to ten days. The dry skin around the beans is removed by milling and polishing, leaving shiny blue or grayish blue beans. The characteristic brown color is produced by roasting.

Laetsch, Plants: Basic Concepts in Botany.

Topic: _____

2. Many long lists of emotional motives like security, curiosity, ego, comfort, recreation, emulation, pride, sex, and many others have been put forth. Any attempt to develop a complete classification of emotional buying motives is doomed to failure, however, because to make it both complete and mutually exclusive is impossible. One's emotions are such complex phenomena that it is presumptuous to attempt to single out and classify them. Two families may purchase the same model automobile for ostensibly the same commonly mentioned motive, "keeping up with the Joneses." Nevertheless, the exact motive-mixes underlying the purchase of the two cars may be different. One family may have bought its car because everyone else in the neighborhood had a new car. The other family may have acquired its new car because the husband felt his status in the community demanded that he drive a better car. Though both of these purchases would be lumped together in the broad category of "keeping up appearances," they were nevertheless made for different reasons.

Buskirk, *Principles of Marketing, The Management View.*

Topic: _____

3. It was a medieval custom to *swaddle* infants during their first year. Swaddling involved wrapping the infant in cloth bandages with arms and legs pressed closely to the body. Parents feared that infants might scratch their eyes and distort their tender limbs by bending them improperly. Swaddling also kept them from touching their genitals and from crawling "like a beast." However, De Mause, a historian who has studied concepts of childhood and child-rearing practices of the past, has found evidence that the main purpose of swaddling was adult convenience. Swaddled infants tend to be quiet and passive; they sleep more, their heart rate slows, and they cry less. Swaddled infants might be laid for hours "behind a hot oven, or hung on pegs on the wall," and leading-strings were sometimes used to "puppet" the infant around for the amusement of adults.

Gander and Gardiner, *Child and Adolescent Development.*

Topic: _____

4. Before we started radio communication in the last century, people had suggested ingenious ways of signaling our presence to other worlds in the solar system: huge bonfires in simple geometric patterns such as squares or triangles; planting a 16-kilometer-wide strip of pine forest in Siberia in the form of a right triangle; huge mirrors to reflect sunlight; a 30-kilometer circular ditch filled with water over which kerosene would be poured and set burning; a powerful concave mirror

to focus sunlight on Mars and burn simple numbers on the desert sands of the planet; a network of large sunlight-reflecting mirrors strategically positioned in several European cities forming the shape of the Big Dipper in Ursa Major.

Berman and Evans, *Exploring the Cosmos.*

Topic: _____

5. An understanding of the eye's ability to form images of both near and distant objects requires a basic knowledge of certain principles of optics. Light travels through air at an incredibly fast rate, approximately 300,000 kilometers/second. Light also travels through other transparent media, such as water and glass, but more slowly. When light rays pass from one medium into another of a different density, the rays are bent unless they strike the surface of the second medium at a perfectly perpendicular angle. The extent of this bending, or refraction, of light varies with the angle between the light rays and the surface of the medium . . . .

Davis, Holtz, and Davis, *Conceptual Human Physiology.*

Topic: _____

## ■ FINDING THE MAIN IDEA

When you make phone calls have you found it helpful to state the general purpose of your call as you begin your conversation? Have you found that in answering a help-wanted ad, it is useful to begin by saying, "I'm calling about your ad in . . . " Or, when calling a doctor's office to make an appointment, you might say, "I'm calling to make an appointment to see Dr. —." Beginning with a general statement such as these helps your listener understand why you are calling and what you want. It also allows the listener time to focus his or her attention before you begin to give the details of your situation. The general statement also gives the listener a chance to organize himself or herself or to get ready to receive the information.

Writers also need to help the reader understand the purpose and organization of a written message. Readers, like listeners, sometimes need assistance in focusing and organizing their thoughts and in anticipating the development of the message. Writers, therefore, often provide a general, organizing statement of the main idea of each paragraph. The sentence that most clearly states this main idea is called *the topic sentence.*

Depending on its placement within the paragraph, the topic sentence provides the reader with different clues. In this section several of the most common placements of topic sentences and the clues that each offers the reader about paragraph development and organization are discussed. Each type has been diagrammed to help you visualize how it is structured.

## ■ Topic Sentence First

The most common location of the topic sentence is the beginning of the paragraph. It may appear as the very first sentence of after an introductory or transitional sentence (one that connects this paragraph to the previous paragraph). In cases with topic sentence first, the author states his or her main idea and then goes on to explain and develop that idea, as in the following paragraph.

> <u>Communication is essential to any kind of social system</u>. Even the apparently solitary male orangutan starts the day with a booming cry that tells other orangutans where he is. Sounds of this kind are common among the primates and many other mammals. Where primates live in social groups, communication is much more complicated. The animals must judge others' emotions, which are conveyed by gestures and sounds. Bluffing is very important, and all the apes have biological structures adapted for bluffing. Gorillas, for example, pound their chests. Chimpanzees charge, hoot, and throw objects. In orangutans there are very large sacs connected with the larynx, and these make the territorial noises possible. When an ape and some monkeys are demonstrating aggressively, the hair on the heads and around the shoulders stands up. This has the effect of making the creature look two or three times its normal size, and being subject to a sudden bluff of this kind can be a scary experience.
>
> Washburn and Moore, *Ape into Human*.

● ● ●

Notice that the author begins by stating that communication is an important part of any social system. Then, throughout the remainder of the paragraph, he explains the importance of communication by showing how it operates within the social structure of primates. When the topic sentence appears first in the paragraph, it announces what the paragraph will be about and what to expect in the remainder of the paragraph.

## ■ Topic Sentence Last

The second most likely place for a topic sentence to appear is the end of the paragraph. However, on occasion you may find that it is expressed in the second-to-last sentence, with the last sentence functioning as a restatement or as a transition to connect the paragraph with what follows. When the topic sentence occurs last, you can expect the writer to build a structure of ideas and offer the topic sentence as a concluding statement. Commonly used in argumentative or persuasive writing, this structure uses sentences within the paragraph as building blocks that support the topic sentence. Notice in the following paragraph that the author leads up to the main idea and states it at the end of the paragraph.

> We can measure the radioactivity of plants and animals today and compare this with the radioactivity of ancient organic matter. If we extract a small, but precise, quantity of carbon from an ancient wooden ax handle, for example, and find it has one-half as much radioactivity as an equal quantity of carbon extracted from a living tree, then the old wood must have come from a tree that was cut down or made from a log that died 5730 years ago. <u>In this way, we can probe into the past as much as 50,000 years to find out such things as the age of ancient civilizations or the times of the ice ages that covered the earth.</u>
>
> Hewitt, *Conceptual Physics.*

● ● ●

In this paragraph the author begins by explaining that radioactivity of plants and animals can be measured and can be compared with older organic matter. Then he uses an example describing how the radioactivity of an ancient ax handle can be measured and how its age can be determined. In the last sentence the author states the main idea, that this procedure can be used to learn about the past.

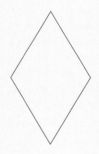

## ■ Topic Sentence in the Middle

If it is neither first nor last the topic sentence will, of course, appear somewhere in the middle of the paragraph. In this case, the topic sentence splits the paragraph into two parts: those sentences preceding it and those that follow it. The sentences that precede the topic sentence often lead up to or introduce the main idea. At other times, the preceding sentences may function as a transition, connecting the ideas to be expressed in the paragraph with ideas in previous paragraphs. The sentences that follow the topic sentence usually explain, describe, or provide further information about the main idea. Notice the placement of the topic sentence as you read the following paragraph.

> Chinese and Japanese Americans have a higher percentage of high school and college graduates than whites or than other minorities. Asians make up 3 percent of the population of the United States, but they make up 21 percent of the student body at the University of California at Berkeley. At Harvard, 8 percent of the students are Asian Americans. <u>In fact, in terms of education and career advancement, Asian Americans are among the most successful minorities in the United States today.</u> In the professional fields of science and engineering, a higher percentage of Asian Americans than whites hold doctoral degrees. Asian American professors have more publications than their white counterparts. Moreover, Asian Americans have a higher average family income than whites.

● ● ●

The paragraph begins by offering some statistics that compare Chinese and Japanese Americans with whites and other minorities. In the middle of the paragraph the writer makes a general statement about what these statistics show. This is the topic sentence of the paragraph. The author then offers additional facts that support the topic sentence.

### ■ Topic Sentence First and Last

Occasionally you may find a paragraph in which the main idea is stated at the beginning and again at the end. This structure is often used for emphasis or clarification. If a writer wants to emphasize an important idea, he or she may repeat it at the end of the paragraph. Or, a writer who thinks an idea needs to be said another way to ensure that the reader understands it may repeat it at the end of the paragraph. In the following paragraph notice that both the first and last sentences state, in different words, the same idea.

> <u>The study of prehistoric humans is, of necessity, the study of their fossil remains.</u> To begin to understand who our ancestors were and what they were like, we must be able to interpret the fragments of them that are coming to the surface in increasing numbers. Given fairly reliable methods to determine their age, we can now turn with more confidence to primate fossils for an answer to the all-important question: How do we tell monkeys, apes, and humans apart? For present-day species this is no problem; all have evolved sufficiently so that they no longer resemble one another. But since they all have a common ancestor, the farther back we go in time, the more similar their fossils begin to look. There finally comes a point when they are indistinguishable. <u>The construction of a primate fossil family tree is essential if we are ever going to discover the line of descent from early hominid to modern human.</u>
>
> Campbell, *Humankind Emerging.*

● ● ●

In the preceding paragraph, both the first and last sentences state that the study of fossils enables us to study prehistoric man. The other sentences explain why fossils are important and how they can be used to distinguish stages in the development of man.

## EXERCISE 4–3

*DIRECTIONS:* Read each of the following paragraphs and then select the main idea of each from the choices given.

1.  If legislation can compel people to give up discrimination, what about their prejudice? It is true, as many lawmakers believe, that we cannot legislate against prejudice because such legislation is practically unenforceable. That is probably why we do not have any antiprejudice law.

But by legislating against discrimination, we can gradually eliminate prejudice. Sample research has long established that people tend to change their attitude if it has been inconsistent for some time with their behavior. This usually involves changing their attitude so that it becomes consistent with their behavior. Thus, people can be expected to gradually change their prejudicial attitude into an unprejudicial one after they have been legally forced to develop the habit of behaving nondiscriminatory. Indeed, since 1954 a series of civil rights laws and court rulings have caused many whites to stop their discriminatory practices and to reevaluate their attitude toward blacks. Today fewer whites are prejudiced. They do not express their prejudice in the traditional stereotypical "redneck" way but in a more indirect, subtle manner.

Thio, *Sociology.*

a. Prejudice can be defeated by passing laws against discrimination.
b. Civil rights laws have stopped whites from discriminating against blacks.
c. Most white Americans are prejudiced.
d. We cannot legislate against prejudice.

2. The major benefit of steroids seems to be to allow muscles to recover more quickly from exercise, so that the athlete can train harder. As athletes were reporting remarkable results with steroids, the medical community began testing the effects of the drugs and the drugs were soon banned. Medical researchers reported a variety of serious side effects of steroid use, including liver cancer, heart disease, and kidney damage. One problem with the drugs is that, along with tissue building, they also "masculinize." The masculinization is particularly acute for women, who may grow facial hair as their voices deepen and their breasts decrease in size. They may, indeed, gain muscle mass, but the masculinizing effects may be impossible to reverse. In adolescents, steroids hasten maturation and may cause growth to stop and the loss of hair in boys. Strangely, in men, the high levels of steroids in the body may cause the body's own production of male hormone to cease, resulting in enlarged breasts and shrunken testes.

Wallace, *Biology: The World of Life.*

a. Muscle recovery from exercise is aided by steroids.
b. The medical community recently began testing the results of steroids.
c. There are a number of serious side effects from steroid use.
d. Some women grow facial hair as a result of steroids.

3. Americans are deeply divided on the issue of abortion. Polls can be found indicating strong support for a woman's right to choose, while

others indicate strong majorities opposing unlimited abortion. Proponents of choice believe that access to abortion is essential if women are to be fully autonomous human beings. Opponents call themselves pro-life because they believe that the fetus is fully human; therefore, an abortion deprives a fetus of the right to life. These positions are irreconcilable, making abortion a politician's nightmare. Wherever a politician stands on this divisive issue, a large number of voters will be enraged.

Edwards et. al., *Government in America.*

a. Strong majorities of Americans oppose abortion.
b. Politicians have trouble with the issue of abortion.
c. Pro-life opponents believe a fetus is a complete human being.
d. Abortion is a matter that seriously divides America.

4. Assertive people are willing to assert their own rights. Unlike their aggressive counterparts, however, they do not hurt others in the process. Assertive people speak their minds and welcome others doing likewise. Robert Alberti and Michael Emmons (1970), in *Your Perfect Right,* the first book on assertiveness training, note that "behavior which enables a person to act in his own best interest, to stand up for himself without undue anxiety, to express his honest feelings comfortably, or to exercise his own rights without denying the rights of others we call assertive behavior." Furthermore, "The assertive individual is fully in charge of himself in interpersonal relationships, feels confident and capable without cockiness or hostility, is basically spontaneous in the expression of feelings and emotions, and is generally looked up to and admired by others." Surely this is the picture of an effective individual.

DeVito, *Messages: Building Interpersonal Communication Skills.*

a. Assertive people stand up for themselves without hurting others.
b. Aggressive individuals do not care if they hurt other people.
c. Alberti and Emmons wrote the first book on assertiveness training.
d. Effective individuals are the result of assertiveness training.

5. Like all the topics covered in this text, power too has an important cultural dimension. In some cultures power is concentrated in the hands of a few and there is a great difference in the power held by these people and by the ordinary citizen: These are called high power distance cultures; examples include Mexico, Brazil, India, and the Philippines (Hofstede, 1984). In low power distance cultures, power is more evenly distributed throughout the citizenry; examples include Denmark, New Zealand, Sweden, and to a lesser extent, the United States. These differences impact on communication in a number of ways. For example, in high power distance cultures there is a great power distance

between students and teachers; students are expected to be modest, polite, and totally respectful. In the United States, on the other hand, students are expected to demonstrate their knowledge and command of the subject matter, participate in discussions with the teacher, and even challenge the teacher, something many African and Asian students wouldn't even think of doing.

DeVito, *Messages: Building Interpersonal Communication Skills.*

a. Low power distance cultures distribute power evenly.
b. African and Asian students would never challenge the teacher.
c. How power is distributed in a culture determines people's behaviors.
d. Only a few people possess power in Mexico, Brazil, India, and the Philipines.

## EXERCISE 4–4

*DIRECTIONS:* Read the following paragraphs and underline the topic sentence in each.

1. Many Americans with disabilities have suffered from both direct and indirect discrimination. They have often been denied rehabilitation services (a kind of affirmative action), education, and jobs. Many people with disabilities have been excluded from the workforce and isolated without overt discrimination. Throughout most of American history, public and private buildings have been hostile to the blind, deaf, and mobility-impaired. Stairs, buses, telephones, and other necessities of modern life have been designed in ways that keep these individuals out of offices, stores, and restaurants. As one slogan said: "Once, blacks had to ride at the back of the bus. We can't even get on the bus."

Edwards, et. al., *Government in America.*

2. A few years ago it was said that a biologist is one who thinks that molecules are too small to matter, a physicist is one who thinks that molecules are too large to matter, and anyone who disagrees with both of them is a chemist. Many biologists, though, are in fact chemists, and vice versa. Perhaps it is true that the biologist whose scope is limited to molecules must periodically be convinced of the existence of the platypus, but no one else has been able to tell us how tiny hummingbirds are able to make it across the Gulf of Mexico. Fortunately, the sharp lines of division between such disciplines are becoming blurred and indistinct as scientists become more broadly trained and able to handle more kinds of ideas in their continuing effort to solve the "Great Puzzle of Life."

Wallace, *Biology: The World of Life.*

3. When frustrations arising from nonproductive behaviors are kept to a minimum, groups can function in an efficient and effective manner. There are, however, times when a group's task and social needs come into direct conflict. If, for example, a group becomes unhappy with its leadership, task-related activities may grind to a halt while members concentrate on the social atmosphere. The group may need to reorganize by appointing new leaders or reassigning responsibilities in order to refocus its attention on task issues. A group also may assume a "know nothing" attitude, in which it despairs of ever having enough information to make a decision (hence relieving it of the responsibility for acting). In this social atmosphere the group may appoint ad hoc study groups to gain new information or postpone consideration of an issue until new information is forthcoming from outside the group. In both cases, task activities are inhibited by a negative social atmosphere that promotes apathy and indifference at the expense of involvement and commitment.

Benjamin and McKerrow, *Business and Professional Communication: Concepts and Practices.*

4. This basic division of labor has been accompanied by many popular stereotypes—oversimplified mental images—of what women and men are supposed to be, and to some extent these stereotypes persist. Women are supposed to be shy, easily intimidated, and passive; men, bold, ambitious, and aggressive. Women should be weak and dainty; men, strong and athletic. It is not bad form for women, but it is for men, to worry about their appearance and aging. Women are expected to be emotional, even to cry easily, but men should hold back their emotions and must not cry. Women are expected to be sexually passive and naive; men, aggressive and experienced. Women are believed to be dependent, in need of male protection; men are supposed to be independent, fit to be leaders. Women are expected to be intuitive and inconsistent; men, logical, rational, and objective.

Thio, *Sociology.*

5. If you are a member of an ethnic group, the assumption of a company that all employees are the same and are treated the same may not hold true in your experience. The fact, for example, that there are associations solely for the support of African-American employees suggests that we still have a ways to go in removing obstacles. In reacting to issues, companies employ a variety of strategies, based on face-to-face communication. Mobil Oil Corporation, for example, did not sit on the assumption that all was well. Instead, it formed two sets of training programs, with one expressly for minority professionals. This gave the minority employees a forum in which to air their perceptions and a means of using communication positively to arrive at solutions. Other

companies initiate informal group discussions to ascertain the nature of problems. Out of these, as in the case of Michigan Bell, can come more formalized groups that meet to consider issues that have an impact on ethnic relations.

Benjamin and McKerrow, *Business and Professional Communication: Concepts and Practices.*

## EXERCISE 4–5

*DIRECTIONS:* The following excerpt is taken from a biology textbook chapter titled "Bioethics, Technology, and Environment." Read the excerpt and underline the topic sentence in each paragraph.

### POLLUTION BY PESTICIDES

Pesticides are biologically rather interesting substances. Most have no known counterpart in the natural world, and most didn't even exist fifty years ago. Today, however, a metabolic product of DDT, called DDE, may be the most common synthetic chemical on earth. It has been found in the tissues of living things from polar regions to the remotest parts of the oceans, forests, and mountains. Although the permissible level of DDT in cow's milk, set by the U.S. Food and Drug Administration, is 0.05 parts per million, it often occurs in human milk in concentrations as high as five parts per million and in human fat at levels of more than twelve parts per million.

**Pesticides,** of course, are products that kill pests. But what is a pest? Biologically, the term has no meaning. The Colorado potato beetle, for example, was never regarded as a pest until it made its way (carried by humans) to Europe, where it began to seriously interfere with potato production. Perhaps this episode best illustrates a definition of a pest: it is something that interferes with humans.

It seems that the greatest pesticidal efforts have been directed at insects and, clearly, much of it has been beneficial. The heavy application of DDT after World War II decreased malaria and yellow fever in certain areas of the world. But DDT and other chlorinated hydrocarbons have continued to be spread indiscriminately any place in which insect pests are found. The result of course, is a kind of (is it artificial or natural?) selection. The problem was that some insects had a bit more resistance to these chemicals than did others. These resistant ones then reproduced and, in turn, the most resistant of their offspring continued the line. The result is that we now have insects that can almost bathe in these chemicals without harm, and malaria is again on the rise.

There are also other risks involved in such wide use of insecticides. For example, most are unselective in their targets; they kill virtually *all* the insect species they contact. Many insects, of course, are beneficial and may form an important part of large ecosystems. Also, some chemical insecticides move easily through the environment and can permeate far larger areas than intended. Another particularly serious problem with pesticides is that many of them persist in the environment for long periods.

In other words, some chemicals are very stable and it is difficult for natural process-es to break them down to their harmless components. Newer chemical pesticides are deadly in the short run, but quickly break down into harmless by-products.

In the past, the tendency of DDT to be magnified in food chains has been par-ticularly disastrous for predators that fed high on the food pyramid. This is because as one animal eats another in the food chain, the pesticide from each level is added to the next. Thus, species high on the food chain, the predators, tend to accumu-late very high levels of these chemicals. In this light, recall that humans are often the top predator in food chains. Before it was banned in the United States, the effects of accumulated DDT on predatory birds was substantial. Reproductive fail-ures in peregrine falcons, the brown pelican, and the Bermuda petrel have been attributed to ingesting high levels of DDT. The problem is that the pesticide inter-feres with the birds' ability to metabolize calcium. As a result, they were laying eggs with shells too thin to support the weight of a nesting parent. With the decline in the use of the pesticide, many bird populations have recovered.

## EXERCISE 4–6

*DIRECTIONS:* Read each of the following paragraphs, and then, in the space provided, write a statement that expresses the main idea of the paragraph.

1. While love is private, marriage is public. And since dating often leads to marriage, parents are concerned about their sons' and daughters' dating partners. Although college students perceive that their parents have very little or no control over whom they date, parental influence on dating may be both direct and indirect. Parents who have resources (car, money) that their offspring want may make them available in exchange for compliance from their offspring or withhold them for noncompliance. Such withholding of resources is at considerable cost to the parent-child relationship since college students regard it as a threat to their independence. They also resent parental involvement in their dating relationships and regard it as a serious violation of their right to choose their own date and mate.

   Knox, *Exploring Marriage and the Family.*

   Main Idea: _____

   _____

2. Earth is only one example of a planet. We must study different planets, each with its own complexity, to see how their differences have evolved from the same set of dynamic processes out of different initial conditions that led to their various structures. Earth does not exhibit all these processes. The planets are natural laboratories for observing phenomena beyond the range, in both time and processes, of our ter-

restrial limitations. To understand our own planet better, we must gain a perspective that can be acquired by a comparative study of other planets. The global processes on Earth are now beginning to be understood in the light of processes on other planets.

Berman and Evans, *Exploring the Cosmos.*

Main Idea:_____

_____

3. One's self-concepts are not fixed. They constantly change with experience and changes in attitudes, philosophies, and goals. It is a heartwarming experience to observe a young man in the process of upgrading his Ideal Self. Perhaps through a series of unfortunate academic selections he has been forced to conclude that he is a mediocre student at best: his Ideal Self requires only that he graduate from college. Then he encounters a subject area that appeals to him. His interest and grades soar. But at the same time the upgrading of his Ideal Self becomes perceptible. He may start thinking of graduate school. He starts making noises like a scholar instead of a playboy; he wants to alter his Real and Ideal Other. His consumption habits may also change; he may even rashly buy some nonrequired books.

Buskirk, *Principles of Marketing, The Management View.*

Main Idea:_____

_____

4. Any discussion of sex among the Puritans would not be complete without reference to bundling, also called tarrying. Although not unique to the Puritans, bundling was a courtship custom which involved the would-be groom's sleeping in the girl's bed in her parents' home. But there were rules to restrict sexual contact. Both partners had to be fully clothed, and a wooden bar was placed between them. In addition, the young girl might be encased in a type of long laundry bag up to her armpits, her clothes might be sewn together at strategic points, and her parents might be sleeping in the same room.

Knox, *Exploring Marriage and the Family.*

Main Idea:_____

_____

5. While parents get the child first and provide the most pervasive influence, teachers represent a major source of influence outside the home. In a study of how and when preschool teachers spoke to the children in their classroom, the researchers observed that the teachers rewarded boys for being aggressive (by showing attention when they were rowdy), rewarded girls for being dependent (by showing attention

when they were near), and gave more individual instruction to boys. And all of the fifteen teachers who were being observed were unaware that they were treating the sexes differently.

Knox, *Exploring Marriage and the Family.*

Main Idea:_____

_____

## ■ Paragraphs Without a Topic Sentence

Although most paragraphs do have a topic sentence, occasionally you will encounter a paragraph without one sentence that clearly expresses the main idea. This structure is used most commonly in descriptive or narrative writing. In these paragraphs you must form your own statement or impression of the main idea. Although the paragraph contains numerous clues, the reader must piece together the information to form a generalized statement.

Here is a paragraph that does not contain a topic sentence.

> For some people, carrying on the family name is important. Others want a child for its love or to prevent loneliness in old age. Some couples are curious about the result of their mixture of genes. Many of us have children because we want to give them opportunities that we never had or to treat them as we wish we had been treated: this may amount to living vicariously through our children. Some individuals have a child in order to hold their marriage together: this is unwise because it usually adds strain to an already failing relationship, and the child is often affected most.

Gander and Gardiner, *Child and Adolescent Development.*

● ● ●

This paragraph discusses the reasons people have children. The first sentence offers one reason (carrying on the family name), and the second presents another (love or the prevention of loneliness), and so forth. Each sentence is concerned with a different reason for having children. Although this paragraph lacks a topic sentence that explains what the paragraph is about, the main idea is quite clear: "People have children for numerous reasons."

Here is another example:

> For most of earth's history, the land was bare. A billion years ago, seaweeds clung to the shores at low tide and perhaps some gray-green lichens patched a few inland rocks. But, had anyone been there to observe it, the earth's surface would generally have appeared as barren and forbidding as the bleak Martian landscape. According to the fossil record, plants first began to invade the land a mere half billion years ago. Not until then did the earth's surface truly come to life. As a film of green spread from the edges of the waters, other forms of life—the heterotrophs—were able to

follow. The shapes of these new forms and the ways in which they lived were determined by the plant life that preceded them. Plants supplied not only their food—their chemical energy—but also their nesting, hiding, stalking, and breeding places.

Aceves and King, *Introduction to Anthropology.*

● ● ●

The paragraph describes the evolution of plants on earth. Each sentence contributes a piece of information about their development. Taken together, the facts indicate that plants evolved slowly, in stages, and other life forms followed them.

From these examples you can see that in some paragraphs the topic sentence is not necessary—the reader can easily "add up" the facts and arrive at his or her own statement of the main idea. If you encounter a paragraph in which the main idea is unstated and not immediately evident, first identify the topic, then ask yourself this question: "What does the writer want me to know about the topic?" In most cases, your answer will be a statement of the writer's main idea.

Once you have identified the main idea in a paragraph in which it is unstated, it may be useful to make a marginal note that summarizes the main idea of that paragraph. Then, when you are reviewing the material, it will not be necessary to reread the entire paragraph.

## EXERCISE 4–7

*DIRECTIONS:* Read the following paragraphs, which contain no topic sentences, and then select the main idea of each from the choices given.

1. Much like others form images of you based on what you do, you also react to your own behavior; you interpret it and evaluate it. For example, let us say you believe that lying is wrong. If you lie, you will evaluate this behavior in terms of your internalized beliefs about lying. You will thus react negatively to your own behavior. You may, for example, experience guilt because your behavior contradicts your beliefs. On the other hand, let's say that you pulled someone out of a burning building at great personal risk. You would probably evaluate this behavior positively; you will feel good about this behavior and, as a result, about yourself.

   DeVito, *Messages: Building Interpersonal Communication Skills.*

   a. If you feel good about your behavior you will feel good about yourself.
   b. How you react to your own behavior helps you to form a self-concept.
   c. You feel guilt when your behavior contradicts your beliefs.
   d. You need to take risks to feel good about yourself.

2. If you are using an object, bring it into view as it becomes the "center" of your speech, and then take the time to remove it from view. Otherwise, your audience's attention both before and after the demonstration will be focused on the object rather than the message. If your speech concerns steps in a process, and using objects helps clarify the methods employed, bring samples of finished stages with you. Do not attempt to work through a complex procedure on a single object. If you need to pass the object around the room, realize that as it moves from person to person less attention will be focused on your message. If you have the time and can continue discussing features of the object as it is passed around, you can focus the listeners' attention on your comments. You will find this approach makes it easier to move on to other phases of your message as you retrieve the object and place it out of sight. If this approach is impractical, and you have to leave the object in plain view, you can refocus attention by using other visual aids.

   Benjamin and McKerrow, *Business and Professional Communication: Concepts and Practices.*

   a. When giving a speech about a physical object, pass it around the room.
   b. Use objects when giving speeches about steps in a process.
   c. Use other visual aids to refocus attention during speeches involving objects.
   d. When giving a speech involving an object, plan how you will use it in advance.

3. People's acceptance of a product is largely determined by its package. The very same coffee taken from a yellow can was described as weak, from a dark brown can too strong, from a red can rich, and from a blue can mild. Even our acceptance of a person may depend on the colors worn. Consider, for example, the comments of one color expert "If you have to pick the wardrobe for your defense lawyer heading into court and choose anything but blue, you deserve to lose the case . . . ." Black is so powerful it could work against the lawyer with the jury. Brown lacks sufficient authority. Green would probably elicit a negative response.

   DeVito, *Messages: Building Interpersonal Communication Skills.*

   a. Colors have an influence on how we think and act.
   b. A product's package largely determines how we accept it.
   c. How effective lawyers are depends on their wardrobe colors.
   d. Color experts rank blue as the most influential to be worn.

4. Bonds hold atoms together, forming molecules. An ionic bond, due to the attractive force between two ions of opposite charge, is formed when electrons are transferred from one atom to another. A covalent bond is formed when atoms share electrons. In some molecules shared electrons are more strongly attracted to one of the atoms, polarizing the molecule. A hydrogen bond is a weak bond formed when the positive end of a hydrogen atom that is covalently bonded to one molecule is attracted to the negative end of another polar molecule. Hydrogen bonding between water molecules gives water some of its unusual characteristics.

Wallace, *Biology: The World of Life.*

   a. Ionic bonds involve the transfer of electrons between atoms.
   b. A number of bonds can be involved in molecule formation.
   c. The attraction between electrons and atoms causes bonds.
   d. Covalent bonds are formed when atoms share electrons.

5. The United States, Western European countries, and Japan are core countries, the world's upper class, the most industrialized and richest societies, popularly known as industrial or developed countries. They have highly diversified economies, producing practically anything from corn to microchips. They also have a very high standard of living, stable governments, and a great deal of individual freedom. Countries with the least influence in the world are called peripheral countries—the world's lower class, relatively poor societies, popularly known as developing countries. These are the predominantly agricultural countries in Africa, Asia, and Latin America. Their economies are highly specialized, producing and exporting to core countries only a few raw materials or foodstuffs, such as oil, copper, sugar, or coffee. Their governments tend to be unstable.

Thio, *Sociology.*

   a. The United States, Western Europe, and Japan are the world's upper class.
   b. The developing countries are known as peripheral countries.
   c. There are many differences between core and peripheral countries.
   d. The core countries are also known as industrialized or developed countries.

## EXERCISE 4–8

*DIRECTIONS:* Read each of the following paragraphs, none of which has a topic sentence. For each, write your own statement of the main idea of the paragraph.

1. Some physical anthropologists specialize in unearthing the fossil remains of our early ancestors. These *human paleontologists* dig in the earth for skeletons which they then reconstruct. They may also work with physicists and geologists, using various chemicals and radioactive substances, to determine the ages of the specimens removed from the earth. Other physical anthropologists are more closely related to biochemists in that they do the bulk of their work in laboratories, analyzing substances found in the bodies of primates, including humans. These scientists use microscopes and other laboratory equipment to study blood, urine, and other biochemicals. Their aim is to find variations in these substances—and the causes of the variations—among different human and nonhuman primates.

   Aceves and King, *Introduction to Anthropology.*

   Main Idea:_____

   _____

2. Today in America, $2 out of every $5 spent for food is spent eating away from home. In 1954 it was nearer $1 out of every $10. Based on these facts it is not difficult to see the tremendous opportunity that has existed in the foodservice industry during the past 20 years. Yet, from my vantage point as a keen observer of industry trends and events, I've seen hundreds of people and thousands of restaurants go broke. At the same time, I am personally aware of over 100 different people who have become millionaires in their endeavors in the foodservice field.

   Fox and Wheatly, *Modern Marketing.*

   Main Idea:_____

   _____

3. Overweight children are frequently rejected by their peer group because they do not do well in sports and because they may be ungainly. A teen-age girl who is overweight, unless she has an unusual personality, may be ostracized by her peers. She is not asked to dance at parties and may not have dates. The results can be very serious, for these social activities are a normal part of growing up. Both men and women may become the butt of jokes by their friends because of their obese condition. Although they may appear to take it good naturally, the sting remains.

   Flack, *Introduction to Nutrition.*

   Main Idea:_____

   _____

4. Traffic is directed by color. Pilot instrument panels, landing strips, road and water crossings are regulated by many colored lights and signs.

Factories use colors to distinguish between thoroughfares and work areas. Danger zones are painted in special colors. Lubrication points and removable parts are accentuated by color. Pipes for transporting water, steam, oil, chemicals, and compressed air, are designated by different colors. Electrical wires and resistances are color coded.

Gerritsen, *Theory and Practice of Color.*

Main Idea:_____

_____

5. There can be no doubt that the reaction sought by the after-dinner speaker at a social banquet differs materially from that sought by a legislator urging the adoption of a bill, or that both of these desired responses differ from the response a college professor seeks when he addresses a class. The first speaker wants his audience to enjoy themselves; the second wants them to act, to vote "aye"; the third wants them to understand.

Monroe and Ehninger, *Principles and Types of Speeches.*

Main Idea:_____

_____

## EXERCISE 4–9

*DIRECTIONS:* From a chapter of one of your textbooks, select a headed section of at least five substantial paragraphs and for each paragraph, identify the topic sentence. If there is no clear topic sentence, write your own statement of the main idea of the paragraph.

## ■ DEVELOPING EXPECTATIONS AS YOU READ

To be an effective reader you must become mentally active as you read. Rather than just taking in facts and ideas as you encounter them, you should be reacting to and thinking about what you are reading. In fact, there are certain mental activities that should occur almost automatically as you read. For instance, you should be thinking about what you have just read, following the author's pattern of thought, and trying to relate the ideas. Also, as you read a paragraph you should be developing expectations about how the writer will develop his or her ideas and what will come next in the paragraph. In other words, you should not only keep up with the writer, you should try to stay one jump ahead.

At the beginning of a conversation you can often predict in what direction the conversation is headed. If a friend starts a conversation with "I can't decide whether I can afford to quit my part-time job at Sears," you can guess what you will hear next. Your friend will discuss the pros and cons of quitting the job as it relates to his financial situation.

Similarly, as you begin to read a paragraph, often you will find sufficient clues to enable you to know what to expect throughout. The topic sentence, especially if it appears first in the paragraph, will often suggest how the paragraph will be developed. Suppose a paragraph were to begin with the following topic sentence:

> The unemployment rate in the past several years has increased due to a variety of economic factors.

What do you expect the rest of the paragraph to include? It will probably be about the various economic factors that cause unemployment. Now, look at this topic sentence:

> Minorities differ in racial or cultural visibility, in the amount of discrimination they suffer, in the character of their adjustment, both as individuals and as groups, and in the length of time they survive as identifiable populations or individuals.

This sentence indicates that the paragraph will contain a discussion of four ways that minority groups differ. This topic sentence also suggests the order in which these differences will be discussed. The factor mentioned first in the sentence (visibility) will be discussed first, the second idea mentioned will appear next, and so forth.

## EXERCISE 4–10

*DIRECTIONS:* Assume that each of the following statements is the topic sentence of a paragraph. Read each sentence, then decide what you would expect a paragraph to include if it began with that sentence. Summarize your expectations in the space provided after each sentence. In some cases, more than one correct set of expectations is possible.

1.  Conventional musical instruments can be grouped into three classes.

_____

2.  The distinction between storage and retrieval has important implications for memory researchers.

_____

3.  When Charles Darwin published his theories of evolution, people objected on scientific and religious grounds.

_____

4. Narcotics such as opium, morphine, and heroin are derived from different sources and vary in strength and aftereffects.

5. Not all factors that contribute to intelligence are measurable.

## ■ MAJOR AND MINOR SUPPORTING DETAILS

In conversation you can explain an idea in a number of ways. If you are trying to explain to someone that dogs make better pets than cats, you could develop your idea by giving examples of the behaviors of particular dogs and cats. You could also give the basic reasons why you hold that opinion or you could present facts about dogs and cats that support your position. As in conversation, a writer can explain an idea in many ways. In a paragraph a writer includes details that explain, support, or provide further information about the main idea.

Once you have identified the topic sentence, you should expect the rest of the paragraph to contain supporting information. Not all details are equally important, however. For example, in the following paragraph the underlined ideas provide very important information about the main idea. As you read the paragraph notice how these ideas directly explain the topic sentence (double underlined).

> There are potential disadvantages to group therapy. Many psychologists feel that the interactions in group situations are too superficial to be of much benefit. A patient with deep-seated conflicts may be better treated by a psychotherapist in individual therapy; the therapist can exert consistent pressure, refusing to let the patient avoid the crucial issues, and she or he can control the therapeutic environment more effectively. Another criticism of groups is that they are too powerful. If the group starts to focus on one individual's defense mechanisms—which are used for a reason, remember—that individual might break down. If no trained therapist is present—which is often the case in encounter groups—the result can be disastrous.
>
> Geiwitz, *Psychology: Looking at Ourselves.*

● ● ●

Each of the underlined details states one of the disadvantages of group therapy. These are called *major details* because they directly explain and support the main idea. Now look back at the details that were not underlined. Can you see that they are of lesser importance in relation to the main idea? You can think of these as details that further explain details. These details are called *minor details.* They provide information that qualifies, describes, or explains the major details. For example, the third sentence further explains the disadvantage described in the second sentence. Also, the sentences that follow the second group of sentences explain what may happen as a result of a group becoming too powerful.

Especially if you are a visual learner, it may be helpful to visualize a paragraph as organized in the following way.

Main Idea
    Major Detail
        minor detail
        minor detail
    Major Detail
        minor detail
    Major Detail

To find the most important, or major, supporting details, ask yourself this question: "Which statements directly prove or explain the main idea?" Your answer will lead you to the important details in the paragraph. Now apply this question to the following paragraph. As you read it, first identify the main idea, then try to locate those details that *directly* explain this idea.

We have seen that inequality has been a problem in human societies for a long time. Poverty has been explained several ways. The *personal view* blames the poor individuals for their poverty. Proponents of this view believe, in effect, that the poor are poor because they are morally or personally defective—lazy, apathetic, good for nothing. The *cultural view* also blames the poor individual for his poverty, but not directly. Rather, it blames the socialization process, which indoctrinates the children of the poor into a way of life that perpetuates their condition. In other words, the poor learn behavior patterns that prevent their upward mobility, patterns that are passed from generation to generation in a vicious circle. Finally, the *economic view* is somewhat noncommittal: it maintains that the poor are poor because they have little or no money. They have little money because they are unemployed, underemployed, or kept in low-paying jobs. Consequently, they have little purchasing power and are underconsumers. The poor themselves are not at fault; our economic structure is.

Perry and Perry, *Face to Face: The Individual and Social Problems.*

● ● ●

In this paragraph you should have identified the three views of poverty as key supporting details. Other sentences in the paragraph further explain each view and can be considered less important.

## EXERCISE 4–11

*DIRECTIONS:* Each of the following statements could function as the topic sentence of a paragraph. After each statement are sentences containing details that may be related to the main idea statement. Read each sentence and put a checkmark beside those with details that do not directly support the main idea statement.

1. *Topic Sentence:*
   From infancy to adulthood women demonstrate marked superiority in verbal and linguistic abilities.
   *Details:*
   _____ a. Girls begin to talk at an earlier age than boys and also learn to speak in sentences earlier.
   _____ b. Males excel in the area of arithmetic reasoning as evidenced by their higher test scores.
   _____ c. Women learn foreign languages much more rapidly and are more fluent in them than men.
   _____ d. The incidence of reading disabilities is much lower for girls than for boys.

2. *Topic Sentence:*
   Employment opportunities for college graduates are plentiful in the technical and business fields but prospects are bleak for the liberal arts areas.
   *Details:*
   _____ a. Career counseling is provided too late in their college careers to assist students in making effective career decisions.
   _____ b. The competition for jobs in journalism and sociology is highly aggressive and can be characterized as frantic.
   _____ c. Over the last year, the demand for accountants and computer programmers and technicians has increased by more than 16 percent.
   _____ d. There is only one position available for every 10 job applicants in the liberal arts field.

3. *Topic Sentence:*
   Quality and content are not the only factors that determine whether a book can achieve best seller status.
   *Details:*
   _____ a. Name recognition of the author exerts a strong influence on sales.
   _____ b. The timing of a book's release during the appropriate season or in conjunction with major news events plays a major role.
   _____ c. Readers appreciate well-crafted books that are both literate and engaging.
   _____ d. The book buying public clearly responds well to well-conceived advance publicity.

4.  *Topic Sentence:*
    Showing how a theory can be developed may be the best way to describe one.
    *Details:*
    _____ a.  Careful testing of a hypothesis leads to more confidence being placed in the idea.
    _____ b.  After carefully describing the idea and defining its premises, it becomes a hypothesis.
    _____ c.  One first comes up with an idea that could explain something that can be observed in nature.
    _____ d.  A hypothesis is a provisional statement or possible explanation to be tested.

5.  *Topic Sentence:*
    The vibrations of objects produce longitudinal waves that result in sounds.
    *Details:*
    _____ a.  Infrasonic and ultrasonic waves cannot be detected by human hearing.
    _____ b.  Sound travels more slowly in more dense mediums, such as water, than it does in less dense ones like air.
    _____ c.  Plucking the strings of a guitar or the striking of a piano's sounding board are good examples.
    _____ d.  The vibration of the vocal cords is what produces human voice.

## EXERCISE 4–12

*DIRECTIONS:* Place brackets around the topic sentence in each of the following paragraphs. Then underline the major supporting details in each. Underline only those details that directly explain or support the main idea.

1.  What is the study of politics? One thing you will notice about political science is that it's a lot like other social sciences such as history, economics, sociology, and psychology. Each studies aspects of the interactions among people. In any large group of people many social relations are going on. Each of these disciplines may look at the same group and ask different questions about the relationships going on there. This division of labor is partly traditional and partly a way of separating complicated human relations into more easily understood parts. Political science fits in by studying one type of interaction between people—that involving power and authority. An example may make the approaches of the other disciplines clearer and distinguish them from political science.

Wasserman, *The Basics of American Politics.*

2. By regularly rewarding good actions and punishing bad ones, the agents of social control seek to condition us to obey society's norms. If they are successful, obedience becomes habitual and automatic. We obey the norms even when no one is around to reward or punish us, even when we are not thinking of possible rewards and punishments. But human beings are very complicated and not easily conditioned, as animals are, by rewards and punishments alone. Thus, sanctions are not sufficient to produce the widespread, day-to-day conformity to norms that occurs in societies all over the world.

Thio, *Sociology.*

3. The skin itself is the largest organ of the body, is composed of epithelial and connective tissue components, and forms a pliable protective covering over the external body surface. It accounts for about 7 percent of the body weight and receives about 30 percent of the left ventricular output of blood. The term protective, as used here, includes not only resistance to bacterial invasion or attack from the outside, but also protection against large changes in the internal environment. Control of body temperature, prevention of excessive water loss, and prevention of excessive loss of organic and inorganic materials are necessary to the maintenance of internal homeostasis and continued normal activity of individual cells. In addition, the skin acts as an important area of storage, receives a variety of stimuli, and synthesizes several important substances used in the overall body economy.

Crouch and McClintic, *Human Anatomy and Physiology.*

4. Assume you are an industrial/organizational psychologist hired by a company to help select a manager for one of its retail stores in a local shopping center. You cannot begin to tell your employers what sort of person they were looking for until you had a complete description of the job this new manager was to do. You would have to know the duties and responsibilities of a store manager in this company. Then, you could translate that job description into measurable characteristics a successful store manager should have. That is, you would begin with a job analysis, "the systematic study of the tasks, duties, and responsibilities of a job and the knowledge, skills, and abilities needed to perform it."

Gerow, *Psychology: An Introduction.*

5. No part of the Earth's surface is exempt from earthquakes, but since the start of systematic recording many large areas have had only occasional shocks of small or moderate intensity. By contrast, several large tracts are subject to frequent shocks, both strong and weak, and are known as seismic belts. The most prominent, aptly called the Circum-Pacific

belt, follows the western highlands of South and North America from Cape Horn to Alaska, crosses to Asia, extends southward along the eastern coast and related island arcs, and loops far to the southeast and south beyond New Zealand. Next in prominence is the broad east-west zone extending through the high mountains of southern Asia and the Mediterranean region to Gibraltar. A third long belt follows the Mid-Atlantic Ridge from Arctic to Antarctic waters, and a fourth runs along the Mid-Indian Range to unite with a belt in eastern Africa. Smaller seismic areas include island groups in the Pacific and Atlantic.

Longwell and Flint, *Introduction to Physical Geology.*

## EXERCISE 4–13

*DIRECTIONS:* Select a section of five or more paragraphs from one of your textbooks and place brackets around the topic sentence in each paragraph. If there is no topic sentence, write a brief statement of the main idea in the margin. Then underline only the major supporting details in each paragraph.

## ■ TYPES OF SUPPORTING DETAILS

A writer can use many types of details to explain or support a main idea. As you read you should notice the type of details a writer uses and be able to identify the details that are most important. As you will see in later chapters on evaluating and interpreting, the manner in which a writer explains and supports an idea may influence how readily you will accept or agree with the idea. Among the most common types of supporting details are illustrations and examples, facts and statistics, reasons, and descriptions. Each is discussed briefly.

### ■ Illustrations and Examples

One way you will find ideas explained is through the use of illustrations or examples. Usually a writer uses examples to make a concept, problem, or process understandable by showing its application in a particular situation. In the following paragraph, numerous examples are provided that explain how various cultures carry labels or stereotypes.

All of us live within a *culture,* one that is qualified by a label like "middle-class American," "Roman," or "Aztec"—a label that conjures up certain objects or behavior patterns typical of this particular culture. For instance, we associate hamburgers with middle-class American culture, and skin canoes with Eskimos. Romans are thought to have spent their time conquering the world, Sioux Indians wandering over the Great Plains. But such stereotypes are often crude, inaccurate generalizations. Though we think of American Indians as legendary, feathered braves, only a few Indian groups ever wore such head-dresses. In fact, the label "American Indian" includes an incredibly diverse set of peoples, ranging from family size hunter-gatherer bands to large, complex civilizations.

Fagan, *World Prehistory: A Brief Introduction.*

● ● ●

In this paragraph the author uses examples from specific cultures—Eskimo, Roman, and American Indian—to illustrate that labels exist. As you read illustrations and examples, try to see the relationship between the illustration or example and the concept or idea it illustrates.

## ■ Facts and Statistics

Another way a writer supports an idea is by including facts or statistics that further explain the main idea. Notice how, in the following paragraph, the main idea is explained by the use of statistics.

The United States became urbanized when it underwent its industrial revolution. New York, Chicago, and later San Francisco easily passed the 1 million mark. Today 235 cities have a population of over 1 million, and 118 of these huge cities are in Third World nations. It is predicted that the urbanization of developing nations will continue. By the year 2000, Mexico City will double in size to 26.3 million; São Paulo, Brazil, will increase to 24 million; Calcutta will grow to 16.6 million; and Cairo will have more than 16.3 million residents (Palen, 1992). By that year, 77 percent of Latin America's population, 41 percent of Africa's, and 35 percent of Asia's will be urbanized. Meanwhile, industrialized cities such as Tokyo, London, Paris, St. Petersburg, Moscow, Vienna, New York, Chicago, Los Angeles, Miami, and Dallas will also continue to grow.

Thompson and Hickey, *Society in Focus: An Introduction to Sociology.*

● ● ●

These authors used population statistics and projections to indicate that Third World cities will become urbanized. When reading paragraphs developed by the use of facts and statistics, you can expect that these details will answer questions such as what, when, where, or how about the main idea.

## ■ Reasons

Certain types of main ideas are most easily explained by giving reasons. Especially in argumentative and persuasive writing, you will find that a writer supports an opinion, belief, or action by discussing *why* the thought or action is appropriate. In the following paragraph the writer provides reasons for the growth of public colleges and universities.

> The growth in American higher education is taking place largely in the public colleges and universities. These colleges are usually more responsive than private colleges to state and local demands, and provide training for the increasingly numerous occupations that require advanced skills. They are relatively inexpensive, often easy to enter, and conveniently located to serve large numbers of students. The rapid expansion of college attendance among job-oriented young people of lower social origins is chiefly in these service-minded institutions.
>
> Broom and Selznick, *Sociology.*

● ● ●

You can see that the writer offers numerous reasons for the growth trend, including response to local demands, cost, ease of entrance, location, and so forth.

### ■ Description

If the purpose of a paragraph is to help the reader understand or visualize the appearance, structure, organization, or composition of an object, then descriptions are often used as a means of paragraph development. Descriptive details are facts that help you visualize the person, object, or event being described. The following paragraph contains descriptive details to enable you to create a visual image of a person.

> A newly married pair had boarded this coach at San Antonio. The man's face was reddened from many days in the wind and sun, and a direct result of his new black clothes was that his brick-colored hands were constantly performing in a most conscious fashion. From time to time he looked down respectfully at his attire. He sat with a hand on each knee, like a man waiting in a barber's shop. The glances he devoted to other passengers were furtive and shy.
>
> Hall and Hall (eds.), *The Realm of Fiction.*

● ● ●

Notice how each detail, by itself, does not contribute much to your understanding of the bridegroom, but when all details are added together you are able to visualize him. Small details such as sitting "with a hand on each knee," contribute to your overall impression and help you realize that the author is trying to suggest that the man is awkward and uncomfortable. In reading descriptive details, you must pay close attention to each detail as you try to form a visual impression of what is being described.

## EXERCISE 4–14

*DIRECTIONS:* For each of the following topic sentences, predict what types of supporting details you would expect to be used to develop the paragraph.

1. It is much easier to sell a product to a buyer who possesses complete purchasing authority than to sell to one who has little authority.
   Type of Detail: _____
   _____

2. The concept of insurance is an ancient one, beginning with the Babylonians.
   Type of Detail: _____
   _____

3. It was cold in the fall in Rome, and the evening fell suddenly and with great importance.
   Type of Detail: _____
   _____

4. Government documents indicate that the total number of Americans living in poverty has decreased, but the definition of the poverty line has also been changed.
   Type of Detail: _____
   _____

5. A sudden explosion at 200 decibels can cause massive and permanent hearing loss.
   Type of Detail: _____
   _____

## ■ USING TRANSITIONS

Have you ever tried to find your way to an unfamiliar place without any road signs to guide you? Do you remember your relief when you discovered one sign post and then another and finally realized you were being led in the right direction? Like road signs, transitions in written material can help you find your way to a writer's meaning. *Transitions* are linking words or phrases writers use to lead the reader from one idea to another. If you get in the habit of recognizing transitions, you will see that they often guide you through a paragraph, helping you read it more easily.

In the following paragraph, notice how the italicized transitions lead you from one important detail to the next.

As a speaker, you should consider the dominant attitudes of your listeners. Audiences may have attitudes toward you, your speech subject, and your speech purpose. Your listeners may think you know a lot about your topic, and they may be interested in learning more. This is an ideal situation. *However,* if they think you're not very credible and they resist learning more, you must deal with their attitudes. *For example,* if a speaker tells you that you can earn extra money in your spare time by selling magazine subscriptions, you may have several reactions. The thought of extra income from a part-time job is enticing. *At the same time,* you suspect that it might be a scam and you feel uncomfortable because you don't know the speaker well. These attitudes toward the speech topic, purpose, and speaker will undoubtedly influence your final decision about selling subscriptions.

Gronbeck, et al., *Principles of Speech Communication.*

● ● ●

Not all paragraphs contain such obvious transitions, and not all transitions serve as such clear markers of major details. Transitions may be used to alert you to what will come next in the paragraph. If you see the phrase *for instance* at the beginning of a sentence, then you know than an exam-

| Type of Transition | Example | What They Tell the Reader |
|---|---|---|
| Time—Sequence | first, later, next, finally, then | The author is arranging ideas in the order in which they happened. |
| Example | for example, for instance, to illustrate, such as | An example will follow. |
| Enumeration | first, second, third, last, another, next | The author is marking or identifying each major point (sometimes these may be used to suggest order of importance). |
| Continuation | also, in addition, and, further, another | The author is continuing with the same idea and is going to provide additional information. |
| Contrast | on the other hand, in contrast, however | The author is switching to a different, opposite, or contrasting idea than previously discussed. |
| Comparison | like, likewise, similarly | The writer will show how the previous idea is similar to what follows. |
| Cause-Effect | because, thus, therefore, since, consequently | The writer will show a connection between two or more things, how one thing caused another, or how something happened as a result of something else. |

**FIGURE 4.1** Common Transitions

ple will follow. When you see the phrase *on the other hand,* you can predict that a different, opposing idea will follow. Figure 4.1 lists some of the most common transitions used within paragraphs and indicates what they tell you. In the next chapter you will see that these transitional words also signal the author's organization.

## EXERCISE 4–15

*DIRECTIONS:* Underline each transition used in the paragraphs in Exercise 4–12.

## EXERCISE 4–16

*DIRECTIONS:* Circle the transitional words or phrases used in each paragraph of the text selection you chose for Exercise 4–13.

**Critical Thinking Tip #4**

**Recognizing Your Own Bias**

In this chapter you are sharpening your skills in understanding an author's message—topic, main idea, and supporting details. Did you know that research studies suggest you will more easily comprehend and recall a message you agree with than one with which you disagree? Suppose you are reading a section in your biology book about the need for tighter controls on industrial pollution. Suppose you once lived next to a factory and feel strongly that tighter controls are needed. You are more likely to understand and recall the information than another student who is opposed to tighter controls. In fact, readers who disagree with an idea tend to miss or overlook ideas that do not support their beliefs.

How do these findings affect the way you read? You need to take extra care when reading ideas with which you think you disagree. Try the following suggestions:

1. Keep an open mind until you've read what the author has said and have evaluated the evidence provided.
2. Work harder than usual to follow the writer's development and reasoning process.
3. Outline the writer's main points so you don't overlook anything.

Then, once you've grasped the writer's ideas, feel free to evaluate these ideas and disagree with them.

## SUMMARY

**1. What is a paragraph?**

A paragraph is a group of related sentences about a single topic. It explains, supports, or gives information for a main idea about a particular topic.

**2. What are the essential elements of a paragraph?**

A paragraph has three essential parts:
- Topic—the common subject of the paragraph.
- Main Idea—the most important idea expressed about the topic.
- Details—the information that explains or supports the main idea.

**3. Where is the topic sentence most likely to be found?**

The topic sentence expresses the main idea of the paragraph. It may be located anywhere in the paragraph, but the most common positions are first and last.

**4. How can you identify main ideas that are not stated in a topic sentence?**

Sometimes you will encounter a paragraph that has no single sentence stating the main idea. In this case, it is up to the reader to figure out the main idea. To find an unstated main idea, ask yourself: What does the writer want me to know about the topic?

**5. What are the most common types of details used to explain or support a main idea?**

Both major details that directly support the main idea and minor details that provide less essential information are of four types:
- Illustrations and examples
- Facts and statistics
- Reasons
- Descriptions

**6. What clues in paragraphs can help you anticipate the writer's ideas?**

Clues to a writer's direction are often evident in the topic sentence, which can suggest how the paragraph will be developed. Further clues can be seen in transitional words or phrases that signal what will come next in the paragraph.

PSYCHOLOGY

# READING SELECTION 7
## THE APPRECIATION OF HUMOR

Mary J. Gander and Harry W. Gardiner
*From Child and Adolescent Development*

*Even very young children love to laugh. Taken from a psychology textbook, this reading explores the development of humor in children. Read it to discover the four stages through which children pass in the development of humor.*

1     One example of the growing thinking capacity in middle childhood is children's appreciation of humor. Consider the joke: "Mr. Jones went into a restaurant and ordered a whole pizza for dinner. When the waiter asked if he wanted it cut into six or eight pieces, Mr. Jones said: 'Oh you'd better make it six! I could never eat eight!'"

2     Why do first graders who have just attained conservation of substance find this joke funnier than do nonconserving first graders or fifth graders who mastered this ability several years before? McGhee believes it is because this joke provokes a moderate amount of cognitive challenge, perfect for the conserving first graders.

3     Although many researchers have investigated children's humor, only Paul McGhee has conducted a longitudinal study of the development of humor. In his work at the Fels Institute, McGhee has proposed a fairly comprehensive theory of humor as part of his ongoing research on child development.

4     McGhee proposes that some incongruity (for example, something unexpected, absurd, inappropriate, or out of context) is usually the basis for humor. However, an incongruity in itself is insufficient; children must know enough about a situation so that the incongruity can be recognized, and they must be in a playful frame of mind. Incongruous events are funny to children precisely because these events are at odds with

reality and they know it! Therefore, the kind of humor children appreciate depends on their underlying cognitive development.

5     When the father of three-year-old Paul put on a beard, glasses, and a large plastic nose, the child became frightened and began to cry, but his nine-year-old brother considered the disguise hilarious. The older boy had reached the concrete operational level and could imagine his father as he was; moreover, he knew that the disguise had not really changed him.

6     Precursors of humor may be observed early. Laughter may be induced in four-month-old infants by tactile stimulation such as blowing against the baby's belly; at eight months, peek-a-boo; and at one year, Dad pretending to cry over a "hurt" finger.

7     McGhee proposes that true humor begins during the second year, or after the child has begun to be capable of fantasy and make-believe. It develops in an invariant sequence of stages related to cognitive development.

## Stage 1: Incongruous Actions Toward Objects

8     Sometime between the ages of one and two years, toddlers begin to pretend that one object is another. Object number 1 somehow evokes their scheme for Object number 2, and they act on number 1 with the number 2 scheme, though fully aware that number 1 is *not* number 2. In a playful mood they find it funny. For example, eighteen-month-old Sally put one of her blocks to her ear as if it were a phone, then "hung up" and laughed. She laughed too when her mother "ate" her toes and found their "taste" terrible.

## Stage 2: Incongruous Labeling of Objects, Events, People

9    This stage usually begins around two years of age, or after children have developed some vocabulary. In it, the commonest type of humor consists of simply giving the wrong names to familiar objects, events, people, and parts of the body. A two-and-a-half-year-old girl told a visitor that she was going to a Winnie-the-Pooh movie. The visitor, trying to be funny, said, "Oh, Winnie-the-Pooh is an elephant, isn't he?" The child collapsed in laughter.

10    Stages 1 and 2 humor do not disappear as the next stage begins, but become incorporated into it in more sophisticated ways.

## Stage 3: Conceptual Incongruity

11    This stage may begin sometime between the ages of three and four and is heavily influenced by development of language and concepts. A distortion of a reality that children conceptually understand as a distortion is funny at this age; accordingly children may point and laugh at handicapped or deformed individuals because their strong egocentrism prevents consideration for others' feelings. Rhyming and creating non-

sense words (Billy, pilly, dilly, silly, gilly) are considered great fun at this stage. So are puppets, such as a talking frog and a monster that devours cookies. Children also begin to find humor in taboo subject matter concerning toilets and physical differences between girls and boys. Within the context of a joke, such topics can release tension and excite much laughter in preschoolers as well as older children.

## Stage 4: Multiple Meanings and the Beginnings of Adult-Type Humor

12    This stage usually comes around ages seven and eight, when concrete operations and other cognitive skills permit appreciation of more sophisticated jokes. Concrete operational children can keep two ideas in mind at once and thus have no problem with double or multiple meanings, as long as they are familiar with the concepts involved. For example, eight- to ten-year-olds find this funny: "What did the man do when he stubbed his toe and broke it?" Answer: "He called a tow truck!" Riddles and "knock-knock" questions also gain popularity. According to McGhee, stage 4 humor can extend into adolescence and adulthood, although it usually becomes more complex and abstract.

## Comprehension Test 7

*Directions: Circle the letter of the best answer.*

**Checking Your Comprehension**

1. Children's appreciation of humor
   a. is an area of child development that has not been studied
   b. develops along with their thinking ability
   c. does not occur until age 7 or 8
   d. occurs earlier for girls than for boys

2. When children pass to stage 3 of humor, what they found to be funny in stage 2
   a. is no longer funny
   b. becomes incorporated into stage 3

   c. remains just as funny for them
   d. is forgotten

3. The basis for humor is usually
   a. one's fear of injury
   b. unusual sounding words
   c. a situation that is incongruous
   d. other people's weaknesses

4. "True humor" usually begins around the age of
   a. 4 months
   b. 2 years
   c. 4 years
   d. 9 years

5. Around the age of 3 or 4, children would most appreciate humor based on
   a. "knock-knock" jokes
   b. cartoon characters and animals
   c. double meanings
   d. nonsense words and rhymes

6. In the phrase "precursors of humor" (paragraph 6), "precursors" most closely means
   a. beginnings
   b. uses
   c. problems
   d. causes

**Thinking Critically**

7. A child that pretends that his or her dresser is a refrigerator is at least
   a. 1 year old
   b. 6 years old
   c. 8 years old
   d. 12 years old

8. A child who enjoys calling his or her dog "Tommy Turtle" is operating at
   a. Stage 1: Incongruous Actions Toward Objects
   b. Stage 2: Incongruous Labeling
   c. Stage 3: Conceptual Incongruity
   d. Stage 4: Multiple Meaning

9. The joke "What did the father chimney say to his son? You're too young to smoke!" would probably be funniest to a
   a. 2 year old
   b. 4 year old
   c. 8 year old
   d. 16 year old

10. The information in this passage is presented by
    a. describing the stages in their order of occurrence
    b. comparing and contrasting the stages with one another

c. presenting the stages in the order of their importance
d. listing problems and solutions with each stage

**Questions for Discussion**

1. Why is humor important? What does it do for us?

2. Does humor serve the same functions for adults and children?

3. Think of an adult joke. Analyze it and describe its incongruity or multiple meanings.

4. How does the article confirm the statement that the truest test of your knowledge of a foreign language is your ability to understand and tell jokes in that language?

---

Selection 7:                   853 words

Finishing Time: _____ _____ _____
                  HR.    MIN.    SEC.

Starting Time: _____ _____ _____
                  HR.    MIN.    SEC.

Reading Time:          _____ _____
                        MIN.    SEC.

WPM Score:             _____

Comprehension Score:   _____%

ZOOLOGY

## READING SELECTION 8
## THE FUTURE OF ZOOS*

Vicki Croke
*From The Modern Ark*

*This reading was taken from a book titled The Modern Ark: The Story of Zoos: Past, Present, and Future. This excerpt focuses on zoos of the future. Read it to answer the following questions:*

1. *What problems and issues do modern zoos face?*
2. *What changes have been proposed for zoos of the future?*

1. It is the year 2020, and a raven-hared matriarch named Gigi had become a media sensation. She has five children, each with a different father. She bore seven, but lost two in infancy. She has lived through good times and bad. She has survived famine and enjoyed plenty. She has seen leaders come and go, coalitions built, and dynasties destroyed. Today, she is pleased that her oldest son rule the community after a very rough campaign. Though she is surrounded by grandchildren, she is still sought after and quite active sexually, She is patient, kind, loving, wise and, above all strong—perhaps three times stronger than a man.

2. Gigi is a chimpanzee in Tanzania, and her daily existence is carried via satellite to huge theater screens in zoos around the world. Her life is one of many that the zoo channel zooms in on. There are polar bears hunting in the Arctic. Penguins waddling off Patagonia. Hyenas waging war in the Masai Mara. Giant pandas nursing young in China. The zoo channel is dramatic, immediate and ever-changing. And though the airwaves may be invisible, they are the strongest link imaginable between vulnerable wild places

and powerful civilization. The zoos that pick up the network have a financial stake in the protection of habitat. The viewers, people who have always shown a remarkable capacity for the care of individual animals, have an emotional stake in their well-being.

3. There are currently plans for just such a high-tech zoo in London, but even if this exact scheme never comes to pass, we know that if zoos are to survive in the coming century, they must zealously make conservation their most urgent priority.

### The World on a String

4. There is a monster loose in the world that is gobbling up every green inch and chopping down every forest. The beast, of course, is the planet's human population. Every year another 97 million human beings join the crowd—90 percent of whom are born in less developed tropical countries, where the bulk of the remaining wildlife lives. By 2050 the world's population could reach 12 billion. That's 12 billion people who need roads and houses and land for crops and domestic animals. Who need fuel and food and wood.

5. Because of that, the nonhuman, nondomesticated animal portion of the plant's biomass is being squeezed out of existence. The statistics are too much a fathom. According to E. O. Wilson, we are reducing biological diversity to its lowest level in 65 million years. We have probably named about 1.4 million species of animals, but that is a tiny fraction of the 4 to 30 million

*Due to the length of this reading, timing is inappropriate and words-per-minute conversions are not provided.

species that actually exist. Through deforestation we may be killing off four to six thousand species a year, with perhaps six species of plant and animals being doomed to extinction each hour, according to Wilson. William Conway, president and general director of NYZS [New York Zoological Society] and WCS [Wildlife Conservation Society] has made up a staggering laundry list of our consumption: We pull 100 million tons of fish from our seas each year. More than 5 billion animals are killed for food each year in the United States. Worldwide, 10 to 15 billion domestic animals are using up space that was once wildlife habitat. Cows and other ruminants have staked out turf nearly the size of Africa. Half that amount again is dedicated to crops. Only about 4 percent of the earth is protected land. Each year, Wilson says, we are losing rain forest cover at the rate equal to the area of Switzerland and the Netherlands combined.

6    Can we console ourselves with the thought that many of these species are just little bugs we don't even have names for? It's even more frightening to think that we'll never know the magnitude of our loss. But the clues are everywhere. Many very big, very charismatic animals are in decline. There are fewer than one thousand giant pandas alive today. Not one species of rhino can be counted in numbers higher than five thousand. Half of the bird species in Polynesia have disappeared. There may have been as many as 10 million elephants in Africa in 1930, but poaching and habitat loss have hacked that figure down to just half a million.

7    It is all completely irreversible. The great, huge pool of genes is now a puddle. And vast tracts of land are just fractured and fragmented pockets of wilderness. Increasingly, these pockets are "managed" areas, where soldiers guard against poaching and biologists monitor the health of the inhabitants. The wild world is becoming a series of megazoos.

8    The zoo community is uniquely qualified to manage and preserve these precious pools of biodiversity. Nutritionists, biologists, wildlife veteri-

narians, population specialists, geneticists and behaviorists are already on staff. Zoos can be what Bill Conway calls "your full-service conservation organization." And who else should be doing this? As Conway also points out, "No powerful government anywhere on earth had placed environmental conservation among its top priorities."

9    Saving and preserving a wild area is complicated business. Conway uses the example of Florida's Everglades National Park. In 1947, the park was established. Hunting stopped. Encroachment ceased. But shockingly, by 1989, the population of large wading birds had been reduced by 90 percent. "Refuge management by benevolent neglect does not save wildlife communities when their ecosystems are too small or are modified by activities outside their border." says Conway.

10    In 1976, it was discovered that three to five Javan tigers, a species previously thought to be extinct, were alive in the MeriBetiri Reserve in eastern Java. The 190-square-mile park is the last area of lowland rain forest in Java. A plan was proposed for their survival, but by the early eighties, none of the these tigers, known for their distinctive narrow stripes, was alive. The Javan tiger slipped through our fingers and is gone forever.

11    "All kinds of conservation activities ultimately come down to buying time," Conway says during an interview in his office at the Bronx Zoo. "And in some instances all we can do is buy time. We successfully bought time for the American bison. Successfully bought time for Arabian oryx. There aren't many example [but] there are others—we may have been successful in buying time for the Mongolian wild horse, Przewalski's horse. When you can buy time for land itself, for nature, then you're not simply buying time for the species, you're buying time for an entire community of species. If you are successful in getting large spaces, you may even be able to help save functioning ecosystems, which is what you want to do. The living animals in your collections, for the vast majority of human beings, provide the only contact they're

ever really going to have with wild animals. So the significance of the zoo animal in a municipality can do nothing but increase. They will become rarer and rarer. And the horrible thing is that as they become more valuble in human eyes, they become less valuble ecologically, because they can no longer fulfill ecological functions as their numbers decline. This gets into a catch-22 situation.

12 "I believe that we are moving away from a time when people can afford to simply sit back and care about animals; we have to care *for* them. Increasingly, the wildlife reserves will be too small to maintain viable populations of animals. Those that are big enough will have to be managed with increasing intensity. Because within the limited spaces we are able to accord them due to our own overprocreation, they cannot sustain their numbers in relation to one another in viable ways. In many a reserve today there can be a male rhino who dominates a whole reserve. No other male can breed. He'll kill them. He'll run them out. So the population will not be viable. If we continue to modify the environment adjacent to our reserves, we're going to run into all kinds of problems."

### Standing at the Crossroads

13 Zoos have the potential to save more biodiversity than any other private organization. But it is a huge responsibility, and the commitment in money and labor is staggering. And the overwhelming majority of zoos are financially strapped. The roof of the ape house is leaking. The elephant has a foot infection. A zoogoer who tripped in the bathroom is suing. The keepers aren't being paid enough. The giraffe fencing blew over in a storm. And yet they are being asked to save the entire planet.

14 Zoos have the weight of the world on their shoulders, and they may shrug it off. The zoo community is at a dramatic crossroads. It is truly a time for a new direction, and not everyone in the zoo community is willing to go.

15 Bill Conway, the visionary of the zoo world, the man referred to as "god" without a trace of sarcasm, says the mission is clear. "There isn't any question about the future of zoos at all," Conway says with confidence. "It is not to be a simple museum of living creatures. It is to be a proactive conservation organization that is directly acting to preserve nature and wildlife." Conway asserts the way to accomplish that is not the issue; the hardest part, the most important part, is deciding to try. "The situation has become so desperate with regard to wildlife and nature that the future of zoos is evolving very, very rapidly, and they are destined to become conservation organizations attempting to preserve wildlife and nature. And that is very straight forward and simple, and after you've gotten that far in you thinking, it's simply a matter of detail.

16 But it may take precious time. Michael Hutchins is pushing his organization toward the future and he may be a little frustrated. "Anything that is that revolutionary takes some time to trickle down to the lowest common denominators, and this is going to take some time. Cultures don't change very fast generally, and we're talking about a culture that has evolved out of the sixteenth centuries. There will have to be some major changes if the institution is to survive. And I personally have strong feelings that it can make the transition, at least in North America."

17 Whether it is a matter of design or detail, most zoos simple don't come near New York—in zeal or impact. The AZA [American Zoo and Aquarium Association] boasts of hundreds of field projects run by accredited zoos. But if one were to weed out the baggage—projects listed several times because many zoos participate in it; or those of only marginal conservation value—Conway estimates that, in 1993, there were only 425 legitimate field projects left to count and 272 belong to New York; the rest were scattered among the nation's zoos and aquariums. Conway is blazing a trail, but his parishioners are a bit timid.

18    In a pamphlet entitled "A Hidden Value," celebrating its upcoming eightieth birthday, the San Diego zoo points out—in facing pages in bold red type—that it has spent $55 million in the last ten years on public relations and in that same amount of time only $17.6 million "in support of internationally acclaimed wildlife conservation conducted by scientists."

19    Michael Hutchins, the respected director of conservation and science at the AZA, concedes that these figures "are probably true," but maintains that the scenario is "changing very rapidly."

20    Rick Barongi, director of Disney's planned five-hundred-acre Animal Kingdom theme park in Orlando, Florida, and has served as director of the children's zoo within the San Diego Zoo, also believes the zoo world is evolving in the direction of conservation work, but he is blunt in his assessment of the current situation. "The Bronx had pretty much done it alone. And Conway is strong enough and smart enough and powerful enough that he can insulate his researchers from the day-to-day, mundane problems that zoos have to deal with. But a Conway comes along only once in a generation. Zoos need to concentrate on a conservation more than preservation and Conway is definitely the true visionary of the field."

21    Tony Vecchio, director of the Roger Williams Park Zoo in Providence, Rhode Island, says, "Most zoos are not doing enough in situ work. And yet the biggest crisis in conservation. We're running out of time and losing more than we're winning. So there's a great sense of urgency."

22    Yet it is clear that many in the zoo world are stuck in the past. In contemplating "the challenges of the twenty-first century," one zoo director spoke, at the 1991 AAZPA [American Association of Zoological Parks and Aquariums] annual meeting, about the importance of entertainment. "Let us also not forget animal rides such as elephant, camel, or even pony rides. Although they may seem like pure entertainment, there is an element of education through the impressions that are gained by the close association of man and beast."

23    The serious, not the silly, will survive in the next century. In a prescient paper deliverd in 1972 at the AAZPA annual meeting, naturalist Roger Caras asked, "The world is changing, are you?" Caras, who has written more than sixty books on nature, said, "If you think you are going to remain the same while all institutions and all values around you evolve with the speed of an atomic explosion, you are in for a shock. You may wake up and find your zoo is not only obsolete in architecture but in purpose." Caras stood before zoo leaders and took them to task for not having a futuristic think tank, for not being and educational institution, for not listening to the concerns of zoogoer, for not marketing and merchandising themselves and for not reaching out to the community. "I know many of you who are fifty years behind the times at a time in history when the only way to survive is to be ten years ahead of the time in which you live. . . . I look ahead and see how many of you could be phased out. Because, with many of my affiliations, I deal with gift and bequest situations, and I see where that money is going. When it doesn't go to you, I despair." Cara's comments are all true today. Zoos that think they cannot afford to change will ultimately find out they can't afford not to.

## Comprehension Test 8*

### Checking Your Comprehension

1. Identify and explain one reason why the aminal population is decreasing.

2. Explain the effects of deforestation.

3. What caused most of the large wading birds in Florida's Everglades National Park to be wiped out by 1989?

4. According to Bill Conway, what is the mission of a zoo?

### Thinking Critically

1. Why are public zoos in a better position to manage biodiversity than government organizations?

2. What can be concluded that zoos must do in order to survive into the twenty-first century?

3. What did the author hope to accomplish by writing this article?

4. What tone does the author take in writing this article?

### Questions for Discussion

1. If you could do one thing to improve your local zoo, what would it be? Why?

2. What role do rainforests play in the matter of biodiversity?

3. What can the average citizen do to prevent the extinction of the world's wildlife?

4. What is the value of protecting the world's diverse animal and plant populations?

---

### Visit the Longman English Pages

For additional readings and exercises, visit the Longman English Skills Web page at:

**http://longman.awl.com/englishpages**

For a username and password, please see your instructor.

---

*Multiple-choice questions are contained in Appendix B (page A10).

# CHAPTER 5
# Patterns: Relationships Among Ideas

IN THIS CHAPTER YOU WILL LEARN:

1. To recognize common organizational patterns.
2. To use patterns to increase your reading efficiency.

Many of our personal daily activities involve following a pattern or an organizing principle. For instance, when you change a flat tire, bake a batch of cookies, assemble a toy, or write a term paper, you use some organized approach or method. Community activities are also organized. Think of a television talk show, a football game, or a meal in a restaurant. Things happen in a particular order, and at any point you can predict with some confidence what is going to follow.

Why do so many activities and events have a pattern? Many things, of course, won't work unless a particular order is followed. In changing a flat tire, for instance, you cannot put on the new tire until you take the flat tire off, you cannot take it off until you remove the hubcap, and so forth. Other events, however, have no inherent order, yet they also follow a pattern. Religious services or ceremonies are examples; they proceed in a predictable, systematic way. In these situations, the order often allows participants or spectators to know what to do or expect next. Humans have a basic need to make sense out of things and to understand how things are done.

Written language often follows a pattern for similar reasons. Many ideas or events have a natural order, and this order is often followed as the idea is explained. For example, in writing that describes how to change a flat tire, the simplest way to arrange the details is the order in which the task is done. In other more abstract cases, a pattern allows the reader to follow the ideas more easily, to remember them more easily, and to see the relationship between the ideas. In this chapter you will look at the most common organizational patterns and see how recognizing these patterns can improve recall.

147

## ■ HOW RECOGNIZING A PATTERN IMPROVES RECALL

Which of the following phone numbers would be easier to remember?

876–5432
792–6538

Which of the following sets of directions would be easier to remember?

After you pass two signals turn left. Then pass two more signals, and turn right. Next, pass two more signals and turn left.
After you pass two streets, turn left. Then after you pass three more streets, turn right. Next, pass one more street, and turn right.

Which of the following shopping lists would be easier to remember if you forgot your list?

paint, brushes, paint remover, drop cloth
milk, deodorant, nails, comb

In each example, you probably selected the first choice as easier to remember. Now, let us consider *why* each is easier to remember than the other choice. The first choices each had a pattern. The items were connected in some way that made it possible to remember them together. The phone number consists of consecutive digits in reverse order; the directions consist of two left—two right—two left; the shopping list contains items related to a particular task—painting. From these examples you can see that items are easier to remember if they are related in some way.

Lists A and B each contain five facts. Which would be easier to learn?

### List A

1. Cheeseburgers contain more calories than hamburgers.
2. Christmas cactus plants bloom once a year.
3. Many herbs have medicinal uses.
4. Many ethnic groups live in Toronto.
5. Fiction books are arranged alphabetically by author.

### List B

1. Effective advertising has several characteristics.
2. An ad must be unique.
3. An ad must be believable.
4. An ad must make a lasting impression.
5. An ad must substantiate a claim.

Most likely, you chose list B. There is no connection between the facts in list A; the facts in list B, however, are related. The first sentence made a general statement, and each remaining sentence gave a particular characteristic of effective advertising. Together they fit into a pattern.

The details of a paragraph, paragraphs within an essay, events within a short story, or sections within a textbook often fit a pattern. If you can recognize the pattern, you will find it easier to remember the content. You will be able to remember a unified whole rather than independent pieces of information. The rest of this chapter examines the most common patterns.

## ■ COMMON ORGANIZATIONAL PATTERNS

The most common organizational patterns are chronological order, comparison-contrast, cause-effect, and enumeration. For each of these patterns we give examples and list frequently used directional words. To help you visualize these patterns, a diagram called a *map* is presented for each. You will see that these maps are useful ways to organize information for study and review, especially if you are a visual learner. If you are an applied learner, you may find that maps make abstract ideas more tangible and concrete. In learning and working with these organizational patterns, focus your attention on the relationships among the ideas, rather than on naming the pattern correctly. As you will see in the section titled Mixed Patterns, patterns sometimes overlap.

### ■ Chronological Order

One of the most obvious patterns is time order, also called sequence of events or chronological order. In this pattern, ideas are presented in the order in which they occur in time. The event that happened first appears first in the paragraph, the event that occurred next in time appears next, and so on. The chronological order pattern can be visualized or mapped as follows:

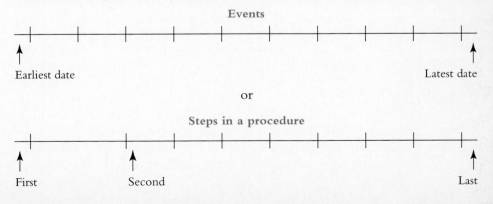

Chronological order is used frequently in reporting current events and appears commonly in news articles and magazines. Directions and instructions are often written using this pattern. It is also used to recount historical events or to provide a historical perspective, and can be found in textbooks and reference sources. The following paragraph, taken from a western civilization text, is organized using chronological order:

Modern computers have evolved rapidly through four generations of technology, each representing such a major advance that it made computers of previous generations obsolete. First-generation machines (1946–1958), based on vacuum tubes, were slow, unreliable, difficult to program, and difficult to use. Second-generation computers (1958–1964), based on transistors, were faster and more reliable. High-level programming languages made them much easier to program. Third-generation computers (1964–1971), based on integrated circuits, were even faster and more reliable than second-generation machines, and they were dramatically cheaper too. Improvements in system software and peripherals (such as time-sharing and interactive processing) made it possible for thousands of people to use a single machine, each having the impression of full and exclusive control of its resources. Users began to demand that computers come equipped with a range of application software. Fourth-generation computers, based on very large scale integration (VLSI) technology, saw further dramatic price drops, rising minicomputer popularity, and the origin of the microcomputer. Further evolution of computer technology may result in a fifth generation of intelligent computers, but for now the demand for useful application software keeps even technologically outmoded computers on the market.

Pfaffenberger, *Personal Computer Applications: A Strategy for the Information Society.*

● ● ●

This excerpt could be mapped by using a timeline:

| 1946 | 1958 | 1964 | 1971 | Present |
|------|------|------|------|---------|
| First generation Vacuum tubes | Second generation Transistors | Third generation Integrated circuits | Fourth generation VLSI technology | Fifth generation Intelligent computers |

Entire passages and chapters, or even books, may be organized using the chronological order pattern. Here are the section headings from a chapter in an advertising textbook. Notice how the topics proceed in order by time.

**THE HISTORY OF ADVERTISING**

Early History
How the Advertising Agency Grew Up
Early Twentieth Century Advertising
Advertising Today

Cohen, *Advertising.*

● ● ●

A chronological order pattern is often evident within each section. For example, the following subheadings appear:

**ADVERTISING TODAY**

Advertising in the Seventies
Advertising in the Eighties
Advertising in the Nineties

● ● ●

One of the clearest ways to describe how to do something is to use steps that follow the order in which it is to be done. This is why chronological order is often used to describe the steps in a process or to outline a method or procedure. The following excerpt from a personal computer applications text describes the process of printing text.

**PRINTING THE TEXT**

Once your document has been formatted, printing is a straightforward, almost automatic process.

**Selecting Printing Options**

You can inform the program what kind of paper you're using, and it will adjust the printing process automatically. If you're using continuous or **tractor feed paper,** for example, the program will not pause for page breaks. If you're using single or **cut sheets,** however, it will pause to let you insert a new page. (Printers equipped with a **cut sheet feeder** do this job automatically.)

**Preparing The Printer And Starting Printing**

Before you give the command that starts printing the document, be sure the printer is turned on and that it's on-line or selected (that is, directly connected to the computer and ready to receive the computer's signals). Then use the command that initiates the printing process.

**Stop Printing Command**

When the printer starts printing, inspect the first page. You may find a gross error of some sort (for example, single spacing when double spacing is required). In such cases, when there's no sense in printing the whole document until the error is fixed, the stop printing command is very useful.

**Printing Selected Pages Or Printing Multiple Copies**

Most programs let you print selected portions of your document. If you wish, you can print more than one copy.

Pfaffenberger, *Personal Computer Applications: A Strategy for the Information Society.*

● ● ●

Materials organized by chronological order use signal words or phrases to connect the events or steps in the process. Examples of such directional words and phrases include:

CHRONOLOGICAL ORDER DIRECTIONAL WORDS/PHRASES

*in* the Middle Ages . . .
the *final* stage . . .
*before* the Civil Rights Act . . .
*on* December 7 . . .

Other directional words/phrases are

first, second, later, next, as soon as, after, then, finally, meanwhile, last, during, when, by the time, until

When you realize that a piece of writing is organized using time order, you can expect that whatever event appears next will have happened next. You will find it easier to remember facts, details, dates, or events because they are organized and connected by their occurrence in time.

## EXERCISE 5–1

*DIRECTIONS:* Which of the following topic sentences suggest that their paragraphs will be developed by using chronology?

1. The human brain is divided into two halves, each of which is responsible for separate functions.
2. Advertising has appeared in magazines since the late 1700s.
3. The life cycle of a product is the stages it goes through from when it is first created to when it is no longer produced.
4. There are really only two ways to gather information from human beings about what they are currently thinking or feeling.
5. To select a presidential candidate you will vote for, you should first examine his or her philosophy of government.

## EXERCISE 5–2

*DIRECTIONS:* Read the following excerpt from a political science textbook and answer the questions that follow.

### POLITICAL BACKGROUND OF SEGREGATION

The end of the Civil War and the emancipation of the slaves did not give blacks the full rights of citizenship. Nor did the passing of the Thirteenth Amendment in 1865 (which outlawed slavery); or the Fourteenth Amendment in 1868 (which extended "equal protection of the laws" to all citizens); or the Fifteenth Amendment in 1870 (which guaranteed the right to vote to all citizens regardless of "race, color, or previous condition of servitude").

Between 1866 and 1877 the "radical Republicans" controlled Congress. "Reconstruction" governments were established in the South to put through reforms in the former Confederate states, and also to bring in votes for the Republicans. Although the sometimes corrupt period of Reconstruction partly deserves the bad name it has gotten in the South, it was a time when blacks won a number of both civil and political rights. The radical Congress passed five civil rights and Reconstruction acts aimed at granting blacks immediate equality and preventing states from curbing these rights.

Then in 1875 Congress passed a civil rights act designed to prevent any public form of discrimination—in theaters, restaurants, transportation, and the like—against blacks. Congress's right to forbid a *state* to act contrary to the Constitution was unquestioned. But this law, based on the Fourteenth Amendment, assumed that Congress could also prevent racial discrimination by private individuals.

The Supreme Court disagreed. In 1883 it declared the Civil Rights Act of 1875 unconstitutional. The majority of the Court ruled that Congress could pass legislation only to correct *states'* violations of the Fourteenth Amendment. Congress had no power to enact "primary and direct" legislation on individuals; that was left to the states. This decision meant the federal government could not lawfully protect blacks against most forms of discrimination. In other words, white supremacy was beyond federal control.

Wasserman, *The Basics of American Politics.*

● ● ●

1. Draw a map of the major events discussed in this article in the order in which they occurred.

2. List the directional words used in this excerpt.

_____

_____

## ■ Definition

Each academic discipline has its own specialized vocabulary. One of the primary purposes of introductory textbooks is to introduce students to this new language. Consequently, definition is a commonly used pattern throughout most introductory-level texts.

Suppose you were asked to define the word *comedian* for someone unfamiliar with the term. First, you would probably say that a comedian is a person who entertains. Then you might distinguish a comedian from other types of entertainers by saying that a comedian is an entertainer who tells jokes and makes others laugh. Finally, you might mention, by way of example, the names of several well-known comedians who have appeared on television. Although you may have presented it informally, your definition would have followed the standard, classic pattern. The first part of your definition tells what general class or group the term belongs to (entertainers). The second part tells what distinguishes the term from other items in the same class or category. The third part includes further explanation, characteristics, examples, or applications.

Here are two additional examples:

| Term | General Class | Distinguishing Characteristics |
|------|---------------|-------------------------------|
| Stress | Physiological reaction | A response to a perceived threat |
| Mutant | Organism | Carries a gene that has undergone a change |

You can map the definition pattern as follows:

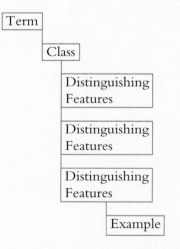

In the following excerpt, the writer defines the term *lipids*:

The **lipids** are a diverse group of energy-rich organic compounds whose main common feature is that they do not dissolve in water. They do, however, dissolve in various organic solvents such as ether, chloroform, and benzene. They include the fats, oils, waxes, and steroids. Their structures vary widely, and they are employed as energy storage molecules (especially in animals), components of cell membranes, insulators for the nervous system, and hormones—just to mention a few. We will focus next on two of the major lipid categories.

Rischer and Easton, *Focus on Human Biology.*

• • •

In this paragraph, the general class of lipids is "organic compounds." Their distinguishing feature is that they do not dissolve in water but do dissolve in organic solvents. The remainder of the paragraph gives examples and explains their structure and use.

Writers often use the directional words shown here to indicate that a definition is to follow.

#### DEFINITION PATTERN DIRECTIONAL WORDS/PHRASES

nepotism *is.* . .
classical conditioning *refers to.* . .
acceleration *can be defined as.* . .
empathy means. . .

Other directional words/phrases are:

consists of, is a term that, involves, is called, is characterized by, that is, occurs when, exists when, are those that, entails, corresponds to, is literally

## EXERCISE 5–3

*DIRECTIONS:* From the following textbook chapter headings select those that are most likely to use the definition pattern.

1. The Nature Of Culture
2. What Is Conditioning?
3. Stressors: The Roots of Stress
4. The Origin of Life
5. Second Law of Thermodynamics

## EXERCISE 5–4

*DIRECTIONS:* Read the following excerpt from a geography textbook and answer the questions that follow.

#### SHIFTING CULTIVATION

The native peoples of remote tropical lowlands and hills in the Americas, Africa, Southeast Asia, and Indonesia practice an agricultural system known as **shifting cultivation.** Essentially, this is a land-rotation system. Using machetes or other bladed instruments, farmers chop away the undergrowth from small patches of land and kill the trees by cutting off a strip of bark completely around the trunk. After the dead vegetation has dried out, the farmers set it on fire to clear the land. These clearing techniques have given shifting cultivation the name of "slash-and-burn" agriculture. Working with digging sticks or hoes, the farmers then plant a variety of crops in the clearings, varying from the corn, beans, bananas, and manioc of American Indians to the yams and nonirrigated rice grown by hill tribes in Southeast Asia. Different crops are typically planted together in the same clearing, a practice called **intertillage.** This allows taller, stronger crops to shelter lower, more fragile ones from the tropical downpours and reveals the rich lore and learning acquired by shifting cultivators over many centuries. Relatively little tending of the plants is necessary until harvest time, and no fertilizer is applied to the fields. Farmers repeat the planting and harvesting cycle in the same clearings for perhaps four or five years, until the soil has lost much of its fertility. Then these areas are abandoned, and the farmers prepare new clearings to replace them. The abandoned fields lie unused and recuperate for 10 to 20 years before farmers clear and cultivate them again. Shifting cultivation is one form of **subsistence agriculture**— that is, involving food production mainly for the family and local community rather than for market.

Jordan, Domosh and Rowntree, *The Human Mosaic:*
*A Thematic Introduction to Cultural Geography.*

● ● ●

1. In your own words, write a definition for each of the three terms defined in the paragraph (see **boldface print**).
2. For each definition, identify the general class and distinguishing characteristics as given in the passage.
3. Underline any directional words used in the passage.

■ **Classification**

If you were asked to describe types of computers, you might mention mainframes, minicomputers, and microcomputers. By dividing a broad topic into its major categories, you are using a pattern known as *classification*.

This pattern is widely used in many academic subjects. For example, a psychology text might explain human needs by classifying them into two categories: primary and secondary. In a chemistry textbook, various compounds may be grouped and discussed according to common characteristics such as the presence of hydrogen or oxygen. The classification pattern divides a topic into parts that are based on common or shared characteristics.

Here are a few examples of topics and the classifications or categories into which each might be divided.

Trees: deciduous, evergreen
Motives: achievement, power, affiliation, competency
Communication: verbal, nonverbal

You can visualize the classification pattern by drawing a map like this:

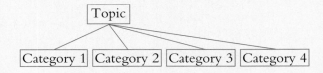

Read the following paragraph to discover how the author classifies muscles:

**TYPES OF MUSCLES IN HUMANS**

Human muscles can be divided into three groups according to their structure and the nerves that activate them. **Smooth muscle** is found in a number of internal structures, such as the walls of the digestive tract, around some blood vessels, and in certain internal organs. **Cardiac muscle** is found in the walls of the heart. Both of these are involuntary, since they function without conscious control. Thus, you don't have to lie awake nights keeping your heart beating. There is some fascinating evidence that "involuntary" responses can be voluntarily controlled to a degree[. . . . ]**Skeletal muscles** are the voluntary muscles.

Wallace, *Biology: The World of Life.*

● ● ●

This paragraph classifies muscles into three types: smooth, cardiac, and skeletal. The classification is based on their structure and the nerves that activate them.

Directional words commonly used to signal this pattern are shown here.

CLASSIFICATION PATTERN DIRECTIONAL WORDS/PHRASES

There are *several types of* bones. . .
An S-corporation *is composed of.* . .
*another kind* of memory is. . .
Societies can be *classified as.* . .

Other directional words/phrases are:

comprises, one, first, second, finally, last, several varieties of, different stages of, different groups that, include

## EXERCISE 5–5

*DIRECTIONS:* Identify and circle the topics listed that might be developed by using the classification pattern.

1. Types of utility
2. The staffing process
3. Growth of plant life
4. Functions of dating
5. Theories of evolution
6. The discovery of DNA
7. Formal organizations
8. Animal tissues
9. Effects of negative feelings
10. Classifying emotions

## EXERCISE 5–6

*DIRECTIONS:* Read the following excerpt from a biology textbook and answer the questions that follow.

### ANGIOSPERMS

All plants that develop a *true flower* are classified as **angiosperms.** The angiosperms vary with respect to their number of floral parts, but all **flowers** are reproductive structures that contain both male and female reproductive parts, and their seeds develop within fruits. More than 300 families of angiosperms are separated into two major classes, monocots and dicots.

### Monocots

**Monocots** develop from germinated seeds that have a single embryonic leaf (called a cotyledon) and grow into plants with parallel leaf venation and floral parts that occur in threes or multiples of three. The vascular tissues in cross sections of monocot stems appear as scattered bundles of cells.

Monocots include most species that are cultivated as food crops by humans. The grass family is by far the largest and most important; it includes rice, wheat, barley, oats, other grains, and the grasses on which most animal *herbivores* feed[. . . . ] The largest monocot species belong to the pineapple, banana, and palm families.

Many spring wildflowers are monocots in the lily, iris, and orchid families. The orchid family has the largest number of flowering plants, over 20,000 species, most of which grow in tropical or subtropical regions of the world.

### Dicots

**Dicots** develop from germinated seeds that have two cotyledons, grow into plants with nested leaf venation, and produce flowers with parts in fours or fives or multiples of four or five. The vascular tissue in the dicot stem forms a circular pattern when viewed in cross section.

Mix, Farber and King, *Biology: The Network of Life.*

● ● ●

1. What is the subject of the classification?

   _____

2. How is it divided?

   _____

3. Circle the directional words used in this excerpt.

   _____

## EXERCISE 5–7

*DIRECTIONS:* Select a brief section from a textbook chapter you are currently studying that uses either the chronological, definition, or classification pattern. State which pattern is being used and list the directional words or phrases that provided you with clues to the type of pattern.

## ■ Comparison-Contrast

Often a writer will explain an object or idea, especially if it is unfamiliar to the reader, by showing how it is similar to or different from a familiar object or idea. At other times, it may be the writer's purpose to show how two ideas, places, objects, or people are similar or different. In each of these situations a writer commonly uses a pattern called comparison-contrast. In this pattern the material is organized to emphasize the similarities or differences between two or more items. There are several variations on this pattern: a paragraph may focus on similarities only, differences only, or both. The comparison-contrast pattern can be visualized and mapped as follows:

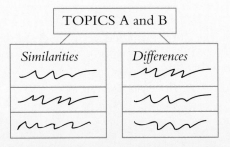

For material that focuses on differences, you might use a map like this:

|  | Topic A | Topic B |
|---|---|---|
| Feature #1 | ⌇ | ⌇ |
| Feature #2 | ⌇ | ⌇ |
| Feature #3 | ⌇ | ⌇ |

The following passage compares the work of Darwin and Mendel. The first paragraph discusses their use of deductive reasoning, and the second describes the compatibility of their theories.

In their original work both Darwin and that other great innovator who followed him, Gregor Mendel, used deductive reasoning to great effect. Both these giants of biology had been trained in theology. As a result, they were well acquainted with an intellectual tradition based on deduction. And since induction is difficult to apply in a field where so little can be directly observed, perhaps theology provided some of the essential intellectual tools both men needed to develop a viewpoint so different from prevailing theological thinking.

Darwin and Mendel are linked in another fundamental way. Darwin could not explain how successful traits are passed on to successive generations, exposing his theory of natural selection to growing criticism. When Mendel was rediscovered, geneticists were paying a lot of attention to mutations. They still felt that natural selection of variants had a minor part in evolution. The major factor, they believed, was sudden change introduced by mutation. Not until the 1930s did biologists realize, at last, that Darwin's theory of natural selection and Mendel's laws of genetics were fully compatible. Together the two form the basis of population genetics, a major science of today.

Laetsch, *Plants: Basic Concepts in Botany.*

● ● ●

A map of the passage could look like this:

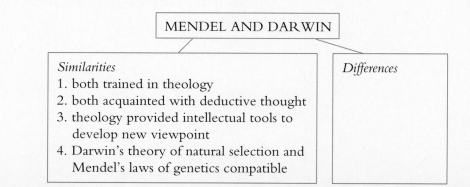

Once you become aware of the comparison-contrast pattern, look for both similarities and differences. First establish what is being compared or contrasted to what. Next determine whether similarities, differences, or both are presented. Often the title, heading, or topic sentence will express the basic relationship between the items or ideas discussed. A topic sentence that states, "It is important to make a distinction between amnesia and forgetting," indicates that the paragraph is primarily concerned with differences. On the other hand, a heading such as "Two Compatible Proposals for Economic Development" emphasizes similarities. Finally, decide whether the comparison or the contrast is the author's central purpose or whether it is used only as a means of support for the main idea.

You will find that directional words help you identify the pattern. They also help you decide whether the paragraph focuses on similarities, differences, or both.

### COMPARISON-CONTRAST DIRECTIONAL WORDS/PHRASES

*both* Faulkner and Williams. . .
*unlike* primary groups, secondary groups. . .
a drive *differs from* a need in that. . .
values, norms, and ethics *share*. . .

Other directional words/phrases are

in contrast, similarly, likewise, however, in comparison, to compare, on the other hand, like, resembles, is similar, as opposed to, whereas, in the same way, correspondingly, instead, in spite of, as well as

## EXERCISE 5–8

*DIRECTIONS:* Which of the following topic sentences suggest that its paragraph will be developed by using comparison-contrast?

1.  Sociology and psychology both focus on human behavior.

2.  The category of mammals contains many different kinds of animals.

3.  Two types of leaders can usually be identified in organizations: informal and formal.

4.  Interpersonal communication is far more complex than intrapersonal communication.

5.  The first step in grasping a novel's theme is to read it closely for literal content, including plot and character development.

## EXERCISE 5–9

*DIRECTIONS:* Read the following excerpt and answer the questions that follow.

Social institutions are often confused with social groups and social organizations, which are described in the next chapter. They are not the same, however. Like institutions, groups and organizations exist to meet some goals, but groups and organizations are deliberately constructed bodies of individuals, whereas institutions are systems of norms. Thus education is an institution; the University of Vermont is an organization. Religion is an institution; the Baptist church is an organization.

The confusion between institutions and organizations stems in part from the fact that the names of institutions can often be used to describe concrete entities as well. In its abstract sense, for example, the word "family" is used to refer to an institution. Using the word in this way, we might say, "During the 1960s, the family in the United States began to undergo important changes." We can also use the word "family" to refer to an actual group of people, however. Using the word in this concrete sense, we might say, "I am going to spend my vacation with my family." The speaker is referring to an existing group of individuals—mother, father, sisters, and brothers. The two meanings of the word are closely related but nevertheless distinct. The word "institution" is an abstraction; the word "organization" refers to an existing group. The distinction should become clearer as we discuss social groups and social organizations in the next chapter and specific institutions in Chapters 12 through 17.

Eschelman and Cashion, *Sociology: An Introduction.*

• • •

1. Identify two topics that are discussed in the excerpt. Does the excerpt compare, contrast, or compare *and* contrast these two topics?

   _____

   _____

2. Draw a map of the similarities or differences between the two topics.

3. List any directional words used in the selection.

   _____

   _____

## ■ Cause-Effect

The cause-effect pattern describes or discusses an event or action that is caused by another event or action. Four possible relationships are described by the cause-effect pattern:

1. **Single Cause-Single Effect.** One cause produces one effect.

   Example: Omitting a key command will cause a computer program to fail.

   Map: Cause ——— ⤍ → Effect

2. **Single Cause-Multiple Effects.** One event produces several effects.

   Example: The effects of inflation include shrinkage real income, increasing prices, and higher interest rates.

   Map:

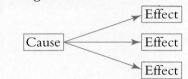

3. **Multiple Causes-Single Effect.** Several events work together to produce single effects.

   Example: Attending class regularly, reading assignments carefully, and taking good lecture notes produce good exam grades.

   Map:

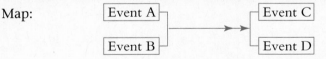

4. **Multiple Causes-Multiple Effects.** Several events work together to produce several effects.

   Example: Because you missed the bus and couldn't get a ride, you missed your first class and did not stop at the library.

   Map:

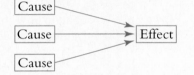

Read the following excerpt and determine what type of cause-effect relationship it illustrates.

#### EXTERNAL FACTORS IN OBESITY

The external cue theory holds that environmental cues prompt us to eat. This means that rather than relying on internal physical hunger cues, we repond to sight, color, and availability of food or to the time of day when we are programmed to eat. This is further complicated by the fact that food is available around the clock—at home, at work, in restaurants and grocery stores (some restaurants even offer home delivery!).

Other factors that may contribute to people's attitudes toward food are the way in which individual families perceive food. Some families are "food centered," which means they tend to overeat at mealtime, eat rapidly, snack excessively, eat for reasons other than hunger, or eat until all their dishes are empty. Unwittingly, family members may become involved as codependents in the exercise of overeating, and serve as enablers for a person whose eating habits are out of control. Overeating by children may be an imitation of overeating by parents. Obese children, over a given time interval, tend to take more bites of food and chew their food less thoroughly than nonobese children. Some parents preach the "clean plate ethic" by which they praise their children for eating all the food on their plates as a token of thanks for having enough food to eat.

Some people eat in response to stress, boredom, insecurity, anxiety, loneliness, or as a reward for being good. Parents who console a child with food may be initiating a life-long behavior pattern. Some people use food as an inappropriate response to psychological stimuli. As you experience pain, anxiety, insecurity, stress, arousal, or excitement, the brain responds by producing substances that soothe pain and lessen arousal. Another effect of these substances is that they enhance appetite for food and reduce activity. If, in addition, you are unusually sensitive to stress, you are likely to eat to compensate for stress, whether negative or positive. Eating may be an appropriate response to all of these stimuli on occasion, but the person who uses them to overeat creates a whole new set of emotional problems relating to his or her overeating. They may get caught in a vicious cycle—depression causing overeating and vice versa.

Byer and Shainberg, *Living Well: Health in Your Hands.*

● ● ●

The first paragraph discusses environmental cues that may stimulate people to eat. The second paragraph examines how a family's perceptions of food can contribute to overeating. The third paragraph explains how some people eat in response to emotional stimuli. It could be mapped as follows:

### External Factors in Obesity

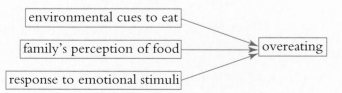

When reading material is organized in the cause-effect pattern, pay close attention to the topic sentence. It usually states the cause-effect relationship that is detailed throughout the paragraph. As you read through the paragraph, read to find specific causes and specific effects. Determine the connection between causes and effects: Why did a particular event or action occur? What happened as a result of it?

Directional words can help you identify the pattern as well as determine the exact nature of the cause-effect relationship. The following list contains directional words that most commonly indicate a cause-effect pattern.

### CAUSE-EFFECT DIRECTIONAL WORDS/PHRASES

hypertension *causes*. . .
Napoleon was defeated at Waterloo, *consequently*. . .
an interest rate increase *resulted in*. . .
hatred *breeds*. . .

Other directional words/phrases are

therefore, hence, for this reason, since, leads to, creates, yields, stems from, produces, for, because, as a result, due to, thus

## EXERCISE 5–10

*DIRECTIONS:* Predict and circle the textbook chapter headings that are most likely to use the cause-effect pattern.

1. The Nature of the Judicial System
2. Why Beauracracies Exist
3. Explaining the Increase in Homelessness
4. How Walt Whitman Uses Imagery
5. Types of Special Interest Groups

## EXERCISE 5–11

*DIRECTIONS:* Read the following excerpt and answer the questions that follow.

### DEPRESSANTS

Alcohol is the most popular of the depressants, which generally reduce activity in the central nervous system. In small amounts depressants act as stimulants by producing relaxation and loosening inhibitions, but in larger quantities they severely impair sensory functions and coordination. Concentrations of .10 to .15 percent of alcohol in the blood (10 to 15 parts in 10,000), which would result from imbibing three bottles of beer, can cause such impairment. At .20 percent a person is severely impaired, and at levels of .40 percent death can occur[. . . . ]

Small amounts of alcohol often produce a pleasurable, relaxed state of consciousness, but larger amounts may cause many people to become belligerent and angry, as well as disoriented and confused. Severe abuse of alcohol may induce hallucinations. They are thought to occur by action of drugs (and their withdrawal) on the central nervous system[. . . . ] Addicts who are withdrawn from alcohol often suffer *delirium tremens,* or, popularly, the D.T.'s. Its most noticeable effect is hand tremors, but the addict also suffers hallucinations, usually visions of terrifying animals such as snakes or surreal monsters. The D.T.'s may be fatal.

Roediger, et al., *Psychology.*

• • •

1. Underline the sentence that states the central cause-effect relationship discussed throughout this excerpt.

2. List or draw a map of the various effects of different amounts of alcohol.

_____

_____

3. Underline the directional words used in this excerpt.

## ■ Enumeration

The enumeration pattern is a list of information. The information listed may be facts, statistics, characteristics, examples, features, or properties. For example, a section in an anthropology text may list and describe characteristics of an ancient culture, or a psychology text may present facts about aggressive behavior. Usually the characteristics need not appear in any particular order.

Often the writer chooses to present the items in a way that is easiest to explain or that is easiest for the reader to understand. Even if this is done, there is still no obvious pattern that will help you organize and remember the information. The following excerpt is an example of a paragraph that lists information.

Cinnamon comes from the bark of *Cinnamomum zelyanicum,* an evergreen tree in the family Lauraceae. Others in the family are mainly aromatic evergreen trees and shrubs, among them camphor and avocado. Cinnamon is native to Ceylon, where all commercial production of the spice is still carried on; attempts to introduce it elsewhere have never been entirely successful. Cinnamon flavors desserts, cakes, and candy, and it is part of curry powder; its oil, distilled from the leaves, is used medicinally.

Laetsch, *Plants: Basic Concepts in Botany.*

• • •

As you can see, the paragraph listed information about cinnamon—its source, its origin, and its uses.

The listing pattern can be visualized and mapped as follows:

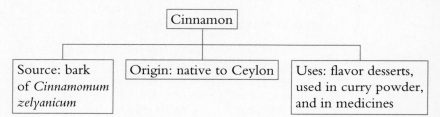

The brief sample paragraph on cinnamon could be mapped as follows:

Directional words are extremely useful in locating items in the list. Usually, as a writer moves from one item in the list to another, he or she will indicate the change. Common examples of directional words for lists are given in the list.

### ENUMERATION PATTERN DIRECTIONAL WORDS/PHRASES

there are *several* characteristics of. . .
*one feature of* families is. . .
Government serves *the following* functions. . .
*Most importantly,* government. . .

Other enumeration pattern directional words/phrases are

first, second, third, numerals (1., 2., 3.), letters (a., b., c.), another, also, too, for instance, for example, finally, the largest, the least

## EXERCISE 5–12

*DIRECTIONS:* Identify and circle the topics listed that might be developed by using the enumeration pattern.

1. Freud's versus Jung's theories
2. Consumer research technology
3. Varieties of theft
4. Purposes of legal punishment
5. The process of gene splicing
6. Learning theories
7. Hormones and reproduction

8. Pastoral society
9. How acid rain occurs
10. The impact of environment on intelligence

## EXERCISE 5–13

*DIRECTIONS:* Read the following excerpt and answer the questions that follow.

### THE STIMULUS FOR HEARING: SOUND

The stimulus for vision is light; for hearing, the stimulus is sound. Sound consists of a series of pressure of air (or some other medium, such as water) beating against our ear. We can represent these pressures as sound waves. As a source of sound vibrates, it pushes air against our ears in waves. As was the case for light waves, there are three major physical characteristics of sound waves: amplitude, frequency (the inverse of wavelength), and purity. Each is related to a different psychological experience. We'll briefly consider each in turn.

The amplitude of a sound wave depicts its intensity—the force with which air strikes the ear. The intensity of a sound determines the psychological experience we call loudness. That is, the higher the amplitude, the louder we perceive the sound. Quiet, soft sounds have low amplitudes.

Measurements of the physical intensity of sound are given in units of force per unit area (or pressure). Loudness is a psychological characteristic. It is measured by people, not by instruments. The decibel scale of sound intensity reflects perceived loudness. Its zero point is the lowest intensity of sound that can be detected, the absolute threshold. Our ears are very sensitive receptors and respond to very low levels of sound intensity. Sounds louder than those produced by jet aircraft engines or fast-moving subway trains (about 120 decibels) are experienced more as pain than as sound. Prolonged exposure to loud sounds causes varying degrees of deafness.

The second physical characteristic of sound to consider is wave frequency, the number of times a wave repeats itself within a given period. For sound, frequency is measured in terms of how many waves of pressure are exerted every second. The unit of sound frequency is the hertz, abbreviated Hz. If a sound wave repeats itself 50 times in one second, it is a 50-Hz sound; 500 repetitions is a 500-Hz sound, and so on.

The psychological experience produced by sound wave frequency is pitch. Pitch is our experience of how high or low a tone is. The musical scale represents differences in pitch. Low frequencies correspond to bass tones, such as those made by foghorns or tubas. High-frequency vibrations give rise to the experience of high-pitched sounds, such as musical tones produced by flutes or the squeals of smoke detectors.

A third characteristic of sound waves is wave purity, or wave complexity. You'll recall that we seldom experience pure, monochromatic lights. Pure sounds are also uncommon in our everyday experience. A pure sound would be one in which all waves from the sound source were vibrating at exactly the same frequency. Such sounds can be produced electronically, and tuning forks produce approximations, but most of the sounds we hear every day are complex sounds consisting of many different sound wave frequencies.

The psychological quality or characteristic of a sound, reflecting its degree of purity, is called timbre. For example, each musical instrument produces a unique variety or mixture of overtones, so each type of musical instrument tends to sound a little different from all others. If a trumpet, a violin, and a piano were to play the same note, we could still tell the instruments apart because of our experience of timbre. In fact, any instrument can display different timbres, depending on how it is constructed and played.

Gerow, *Psychology: An Introduction.*

● ● ●

1. Underline the sentence that states what the entire passage will discuss.
2. Explain in your own words the three major physical characteristics of sound waves and their related psychological experiences.
3. Underline the directional words or phrases used in this excerpt.

## ■ Mixed Patterns

Many texts contain sections and passages that combine one or more organizational patterns. For instance, in listing characteristics of a newly developed computer program, an author may explain it by comparing it with similar existing programs. Or, in describing an event or process, the writer may also include the reasons (causes) an event occurred or explain why the steps in a process must be followed in the prescribed order.

Read the following paragraph, also about our changing ideas of deviance, and determine what two patterns are used.

### VARIATION BY TIME

An act considered deviant in one time period may be considered nondeviant in another. Cigarette smoking, for example, has a long history of changing normative definitions. Nuehring and Markle (1974) note that in the United States between 1895 and 1921, fourteen states completely banned cigarette smoking and all other states except Texas passed laws regulating the sale of cigarettes to minors. In the early years of this century, stop-smoking clinics were opened in several cities and antismoking campaigns were widespread. Following World War I, however, cigarette sales increased and public attitudes toward smoking changed. Through the mass media, the tobacco industry appealed to women, weightwatchers, and even to health seekers. States began to realize that tobacco could be a rich source of revenue, and by 1927 the fourteen states that banned cigarettes had repealed their laws. By the end of World War II, smoking had become acceptable, and in many contexts it was thought socially desirable.

Eschelman and Cashion, *Sociology: An Introduction.*

● ● ●

In this passage, the textbook author is explaining how the meaning of deviance varies with the times. The author uses examples to explain these changes, and these examples are arranged in time sequence. However, the paragraph also uses a comparison-contrast organization because it compares pre- and post-World War I attitudes toward smoking. Thus two patterns—time order and comparison-contrast—are used.

When reading mixed patterns, focus on one of the patterns and use it to guide your reading. Whenever possible, choose the predominant or most obvious pattern. However, regardless of which pattern you choose, it will serve to organize the author's thoughts and make them easier to recall.

Because more than one pattern is evident in mixed patterns, you can expect a mix or combination of directional words as well.

## EXERCISE 5–14

*DIRECTIONS:* Read the following excerpt and answer the questions that follow.

### THE ORGANIZATION OF RELIGION

People have tried to understand the world around them throughout history, but we do not know exactly how or why they began to believe in supernatural beings or powers. Societies such as the Tasaday of the Philippines or the Bushmen of Africa, who rely on hunting and gathering as their primary means of subsistence, often explain things in naturalistic terms. This type of religion is known as *animism,* which is the belief that spirits inhabit virtually everything in nature: rocks, trees, lakes, animals, and humans alike, and that these spirits influence all aspects of life and destiny. Sometimes they help, perhaps causing an arrow to strike and kill a wild pig for food. At other times, they are harmful as when they make a child get sick and die. These spirits can sometimes be influenced by specific rituals or behaviors, however, and pleasing them results in favorable treatment.

Some tribal societies practice a form of religion known as *shamanism,* which revolves around the belief that certain individuals, called shamans, have special skill or knowledge in influencing spirits. Shamans, most of whom are men, are called upon to heal the sick and wounded, to make hunting expeditions successful, to protect the group against evil spirits, and to generally ensure the group's well-being. Shamans receive their power through ecstatic experiences, which might originate from a psychotic episode, the use of a hallucinogen, or deprivation such as fasting or lack of sleep. The American Indians of the northwestern United States hold that ancestral spirits work for the good or ill of the tribe solely through shamans.

A third form of religion among primitive peoples is totemism. *Totemism* is the worship of plants, animals, and other natural objects both as gods and ancestors. The totem itself is the plant or animal believed to be ancestrally related to a person, tribe, or clan. Totems usually represent something important to the community such as a food source or dangerous predator, and the people often wear costumes and perform dances to mimic the totem object. Most readers are probably familiar with the totem pole used by North American Indians. This tall post, carved or painted with totemic symbols, was erected as a memorial to the dead. Totemism is still practiced today by some New Guinea tribes and by Australian aborigines. Durkheim believed that totemism was one of the earliest forms of religion and that other forms of religious organization evolved from it.

Eschelman and Cashion, *Sociology: An Introduction.*

● ● ●

1. What patterns are evident in this excerpt? Which do you think is predominant?

   _____

2. Underline the directional words that suggest these patterns.
3. Draw a map of this excerpt.
4. Explain in your own words each of the three forms of primitive religion.

   _____

   _____

■ **APPLYING ORGANIZATIONAL PATTERNS**

Now that you are familiar with the six basic organizational patterns, you are ready to use these valuable structures to organize your learning and shape your thinking. Patterns give ideas shape or form, thereby making them more readily comprehensible. Table 5.1 on page 172 presents a review of these organizational patterns and of directional words commonly used with each pattern.

Although this chapter focuses on the use of patterns in textbook writing, you will find such patterns in other academic situations as well. Look for these patterns as you read, listen for them in lectures, and use them in completing assignments and writing papers. For example, your professor may organize his or her lecture by using one or more of these patterns and may use directional words to enable you to follow the line of thought. On exams, especially essay exams, you will find questions that require you to organize information in terms of one or more of the organizational patterns.

Organizational patterns and directional words are also useful in organizing your own ideas and presenting them effectively in other situations.

**Table 5.1** A Review Of Patterns And Directional Words

| Pattern | Characteristics | Directional Words |
|---|---|---|
| Chronological Order | Describes events, processes, procedures | first, second, later, before, next, as soon as, after, then, finally, meanwhile, following, last, during, in, on, when, until |
| Definition | Explains the meaning of a word or phrase | is, refers to, can be defined as, means, consists of, involves, is a term that, is called, is characterized by, occurs when, are those that, entails, corresponds to, is literally |
| Classification | Divides a topic into parts based on shared characteristics | classified as, is comprised of, is composed of, several varieties of, different stages of, different groups that, includes, one, first, second, another, finally, last |
| Comparison-Contrast | Discusses similarities and/or differences among ideas, theories, concepts, objects, or persons | *Similarities:* both, also, similarly, like, likewise, too, as well as, resembles, correspondingly, in the same way, to compare, in comparison, share<br>*Differences:* unlike, differs from, in contrast, on the other hand, instead, despite, nevertheless, however, in spite of, whereas, as opposed to |
| Cause-Effect | Describes how one or more things cause or are related to another | *Causes:* because, because of, for, since, stems from, one cause is, one reason is, leads to, causes, creates, yields, produces, due to, breeds, for this reason<br>*Effects:* consequently, results in, one result is, therefore, thus, as a result, hence |
| Enumeration | Organizes lists of information: characteristics, features, parts, or categories | the following, several, for example, for instance, one, another, also, too, in other words, first, second, numerals (1., 2.), letters (a., b.), most importantly, the largest, the least, finally importantly |

As you write papers and complete written assignments, these patterns will provide a basis for relating and connecting your ideas and presenting them in a clear and understandable form. The directional words are useful as transitions, leading your reader from one idea to another.

## EXERCISE 5–15

*DIRECTIONS:* Read each of the following paragraphs and identify the predominant organizational pattern used. Write the name of the pattern in the space provided. Choose from among the following patterns: chronological order, definition, classification, comparison-contrast, cause-effect, and enumeration. Draw a map of each paragraph.

1. Lions in the great grasslands of Africa are very fond of zebras. When a lion kills and feasts on zebra flesh, it is filled with new energy, which enables it to live, sire offspring, and hunt more zebras. For their part,

the zebras find food in the grasses and other plants. Taking in energy from the plants, the zebras can live and multiply. But the lions limit the number of zebras by hunting and killing them; if they did not kill the zebras, there might be more zebras than grass to support the zebras. The quantity of grass limits the lion population, too, because the number of lions that can survive depends on the quantity of zebras available as food, as energy. And thus there exists, between lions, zebras, and plants, a balance of energy—a balance of life.

Laetsch, *Plants: Basic Concepts in Botany.*

Pattern: _____

2. The national government, as we have seen, is based on a system of dividing or *decentralizing* power. Political parties, on the other hand, are a means of organizing or *centralizing* power. The framers of the Constitution decentralized power in separate branches and a federal system partly to avoid the development of powerful factions that could take over the government. This very decentralization of power, however, created the need for parties that could pull together or centralize that power.

Wasserman, *The Basics of American Politics.*

Pattern: _____

3. After the Constitution was ratified, the Federalist faction grew stronger and more like a political party. Led by Alexander Hamilton, secretary of the treasury under President George Washington, the Federalists championed a strong national government that would promote the financial interests of merchants and manufacturers. After Thomas Jefferson left President Washington's cabinet in 1793, an opposition party began to form under his leadership. The new *Democratic-Republican* party drew the support of small farmers, debtors, and others who did not benefit from the financial programs of the Federalists. Under the Democratic-Republican label, Jefferson won the presidential election of 1800, and his party continued to control the presidency until 1828. The Federalists, without power or popular support, gradually died out.

Wasserman, *The Basics of American Politics.*

Pattern: _____

4. *Homeostasis* refers to an organism's tendency to maintain a relatively constant internal environment. When we are well, our body temperature is approximately 98.6° Fahrenheit. Organisms, in order to stay alive, must maintain a somewhat constant internal equilibrium. Some departures from homeostasis are brief and not injurious—exercise, for

example. But prolonged departure from homeostasis can mean illness and threaten the survival of the organism.

Wright and Weiss, *Social Problems.*

Pattern: _____

5. Every day the mass media tell us in some new way that the American family is in trouble. The divorce rate is rising rapidly—in California it is supposedly already over 50 percent. And it is going up fastest among people who have been married 20 years or longer. About a million legal abortions are done each year, sending the birthrate below the replacement level. Almost 50 percent of all adult women work at least part time, a parameter that implies, among other things, many children are being cared for largely by people other than their parents. And the women's liberation movement seems to be putting down most traditional ideas about how men and women should deal with each other. The family seems to be facing a major crisis and some observers think it may be so seriously weakened that it can never fully recover.

Wright and Weiss, *Social Problems.*

Pattern: _____

---

### Critical Thinking Tip #5

#### Analyzing Cause-Effect Relationships

Cause and effect relationships are complex and often can be misleading. Here's a sample situation:

Sarah earned her bachelor's degree in three years instead of four by attending summer sessions. Since she graduated, she has never held a job for longer than three weeks. Obviously, condensing her studies was not a good idea.

In this situation, the writer assumed that a cause-effect relationship existed: Sarah cannot hold a job *because* she condensed her studies. Although education and job skills may be related, one is not necessarily the cause of the other. Sarah may not be able to hold a job because she is lazy, frequently late, or cannot get along with other employees.

A common reasoning error is to assume that because two events are related or occur close in time, one event caused the other. Some advertising encourages this type of erroneous thinking. For example, an ad may show a happy family eating a particular brand of breakfast cereal. It implies that you will have a happy family if you buy that particular brand.

Always analyze cause-effect relationships; look for evidence that one event or action is the direct cause of another.

## EXERCISE 5–16

*DIRECTIONS:* Choose one of the selections at the end of the chapter. Read the selection and answer the multiple-choice questions. Then review the selection and identify the organizational pattern of each paragraph. In the margin next to each paragraph, write, in abbreviated form, the name of the organizational pattern: CO for chronological order, CC for comparison-contrast, D for definition, CL for classification, CE for cause-effect, and E for enumeration. Underline any directional words that you find.

## EXERCISE 5–17

*DIRECTIONS:* Suppose your instructor asked you to write a paper on one of the following topics. Discuss which organizational pattern(s) might be useful in developing and organizing a paper for each topic.

1. Types of hairstyles worn by African-American women
2. How a child's brain develops
3. A study of what is "cool"
4. An explanation of extreme sports
5. An explanation of attention deficit disorder

## EXERCISE 5–18

*DIRECTIONS:* Choose a section from one of your current textbook chapters. Identify the organizational pattern used in each paragraph by writing CO, CC, D, CL, or CE in the margin beside each paragraph. Underline the directional words in each paragraph.

## SUMMARY

**1. Why is it helpful to recognize the organizational pattern of a paragraph or passage you are reading?**

When you recognize the specific pattern of the material you are reading, you will be better able to follow the ideas being presented and to predict what will be presented next. You will find that you have made connections among the important ideas so that recalling one idea will help you to recall the others. As a result, you will find it easier to learn and remember them.

**2. What are the six common organizational patterns?**

The six common organizational patterns are:

- Chronological Order—events or procedures are described in the order in which they occur in time.
- Definition—an object or idea is explained by describing the general class or group to which it belongs and how the item differs from others in the same group (distinguishing features).
- Classification—an object or idea is explained by dividing it into parts and describing or explaining each.
- Comparison-Contrast—a new or unfamiliar idea is explained by showing how it is similar to or different from a more familiar idea.
- Cause-Effect—connections between events are explained by showing what caused an event or what happened as a result of a particular event.
- Enumeration—information is organized into lists on the basis of characteristics, features, parts, or according to categories.

**3. What are directional words or phrases?**

Directional words or phrases guide you from one important idea in a paragraph or passage to another. These linking words or phrases are signals or clues to the way a piece of writing is organized and allow you to more easily follow a writer's thoughts.

SOCIOLOGY

## READING SELECTION 9
### EYE LANGUAGE
Julius Fast
From *Family Health*

*Why does everyone stare at the ceiling in an elevator? Why are you uncomfortable if someone stares at you? This article, written by Julius Fast, an expert in body language, describes how eyes communicate.*

1    The cocktail party was almost over when Lynn came to say goodbye. "Are you leaving alone?" I asked, surprised. Lynn is an attractive woman, and there were several good-looking men at the party.

2    Lynn shook her head. "See that tall blond guy near the kitchen? He'll take me home."

3    "You mean Jim?"

4    "I guess so. We haven't been introduced."

5    "Then how do you know he'll take you home?" I demanded.

6    "We've made eye contact." She grinned. "We haven't said a word, but we've been communicating for the last ten minutes."

7    "Across a crowded room? Honestly, Lynn. . . . "

8    But Lynn wasn't listening to me. She was looking at Jim, as he stood talking to another man. While I watched, she caught Jim's eye, smiled, glanced at the clock and then looked at the door of the bedroom where the coats were. A moment later, as Lynn pecked my cheek and sauntered toward the bedroom, I saw Jim smile, clap his companion cheerfully on the shoulder and turn away. He and Lynn reached the front door at virtually the same moment.

9    Coincidence? Not at all. As I realized later, the two of them were merely advanced practitioners in the fine art of eye contact, the single most significant element of body language. With people like Lynn and Jim, more can be communicated with one glance than with a dozen words. Mankind has used this silent skill since the first Stone-Age beauty looked back over her shoulder at a hairy, skin-clad hunter. Writers are fond of describing steely gazes and soft, tender ones, shy looks and challenging stares. Yet the eyeball itself, except for pupil size, can hardly change. It remains essentially the same through every type of glance.

10    What does change, then? The skin around the eye, the muscles, the lid and the eyebrow, all form a constantly mobile container for the eye itself. This expressive container, plus the tilt of the head, makes it possible for the eye to convey hundreds of different expressions and signals. The length of a look, too, is especially significant.

11    Look at someone, then look away. You have made a statement. Hold the glance for a second longer and you've made a different statement. Hold it for two seconds and the meaning has changed again. For every situation, there is a *moral looking time,* the amount of time that you can hold someone else's gaze without being rude, aggressive or intimate.

12    In an elevator, for example, the moral looking time is zero. You look up at the indicator lights, down at the floor, anywhere but into the eyes of a fellow passenger. The moral looking time is a little longer in a crowded subway or bus, and still longer out on the street. There we may catch someone's eye as we walk toward him, but we mustn't hold his glance for longer than three seconds. A glance, if it's held for less than three seconds, signals *You are another human being. I recognize you as such.* If you hold the stranger's eye for longer than three seconds, you signal: *I am interested in you.*

13    This interest can be a straight man-woman thing. Most men will give an attractive woman a three-seconds-plus look, and most attractive women accept it comfortably. But if one man gives another man a three-seconds-plus stare, he signals: *I know you* or *I am interested in you because you look different, strange, peculiar.* Because this glance is so ambiguous—it could imply anything from idle curiosity to sexual interest—the reaction is often hostile.

14    The eye game is used by men to pick up women and, more subtly, by women to pick up men. Homosexuals often identify each other on the street via extended eye contact, followed by a backward glance after a few paces. If the other glances back, too, a pickup is in the offing. The eye game is also used by lonely people who would merely like to exchange a word of greeting with another human being. I've played the eye game in big cities and small towns. Holding the eye of another man a bit beyond the moral looking time in a city usually brings a frown of annoyance. In a small town it will just as readily bring a smile, a nod and a word or two of greeting.

15    Try it yourself, when you feel adventurous. Walk down the street playing the eye game, and see what sort of reactions you get. But be prepared for just about anything!

16 Just as many messages can be signaled by holding someone's gaze, others can be sent by lowering the eyes or using other means of stare. In many animal species, and in man, a prolonged gaze can be a sign of hostility. Cutting off your own gaze is a gesture of appeasement that disarms the other person's aggression.

17 I remember an evening I spent in a bar when I was a young soldier. I happened to catch the eye of a marine across the room. We had both had a few drinks, and the idle glance suddenly turned into a contest. Who was going to outstare the other? After a short, angry locking of eyes, I told myself: *This is silly unless I want a fight.* I broke eye contact first, the marine took it as an appeasing signal and, with a cheerful grin, came over to my table and clasped my hand. We spent a pleasant evening talking.

18 How do we learn the different moral looking times that enable us to function in our society? We pick them up as we do all body language, from the people around us—our parents and family first, then our friends and finally strangers. The specific rules of eye contact depend on the culture in which we live. Every group has its own regulations. Latin Americans and Arabs have longer looking times than ours; Asians and Northern Europeans have shorter ones. North African Tuaregs search each other's eyes avidly as they talk, while the Japanese pay little attention to eye contact.

19 Real problems can arise when the rules of different cultures get confused. For example, in America we consider a forthright glance a sign of truth, and assume that a liar avoids eye contact. But this assumption does not necessarily hold in other cultures. Take this example: In an American high school, a group of girls who had been caught smoking in the restroom were suspended by the principal, though he was troubled about one Spanish-speaking girl who had never been in trouble. "She said she wasn't involved," the principal told her teacher. "I would have believed her except that the whole time she talked to me, she didn't meet my eyes. She must have been lying."

20 Fortunately, the teacher, like the student, was Puerto Rican. She was able to explain to the principal that a "good" Puerto Rican girl invariably lowers her eyes as a sign of respect and obedience when she is being questioned by someone in authority. The principal promptly reinstated the girl.

## Comprehension Test 9

*Directions:   Circle the letter of the best answer.*

**Checking Your Comprehension**

1. Each time you look at someone you are
   a. making a statement
   b. violating the moral looking time
   c. not practicing body language
   d. trying to "pick up" that person

2. When riding in an elevator, people usually
   a. try to make conversation with other passengers
   b. stand in the middle of the elevator
   c. look at the floor
   d. make eye contact with the other passengers

3. If a gaze is prolonged beyond the moral looking time, it may be taken as
   a. a sign of hostility
   b. a sign of appeasement
   c. a joke
   d. unimportant

4. Fast states that the eye game is learned first from
   a. friends
   b. strangers
   c. parents and family
   d. teachers

5. In American culture, when a person is telling a lie, he or she will usually
   a. seek eye contact
   b. avoid eye contact
   c. use other body language cues
   d. close his eyes

6. An *ambiguous* glance (paragraph 13) is one that is
   a. very definite
   b. unclear
   c. promiscuous
   d. strange

### Thinking Critically

7. If the author had not broken eye contact with the marine in the bar, probably
   a. the marine would have walked away
   b. a fight would have broken out
   c. the marine would have been appeased
   d. a conversation would have started

8. If you want to meet someone in your sociology class, you should
   a. make direct eye contact and hold the glance for a little longer than for a stranger
   b. sit as close as possible to him or her
   c. glance at the person and follow with a backward glance
   d. avoid eye contact and rely on body movement

9. If a Tuareg from North Africa looked into your eyes throughout a conversation with him, you could assume that he
   a. was sexually attracted to you
   b. meant nothing by this
   c. wanted to fight with you
   d. was lying to you

10. The author used the example of the cocktail party to illustrate that eye language is
    a. used only by members of the opposite sex
    b. a lost art in our society
    c. misunderstood by most people
    d. a very effective means of communicating

### Questions for Discussion

1. Why do eyes and eye contact seem so important in our culture? What is it about eyes that make them so communicative?

2. Why do you think that a long stare is often interpreted as hostile? Why does it make us uncomfortable?

3. Describe several recent situations in which eye language was important.

4. What messages, other than those mentioned in the article, can be sent through eye contact?

5. What type of evidence does the author offer to validate his claims about eye language?

| Selection 9: | | 1171 words |
|---|---|---|
| Finishing Time: | | |
| | HR.　MIN. | SEC. |
| Starting Time: | | |
| | HR.　MIN. | SEC. |
| Reading Time: | | |
| | MIN. | SEC. |
| WPM Score: | | |
| Comprehension Score: | | % |

**EDUCATION**

# READING SELECTION 10
## HOW STUDENTS GET LOST IN CYBERSPACE

Steven R. Knowlton
From *the New York Times*

*The Internet contains a wealth of information, but as this article explains, it is easy to get lost. Preread and then read this article from* Education Life *to answer the following questions.*

*1. Why is it easy to get lost on the Internet?*
*2. What precautions should students take to be sure they obtain reliable information?*

1   When Adam Pasick, a political science major at the University of Wisconsin at Madison, started working on his senior honors thesis this fall, he began where the nation's more than 14 million college students increasingly do: not at the campus library, but at his computer terminal.

2   As he roamed the World Wide Web, he found journal articles, abstracts, indexes and other pieces of useful information. But it wasn't until he sought help from his professor, Charles H. Franklin, that he found the mother lode.

3   Dr. Franklin steered Mr. Pasick to thousands of pages of raw data of a long-term study of political attitudes, information crucial to Mr. Pasick's inquiry into how family structure affects political thinking.

4   The Web site containing all this data is no secret to political scientists, Dr. Franklin said, but can be hard for students to find.

5   "It is barely possible that if you did a Web search, you would show it up," he said. "Whether the average undergraduate could is another question." It would be even harder for the uninitiated to find their way around the site, he said. "One of the things you're missing on the Web is a reference librarian."

6   It is just such difficulties that worry many educators. They are concerned that the Internet makes readily available so much information, much of it unreliable, that students think research is far easier than it really is. As a result, educators say, students are producing superficial research papers, full of data—some of it suspect—and little thought. Many of the best sources on the Web are hard to find with conventional search engines or make their information available only at a steep price, which is usually borne by universities that pay annual fees for access to the data.

7   Mr. Pasick, 21, of Ann Arbor, Mich., whose conversation is filled with computer and Web search terms, admits that he would have never found the site, much less the data, on his own.

8   "All the search engines are so imprecise," Mr. Pasick said. "Whenever I have tried to find something precise that I was reasonably sure is out there, I have had trouble."

9   Dr. David B. Rothenberg, a philosophy professor at the New Jersey Institute of Technology, in Newark, said his students' papers had declined in quality since they began using the Web for research.

10   "There are these strange references that don't quite connect," he said. "There's not much sense of intelligence. We're indexing, but we're not thinking about things."

11   One way to improve the quality of student's research is to insist that students be more thorough, said Elliot King, a professor of mass communication at Loyola College of Maryland and author of "The Online Student," a textbook for on-line searching.

12   "Because information is so accessible, students stop far too quickly," he said. If a research paper should have 15 sources, he said, the professor should insist students find, say, 50 sources

and use the best 15. When Dr. King assigns research papers in his own classes, he insists that students submit all the sources they did not use, along with those they finally selected.

13    The jumble in Web-based student papers mirrors the information jumble that is found on line, said Gerald M Santoro, the lead research programmer at the Pennsylvania State University's Center for Academic Computing in State College, Pa.

14    The Internet, he said, is commonly thought of as a library, although a poorly-catalogued one, given the limitations of the search engines available. But he prefers another analogy.

15    "In fact, it is like a bookstore," Dr. Santoro said, explaining that Web sites exist because someone wants them there, not because any independent judge has determined them worthy of inclusion.

16    Dr. William Miller, dean of libraries at Florida Atlantic University in Boca Raton, and the immediate past president of the Association of College and Research Libraries, cautioned that free Web sites were often constructed "because somebody has an ax to grind or a company wants to crow about its own products." And he said that the creators of many sites neglect to keep them up to date, so much information on the Web may be obsolete.

17    "For the average person looking for what is the cheapest flight to Chicago this weekend, or what is the weather like in Brazil, the Web is good," Dr. Miller said. But much of its material, he added, is simply not useful to scholars.

*Adam Pasick, a political sicience major at the University of Wisconsin at Madison, with Dr. Charles H. Franklin, as he used the Internet to research his thesis.*

18     Yet despite the Web's limitations, educators like Dr. King still see it as a way to "blast your way out of the limitations of your own library."

19     Some of the most valuable information comes from home pages set up by the government and universities. One example, said Dr. King, was research conducted by a student trying to find information on cuts in financing for the Corporation for Public Broadcasting. The relevant books in the college's library were few and outdated, he said, but, with his help, the student found full texts of Congressional hearings about public broadcasting's budget.

20     "Her essay no longer consisted of relying on books or magazines," he said, "but in getting raw data on which the books and magazines are based."

21     On the Web, students can also find electronic versions of the most popular academic journals, the mainstay of research for faculty and advanced students. Most university libraries now have electronic subscriptions to a few hundred journals. Dr. Miller warned, however, that while that may be a tenth of the journals in the library of a small liberal arts college, it is a tiny fraction of the journals subscribed to by a large research university, which may order more than 100,000. The trend is clearly toward electronic versions of academic journals, he added, but most are still not on line and the ones that are tend to be expensive. On-line subscriptions, for instance; can often run into thousands of dollars a year.

22     The time will surely come, Dr. Miller said, when most academic journals are on line, "but you'll need either a credit card number or a password" from an institution that has bought an electronic subscription. "And if you don't have one or the other, you won't get in," he said.

23     When Mr. Pasick turned to Dr. Franklin for help, the professor's expertise was only one of the necessary ingredients for success. The other was the University of Wisconsin's access to the Web site, as one of 450 research institutions that pay up to $10,000 a year for the privilege. (The site is operated by the Interuniversity Consortium for Political and Social Research, at http://www.icpsr.umich.edu.)

24     Even at an institution with the resources to take full advantage of cyberspace, there are some forms of assistance that the Web will never provide, some educators say.

25     Dr. Santoro describes academic research as a three-step process: finding the relevant information, assessing the quality of that information and then using that information "either to try to conclude something, to uncover something, to prove something or to argue something." At its best, he explained, the Internet, like a library, provides only data.

26     In the research process, he said, "the Internet mainly is only useful for that first part, and also a little bit for the second. It is not useful at all in the third."

---

## Comprehension Test 10*

### Checking Your Comprehension

1. How did Adam Pasick finally find the information he needed on the Internet?

2. What are the major problems with students doing research on the Internet?

3. One professor complained that because "information is so accessible, students stop far too quickly" when doing research. How did this professor solve this problem?

4. This reading discusses online subscriptions to academic journals. According to the reading, why are most journals not available online at many colleges?

*Multiple-choice questions are contained in Appendix B (page A12).

**Thinking Critically**

1. Should students rely on the Internet exclusively to do academic research? Why or why not?

2. How can a student tell if information on the Internet is reliable?

3. Explain what Dr. Santoro means when he makes the statement that the Internet is more "like a bookstore" than a library.

4. Do you agree with the author's advice about the best place to begin a research project? Why?

**Questions for Discussion**

1. In the reading, Dr. Santoro states that one of the reasons students do academic research is to "prove something or to argue something," and he goes on to state that the Internet "is not useful at all" to this end. Do you agree or disagree with Dr. Santoro? Justify your answer.

2. The reading suggests that in many ways the Internet is not useful for academic research.

Are there better alternatives to the Web? What are they?

3. How would you proceed with a research project on "solutions to homelessness" for a sociology class? Would you use the Internet? How would you begin the project? What search engines might you use to find the information you need? At what point might you use the library and for what specific reason(s)?

| Selection 10: | | 1219 words | |
|---|---|---|---|
| Finishing Time: | | | |
| | HR. | MIN. | SEC. |
| Starting Time: | | | |
| | HR. | MIN. | SEC. |
| Reading Time: | | | |
| | | MIN. | SEC. |
| WPM Score: | | | |
| Comprehension Score: | | | % |

**Visit the Longman English Pages**

For additional readings and exercises, visit the Longman English Skills Web page at:

**http://longman.awl.com/englishpages**

For a username and password, please see your instructor.

# CHAPTER 6
# Reading Essays and Articles

IN THIS CHAPTER YOU WILL LEARN:

1. To recognize the parts of formal essays.
2. To read narrative, descriptive, and expository essays.
3. To read popular press articles.
4. To read scholarly journal articles.
5. To critically analyze essays and articles.

While textbooks are your primary source of information in a college course, they are by no means your only source. Many instructors assign supplemental readings, often in the form of essays and articles. They may be from current popular magazines and may illustrate concepts, principles, or issues you are studying. They may be readings from scholarly journals assigned to update you on new research or to acquaint you with current issues. You also need to read essays and articles when you research a topic for a research paper, prepare for a panel discussion, or provide support for your own ideas in your essays. In English and literature classes you will read a wide variety of essays and be expected to respond to them in discussions and to react to them in writing.

This chapter discusses various types of essays and articles and offers approaches for reading each. The information you learn in this chapter will also be helpful to you in your own writing. For example, as you learn the structure of an essay, you can use that structure to write more effective essays. As you learn the characteristics of each essay type, you will be better prepared to write them. Likewise, as you learn the structures of various types of articles you will enhance your ability to write them.

## ■ Comparing Essays and Articles

Both essays and articles will be part of the reading assignments in many of your courses. You will encounter them in your textbooks as special features within chapters, or in scholarly journals, newspapers, and magazines, as outside reading assignments, or as part of researching a topic for a paper.

Essays differ from articles in that essays present the personal views of an author on a subject. They are more subjective than articles because they frequently emphasize the author's individual feelings and perceptions about a particular topic. Articles, on the other hand, are generally more objective. When writing an article the author assumes the role of a reporter. He or she avoids expressing personal feelings or viewpoints and concentrates on directly stating the facts. This does not mean that essays are not factual or accurate. Essays simply provide a personal approach to the information presented. Essays allow a writer to describe things as he or she pictures them, to tell a story as if he or she were there, or to present information as he or she understands it. In short, essays and articles differ mainly in their viewpoints.

## ■ READING ESSAYS

Essays usually have a different structure than articles. Understanding how they are organized will help you read them more effectively and efficiently. This section will examine how essays are organized and will help you become aware of their common parts and what is contained in each part. We will then look at three types of essays and how to read them.

### ■ Examining the Structure of Essays

**Essays** are short pieces of writing that examine a single topic and focus on a single idea about that topic. They may be encountered in anthologies, newspapers, and magazines of all types. Essays follow a standard organization and have the following parts:

- title
- introduction
- thesis statement
- supporting information
- summary or conclusion

The structure of an essay is similar to that of a paragraph. Like a paragraph, an essay has a topic. It also explores a single idea about the topic; in an essay this is called the thesis statement. Like a paragraph, an essay provides ideas and details that support the thesis statement. However, unlike a paragraph, an essay deals with a broader topic and the idea which it explores is often more complex. You can visualize the structure of an essay as follows:

The Structure of an Essay

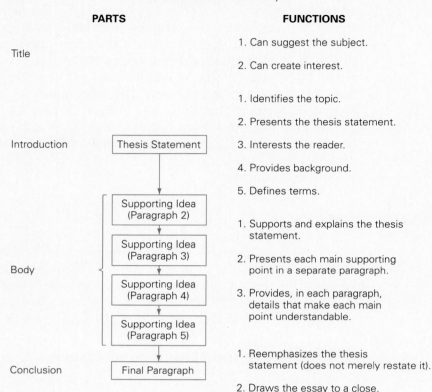

| PARTS | | FUNCTIONS |
|---|---|---|

Title
1. Can suggest the subject.
2. Can create interest.

Introduction — Thesis Statement
1. Identifies the topic.
2. Presents the thesis statement.
3. Interests the reader.
4. Provides background.
5. Defines terms.

Body — Supporting Idea (Paragraph 2), Supporting Idea (Paragraph 3), Supporting Idea (Paragraph 4), Supporting Idea (Paragraph 5)
1. Supports and explains the thesis statement.
2. Presents each main supporting point in a separate paragraph.
3. Provides, in each paragraph, details that make each main point understandable.

Conclusion — Final Paragraph
1. Reemphasizes the thesis statement (does not merely restate it).
2. Draws the essay to a close.

Note: There is no set number of paragraphs that an essay contains. This model shows six paragraphs, but in actual essays, the number will vary greatly.

Let's examine the function of each of these parts of an essay in greater detail by referring to an essay titled "Citizenship or Slavery? How schools take the volunteer out of volunteering." It was written by Andrea Martin and first appeared in the *Utne Reader*.

## CITIZENSHIP OR SLAVERY?
### HOW SCHOOLS TAKE THE VOLUNTEER OUT OF VOLUNTEERING

*Introduction*

"Service-learning" is a new buzzword for sending high school students into the community to do volunteer work. Service-learning isn't really volunteering, though, when it is required for high school graduation—and there's the rub. Americans generally applaud community service, but make that service mandatory and sizzling controversy erupts.

*definition*

*Thesis Statement*

George Bush promoted the notion of mandatory youth services as a means of reinvigorating responsible citizenship. The hotly debated issue of a national community service draft was finally settled in 1993 with the creation of the voluntary AmeriCorps. Locally, though, requirements for mandatory community service are on the increase, and they're being met with sturdy opposition.

Community service as an adjunct to classroom education is not new. Elective programs began to draw attention about 10 years ago, and both educators and students are generally pleased with them. Students develop new skills, greater self-esteem, and more enthusiasm for school. Communities benefit as energetic young people help in nursing homes and day care centers, lend a hand in nonprofits, and plant trees and pick up roadside trash. Noting these benefits, some enthusiasts began to make the case for required service.

The National Service-Learning Cooperative Clearinghouse estimates that more than a million high school students did community work through their schools in 1993, reports Suzanne Goldsmith in the liberal political journal *The American Prospect* (Summer 1995). Some of that is voluntary, but one quarter of America's public schools now impose a service requirement, according to Educational Research Service findings cited by Eric Felten in a critical article in the conservative newsweekly *Insight on the News* (Aug. 15, 1994). Washington, D.C., for example, requires 100 hours of service for high school graduation.

Before service-learning entered the schools, community service was an individual undertaking or was organized by scouts, churches, and other groups for their members. Many question the intrusion of education into what should be a private matter. Amitai Etzioni, a noted communitarian and a vocal advocate of volunteerism, argues in *Insight on the News* that the "public schools have moved beyond their mission by requiring community service." Politics becomes entangled in the educational process when schools encourage lobbying for specific causes or approve some forms of service and exclude others. (For example, in one community, service to Planned Parenthood was approved but service to an anti-abortion group was not.) As Goldsmith notes, opposition to an educational system perceived as setting a social agenda may ultimately be the most serious threat to service-learning.

There are also legal objections to mandatory service. Three high school students in Bethlehem, Pennsylvania, sued the school board on the grounds that the service requirement violated the constitutional prohibition of slavery. The students were represented by the Institute for Justice, a libertarian group that also represented students in similar cases in Mamaroneck, New York, and Chapel Hill, North Carolina. All three cases have failed in the courts. In denying the North Carolina slavery case, U.S. District Judge Frank W. Bullock cited the argument made

*(margin annotations: body; background information; authority; statistics & sources; authority; fact; supporting idea; authority; quote; example; indirect quote; supporting idea; descriptions & facts)*

*[margin annotation: body]*

by the American Alliance for Rights and Responsibilities that service-learning is an educational initiative that prepares students for participation in society.

*[margin annotation: supporting idea]*

Whether or not mandatory service is moral or legal, some educators question its merit. In the short run, it diverts diminishing resources from teaching basic skills to covering the costs of administering programs and transporting students to their work sites. When they work after the school day is over, students who live in far-flung rural areas are at a disadvantage, as are those who have after-school jobs or whose parents can't provide transportation. In the long run, making volunteer work just one more demand imposed on students may create a backlash, prejudicing them against future volunteer work. Critics of education often point out that schools diminish the joy of learning. Now they run the risk of diminishing the joy of community service too.

*[margin annotation: reasons]*

*[margin annotation: conclusion]*

Writing in the National Civic Review (Summer/Fall 1995), Matthew Moseley describes the enormous resurgence of volunteerism among American youth—a movement that, as witnessed and supported by magazines such as *Who Cares* is proving to be a major social force. And Goldsmith, in *The American Prospect,* holds up as models schools that have made community service an appealing elective course; these programs usually generate enthusiasm and plenty of participation. It all suggests that communities should urge their schools to stimulate young people's natural urge to be useful by ensuring that service remains a genuine choice.

*[margin annotation: authority]*

*[margin annotation: authority]*

*[margin annotation: further direction, refers back]*

• • •

## *The Title*

The title usually suggests the subject of the essay and is intended to capture the reader's interest. Some titles are highly descriptive and announce exactly what the essay will be about. For example, an essay titled "Television Addiction" announces the subject of the essay. Other titles are less directly informative. The title "It Begins at the Beginning" reveals little about the subject matter and only becomes meaningful within the context of the essay itself. (It is an article about differences in how males and females communicate and how those differences begin in childhood years.)

Some essays have both a title and a subtitle. In these essays, the subtitle usually suggests the subject matter more directly. In the sample essay, the title "Citizenship or Slavery?" is mainly intended to capture your interest rather than to directly announce the subject. The subtitle "How schools take the volunteer out of volunteering" focuses you more clearly on what the essay will be about.

## EXERCISE 6–1

*DIRECTIONS:* What would you expect to be discussed in essays with each of the following titles?

1. Animal Rights: Right or Wrong
2. Firearms, Violence, and Public Policy
3. The Price of Power: Living in the Nuclear Age
4. The Nature and Significance of Play
5. Uncivil Rights—The Cultural Rules of Anger

## EXERCISE 6–2

*DIRECTIONS:* Read the following title and subtitle of an essay. Predict what you think the essay will discuss.

"Attention Must Be Paid—New Evidence for an Old Truth: Babies need love that money can't buy"

### The Introduction

The introduction, usually one or two paragraphs long, sets the scene for the essay and places the subject within a framework or context. The introduction may

- present the thesis statement of the essay
- offer background information (explain television addiction as an issue, for example)
- define technical or unfamiliar terms (define addiction, for example)
- build your interest (give an instance of an extreme case of television addiction)

Notice how the sample essay, "Citizenship or Slavery?" accomplishes these goals in its first two paragraphs. It opens by defining "service learning," the topic of the essay, and then in the second sentence states its thesis—that service learning isn't true volunteerism when it is required. The remainder of the first two paragraphs provides background for the controversy over mandatory community service programs.

## EXERCISE 6–3

*DIRECTIONS:* Read only the first two paragraphs of the essay "Attention Must Be Paid" by Mortimer Zuckerman. What types of information do they provide?

## ATTENTION MUST BE PAID

Later than I might have expected, I have begun learning about parenthood first-hand. On July 7, Abigail Jane Zuckerman was born. Now I understand what all the excitement has been about.

Looking at a newborn in her crib, anyone must have a sense of the many things that have been determined about her life, by genes and circumstances, but also of the countless decisions and shaping experiences that lie ahead. Parents of every era have worried about making these choices in the right way. Recent scientific findings give new reason for concern—in particular, about whether children can thrive under the modern belief that parents can contract out their basic responsibilities for care.

Every day a newborn baby's brain is developing with phenomenal speed. Billions of nerve cells—neurons—are growing and specializing. By age 2, the number of synapses, or connections among the neurons, approaches adult levels, and by age 3 a child's brain has 1 quadrillion such connections. The synapses are the basic tools of processing within the brain.

Is inherited ability the main factor in establishing these connections? Apparently not. Interactions with an attentive adult—in most cases, a mother—matter most. The sight, sound, touch, smell, and especially, the intense involvement, through language and eye contact, of parent and child affect the number and sophistication of links within the brain. These neural patterns—again, set by age 3—seem to be more important than factors we usually emphasize, such as gender and race. In their book *Meaningful Difference in the Everyday Experience of Young American Children,* professors Todd Risley and Betty Hart say that the number of words an infant hears each day may be the single most important predictor of later intelligence and economic and social success.

This should be hopeful news, for it suggests that rich possibilities are open to every child. But the same research shows that verbal stimulation differs by income and education. On average, the child of professional parents hears about 2,100 words an hour; of working-class parents, 1,200 words. Parents on welfare speak about 600 words an hour. Professional parents give their children emotional encouragement 30 times an hour—twice as often as the working-class baby and five times as often as the welfare baby. This word play is so important that those left behind at age 2 may never catch up.

These findings come when many subscribe to the notion that there is no harm in a mother's leaving her baby in someone else's care and returning to work. More than half of all mothers are back at work before their baby is 1. The working mother is a fundamental feature of this era. But what will parents do when they learn that absence in the first three years may have a significant effect on their baby's future? Most working parents know in their hearts that "quality time" is no substitute for quantity time—the time that a child requires for emotional and, it now seems, intellectual development.

What children need is the touching, holding, cooing, rocking, and stimulation that come traditionally from a mother. In some households a stay-at-home father will fill the role of the absentee mother, but that is rare. In most families, if it is not the mother spending those three years with an infant, it will be a baby sitter or day-care worker. Often there are class, educational, and—increasingly—language differences between the parents and the hired caretaker. Parents are therefore going to be challenged to find a better balance between raising their children and working, especially parents who are too tired and emotionally drained to give children the stimulus and engagement they need. When babies are cared for by caring adults, they become much better learners and are much more confident to take over the world. Attention is the greatest gift that parents can bestow.

● ● ●

### The Thesis Statement

The thesis statement of an essay is its main point. All other ideas and paragraphs in the essay support this idea. Once you identify an essay's thesis, you have discovered the key to its meaning. The thesis is usually stated in a single sentence and this sentence appears in the introductory paragraphs. It often follows the background information and the attention-getter. In our sample essay, "Citizenship or Slavery?," the thesis is stated early in the first paragraph and is followed by background information. Occasionally, an author will first present evidence in support of the thesis and finally state the thesis at the end of the essay. This organization is most common in argumentative essays (see Chapter 12). You may also find, on occasion, that an author implies rather than directly states the thesis; the thesis is revealed through the supporting paragraphs. When you cannot find a clear statement of the thesis, ask yourself this question: "What is the one main point the author is making?" Your answer is the implied thesis statement.

Here are a few sample thesis statements.

- Due to its negative health effects, cigarette smoking is once again being regarded as a form of deviant behavior.

- Career choice is influenced by numerous factors including skills and abilities, attitudes, and life goals.

- Year-round school will provide children with a better education that is more cost effective.

## EXERCISE 6–4

*DIRECTIONS:* Read the entire essay "Attention Must Be Paid" on pp. 190–191 and identify its thesis statement.

### Body

The body of the essay contains sentences and paragraphs that explain or support the thesis statement. This support may be in the form of

- examples
- descriptions
- facts
- statistics
- reasons
- anecdotes (stories that illustrate a point)
- personal experiences and observations
- quotations from or references to authorities and experts
- comparisons

Most writers use various types of supporting information. In the sample essay "Citizenship or Slavery?" on pp. 186–188 the author uses several types of information in her supporting paragraphs. Notice how she uses *facts* and *statistics* in the third paragraph to show how widespread community service requirements are. Her fourth paragraph refers to *authorities* and *quotes* them directly and indirectly. She also includes an *example* of politics at work in these programs. The fifth paragraph concentrates on *descriptions* of and facts about legal cases on required community service programs and the results of these cases. The final paragraph of the body of this essay provides *reasons* against mandatory service.

## EXERCISE 6–5

*DIRECTIONS:* Review the essay "Attention Must Be Paid" and mark where the body begins and ends. Then, in the margin beside each supporting paragraph, label the type(s) of supporting information the author used.

### Conclusion

An essay is brought to a close with a brief conclusion, not a summary. (A summary provides a review of the key ideas presented in an article. Think of a summary as an outline in paragraph form. The order in which the information appears in the summary reflects the order in which it appears in the article itself.) A **conclusion** is a final statement about the subject of the essay. A conclusion does not review content as a summary does. Instead, a conclusion often refers back to, but does not repeat, the thesis statement. It may also suggest a direction of further thought or introduce a new way of looking at what has already been said. The sample essay, "Citizenship or Slavery?" on pp. 186–188 ends with a conclusion that strengthens the case in favor of volunteerism and elective courses rather than required community service courses. It refers back to the thesis statement by encouraging communities to allow service learning to be a matter of choice.

## EXERCISE 6–6

*DIRECTIONS:* Explain how the conclusion of "Attention Must Be Paid" draws this essay to a close.

## ■ Reading Various Types of Essays

There are four common types of essays: narrative, descriptive, expository, and argumentative. Each has a distinct purpose and unique characteristics. This section will discuss only narrative, descriptive, and expository essays. Argumentative essays are discussed in detail in Chapter 12, "Arguments and Persuasive Writing."

### *Narrative Essays*

Narrative essays relate a sequence of events, often in the form of a story. They review events that have happened, usually in the order in which they occurred. A narrative uses the time order thought pattern discussed in Chapter 5 as a means of organization. A narrative, however, goes beyond an ordering or listing of events. A narrative makes a point, communicates an attitude or feeling, or explains an idea. It has a thesis—a central idea that grows out of the story. Narrative essays often use vivid descriptions to bring to life the story being told and the point being made. In this sense, the categories of narrative and descriptive essays may often seem to overlap.

If you write an essay describing an important event or telling how someone influenced your life, you may use the narrative form. You describe events as they happened, showing how or why they were important or meaningful. Follow these steps when reading narratives:

1. **Establish the setting.** Determine when and where the events are taking place.

2. **Notice how the story is told and who is telling it.** The perspective or point of view of the person relating the events is often important.

3. **Look beyond the specific events to discover their overall meaning.** Ask yourself why the writer is telling the story. What point is the author trying to make? What is his or her thesis?

4. **Watch for the writer's commentary as he or she tells the story.** This commentary provides clues about the author's overall message or purpose for writing.

The following narrative essay is taken from a book titled *Mortal Lessons,* written by Richard Selzer, a medical doctor. This essay tells the story of a patient who is recovering from surgery that left her face deformed.

I stand by the bed where a young woman lies, her face postoperative, her mouth twisted in palsy, clownish. A tiny twig of the facial nerve, the one to the muscles of her mouth, has been severed. She will be thus from now on. The surgeon had followed with religious fervor the curve of her flesh; I promise you that. Nevertheless, to remove the tumor in her cheek, I had cut the little nerve.

Her young husband is in the room. He stands on the opposite side of the bed, and together they seem to dwell in the evening lamplight, isolated from me, private. Who are they, I ask myself, he and this wry-mouth I have made, who gaze at and touch each other so generously, greedily? The young woman speaks.

"Will my mouth always be like this?" she asks.

"Yes," I say, "it will. It is because the nerve was cut."

She nods, and is silent. But the young man smiles.

"I like it," he says. "It is kind of cute."

All at once I *know* who he is. I understand, and I lower my gaze. One is not bold in an encounter with a god. Unmindful, he bends to kiss her crooked mouth, and I so close I can see how he twists his own lips to accommodate to hers, to show her that their kiss still works. I remember that the gods appeared in ancient Greece as mortals, and I hold my breath and let the wonder in.

● ● ●

The incident takes place in a hospital where a woman is recovering from surgery to remove a tumor on her cheek. The author, who is the surgeon, is relating the events. Imagine how differently the events might have been told by the woman herself or by her husband. The article describes the occasion when the woman learns her mouth will be permanently twisted. The surgeon's purpose in writing becomes clear in the last paragraph. His main point is that the husband's kiss is godlike—it determines the woman's response to and acceptance of her deformity. Through his narrative of these events, the surgeon is making a comment on life: A person's limitations and handicaps are not as important as how they are perceived by and reacted to by others.

## EXERCISE 6–7

*DIRECTIONS:* Read the following narrative essay by Lucinda Franks and answer the questions that follow.

### THE STORY OF "JAMES B"

The gentleman in the corner had been regarded as a true American success, lanky and deep-voiced, brilliant and beloved, the master of all he surveyed. Now, he gazed out defiantly, as if still on the summit, too high to see the cat feces at his feet or the unopened mail or the mirror that would have told him he was master of nothing but his own delusions.

Those who were to thrust the mirror in front of the 62-year-old man, whom I will call James B, were his daughter Isabel, myself and three of the friends who loved him best. Isabel and I had been inseparable summertime friends, and James B, through an enormous white telescope in his backyard, had first introduced me to the stars in their firmament. His whimsies about what lay beyond them still quickened the heart of the child in me. Now, I was sitting impertinently in his living room, preparing to tell him that it didn't matter if he could no longer ponder eternity—he would soon be part of it.

If James B had denied his problem, so had we. He had been depressed over the death of his wife and the loss of his architectural business. He had been presenting different excuses to each of us for his growing isolation. He had kept us at bay by clever use of the telephone, until it was cut off for nonpayment of a bill he had never opened.

Yet at last we had gathered into a crisis intervention team and surprised him, hung-over, before he could perfect his alibis. Dr. Nicholas Pace, of New York's Pace Health Services, who helped refine the crisis intervention technique, had advised us to use reason, histrionics and even threats to strip James B of his defenses and deliver him to a treatment center. We were not to leave without him. The effectiveness with which we played our parts might mean the difference between his life and death.

"Daddy, we are here because we love you." Isabel's voice wavered, but the 9-month-old baby on her knee stared at her grandfather unblinkingly. James B, very gingerly, poured out coffee. "I can understand your concern," he said. He had thrown on a shirt—even a tie—but below his bathrobe, his thin, red legs had the look of arms flung down in defeat. "I've had this local flu. I've been going to my doctor for shots every day."

"I checked with your doctor, Daddy, and he hasn't seen you for two years. We think your disease is alcoholism."

All of James B's roles now seemed to collide and fall away, revealing the obsession which shone in his eyes like unrequited love. "That's preposterous! My problems have nothing to do with alcohol."

Mel, his former business partner, said he had watched the most brilliant man he had ever known become addled into dull predictability. George, his former chess opponent, blushed and said that James B had begun to cheat at the game. Lisa, his former lover, tremulously said she was going to marry a man she didn't love because the one she did had not preferred her to the bottle. I reminded him of the stars, and of all the people, including my baby and Isabel's who could still learn from him.

Coached about the new science of alcohol and the liver, we tried to convince James B that there was no shame in being an alcoholic.

"Look, can't you understand?" James B said. "I'm sick, yes; depressed, yes; getting old, yes. But that's all."

"Jim," Mel said, in a voice that resonated with the tension we all felt, "it sounds like you would rather be anything at all than an alcoholic."

After 14 hours of this scenario, some of us began to question whether he really *was* an alcoholic. Maybe it was some other illness. Then he let spill a few words. "Geez, if I couldn't go down to the pub for a few, I think I'd go nuts!"

"Aaah," Isabel said. "You just admitted it." She put the baby on her father's knee. "Look at your granddaughter. This is your immortality, Daddy, and she needs you. Please don't die. Please choose life, for us."

James B put his face, the color of gravel, in his hands. No one spoke. When he looked up, he said he would go to a local hospital.

At the emergency room, the doctor couldn't feel James B's liver and doubted whether the blood test, which could only measure severe damage, would show anything. "You're wasting time. An alcoholic won't stop drinking unless he wants to, and I've got dying patients here."

"But if we don't get him help, my father *is* going to die," Isabel said. "You can always bring him back when he starts hemorrhaging," the doctor said. Nevertheless, he agreed to do a blood test. Three hours later, the doctor came over to us with a sheepish look. Over the cries of James B's overtired granddaughter, he told us the test showed extensive liver damage. James B, who had been sitting stonily, swallowed hard. It was probably his diet, he argued at first, but finally he said he would enter a treatment center. We all cheered and shook his hand; he could have been a POW come home.

That very night, we drove him to the Edgehill treatment center in Newport, R.I. After 28 days, he emerged looking considerably changed. Over the next few months, he managed to restore order to his house. Though not yet emotionally able to handle frequent family meetings, he sent his granddaughter a toy a week.

Isabel, having learned that alcoholism is a family disease, afflicting each member to some degree, attended Al-Anon meetings, for the family and friends of alcoholics, where she was told that to cover up for her father was to destroy him. At Adult Children of Alcoholics, she got help in dealing with the deep scars of having grown up with an alcoholic parent.

"My father was so strong a figure and my identification with him was so intense that I always accepted his masks and his manipulations," Isabel said. "But I was suffering inside my own mask, and the games we played were killing us both."

James B, now about half-way through the long recovery process, looks back at the crisis intervention with bitter gratitude. "They stripped me of my skin and I'm still bleeding, but they saved my life," he says. "A person I haven't known for years is taking the place of alcohol. I like and respect him, and I never want to lose him, or my family, again."

● ● ●

1. What sequence of events does this article recount?

_____

2. Who is recounting the story?

_____

3. How does the writer feel about the events she describes? Substantiate your answer with references to the essay.

4. Why do you think the author wrote the essay?

5. What did you learn about the disease of alcoholism from reading the essay?

## EXERCISE 6–8

*DIRECTIONS:* Reading Selection #2, "Hispanic, USA: The Conveyor-Belt Ladies," is another example of a narrative essay. Read or review the essay and answer the following questions.

1. What is the setting of this essay?
2. From whose point of view is the story told?
3. How do you think the story would change if it were told from the point of view of one of the other women working in the plant?
4. What is the overall message of the essay?

### Reading Descriptive Essays

Descriptive writing appeals to the senses—to your sense of touch, taste, smell, sight, and sound. Descriptive essays provide extensive sensory details about the characteristics of people, objects, events, or places. The details are intended to appeal to your senses and to help you create a mental picture. The writer usually provides the sensory details to create a single impression that becomes the author's thesis. Descriptive writing is used in many forms of writing, including advertising. In the following travel advertisement, notice how the writer helps you form a visual image and impression of Bermuda.

> For more than a century, people who value relaxation have been returning to Bermuda year after year. They appreciate the pink-tinted beaches, the flower-laden garden paths, the cozy pubs, and the clear, turquoise waters.

• • •

Do the phrases "pink-tinted beaches," "flower-laden garden paths," and "clear, turquoise waters" help you picture a beach in Bermuda? Do you have an impression of Bermuda as a beautiful tropical paradise?

In reading descriptive writing, be sure to follow these steps:

1. **Identify the subject of the essay.** Ask yourself: "Who or what is being described?"

2. **Pay close attention to the writer's choice of words.** Notice sensory details; the writer often paints a picture with words. Through word choice, a writer tries to create an attitude or feeling. Try to identify that feeling.

3. **Establish the overall impression the writer is trying to create.** Ask yourself these questions: What do all these details, taken together, suggest about the subject? What is the writer trying to say? How am I supposed to feel about the subject?

4. **Pay particular attention to the first and last paragraphs.** They will probably provide the most clues about the writer's main points and purpose for writing.

Now read the following excerpt from an essay titled "Aging in the Land of the Young" by Sharon Curtin, and apply the steps listed. As you read, mark words that are particularly descriptive.

Old men, old women, almost 20 million of them. They constitute 10 percent of the total population, and the percentage is steadily growing. Some of them, like conspirators, walk all bent over, as if hiding some precious secret, filled with self-protection. The body seems to gather itself around those vital parts, folding shoulders, arms, pelvis like a fading rose. Watch and you see how fragile old people come to think they are.

Aging paints every action gray, lies heavy on every movement, imprisons every thought. It governs each decision with a ruthless and single-minded perversity. To age is to learn the feeling of no longer growing, of struggling to do old tasks, to remember familiar actions. The cells of the brain are destroyed with thousands of unfelt tiny strokes, little pockets of clotted blood wiping out memories and abilities without warning. The body seems slowly to give up, randomly stopping, sometimes starting again as if to torture and tease with the memory of lost strength. Hands become clumsy, frail transparencies, held together with knotted blue veins.

● ● ●

This essay discusses the process of aging. Words and phrases such as "fading rose," "filled with self-protection," "paints every action gray," "ruthless," "torture," "exhausts," and "hoard greedily" create a feeling of depression, dread, and despair. The overall impression is that aging is something to dread. This author shows us nothing positive about aging—no reference to a golden age, to inner peace, to depth or wisdom.

## EXERCISE 6–9

*DIRECTIONS:* Read the following descriptive essay by Brenda Peterson and answer the questions that follow.

### SEAGULL SONG

"Seagulls memorize your face," the old man called out to me as he strode past on his daily walk. I stood on the seawall feeding the flock of gray-and-white gulls who also make this Puget Sound beach their home. "They know their neighbors." He tipped his rather rakish tweed motoring cap and kept walking fast. "Can't let the heartbeat stop," he explained.

I met this man many days on the beach. We rarely talk; we perform our simple chores; I feed the seagulls and say prayers, he keeps his legs and his heart moving. But between us there is an understanding that these tasks are as important as anything else in our lives; maybe they even keep us alive. Certainly our relationship with each other and with this windswept Northwest beach is more than a habit. It is a bond, an unspoken treaty we've made with the territory we call home.

For twelve years I have migrated from beach shack to cabin, moving along the shore like the Native tribes that once encircled all of Puget Sound. But unlike the first people who loved this wild, serpentine body of cold water, my encampments have changed with the whim of my landlords rather than with the seasons. Somehow mixed up in my half-breed blood is a belief that I may never own land even if one day I might be able to afford it. Ownership implies possession; as much as I revere this inland sea, she will never belong to me. Why not, then, belong to her?

*Belong.* As a child the word mesmerized me. Because my father's forestry work moved us every other year, the landscape itself seemed in motion. To *be long* in one place was to take deep root like other settled folk, or like the trees themselves. After I have lived a long life on this beach, I hope that someone might someday say, "She belonged here," as much as the purple starfish that cling to rock crevices covered in algae fur.

The Hopi Indians of Arizona believe that our daily rituals and prayers literally keep this world spinning on its axis. For me, feeding the seagulls is one of those everyday prayers. When I walk out of my front door and cross the street to the seawall, they caw-welcome, their wings almost touching me as they sail low over my shoulders, then hover overhead, midair. Sometimes if it's been raining, their feathers flick water droplets onto my face like sprinklings of holy water. The brave fliers swoop over the sea and back to catch the bread in their beaks inches above my hand. Then the cacophonic choir—gulls crying and crow *kak-kak*-ing as my special sidearm pitch sends tortillas whizzing through the air, a few of them skipping across the waves like flour Frisbees.

I am not the only neighbor who feeds these gulls. For the past three years, two afternoons a week, a green taxi pulled alongside the beach. From inside, an ancient woman, her back bent like the taut arch of a crossbow, leaned out of the car window and called in a clear, tremulous soprano. The seagulls recognized the sun-wrinkled, almost blind face she raised to them. She smiled and said to the taxi driver, "They *know* I'm here."

It was always the same drive, the same ritual—a shopping bag full of day-old bread donated by a local baker. "She told me she used to live by the sea," the driver explained to me once. "She don't remember much else about her life . . . not her children, not her husband." Carefully the driver tore each bread slice into four squares the way the woman requested. "Now she can't hardly see these birds. But she hears them and she smells the sea. Calls this taking her medicine."

Strong medicine, the healing salt and mineral sea this old woman took into her body and soul twice a week. She lived in the nursing home at the top of our hill, and every time I saw the familiar ambulance go by I prayed it was not for Our Lady of the Gulls.

Several years ago, when wild hurricanes shook the South and drought seized the Northwest, the old woman stopped coming to our beach. I waited for her all autumn, but the green taxi with its delighted passenger never came. I took to adding two weekly afternoon feedings to my own morning schedule. These beach meetings are more mournful, in memory of the old woman who didn't remember her name, whose name I never knew, who remembered only the gulls.

Not long afterward my landlady called with the dreaded refrain: "House sold, must move on." I walked down to the beach and opened my arms to the gulls. With each bread slice I said a prayer that Puget Sound would keep me near her. One afternoon I got the sudden notion to drive down the sound. There I found a cozy cottage for rent, a little beach house that belongs to an old man who's lived on this promotory since the 1940s. A stroke had sent him to a nursing home, and the rent from the cottage would pay for his care.

Before I moved one stick of furniture into the house, I stood on the beach and fed the gulls in thanksgiving. They floated above my head; I felt surrounded by little angels. Then I realized that these were the very same gulls from two miles down the beach near my old home—there was a bit of fishline wrapped around a familiar webbed foot, that wounded wing, the distinct markings of a young gray gull, one of my favorite high fliers.

Who knows whether the old man was right? The seagulls may have memorized my face and followed me—but I had also, quite without realizing it, memorized them. And I knew then that I was no newcomer here, not a nomad blown by changeable autumn winds. It is not to any house, but to this beach I have bonded. I belong alongside this rocky inlet with its salt tides, its pine-tiered, green islands, its gulls who remember us even when we've forgotten ourselves.

● ● ●

1. In the fifth paragraph the author describes her daily ritual of feeding the seagulls. Underline words or phrases that you think are especially descriptive.

2. What is the main point the author is making in this essay?

_____

_____

3. How does the author use the last paragraph to conclude this essay? What does she do to tie this essay all together?

_____

_____

4. This essay conveys a feeling of reverence for the Puget Sound. Which words and phrases does the author use to achieve this feeling of almost religious awe?

_____

_____

## EXERCISE 6–10

*DIRECTIONS:* Brent Staples in his essay "Just Walk on By: A Black Man Ponders His Power To Alter Public Space" (Reading Selection #4, pp. 60–62), uses descriptive detail to effectively convey his message. Read or review the essay and highlight sentences or paragraphs that are particularly descriptive.

### *Expository Essays*

An **expository essay** presents information on a specific topic from a particular writer's point of view. Its purpose is to present the facts as the author understands them on a given topic and to explain them to the reader. For example, a story in *Time* magazine that reports a new method of gene therapy is expository. It is written to explain the new method. An essay titled "What Causes Earthquakes?" is written to explain the changes in the earth that produce earthquakes.

The essay "Attention Must Be Paid" is also an example of an expository essay. Its purpose is to present and explain new findings about the effects of hired child care on the development of young children. The author accomplishes this by giving facts and statistics and by referring to authorities on the subject. This essay does reflect the author's individual interpretation of recent findings on the topic, but its central purpose is to inform the reader about the importance of more direct care of young children by parents rather than by babysitters or day care workers.

Expository essays are often organized using one or more of the thought patterns described in Chapter 5, "Patterns: Relationships Among Ideas." Depending on a writer's purpose, he or she may choose a specific pattern, as shown here.

| If a Writer's Purpose Is To | The Pattern Used Is |
| --- | --- |
| Trace the history or sequence of events | Chronological order |
| Explain how something works | Chronological order |
| Explain a subject by describing types or parts | Classification |
| Explain why something happened | Cause-Effect |
| Explain what something is | Definition |
| Emphasize similarities or differences between two or more things | Comparison-Contrast |

When reading expository essays, use the following guidelines.

1. **Establish the authority of the author whenever possible.** In order to trust that the author presented accurate, reliable information, make sure he or she is knowledgeable about or experienced with the subject.

2. **Pay attention to background information the author provides.** Especially if the subject is one with which you are unfamiliar, you must fill in gaps in your knowledge. If the background supplied is insufficient, consult other sources to get the information you need.

3. **Identify the author's thesis.** Determine exactly what information the author is presenting about the subject. Test your understanding by expressing it in your own words.

4. **Pay attention to new terminology.** Mark or underline new terms as you read them. If some are not defined and you cannot determine their meaning from context, be sure to look them up.

5. **Highlight as you read.** Mark the thesis statement and each major supporting detail.

6. **Outline, map, or summarize the essay.** To ensure recall of the information, as well as to test your understanding of it, use some form of writing.

## EXERCISE 6–11

*DIRECTIONS:* Read the following expository essay by Andrea Martin and highlight it as suggested in the guidelines above. Circle any new terminology you encounter, then either outline, map, or summarize the essay.

### WHY GET MARRIED?
#### MORE COUPLES FIND "LIVING IN SIN" A GOOD FAMILY VALUE

About 3.5 million unmarried opposite-sex couples are living together in the United States today, up from 2 million a decade ago. If you think this is merely an explosion of passionate anti-authoritarianism, guess again: Many of the couples who are joining the boom may simply be making a sound fiscal decision.

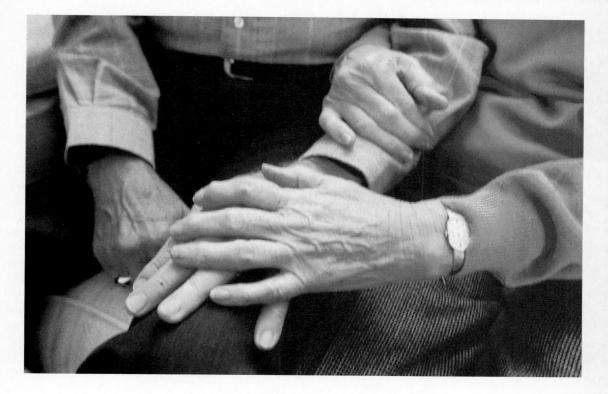

Some observers link the widespread acceptance of cohabitation with recognition that the economics of marriage are often unfavorable. To begin with, there's a 50 percent chance that a marriage will fail, and divorce is expensive. Beyond that, tax laws and other governmental policies—in a country that says it wants strong families—may actually be discouraging marriage.

It's well known that the poor are often victims of tax and government-benefit marriage penalties. When marriage reduces welfare eligibility, many decide against it. In addition, as Joseph Spiers noted in *Fortune* (July 11, 1994), married low-wage workers may be at an income-tax disadvantage. For example, the standard deduction and Earned Income Credit are often lower for working couples than for two singles. Spiers concludes that "the task of welfare reform might get easier if government first removes this disincentive to build stable families."

The problem persists higher up on the economic ladder, too. In *Forbes* (May 22, 1995), Janet Novack describes tax penalties that affect well-to-do couples, including income taxes higher than singles pay and business expense ceilings that don't double for marrieds. "[Had] Congress set about to create a tax code to encourage people to avoid marriage, it could scarcely have done a better job," says Novack. She concludes: "We hate to say it, but if you are a prosperous person contemplating marriage with a well-heeled partner, maybe you should forget the ceremony and just move in together."

Middle-aged couples of more modest means face another hurdle if either partner is divorced or widowed and has college-age children. Colleges routinely include stepparents' income in calculating whether a student will receive financial aid and, if so, how much. This forces potential stepparents to take on burdensome responsibilities for children who are not their own, and it may result in the denial of aid. Divorced parents have to decide between remarriage and their children's education.

In the American Association of Retired Persons magazine *Modern Maturity* (May/June 1995), Linda Stern describes the various marriage and remarriage penalties that threaten older people: Social Security earnings limits, capital gains exclusions on home sales, and Medicaid eligibility limits, for example. As a result, unmarried couples quietly move in together and enjoy companionship, while long-married couples sometimes divorce in order to avoid financial disaster.

Are these penalties causing cohabitation? It's impossible to say for sure, but the fact that older couples are an important part of the boom suggests a connection. "The Census Bureau estimates that the percentage of cohabiting unmarried couples has doubled since 1980, and older couples are keeping pace," writes Stern. "In 1993 some 416,000 couples reported that they were unmarried, living together, and over 45. That compares with 228,000 who fit the description in 1980." And in the *New York Times* (July 6, 1995), Jennifer Steinhauer reports on the research of Professor Larry Bumpass of the University of Wisconsin, who found that the biggest increase in couples choosing to live together was not among twenty-somethings, but among people over 35. Bumpass found that 49 percent of his subjects between 35 and 39 are living with someone, up from 34 percent in the late 1980s. Among people 50 to 54, the practice has doubled. Using data from his survey, Bumpass showed that only a small segment of people disapprove of cohabitation and sex outside marriage. He concluded that "the trends we have been observing are very likely to continue, with a declining emphasis on marriage."

Of course, marriage still has its advantages, beyond obvious ones like greater emotional security and social and religious approval. It can be a social welfare system, providing health insurance and retirement security to a spouse who otherwise would have none. For couples in which one person earns most of the family income, tax laws are favorable to marriage.

But overall, official economic policy makes marriage a bad option for too many people. Those who determine our income taxes, government benefits, and institutional practices must remember that marriage is an economic as well as a social arrangement. In a society in which many marriages have failed, financial security is tenuous, and living together is acceptable, we can no longer assume that the institution of marriage will survive the burdens it has carried in the past. Moving toward marriage-neutral tax and benefit policies would, in the long run, lay a better foundation for true family values.

● ● ●

## EXERCISE 6–12

*DIRECTIONS:* The essay "How To Brag About Yourself To Win and Hold a Job" (Reading Selection #1, pp. 17–18) is an example of an expository essay. Read or review the essay and answer the following questions.

1. Why is the essay an example of an expository essay?
2. To what extent does the essay include the author's opinions and interpretations?
3. Do you feel Challenger is qualified to write an essay on the subject? Why?
4. Write a list of job-seeking and job-holding advice that summarizes Challenger's suggestions.

# ■ READING ARTICLES

Articles, like essays, can tell a story, describe, or inform. Unlike essays, they do this with little personal involvement of the author. Also, they have structures that are somewhat different from that of an essay. Three types of articles are discussed in this section: popular press articles, feature articles, and scholarly articles. The structure of an article depends upon its type. Each has special features that will help you to locate the information you want more efficiently.

## ■ Reading Popular Press Articles

Articles that appear primarily in magazines and newspapers assume a different style and format from most essays. While popular press articles examine a topic and focus on an aspect of a topic, they tend to be more loosely or informally structured than most essays and scholarly journal articles. The title is usually eye catching and descriptive. The introductory section may be less fully developed and a formal paragraph conclusion may not be used.

The two most common types of popular press articles found in both newspapers and magazines are hard news articles and feature articles. They have essentially the same form, consisting of a beginning, called the *lead,* the story itself, called the *body or development,* and sometimes a formal *conclusion* as an ending.

### *Hard News Articles*

Articles that directly report the serious news are known as hard news articles. They are stories about conflict, death, and destruction as well as items of interest and importance in government, politics, science, medicine, business, and the economy. Articles of this type may be organized in one of two ways.

*Inverted Structure* The traditional structure used in newspaper articles is known as the *inverted pyramid,* because the article moves from general to more specific information. It contains the following parts:

- *Title*. Titles, or headlines, used in hard news stories are brief and directly informative about the article's content. They are usually expressed in active language, somewhat in the form of a telegraph message: "President Threatens Veto Over Budget" or "Diet Drug Thought To Be Health Risk." Reading the title is usually sufficient to help you decide whether or not to read the article.

- *Datelines*, *Credit Lines*, **and** *Bylines*. These follow the title and come just before the *summary lead*. *Datelines* appear on all but local news stories and generally only give the place where the story came from; occasionally the date will be given. *Credit lines* may also appear before the lead and supplement datelines. They give the name of the wire service or newspaper from which the story was taken, such as "Associated Press" or *Washington Post*. *Bylines* name the writer of the article and are sometimes also included between the title and the lead.

- *Summary Lead*. This opening paragraph contains a summary of the most essential information in the story. It is similar to the *thesis statement* in an essay and the *abstract* in a scholarly article. Reading this lead alone may provide you with all the information you need from the article and will help you to determine if you need to read further to get the information you want.

- *Body or Development*. The supporting facts are presented here—arranged in descending order of importance or interest. The most important details are placed first, followed by those second in importance or interest, and so on, until those facts most easily dispensed with are placed at the end of the story. If the lead paragraph doesn't contain the information you need, this type of organization will permit you to locate it easily. Since the *inverted pyramid* structure contains no conclusion there is no need to skip to the end of the article when pre-reading it.

Look at the following news article and note where its parts are located.

*Title or Headline* ____

## Lawsuits seek heart monitoring for users of withdrawn diet drugs

*Byline* ———————— By Beth Powell

*Credit line* ———————— *Associated Press*

*Dateline*

*Summary lead*

WASHINGTON—Class-action suits demanding payment for heart monitoring for former diet drug users have been filed in five states against the makers of prescription drugs pulled off the market a week ago.

*Body*

The suits were filed last week in New York, Utah, Colorado and Hawaii and earlier in California on behalf of patients who might have been injured by using fen-phen, the popular name for a combination of prescription diet drugs, attorney Gary Mason said.

After studies linked the diet pills to serious heart damage, drug makers withdrew from the market fenfluramine and dexfenluramine, sold under the brand names Pondimin and Redux, respectively.

The Food and Drug Administration urged millions of dieters to stop taking both drugs immediately.

The FDA said phentermine, which combined with fenfluramine made the once-popular fen-phen combination, appears safe when used by itself. But doctors said phentermine has only mixed results when taken alone.

The lawsuits seek medical monitoring, emergency notification and updated patient warnings for class members, Mason said. Some suits seek specific monetary damages for individuals.

Mason, whose law firm Cohen, Milstein, Hausfeld & Toll is coordinating the class-action suits, said similar actions would be filed in all 50 states within the next few weeks.

The nine defendants in the suits are Wyeth-Ayerst Laboratories Co., division of American Home Products Corp.; Interneuron Pharmaceuticals; Gate Pharmaceuticals, a division of Teva Pharmaceuticals, USA; Smithkline Beecham Corp.; Abana Pharmaceuticals; Richwood Pharmaceutical Co.; Ion Laboratories; Medeva Pharmaceuticals; and A. H. Robins Co.

*Body*

● ● ●

*Action Story* A second common format for hard news articles is the *action story*. It contains all the parts of the inverted pyramid with a few variations. It also begins with a telegraphic title that can be followed by a byline, credit line, and dateline. Its opening paragraph is also in the form of a summary lead. However, its body presents the events in chronological order of their occurrence, rather than in order of importance or interest. Furthermore, this format includes a conclusion that contains additional information that does not fit within the chronology used in the body.

## EXERCISE 6–13

*DIRECTIONS:* Locate a hard news article from a newspaper or magazine. Determine which format is used, the inverted pyramid or the action story. Then label the article's parts.

### Feature Articles

A second type of popular press article is the feature article. Found in both newspapers and magazines, the feature article is longer and goes into greater depth than the usual hard news article. It usually deals with larger issues and subjects. Because of its length, this type of article requires a different structure than hard news articles.

It also begins with a *title* that is often in the form of a complete sentence and may contain a byline, credit line, and dateline. Its other parts may differ, though.

- *Feature Lead*. The lead in a feature article does not usually summarize its contents. Instead, it is intended to spark your interest in the topic being presented. It may begin with an interesting anecdote, present some highlight of the article, or offer an example of something you will learn more about later. Since the feature lead is primarily an interest builder, you may be able to skim through it quickly when reading the article.

- *Nut Graph*. The nut graph explains the nature and scope of the article. Depending upon the length of the article it may be one paragraph, or it may run to several paragraphs. When reading feature articles, read this section carefully. It will offer clues to the organization and content of the article and help you to grasp its main points.

- *Body or Development*. This is where the detailed information of the article is presented. Unlike hard new stories, the information can be organized in more than one way. Each paragraph or section may use a different thought pattern to develop its ideas, much like the expository essay. Mark and annotate this section as you read it, sifting through the main and secondary points.

- *Conclusion*. Feature articles often end with a conclusion, which, like the conclusion of a formal essay, makes a final statement about the subject of the article. Rather than summarizing the information presented, it may refer back to the nut graph, introduce a new way of looking at it, or suggest a direction for further thought.

Refer to the following feature article to see an example of this structure.

*Title* ——————— # WHY DO DOGS BARK?

*Byline* ——————— By Richard Folkers

*Feature lead*

Dogs can be pretty good communicators. A yelp is easy to recognize as a sound of distress. Growls are obvious. A whine, coupled with a scratch at the door, may just keep the carpet clean and dry.

*Nut Graph*

But what about barking? Is a dog sounding an alarm? Defining its territory? Just playing? The principles of evolution dictate that animals retain traits through natural selection. They hang on to functions that contribute to their survival, and that applies to making sounds no less than anything else. Scientists believe male birds sing, for example, to mark their territory, to attract mates, to maintain pair relationships, and to warn of impending predatory doom. But barking seems to defy all the rules of biological necessity.

*Body or Development*

Biologists Raymond Coppinger and Mark Feinstein, who have studied this puzzle, say dogs often seem to bark extravagantly and for no apparent reason at all. The two Hampshire College scientists once spent the night in a Minnesota field listening to a guard dog bark continuously for seven hours. There were no other dogs around, no humans responding, no predators lurking. It just barked. Feinstein recently came upon two dogs in a hot car. "One was barking like crazy, the other staring out the window. They were under the same conditions," he says. "They've got this capacity which doesn't play any necessary function in their lives."

Those dogs, like all domestic dogs, are descended from the wolf, and wolves don't bark much. But their puppies do, and Coppinger and Feinstein believe that may help explain the mystery of barking. Early dogs (wolves really) were scavengers, hanging around human habitations—and their plentiful heaps of garbage. Humans, in turn, tended to tolerate the tamer ones; it was they that became the sires of what would become the domestic dog. Experiments in a number of animals have shown that breeding for tameness breeds animals that are, in effect, perpetual adolescents, displaying many youthful traits into adulthood. "You get an animal more like a juvenile wolf," says Feinstein.

*Body or Development*

So why do juveniles bark? Feinstein and Coppinger believe wolf pups are in a transition period; a bark is acoustically halfway between an infantile attention-seeking whine and an adult, hostile growl.

Adult dogs do find ways to use their barks to communicate; they might be asking to go in or out, defending territory, or just playing. But as Feinstein notes, precisely because barking has no biological necessity for dogs, "they can adapt it to use under almost any circumstance."

*Conclusion*

Ultimately, science's best answer may be the punch line of the old joke about why dogs chase their tails and lick themselves: because they can.

● ● ●

## EXERCISE 6–14

*DIRECTIONS:* Select a feature article from the periodicals available to you. Label its parts, then mark and annotate it.

### ■ Reading Articles from Scholarly Journals

Scholarly journals are publications by professional societies or college and university presses that report developments and research in a particular academic discipline. For example, in the field of psychology, scholarly journals include *American Journal of Psychology*, *Journal of Abnormal Psychology*, and *Psychological Bulletin*. Articles published in scholarly journals are usually peer reviewed. That is, before an article is published, other professionals in the field read the article and confirm that it is legitimate, accurate, and worthwhile.

You need to read articles from scholarly journals when you research a topic for a paper or write a research paper. Some professors distribute a reading list each semester, of which scholarly articles are part. Others supplement text assignments by assigning articles and placing copies of them on reserve in the library. Many scholarly articles, especially those that report research conducted by the author, follow a similar format and often include the following parts, although different journals use different headings to organize their articles, or may not label all sections with headings.

- **Abstract.** An abstract is a brief summary of the article and its findings and is sometimes labeled as "Summary." It usually appears at the beginning of the article following the title and author. Read the abstract to get an overview of the article, and, when doing research, to determine if the study or report contains the information you need.

- **Summary of Related Research.** Many research articles begin by summarizing research that has already been done on the topic. Here authors will cite other studies and briefly report their findings. This summary brings you up to date on the most current research as well as suggests a rationale for why the author's study or research is necessary and appropriate. In some journals, this rationale may appear in a section called *Statement of the Problem*.

- **Description of Research.** In this section, which may also be labeled "Method," the author describes his or her research or explains his or her ideas. For experimental research, you can expect the author to present the research design, including the purpose of the research, description of the population involved, sample size, methodology, and statistical tests applied.

- **Results.** Results of the research are presented in this section.

- **Implications, Discussion, and Conclusions.** Here the author explains what the results mean and draws possible implications and conclusions.

- **Further Research.** Based on his or her findings, some authors end the article by suggesting additional research that is needed to further explain the problem or issue being studied.

Here is a sample scholarly article from *Psychological Reports*. Read the article and study the annotations.*

# SEX DIFFERENCES IN HUMOR[1]

Scott A. Myers

*Department of Speech and Theatre Arts
McNesse State University*

Barbara Lorene Ropog,
R. Pierre Rodgers

*School of Communication Studies
Kent State University*

*Abstract*

*Summary*—This study <u>examined how</u> 48 <u>men</u> and 88 <u>women</u> at a small southern university <u>differed</u> in their <u>orientation toward</u> and their <u>uses of humor</u>. They completed two self-report scales with reference to their general use of humor. Analysis indicated that the <u>men</u> reported a <u>greater frequency</u> of <u>attempts at humor</u> than women; <u>men perceived</u> these <u>attempts as more effective</u> than did the women; and the <u>men</u> reported <u>using humor for negative affect more often</u> than women.

} *What studied*

} *Results*

*Summary of related research*

Humor provides utility of communication in every day interactions (Graham, Papa, & Brooks, 1992), in part because everyday conversation thrives on wordplay, sarcasm, anecdotes, and jokes (Norrick, 1993). And as noted by Booth-Butterfield and Booth-Butterfield (1991), a sense of humor is highly valued in American society; however, some research suggests that men and women differ in their approach to the use of humor. In general communicative interactions, men's humor is characterized by aggression, hostility, and competition (Palmer, 1994; Walker & Dresner, 1988) that often targets women for disparagement (Cantor, 1976, Crawford & Gressley, 1991; Palmer, 1994). Women, on the other hand, are more inclined to use understatement, irony, and self-deprecation (Walker & Dresner, 1988) as forms of humor.

*Description of research*

Studies of humor in general and men's humor in particular have provided a large body of data regarding how and why humor is used (e.g., Morris, 1994; Walker & Dresner, 1988) but in incomplete regarding the humor used by women and the difference in use of humor by men and women (e.g., Crawford & Gressley, 1991). Therefore, we were inter-

---

* Reproduced with permission of authors and publishers from Myers, S.A., Ropog, B.L., and Rodgers, R.P., "Sex Differences in Humor." *Pyschological Reports,* 1997, 81, 221–222. © Pschological Reports 1997.

[1] An earlier version of this paper was presented at the 1997 Central States Communication Association meeting in St. Louis, Missouri. Address enquires to S. A. Myers, Ph.D., Department of Speech and Theatre Arts, POB 90420, McNesse State University, Lake Charles, LA 70609–0420 or e-mail (smyers@acc.mcneese.edu).

ested in whether men and women differ in their frequency and effectiveness of attempted humor and in their uses of humor for positive affect, expressiveness, and negative affect.

*Purpose of study*

*Method.*—Participants were 136 undergraduate students (48 man and 88 women) from a small southern university. The ages of the respondents ranged from 17 to 43 years ($M = 20.7$, $SD = 4.4$). Participants were asked to complete two self-report scales in reference to their general use of humor, the Humor Orientation Scale (Booth-Butterfield & Booth-Butterfield, 1991) and the Uses of Humor Index (Graham, *et. al.*, 1992). Responses for all items were solicited using a 5-point rating scale anchored by strongly agree (5) and strongly disagree (1).

*Sample population & size*

*How data was obtained*

*Description of research*

The Humor Orientation Scale is a 17-item measure that asks respondents to assess both the perceived frequency , i.e., the rate at which humor attempts are made—"I regularly tell jokes and funny stories when I am with a group," and the perceived effectiveness, i.e., whether the actor believes the attempt was perceived as humorous—"People usually laugh when I tell a joke or story," of the attempts. A coefficient alpha of .80 ($M = 32.0$, $SD = 5.7$) was reported for the frequency dimension and also for the effectiveness dimension ($M = 29.0$, $SD = 4.8$).

*Description of scales used*

*Data reliability*

The Uses of Humor Index is an 11-item measure on which respondents report their reasons for use of humor across three dimensions: (a) positive affect, i.e., prosocial use—"I use humor to make light of a situation," (b) expressiveness, i.e., self-disclosure, emotional expression—"I use humor to let others know my likes and dislikes," and (c) negative affect, i.e., anti-social use—I use humor to demean and belittle others." A coefficient alpha of .78 was reported for the positive affect dimension ($M = 12.2$, $SD = 2.0$), of 4.7 for the expressiveness dimension ($M = 15.5$, $SD = 3.1$), and .84 for the negative affect dimension ($M = 6.9$, $SD = 3.0$).

*Data reliability*

*Results.*—Three significant finding emerge from the study. First, men ($M = 33.4$) reported more frequent attempts at humor than women ($M = 31.2$, $F_{1,134} = 5.16$, $p < .05$). Second, men ($M = 30.6$) perceived their humor as more effective than women ($M = 28.1$; $F_{1,134} = 8.86$, $p < .01$). Third, men ($M = 7.7$) reported using humor for negative affect more often than women ($M = 6.5$; $F_{1,134} = 5.45$, $P < .05$). No significant sex difference was evident for either positive affect ($F_{1,134} = 1.39$, ns) or expressiveness ($F_{1,134} = .06$, ns).

*Results*

*Moderately significant*

*Highly significant*

*Moderately significant*

Because the data were gathered using self-report ratings rather than behavioral or objective measures, the results should be interpreted with caution. However, the findings indicate that not only do men engage in more frequent attempts at humor than women, but that they perceive these attempts as more effective and use humor for expression of negative affect. These findings support the notion advanced by Crawford and Gressley (1991) that perhaps women do not incorporate humor into their repertoire of interpersonal communication behaviors as readily as men. White (1988) posited that women do no use humor regularly due to the social norms that govern communication. Because women

*Conclusions, Implications, Discussion*

*Conclusion*

*Why this may be so*

are conditioned to not complain, to accept existing social norms, and to not express objections to male attitudes (Rowe, 1995), women may be reluctant to violate social norms against being negative, which may naturally contribute toward a reluctance to use humor. In addition, Walker and Dresner (1988) posited that women are conditioned to accept subordinate and passive roles, which subsequently affects the situations in which they use humor.

## References

BOOTH-BUTTERFIELD, S., & BOOTH-BUTTERFIELD, M. (1991) Individual differences in the communication of humorous messages. *Southern Communications Journal,* 56, 205–218.

CANTOR, J. R. (1976) What is funny to whom? The role of gender. *Journal of Communication,* 26, 110–118.

CRAWFORD, M., & GRESSLEY, D. (1991) Creativity, caring, and context; women's and men's accounts of humor preferences and practices. *Psychology of Women Quarterly,* 15, 217–231.

GRAHAM, E. E., PAPA, M. J., & BROOKS, G. P. (1992) Functions of humor in conversation: conceptualization and measurement. *Western Journal of Communication,* 56, 161–183.

MORRIS, L. A. (Ed.)(1994) *American women humorists.* New York: Garland.

NORRICK, N. R. (1993) *Conversational joking: humor is everyday talk.* Bloomington, IN: Indiana Univer. Press.

PALMER, J. (1994) *Taking humor seriously.* New York: Routledge.

ROWE, K. (1995) *The unruly woman: gender and the genres of laughter.* Austin, TX: Univer. of Texas Press.

WALKER, N., & DRESNER, Z. (Eds.) (1988) *Redressing the balance: American women's literary humor from colonial time to the 1980's.* Jackson, MS: Univer. Press of Mississippi.

WHITE C. L. (1988) Liberating laughter: an inquiry into the nature, content, and functions of feminist humor. In B. Bate & A. Taylor (Eds.), *Women communicating: studies of women's talk.* Norwood, NJ: Ablex. Pp. 75–90.

*Accepted June 9, 1997.*

● ● ●

When reading scholarly journals, keep the following tips in mind.

1. **Be sure you understand the author's purpose.** Determine why the study was conducted.

2. **Highlight as you read.** You may need to refer back to information presented earlier in the article.

3. **Use index cards.** If you are reading numerous articles keep a $4 \times 6$ index card for each. Write a brief summary of the purpose and findings.

4. **Use quotations.** If you take notes from the article, be sure to place in quotations any information you copy directly from the article. If you fail to do so, you may inadvertently plagiarize. Plagiarism is presenting someone else's ideas as your own, and carries stiff academic and legal penalties.

## ■ ANALYZING ESSAYS AND ARTICLES

Essays and articles require close analysis and evaluation. While textbooks usually present reliable, unbiased factual information, essays and even some articles often express opinions and represent particular viewpoints; consequently, you must read them critically. Use the following questions to guide your analysis.

1. **Who is the author?** Check to see if it is a name you recognize. Try to discover whether or not the author is qualified to write about the subject.

2. **What is the author's purpose?** Is the writer trying to present information, convince you of something, entertain you, or express a viewpoint?

3. **What does the introduction or lead add to the piece of writing?** Does it interest you or supply background information, for example.

4. **What is the author's thesis?** Try to express it in your own words. By doing so, you may find bias or discover a viewpoint you had not previously recognized.

5. **Does the author adequately support the thesis?** Is a variety of supporting information provided? An article that relies entirely upon the author's personal experiences, for example, to support a thesis may have limited usefulness.

6. **Does the author supply sources, references, or citations for the facts and statistics presented?** You should be able to verify the information presented and turn to those sources should you wish to read more about the subject.

For more information on thinking critically about essays and articles, refer to Chapters 10, 11, and 12 in Unit Four, "Reading Critically."

## EXERCISE 6–15

*DIRECTIONS:* Evaluate the expository essay "How To Brag About Yourself To Win and Hold a Job" (p.17–18) by answering each of the questions listed above.

## EXERCISE 6–16

*DIRECTIONS:* Use an Internet source to locate an article or essay. Try to locate one from an electronic magazine, rather than from an electronic version of a print magazine. Then answer the following questions.

1. Answer questions 1–6 for analyzing essays and articles.
2. In what ways is the article similar to print magazine articles and in what ways is it different?
3. What are the advantages of electronic magazines over print magazines?

## EXERCISE 6–17

*DIRECTIONS:* Compile a list of articles and essays that you have been assigned to read this semester. For each assignment indicate its source: popular press, scholarly journal, or in-text reading.

---

### Critical Thinking Tip #6

#### Evaluating Research Sources

When you conduct research, you will read a variety of articles and essays, as well as other source material. Not all sources you encounter while preparing a research paper are equally worthwhile or appropriate. Therefore, it is essential to critically evaluate all sources when conducting research. The following suggestions will help you to evaluate reference sources:

1. Check your source's copyright date. Make certain you are using a current source. For many papers such as those exploring controversial issues or scientific or medical advances, only the most up-to-date sources are useful.
2. Be sure to use an authoritative source. The material should be written by a recognized authority or by someone who is working within his or her field.
3. Choose sources that provide the most complete and concrete information.
4. Select first-hand accounts of an event or experience rather than second- or third-hand accounts whenever possible.
5. Avoid using sources that present biased information and be wary of those that include personal opinion and reactions.

## SUMMARY

**1. How do essays and articles differ?**

Essays and articles differ mainly in viewpoint. Essays are written from a personal perspective while articles are more objective in their presentation of information.

**2. What are the parts of an essay?**

Essays have five essential parts with different functions.
- Title—suggests the subject and attracts the reader.
- Introduction—offers background, builds interest, defines terms, and states the thesis.
- Thesis Statement—clearly and sufficiently expresses the main point of the essay.
- Body—presents, in a number of paragraphs, information that supports or explains the thesis.
- Conclusion—brings the essay to a close by making a final statement of the subject.

**3. What should you look for when reading narrative essays?**

Narrative essays present a series of events, often in story form and vividly described. When reading them look for:
- the time and place of the events.
- the point of view from which it is told.
- the overall meaning or thesis of the narrative.
- any commentary by the author that helps reveal his or her point.

**4. What should you focus on in descriptive essays?**

Descriptive essays emphasize sensory impressions to create a vivid picture of a person, object, event, or place. It is useful to focus on:
- who or what is being described.
- the writer's choice of words and the feeling they convey.
- the overall impression the description leaves you with.
- the first and last paragraphs for clues to the writer's purpose or main point.

**5. What can you do to improve your reading of expository essays?**

Expository essays are meant to inform you about a particular viewpoint. When reading such essays you should:

- check that the author can be trusted to present the facts fairly and accurately.
- be sure the background information given is complete.
- get the writer's thesis clearly in mind.
- focus on new terminology used.
- mark and highlight the thesis statement and important terms.
- make an outline, map, or summary to ensure your recall.

**6. How are popular press articles organized?**

Articles found in magazines and newspapers have a different style and format than essays. Hard news stories, action stories, and feature articles have some differences in format but can contain the following parts:

- Title—often eye catching and descriptive.
- Dateline—the location and date of the story.
- Credit Line—the wire service or newspaper the story came from.
- Byline—the name of the writer.
- Lead—an opening paragraph that either summarizes major information (news stories) or sparks interest in the topic (feature stories).
- Nut Graph—one or more paragraphs that define a feature article's nature and scope.
- Body or Development—the section that presents the supporting facts.
- Conclusion—the final statement about the subject of the article.

**7. What are the parts of most scholarly journal articles?**

Professional societies publish journals that report research and developments in their fields. They often contain the following six parts which may or may not be labeled:

- Abstract or Summary—follows the title and author.

- Summary of Related Research—reviews current research on the topic.
- Description of Research—also called "Method," tells how the research was carried out or explains the author's ideas, including the purpose of the study.
- Results—states the outcomes of the study.
- Implications, Discussion, and Conclusions —explains the meaning and implications of the study's results.
- Further Research—suggestions for additional studies needed.

**8. How can you read essays and articles more critically?**

To closely analyze and evaluate essays and articles, ask these questions:
- Who is the author?
- What is his or her purpose?
- What does the introduction or lead add to the piece of writing?
- What is the thesis?
- Is it adequately supported?
- Are sources, references, or citations given for the facts and statistics used?

## READING SELECTION 11
### MEDICAL PRIVACY

From *Money*

*Are your medical records accessible by others? Read this article to discover more about the issue of medical privacy and how to protect yourself and your family.*

### Medical Privacy

1　Of all the aspects of American life where privacy is invaded, the area of medical privacy is unquestionably the most disturbing. "Many people imagine that their doctor keeps their medical records and no one else sees them," says Robert Gellman, a leading privacy expert who is advising the Department of Health and Human Services on the development of medical privacy standards. "That's a joke."

2　Case in point: The private Medical Information Bureau houses files on some 15 million Americans, which are used by MIB's member insurance companies to help determine who gets life and health insurance and what they'll pay. Medical personnel in managed-care networks can read your files that aren't kept at MIB too. So can pharmacy benefits-management companies and some employers. In a new study of the privacy practices of 300 Fortune 500 companies by University of Illinois professor David Linowes, 35% of employers said they use personal medical information as a basis for hiring, promotion, and firing decisions.

3    Jane Gass learned about the sharing of employee medical records the hard way. After the nurse was fired by her longtime employer for refusing to give her new boss the keys to employees' private medical files, she sued the company for wrongful termination. A federal district court judge has since held that the law did not limit an employer's ability to designate who holds those keys. Complains Gass: "I try to uphold a code of ethics. But when I do, I get fired."

4    The drive by managed-care companies to hold down medical costs has led some of these firms to demand ever more detailed medical records from doctors to justify—or refuse—coverage. Psychiatrist Denise Nagel, executive director of the National Coalition for Patient Rights, tells of one psychiatric patient who was horrified to learn that explicit reports of his sexual fantasies were available online to his dermatologist, podiatrist and anyone with access to his health maintenance organization's computers. While that HMO has since limited online file sharing, Nagel says: "The practice is still widespread throughout the health-care industry."

5    Similarly, employers regularly get reports from pharmacies and pharmaceutical benefit managers about their worker's prescription-drug use and, increasingly, employers are strong-arming insurers for their workers' medical histories and the nature of their office visits. For instance, in November 1992, the Rite Aid drugstore chain gave the Southeastern Pennsylvania Transportation Authority (SEPTA) a list of employees taking more than $100 worth of drugs a month, enabling a supervisor to single out workers on Retrovir, a drug used to treat AIDS. Says Philadelphia lawyer Clifford Boardman, who sued SEPTA and Rite Aid on behalf of an HIV-positive employee: "My impres-

sion is that this is a standard approach in the pharmaceutical industry." Rite Aid settled, but SEPTA won an appeal after the judge ruled that the harm inflicted to the employee was minimal.

6    The prognosis for the future looks even more alarming, since the dawn of genetic testing is creating medical records that contain information not only on actual ailments but also on patients' genetic predisposition to diseases like breast cancer, Alzheimer's and Parkinson's. Think your employers can't order up this stuff? Think again. In a recent landmark ruling, a California judge dismissed a lawsuit filed by seven employees against Lawrence Berkeley Laboratory for secretly testing them for sickle-cell anemia, a genetic disease prevalent among African Americans, during a routine physical.

**How to Protect Yourself**

7    Call the Medical Information Bureau (617–426–3660) to find out whether it has your medical records. If it does, get a copy to check their accuracy. Should you find mistakes, MIB will investigate and, if the bureau agrees that any records are inaccurate, it will edit or delete them. Otherwise you can put a statement of dispute in the file, which will come up whenever the report is pulled. If you get in touch with MIB within 30 days of having been denied insurance or charged a new, higher premium because of an MIB report, the copy of your file is free. Otherwise you'll pay $8.

8    Interview potential doctors, particularly mental-health practitioners, about their policy on reporting your medical condition and treatment to managed-care companies and employers.

9    You can minimize the risk that results of a medical test, mental-health consultation or prescription-drug purchase will appear in your records. If possible, don't file for reimbursement from your insurer, and go to a practitioner or druggist who agrees not to report the results to your insurer or employer. Says Bryant Welch, a Washington D.C. clinical psychologist and attorney: "That's not paranoid. It's pragmatic."

## Comprehension Test 11

*Directions: Circle the letter of the best answer.*

**Checking Your Comprehension**

1. This reading is mostly about
   a. privacy in your home.
   b. privacy of your health records.
   c. your financial privacy.
   d. privacy as it relates to your work.

2. Which of the following best describes the main idea of this selection?
   a. Your medical history is available to a number of people and agencies.
   b. Your health care insurer can deny you coverage based upon your medical history.
   c. Your medical history can become available through the Internet.
   d. Your boss has a right to review your medical records.

3. Jane Gass, a nurse, was fired from her job because
   a. she was found infringing on the privacy rights of patients.
   b. her boss discovered she had a contagious disease.
   c. she was snooping in other people's medical records.
   d. she refused to give her new boss access to employees' medical files.

4. The result of Jane Gass' case was that
   a. the case never went to court.
   b. her lawsuit was upheld and she was reinstated.
   c. she lost and was fired from her job.
   d. the case is still pending in federal district court.

5. The case of the psychiatric patient was presented in order to illustrate invasion of privacy by
   a. a managed care company.
   b. a medical laboratory.
   c. an employer.
   d. a drugstore.

6. As used in paragraph 3 in the reading, the word "designate" means
   a. share.
   b. select.
   c. deny.
   d. realize.

**Thinking Critically**

7. From this article, the reader may conclude that
   a. people's medical records are kept under lock and key.
   b. a person's medical history is difficult to obtain.
   c. medical records are widely available to many people.
   d. it is illegal to obtain another person's medical records without permission.

8. The author's attitude toward the issue of medical privacy is that
   a. individuals' privacy should be protected.
   b. insurance companies have a right to view all medical records.
   c. employees should understand why their boss needs to read their medical files.
   d. what people don't know won't hurt them.

9. With which of the following statements would the author of this article agree?
   a. There is no way to prevent others from obtaining your medical records.
   b. By taking the matter to court, you can make your medical records unavailable to others.
   c. With careful planning, it is possible to limit access to your medical records.
   d. No one should ever have access to your medical records.

10. From this article it is clear that in the future, invasion of privacy as it relates to medical records will
    a. get better.
    b. get worse.
    c. stay the same.
    d. not be an issue.

**Questions for Discussion**

1. What can be done to prevent abuses resulting from access to the medical records of individuals?

2. Do you think it should be legal for insurance companies to obtain a person's medical records? Why?

3. Do you think that information technology such as computers and the Internet have extended our freedoms or placed more limits on them? Explain why.

4. Who should have access to your medical records and for what reason? Justify your answer.

EDUCATION

# READING SELECTION 12
## CHANGING THE PATTERN OF GENDERED DISCUSSION: LESSONS FROM SCIENCE CLASSROOMS*

Barbara J. Guzzetti and Wayne O. Williams
From *Journal of Adolescent and Adult Literacy*

*Do girls respond differently in classroom discussions? This scholarly journal article explores the question of how male and female students are influenced by each other in class participation and discussion in a science classroom. Read the article to discover the outcomes of a research study designed to answer these questions.*

1    A plethora of research shows that the true discussion of the concepts in texts facilitates students' learning. True discussion occurs when students' voices dominate, when students interact with each other, and when students talk in phrases and sentences (Alvermann, Dillon & O'Brien, 1987). Discussion is particularly effective in changing students' alternative concep-

tions (ideas that vary from scientifically accepted concepts) when individuals are asked to provide evidence from the text to support their opinions (Guzzetti, Snyder, Glass, & Gamas, 1993) Hence, discussion that disenfranchises females is especially detrimental in science because it is important to discuss ideas when students' theories are contradicted by scientific thought (Alvermann & Hynd, 1989).

2    Students seem to agree with researchers who find discussion necessary, because they self-report that discussion is one of the most effective ways to learn science material (Tobin & Garnett, 1987). Yet, both true discussion and the more typical recitation-type discussion, where the teacher asks a question and a student provides the answer, (Alvermann et al., 1987), are dominated by males

---

* Due to the length of this reading, timing is inappropriate and word-per-minute conversions are not provided.

(Tobin & Garnett, 1987). Some researchers believe that the tendency for boys to achieve more than girls in science may be a result of greater opportunities to engage in academic activities, like discussions (Tobin & Garnett, 1987).

3 These insights from research in reading education and science education focused mainly on observations of verbal interactions between teachers and students. Researchers from science education agree that teachers have disparate expectations for students' responses in teacher-led discussion. For example, in teacher-led, whole-class discussion, boys are spoken to and are asked higher level questions more frequently (Becker, 1981; Hall & Sadler, 1982). Science teachers elaborate more on males' responses than females' responses in large-group discussions of scientific concepts (Jones & Wheatley, 1990). Teachers will take a student's argument on a position more seriously when it comes from a male (Lemke, 1990).

4 This research from science education focuses on the teacher's behavior that fosters gender disparity in classroom discussion. But, teachers aren't the only ones whose behaviors constrain girl's contributions to discussions. Students may well constrain or enable each other. Hence, we (the university researcher, Guzzetti, and the participating physics teacher, Williams) decided to examine interactions between students in discussion.

5 Recent research in gender and literacy (conducted in other subject areas) provides evidence that who talks in discussion, how much, and what is said are influenced by changing relationships of power among students (Alvermann & Anders, 1994). Researchers from reading education (Alvermann, 1993; Alvermann & Anders, 1994) have directed teachers to examine "the reasons behind the silence," like students' self-confidence and peer relationships.

6 Sociolinguists identify other social norms in classrooms that favor males in instructional conversations. Males are enabled by females to dom-

inate instructional talk because females respond to social pressures that women be good listeners who are valued for their ability to be attentive to others (Lafrance, 1991). Hence, there is a cultural proclivity to see any talk by females as too much talk (Tromel-Plotz, 1985). As a result, language practices have been cited as key influences contributing to the domination and oppression of young women in classrooms (Gilbert, 1989).

## Why we did the study

7 Stimulated by our readings from four fields (reading/literacy education, science education, sociolinguistics, and feminist pedagogy) and in response to calls for descriptions of students' interactions that perpetuate gender disparity (Krockover & Shepardson, 1995; Tobin 1988), we conducted this investigation. We wanted to know specifically how students were influenced by each other in their talk about science concepts.

8 In addition to whole-class discussion, we wanted to examine students' interactions in small groups because some researchers recommend this structure to address gender disparity (Tannen, 1992), while others warn that males dominate science talk, whatever the structure or activity (Lemke, 1990; Morse & Handley, 1985).

9 We also decided to explore students' interactions in various types of discussion, as well as various structures. The range of interactions we sought to examine included debate or refutational discussion in whole-class settings and collaborative discussion for team work in small groups. We anticipated making comparisons of verbal interactions between genders from one form and structure to another.

## How we did the study

10 This article presents an overview of our findings from a 2-year study and provides recommendations for fostering equitable participation in discussion. In the first year, we identified and described the types of behaviors and language

patterns that characterized gender disparity, without changing the normal structure of the class (Guzzetti & Williams, 1996). To accomplish this, we (Guzzetti and two graduate assistants) observed the same two sections of physics (juniors and seniors, 9 females and 15 males) and honors physics (juniors and seniors, 14 females and 17 males) daily for almost the entire school year (commencing in August and ending in March).

11    We also administered a questionnaire that assessed students' preferences for classroom structure, their perceptions of gender differences in talk, and their individual participation. Finally, we conducted informal interviews with those students whose academic performance was affected by their gendered interactions.

12    In the second year of our study, we used the knowledge we had gained from our first year's observations to change the structure of the physics classroom. In response to the gender disparity we described during the first year, we implemented same-sex lab groups and small-group discussions. In doing so, we were influenced by our reading of The American Association of University Women's (AAUW) 1992 report, *How Schools Shortchange Girls.* This synthesis of research states that although girls often perform better in same-sex work groups, researchers have not yet described the dynamics of participants' interactions, or the circumstances under which single-sex groups are most beneficial.

13    Hence, we wanted to identify how same-sex grouping might diminish gender bias in science activity and talk about that activity. We also hoped to change student interaction that impeded female participation. We wondered if enabling females to participate in small-group, single-sex discussions would have an influence on their participation in whole-class, dual-sex discussions.

14    To accomplish these goals, the second year of our study consisted of daily observation of two related units—gravity and projectile motion. We chose these units because they represent counterintuitive concepts (i.e., contrary to logic and common sense). Students typically have alternative conceptions for these concepts, and are often found discussing their ideas with each other. Hence, we anticipated that we would be able to observe a myriad of discussions forms and participation styles in these units.

### What we found

15    Listed and explained below are five findings from our 2-year study. These findings were evidenced in at least three sources—observations of whole-class or small-group discussions, formal or informal interviews, and students' questionnaire responses. Each finding complements or extends other research on gender disparity in discussion and has direct implications for instructional practice.

16    1. *Refutational discussions favor males.* We had frequent opportunities to observe students arguing their ideas because Williams structured a whole-class, refutational discussion (called "inquiry training") during each unit. Williams would choose a counterintuitive concept, formulate a question about it, and, before class started, would secretly select a student to be a "shill" during the discussion. Williams provided this student with a logical but scientifically incorrect idea as a response to the question, and a logical but faulty explanation for that idea. The shill was awarded extra credit points if he or she could convince others of that position.

17    Few females were shills, as Williams selected shills from students' responses to a questionnaire indicating their desire to assume this role. Not many females desired to be shills; large numbers of boys did, however. Two females we interviewed who had been shills before our observations either thought their assertions were ineffectual or did not remember the details of the discussions.

18 Inquiry training was particularly interesting to us because we knew from past research that written forms of refutation are effective in learning counterintuitive science concepts (Guzzetti et al., 1993). Hence, we anticipated that oral forms of refutation would be potentially powerful in changing students' alternative conceptions. We believed that equal access to this type of discussion would be especially necessary for students to evolve an understanding of these concepts. We also knew however, from past research that whole-class discussion typically favors males (Tannen, 1992).

19 Examination of our observation notes during both years of our study documented that girls spoke only rarely in whole-class, refutational discussions. In these discussions, it was always the same few girls who volunteered to speak. When girls did refute, they tended to pose their refutation as a question, like "Have you thought about this . . ." or "Shouldn't that be. . . ?" Boys, however, would argue directly with each other, making assertions like "That's wrong because . . .". Males were also most likely to display aggressive language behavior, like interruptions, louder vocalizations, and emphatic intonations.

20 This contrast in language styles was perceived by the males as an indicator that girls didn't understand physics as well as the boys did. Males made this inference because, in the words of one boy in honors physics, "Girls ask a lot of questions, but I think the guys know the basic facts, so they don't need to." Another male in the class, John (pseudonym), volunteered that "Girls don't seem to grasp the concepts as the guys do"; when asked why he thought so, he stated, "Because they're the ones asking most of the questions. . . . Most of the time, when I have something to say, it's usually an argument about air resistance or friction."

21 This perception on the part of the males that the girls' questioning indicated their lack of knowledge was consistent across sections of physics.

22 Girls' explanations for their differential participation in whole class, refutational discussions alluded to issues of self-confidence and social norms. In response to the questionnaire item "How likely are you to argue with a shill in class discussion?" in the first year without intervention, the majority (across sections) of the females (78%) stated that they were not likely to argue. In comparison, less than half (40%) of the males stated they wouldn't debate. Comments from girls included statements like "I'm not confident enough in my knowledge of physics to debate about it," "I don't know enough to argue about it," and "I'm not too sure of the answer." In contrast, comments from boys were typically a remark like "I'll argue with anyone about anything, especially if I disagree with them."

23 In our second year (after the interventions of same-sex lab groups and small group discussions), more females were likely to debate, although refutational discussions still favored males. Less than half of the girls (45%) stated they might or would argue, in contrast to about two thirds of the boys (66%) across sections. Comments from girls still indicated a lack of self-confidence, like "I have doubts about my thoughts" and "I'm not very likely to argue because I probably wouldn't know if they were right or wrong." In response to the query "Do you talk very much in whole-class discussions?" an Asian female in a single-sex lab group replied, "Mostly in small groups I don't have a problem. I talk as much as possible. But, in a bigger class I don't talk as much unless I'm very sure about what I'm saying."

24 These students' remarks that refer to gender differences in self-confidence are consistent with observations by researchers. Writers on gender and language characterize women's speech as insecure or lacking in confidence (Lakoff, 1975). Others argue that questions rather than assertions provide social grace (Dubois & Crouch, 1975; Edelsky, 1979) and typify females' inclusive conversational style (Tromel-Plotz, 1985). Hence, by refuting less often and by posing their

refutations as a query, the girls were being consistent with socially learned norms of gender-appropriate language.

25 Females who were inclined to voice their opinions during refutational discussions reported feeling ineffectual and having their opinions dismissed by the boys. One female, Barbara (pseudonym), in honors physics (during year 2) stated:

> It's really hard to get what you think across. [Boys think] "Oh, you're a girl, I'm going to listen to my buddy over here. He knows what he's talking about; I'm going to be cool." It's such a male-dominated class that I definitely notice a difference. I may talk out a lot, but I don't fell like they're even listening to my ideas.

26 Barbara's perception of being ignored in whole-class discussion is consistent with Tromel-Plotz's (1985) observation that women are forced into subservient positions in discussion by males not giving females a chance to talk, disregarding what they say when they do get a chance, and not taking women seriously as equal participants in the discussion. Tannen (1994) explains that women who use conversational strategies (like being indirect) that are designed to take others' feelings into account may perceive that they are not being listened to. They also may be seen by others as less competent and confident than they really are.

27 Comments from females who did not participate in refutational discussions alluded to conversational preferences that reflect social norms, like "I'm not very likely to argue because I don't enjoy trying to prove myself in this class" or "I hate arguing." These remarks about conversational style (proclivity to argue or not argue) are consistent with research citing girls' socialization to avoid arguments. Researchers identify social norms like these as a constraining influence on girls' participation in scholarly debate (Meyer & Fowler, 1993). Girls feel a social expectation as females to avoid sounding intellectually threatening (equal or superior) around young men (Johnson, 1995). Our findings agree with Tannen's (1992) conclusion that "debate-like formats as learning tools make classrooms more hospitable to men" (p. 4).

28 2. *Females do not participate in whole-class discussions because they are afraid.* In both years of our study, females' reasons for not speaking out were not only because of their lack of self-confidence or fear of violating social conventions, but also because they felt intimidated. Their comments focused on their fears of repercussions from the male students, such as "I like working with all girls because you don't have to worry about your reputation"; "I wouldn't argue in class because they [boys] would probably bite off my head if I did"; and "Guys tend to be hostile—if you're wrong, you're stupid, according to them."

29 Comments like these were more likely to be heard in classes where the proportion of males to females was most asymmetrical, and in classes where there were no groupings by gender.

30 3. *Small groups do not necessarily facilitate females' participation unless grouped by gender.* Observation notes from our first year showed that merely putting students into small groups did not facilitate females' participation in instructional activity or talk about that activity. Most often, the males were the ones in lab groups who were engaged in manipulating the equipment, giving directions, and making verbal inferences about their observations. Females were most likely to be confined to setting up the equipment and passively recording data the boys had actively generated by conducting the experiment. A summary of observation notes by a research assistant reads "Only the boys in each team operate the experiment, whereas the girls just sit there and record the data."

31 Observations and interviews from our second year (when most students were grouped by gender for lab assignments—uneven numbers of males and females prevented total division) showed that females became more active participants when placed in same-sex groups, and they engaged more often in a wider range of verbal interactions.

Our observation notes document girls' discussion while setting up the equipment, manipulating the experiment, identifying errors and resolving them, measuring, making observations, recording the data, and negotiating their meaning.

32    Females' talk during these events was characterized by collaborative inquiry and equal participation. In contrast, when only one male was present in a group, that male was most likely to give orders, to ask only assumptive questions (assuming agreement), and to talk to demonstrate or show girls how to proceed. Girls' voices were generally silenced.

33    4. *Males and females display different conversational styles in small groups as well as in large groups.* Female students characterized their discussions with each other as more interactive, more concerned about consensus, more willing to consider others' opinions, more prone to question, and more likely to consult authority to settle disagreements. In response to the questionnaire item "Do you notice any differences in the way boys talk in class versus the way girls talk in class, and, if so, what?" females supported our inferences with statements like "Guys are hostile," "Girls are likely to listen to opinions," and "Guys are more direct and narrow minded." Males made comments like "The boys generate ideas faster than the girls," "Most of the girls seem timid and shy compared to the boys," and "The boys make it sound technical, and the girls say it in words they understand."

34    Females' collaborative discussion style was in sharp contrast to the males' independent discussion style. Even in small-group discussions, we found males more assertive or aggressive in their verbal interaction and less likely to negotiate shared meanings (except when required to find evidence for their opinions from the text). This pattern may be consistent across both large and small groups because males have been characterized as having more self-confidence and less need for dependence on others (American Association of University Women, 1992). Boys

recognized this disparity, as they wrote comments on their questionnaires like "Boys are more opinionated," "Boys are louder and more confident," "Boys are always right," and "Girls ask questions; boys express what they think."

35    We also found males to be competitive and, on the whole, unlikely to incorporate verbal suggestions from females. Guzzetti's observation notes during an experiment on projectile motion read (pseudonyms used):

> I notice that a lab group of boys next to a lab group of girls has marks all over their paper [indicating many trials and errors]. Bryan tells me it's because their steel ramp is "drunk"; it keeps moving [causing error]. I tell them that happened to Janice's group yesterday. Immediately, Bryan asks Janice's group how they fixed that. Amanda tells Bryan that they didn't, they just put a mark on the table to align the ramp each time. Bryan says they'll start to do that. Amanda informs him that they have a patent on it [entitlement to extra credit points if others use their idea]. Upon hearing this, the other two boys in Bryan's group retort "Oh! Never mind!" Bryan tells me that he doesn't care if the girls get extra credit just so long as his group gets the experiment right. Bryan's group, however, does not incorporate the girls' idea.

36    5. *Students are well aware of gender disparity in classroom discussion.* One of the most common findings from prior research is that teachers are usually unaware of gender bias in classroom activity and talk about that activity (Jones & Wheatley, 1990; Tobin, 1988). For example, Williams was not aware of any gender inequities in his classes prior to reading our data and believed he was gender fair in his interactions with students. Our observations confirmed that Williams used the seating chart to call on fairly proportional numbers of males and females. He reported that in his 30 years of teaching, girls and boys achieved equally in his classes, and that some of his best students (selected for honors or awards in science) had been girls. Prior to our study, Williams was looking for gender bias only in his own attitudes and behaviors.

37    Our investigation provided a plethora of evidence, however, that teachers like Williams may be unaware of gender disparity in their own or their students' actions, students are not unaware. Both males and females consistently reported males' domination of science activity and talk about that activity before we changed the classroom structure. In the first year of our study, 100% of the girls in physics reported gender differences in how often and the ways boys talk in class, and all of the girls nominated a male as the person who talked the most.

38    Although only 50% of the males in the class reported gender differences in classroom talk, 94% of them nominated a boy as the person who talked the most in class. In honors physics that year, 80% of the females and 60% of the males reported that males dominated discussions. (In year 2, after our intervention, these numbers were reduced to about half of the females and a third of the males across sections who noticed gender differences in discussion.) These data also indicate that students who do not notice gender inequities are most likely to be males.

## What can be done

39    These data show us that teachers not only need to be concerned with their own language that fosters gender inequity in discussion, but must also monitor their students' ways of talking. Teachers must provide conditions that foster gender equity among students in instructional activity and talk about that activity. In our research, students were the major contributors to gender inequities in discussion. It was their interactions with each other that intimidated and threatened the girls, made them afraid of repercussions, and silenced their voices.

40    The following four suggestions for addressing gender disparity in classroom discussion are based on our experiences during the 2 years of our study and on our readings in the literature on gender bias.

41    1. *Recognize gender bias in discussion.* Because teachers are generally unaware of gender inequities among students in their verbal interactions, teachers will need to become active observers for gender bias. Teachers must consciously observe to identify students who dominate the discussion and be aware of those who practice covert or overt tactics to gain control. Although awareness is not sufficient for change (Taylor, 1989; Tobin, 1988), teachers must be able to recognize the problem to take steps to alleviate it.

42    Teachers can observe gender bias in discussion by looking for specific behaviors that characterize it. Ploys that indicate gender bias include both verbal and nonverbal behaviors that ultimately inhibit equitable discussion (Tromel-Plotz, 1985). Verbal ploys to gain control include interruptions, call outs, and increased vocal pitch, tone, or loudness. Nonverbal tactics include withholding active feedback, using elaborate gestures (e.g., jumping out of a seat, wildly waving a hand) to gain attention, and body language (e.g., frowns, looks of disapproval, and gaze aversion) to stifle discussion of a verbalized idea.

43    In addition to noticing the quality of verbal interactions, it is also necessary to notice the quantity of talk between genders. Power relationship often depend more on who is doing the talking than on what is actually said. When one gender consistently has the floor over another, power relationships between genders are unbalanced (Edelsky, 1981).

44    2. *Group by gender in small groups for refutational discussion.* Since whole-class and refutational discussions favor males, teachers can encourage females' participation by grouping by gender to debate views. These types of discussions are useful in learning new concepts and should, therefore, be made gender-fair. Conditions that encourage females to participate in discussion can be established by allowing girls to debate with each other and to elect a

spokesperson to report their group's view to the total class.

45 We recommend incorporating a Discussion Web (Alvermann, 1991) for these debates. We suggest adapting this procedure by pairing students by gender to reach consensus on a response to a central question. Students may be required to provide evidence from the textbook, trade books, or labs to support their views. After reaching agreement, this group of two then joins another group of two and again attempts to reach consensus through substantiated persuasion. This group of four may join another group of four and repeat the process. Finally, the group of eight students elects a spokesperson who reports the group's view to the whole class, stimulating whole-class discussion and consensus.

46 By using a Discussion Web, females will be given the opportunity to be discussion leaders in smaller groups. They will also gain more condence in their opinions because they will have textual or external support for their views. Based on our observations, we believe that this type of leadership in small groups may assist females in asserting their opinions more freely in whole-class discussion, give them practice in being leaders in discussion, and make debates less biased toward males.

47 3. *Promote self-confidence by providing an intellectually safe environment.* Teachers can encourage girls' participation in discussion by calling on them more often (prompting), restating or elaborating on their remarks, and by giving positive reinforcement for their comments and questions (Morse & Handley, 1985). By doing so, teachers can demonstrate that they value females' participation and take their comments seriously. If the teacher models these behaviors, students may be inclined to emulate them.

48 Teachers, together with their students, can also establish rules for discussion. In the classes we observed during our second year, Williams monitored interruptions and call outs in whole-class discussion and did not allow them. In a similar way, teachers and students, by having discussions together, may create a list of unacceptable tactics (like those identified in our first recommendation) and expect that all students, whatever their gender, avoid them.

49 4. *Expand acceptable notions of science and ways of talking about science.* Teachers can present a view of science as active questioning and exploration, dispelling the misconception of science as passive observation and memorization of facts (Carey, Evans, Honda, Jay, & Unger, 1989), while at the same time publicly valuing feminine ways of talking. Teachers can demonstrate that they value females' language strategies by presenting women's tendencies to question as positive rather than negative, and modeling questioning as a legitimate way to "talk science." Teachers can remind students that questions are the first step in scientific inquiry, that scientists frequently form new theories by questioning, and that science is not static and stable, but constantly changing due to questioning and requestioning prior assumptions. Teachers can model this behavior in discussion by sharing with the class questions they and other scientists still have about the concepts under study.

50 Hence, teachers can demonstrate sensitivity to gender by expanding their philosophies of science and what counts as science talk. Discursive practices that emphasize objectivity, logic, and rationality may well disenfranchise women. Rather that creating a dichotomy between objective and subjective, teachers can strive for a holistic way of approaching science inquiry and talk about that inquiry.

51 Teachers can also demonstrate that they value feminine ways of talking about science by modeling and rewarding collaborative (rather than authoritative) discussion styles. We believe that recommendations for addressing gender bias should not simply focus on ways to make women sound more like men in instructional conversations, but should expand the possibili-

ties for each gender. For when males are not socialized to listen to others, they, too, are disenfranchised, denied a strategy that enables learning through collaboration, by talking with rather than to others.

## Reflections

52    These suggestions are only first steps in creating gender-fair discussions. Teachers and their students may together find other more contextually appropriate ways to address gender disparity in their own classroom activity and talk. Whatever teachers choose to do, we agree with Tobin (1988) that students should be involved in creating solutions to a problem that so directly affects their opportunities for learning and their views of each other.

## References

Alvermann, D. E. (1991). The discussion web: A graphic aid for learning across the curriculum. *The Reading Teacher,* 45, 92–99.

Alvermann, D. E., & Anders, P. A. (1994, July). *New directions for inquiry and practice: Content area literacy from a feminist/critical perspective.* Paper presented at the International Reading Association's 15th World Congress on Reading, Buenos Aires, Argentina.

Alvermann, D. E., Dillon, D. R., & O'Brien, D. G. (1987). *Using discussion to promote reading comprehension.* Newark, DE: International Reading Association.

Alvermann, D. E., & Hynd, C. R. (1989, November). *The influence of text and discussion on the learning of counter-intuitive science concepts.* Paper presented at the annual meeting of the National Reading Conference, Austin, TX.

American Association of University Women. (1992). *How schools shortchange girls: A study of major findings on girls and education.* Washington DC: Author.

Becker, J. R. (1981). Differential treatment of females and males in mathematics classes. *Journal for research in Mathematics Education,* 12, 40–53.

Carey, S., Evans, R., Honda, M., Jay, E., & Unger, C. (1989). An experiment is when you try it and see if it works: A study of grade 7 student's understanding of the construction of scientific knowledge. *International Journal of Science Education,* 11, 514–529.

Dubois, B. L., & Crouch, I. (1975). The question of tag questions in women's speech: They don't really use more of them, do they? *Language in Society,* 4, 289–294.

Edelsky, C. (1979). Question intonation and sex role. *Language in Society,* 8, 15–32.

Edelsky, C. (1981). Who's got the floor? *Language in Society,* 10, 383–421.

Gilbert, P. (1989). Personally (and passively) yours: Girls, literacy and education. *Oxford Review of Education,* 15, 257–265.

Guzzetti, B. J., Snyder, T. E., Glass, G. V. & Gamas, W. S. (1993). Promoting conceptual change in science: A comparative meta-analysis of interventions from reading education and science education. *Reading Research Quarterly,* 28, 116–159.

Guzzetti, B. J., & Williams, W. O. (1996). Gender, text, and discussion: Examining intellectual safety in the science classroom. *Journal of Research in Science Teaching,* 33, 5–20.

Hall, R., & Sadler, B. R. (1982). *The classroom climate: A chilly one for women? Project on the status of women.* Washington, DC: Association of American Colleges. (ERIC ED 215 628)

Jones, M. G., & Wheatley, J. (1990). Gender differences in teacher-student interactions in science classrooms. *Journal of Research in Science Teaching,* 27, 861–874.

Krockover, G. H, & Shepardson, S. D. P. (1995). The missing links in gender equity research. *Journal of Research in Science Teaching,* 32, 223–224.

Lafrance, M. (1991). School for scandal: Different educational experiences for females and males. *Gender and Education.* 3(12), 312.

Lakoff, R. (1975). *Language and women's place.* New York: Harper and Row.

Lemke, J. (1990). *Talking science: Language, learning and values.* Norwood, NJ: Ablex.

Meyer, D. K., & Fowler, L. A. (1993, December). *Is gender related to classroom discourse across content areas?* Paper presented at the annual meeting of the National Reading Conference, Charleston, SC.

Morse, L. W., & Handley, H. M. (1985). Listening to adolescents: Gender differences in science classroom interaction. In L. C. Wilkinson & C. B. Marrett (Eds.), *Gender influences in classroom interaction* (pp. 37–56). New York: Academic Press.

Tannen, D. (1992). How women and men use language differently in their lives and in the classroom. *The Chronicle of Higher Education,* 3–6.

Tannen, D. (1994). *Talking from 9 to 5: How women's and men's conversational styles affect who gets heard, who gets credit, and what gets done at work.* New York: Morrow.

Taylor, S. (1989). Empowering girls and young women: The challenge of the gender-inclusive curriculum. *Journal of Curriculum Studies,* 21, 441–456.

Tobin, K. (1988). Differential engagement of males and females in high school science. *International Journal of Science Education,* 10(3), 239–252.

Tobin, K., & Garnett, P. (1987). Gender related differences in science activities. *Science Education,* 71(1), 91–103.

Tromel-Plotz, S. (1985, September). *Women's conversational culture: Rupturing patriarchal discourse.* Unpublished manuscript. Roskilde Universitetscenter, Roskilde, Denmark.

## Comprehnsion Test 12*

### Checking Your Comprehension

1. What was the basic purpose of this study?

2. What was the goal of the first year of this study? The second year?

3. What was the purpose of "shills" in the whole class refutational discussions?

4. What were the basic findings of this study?

### Thinking Critically

1. In what ways do the authors believe teachers can alter their own behaviors to help eliminate gender bias in science classrooms?

2. Why do the authors favor the "Discussion Web" as a means of involving females in science debates?

3. What do the authors think is the major cause of gender inequality in science discussions? Why?

---

* Multiple-choice questions are contained in Appendix B (page A13).

## Questions for Discussion

1. It appears that males are given more opportunities to excel in high school science than females. Name and discuss a situation in which the opposite is true—that females are given an advantage over males in other academic areas.

2. If you had to come up with one additional suggestion for science teachers to soothe the gender bias problem, what would it be?

3. Do you agree that separating boys from girls in small groups results in better learning? Why?

---

**Visit the Longman English Pages**

For additional readings and exercises, visit the Longman English Skills Web page at:

**http://longman.awl.com/englishpages**

For a username and password, please see your instructor.

# Task Performance Assessment
# UNIT TWO

The following task is designed to assess your ability to use and apply the skills taught in this unit.

## THE SETTING

Assume you are taking a child and adolescent psychology course. This week you are studying the stages of cognitive development in children. Your instructor has assigned Reading Selection #7, "The Appreciation of Humor" (pp. 139–140) as an outside reading. Your next exam will be next week, and you suspect it will include a question on this reading. Read this article carefully before completing the following tasks.

## THE TASKS

1. State the thesis of this article.
2. Identify the *overall* organizational (thought) pattern used in this reading.
3. Underline the topic sentences of paragraphs 8, 9, 11, and 12.
4. Identify four transitional words or phrases in paragraphs 4 through 8.

# UNIT 3
# Reading and Learning from College Texts

College textbooks are the primary information sources in most of your college courses. The purpose of this unit is to present techniques that will enable you to read and learn from them more efficiently. First, the unit presents strategies for reading graphic and visual material within your textbooks and for becoming familiar with electronic media that accompany them. Next, it considers the organization common to most textbooks and identifies effective learning and retention systems. Finally, it describes techniques for selecting important information and for organizing that information. These techniques will improve your ability to learn most textbook material.

Chapter 7 presents strategies for using visuals, graphics, and electronic sources and for integrating them with the text of the chapters you are studying. Chapter 8 focuses on reading and recall strategies that take advantage of the organization within textbooks. Chapter 9 presents techniques for highlighting and marking textbooks, annotating and making marginal notations, as well as other methods of organizing information including paraphrasing, outlining, mapping, and summarizing.

# CHAPTER 7

# Graphic, Visual, and Electronic Literacy

IN THIS CHAPTER YOU WILL LEARN:

1. To read graphics effectively.
2. To integrate text and graphics.
3. To use electronic and multimedia sources.
4. To interpret and evaluate graphic and visual sources.

Today's textbooks and other academic sources are enhanced with a larger number of graphics than ever before. To read a textbook effectively, you must read not only the prose material, but also graphs, charts, tables, cartoons, photographs, and flowcharts. As you read and research sources outside your textbooks, you may view videotapes, visit Web sites, or use computer software and CD-ROMs. All of these learning sources require skills in reading and interpreting visual and graphic material and in integrating this material with the accompanying text. The purpose of this chapter is to equip you with visual and graphic literacy skills that will improve your reading of textbook and research materials.

For the purpose of the discussions in this book, we will define *graphics* as any visual representation that accompanies text. Graphics, then, includes all of the following: maps, charts, tables, graphs, flowcharts, cartoons, diagrams, drawings, and photographs. In addition to graphics found in books, we will also consider stand-alone visual sources of information that are not usually accompanied by print text such as films, videotapes, Web sites, CD-ROMs, and other computer software.

## ■ WHY GRAPHICS ARE USED

Graphics are typically included in textbooks, resource materials, and class instruction in order to clarify complex information and to help you further interpret it. They serve a number of important functions that enhance your reading and learning efficiency. Graphics can consolidate information, explain and illustrate ideas, or display trends, patterns, and variations.

## ■ Graphics Consolidate Information

Most graphics display information in a condensed, more easily accessible form than written material. Try this experiment. Look at Fig. 7.1 and imagine presenting the information contained in it in sentence and paragraph form. The result might be as follows:

Among adults in the United States, 91 percent identify themselves with a specific religion while 9 percent report no religious affiliation. Of those who can be identified with a specific religion, 60 percent say they are Protestants, 25 percent Catholics, 2 percent Jews, and 4 percent are affiliated with various other religions. Among Protestants, Baptists are the largest group, representing 21 percent of total U.S. religious affiliation. Methodists represent 9 percent, Lutherans 7 percent, Presbyterians 5 percent, and Episcopalians 2 percent. Other Protestant groups comprise the remaining 16 percent of U.S. adults.

You probably found this paragraph to be repetitious and tedious to read. Certainly reading this paragraph is more time consuming than studying the pie chart in Fig. 7.1. Moreover, the pie chart presents the same information more concisely and in a form that clearly shows the relationships between the individual pieces of information. To determine these relationships from the paragraph alone would require you to read closely and reread frequently.

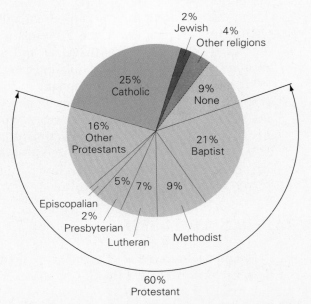

*Source:* Data from National Opinion Research Center, 1994.

**FIGURE 7.1** Religious Affiliations in the United States

## ■ Graphics Explain and Illustrate

Imagine trying to set up a computer system or to assemble a ten-speed bicycle without a schematic diagram. In a human biology course, imagine trying to understand the digestive system without diagrams to assist you. The purpose of some graphics, especially drawings, diagrams, and flowcharts, is to explain an unfamiliar and complex object or process by showing relationships among the various parts.

## ■ Graphics Dramatize Information

What could more dramatically illustrate the economic rewards of education than the following bar graph?

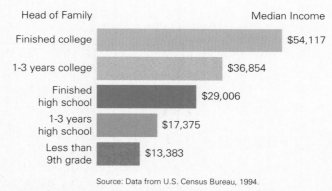

Head of Family                    Median Income

Finished college                  $54,117
1-3 years college                 $36,854
Finished high school              $29,006
1-3 years high school             $17,375
Less than 9th grade               $13,383

Source: Data from U.S. Census Bureau, 1994.

**FIGURE 7.2**  The More Education People Have, the Bigger Their Earnings.

This visual representation of income related to education level is much more powerful than simply presenting in prose form the median incomes that correspond to different educational levels. The difference between the sizes of bars in this graphic makes an immediate visual impact on the reader.

## ■ Graphics Display Trends, Patterns, and Variations

Graphics make it easy to see differences and changes. As a result, trends and patterns become clearer and more noticeable. For example, in Fig. 7.3 on the next page, you can clearly see that the more hours children watch TV per week, the lower their school achievement is. The steady descent of the trend line in this line graph after 15 hours of viewing time makes obvious this pattern of declining school achievement.

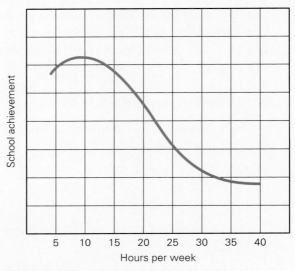

**FIGURE 7.3** Television Viewing and School Achievement

## EXERCISE 7–1

*DIRECTIONS:* Locate one graphic in one of your textbooks or in a newspaper (*USA Today* frequently includes numerous graphics). Identify which function the graphic fulfills.

## ■ A STRATEGY FOR READING GRAPHICS

When trying to read an assignment quickly, many students skip over or quickly glance at the graphics. You may tend to rely on the text that accompanies a graphic to convey its meaning, especially if you are a verbal rather than spatial learner. Doing so usually costs more time than it saves. Because graphics clarify, summarize, or emphasize important facts, concepts, and trends, you need to study them closely. Here are some general suggestions that will help you get the most out of graphic elements in the material you read.

1. **Read the title or caption**. The title tells you what situation or relationship is being described.

2. **Read the legend.** It is the explanatory caption that may accompany the graphic. The legend may also function as a key, indicating what particular colors, lines, or pictures mean.

3. **Determine how the graphic is organized.** If you are working with a table, note the column headings. For a graph, notice what is marked on the vertical and horizontal axes (top to bottom and left to right lines).

4. **Determine what variables the graphic is concerned with.** Identify the pieces of information that are being compared or the relationship that is being shown.

5. **Note any symbols and abbreviations used.**

6. **Determine the scale or unit of measurement.** Note how the variables are measured. For example, does a graph show expenditures in dollars, thousands of dollars, or millions of dollars?

7. **Identify the trend(s), pattern(s), or relationships the graphic is intended to show.** The following sections discuss this step in greater detail.

8. **Read any footnotes.** Footnotes, printed at the bottom of a graph or chart, indicate how the data were collected, explain what certain numbers or headings mean, and describe the statistical procedures used.

9. **Check the source.** The source of data is usually cited at the bottom of the graph or chart. Unless the information was collected by the author, you are likely to find a research journal or publication from which the data were taken. Identifying the source is helpful in assessing the reliability of the data.

10. **Make a brief summary note.** In the margin, jot a brief note about the trend or pattern the graphic emphasizes. Writing will crystallize the idea in your mind, and your note will be useful when you review.

## ■ INTEGRATING TEXT AND GRAPHICS

In both textbooks and reference sources, most graphics do not stand alone; they have corresponding printed text that may explain, summarize, or analyze the graphic. Be sure to consider the text and the graphic together to get their complete meaning.

Here are some guidelines for integrating text and graphics.

1. **Notice the type and number of graphics included in the material as you preread the chapter (see Chapter 2).**

2. **Refer to the graphic when the author directs you to.** Writers tell you when they want you to look at the graphic by saying, "See Figure 17.2" or by introducing the graphic, "Table 9.7 displays. . ."

3. **Read the graphic, using the previously listed steps**.

4. **Move back and forth between the text and graphic**. As you study the graphic, especially if it is a diagram or illustration, refer back to the text as needed, checking the meaning or function of particular terms or parts.

5. **Determine why the text writer included the graphic**. Ask these questions:
   - What am I supposed to learn from this graphic?
   - Why was it included?
   - What new information does the graphic contain?
   - On what topic did the graphic provide more detail or further explanation?

Let's look at an example. The following passage and its corresponding graphic were taken from an anatomy textbook chapter on accessory organs of the skin. Read the passage and study the corresponding diagram using the suggested techniques.

*Hairs* or *pili* are variously distributed over the body. Their primary function is protection. Hair on the head guards the scalp from injury and the sun's rays; eyebrows and eyelashes protect the eyes from foreign particles; hair in the nostrils protects against inhaling insects and foreign particles.

Each hair is a thread of fused, keratinized cells that consists of a shaft and a root [Figure 7.4]. The *shaft* is the superficial portion, most of which projects above the surface of the skin. The *root* is the portion below the surface that penetrates into the dermis and even into the subcutaneous layer. Surrounding the root is the *hair follicle,* which is composed of two layers of epidermal cells: external and internal root sheaths surrounded by a connective tissue sheath.

The base of each follicle is enlarged into an onion-shaped structure, the *bulb.* This structure contains an indentation, the *papilla of the hair,* which contains many blood vessels and provides nourishment for the growing hair. The bulb also contains a region of cells called the *matrix,* which produces new hairs by cell division when older hairs are shed.

Each hair follicle goes through a *growth cycle,* which consists of a *growth stage* and a *resting stage.* During the growth stage, a hair is formed by cells of the matrix that differentiate, become keratinized, and die. As new cells are added at the base of the hair root, the hair grows longer. In time, the growth of the hair stops and the resting stage begins. During this time, the matrix is inactive and the hair follicle shortens. After the resting stage, a new growth cycle begins in which a new hair

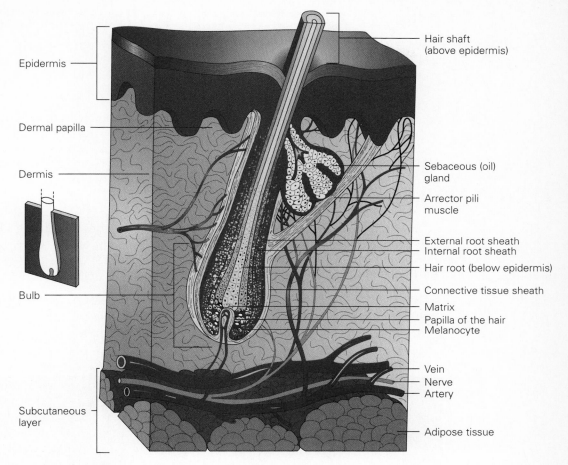

Longitudinal section of a hair

**FIGURE 5.4**  Principal Parts of a Hair Root and Associated Structures

replaces the old hair and the old hair is pushed out of the hair follicle. In general, scalp hair grows for about three years and rests for about one to two years.

Associated with hairs is a bundle of smooth muscle called *arrector pili.* It is located along the side of the hair follicle. These muscles contract under stresses of fright and cold, pulling the hairs into a vertical position and resulting in "goosebumps" or "gooseflesh."

Tortora, *Introduction to the Human Body.*

● ● ●

Did you find yourself going back and forth frequently between the text and the diagram? This text excerpt and diagram illustrate the back-and-forth reading that is often necessary when reading detailed information.

## EXERCISE 7–2

*DIRECTIONS:* Answer the following questions in reference to the text "Hair" and its corresponding diagram.

1. What was the purpose of the diagram?
2. What did you learn from it that was not stated in the text?
3. What ideas stated in the text did the diagram make easier for you to understand?

## ■ TYPES OF GRAPHICS

Many types of graphics are used in textbooks. Besides describing some type of relationship, each type achieves particular purposes for the writer.

### ■ Photographs

Photographs are included in texts for a variety of reasons. A writer may include photographs to add interest or to help you visualize an event, concept, or feeling. Photographs may provide an example of a concept.

**FIGURE 7.5** What is considered abnormal or deviant in one culture may be viewed as quite normal and acceptable in another. One simple example is how people of various cultures dress.

Photographs in a biology textbook may be used to illustrate variation among species, for instance. Photographs may be used to create emotional responses. For example, in discussing the problem of poverty and famine in developing countries, a writer may include a photograph of a malnourished child to help readers visualize those conditions and sympathize with the victims. Or, to create an appreciation of the intricate and beautiful carvings discovered at an archaeological site, a photograph of the carvings may be included. Take time to study photographs to determine what ideas or concepts they illustrate. These visual aids provide important clues to what the author considers to be important.

When studying photographs, read the caption. It may provide clues to the importance or meaning of the photograph. The pair of photographs in Figure 7.5 could be confusing without the captions. This caption helps you to visualize the dramatic contrast between what different cultures regard as normal dress.

## EXERCISE 7–3

*DIRECTIONS:* Study the photograph shown in Fig. 7.6 and answer the questions that follow.

1. What is this photograph intended to illustrate?
2. What does it show that a verbal description could not?

**FIGURE 7.6**  Children can inherit the debts of their parents and be forced to work alongside them in debt slavery. This Pakastani child will spend his life in fields of mud, making bricks.

## ■ Maps

There are two types of maps: locational and thematic. Locational maps are intended to show the exact positions of physical objects: countries, cities, states, rivers, mountains, and so forth. You will find these maps in history, astronomy, geography, archaeology, and anthropology texts. To read these types of maps, concentrate on each item's position in relation to other objects. For instance, when referring to a map of our galaxy in an astronomy text, concentrate on the locations of planets relative to each other, of the planets to the sun and moon, and so forth.

Thematic maps provide statistical or factual information about a particular area or region. A color coded map of the United States may be used to show mean income levels within each state. A map of Africa may be coded to represent the form of government of each country.

When reading thematic maps, look for trends or patterns. When studying a map of the United States showing mean income levels, you should look for regional clusters or patterns. Are incomes higher in the North or South? Are they higher in highly populated states such as New York and California or in lower population states such as Montana or Idaho? When reading the map of Africa showing types of government, you should look for most and least common forms and try to discover regional similarities. Do the northern or eastern countries, for example, have similar forms of government?

## EXERCISE 7–4

*DIRECTIONS:* Study the map shown in Fig. 7.7 and answer the questions that follow.

1.  What is the purpose of this map?

2.  What type of map is this?

3.  Which had the larger number of female congressional members in 1970, the east coast or west coast states?

4.  Which had the larger number in 1994?

5.  About what percent of the states had female Congress members by 1994?

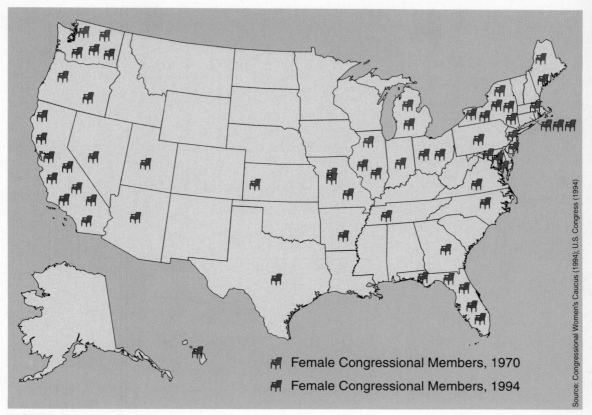

Female Congressional Members, 1970

Female Congressional Members, 1994

Source: Congressional Women's Caucus (1994); U.S. Congress (1994)

**FIGURE 7.7**   Females in Congress, 1970 and 1994

## ■ Tables

A table displays facts, figures, statistics, and other data in a condensed orderly sequence for convenience of reference and clarity. The information in tables is classified or organized so that the data can easily be compared.

Use the following steps when reading tables:

1. Determine how the data are classified or divided.

2. Make comparisons and look for trends.

3. Draw conclusions.

Figure 7.8 on page 246, a table taken from a sociology text, displays three sets of data that compare Japan with four other countries. By scan-

How Japan Compares with Others

Japan is ahead in national economic power:

| | Average GNP* Per Person |
|---|---|
| Japan | $27,300 |
| Germany | $24,700 |
| United States | $22,200 |
| France | $21,300 |
| Britain | $17,600 |

But the Japanese individual's welfare falls behind:

| Amount of housing space per person, in square meters | | Average working hours per year | |
|---|---|---|---|
| United States | 61.8 | Germany | 1,590 |
| Germany | 37.2 | France | 1,680 |
| Britain | 35.2 | United States | 1,940 |
| France | 30.7 | Britain | 1,950 |
| Japan | 25.0 | Japan | 2,210 |

*Gross National Product
*Source:* Japanese and German government reports

**FIGURE 7.8**  A Sample Table

ning the table you can easily see that Japan is a leader in economic growth, as measured by GNP (gross national product), but lags behind other countries in housing space and leisure time.

# EXERCISE 7–5

*DIRECTIONS:* Answer the following questions based on the table shown in Fig. 7.9.

1. How are the data in this table organized?
2. In which city can you buy the cheapest cup of coffee?
3. In which city do clothing items appear to be most expensive?

**Shopper's Guide**

| | New York | London | Paris | Tokyo | Mexico City |
|---|---|---|---|---|---|
| Aspirin (100 tablets) | $0.99 | $1.23 | $7.07 | $6.53 | $1.78 |
| Cup of coffee | $1.25 | $1.50 | $2.10 | $2.80 | $0.91 |
| Movie | $7.50 | $10.50 | $7.89 | $17.29 | $4.55 |
| Compact disc | $12.99 | $14.99 | $23.16 | $22.09 | $13.91 |
| Levi's 501 jeans | $39.99 | $74.92 | $75.40 | $79.73 | $54.54 |
| Ray-Ban sunglasses | $45.00 | $88.50 | $81.23 | $134.49 | $89.39 |
| Sony Walkman (mid-range) | $59.95 | $74.98 | $86.00 | $211.34 | $110.00 |
| Nike Air Jordans | $125.00 | $134.99 | $157.71 | $172.91 | $154.24 |
| Gucci men's loafers | $275.00 | $292.50 | $271.99 | $605.19 | $157.27 |
| Nikon camera | $629.95 | $840.00 | $691.00 | $768.49 | $1,054.42 |

Source: M. D. Fefer, "Tourists and Bargains Galore," Fortune, June 13, 1994, p. 12.

**FIGURE 7.9**  Comparison of Prices for Selected Items in Five World Capitals

4. Of these five cities, which one is generally the least expensive to shop in?
5. Which is generally the most expensive?

## ■ Graphs

A graph clarifies the relationship between two or more sets of information. A graph often reveals a trend or pattern that is easily recognizable in visual form but not as obvious when the data appear in list or paragraph form. Several types of graphs are described in the following sections.

### Bar graphs

A bar graph is often used to compare quantities or amounts. It is especially useful in showing changes that occur over time. Bar graphs are often included in texts to emphasize differences. The graph shown in Fig. 7.10 displays the number of communication appliances owned per 1000 people in five different countries and emphasizes the differences in ownership among them.

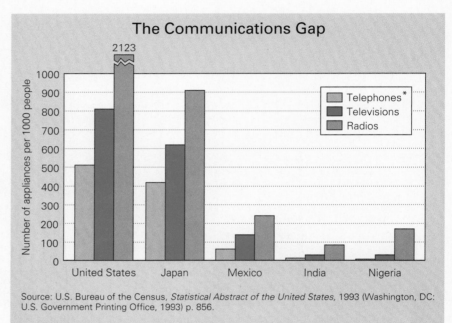

Source: U.S. Bureau of the Census, *Statistical Abstract of the United States,* 1993 (Washington, DC: U.S. Government Printing Office, 1993) p. 856.

*Indicates telephone lines, not individual telephones.

**FIGURE 7.10** The Communications Gap

When reading bar graphs, pay particular attention to differences in amount between the variables. Notice which variables have the largest and smallest differences and try to think of reasons that account for the differences.

## EXERCISE 7–6

*DIRECTIONS:* Study the bar graph shown in Fig. 7.11 and answer the following questions.

1. What is the purpose of this graph?

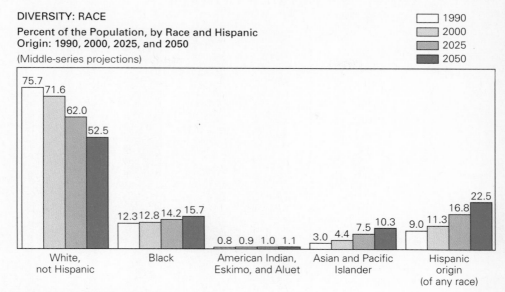

DIVERSITY: RACE

Percent of the Population, by Race and Hispanic
Origin: 1990, 2000, 2025, and 2050

(Middle-series projections)

□ 1990
▨ 2000
▨ 2025
▨ 2050

*Source:* Bureau of the Census, 1995.

**FIGURE 7.11** Diversity: Race
Percent of the Population, by Race and Hispanic Origin: 1990, 2000, 2025, and 2050

2. Which group will decrease in percent of the U.S. population between 1990 and 2050?
3. Which group will show the largest percentage increase over these years?
4. Which group will have the smallest percentage increase over these years?

### Stacked bar graphs

In a stacked bar graph, instead of arranging bars side by side, they are placed one on top of the other as in Fig. 7.12 on page 250.

The stacked bar graph is often used to emphasize whole/part relationships. That is, it shows the component parts that make up a total. In Fig. 7.12 the whole represents all employment in the United States from 1900 to 2000, while the parts are the four categories of possible jobs: white collar, service, blue collar, and farm.

Because stacked bar graphs are intended to make numerous comparisons, study the graph carefully to be sure you "see" all possible relationships. For example, in Fig. 7.12 be sure you see the decline in blue collar and farm jobs as well as the increase in white collar positions.

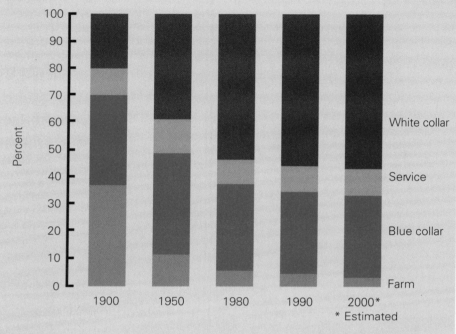

Source: *Employment and Training Report of the President* (Washington, D.C.: Government Printing Office, various years).

**FIGURE 7.12** White-collar positions are increasing while blue-collar and farm jobs are declining.

### Line graphs

In line graphs, information is plotted along a vertical and a horizontal axis, with one or more variables plotted on each. A line graph plots and connects points along these axes. A line graph usually includes more data points than a bar graph. Consequently, it is often used to present detailed and/or large quantities of information. If a line graph compares only two variables, then it consists of a single line. More often, however, line graphs compare two or more variables, and multiple lines are used. The line graph in Fig. 7.13 compares four categories of expenditures in the United States budget.

Line graphs are often used to display continuous data—data that connects time or events that occur in a sequence. You can see this in Fig. 7.13, which displays the levels of expenditures from 1967 to 1997.

Line graphs can display one of three general relationships: positive, negative, or independent. Each of these is shown in Fig. 7.14.

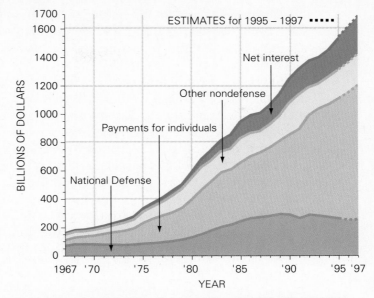

*Source: Budget of the United States Government, Fiscal Year 1996: Historical Tables.*

**FIGURE 7.13**   Federal Expenditures

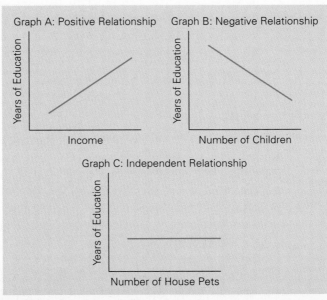

**FIGURE 7.14**   Linear Graphic Relationships

*Postive relationships.* When the variables increase or decrease at the same time, the relationship is positive and is shown by a line that climbs up from left to right. In graph A, as years in school increase, so does income.

*Inverse (or negative) relationships.* When one variable increases and the other decreases, the relationship is inverse or negative. In graph B, as the years of education increase, the number of children decreases.

*Independent relationships.* When the variables have no effect on each other, the relationship is independent. In graph C, years in school have no effect on number of house pets. Once you discover the trend and the nature of the relationship a linear graph describes, jot them down in the margin for review later.

To read line graphs, look for upward or downward trends and positive or negative relationships. Notice when the line(s) begin to rise or fall and try to think of reasons that may account for the increase or decline.

## EXERCISE 7–7

*DIRECTIONS:* What type of relationship (positive, inverse, or linear) would each of the following linear graphs show?

1. In a graph plotting effective use of study time versus college course grades, what type of relationship would you expect?
2. In a graph plotting time spent reading versus time spent playing tennis, what relationship would you predict?
3. What type of relationship would be shown by a graph plotting time spent checking a dictionary for unknown words versus reading speed?

### Circle graphs

A circle graph, also called a pie chart, is used to show whole/part relationships or to show how parts of a unit have been divided or classified. They illustrate what part of a total a particular variable represents. Circle graphs often emphasize proportions or emphasize the relative size or importance of various parts. The whole circle represents 100 percent or the total amount of something. The pieces of the pie show the relative size or proportion of particular parts of that whole. The larger the piece of the pie, the larger portion of the total it represents.

Figure 7.15 shows the racial composition of the United States. It shows the various racial groups and portions of our population comprised by them.

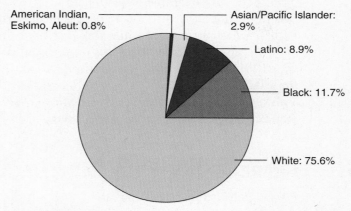

## A GROWING DIVERSITY

American Indian, Eskimo, Aleut: 0.8%

Asian/Pacific Islander: 2.9%

Latino: 8.9%

Black: 11.7%

White: 75.6%

*Source: Washington Post,* 1991.

**FIGURE 7.15** Racial Composition of the United States: A Growing Diversity

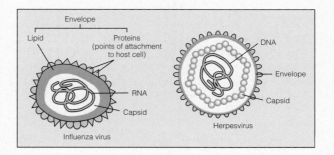

Envelope

Lipid

Proteins (points of attachment to host cell)

DNA

RNA

Envelope

Capsid

Capsid

Herpesvirus

Influenza virus

**The Structure of Viruses**
Viruses are extremely small particles that infect cells and cause many human diseases. Their basic structure includes an outer envelope, composed of lipid and protein, a protein capsid, and genetic material that is enclosed within the capsid.

**FIGURE 7.16** The Structure of Viruses

### *Diagrams*

A diagram is a drawing that explains an object, idea, or process by outlining, in visual form, parts or steps or by showing the item's organization. The purpose of a diagram, as with tables and charts, is to simplify and clarify the writer's explanation and to help you visualize the item diagrammed. For example, the diagram from a biology text in Fig. 7.16 describes the structure of two common viruses. This diagram clearly explains their structures while showing their differences.

To read a diagram, focus on its purpose. What is it intended to illustrate? Why did the author include it? To study a diagram, cover the diagram and try to draw it and label its parts without reference to the text. This activity will provide a good test of whether or not you truly understand the process or concept illustrated.

## EXERCISE 7–8

*DIRECTIONS:* Study the diagram shown in Figure 7.17 and answer these questions.

1. What is the purpose of the diagram?

   _____

2. What does it reveal about the lifestyle of wealthy Muslim families?

   _____

3. Why is this diagram more useful than a verbal description?

   _____

## EXERCISE 7–9

*DIRECTIONS:* Draw a diagram that illustrates one of the following.

a. the registration process at your college
b. a process explained in one of your textbooks
c. the floor plan of your library's reference section
d. an object described in one of your textbooks

## ■ Charts

Three types of charts are commonly used in college textbooks: organizational charts, flowcharts, and pictograms. Each is intended to display a relationship, either quantitative or cause-effect.

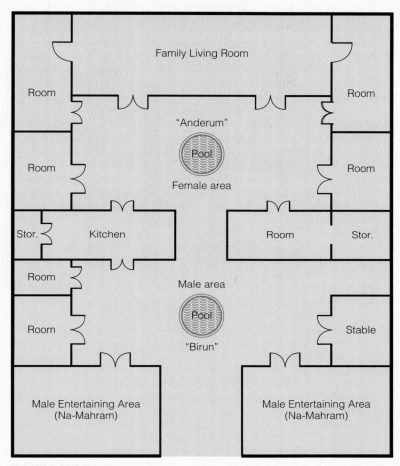

**FIGURE 7.17** Plan of a traditional wealthy Muslim family home. The female area of the house (*anderum*) is located in the more private portions of the house toward the back, while the male area (*birun*) is in the more public, anterior portion of the house.(*Source: Daphne Spain, Gendered Spaces*)

## *Organizational Charts*

An organizational chart divides an organization, such as a corporation, hospital, or university, into its administrative parts, staff positions, or lines of authority. Figure 7.18 on page 256 shows a particular type of departmental organization in a corporation called matrix departmentalization. It shows levels of authority from the level of general manager to department

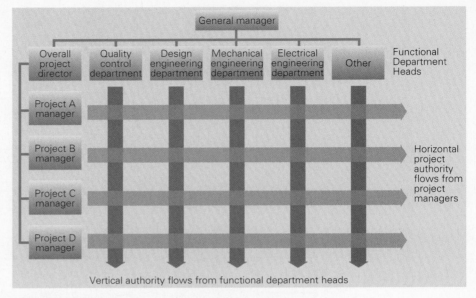

**FIGURE 7.18** Example of Matrix Departmentalization

heads and finally to project managers. It depicts how authority flows in this special type of organization.

### Flowcharts

A flowchart is a specialized type of chart that shows how a process or procedure works. Lines or arrows are used to indicate the direction (route or routes) through the procedure. Various shapes (boxes, circles, rectangles) enclose what is done at each stage or step. You could draw, for example, a flowchart to describe how to apply for and obtain a student loan or how to locate a malfunction in your car's electrical system. The flowchart shown in Fig. 7.19 taken from a management textbook, describes how a business is formed and operated. The chart provides you with a road map of the entrepreneurial process and describes the parts of this process and the steps to be followed.

To read flowcharts effectively, use the following suggestions.

1. Decide what process the flowchart shows.

2. Next, follow the chart, using the arrows and reading each step. Start at the top or far left of the chart.

3. When you've finished, describe the process in your own words. Try to draw the chart from memory without referring to the text. Compare your drawing with the chart and take note of anything you forgot or misplaced.

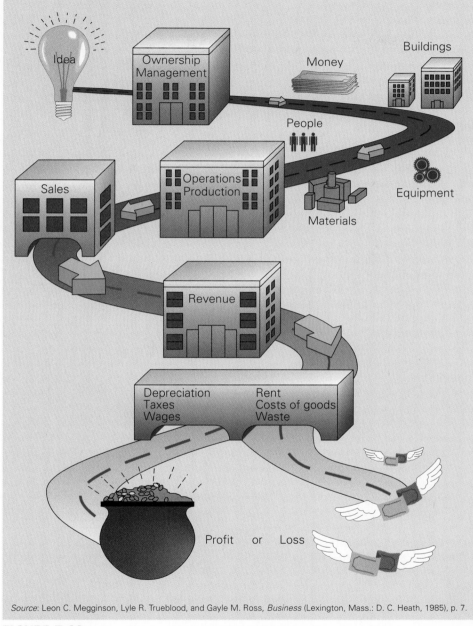

*Source*: Leon C. Megginson, Lyle R. Trueblood, and Gayle M. Ross, *Business* (Lexington, Mass.: D. C. Heath, 1985), p. 7.

**FIGURE 7.19**    How a Business is Formed and Operates

### Pictograms

A pictogram is a combination of a chart and graph, and uses symbols or drawings (such as books, cars, or buildings) instead of lines, bars, or numbers to represent specified amounts. This type of chart tends to be visually appealing, makes statistics seem realistic, and may carry an emotional impact. For example, a chart that uses stick figure drawings of children to indicate the infant mortality rate per country may have a more significant impact than statistics presented in table form. A sample pictogram is shown in Fig. 7.20. This pictogram uses coins to represent thousands of dollars of per capita income. It compares the incomes of individuals in three industrialized countries with those in three less developed countries.

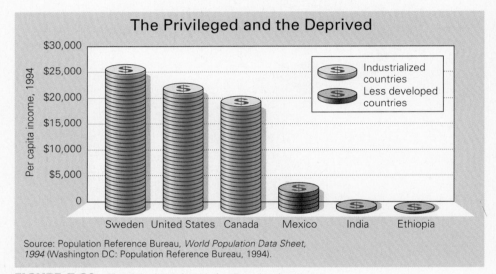

Source: Population Reference Bureau, *World Population Data Sheet, 1994* (Washington DC: Population Reference Bureau, 1994).

**FIGURE 7.20** The Priveleged and the Deprived

### Cartoons

Cartoons are included in textbooks to make a point quickly or simply to lighten the text by adding a touch of humor about the topic at hand. Cartoons usually appear without a title or legend and there is usually no reference within the text to the cartoon.

Cartoons can make abstract ideas and concepts concrete and real. Pay close attention to cartoons, especially if you are a visual-oriented learner. They may help you recall ideas easily by serving as a recall clue that triggers your memory of related material.

FAMILIES

"I guess we'd be considered a family. We're living together, we love each other, and we haven't eaten the children yet."

Drawing by S. Gross; © 1993 The New Yorker Magazine, Inc.

**FIGURE 7.21**

The cartoon shown in Fig. 7.21 appears in a cultural anthropology textbook chapter titled "Families." It appears on a text page that defines the family and discusses types of families, nuclear and extended.

## EXERCISE 7–10

*DIRECTIONS:* Indicate what type of graphic(s) would be most useful in presenting each of the following sets of information.

1. The effects of flooding on a Midwestern town.
2. The top five soft drink brands by percent of marketshare.
3. Changes in yearly per capita income from 1975 to 1995 in Germany, France, Japan, and the United States.

4. The suicide rates for various age groups.
5. The top 20 places to live in the United States and their average income, cost of housing, quality of schools, level of taxes, amount of crime, and availability of cultural and recreational activities.
6. Government spending in 1992 and 1996 for payments to individuals, defense, interest on debt, grants to state and local governments, and all other spending.
7. The basic parts of a solar powered automobile.
8. A description of how acid rain affects the environment.
9. The main areas of earthquakes and volcanic activity throughout the world.
10. Book sales in each of 10 categories for the years 1993 through 1997.

## ■ STRATEGIES FOR LEARNING FROM VISUAL AND ELECTRONIC MEDIA

College instructors are increasingly using a variety of instructional media to supplement their textbook and lecture material. These include television, film, video, CD-ROM, computer tutorials, and the Internet. In fact, some college texts are accompanied by a CD-ROM or computerized tutorial for student use outside the classroom. In other courses you may be encouraged or required to use Internet sources or to communicate with your instructor by e-mail. Technology is playing an increasingly important role in education. This section provides suggestions for working with and learning from electronic learning sources and resources.

### ■ Film, Video, and Television

Your instructor may show a video, film, slide presentation, or television program segment in class. Others might assign the class to view it on their own time and could require a brief written summary or critique. The most important step in viewing and learning from these sources is to determine what you are supposed to learn from them. Instructors use visual media to accomplish a variety of purposes. Among the most common are:

- **to make abstract ideas concrete and tangible.** To illustrate how an infant learns language, a child development instructor may show a series of film clips of the child speaking at different ages.

- **to demonstrate principles or procedures.** A nursing instructor may show a video of the correct procedure for drawing a blood sample.

## Computer Tutorials

Computer tutorials accompany some textbooks. This software is usually available from your instructor or the college's academic computer lab. Their main purpose is often to provide practice and application of skills or concepts taught in the textbook. For example, a physiology textbook may have software that helps you learn the functions and parts of each of the body's systems (circulatory, digestive, immune, and so forth). Software for an algebra text may contain review of various algebraic functions, activities and games, and review quizzes. Here are some suggestions for making the best use of available software.

1. **Try whatever is available.** Even if you've never used a computer before, if software is available, try it out. College computer labs are usually staffed with friendly, helpful people (sometimes other students) who can show you how to get started.

2. **Keep a record of your progress on quizzes.** Many programs will do this for you and allow you to print a progress report. This record will enable you to see your strengths and weaknesses, plan further study, and review troublesome topics.

3. **Space out your practice.** Because many software programs are fun and engaging, some students work on them for hours at a time. To get maximum benefit from the time you are spending, limit your work to an hour or so. Beyond that, many activities become routine, your mind switches to "automatic pilot," and learning ceases to occur.

4. **Consolidate your learning.** When you finish a module or program segment, do not just exit and shut the machine off. Stop and reflect on what you have learned. If you worked on an algebra module about the multiplication of polynomials, then stop and recall the techniques you've learned. Write notes or summarize the process in a separate section of your course notebook reserved for this purpose.

## ■ Internet Sources

The Internet is a worldwide network of computers through which you can access a wide variety of information and services. Through the Internet, you can access the World Wide Web (a network of networks), a service that connects this vast array of resources. Many instructors use the Internet and have begun requiring their students to do so. In many cases, the Internet has become a visual medium. Many sources use graphics and photographs to present and display information. Here is an overview of the services your instructor may ask you to access:

### *E-Mail (electronic mail)*

E-mail (electronic mail) enables you to send messages from one person or place to another by using your computer. A variety of computer programs are available that allow you to send and receive messages electronically, as well as to print them for future reference. There are many academic uses for e-mail. Students in a class may collaborate on a project or critique each others' papers using e-mail. Other times, instructors and students may communicate through e-mail. In completing a research paper, it is possible to contact professors or other students doing research on the topic you are studying. It is also possible to transmit word processing files by attaching them to an e-mail message.

Most e-mail follows a consistent format and, consequently, is easy to read. Messages begin with a memo format in which the topic of the message, date the message was sent, sender, and receiver are identified as "Subject" or "Re," "Date," "From," and "To." The message follows this introductory identifying information. Following the message is transmittal information that tracks the electronic path through which the message was sent. This information can be ignored unless you wish to verify the source of the sender.

The style of e-mail messages tends to be more casual and conversational than the traditional print forms of communication (letters and memos) but more formal than phone or in-person conversations. Because e-mail is intended to be a rapid, expedient means of communication, some formalities of written communication are relaxed. Expect to find a briefer introduction, more concise sentences, and few or no concluding remarks. Consequently, e-mail requires close attention; unlike print forms of communication, there is little repetition and fewer cues as to what is important.

---

Subj:    Research on learning styles
Date:    98-02-23  11:49:34 EST
From:    Maryrod@daemon.edu   (Mary Rodriguez)
Reply to: Maryrod@daemon.edu
To:      KateApp@daemon.edu


Dear Kate,
In response to your request for recent research on the learning styles of university versus community college students, I do know of one article that may be useful as a starting point:
Henson, Mark and Schemeck, R.R.   "Learning Styles of Community College Versus University Students." <u>Perceptual Motor Skills,</u> 76(1),  118.
Good luck on your research project.
Mary

---

**FIGURE 7.22**   A Sample E-Mail Message

Reading lengthy e-mail messages may be easier if you print them first. Figure 7.22 shows a sample e-mail message. Notice that the message is a concise yet effective form of communication.

### Web Sites

A Web site is a location on the World Wide Web where you can obtain information on a particular subject. It is a collection of related pages stored together. You can move around the site from page to page by clicking on specially marked pages on the screen called *links*. Each page is called a *Web page* and stands for a set of information. (It can be any length and is not restricted to a single screen or printed page.) The first page you see when you access a Web site is called its home page.

Major corporations such as Hertz, Burger King, and General Motors have Web sites, as do many universities, government agencies, and local businesses. A sample homepage for Nike footwear is shown in Figure 7.23. Notice that this site offers news and information as well as product descriptions.

**FIGURE 7.23** A Sample Homepage

Web sites have recently been established by textbook publishers and authors to provide information and activities that supplement the text. A Web site for a biology text, for example, may contain reviews of recent research and discoveries not included in the text. A Web site for an English composition textbook may contain additional current readings or up-to-date information on using and evaluating electronic sources or exercises that relate to specific portions of the textbook. Web sites also provide interesting links, or connections, that direct you to other Web sites that offer related information. Web sites are useful sources of information when researching a topic. An excerpt from a Web site sponsored by Saint Mary's College is shown in Figure 7.24. It is intended as a resource for students to help them locate library resources in the field of sociology.

**Faculty and Academics** — Saint Mary's College

### Sociology

"The focus of sociology is the structure and the process of social life in contemporary American society. It addresses pressing social issues such as race, gender, age, and poverty, and examines the impact that cultural, structural, and socio-historical forces have on society, the group, and the individual". Saint Mary's College 1995-1997 Catalog.

**Saint Mary's College Library Resources**

- Albert - search for book, periodical, video, & multimedia holdings at Saint Mary's College Library
- Infotrac - search for articles in periodicals at Saint Mary's College Library
- Information available at saint Mary's College Library
  - Sociology

**Internet Resources**

- General Resources
- Journals
- Statistics, Polls, and Social Science Date Sets
- Special Topics
  - Aging
  - Crime
  - Demography and Population
  - Family and Children

**General**

- A Sociological Tour Through Cyperspace - a web document with information and many links to WWW resources in Sociology. Created by Michael Kearl, Professor of Sociology, Trinity University, TX. A great starting point!

- SocioSite - (Sociological Institute, University of Amsterdam) A comprehensive collection of WWW Sociology Links. Select "Subject Areas" for links to resources in a broad array of subjects related to Soc iology.

- SocioWeb - also provides access to many useful Sociology sites.

- Sociologists Page - Links to information about major sociological thinkers including excerpts from their writings. (Sociological Institute of the University of Amsterdam).

**FIGURE 7.24** A Sample Web Site

## EXERCISE 7–12

*DIRECTIONS:* Visit a Web site sponsored by an educational institution and a Web site sponsored by a corporation. Then answer the following questions.

1. What is the purpose of each site?
2. In what ways are they similar and in what ways do they differ?

### Web Site Addresses

Each Web site has its own address, known as its URL (Uniform Resource Locator). Here's how to read a URL for the *San Francisco Chronicles:*

transfer format    host computer    directory path    file name

http: // www. sfgate.com / chronicle / index.shtmL

The transfer format identifies the type of server the document is located on and indicates the type of transfer format that is to be used. The second names the host computer. The directory path is the "address" part of the Web site. The last is the document name.

Many sites can be contacted using only the transfer format and the host computer address. Then once you've contacted the site, you can move to different directions and files within the Web site.

Anyone can place a Web site on the Internet. Consequently, you must be cautious and verify that the sources are reliable. See "Evaluating Internet Sources," on page 268.

Examining a Web site address can help you evaluate the source. Commercial sources usually have < .com > as part of the host computer address; colleges and universities and other educational institutions are labeled < .edu >, government agencies are identified by < .gov >, < .net > refers to a network, and < .org > refers to an organization. Thus the URL can help you distinguish educational, governmental, and commercial sources.

### Reading a Web site

The home page, which is the master directory of the Web site, is the key to reading and using the site effectively. It may contain an identifying logo and will offer an overview of what you will find on other connected pages at the site and may suggest links to other Web sites.

A Web page usually contains a heading, called a header, that serves as a title for the information on that page. It usually appears in bigger, bolder type than the rest of the text on the page. These headers serve as valuable, concise descriptions of the contents of the page. Use them to decide whether the page contains the information you need and if it is worth reading.

Web sites are well suited for skimming; see Chapter 13. You can scroll through a Web page by using the down arrow ( ↓ ) or page down key.

### Newsgroups

Newsgroups are collections of people interested in a particular topic or issue and who correspond and discuss it. Participants post messages on a given topic; other participants read and respond. Read postings with a critical mind-set. Most postings are written by average people expressing their opinions; their ideas may be informative, but they may also contain incorrect information, bias, and unsubstantiated opinion. At times, you also may find postings that are mindless ranting and raving. Here are some tips for reading newsgroup postings.

- Separate fact from opinion. (See Chapter 11, p. 392)

- Take into account the bias, motivation, and prejudices of the poster.

- Verify any information you get from a newsgroup with a second source.

Usually newsgroups are open forums; anyone can lurk or "listen in" to the discussion. Newsgroups can yield additional sources of information, as well as a variety of interesting perspectives on a topic.

Electronic Application

## EXERCISE 7–13

*DIRECTIONS:* Visit a newsgroup and either lurk or participate in the discussion. Then answer the following questions.

1. What was the topic of discussion?
2. Were the postings largely fact or opinion?
3. Did you detect bias or prejudice?
4. How useful is the newsgroup as a source of information?

## ■ Evaluating Internet Sources

While the Internet contains a great deal of valuable information and resources, it also contains rumor, gossip, hoaxes, and misinformation. In other words, not all Internet sources are trustworthy. You must evaluate a source before accepting it. Here are some guidelines to follow when evaluating Internet sources.

1. **Check the author.** For Web sites, look for professional credentials or affiliations. If no author is listed, you should be skeptical. For newsgroups or discussion groups, check to see if the author has given his or her name and a signature (a short biographical description included at the end of messages).

2. **Discover the purpose of the posting.** Many Web sites are written with an agenda such as to sell a product, promote a cause, advocate a position, and so forth. Look for bias in the reporting of information.

3. **Check the date of the posting.** Be sure you are obtaining current information. Web sites usually include the date on which it was last updated.

4. **Check the sponsoring organization of the site.** If a site is sponsored or provided by a well-known organization, such as a reputable newspaper such as *The New York Times,* the information is apt to be reliable.

### Critical Thinking Tip #7

### Analyzing Statistics

The purpose of many graphs, charts, and tables, whether in electronic or print sources, is to display statistics in an easy-to-read format. A critical reader should look as closely at statistics as at any other type of information. Although statistics may seem like "hard facts," they can be misleading and deceiving.

Here is an example: Many graphics report averages—average salaries, average costs, average weights, or average educational levels. Did you know that an average can be computed three different ways with, at times, three very different results? The terms *median, mode,* and *mean* all are used to report averages. Let's say you want to report the average temperature for one week in your town or city. The daily temperatures are 69, 70, 70, 94, 95, 95, and 96.

The mean temperature is 84.1.

The median temperature is 94.

The mode is 70.

These are very different numbers. Here's how they are calculated:

*Mean*—total the daily temperatures and divide by 7.

*Median*—arrange the temperatures from low to high and take the middlemost temperature (the one with three higher and three lower temperatures.)

*Mode*—choose the temperature that occurs most frequently.

This is just one example of why caution is needed when interpreting statistics. There are many others. (In the example, for instance, how was the daily temperature calculated? Was it the daily high, daily low, 24-hour "average"?)

Because statistics are subject to manipulation and interpretation, study graphics with a questioning and critical eye.

5. **Check links (addresses of other sources suggested by the Web site.)** If these links are no longer working, the Web site you are visiting may be outdated or not reputable.

6. **Cross-check your information.** Try to find the same information in, ideally, two other sources, especially if the information is vitally important (issues dealing with health, financial discussion, etc.) or if it is at odds with what seems logical or correct.

## EXERCISE 7–14

*DIRECTIONS:* Visit a Web site and become familiar with its organization and content. Evaluate it using the suggested criteria. Then write a brief paragraph explaining why the Web site is or is not a reliable source.

## SUMMARY

**1. Why are graphics included in your courses?**

Graphics serve a number of different functions in your courses. They are used to:
- consolidate information
- explain and illustrate ideas
- dramatize information
- display trends, patterns, and variations

**2. What steps should you take to read graphics more effectively?**

To get the most from all types of graphics you should begin by reading the title or caption and determining how the graphic is organized; what symbols, abbreviations, and variables are presented; and what scale, values, or units of measurement are being used. You should then study the data to identify trends, patterns, and relationships within the graphic. Note any explanatory footnotes and the source of the data. Finally, making marginal notes will aid your further reading or review.

**3. How can you integrate graphics with their corresponding printed text?**

To integrate text and graphics:
- Be alert to the graphics as you preread chapters.

**4. What types of graphics are commonly used in textbooks and academic sources?**

**5. What types of visual and electronic media are used in college courses?**

- Refer to each graphic when you are directed to.
- Read the graphic carefully.
- Move back and forth between text and graphic frequently.
- Find out why the graphic was included.

Many types of graphics are used in conjunction with print materials. They include photographs, maps, tables, graphs, diagrams, charts, pictograms, and cartoons.

College instructors are using a wide range of visual media to supplement textbooks and their lectures. These include the more traditional films, videos, slides, and television programs, as well as electronic learning aids such as CD-ROM, computer tutorials, and Internet sources such as Web sites, e-mail, and newsgroups.

BIOLOGY

## READING SELECTION 13
### HOMEOSTASIS

Carl E. Rischer and Thomas A. Easton
*From Focus on Human Biology*

*How does the human body regulate itself? This reading, taken from a biology textbook, explains the principle of homeostasis. Read the excerpt to discover what homeostasis is and how it controls bodily functioning.*

1    The basic principle of homeostasis has made it possible to understand a great deal about how the body works. **Homeostasis** is the balance maintained when several systems operate to keep the conditions inside the body roughly constant. That is, the body maintains its temperature and levels of mineral salts, nutrients, wastes, oxygen, and water within the narrow limits that support human life.

2    Many different diseases can result when various aspects of homeostasis fail. For instance, the human body uses the sugar glucose as its main fuel. Thus, it is extremely important to keep just enough sugar in circulation so that the cells can draw on it to power their own activities; normally that is 90 milligrams (mg) of glucose in each 100 milliliters (ml) of blood. If a person's blood sugar falls too low, he or she suffers from *hypoglycemia* (*hypo* = under, beneath; *glyc* = sweet) and lack of energy. If, on the other hand, the blood sugar is too high, the problem is *hyperglycemia* (*hyper* = over, above) or diabetes mellitus (sugar diabetes). Excess blood sugar is excreted in the urine; in severe cases, the body's

cells lose water, the brain stops working, and the patient goes into a coma.

## Negative Feedback and Homeostatic Control

### Controlling Sugar Level in the Blood

3　How does the body prevent hypo- and hyperglycemia? After a meal, when sugar is being absorbed from the digestive system, spe-

cific cells in a gland called the pancreas sense the rising sugar level in the blood and secrete *insulin*. Insulin causes cells in the muscles and liver to quickly absorb this excess sugar from the blood, reducing its level back to the normal 90 mg/100 ml [Figure 1.4].

4　Between meals, the blood sugar level falls as the cells use the sugar for energy. The pancreas responds by secreting another substance called *glucagon*, which signals the liver to release some of the extra sugar stored there. This hormone raises the sugar level back up to the normal level (see Figure 1.4).

5　This type of control mechanism is called **negative feedback.** Such feedback mechanisms use the level of the substance or the physical condition being controlled as the indicator for turning off or on the homeostatic response. Negative-feedback mechanisms measure the level of whatever is being controlled against some "set point," or specific level determined in advance. When the variable departs from the set point, the mechanism switches on to counteract the

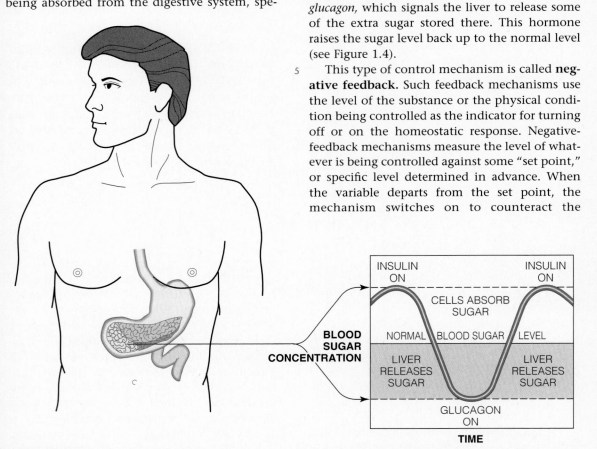

**FIGURE 1.4** Homeostatic control of blood sugar concentration. Many of the body's systems are controlled by feedback systems. In this oversimplified diagram, the level of sugar circulating in the blood is regulated by the pancreas. When the sugar level drifts far enough above the normal set point, it stimulates the pancreas to release insulin, which causes many of the body's cells to take up and use or store the excess sugar, causing the level to decline back toward the set point. When the sugar level drops below the set point, the pancreas releases glucagon, which encourages cells that store sugar to release some of their reserve into the blood, thus raising the level back toward the set point.
**Question:** Which hormone—insulin or glucagon—will be secreted after you eat a candy bar?

change, returning the variable to the set point [Figure 1.5].

6    In contrast, *positive feedback* acts in the opposite way: it increases the departure of some variable from its starting point. Once activated, positive-feedback systems are often destructive. An example is the positive-feedback squeal, of increasing intensity, produced by public address systems when a microphone is placed in front of the speaker. (Why does such a situation produce louder and louder squeals?)

7    Why is it hard to think of any examples of positive-feedback systems existing in a living body?

### Mechanical Negative-Feedback Controls

8    A simple example of a negative-feedback mechanism is the thermostat that controls room temperature by turning a heater off and on. As the temperature goes up, a temperature-sensitive

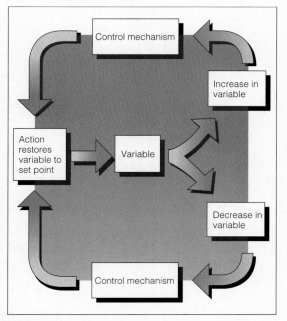

**FIGURE 1.5** In negative-feedback systems, the "effects" feed back on their cause to keep variation within a narrow range around a "set point." **Question:** "To negate" means to undo. Relate this information to "negative feedback."

switch opens, turning off the heater. As the room temperature cools again, the temperature sensor changes until it turns the heater back on. Thus, by alternately turning the heater off and on, the thermostat keeps the room temperature fairly constant.

### Body Temperature Control

9    A similar thermostat works to control human body temperature. Located in the brain, it activates sweating, panting, and rerouting the blood to the superficial vessels of the skin when the body is overheated. In light-complexioned people, this change in blood flow results in a reddening (flushing) of the skin and quickly dissipates the excess heat. When the body is chilled, it routes the blood away from the skin, conserving the body heat, and activates shivering—releasing small pulses of heat as the tiny muscle fibers quiver (raising the body's temperature).

### Negative Feedback in Other Body Systems

10    Negative-feedback mechanisms also work to maintain blood pressure, heart rate, fluid volume, and blood levels of oxygen, carbon dioxide, calcium, sodium, and other substances. The composition of the blood thereby remains constant (within limits) and the body cells remain in an environment that allows them to survive. Extreme changes in blood composition, the availability of nutrients (food molecules), body temperature, or heart function can be fatal.

11    The principle of homeostasis helps us to understand how various aspects of body functions are interrelated. It also tells us that whenever we find a substance or activity in the body that maintains a steady level, we can then expect to find a control mechanism. The concept of homeostasis, therefore, serves both as an organizing principle for our knowledge of the body and as a guide to further research.

1. Explain homeostasis and how it contributes to survival.

2. Diagram and explain how a negative-feedback mechanism operates.

## Comprehension Test 13

*Directions: Circle the letter of the best answer.*

**Checking Your Comprehension**

1. This reading is primarily about
   a. controlling blood sugar
   b. how the body maintains balanced conditions
   c. how negative feedback is beneficial
   d. the human body's feedback mechanisms

2. The principle of homeostasis
   a. explains why people suffer strokes
   b. describes how the body reacts to disease
   c. describes how the body evolved to its present state
   d. explains how the body reacts to and survives changes in its environment

3. Negative feedback is a system in which the body
   a. absorbs excess substances
   b. regulates overproduction of chemicals
   c. increases its functioning in response to disease
   d. restores its functioning to a set level

4. The author compares the body's regulation of temperature to a
   a. heater
   b. thermometer
   c. thermostat
   d. fuel

5. When a person's blood sugar decreases,
   a. the pancreas alerts the liver
   b. the pancreas overproduces sugar
   c. the pancreas releases glucagon
   d. the pancreas releases insulin

6. The term activated (paragraph 6) means
   a. organized
   b. accelerated
   c. set in motion
   d. regulated

**Thinking Critically**

7. Which of the following statements can be assumed to be true based on information presented in the reading?
   a. Negative feedback regulates the production of hormones.
   b. Negative feedback is responsible for coronary disease.
   c. Body temperature control is an example of positive feedback.
   d. Hyperglycemia is caused by water loss.

8. It is reasonable to assume that
   a. the body uses few or no positive-feedback systems
   b. The body continually exists in a static, unchanging state
   c. the principle of homeostasis can explain why cancer spreads
   d. a positive-feedback system operates in a similar way to a negative-feedback system

9. Homeostasis explains which of the following?
   a. organ growth
   b. lung collapse
   c. pain
   d. perspiration

10. If your blood pressure were regulated by a positive-feedback system, once your blood pressure fell and the system was activated, your blood pressure would
   a. return to a normal level
   b. remain low
   c. rise to a dangerous level
   d. decrease

**Questions for Discussion**

1. Do all people who suffer from sugar diabetes need to take insulin? If not, why not?

2. The author implies that the body uses few or no positive feedback systems. Explain why this is so.

3. Explain how certain extreme changes in the body can be fatal. Give a specific example.

4. How useful are the diagrams included in this reading?

| Selection 13: | 999 words |
| --- | --- |

Finishing Time: _____ _____ _____
HR.   MIN.   SEC.

Starting Time: _____ _____ _____
HR.   MIN.   SEC.

Reading Time: _____ _____
MIN.   SEC.

WPM Score: _____

Comprehension Score: _____%

ECONOMICS

# READING SELECTION 14
## SO FEW FARMERS, SO MANY BUREAUCRATS

Roger LeRoy Miller
*From Economics Today*

*The issue of government bureaucracy concerns many citizens. Taken from an economics textbook, this reading examines the Department of Agriculture and its relationship to farmers. Read the excerpt to figure out why there are so few farmers and so many bureaucrats.*

1    Here is one of the great seeming paradoxes of the twentieth century: Farming occurs in 16 percent of the 3,042 counties in the United States. Nonetheless, the Department of Agriculture maintains 11,000 offices in 2,859 of these counties, or 94 percent. We must wonder what employees in the Agriculture Department in the 2,372 counties that do not have any farmers actually do. "Nice work if you can get it" is perhaps the best answer to that.

**A Few Numbers**

2    In Figure 27.2 you see the ratio of farmers to agricultural employees from 1950 to 1990 plus some estimates made to the year 2015 by economist David L. Littmann. Using the estimates in Figure 27.2 on page 276, we come to the fateful prediction that in the year 2001 there will already be more bureaucrats in the Department of Agriculture than there are U.S. farmers.

**Why There Are So Few Farms and Farmers**

3    From Figure 27.3 on the next page you can see that the number of farms in the United States rose from 1.4 million in 1850 to a high of 6.8 million in 1935. Since then the number has declined

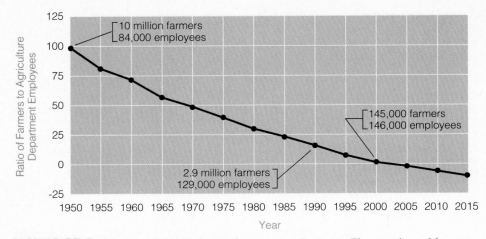

**FIGURE 27.2** Farmers disappearing as bureaucrats increase. The number of farmers in the United States has decreased steadily since 1950, yet the number of employees in the U.S. Department of Agriculture has steadily increased and may actually exceed the number of working farmers by the year 2001. (Figures for 1995–2001 are estimates.) *Source:* USDA Economic Research Service

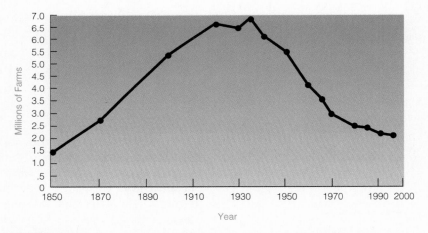

**FIGURE 27.3** Farms in the United States, 1850–1995. The number of farms in the United States rose from 1.4 million in 1850 to a high of 6.8 million in 1935. Today there are just over 2 million farms. *Source:* U. S. Bureau of the Census

fairly steadily to its present level of around 2.1 million. During this time the nature of the average farm has also changed sharply. Since 1960 alone, the size of the average farm has grown by almost 65 percent. Although the typical farm is still run by an individual owner-

operator, the economic importance of such farms is shrinking rapidly. About 65 percent of all American farms have annual sales of less than $25,000. Together they count for only 6 percent of national farm output. In contrast, farms with sales in excess of $250,000 make up about 4 percent of all farms. They, however, account for about 50 percent of all U.S. farm output. Agriculture is rapidly becoming agribusiness. There are two major reasons why this is occurring.

### Increased Productivity

4   The first reason is increased productivity in the farming sector. Between 1935 and 1950 agricultural output per worker-hour doubled. Between 1950 and 1965 it more than doubled again. As you read this book it is doubling once more. A given amount of labor will now produce 10 times as much agricultural output as it did 60 years ago!

### A Limit To The Amount of Food That People Can Eat

5   The second explanation has to do with the fact that there are limits to the amount of food that people can eat. As families get richer, they do not keep buying more and more food. The income elasticity of demand for food is less than 1. As income rises, food expenditures become less important in each person's budget.

### Why So Many Farm Bureaucrats?

6   As farm productivity has reached higher and higher levels, the pressure for market prices to fall has increased. Enter the farm lobbies. They have attempted to slow the progress in the reduction of the existing levels of farm labor and capital. They have asked for and received large taxpayer subsidies.* The estimate for 1993 alone is $22 billion, much of which has gone into subsidies that have kept farm prices up (and consumer spending on food about 14 percent higher than it would be otherwise).

7   Farmers are an odd lot. The majority of them take the extra profits they earn from the subsidy and plow it back into their farms. They continue to increase productivity. But then they produce even more, putting more downward pressure on farm prices. A vicious circle ensues in which well-to-do farmers pour in additional dollars lobbying for more federal government help. But along with federal government help comes, of course, more bureaucrats.

### If It Is So Obvious, Why Doesn't It Go Away?

8   Anybody can read the meaning of Figure 27.2. The president, members of Congress, and even those wily bureaucrats working in Agriculture Department offices hundreds or even thousands of miles from the closest farm know the story. So why isn't something done? Why doesn't Congress eliminate, at a minimum, all of the wasted resources in the Department of Agriculture? Surely the federal government could subsidize the farming sector without such a large bureaucracy. The answer, of course, has to do with the theory of public choice. The bureaucrats in the Department of Agriculture have formed a coalition. They are part of an "iron triangle" that includes their own department, members of Congress who are involved in agricultural affairs, and agribusiness men and women. The members of this iron triangle have a clear-cut vested interest in preserving the status quo. You as a consumer of farm products have an interest also. But your interest is trivial compared to those in the iron triangle. If you spent time and effort to reduce the bloated bureaucracy in the Department of Agriculture, your tax liability might go down a few cents. Each employee in the Department of Agriculture is looking at the loss of a very well-paid job (per constant-quality unit of effort). Who do you think is going to spend more time on this issue?

---

* payments

## Comprehension Test 14*

*Directions:* *Circle the letter of the best answer.*

### Checking Your Comprehension

1. Explain the paradox in farming the author refers to in the beginning of the article.

2. According to statistics in the article, what do economists predict will happen in the year 2001?

3. How has the average farm changed in size since 1960?

4. What do most farmers do with the extra profits they earn from government subsidies?

### Thinking Critically

1. Explain in your own words why this country has proportionately more agricultural bureaucrats than farmers today.

2. The author states that "agriculture is rapidly becoming agribusiness." What is meant by this?

3. Why doesn't Congress choose to eliminate some of the bureaucratic positions in the Department of Agriculture when they are clearly not needed?

4. Why do the members of the "Iron Triangle" have a greater interest than the average taxpayer in keeping the status quo when it comes to the disproportionate number of employees in the Department of Agriculture?

### Questions for Discussion

1. Does the government seem to play a larger role than it should in areas other than agriculture?

2. Discuss the probable reasons for the significant increase in productivity among farmers over the last 60 years.

3. Explain what the author means when he states that "as income rises, food expenditures become less important in each person's budget." Do you agree with this statement? Why or why not?

4. Why do you think the number of farms in the United States increased by more than 5 million from 1850 to 1935 only to decrease by more than 4 million since then?

| Selection 14: | | 952 words | |
|---|---|---|---|
| Finishing Time: | _____ | _____ | _____ |
| | HR. | MIN. | SEC. |
| Starting Time: | _____ | _____ | _____ |
| | HR. | MIN. | SEC. |
| Reading Time: | | _____ | _____ |
| | | MIN. | SEC. |
| WPM Score: | | _____ | |
| Comprehension Score: | | _____ | % |

---

### Visit the Longman English Pages

For additional readings and exercises, visit the Longman English Skills Web page at:

http://longman.awl.com/englishpages

For a username and password, please see your instructor.

---

* Multiple-choice questions are contained in Appendix B (page A15).

# CHAPTER 8

# Learning and Retention Strategies

IN THIS CHAPTER YOU WILL LEARN:

1. To use textbook structure to guide your reading.
2. To increase your retention and recall using new techniques and systems.
3. To read scientific and technical material more efficiently.

The purpose of this chapter is to help you understand the structure and distinguishing features of textbooks and how to use them to your advantage in reading and recalling information. A textbook is a unique, highly specialized information source. It is very different from any other type of printed material. One feature distinguishes it from all other forms of written expression: It is designed to teach.

A textbook also has a consistent, tight organization not always found in other types of factual material. The first section of this chapter shows you how to use this structure and the learning aids associated with it to guide your learning. The second section discusses a number of strategies for improving your ability to retain information. Next, this chapter presents SQ3R, an effective system for reading and studying factual material. The last section offers suggestions for reading scientific and technical material.

## ■ USING THE ORGANIZATION OF TEXTBOOK CHAPTERS

Have you ever entered a large new discount store or supermarket and felt confused and disoriented? If you are an efficient shopper, you would look for the signs that hang over the aisles and indicate what products are shelved in that section so you could quickly find what you need. It is just as easy to become confused and disoriented when reading a textbook chapter unless you identify its organization and follow the signs the author gives you to locate what you need. You will find the headings to be essential guideposts that lead you through each chapter, especially if you are a pragmatic learner who appreciates order and systems.

## ■ Headings

The signs used in textbooks are the headings that organize each chapter by dividing it into topics. Headings are labels that indicate the contents of the material that follows. Most chapters use several types of headings, each distinguished by different size and style of print. Heading positions can also vary.

The various kinds and positions of headings suggest differing degrees of importance. Table 8.1 shows an excerpt from a chapter on punishment and imprisonment in an introductory criminology textbook. Much of the material between headings has been deleted in order to emphasize the function of the headings.

In Table 8.1 you can see three levels of headings, each distinguishable by its size and location:

1. The largest heading announces a broad, general subject—the effects of imprisonment.

2. The headings at the next level are more detailed and announce topics into which the subject has been divided.

3. The third level of headings provides subtopics—in this excerpt a listing of the various types of victimization.

When headings are considered together, they form an outline of the chapter content as shown here:

> The Effects Of Imprisonment: A Closer Look
>    The "Pains Of Imprisonment"
>       Victimization of Prisoners
>          Biological Victimization
>          Psychological Victimization
>          Economic Victimization
>          Social Victimization
>    Prison Subcultures And Prisonization

Often in a text, the table of contents provides a listing of headings and more important subheadings. Develop the habit of using headings as guideposts to understanding the organization and important contents of a chapter. Use the following suggestions before reading a chapter:

1. **Study the entry for a chapter in the table of contents before beginning to read the chapter.** Notice how the topics are connected and how the author proceeds from topic to topic.

**Table 8.1** The Function of Headings

**The Effects of Imprisonment: A Closer Look**

As we observed in the preceding chapter, America's prison population has been increasing over the past few years. Whatever the merits of decarceration and community corrections, . . .

The "Pains of Imprisonment"

In a study of life in a maximum security prison, Gresham Sykes wrote about the "pains of imprisonment." He observed, as others had before him, . . .

The fifth and final pain of imprisonment identified by Sykes is forced association with other criminals, . . .

Victimization of Prisoners

Sociologist Lee Bowker has depicted the inmate experience as one of victimization. . . .

*Biological Victimization* Included here are murder, rape, and assault. Bowker contends. . . .

Homosexual rape and other sexual assaults have long been associated with prison life. . . .

Bowker suggests that there may be even more violence in juvenile institutions than in adult ones. . . .

*Psychological Victimization* Combined with other forms of victimization, this primarily consists of manipulation and intimidation for the purposes of achieving status, prestige, authority, and power. . . .

*Economic Victimization* Bowker correctly observes that '"enforced material deprivation encourages the formation of a sub rosa. . . .

Public discussion on the uses of prison labor have tended to emphasize one or more of the following as governing principles. . . .

Even so, it is worth pointing out that economic victimization through the prison labor system is not inevitable. . . .

*Social Victimization* By this Bowker means the victimization of prisoner groups rather than specific individuals. He identifies three bases. . . .

In Bowker's view racial and ethnic group victimization is the most significant. . . .

Certain offenders are singled out for special victimization by other inmates. . . .

Prison Subcultures and Prisonization

We have reviewed some pretty unpleasant facets of prison life in the last few pages. . . .

2. **Preread the chapter to get a more detached picture of its structure and focus.**

3. **Use the chapter's headings to identify its overall organizational pattern (see Chapter 5). For example, does the chapter follow a time sequence?**

## EXERCISE 8–1

*DIRECTIONS:* Study the following outlines of chapter headings and answer the questions that follow each.

I. Text: *Sociology: An Introduction*
   A. CHAPTER: **DEVIANCE AND SOCIAL CONTROL**
      1. Major Heading: **What is Deviance?**
         a. Minor Heading: **Traditional Views of Deviance and Deviants**
            (1) Subtopic: **The Absolutist View**
            (2) Subtopic: **The Moral View**
            (3) Subtopic: **The Medical and Social Pathological View**
            (4) Subtopic: **The Statistical View**
         b. Minor Heading: **The Relative Nature of Deviance**
            (1) Subtopic: **Variation by Time**
            (2) Subtopic: **Variation by Place**
            (3) Subtopic: **Variation by Situation**
            (4) Subtopic: **Variation by Social Status**

1. What is the main purpose of the portion of the chapter summarized by the headings shown?

   _____

   _____

2. According to what factors does the meaning of deviance vary?

   _____

   _____

3. What organizational pattern(s) does this chapter seem to reflect?

   _____

   _____

II. Text: *The Basics of American Politics*
   A. CHAPTER: **WHO WINS, WHO LOSES: PLURALISM VERSUS ELITISM**
      1. Heading: **Pluralism**
      2. Heading: **Power Elite**
      3. Heading: **The Debate**
      4. Heading: **Wrap Up**

4. What organizational pattern does this chapter title suggest?

   _____

   _____

5. What content do you predict the section titled "Wrap Up" will contain?

_____

_____

## ■ Textbook Learning Aids

Because a textbook is intended to help you learn, it contains various features designed to help you learn its content in the most efficient and effective way. Table 8.2 provides a brief review of common textbook learning aids and their uses.

**Table 8.2** Textbook Learning Aids

| Feature | Use |
| --- | --- |
| Learning Objectives | Focus your attention on what is important in the chapter |
| Chapter Outline | Enables you to see sequence and organization of ideas |
| Chapter Overview | Explains purpose and focus of chapter |
| Special Interest Boxes | Provide perspectives or application of important concepts |
| Marginal Notations | Offer commentary, pose questions, provide illustrations and examples, identify key terms |
| Summary | Condenses and consolidates chapter content |
| Vocabulary Lists | Identify terminology to learn |
| Review Questions | Test your knowledge of key concepts and ideas |
| Discussion Questions | Provoke thought; enable you to think critically |
| Suggested Readings or References | Provide additional sources of information |
| Glossary | Offers easy-to-use mini-dictionary of key terminology |
| Appendix | Contains useful additional materials |

## EXERCISE 8–2

*DIRECTIONS:* Review one of your textbooks to discover the learning aids it contains. Make a list of the "Textbook Learning Aids" from Table 8.2 that it contains.

## ■ APPLYING EFFECTIVE RECALL STRATEGIES

### ■ Using Review To Increase Recall

Review refers to the process of going back over something you have already read. There are two types of review: immediate and periodic. Both types can greatly increase the amount you can remember from a printed page.

#### Immediate Review

When you finish reading an assignment, your first inclination may be to breathe a sigh of relief, close the book, and go on to another task. Before you do this, however, take a few minutes to go back over the material. Briefly review the overall organization and important ideas presented. Think of review as a postreading activity, similar to prereading. In reviewing you should reread the parts of the article or chapter that contain the most important ideas. Concentrate on titles, introductions, summaries, headings, graphic material, and, depending on the length of the material, topic sentences. Also review any notes you made and any portions of the text that you highlighted.

Considerable research has been conducted on how individuals learn and remember. These experiments have shown that review immediately following reading greatly improves the amount remembered. However, the review must be *immediate;* it will not produce the same effects if you do it after a 10 minute break or later in the evening. To get the full benefit, you must review while the content of the article or chapter is still fresh in your mind. Review before you have had a chance to forget and before other thoughts and ideas interfere or compete with what you have read.

#### Periodic Review

Although immediate review is very effective and will increase your ability to recall information, it is not sufficient for remembering material for long periods. To remember facts and ideas permanently, you need to review them periodically, going back and refreshing your recall on a regular basis. For example, suppose you are reading a chapter on criminal behavior in your sociology text, and a midterm exam is scheduled in four weeks. If you read the chapter, reviewed it immediately, and then did nothing with it until the exam a month later, you would not remember enough to score well on the exam. To achieve a good grade, you need to review the chapter periodically. You might review the chapter once several days after reading it, again a week later, and once again a week before the exam.

### Why Review Is Effective

Immediate and periodic reviews are effective for two reasons:

1. **Review provides repetition.** Repetition is one important way that you learn and remember information. Think about how you learned the multiplication tables or why you know the phone numbers of your closest friends. In both cases, frequent use enables you to remember.

2. **Review consolidates, or draws together, information into a unified whole.** As you read a chapter, you are processing the information piece by piece. Review, both immediate and periodic, provides a means of seeing how each piece relates to each other piece and to the material as a whole.

## EXERCISE 8–3

*DIRECTIONS:* Read one of the selections at the end of the chapter and review it immediately. Highlight the parts of the selection that you reread as part of your immediate review. Then answer the questions that follow the selection.

## EXERCISE 8–4

*DIRECTIONS:* Plan a periodic review schedule for one of your courses. Include both textbook chapters and lecture notes.

## ■ Other Aids to Recall

Review and repetition are primary methods of increasing retention. Other aids or methods for increasing your recall include the following:

### Building an Intent to Remember

Very few people remember things that they do not intend to remember. Do you remember what color of clothing a friend wore last week? Can you name all the songs you heard on the radio this morning? Can you remember exactly what time you got home last Saturday night? If not, why not? Most likely you cannot remember these facts because at the time you did not see the importance of remembering them. Of course, if you had known that you would be asked these questions, you would have most likely have remembered the items. You can see, then, that you must intend to remember things to be able to do so effectively. The same principle holds true for reading and retention. To remember what you read, you must have a clear and strong intent to do so. Unless you have defined what you intend to remember before you begin reading, you will find that it is difficult to recall specific content.

In Chapter 2 you saw how guide questions can help you keep your mind on what you are reading. Now you can see that they also establish an intent to remember.

Before you begin to read an assignment, define as clearly as possible what you intend to remember. Your definition will depend on the type of material, why you are reading it, and how familiar you are with the topic. For instance, if you are reading an essay assigned in preparation for a class discussion, plan to remember not only key ideas but also points of controversy, application, and opinions with which you disagree. Your intent might be quite different in reviewing a chapter for an essay exam. Here you would be looking for important ideas, trends, guiding or controlling principles, and significance of events.

As you read a text assignment, sort important information from that which is less important. Ask and continually answer questions such as:

1. **How important is this information?**

2. **Will I need to know this for the exam?**

3. **Is this a key idea or is it an explanation of a key idea?**

4. **Why did the writer include this?**

### *Organizing and Categorizing*

Information that is organized, or that has a pattern or structure, is easier to remember than material that is randomly arranged. One effective way to organize information is to *categorize* it, to arrange it in groups according to similar characteristics. Suppose, for example, that you had to remember the following list of items to buy for a picnic: cooler, candy, 7-Up, Pepsi, napkins, potato chips, lemonade, peanuts, paper plates. The easiest way to remember this list would be to divide it in groups. You might arrange it as follows:

| *Drinks* | *Snacks* | *Picnic Supplies* |
| --- | --- | --- |
| 7-Up | peanuts | cooler |
| Pepsi | candy | paper plates |
| lemonade | potato chips | napkins |

By grouping the items into categories, you are putting similar items together. Then, rather than learning one long list of unorganized items, you are learning three shorter, organized lists.

Now imagine you are reading an essay on discipline in public high schools. Instead of learning one long list of reasons for disruptive student behavior you might divide the reasons into groups such as peer conflicts, teacher-student conflicts, and so forth.

### Associating Ideas

Association is a useful way to remember new facts and ideas. It involves connecting new information with previously acquired knowledge. For instance, if you are reading about divorce in a sociology class and are trying to remember a list of common causes, you might try to associate each cause with a person you know who exhibits that problem. Suppose one cause of divorce is lack of communication between the partners. You might remember this by thinking of a couple you know whose lack of communication has caused relationship difficulties.

Suppose you are taking an introductory physics course and are studying Newton's Laws of Motion. The Third Law states: To every action there is always opposed an equal reaction. To remember this law you could associate it with a familiar everyday situation such as swimming that illustrates the law. When you swim you push water backward with your feet, arms, and legs, and the water pushes you forward.

Association involves making connections between new information and what you already know. When you find a connection between the known and the unknown, you can retrieve the new information from your memory along with the old.

### Using a Variety of Sensory Modes

Your senses of sight, hearing, and touch can all help you remember what you read. Most of the time, most of us use just one sense—sight—as we read. However, if you are able to use more than one sense, you will find that recall is easier. Activities such as underlining, highlighting, notetaking, and outlining involve your sense of touch and enable you to reinforce your learning. Or, if you are having particular difficulty remembering something, try to use your auditory sense as well. You might try repeating the information out loud or listening to someone else repeat it. Most of us tend to rely only on our strengths. Visual learners tend to rely on visual skills; and auditory learners tend to depend on their auditory skills, for example. To become a more efficient learner, try to engage additional sensory modes, even if they are not your strengths.

### Visualizing

Visualizing, or creating a mental picture of what you have read, often aids recall. In reading descriptive writing that creates a mental picture, visualization is an easy task. In reading about events, people, processes, or procedures, visualization is again relatively simple. However, visualization of abstract ideas, theories, philosophies, and concepts may not be possible. Instead, you may be able to create a visual picture of the relationship of ideas in your mind or on paper. For example, suppose you are reading about the invasion of privacy and learn that there are arguments for and against the storage of personal data about each citizen in large computer banks. You might create a visual image of two lists of information—advantages and disadvantages.

### Using Mnemonic Devices

Memory tricks and devices, often called mnemonics, are useful in helping you recall lists of factual information. You might use a rhyme, such as the one used for remembering the number of days in each month: "Thirty days hath September, April, June, and November. . . ." Another device involves making up a word or phrase in which each letter represents an item you are trying to remember. If you remember the name Roy G. Biv, for example, you will be able to recall the colors in the light spectrum: **r**ed, **o**range, **y**ellow, **g**reen, **b**lue, **i**ndigo, **v**iolet.

## EXERCISE 8–5

*DIRECTIONS:* Five study learning situations follow. Decide which of the retention aids described in this section—organization-categorization, association, sensory modes, visualization, and mnemonic devices—might be most useful in each situation and list that aid after each.

1. In a sociology course you are assigned to read about and remember the causes of child abuse. How might you remember them more easily?

   _____

2. You are studying astronomy and you have to remember the names of the nine planets: Mercury, Venus, Earth, Mars, Jupiter, Saturn, Uranus, Neptune, and Pluto. What retention aid(s) could help you remember them?

   _____

3. You are taking a course in anatomy and physiology and must learn the name and location of each bone in the human skull. How could you learn them easily?

   _____

4. You have an entire chapter to review for a history course, and your instructor has told you that your exam will contain 30 true-false ques-

tions on Civil War battles. What could you do as you review to help yourself remember the details of various battles?

_____

5. You are taking a course in twentieth century history and are studying the causes of the Vietnam War in preparation for an essay exam. You find that there are many causes, some immediate, others long-term. Some have to do with international politics; others, with internal problems in North and South Vietnam. How could you organize your study for this exam?

_____

## EXERCISE 8–6

*DIRECTIONS:* Find a classmate or group of classmates who are taking one of the same courses you are. (If no one is taking the exact same course, join a group of classmates who are taking a similar course, another social science course, another English course, and so forth.) Discuss how you could use each of the recall strategies described in this section to improve your performance in that course.

## EXERCISE 8–7

*DIRECTIONS:* Read the following excerpt. Then decide which retention aid(s) you might use to learn the four types of groups discussed in the material.

### SOCIAL GROUPS

. . . In our discussion, we will focus chiefly on social groups—those in which people physically or socially interact. Several other types are also recognized by most sociologists, however, and deserve to be mentioned.

*Statistical groups,* or more accurately, statistical groupings, are formed not by the group members but by sociologists and statisticians. In 1990, for example, there were 66,090,000 families in the United States with an average size of 3.17 people per family (*Current Population Reports,* Series P–20, No. 447, 1990). The group of women between 5 feet 1 inch and 5 feet 5 inches tall would be another statistical group.[. . . ]

Another type of group is the *categorical group* in which a number of people share a common characteristic. Teenagers, the handicapped, unwed mothers, interracial couples, millionaires, redheads, students, women, senior citizens, and virgins are all categorical groups.[. . . ]

A third type of group is the *aggregate.* An aggregate is a social group comprising a collection of people who are together in one place. You may join a group of this sort buying an ice cream cone, riding a bus, or waiting to cross a street.[. . . ]

A fourth type is the *associational* or *organizational group,* which is especially important in complex industrialized societies. Associational groups consist of people who join together in some organized way to pursue a common interest, and they have a formal structure.[. . . ]

Eschleman, Cashion and Basirico, *Sociology: An Introduction.*

● ● ●

## ■ READING AND LEARNING WITH THE SQ3R SYSTEM

Throughout this chapter you have become familiar with devices and techniques to improve your ability to remember what you read. You may be wondering how you will be able to use all these techniques and how to combine them most effectively. Many students have asked similar questions. As a result, systems have been developed and tested that combine some of the most useful techniques into a step-by-step procedure for learning as you read.

### ■ The SQ3R Reading-Study System

Developed in the 1940s, the SQ3R system has been used successfully for many years. Considerable experimentation has been done, and the system has proven effective in increasing students' retention. It is especially useful for studying textbooks and other highly factual, well-organized materials. Basically, SQ3R is a way of learning as you read. Each of the steps in the system will be briefly summarized, and you will then see how it can be applied to a sample selection.

1. **Survey.** Become familiar with the overall content and organization of the material. You have already learned this technique and know it as prereading.

2. **Question.** Formulate questions about the material that you expect to be able to question as you read. As you read each successive heading, turn it into a question. This step is similar to establishing guide questions discussed in Chapter 2.

3. **Read.** As you read each section, actively search for the answer to your guide questions. When you find the answers, highlight or mark portions of the text that concisely state the information.

4. **Recite.** Probably the most important part of the system, "recite" means that you should stop after each section or after each major heading, look away from the page, and try to remember the answer to your ques-

tion. If you are unable to remember, look back at the page and reread the material. Then test yourself again by looking away from the page and "reciting" the answer to your question.

5. **Review.** Immediately after you have finished reading, go back through the material again and read titles, introductions, summaries, headings, and graphic material. As you read each heading, recall your question and test yourself to see if you can still remember the answer. If you cannot, reread that section again.

Now, to give you a clear picture of how the steps in the SQ3R method work together to produce an efficient approach to reading-study, the method will be applied to a textbook chapter. Suppose you have been assigned to read the following excerpt, "Meanings and Messages," taken from *Human Communication* by Joseph DeVito for a class that is studying verbal and nonverbal communication. Follow each of the SQ3R steps in reading the selection.

1. **Survey.** Preread the article, noticing introductions, headings, first sentences, and the last paragraph. From this prereading you should have an overall picture of what this article is about and what conclusions the author draws about the listening process.

2. **Question.** Using the headings as a starting point, develop several questions that you might expect the article to answer. You might ask questions such as these:
   How are meanings and messages related?
   How can meanings be "in people"?
   What besides words and gestures makes up meanings?
   What makes meanings unique?
   What is the difference between denotative and connotative meanings?
   How does context affect meaning?

3. **Read.** Now read the entire selection, keeping your questions in mind as you read. Stop at the end of each major section and proceed to step 4.

4. **Recite.** After each section, stop reading and check to see if you can recall the answers to your questions.

5. **Review.** When you have finished reading the entire article, take a few minutes to reread the headings and recall your questions. Check to see that you can still recall the answers.

### MEANINGS AND MESSAGES

Meaning is an active process created by cooperation between source and receiver—speaker and listener, writer and reader. Here are a few important corollaries concerning meaning.

### Meanings Are in People

Meaning depends not only on messages (whether verbal, nonverbal, or both) but on the interaction of those messages and the receiver's own thoughts and feelings. You do not receive meaning; you create meaning. You construct meaning out of the messages you receive combined with your own social and cultural perspectives (beliefs, attitudes, and values, for example). Words do not mean; people mean. Consequently, to discover meaning, you need to look into people and not merely into words.

An example of the confusion that can result when this relatively simple fact is overlooked is provided by Ronald D. Laing, H. Phillipson, and a. Russell Lee in *Interpersonal Perception* and analyzed with insight by Paul Watzlawick in *How Real Is Real?* A couple on the second night of their honeymoon are sitting at a hotel bar. The woman strikes up a conversation with the couple next to her. The husband refuses to communicate with the couple and becomes antagonistic toward his wife as well as the couple. The wife then grows angry because he has created such an awkward and unpleasant situation. Each becomes increasingly disturbed, and the evening ends in a bitter conflict in which each is convinced of the other's lack of consideration. Eight years later, they analyze this argument. Apparently the idea of honeymoon had meant very different things to each of them. To the husband it had meant a "golden opportunity to ignore the rest of the world and simply explore each other." He felt his wife's interaction with the other couple implied there was something lacking in him. To the wife, honeymoon had meant an opportunity to try out her new role as wife. "I had never had a conversation with another couple as a wife before," she said. "Previous to this I had always been a 'girlfriend' or 'fiancée' or 'daughter' or 'sister.'"

One very clear implication of this principle is that meaning is always ambiguous to some extent. Each person's meaning is somewhat different from each other person's, therefore you can never know precisely what any given word or gesture means. Nonverbal gestures—with the obvious exception of emblems—are usually more ambiguous than verbal messages.

### Meanings Are More Than Words and Gestures

When you want to communicate a thought or feeling to another person, you do so with relatively few symbols. These represent just a small part of what you are thinking or feeling, much of which remains unspoken. If you were to try to describe every feeling in detail, you would never get on with the job of living. The meanings you seek to communicate are much more than the sum of the words and nonverbal behaviors you use to represent them.

Because of this, you can never fully know what another person is thinking or feeling. You can only approximate it on the basis of the meanings you receive, which, as already noted, are greatly influenced by who you are and what you are feeling. Conversely, others can never fully know you; they too can only approximate what you are feeling. Failure to understand another person or to be understood are not abnormal situations. They are inevitable, although you should realize that with effort you can always understand another person a little better.

**Meanings Are Unique**

Because meanings are derived from both the messages communicated and the receiver's own thoughts and feelings, no two people ever derive the same meanings. Similarly, because people change constantly, no one person can derive the same meanings on two separate occasions. Who you are can never be separated from the meanings you create. As a result, you need to check your perceptions of another's meanings by asking questions, echoing what you perceive to be the other person's feelings or thoughts, and seeking elaboration and clarification—in general, practicing all the skills identified in the discussion on effective interpersonal perception and listening.

Also recognize that as you change, you also change the meanings you created out of past messages. Thus, although the message sent may not have changed, the meanings you created from it yesterday and the meanings you create today may be quite different. Yesterday, when a special someone said, "I love you," you created certain meanings. But today, when you learn that the same "I love you" was said to three other people or when you fall in love with someone else, you drastically change the meanings you perceive from those three words.

**Meanings Are Both Denotative and Connotative**

To understand the nature of denotative and connotative meaning, consider a word such as *death*. To a doctor this word might mean, or denote, the point at which the heart stops beating. To doctor, *death* is a word signifying an objective description of an event; the word is basically denotative. To a mother whose son has just died, the words means much more. It recalls the son's youth, his ambitions, his family, his illness, and so on. To her the word is emotional, subjective, and highly personal. These emotional, subjective, and personal reactions are the word's connotative meanings.

Nonverbal behaviors may also be viewed in terms of their denotation and connotation. Some nonverbal behaviors are largely denotative (for example, a nod signifying yes) while others are primarily connotative (for example, a smile, raised eyebrows, or a wink).

Another distinction between the two types of meaning has already been implied: the denotative meaning of a message is more general or universal; most people would agree with the denotative meanings and would give similar definitions. Connotative meanings, however, are extremely personal, and few people would agree on the precise connotative meaning of a word or nonverbal behavior. Test this idea by trying to get a group of people to agree on the connotative meanings of such words as *religion, racism, democracy, wealth,* and *freedom* or of such nonverbal behaviors as raised eyebrows, arms folded in front of one's chest, or sitting with one's legs crossed. Chances are very good that it will be impossible to reach an agreement.

**Meanings Are Context-Based**

Verbal and nonverbal communications exist in a context, and that context to a large extent determines the meaning of any verbal or nonverbal behavior. The same words or behaviors may have totally different meanings when they occur in different contexts. For example, the greeting, "How are you?" means "Hello" to someone you pass regularly on the street but means "Is your health improving?" when said to a friend in the hospital. A wink to an attractive person on a bus means something completely different from a wink that signifies a put-on or a lie. Similarly, the meaning of a given signal depends on the behaviors it accompanies or is close to in time. Pounding a fist on the table during a speech in support of a politician means something quite different from that same gesture in response to news of a friends death. Divorced from the context, it is impossible to tell what meaning was intended just from examining signals. Of course, even if you know the context in detail, you still may not be able to decipher the meaning of the verbal or nonverbal message.

● ● ●

### ■ How SQ3R Improves Your Reading Efficiency

The SQ3R system improves your reading efficiency in three ways: It increases your comprehension, increases your recall, and saves you valuable time by encouraging you to learn as you read.

Your comprehension is most directly improved by the S and Q steps. By surveying or prereading you acquire an overview of the material that serves as an outline to follow as you read. In the "Question" step, you are focusing your attention and identifying what is important to look for as you read.

Your recall of the material is improved through the "Recite" and "Review" steps. By testing yourself while reading and immediately after you have finished, you are building a systematic review pattern that will provide the necessary repetitions to ensure learning and recall.

Finally, because you are learning as you are reading, you will save time later when you are ready to study the material for an exam. Because you have already learned the material through recitation and review, you will find that you need much less time to prepare for an exam. Instead of learning the material for the first time, all you need to do is refresh your memory and review difficult portions.

## EXERCISE 8–8

*DIRECTIONS:* Divide the class into two groups. Your instructor will assign a reading selection from the text. One group should read the selection using the SQ3R method. The other group should only read the selection once, *without* using any parts of the SQ3R system. Neither group should highlight or annotate. When both groups have finished, groups may question one another to determine which group learned and recalled more information or compare their scores on the comprehension test that accompanies the reading.

## ■ Adapting the SQ3R System

As mentioned previously, SQ3R is a very popular, well-researched reading-study system. However, to make the best use of SQ3R, you need to adjust and adapt the procedure to fit the material you are studying and your learning style.

### Adapting SQ3R to Suit the Material

Your texts and other required readings vary greatly from course to course. For example, a mathematics text is structured and written quite differently from a sociology text. A chemistry text contains numerous principles, laws, formulas, and problems, whereas a philosophy text contains mostly reading selections and discussions. To accommodate this wide variation in your textbooks and other assigned readings, use the SQ3R system as a base or model. Add, vary, or rearrange the steps to fit the material. For example, when working with a mathematics text, you might add a "Study the Sample Problems" step in which you analyze the problem-solving process. When reading an essay, short story, or poem for a literature class, add a "React" step in which you analyze various features of writing, including the writer's style, tone, purpose, and point of view. For textbooks with a great deal of factual information to learn, you might add "Highlight," "Take Notes," or "Outline" steps.

## EXERCISE 8–9

*DIRECTIONS:* Read one of the selections at the end of the chapter using the SQ3R system and follow each of the steps listed here. Add to or revise the system as necessary. After you complete the "Review" step, answer the multiple-choice questions that follow the selection.

1. **Survey.** Preread the article to get an overview of the organization and content of the article.
2. **Question.** Write the questions you expect to be able to answer when you read the article.

_____

_____

3. **Read.** Read the selection, looking for the answers to your questions. As you find them, write them in this space.

   _____

   _____

4. **Recite.** After each boldface heading, stop and recall your questions and their answers.
5. **Review.** After finishing the article, quickly go back through the article review the major points.

### Adapting SQ3R to Suit Your Learning Style

Throughout this text you have probably found that some techniques work better for you than others. This is perfectly natural and consistent with learning theory. You may also have noted that you learn somewhat differently from others. Both findings are due to variations in personal learning style. Each person finds certain methods for learning easier than others. Just as everyone's personality is unique, so is everyone's learning style. Some students, for example, learn best visually. Seeing charts, diagrams, drawings, or pictures—rather than reading or listening—appeals to them. Other students are auditory learners—they learn best by listening. Such students, for instance, would learn more quickly from an instructor's lecture than from a textbook chapter on the same topic.

As part of the process of developing your own reading-study system, consider your learning style. Ask yourself the following questions:

1. Does repeating things out loud help me to learn?

2. Do organizational charts, lists, and diagrams help me to learn?

3. Is writing and rewriting information a good way for me to learn?

4. Does asking challenging questions and answering them help me to learn?

5. Does writing summaries or outlines help me to remember information?

When you have discovered some features of your own learning style, you can adapt the SQ3R system to suit it. For instance, if writing outlines helps you recall the idea structures, replace the "Recite" step with an "Outline" step and make the "Review" step a "Review of Outline" step. Or, if you have discovered that you learn well by listening, replace the "Recite" and "Review" steps with "Tape Record" and "Listen" steps, in which you dictate and record information to be learned and review it by listening to the tape.

As you are no doubt beginning to see, there are numerous possibilities for developing your own reading-study system. The best approach is to test variations until you find the most effective system for you.

## EXERCISE 8–10

*DIRECTIONS:* List the courses you are taking this semester in the spaces provided. Next to each, indicate what modification(s) in the SQ3R system you would make to suit each course's content and learning requirements:

_____

_____

_____

_____

## ■ READING SCIENTIFIC/TECHNICAL MATERIAL

If you are taking courses in the sciences, technologies, engineering, data processing, or health-related fields, you are working with a specialized type of textbook. In this section you will see how scientific and technical textbooks differ from those used in other classes. You will also learn several specific approaches to reading technical material. The key to reading technical material efficiently is to recognize how it differs from other types of material. You must adapt your reading and study methods to accommodate these differences.

Each of the following paragraphs describes a spice called nutmeg. Read each and decide how they differ.

### PARAGRAPH 1

Nutmeg is the kernel of a tropical fruit of a nutmeg tree. It is added to foods to change their flavor. The tree belongs to the nutmeg family, Myristicacae, genus *Myristica,* species *M. fragrans.* The tree grows to a height of 70 feet and it is evergreen. As the fruit of the tree ripens, it hardens and splits open at the top, showing a bright scarlet membrane. The spice called mace is made from this membrane.

### PARAGRAPH 2

Nutmeg is a pungent, aromatic spice often added to foods to give them a delicious tang and aroma. It adds a subtle spiciness to desserts and perks up the flavor of such bland dishes as potatoes. Nutmeg comes from a tree grown in warm climates. The nutmeg tree is tall and gracious, with long, pale leaves and beautiful yellow flowers.

● ● ●

Did you notice that the first paragraph presented only precise, factual information? The words used have very exact meanings. Some words have technical meanings ("genus," "species," "*Myristica*"). Others are everyday words used in a specialized way ("evergreen," "membrane"). An abbreviation, "M.," was also used. Because of the language, the paragraph does not allow for interpretation or expression of opinion. In fact, you cannot tell if the writer likes or has ever tasted nutmeg. The purpose of the paragraph is to give clear, detailed information about nutmeg.

The second paragraph is written quite differently; it presents fewer facts and more description. Many words such as *delicious*, *beautiful*, *gracious*, and *subtle* allow room for interpretation and judgment. This paragraph helps you imagine how nutmeg tastes and learn about its origin.

Paragraph 1 is an example of scientific/technical writing. It is very precise, exact, and factual. This section discusses the particular features of scientific/technical material and gives suggestions for reading this type of writing.

## ■ Fact Density

Scientific and technical writing is highly factual, dense, and concise. A large amount of information is closely packed together into a relatively small space on the page. Compared to many other forms of writing, technical writing may seem complicated and difficult. Here are a few suggestions for handling densely written material:

1. **Read technical material more slowly and carefully than other textbook content.** Plan to spend more time on a technical reading assignment than on other assignments.

2. **Plan on rereading certain sections several times.** Sometimes it is useful to read a section once rather quickly just to learn what main ideas it contains. Then read it carefully a second time, fitting together all the facts that explain the important ideas.

3. **Keep a notebook of significant information.** In some textbooks you can highlight what is important to remember. (This method is discussed in Chapter 9.) However, because technical books are so highly factual, highlighting is usually not effective. Students who have tried this report that it seems like everything is important and that they end up with most of the page highlighted. Instead, try using a notebook to record information you need to remember. Recording this information in your own words is a useful way of checking whether or not you have really understood it and will increase your retention. Figure 8.1 shows

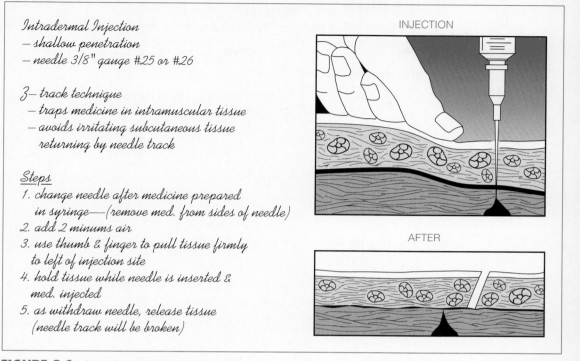

*Intradermal Injection*
*— shallow penetration*
*— needle 3/8" gauge #25 or #26*

*3— track technique*
  *— traps medicine in intramuscular tissue*
  *— avoids irritating subcutaneous tissue*
    *returning by needle track*

*Steps*
*1. change needle after medicine prepared*
   *in syringe—(remove med. from sides of needle)*
*2. add 2 minums air*
*3. use thumb & finger to pull tissue firmly*
   *to left of injection site*
*4. hold tissue while needle is inserted &*
   *med. injected*
*5. as withdraw needle, release tissue*
   *(needle track will be broken)*

INJECTION

AFTER

**FIGURE 8.1**  Sample notebook page

an excerpt from a nursing student's notebook. Notice that this student included definitions and diagrams as well as detail.

## ■ The Vocabulary of Technical Writing

Scientific/technical writing in each subject area is built on a set of very precise, exact word meanings. Each field has its own language, and you must learn the language in order to understand the material. Here are a few sentences taken from textbooks in several technical fields. As you read, notice the large number of technical words used in each.

### ENGINEERING MATERIALS

If the polymer is a mixture of polymers, the component homopolymers (polymers of a single monomer species) and their percentages should be stated.

**AUTO MECHANICS**

Each free end of the three stator windings is connected to the leads of one negative diode and one positive diode.

**DATA PROCESSING**

Another advantage of the PERFORM/VARYING statement is that the FROM value and the BY value may not be any numeric value (except that the BY value may not be zero.)

• • •

In these examples, some words are familiar ones with new, unfamiliar meanings ("FROM," "BY"). Others are words you've probably never seen ("monomer," "stator").

In scientific/technical writing you'll encounter two types of specialized vocabulary. First, everyday words with which you are familiar are given entirely new, technical meanings. Here are a few examples.

1. Institution (sociology): a cluster of values, norms, statuses, and roles that develop around a basic social goal

2. Pan (photography): to follow the motion of a moving object with a camera

3. Cabinet (government): a group of presidential advisers who head executive departments

A second type of specialized vocabulary uses words you may have never heard or seen. These also have very exact, precise meanings. Several examples are listed:

| Field | Technical Word | Meaning |
|---|---|---|
| computer science | modem | an interface (connector) that allows the computer to send and receive digital signals over telephone lines or through satellites |
| astronomy | magnetosphere | the magnetic fields that surround the earth or other magnetized planets |
| biology | cocci | spherically shaped bacteria |

### Tips for Learning Specialized Vocabulary

There are a number of tips that may make it easier for you to learn specialized vocabulary:

1. **Keep a notebook or a notebook section for listing new words in each course.** Add words to the list as they appear in the text.

2. **Use context clues to try to discover the definition of a new term** (refer to Chapter 9 for more information). A definition clue is often provided when the word is introduced for the first time. As each new word is introduced, mark it in your text and later transfer it to your notebook. Organize this portion of your notebook by chapter. Refer to your notebook for review and reference. Use the card system (see Chapter 9) to learn words you are having trouble remembering.

3. **Prefix-root-suffix learning is a particularly useful approach for developing technical vocabulary.** In many fields, the technical words use a particular set of prefixes, roots, and suffixes that are meaningful in that area. For example, fields related to medicine use a set of prefixes, roots, and suffixes in many words. Here are several examples using prefixes:

| Prefix | Meaning | Example | Definition |
|--------|---------|---------|------------|
| cardi- | heart | cardiogram | test that measures contractions of the heart |
| hem-/hema- | blood | hematology | study of the blood |
| hypo- | under | hypodermic needle | needle that goes under the skin |
| osteo- | bone | osteopath | doctor who specializes in treatment of the bones |

In most scientific/technical fields you will find a core of commonly used prefixes, roots, and suffixes. Keep a list of common word parts in your notebook. Add to the list as you work through the course. For those word parts you have difficulty remembering, use a variation of the word card system. Write the word part on the front of the card and its meaning, pronunciation, and an example on the back.

4. **Learn to pronounce each new term you come across.** Pronouncing the word is a good way to fix it in your memory and make you feel confident in its use.

5. **Use the glossary in the back of your text.** A glossary is more useful than a dictionary because it gives the meanings of the words as used in the field you are studying; you won't have to waste time sorting through numerous meanings to find the appropriate one.

6. **If you are majoring in a technical field, consider purchasing a subject-area dictionary.** Many academic disciplines have a specialized dictionary that indexes commonly used terminology particular to that field. Nursing students, for example, often buy a copy of Taber's *Cyclopedic Medical Dictionary*.

## ■ Abbreviation and Notation Systems

Many scientific/technical fields extensively use a set of abbreviations and notations (signs and symbols). These are used as shortcuts to writing out complete words or meanings and are used in formulas, charts, and drawings. Here are a few examples:

| Field | Symbol | Meaning |
|---|---|---|
| chemistry | C | carbon |
| | H | hydrogen |
| | O | oxygen |
| biology | X | crossed with |
| | ♂ | male organism |
| | ♀ | female organism |
| physics | M | mass |
| astronomy | D | diameter |
| | Δ | distance |

To read scientific/technical material efficiently, learn the abbreviation and notation systems as soon as possible. You will save time and avoid interrupting your reading to look up a particular symbol. Check to see if lists of abbreviations and symbols are included in the appendix (reference section) in the back of your text. Also, make a list in your notebook of those symbols you need to learn. Make a point of using these symbols in your class notes whenever possible; regular use is the key to learning them.

## ■ Illustrations

Most scientific/technical books contain numerous drawings, charts, tables, and diagrams. Although these make the text appear difficult and complicated, they actually make things easier to understand. Illustrations give you a visual picture of the idea or process being explained. Figure 8.2 is a diagram taken from a photography text that explains how three types of enlargers work. The accompanying text is given here:

An **enlarger** can produce a print of any size—larger, smaller, or the same size as a negative, so it is sometimes more accurately called a projection printer. Most often, however, it is used to enlarge an image. Although an enlarger is a relatively simple machine, it is a vital link in the photographic process: the best camera in the world will not give good pictures if they are printed by an enlarger that shakes when touched, has a poor lens, or tends to slip out of focus or alignment.

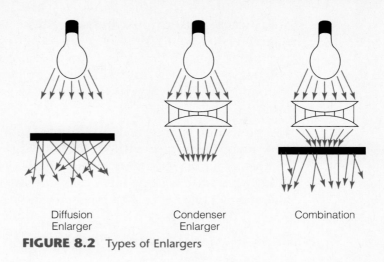

Diffusion Enlarger     Condenser Enlarger     Combination

**FIGURE 8.2** Types of Enlargers

An enlarger operates like a slide projector mounted vertically on a column. Light from an enclosed lamp shines through a negative and is then focused by a lens to expose an image of the negative on printing paper placed at the foot of the enlarger column. Image size is set by changing the distance from the enlarger head (the housing containing lamp, negative, and lens) to the paper; the greater the distance, the larger the image. The image is focused by moving the lens closer to or farther from the negative. The exposure time is controlled by a timer. To regulate the intensity of the light, the lens has a diaphragm aperture with f-stops like those of a camera lens.

An enlarger should spread light rays uniformly over the negative. It can do this in several ways. In a **diffusion enlarger,** a sheet of opal glass (a cloudy, translucent glass) is placed beneath the light source to scatter the light evenly over the negative or the light rays are bounced within a mixing chamber before reaching the negative. In a **condenser enlarger,** lenses gather the rays from the light source and send them straight through the negative. Sometimes a combination of the two systems is used [see Figure 8.2].

Upton and Upton, *Photography.*

● ● ●

Here are a few suggestions on how to learn from illustrations:

1. **Refer back and forth between the text paragraphs and the illustrations.** Illustrations are intended to be used with the paragraphs that refer to it. You may have to stop several times while reading the text to refer to an illustration. For example, when "diffusion enlarger" is mentioned in the example, you should stop reading and check the diagram to see where it is located. You may also have to reread parts of the explanation several times.

2. **Study each illustration carefully.** Notice its title or caption. This tells you what the illustration is intended to show. Then look at each part and try to see how they connect. Note any abbreviations, symbols, arrows, or labels. In the diagram of types of enlargers, the arrows are important. They suggest the direction or order in which the light operates.

3. **Test your understanding of an illustration by drawing and labeling your own illustration without looking at the one in the text.** Then compare your drawing with the text. If you left anything out, continue drawing and checking until your drawing is complete and correct. Make a final drawing in your notebook and use it for review and study.

## ■ Examples and Sample Problems

Technical books include numerous examples and sample problems. Use the following suggestions when working with examples and problems.

1. **Pay more attention to examples than you normally do in other textbooks.** Often, examples or sample problems in technical books help you understand how rules, principles, theories, or formulas are actually used. Creative learners who usually prefer experimentation and avoid rules and examples may find that sample problems simplify an otherwise complex process. Think of examples as connections between ideas on paper and the practical, everyday use of those ideas.

2. **Be sure to work through sample problems.** Carefully make sure that you understand what was done in each step and why it was done. For particularly difficult problems, write a step-by-step list of how to solve that type of problem in your notebook. Refer back to sample problems as guides or models when working problems at the end of the chapter or others assigned by your instructor.

3. **Use the problems at the end of the chapter as a self-test.** As you work through each problem, keep track of rules and formulas that you didn't know and had to look up. Also, notice the types of problems you could not solve without looking back at the sample problems. You'll need to do more work with each of these types.

## EXERCISE 8–11

*DIRECTIONS:* Read the following excerpt from *Conceptual Physics* by Paul Hewitt, an introductory physics textbook and answer the questions that follow.

## REFLECTED LIGHT AND COLOR

Roses are red and violets are blue; colors intrigue artists and physics types too. To the physicist, the colors of objects are not in the substances of the objects themselves or even in the light they emit or reflect. Color is a physiological experience and is in the eye of the beholder. So when we say that light from a rose is red, in a stricter sense we mean that it appears red. Many organisms, including people with defective color vision, will not see the rose as red at all.

The colors we see depend on the frequency of the light we see. Different frequencies of light are perceived as different colors; the lowest frequency we detect appears to most people as the color red, and the highest as violet. Between them range the infinite number of hues that make up the color spectrum of the rainbow. By convention these hues are grouped into the seven colors of red, orange, yellow, green, blue, indigo, and violet. These colors together appear white. The white light from the sun is a composite of all the visible frequencies.

Except for light sources such as lamps, lasers, and gas discharge tubes, most of the objects around us reflect rather than emit light. They reflect only part of the light that is incident upon them, the part that gives them their color.

### SELECTIVE REFLECTION

A rose, for example, doesn't emit light; it reflects light. If we pass sunlight through a prism and then place a deep-red rose in various parts of the spectrum, the rose will appear brown or black in all parts of the spectrum except in the red. In the red part of the spectrum, the petals will appear red, but the green stem and leaves will appear black. This shows that the red rose has the ability to reflect red light, but it cannot reflect other kinds of light; the green leaves have the ability to reflect green light and likewise cannot reflect other kinds of light. When the rose is held in white light, the petals appear red and the leaves green, because the petals reflect the red part of the white light and the leaves reflect the green part of the white light. To understand why objects reflect specific colors of light, we must turn our attention to the atom.

Light is reflected from objects in a manner similar to the way sound is "reflected" from a tuning fork when another that is nearby sets it into vibration. A tuning fork can be made to vibrate even when the frequencies are not matched, although at significantly reduced amplitudes. The same is true of atoms and molecules. Using the spring model of the atom we discussed in the previous chapter, we can think of atoms and molecules as three-dimensional tuning forks with electrons that behave as tiny oscillators that vibrate as if attached by invisible springs (Figure 26.1). Electrons can be forced into vibration (oscillation) by the vibrating (oscillating) electric fields of electromagnetic waves.* Once vibrating, these electrons send out their own electromagnetic waves just as vibrating acoustical tuning forks send out sound waves.

Atoms (and molecules) have their own natural frequencies; electrons of one kind of atom can be set into vibration at frequencies that are different from the frequencies

---

* We use the words oscillate and vibrate interchangeably. Also, the words oscillators and vibrators have the same meaning.

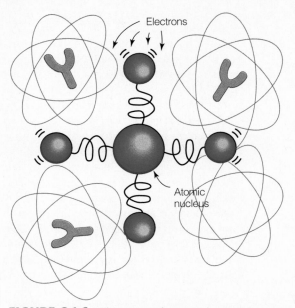

**FIGURE 26.1**   The outer electrons in an atom vibrate as if they were attached to the nucleus by springs. As a result, atoms and molecules behave somewhat like optical tuning forks.

for other atoms. At the resonant frequencies where the amplitudes of oscillation are large, light is absorbed. But at frequencies below and above the resonant frequencies, light is re-emitted. If the material is transparent the re-emitted light can travel through the material. For both opaque and transparent materials, the light re-emitted back into the medium from which it came is the reflected light.

Usually a material will absorb some frequencies of light and reflect the rest. If a material absorbs most visible frequencies and reflects red, for example, the material appears red. If it reflects all the visible frequencies, like the white part of this page, it will be the same color as the light that shines on it. If a material absorbs all the light that shines on it, it reflects none and is black.

When white light falls on a flower, some of the frequencies are absorbed by the cells in the flower and some are reflected. Cells that contain chlorophyll absorb most of the frequencies and reflect the green part of the light that falls on it. The petals of a red rose, on the other hand, reflect primarily red light, with a lesser amount of blue. Interestingly enough, the petals of most yellow flowers, like daffodils, reflect red and green as well as yellow. Yellow daffodils reflect a broad band of frequencies. The reflected colors of most objects are not pure single-frequency colors, but are composed of a spread of frequencies.

An object can only reflect frequencies that are present in the illuminating light. The appearance of a colored object therefore depends on the kind of light used. A candle flame emits light that is deficient in blue; its light is yellowish. An incandes-

**FIGURE 26.2** Color depends on the light source.

cent lamp emits light that is richer toward the lower frequencies, enhancing the reds. In a fabric with a little bit of red in it, for example, the red will be more apparent under an incandescent lamp than when illuminated with a fluorescent lamp. Fluorescent lamps are richer in the higher frequencies, so blues are enhanced under them. With various kinds of illumination, it is difficult to tell the true color of objects. Colors appear different in daylight than they appear when illuminated by either kind of lamp (Figure 26.2).

## SELECTIVE TRANSMISSION

The color of a transparent object depends on the color of the light it transmits. A red piece of glass appears red because it absorbs all the colors that compose white light, except red, which it *transmits.* Similarly, a blue piece of glass appears blue because it transmits primarily blue and absorbs the other colors that illuminate it. The piece of glass contains dyes or *pigments*—fine particles that selectively absorb certain frequencies and selectively transmit others. From an atomic point of view, electrons in the pigment molecules are set into vibration by the illuminating light. Some of the frequencies are absorbed by the pigments, and others are re-emitted from molecule to molecule in the glass. The energy of the absorbed frequencies increases the kinetic energy of the molecules and the glass is warmed. Ordinary window glass is colorless because it transmits all visible frequencies equally well.

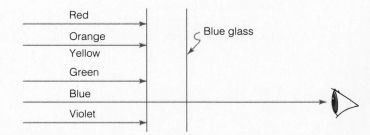

**FIGURE 26.3** Only energy having the frequency of blue light is transmitted; energy of the other frequencies is absorbed and warms the glass.

**QUESTIONS**

1. When red light shines on a red rose, why do the leaves become warmer than the petals?
2. When green light shines on a rose, why to the petals look black?
3. If you hold a match, a candle flame, or any small source of white light in between you and a piece of red glass, you'll see two reflections from the glass: one from the front surface and one from the back surface. What color of reflections will you see?

● ● ●

1. How does this excerpt compare with the psychology textbook excerpt on pp. 55–58 for each of the following characteristics?
   a. fact density _____
   b. number of technical terms _____
   c. number and use of illustrations _____
   d. number of examples _____

2. Underline terminology you would need to learn to pass an exam based on this chapter.

3. Explain the purpose of each of the following figures:
   a. Figure 26.1 _____
   b. Figure 26.2 _____
   c. Figure 26.3 _____

4. Answer the questions that appear at the end of the excerpt.
   1. _____
   2. _____
   3. _____

**Critical Thinking Tip #8**

**Using Your Background Knowledge and Experience**

Your familiarity with a topic can influence how easily you can remember information about it. A brand new topic is more difficult to learn than one you already know something about. In fact, the more familiar a topic, the more easily you can learn new information about it. Your brain establishes connections or links between old and new information. By tying your new learning to the old, you will find you can remember the new information more easily.

When you read the title of a chapter, you may think you know nothing about it, but often you will discover you know more about it than you originally thought. For example, suppose you are ready to begin reading a section of a chapter in your psychology book titled "Aggressive Behavior." At first you may say you know nothing about aggression. However, aggression is something we all witness daily: A man kicks a soda machine when he loses his money; a child slaps another child; a phone salesperson aggressively pursues a conversation until you hang up. Once you realize that you are familiar with aggression, reading the chapter section will become both easier and more interesting.

Sometimes you have to work a bit to discover what you already know. Try the following techniques:

1. Ask yourself: What have I already read or seen that is related to this topic?
2. Brainstorm. Spend two or three minutes thinking about or writing anything that comes to mind about your topic.
3. Try to think of situations or examples from your own experiences that relate to the topic.

Then, apply your prior knowledge. If you are reading about types of aggression, for example, decide which type the soda machine example fits into. Connecting new to old learning will pay off in increased retention and recall!

## SUMMARY

**1. How are textbook chapters organized to help you learn?**

Textbooks are unique information sources and vehicles for learning. Textbook chapters use a system of headings and subheadings to organize information and show what is important. They also use other aids to help you learn, including
- Chapter previews
- Special interest inserts
- Marginal notations
- Summaries
- Lists of new terminology
- Review questions
- Discussion questions
- Chapter outlines
- Suggested readings or references

**2. Describe the two types of review that you can use to increase retention.**

Immediate review is done right after reading while the information is still fresh in your mind. Periodic review is done at a later time to refresh your recall of the material.

**3. What other aids or methods can be used to increase your recall?**

Other aids to retention include
- Intent to remember
- Organization/categorization
- Association
- Use of sensory modes
- Visualization
- Mnemonic devices

**4. What is the SQ3R system for reading and learning?**

The SQ3R system is a method for increasing reading efficiency and flexibility that directly enhances your retention. The steps are
- Survey
- Question
- Read
- Recite
- Review

**5. What should be considered when adapting the SQ3R system?**

To make the best use of the SQ3R method you should adapt it to suit both the material you are reading and how you learn best. You should consider the reading material's structure and content when adapting SQ3R. Also, you should make adjustments that incorporate the methods for learning that work best for you.

**6. How does writing in the scientific/technical fields differ from that in other areas of study?**

Textbooks in scientific/technical fields are highly specialized and differ from other texts in that technical material
- Is factually dense.
- Uses technical vocabulary.
- Uses abbreviations and notation systems.
- Uses a large number of illustrations and examples.
- Contains sample problems.

**POLITICAL SCIENCE**

# READING SELECTION 15
## THE NEWS AND PUBLIC OPINION
George C. Edwards, et al.
*From Government in America*

*How influential is the media in shaping or determining opinions viewers and listeners hold? This excerpt from an American government textbook examines the relationship between news and public opinion.*

1    How does the threatening, hostile, and corrupt world often depicted by the new media shape what people believe about the American political system? This question is difficult to answer. Studying the effects of the new media on people's opinions and behaviors is a difficult task. One reason is that it is hard to separate the media from other influences. When presidents, legislators, and interest groups—as well as news organizations—are all discussing an issue, it is not easy to isolate the opinion changes that come from political leadership from those that come from the news. Moreover, the effect of one news story on public opinion may be trivial; the cumulative effect of dozens of news stories may be quite important.

2    For many years students of the subject tended to doubt that the media had more than a marginal effect on public opinion. The "minimal effects hypothesis" stemmed from the fact that early scholars were looking for direct impacts—for example, whether the media affected how people voted.[34] When the focus turned to how the media affect *what American think about,* more positive results were uncovered. In a series of controlled laboratory experiments, Shanto Iyengar and Donald Kinder subtly manipulated the stories participants saw on TV news.[35] They found they could significantly affect the importance people attached to a given problem by splicing a few stories about it into the news over the course of a week. Iyengar and Kinder do not maintain that

the networks can make something out of nothing or conceal problems that actually exist. But they do conclude that "what television news does, instead, is alter the priorities Americans attach to a circumscribed set of problems, all of which are plausible contenders for public concern."[36]

3    This effect has far-reaching consequences. By increasing public attention to specific problems, the media influence the criteria by which the public evaluates political leaders. When unemployment goes up but inflation goes down, does public support for the president increase or decrease? The answer could depend in large part on which story is emphasized by the media. The fact that the media emphasized the country's slow economic growth in 1992, rather than the good news of low interest rates, was clearly damaging to President Bush's reelection campaign.

4    In another study, Page, Shapiro, and Dempsey examined changes in public attitudes about issues over time. They examined public opinion polls on the same issues at two points in time, carefully coding the news coverage of these issues on the networks and in print during the interim. People's opinions did indeed shift with the tone of the news coverage. The impact of news commentators, such as John Chancellor and David Brinkley, seemed particularly significant in affecting opinion change. Another source of opinion change was presidential statements, though this varied by the popularity of the president. Not surprisingly, popular presidents were much more effective in changing people's opinions than unpopular ones. In contrast, interest groups seemed to have a negative impact on opinion change, suggesting that interest groups' overt activities on behalf of a certain policy position

## The People Speak

### Stories Citizens Have Tuned In and Stories They Have Tuned Out

Since 1986, the monthly survey of the PEW Research Center for the People and the Press has asked Americans how closely they have followed major news stories. As one would expect, stories involving disaster or human drama have drawn more attention than complicated issues of public policy. A representative selection of their findings is presented below. The percentage in each case is the proportion who reported the story "very closely."

| | |
|---|---|
| The explosion of the space shuttle *Challenger* | 80% |
| San Francisco earthquake | 73% |
| Los Angeles riots | 70% |
| Rescue of baby Jessico McClure from a well | 69% |
| Crash of TWA 800 | 69% |
| Iraq's invasion of Kuwait | 66% |
| Hurricane Andrew | 66% |
| Explosion during Atlanta Olympics | 57% |
| Supreme Court decision on flag burning | 51% |
| Opening of the Berlin Wall | 50% |
| Introduction of President Clinton's 1993 economic program | 49% |
| Arrest of O. J. Simpson | 48% |
| Nuclear accident at Chernobyl | 46% |
| Attack on ice skater Nancy Kerrigan | 45% |
| Arrest in the Unabomber case | 44% |
| Iran-Contra hearings | 33% |
| Mass suicide of "Heaven's Gate" cult | 32% |
| Passage of the 1994 Crime Bill | 30% |
| 1996 New Hampshire primary | 22% |
| Congressional debate over NAFTA | 21% |
| Clinton's veto of the bill to ban "partial-birth" abortions | 21% |
| Congressional repeal of catastrophic health insurance | 19% |
| Nomination of Robert Bork to the Supreme Court | 17% |
| Education summit held by President Bush and the nation's governors | 15% |
| Clinton's cabinet choices for his second term | 15% |
| Passage of the 1996 Communications Deregulation Bill | 12% |
| Discussion and debate about expanding NATO into Eastern Europe | 6% |

SOURCE: PEW Research Center for the People and the Press.

may in fact discourage support for that position. Of all the influences on opinion change these researchers examined, the impact of new commentators was the strongest. If Page and his colleagues are correct, the new media today are one of the most potent engines, perhaps the most potent, of public opinion change in America.[37]

5   Much remains unknown about the effects of the media and the news on American political behavior. Enough is known, however, to conclude that the media are a key political institution. The media control much of the technology that in turn controls much of what Americans believe about politics and government. For this reason, it is important to look at the American policy agenda and the media's role in shaping it.

## Comprehension Test 15

*Directions:   Circle the letter of the best answer.*

### Checking Your Comprehension

1. This reading is primarily concerned with how
   a. the media depict violence in the world today.
   b. the media shape our opinions.
   c. the general public feels about the media.
   d. television overdramatizes and sensationalizes situations.

2. The central thought of this selection is that the media
   a. tend to present a biased view of the world.
   b. can persuade the public to believe ideas which are untrue.
   c. should not cover certain political issues and events.
   d. can sway opinions based on what and how they report.

3. It is difficult to study the effects of the news media on people's opinions and behaviors because
   a. people are not honest about their opinions.
   b. the media cover so many events it's impossible to tell what the public thinks.
   c. people sometimes behave in opposition to the media.
   d. it is hard to separate the media from other influences.

4. According to the reading, the media damaged President Bush's re-election by
   a. giving more time and better coverage to Bill Clinton.
   b. depicting Bush's campaign as dishonest and corrupt.
   c. emphasizing the nation's sluggish economic growth rate.
   d. portraying Bush as a weak candidate for re-election.

5. People's opinions are most strongly influenced by the
   a. statements of the president.
   b. activities of interest groups.
   c. presentations of new commentators.
   d. findings of researchers.

6. The word "splicing" in paragraph 2 means
   a. eliminating.
   b. adding.
   c. highlighting.
   d. exaggerating.

### Thinking Critically

7. From the reading it is reasonable to conclude that the author believes the media
   a. play a large role in government policy.
   b. directly affect how people vote.
   c. cannot affect what people think about.
   d. fairly balance good and bad news.

8. It is evident from the reading that the author's attitude toward the media is that they
   a. are fair in their overall coverage of the news.
   b. are unable to influence political opinion.
   c. have too much power and influence.
   d. have become corrupt in recent years.

9. Based on the reading, the reader can assume that
   a. the more popular a president is, the more effective he will be in changing public opinion.
   b. the longer a president is in office, the more likely it is that he can change public opinion.
   c. the less coverage the media give an issue, the more likely it is that viewers will change their minds about that issue.
   d. the greater the coverage provided by the media, the less public opinion will change.

10. According to the reading, which one of the following statements is true?
    a. Television is more effective in changing public opinion than newspapers.
    b. The media may be the strongest means used to change people's political views.
    c. News commentators are always able to sway viewers to their point of view.
    d. A newspaper editorial on a presidential campaign can do more damage than a television editorial.

**Questions for Discussion**

1. Do you think that the media control people? How?
2. What conclusions can you draw about the media and their power over viewers?
3. Which do you think has a stronger influence, television media or the newspapers? Why?
4. What kinds of stories do you think should take precedence in the news? How would this affect the viewer?

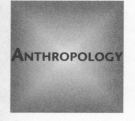

ANTHROPOLOGY

## READING SELECTION 16
## THE DOMESTIC SPHERE OF CULTURE

Marvin Harris
*From Cultural Anthropology*

*Household living arrangements vary from culture to culture. Read this excerpt from a cultural anthropology textbook to learn about cultural variations in domestic ways of life.*

1  All societies have a domestic sphere of life. The focus of the domestic sphere is a dwelling space, shelter, residence, or household, in which certain universally recurrent activities take place. It is not possible to give a simple checklist of what these activities are (Netting, Wilk, and Arnould, 1984). In many cultures, domestic activities include preparation and consumption of food; cleaning, grooming, teaching, and disciplining the young; sleeping; and adult sexual intercourse. However, in no culture are these activities carried out exclusively within domestic settings.

2  In the case of modern industrial cultures, this pattern is evident with respect to enculturation and education. Enculturation and education in contemporary life are increasingly carried out in special nondomestic buildings (schools) under the auspices of specialists (teachers) who live in separate households. Many village and band societies also separate their children and adolescents from the entire domestic scene in order to teach them the lore and ritual of the ancestors, sexual competence, or the military arts. Among the Nyakyusa of southern Tanzania, for example, at age 6 or 7, boys begin to put up reed shelters or playhouses on the outskirts of their villages. The boys gradually improve and enlarge these playhouses, eventually constructing a whole new village. Between the ages of 5 and 11, Nyakyusa boys sleep in their parents' house. But during adolescence, they are permitted to visit only during daylight hours and must sleep in the new village although their mothers still cook for them. The founding of a new Nyakyusa village is

complete when the young men take wives who cook for them and begin to give birth to the next generation.

3  Another famous variation on this pattern is found among the Masai of East Africa, where unmarried men of the same age-set, or ritually defined generation, establish special villages or camps from which they launch war parties and cattle-stealing raids. It is the mothers and sisters of these men who cook and keep house for them.

4  In many societies, married men spend a good deal of time in special men's houses. Food is handed in to them by wives and children, who are themselves forbidden to enter. Men also sleep and work in these "club-houses" although they may on occasion bed down with their wives and children. Among the Fur of the Sudan, for example, husbands usually sleep apart from their wives in houses of their own and take their meals at an exclusive men's mess. One of the most interesting cases of the separation of cooking and eating occurs among the Ashanti of West Africa. Ashanti men eat their meals with their sisters, mothers, and maternal nephews and nieces, not with their wives and children. But it is the wives who do the cooking. Every evening in Ashanti land one sees a steady traffic of children taking their mother's cooking to their father's sister's house.

5  Among the Zumbagua peasants of the Peruvian Andes, households undergo a regular cycle of growth in which varieties of domestic behavior are gradually added to everyday life.

During courtship, couples have sex in the fields at a distance from the houses where they eat and sleep. When they get married they build a small windowless hut that lacks any source of heating for warmth or cooking. This hut adjoins the house of the groom's or bride's parents. Now they sleep and have sex together under one roof, but they continue to cook and eat in the kitchen of their parents. Their first children are brought up and cared for by the couple's parents. With the birth of additional children, the couple adds a kitchen of their own to their hut, which becomes a storeroom, and they gradually begin to sleep, cook, eat, have sex, and nurture their offspring around their new hearth.

Writes anthropologist Mary Weismantel (1989:57): "The existence of a [Zumbagua] household is defined by the presence of a kitchen. The word kitchen in itself implies much more than a room where food is prepared. It is here that meals are made and eaten, male and female heads of households sleep and live, baths are taken, the family meets, guests are entertained, decisions made, wakes held, babies born and the sick nursed back to health. In addition, only kitchens are warm: the hearth is the only source of heat in Zumbagua homes. Cats, guinea pigs, and convalescent sheep demonstrate their innate grasp of the role of the kitchen in the Zumbagua household by their refusal to live in any other building, while chickens and dogs, less privileged, spend most of their lives attempting to join the circle around the kitchen hearth."

## Comprehension Test 16*

### Checking Your Comprehension

1. What is meant by the term *domestic sphere*?
2. Who eats the food that Ashanti children take to their aunt's house every evening?

3. In the Zumbagua community, who raises a couple's first child?
4. At what point is a new village in Nyakyusa considered complete?

---

* Multiple-choice questions are contained in Appendix B (page A17).

**Thinking Critically**

1. Why do six-year-old Nyakyusa boys begin building playhouses and shelters?

2. In the Peruvian Andes, why do the Zumbagua newlyweds build a windowless hut and attach it to their parent's house?

3. At what point does a young Zumbaguan couple add a kitchen to their hut? Why is this a significant social undertaking?

4. What evidence indicates that even cats and guinea pigs enjoy a higher social status than chickens and dogs in a Zumbagua house? Why is this?

**Questions for Discussion**

1. What is the purpose for special men's clubs or houses among certain cultural groups in the Sudan?

2. In Zumbagua, why is the kitchen said to be the center of activity? What room in an American house might be considered equivalent to a Zumbaguan kitchen?

3. What is the significance of the war parties and cattle stealing raids initiated by young Masai men of East Africa? Do young men in the United States have similar "rites of passage"?

4. Compare and contrast the role of women in Tanzania with the role of women in the United States.

| Selection 16: | | | 790 words |
|---|---|---|---|
| Finishing Time: | _____ | _____ | _____ |
| | HR. | MIN. | SEC. |
| Starting Time: | _____ | _____ | _____ |
| | HR. | MIN. | SEC. |
| Reading Time: | | _____ | _____ |
| | | MIN. | SEC. |
| WPM Score: | | _____ | |
| Comprehension Score: | | _____ | % |

**Visit the Longman English Pages**

For additional readings and exercises, visit the Longman English Skills Web page at:

**http://longman.awl.com/englishpages**

For a username and password, please see your instructor.

# CHAPTER 9
# Techniques for Learning Textbook Material

IN THIS CHAPTER YOU WILL LEARN:

1. To use highlighting effectively.
2. To make marginal annotations.
3. To paraphrase text.
4. To use outlining to organize ideas.
5. To summarize information.
6. To draw conceptual maps.

As a college student, you are expected to learn large amounts of textbook material. Rereading to learn is *not* an effective strategy. Writing *is* an effective strategy. In fact, writing is an excellent means of improving both your comprehension and your retention. Many successful students almost always read with a pen in hand ready to highlight, mark, annotate, or paraphrase ideas. Some students use writing to study and review the material after reading. They outline to organize information, write summaries to condense ideas, or draw maps to show relationships.

Writing during and after reading has numerous advantages:

1. **Writing focuses your attention.** If you are writing as well as reading, you are forced to keep your mind on the topic.

2. **Writing forces you to think.** By highlighting or writing you are forced to decide what is important and understand relationships and connections.

3. **Writing tests your understanding.** One of the truest measures of understanding is your ability to explain an idea in your own words. When you have understood an idea, you will be able to write about it, but when an idea is unclear or confusing, you will be at a loss for words.

4. **Writing facilitates recall.** Research studies indicate that information is recalled more easily if it is elaborated on. Elaboration involves expanding and thinking about the material by drawing connections

and associations, seeing relationships, and making applications. As you will see throughout the chapter, writing is a form of elaboration.

This chapter describes six learning strategies that use writing as a learning tool: highlighting, annotating, paraphrasing, outlining, summarizing, and mapping.

# ■ HIGHLIGHTING TECHNIQUES

When reading factual material, the easiest and fastest way to mark important facts and ideas is to highlight them using a pencil, pen, or marker. Many students are hesitant to mark their texts because they want to sell them at the end of the semester. However, highlighting makes the book more useful to you, so try not to let your interest in selling the book prevent you from reading and studying in the most efficient manner.

## ■ How to Highlight Effectively

Your goal in highlighting is to identify and mark those portions of an assignment that are important to reread when you study that chapter. Here are a few suggestions on how to highlight effectively:

1. **Read a paragraph or section first and then go back and highlight what is important.** If you highlight as you read, you run the risk of highlighting an idea that you think is important, only to find out later in the passage that it is less important than you originally thought.

2. **Use your knowledge of paragraph structure to guide your highlighting.** Try to highlight important portions of the topic sentence and any supporting details that you want to remember. Use signal words to locate changes or divisions of thought.

3. **Use headings to guide your highlighting.** Earlier in this book you learned that headings could be used to establish a purpose for reading. In Chapter 8 you saw that turning headings into questions to guide your reading is the Q step in the SQ3R reading-study system. A logical extension of these uses of headings is to use questions to help you identify what to highlight. As you read, you should be looking for the answer to your questions; when you find information that answers the questions, highlight it.

4. **Use a system for highlighting.** You can use a number of systems. They include
   - using two or more colors of ink or highlighters to distinguish between main ideas and details or more and less important information.

- using single underscoring for details and highlighting for main ideas.
- placing brackets around the main idea and using a highlighter to mark important details.

Because no system is the most effective for everyone, develop a system that works well for you. Once you develop that system, however, use it consistently. If you vary systems, your chances for confusion and error while reviewing are greater.

5. **Highlight just enough words to make the meaning clear when rereading.** Avoid highlighting a whole sentence. Usually the core parts of the sentence, along with an additional phrase or two, are sufficient. Notice that you can understand the meaning of the following sentence by reading only the highlighted parts.

Fad diets disregard the necessity for balance among the various classes of nutrients.

• • •

Now, read only the highlighted parts of the following paragraph. Can you understand what the paragraph is about?

### CIGARETTE SMOKING

The person who smokes more than a pack of cigarettes a day runs nearly twice the risk of heart attack, and nearly five times the risk of stroke, as does a nonsmoker. Abstaining from smoking lowers your risk of heart attack twenty-two percent below the norm. Smoking more than a pack a day raises your risk to thirty-two percent above the norm. In addition, as explained in other chapters of this book, smoking greatly increases susceptibility to lung cancer and to such lung diseases as bronchitis and emphysema.

Dorfman et.al., *Well-Being: An Introduction to Health.*

• • •

Most likely you were able to understand the basic message by reading only the highlighted words. You were able to do so because the highlighted words were core parts of each sentence or modifiers that directly explained those parts.

6. **Be sure that your highlighting accurately reflects the content of the passage.** Incomplete or hasty highlighting can mislead you as you review the passage and cause you to miss the main point. As a safeguard against this, occasionally test your accuracy by rereading only what you have highlighted. Does your highlighting tell what the paragraph or passage is about? Does it express the most important idea in the passage?

## ■ Highlighting the Right Amount

If you highlight either too little or too much, you will defeat its purpose. If you highlight too little, you will miss valuable information and your review and study of the material will be incomplete. If you highlight too much, you are not identifying and highlighting the most important ideas. The more you highlight, the more you will have to reread when studying, and the less of a timesaver the procedure will be.

Here is a passage highlighted in three ways. Read the entire passage and then examine each version of the highlighting. Try to decide which version would be most useful if you were rereading it for study purposes.

### Version 1

Alcoholism

Alcoholism is a disease that requires medical treatment, and it is increasingly common. It cuts across all age, class and social strata. Contrary to stereotype, few alcoholics are skid row bums. Most are employed, married, respectable people; women are as vulnerable as men. Approximately seven percent of the population, or ten percent of all drinkers, are alcoholics.

Dr. E. M. Jellinek, a leading researcher into alcoholism, divides the development of alcoholism into four stages: (1) the pre-alcoholic phase, (2) the prodromal phase, (3) the crucial phase, and (4) the chronic phase. Perhaps most important for our purposes here is the pre-alcoholic phase, for it is hoped that some potential alcoholics, recognizing the early warning signals of alcoholism, will seek counseling or other help in time to prevent serious onset of the illness.

Some symptoms of the pre-alcoholic phase are (a) drinking used as a mechanism to escape from problems (in college students, usually academic or social problems); (b) drinking used to bolster courage, as before a test or job interview; (c) development of an increased tolerance for alcohol. There may also be (d) feelings of guilt associated with drinking or (e) feelings of urgency connected with downing the first few drinks. These last two symptoms, however, may not appear until the prodromal phase.

Dorfman et. al., *Well-Being: An Introduction to Health.*

### Version 2

Alcoholism

Alcoholism is a disease that requires medical treatment, and it is increasingly common. It cuts across all age, class, and social strata. Contrary to stereotype, few alcoholics are skid row bums. Most are employed, married, respectable people; women are as vulnerable as men. Approximately seven percent of the population, or ten percent of all drinkers, are alcoholics.

Dr. E. M. Jellinek, a leading researcher into alcoholism, divides the development of alcoholism into four stages: (1) the pre-alcoholic phase, (2) the prodromal phase, (3) the crucial phase, and (4) the chronic phase. Perhaps most important for our purposes here is the pre-alcoholic phase, for it is hoped that some potential alcoholics, recognizing the early warning signals of alcoholism, will seek counseling or other help in time to prevent serious onset of the illness.

Some symptoms of the pre-alcoholic phase are (a) drinking used as a mechanism to escape from problems (in college students, usually academic or social problems); (b) drinking used to bolster courage, as before a test or job interview; (c) development of an increased tolerance for alcohol. There may also be (d) feelings of guilt associated with drinking or (e) feelings of urgency connected with downing the first few drinks. These last two symptoms, however, may not appear until the prodromal phase.

### Version 3

Alcoholism

Alcoholism is a disease that requires medical treatment, and it is increasingly common. It cuts across all age, class, and social strata. Contrary to stereotype, few alcoholics are skid row bums. Most are employed, married, respectable people; women are as vulnerable as men. Approximately seven percent of the population, or ten percent of all drinkers, are alcoholics.

Dr. E. M. Jellinek, a leading researcher into alcoholism, divides the development of alcoholism into four stages: (1) the pre-alcoholic phase, (2) the prodromal phase, (3) the crucial phase, and (4) the chronic phase. Perhaps most important for our purposes here is the pre-alcoholic phase, for it is hoped that some potential alcoholics, recognizing the early warning signals of alcoholism, will seek counseling or other help in time to prevent serious onset of the illness.

Some symptoms of the pre-alcoholic phase are (a) drinking used as a mechanism to escape from problems (in college students, usually academic or social problems); (b) drinking used to bolster courage, as before a test or job interview; (c) development of an increased tolerance for alcohol. There may also be (d) feelings of guilt associated with drinking or (e) feelings of urgency connected with downing the first few drinks. These last two symptoms, however, may not appear until the prodromal phase.

● ● ●

This passage on alcoholism contains two important sets of information. It lists the four stages of alcoholism, and it describes the symptoms of the pre-alcoholic phase. In evaluating the highlighting done in version 1, you can see that it does not contain enough information. The four stages are not highlighted, and some, but not all, symptoms of pre-alcoholism are highlighted.

Version 2, on the other hand, has too much highlighting. Although all of the important ideas are highlighted, many less important details are also highlighted. For instance, in the third paragraph examples of the various symptoms as well as the symptoms themselves are highlighted and appear to be of equal importance. In fact, nearly every sentence is highlighted, and for review purposes it would be almost as easy to reread the entire passage as it would be to read only the highlighting.

Version 3 is an example of effective highlighting. If you reread only the highlighting, you will see that both the four stages of alcoholism and the symptoms of the pre-alcoholic phase are highlighted.

As a general rule of thumb, try to highlight no more than 20 to 30 percent of the passage. Once you exceed this range, you begin to lose effectiveness. Of course, if a particular section or passage is very factual or detailed it may require more detailed highlighting. However, if you find that an entire assignment or chapter seems to require 60 to 70 percent highlighting, you should consider using one of the other notetaking methods suggested later in this chapter.

# EXERCISE 9-1

*DIRECTIONS:* Read and highlight the following excerpt from a chemistry textbook, using the guidelines for highlighting. When you have finished, compare your highlighting to that in the sample on pages 320–321.

## *Excerpt*

### Nucleic Acids

Figure 19.1 is a diagram of a typical cell. The outside is a semi-permeable membrane, which lets specific molecules pass into and out of the cell. Most of the inside is water, with many small molecules dissolved in it. Various solid bodies, called *organelles,* are dotted all around the cell like islands. Each organelle has a function.

A newly formed cell comes with packages of information, called *chromosomes.* The information tells the cell how to make others just like it and also how to make cells with different functions—eye cells, for instance, or liver or leaf cells. The cell makes other cells by first making proteins. Some of the proteins will form the structural parts of the new cells, whereas others will control or regulate the production of other kinds of molecules that provide structure or function. Within the chromosomes are genes—directions for making individual protein molecules. A human being has forty-six chromosomes, which contain over a hundred thousand genes.

The chromosomes are located in the *nucleus,* the organelle that contains the cell's "brains." The molecules in the chromosomes that contain information, plus others found in the nucleus, are called *nucleic acids.*

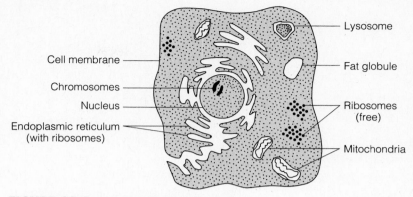

**FIGURE 19.1** A generalized animal cell.

**DNA structure and replication**

As soon as the cell is formed, long slender threads unravel from each chromosome. These threads are the nucleic acid *deoxyribonucleic acid* (DNA). The DNA in human chromosomes, originally contained in a nucleus only $8 + 10^{-4}$ centimeters in diameter, has a combined length of over 2 meters when it's all unraveled.

DNA has two functions. The first, which it performs when the cell isn't dividing, is to direct the synthesis of proteins. Some of these proteins are catalysts called *enzymes.* Every reaction in a cell needs a special enzyme to make it go, and thus enzymes are second in command to DNA when it comes to getting things done in the cell.

DNA's second function is *replication,* or copying itself. It stops directing protein synthesis and starts replicating as soon as the cell is ready to begin dividing. When the DNA has completely replicated itself, the two sets that result pack themselves back up into separate chromosomes and the cell divides. Each of the two new cells will have a copy of the directions.

Newell, *Chemistry.*

## *Sample Highlighting*

Nucleic Acids

Figure 19.1 is a diagram of a typical cell. The outside is a semi-permeable membrane, which lets specific molecules pass into and out of the cell. Most of the inside is water, with many small molecules dissolved in it. Various solid bodies, called organelles, are dotted all around the cell like islands. Each organelle has a function.

A newly formed cell comes with packages of information, called chromosomes. The information tells the cell how to make others just like it and also how to make

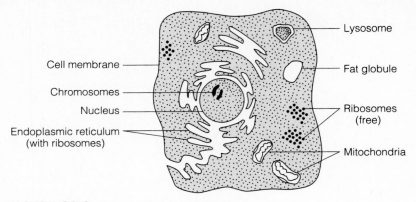

Cell membrane

Chromosomes

Nucleus

Endoplasmic reticulum
(with ribosomes)

Lysosome

Fat globule

Ribosomes
(free)

Mitochondria

**FIGURE 19.1** A generalized animal cell.

cells with different functions—eye cells, for instance, or liver or leaf cells. The cell makes other cells by first making proteins. Some of the proteins will form the structural parts of the new cells, whereas others will control or regulate the production of other kinds of molecules that provide structure or function. Within the chromosomes are *genes*—directions for making individual protein molecules. A human being has forty-six chromosomes, which contain over a hundred thousand genes.

The chromosomes are located in the *nucleus,* the organelle that contains the cell's "brains." The molecules in the chromosomes that contain information, plus others found in the nucleus, are called *nucleic acids.*

## DNA structure and replication

As soon as the cell is formed, long slender threads unravel from each chromosome. These threads are the nucleic acid *deoxyribonucleic acid* (DNA). The DNA in human chromosomes, originally contained in a nucleus only $8 + 10^{-4}$ centimeters in diameter, has a combined length of over 2 meters when it's all unraveled.

DNA has two functions. The first, which it performs when the cell isn't dividing, is to direct the synthesis of proteins. Some of these proteins are catalysts called *enzymes.* Every reaction in a cell needs a special enzyme to make it go, and thus enzymes are second in command to DNA when it comes to getting things done in the cell.

DNA's second function is *replication,* or copying itself. It stops directing protein synthesis and starts replicating as soon as the cell is ready to begin dividing. When the DNA has completely replicated itself, the two sets that result pack themselves back up into separate chromosomes and the cell divides. Each of the two new cells will have a copy of the directions.

● ● ●

## EXERCISE 9–2

*DIRECTIONS:* Choose one of the reading selections at the end of this chapter. Assume that you are reading it as part of a class reading assignment on which you will be tested. As you read, highlight the important ideas. Tomorrow, reread what you have highlighted and then answer the multiple-choice questions that follow the selection.

## ■ ANNOTATING AND MAKING MARGINAL NOTATIONS

If you were reading the want ads in a newspaper in search of an apartment to rent, you would probably mark certain ads. As you phoned for more information, you might make notes about each apartment. These notes would help you decide which apartments to visit. Similarly, in many types of academic reading, making notes, or *annotating,* is a useful strategy. Annotating is a means of keeping track of your impressions, ideas, reactions, and questions as you read. Then, after reading, reviewing your annotations will help you form a final impression of the work. If a writing assignment accompanies the reading, your annotations will serve as an excellent source of ideas for a paper. Annotating should be used in conjunction with highlighting. Highlighting is a means of identifying important information; annotating is a method of recording *your* thinking about these key ideas.

There are no fixed rules about how or what to annotate. In general, try to mark or note any ideas about the assignment that come to mind as you read or reread. Write your annotations in the margins. Use annotations to

- Write questions about the material
- Condense important points
- Identify ideas with which you disagree
- Mark good or poor examples of supporting data
- Jot down inconsistencies
- Locate key terms or definitions
- Consider contrasting points of view
- Summarize arguments
- Mark words with strong connotative meanings
- Identify the author's viewpoints or feelings

Several methods of annotation are discussed in the following sections.

## ■ Using Symbols to Annotate

Symbols can be used to distinguish types of information, to emphasize material to be studied, or to show relationships among ideas. They can be very convenient, for instance, in calling attention to examples or definitions, portions of an assignment that you feel are particularly important to study, or contrasting ideas and opinions.

Develop your own set of symbols and use them consistently. Here is a sample list of commonly used symbols and their meanings.

| Symbol | Meaning |
|---|---|
| ex | an example is included |
| def | an important term is defined |
| ☐ | unknown word to look up in dictionary later |
| T | good test question |
| ? | confusing idea |
| * | very important |
| sum | summary statement |
| ↗ | relates to another idea |

Now read the following passage, paying particular attention to the use of symbols.

### GOVERNMENT HEALTH ORGANIZATION

*def* { Government health agencies, the tax-supported arm of the community health effort, perform an important function in community health practice. They are the official public health and welfare agencies whose areas of jurisdiction and types of service are dictated by law. They coordinate activities that often can be carried out only by group or community-wide action, for example, proper sewage disposal or

*ex* { the provision of sanitary water systems. Government health agencies develop facilities and programs for special groups, such as native Americans, migrant workers, and military personnel and veterans, whose health care is not the direct responsibility of any one state or locality. Many community health activities require an

*3 functions* authoritative legal backing to ensure enforcement (another useful function of official agencies) of control in such areas as environmental pollution, highway safety

*ex* { practices, and harmful use of drugs. Official agencies provide important record-keeping services, which include the collection of vital statistics, research, consultation, and sometimes financial support to other community health groups.

Spradley, *Community Health Nursing.*

● ● ●

## ■ Annotating to Condense Information

Annotating is a helpful technique to use when you work through complicated or lengthy explanations.Often, a few marginal notes can be used to summarize an entire paragraph, as shown in the following example.

*size of market depends on size and value of item*

A *"market"* is a group of buyers with significant buying potential and unfulfilled needs or desires, who have the means to purchase, and whom the marketer can profitably serve. Let's take this definition apart.

First, a market must have significant potential. That is, usually the final amount of the sale will produce a current or future profit for you. Note that we did not specify market size. In the intermediate market the number of actual buyers may be small, but the size of the order may be substantial. The final market, however, can consist of many thousands or millions of individual customers who purchase fewer items. Thus, if you are marketing consumer goods the sale of ten pairs of specially designed athletic shoes to a basketball team would not be significant. But the sale of one atomic reactor with its power-plant complex to a public utility company would represent billions of dollars.

Fox and Wheatley, *Modern Marketing.*

● ● ●

You can see that annotations are a useful timesaving device when ideas are complicated and cannot be reviewed quickly by highlighting.

## ■ Annotating to Record Reactions

Annotations are particularly useful when reading literature, essays, controversial articles, arguments, or persuasive material. Because each type of work is intended to provoke a reader's response, record your reactions and feelings as you read.

The poem "Anecdote of the Jar" follows. Read the poem first, then study the annotations. Notice how the annotations reveal the reader's thinking about the poem.

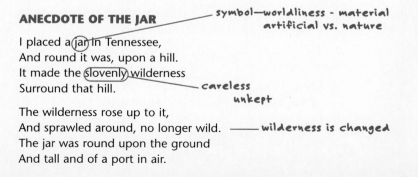

**ANECDOTE OF THE JAR**　　　*symbol—worldliness - material artificial vs. nature*

I placed a jar in Tennessee,
And round it was, upon a hill.
It made the slovenly wilderness　　*careless unkept*
Surround that hill.

The wilderness rose up to it,
And sprawled around, no longer wild.　*wilderness is changed*
The jar was round upon the ground
And tall and of a port in air.

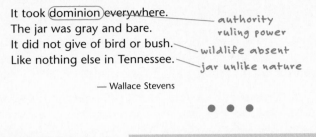

It took (dominion) everywhere. — authority / ruling power
The jar was gray and bare.
It did not give of bird or bush. — wildlife absent
Like nothing else in Tennessee. — jar unlike nature

— Wallace Stevens

• • •

## EXERCISE 9–3

*DIRECTIONS:* Refer to the same reading selection used for exercise 9–2. Review your highlighting and add annotations that clarify or summarize content or record your reactions. Add at least two annotations that reflect your thinking.

## EXERCISE 9–4

*DIRECTIONS:* Highlight and annotate a section from a current chapter in one of your textbooks using the suggestions for effective highlighting and annotating presented earlier in this chapter.

## ■ PARAPHRASING

A paraphrase restates a passage's ideas in your own words. You retain the author's meaning, but you use your own wording. In speech we paraphrase frequently. For example, when you relay a message from one person to another, you convey the meaning but do not use the person's exact words. A paraphrase makes a passage's meaning clearer and often more concise.

Paraphrasing is a useful technique in several situations.

1. **Paraphrasing is a means of recording information from reference sources in note form for later use in writing a research paper.**

2. **Paraphrasing is also useful when dealing with material for which exact, detailed comprehension is required.** For instance, you might paraphrase the steps in solving a math problem or the procedures for a lab set-up in chemistry.

3. **Paraphrasing is also helpful for understanding extremely difficult or complicated passages that must be worked out word by word.**

4. **Paraphrasing is useful when reading material that is stylistically complex, or with an obvious slant, bias, strong tone, or detailed description.**

Study the following example of a paraphrase of the stylistically complex preamble of the United States Constitution. Notice that it restates in different words the intent of the preamble.

**PREAMBLE:**

We the people of the United States, in order to form a more perfect union, establish justice, insure domestic tranquillity, provide for the common defense, promote the general welfare, and secure the blessings of liberty to ourselves and our posterity, do ordain and establish this Constitution of the United States of America.

**PARAPHRASE:**

The citizens of the United States established the Constitution to create a better country, to provide rightful treatment, peace, protection, and well-being for themselves and future citizens.

● ● ●

Notice first how synonyms were substituted for words in the original—*citizens* for *people, country* for *union, protection* for *defense,* and so forth. Next, notice that the order of information was rearranged.

Use the following suggestions to paraphrase effectively.

1. **Read slowly and carefully.** You must understand exactly what is said before you can paraphrase.

2. **Read the entire material before writing anything**.

3. **As you read, focus on both exact meanings and relationships between ideas**.

4. **Begin paraphrasing sentence by sentence**.

5. **Read each sentence and identify its core meaning.** Use synonyms, replacing the author's words with your words. Look away from the original sentence and write in your own words what it means. Then reread the original and add any additional or qualifying information.

6. **Don't try to paraphrase word by word.** Instead, work with clauses and phrases (idea groups).

7. **For words or phrases about which you are unsure of the meaning, check a dictionary to locate a more familiar meaning.**

8. **You may combine several original sentences into a more concise paraphrase.** It is also acceptable to present ideas in a different order than in the original.

9. **Compare your paraphrase with the original for completeness and accuracy**.

## EXERCISE 9–5

*DIRECTIONS:* Provide synonyms for the underlined words or phrases in the following excerpt from Sartre's essay on existentialism. Discuss and compare choices in a class discussion.

The existentialist, on the contrary, thinks it very <u>distressing</u> that God does not exist, because all possibility of finding values in a heaven of ideas disappears along with Him; there can no longer be an *a priori* <u>Good</u>, since there is no <u>infinite</u> and perfect consciousness to think it. Nowhere is it written that the Good exists, that we must be honest, that we must not lie; because the fact is we are on a <u>plane</u> where there are only men. Dostoievsky said, "If God didn't exist, everything would be possible." That is the very <u>starting point</u> of existentialism. Indeed, everything is <u>permissible</u> if God does not exist, and as a result man is <u>forlorn,</u> because neither within him nor without does he find anything to cling to. He can't start making excuses for himself.

Sartre, *Existentialism.*

● ● ●

## EXERCISE 9–6

*DIRECTIONS:* Write a paraphrase of the second paragraph of the following selection from a sociology text.

### THE HOME SCHOOLING MOVEMENT

It is difficult to estimate the number of youngsters involved in **home schooling,** *where children are not sent to school and receive their formal education from one or both parents.* Legislation and court decisions have made it legally possible in most states for parents to educate their children at home, and each year more people take advantage of that opportunity. Some states require parents or a home tutor to meet teacher certification standards, and many require parents to complete legal forms and affidavits to verify that their children are receiving instruction in state-approved curricula.

Supporters of home education claim that it is less expensive and far more efficient than mass public education. Moreover they cite several advantages: alleviation of school overcrowding, added curricular and pedagogical alternatives not available in the public schools, strengthened family relationships, lower dropout rates, the fact that students are allowed to learn at their own rate, increased motivation, higher standardized test scores, and reduced discipline problems. Proponents of home schooling also believe that it provides the parents with the opportunity to reinforce their moral values through education-something they are not satisfied that the public schools will do.

Critics of the home schooling movement contend that it creates as many problems as it solves. They acknowledge that, in a few cases, home schooling offers educational opportunities superior to those found in most public schools, but few parents can provide such educational advantages. Some parents who withdraw their children from the schools in favor of home schooling have an inadequate educational background and insufficient formal training to provide a satisfactory education for their children. Typically, parents have fewer, not more, technological resources at their disposal than do schools. However, . . . the relatively inexpensive computer technology that is readily available today is causing some to challenge the notion that home schooling is in any way inferior to more highly structured classroom education.

Finally, a sociological concern is the restricted social interaction experienced by children who are educated at home. Patricia Lines, a U. S. Department of Education policy analyst, believes that the possiblities provided by technology and the promise of home schooling are greatly exaggerated and insisted that "technology will never replace the pupil-teacher relationship." Also, while relationships with parents and siblings may be enhanced, children taught at home may develop a distorted view of society. Children who live in fairly homogeneous neighborhoods, comprising people of the same race, socioeconomic status, and religious background, do not experience the diversity that can be provided in the social arena of the schools. They may be ill equipped to function successfully in the larger multicultural world.

Thompson and Hickey, *Society in Focus: An Introduction to Sociology.*

• • •

## EXERCISE 9–7

*DIRECTIONS:* Write a paraphrase of the excerpt on p. 327 ("A market is . . . ). When you have finished, compare your paraphrase with that of another student.

## ■ OUTLINING

Outlining is an effective way to organize information and discover relationships between ideas. It forces you to select what is important from each paragraph and determine how it is related to key ideas in other paragraphs. Outlining enables you to learn and remember what you read because the process of selecting what is important and expressing it in your own words requires thought and comprehension and provides for repetition and review. Outlining is particularly effective for pragmatic learners who can learn material that is orderly and sequential.

Outlining is particularly useful in the following situations:

• When reading material that seems difficult or confusing, outlining forces you to sort ideas, see connections, and express them in your own words.

- When you are asked to write an evaluation or a critical interpretation of an article or essay, it is helpful to outline the factual content. The outline reflects development and progression of thought and helps you analyze the writer's ideas.

- In subject matter where order or process is important, an outline is particularly useful. For example, in a data processing course in which various sets of programming commands must be performed in a specified sequence, an outline is a good way to organize the information.

- In the natural sciences, in which classifications are important, outlines help you record and sort information. In botany, for example, one important focus is the classification and description of various plant groups. An outline enables you to list subgroups within each category and to keep track of similar characteristics.

## ■ Developing an Outline

To be effective, an outline must show the relative importance of ideas and the relationship between ideas. The easiest way to achieve this is to use the following format:

I. **First Major Topic**
   A. First major idea
      1. First important detail
      2. Second important detail
   B. Second major idea
      1. First important detail
         a. Minor detail or example
         b. Minor detail or example
      2. Second important detail
II. **Second Major Topic**
   A. First major idea

Notice that the more important ideas are closer to the left margin, and less important details are indented toward the middle of the page. A quick glance at an outline indicates what is most important and how ideas support or explain one another.

Use the following suggestions to write effective outlines:

1. **Read a section completely before writing.**

2. **Be brief and concise; do not write in complete sentences.** Unless the outline is to be submitted to your instructor, use abbreviations, symbols, or shorthand words as you would in lecture notetaking.

3. **Use your own words rather than those in the text.**

4. **Be certain that all information beneath a heading supports or explains it.**

5. **Every heading that is aligned vertically should be of equal importance.**

To illustrate further the technique for outlining, read the following passage and then study the outline that follows it.

### PROTEIN

Protein is essential for the repair and continuous replacement of body tissues and for growth. Proteins are a primary component of much body tissue, in particular of muscle. All enzymes are proteins, and protein is needed for making antibodies and hormones.

The body cannot store protein as it does fat; an adequate daily intake of protein is essential for well-being. A few Americans have diets deficient in protein, but most of us consume more protein daily then we need, as much as two or three times the necessary amount. For example, a woman who orders a twelve-ounce steak at a restaurant consumes about twice her daily protein requirement on the spot. For the average man, that same steak represents about 1.66 times the recommended daily allowance of protein. Although this is not in itself harmful (the excess protein is excreted), the extra calorie intake can lead to weight problems. Even in high-protein foods, such as lean meat or cheese, only twenty to thirty percent of the calories come from protein, the rest come from fat.

Proteins are the most complex molecules found in nature. They are built from smaller units called *amino acids.* Of these, there are two kinds: (1) those which the body cannot make, and which must be ingested, called the *essential* amino acids; (2) those which the body can make, ungratefully called the *nonessential* amino acids. The proteins our bodies use are made up of twenty-two amino acids; eight of these are those which the body cannot make.

Dorfman et. al., *Well-Being: An Introduction to Health.*

● ● ●

Here is the outline for the above selection:

I.  Proteins
    A. essential for body tissue growth
       1. muscle
       2. enzymes
    B. body cannot store protein
       1. most Americans consume too much
       2. can lead to weight problems
    C. proteins build from 2 types of amino acids
       1. essential amino acids
          a. body cannot make
          b. must be ingested
       2. nonessential amino acids made by body

By reading the passage and then reviewing the outline, you can see that it represents, in briefest form, the contents of the passage. Reading an outline is an effective way to reacquaint yourself with the content and organization of a chapter without taking the time that reading, highlighting, or marginal notation requires.

### ■ How Much Information to Include

Before you begin to outline, decide how much information to include. An outline can be very brief and cover only major topics, or, at the other extreme, it can be very detailed, providing an extensive review of information.

The purpose of your outline should determine how much detail you include. For example, if you are outlining a reading assignment for which your instructor asked that you be familiar with the author's viewpoint and general approach to a problem, little detail is needed. On the other hand, if you are outlining a section of an anatomy and physiology text for an upcoming objective exam, a much more detailed outline is needed. To determine the right amount of detail, ask yourself: "What do I need to know? What type of test situation, if any, am I preparing for?"

## EXERCISE 9–8

*DIRECTIONS:* Read the following excerpt from Brian Fagan's *Introduction to Archaeology,* an archaeology textbook, and write a brief outline or summary notes.

#### ARCHAEOLOGY AS A SOCIAL SCIENCE

Archaeologists bring a unique tool to the social sciences of which they are a part: a perspective that enables them to understand how people have dealt with the world around them from the earliest times. This facility contributes to a much better understanding of our own history, as well as that of the environment, the world climate, and the landscape. The long-abandoned settlements that archaeologists study are repositories of precisely dated geological, biological, and environmental data that can add a vital time depth to studies of the contemporary world. In the dry pueblos of Arizona preservation conditions are so good that wood, fossil pollen grains, and other environmental evidence are found in abundance. It is proving to be possible to study the gradual evolution of southwestern agriculture through many centuries and determine how the local people responded to uneven rainfall and other environmental changes. Information from such researchers is invaluable to students of agriculture who are trying to expand crop production in the desert. Archaeological sites are storehouses of information for a host of natural and physical sciences.

Archaeologists have many practical tasks in today's world that further amplify their role as social scientists. One such task is the settling of territorial claims by excavation. In the eighteenth century an archaeological investigation figured in the settling of a border dispute between the British and the Americans over the site of Samuel de Champlain's settlement at Dochet Island on the St. Croix River, between Maine and Canada. An antiquarian dug to find the site of the fort, but the results were inconclusive. Excavations have occasionally featured in disputes over Indian lands and we can expect that archaeologists will provide expert testimony in many future cases.

Recent federal legislation requires that archaeological impact studies be done on all government-funded development projects to ensure that minimal damage is done to archaeological resources during construction work. This legislation has massively expanded archaeological work throughout North America. [ . . . ] It is designed to protect the finite data base of archaeological sites that are studied by archaeologists and by scientists from many other disciplines.

Archaeology has also worked directly for contemporary American society, especially in management of resources and waste. University of Arizona archaeologist William Rathje has studied the garbage dumps in Tucson for a long time (Rathje, 1974). He examines patterns in garbage disposed of by Tucson households, analyzes evidence from the dump with the latest archaeological research designs and techniques, and joins to it data gleaned from interviews with householders and other sources. His study has revealed startlingly wasteful habits in Arizona households of many economic and social backgrounds, information that could be used to suggest better strategies for consumer buying and resource management.

## EXERCISE 9–9

*DIRECTIONS:* Write an outline of "The Home Schooling Movement" on p. 330.

## ■ MAPPING TO SHOW RELATIONSHIPS

Mapping is a process of drawing diagrams to describe how a topic and its related ideas are connected. It is a means of organizing and consolidating information by using a visual format. Maps facilitate learning because they group and consolidate information. Although mapping appeals to visual learners, verbal learners will also find it to be effective in organizing information. This section discusses two types of maps: concept maps and thought pattern maps.

### ■ Concept Maps

Concept maps are visual outlines; they show how ideas within a passage are related. Maps can take different forms. You can draw them in any way that shows the relationships among the ideas. Sketching rather than exact, careful drawing is appropriate. When drawing maps feel free to abbreviate, add lines to show relationships, add notes, or redraw to make

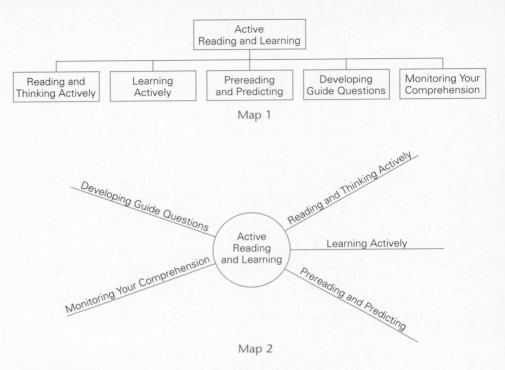

**FIGURE 9.1** Two Sample Concept Maps of Chapter 2.

changes. Figure 9.1 shows two sample maps. Each was drawn to show the organization of Chapter 2 of this text. Refer back to Chapter 2, pp. 24–63, then study each map.

Think of a map as a diagram that shows how ideas are connected. Maps, like outlines, can vary in the amount of detail included, ranging from very general to highly specific. The maps shown in Fig. 9.1 only provide an overview of the chapter and reflect its general organization. A more detailed map of one of the topics, prereading, included in Chapter 2 (p. 36), is shown in Figure 9.2. Use the following steps in drawing a map.

1. **Identify the overall subject and write it in the center or at the top of the page.** How you arrange your map will depend on the subject matter and its organization. Circles or boxes are useful but not absolutely necessary.

2. **Identify the major supporting information that relates to the topic.** State each fact or idea on a line connected to the central topic.

3. **As you discover details that further explain an idea already mapped, draw a new line** branching from the idea it explains.

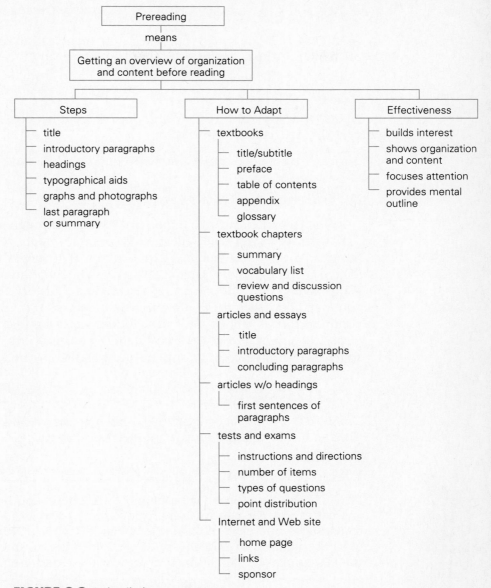

**FIGURE 9.2** A detailed concept map.

# EXERCISE 9–10

*DIRECTIONS:* Draw a map that reflects the overall organization of this chapter.

## EXERCISE 9–11

*DIRECTIONS:* Draw a map that reflects the organization of one of the end-of-chapter readings in this book that you have read this semester.

## EXERCISE 9–12

*DIRECTIONS:* Select a section from one of your textbooks. Draw a concept map that reflects its organization.

### ■ Thought Pattern Maps

When a particular thought pattern is evident throughout a passage, you may wish to draw a map reflecting that pattern. Maps for each common thought pattern are shown in Chapter 5. Now that you are familiar with the idea of mapping, review Chapter 5 paying particular attention to the diagrams shown for each pattern. When reading a history text, for example, you may find it helpful to draw time lines (see p. 150) to organize events within historical periods. Or, when reading a text that compares two works of philosophy or two key political figures, you may find one of the maps shown on p. 160 helpful in distinguishing similarities and differences.

## EXERCISE 9–13

*DIRECTIONS:* Draw a concept map showing the overall organization of Chapter 8, "Textbook Learning and Retention Strategies."

## EXERCISE 9–14

*DIRECTIONS:* Conduct an experiment to see whether outlining or mapping is a better way for you to show relationships between ideas. Choose and read a substantial section from one of your textbooks. Write a brief outline of it, then draw a map of this same section. Which of these two methods was easier for you to do? Which of these will be most useful for you? Why?

## ■ SUMMARIZING INFORMATION

A summary is a compact restatement of the important points of a passage. You might think of it as a shortened version of a longer message. Unlike a paraphrase, a summary does not include all information presented in the original. Instead, you must select what to include. A summary contains only the gist of the text, with limited background, explanation, or detail. Although summaries vary in length, they are often one quarter or less of the length of the original.

Summaries are useful in a variety of reading situations in which a condensed overview of the material is needed. You might summarize information in preparation for an essay exam, or key points of news articles required in an economics class. Some class assignments also require summarization. Lab reports for science courses include a summary of results. A literature instructor may ask you to summarize the plot of a short story.

Use the following steps as a guide when writing a summary.

1. **Read the entire original work first.** Do not write anything until you understand it completely and have a complete picture of the work.

2. **Reread and highlight key points.** Look in particular for topic sentences and essential details.

3. **Review your highlighting.** Cross out all but vital phrases. Eliminate repetitious information.

4. **Write sentences to include all remaining highlighted information.** Condense and combine information wherever possible.

5. **Present ideas in the summary in the same order in which they appeared in the original,** unless you are purposely regrouping ideas.

6. **Revise your summary.** Try to make your summary more concise by eliminating repetition and combining ideas.

Read this selection by Joyce Cary, and study the sample summary.

## ART AND EDUCATION

A very large number of people cease when quite young to add anything to a limited stock of judgments. After a certain age, say 25, they consider that their education is finished.

It is perhaps natural that having passed through that painful and boring process, called expressly education, they should suppose it over, and that they are equipped for life to label every event as it occurs and drop it into its given pigeonhole. But one who has a label ready for everything does not bother to observe any more, even such ordinary happenings as he has observed for himself, with attention, before he went to school. He merely acts and reacts.

For people who have stopped noticing, the only possible new or renewed experience, and, therefore, new knowledge, is from a work of art. Because that is the only kind of experience which they are prepared to receive on its own terms, they will come out from their shells and expose themselves to music, to a play, to a book, because it is the accepted method of enjoying such things. True, even to plays and books they may bring artistic prejudices which prevent them from seeing *that* play or comprehending *that* book. Their artistic sensibilities may be as crusted over as their minds.

But it is part of an artist's job to break crusts, or let us say rather that artists who work for the public and not merely for themselves, are interested in breaking crusts because they want to communicate their intuitions.

● ● ●

### *Sample Summary*

Many people consider their education to be complete at an early age, and at that time, cease to observe and react to the world around them. Art forces people to think and react. For some people, their artistic sensibility may be as stagnant as their minds. It is the artist's responsibility to intervene in order to communicate.

## EXERCISE 9–15

*DIRECTIONS:* Read and summarize the following essay by James Thurber.

### A DOG'S EYE VIEW OF MAN

If Man has benefited immeasurably by his association with the dog, what, you may ask, has the dog got out of it? His scroll has, of course, been heavily charged with punishments: he has known the muzzle, the leash, and the tether; he has suffered the indignities of the show bench, the tin can on the tail, the ribbon in the hair; his love life with the other sex of his species has been regulated by the frigid hand of authority, his digestion ruined by the macaroons and marshmallows of doting women. The list of his woes could be continued indefinitely. But he has also had his fun, for he has been privileged to live with and study at close range the only creature with reason, the most unreasonable of creatures.

The dog has got more fun out of Man than Man has got out of the dog, for the clearly demonstrable reason that Man is the more laughable of the two animals. The dog has long been bemused by the singular activities and the curious practices of men, cocking his head inquiringly to one side, intently watching and listening to the strangest goings-on in the world. He has seen men sing together and fight one another in the same evening. He has watched them go to bed when it is time to get up, and get up when it is time to go to bed. He has observed them destroying the soil in vast areas, and nurturing it in small patches. He has stood by while men built strong and solid houses for rest and quiet, and then filled them with lights and bells and machinery. His sensitive nose, which can detect what's cooking in the next township, has caught at one and the same time the bewildering smells of the hospital and the munitions factory. He has seen men raise up great cities to heaven and then blow them to hell.

• • •

## Critical Thinking Tip #9

### Annotating and Critical Thinking

Annotating is a way of identifying and summarizing key information. It is also a way to facilitate critical thinking. Annotating helps you record your reactions as you read. You might:

- Jot down questions
- Highlight emotionally charged words
- Note opposing ideas
- Mark ideas you question or disagree with
- Note places where you feel further information is needed
- Mark sections you feel are particularly strong or weak

Here is a sample annotation in which a reader recorded her thinking about the passage.

#### TELEVISION AND VIOLENT BEHAVIOR

The basic question is a simple one: Does television veiwing have an impact on the violent behaviors of viewers? By now, you know that such simple questions seldom have simple answers, but in this case, we do seem to have a simple and direct answer: Yes, watching violence on television does have an effect on violent behaviors, particularly for children.

*how is violence defined?*

There is no doubt that television veiwing is a popular pastime among children. In fact, "the average child born today will by the age of 15 have spent more time watching television than going to school" (Liebert, 1986, p. 43). Is watching television related to increased violence?" In the simplest terms, only three possibilities exist in this equation. (1) Television has no significant relationship to aggressive behavior. (2) Television reduces aggressive behavior. (3) Television increases aggressive behavior. Almost all the studies reviewed in the past decade support the third possibility. No studies of any consequence support the second possibility" (Rubenstein, 1983).

*dated?*

*need definition*

*reasons? more info?*

*what about since 1983?*

As you learn more about critical thinking throughout the text, you will get more ideas about what to mark and annotate.

## EXERCISE 9–16

*DIRECTIONS:* Write a summary of "The Home Schooling Movement" on p. 330. Use the outline you constructed in Exercise 9-9 to guide your writing.

## EXERCISE 9–17

*DIRECTIONS:* Select a section of at least five substantial paragraphs from one of your current textbook chapters. Write a paraphrase of its first paragraph, then write a summary of the entire section.

## EXERCISE 9–18

*DIRECTIONS:* Choose one of the reading selections at the end of this chapter. Read the selection, highlight, and annotate it. Then write a brief outline and summary of its content. Be sure to show the relationships between ideas as well as record the most important ideas.

## SUMMARY

**1. Why is writing during and after reading an effective learning strategy?**

Writing during and after reading enhances both your comprehension and recall. Writing activities such as highlighting, annotating, paraphrasing, outlining, summarizing, and mapping can
- focus your attention
- force you to think
- test your understanding
- aid your recall

**2. How can you highlight more effectively?**

To make highlighting an efficient means of identifying what is important within each paragraph you should
- read first, then highlight.
- use paragraph structure to guide you.
- use headings as a guide.
- develop your own highlighting system.
- highlight as few words as possible.
- reread your highlighting to test its accuracy.

**3. Why should you annotate and make marginal notations in conjunction with your highlighting?**

Annotating involves recording ideas, reactions, impressions, and questions as you read. Using symbols and brief phrases as marginal notes is useful in condensing, supplementing, and clarifying passage content because you are adding your own thinking to the highlighted material.

**4. Why is paraphrasing a useful study strategy?**

Paraphrasing is the restatement of a passage's ideas in your own words. It is a particularly useful strategy for recording the meaning and checking your comprehension of detailed, complex, precise, difficult, or unusually written passages. Using your own words rather than the author's expresses the meaning of the passage clearer and more concisely, thereby making study and review easier.

**5. What is an outline and what are its advantages?**

Outlining is a form of organizing information that provides you with a structure that indicates the relative importance of ideas and shows the relationships among them. When done well, it helps you sort out ideas, improves your concentration, and aids your recall.

**6. What is mapping?**

Mapping is a process of drawing diagrams to show the connection between a topic and its related ideas. Both concept maps and thought pattern maps enable you to adjust to both the type of information being recorded and its particular organization. Grouping and consolidating information in this way makes it easier to learn and remember.

**7. What is involved in summarizing?**

Summarizing involves selecting a passage's most important ideas and recording them in a condensed abbreviated form. A summary provides a brief overview of a passage that can be useful in completing writing assignments and reports, preparing for class participation, or in reviewing for exams.

POLITICAL
SCIENCE

## READING SELECTION 17
## THE SUPREME COURT IN ACTION
Edward S. Greenberg and Benjamin I. Page
From *The Struggle for Democracy*

*The Supreme Court of the United States is an important and powerful part of our democratic system. Read this excerpt from an American government textbook to learn the traditions and rules the court follows and how it decides which cases to hear.*

1   The Supreme Court meets from the first Monday in October (set by statute) until late June or early July, depending on the press of business. Let's see how it goes about deciding cases.

### Norms of Operation

2   The Court is a tradition-bound institution defined by many rituals and long-standing norms. Brass spittoons still stand next to each justice's chair; quill pens and inkwells still grace the desks of competing counsel. Pages only gave up knickers in 1963; required formal wear (with tails) for lawyers was only recently abandoned. When the justices meet in public session to hear oral arguments or to announce decisions, they enter the courtroom in the same way: the chief justice is the first to emerge from behind the curtain that is draped behind the bench; the remainder enter in order of seniority.

3   More important than rituals are norms, unwritten but clearly understood ways of behaving. One norm is *secrecy,* which keeps the conflicts between justices out of the public eye and elevates the stature of the Court. Justices do not grant interviews very often. Reporters are not allowed to stalk the corridors for a story. Clerks are expected to keep all memos, draft opinions, and conversations with their justices confidential. Justices are not commonly seen on the frantic Washington, D.C., cocktail party circuit.

When meeting in conference to argue and decide cases, the justices meet alone, without secretaries or clerks. While a breach of secrecy has occurred on occasion, allowing "insider" books like *The Brethren* to be published, they are the exceptions. As a result, we know less about the inner workings of the Court than about any other branch of government.

4   *Courtesy* is another norm. Though justices may sometimes express their displeasure and distaste for each other in private, in public they treat each other with great formality and respect. The justices shake hands before court sessions and conferences. They refer to each other as "my brother" or my "dissenting brother." Differences of opinion are usually respected; justices are allowed every opportunity to make their case to their fellow justices.

5   *Seniority* is another important norm. Seniority determines the assignment of office space, the seating arrangements in open court (the most junior are at the ends), the order of speaking in conference (the chief justice, then the most senior, etc.), and the order of voting (the most junior goes first).

6   Finally, the justices are expected to stick very closely to *precedent* when they are reaching a decision. When the Court departs from precedent, it is essentially overruling its own past actions, exercising judicial review of itself. In most cases, departure from precedent comes in only very small steps over many years, for example, several decisions chipped away at the "separate but equal" doctrine of *Plessy v. Ferguson* before it was decisively reversed in *Brown v. Board of Education.* If there is a significant ideological turnover on the court, however, change can

Oral argument and the announcement of decisions happen here in the main courtroom of the Supreme Court building.

come more quickly. The Rehnquist Court has been particularly aggressive in overturning precedents on the civil rights, criminal justice, and abortion fronts.

## Controlling the Agenda

7    The Court has a number of screening mechanisms to control its agenda and to focus its attention on cases that involve important federal or constitutional questions.

8    Several technical rules help keep down the numbers. Cases must be real and adverse, meaning that they must involve a real dispute between two parties. The Court will not provide "advisory" opinions to guide the other branches. Disputants in a case must have standing, meaning that they must have a real and direct interest in the issues that are raised. The Court

sometimes changes the definition of *standing* to make access easier or more difficult. The Warren Court favored a broad definition of *standing*, inviting litigation. The Rehnquist court tightened the definition, making it harder for people suing in the name of some larger group of affected people—consumers, racial minorities, and so on—to bring cases. Cases must also be ripe, meaning that all other avenues of appeal have been exhausted and that injury has already taken place (it will not accept hypothetical or predicted injury cases). Appeals must also be filed within a specified time limit, paperwork must be proper and complete, and a filing fee of $200 must be paid. The fee can be waived if a petitioner is indigent and files an affidavit *in forma pauperis* (in the manner of a pauper). One of the most famous cases in American history, *Gideon v. Wainwright* (1963), which established the right to counsel in criminal cases, was submitted *in forma pauperis* on a few pieces of lined paper by a Florida State Penitentiary inmate named Clarence Earl Gideon.

9 The most powerful tool that the Court has for controlling its own agenda is the power to grant or not to grant a **writ of certiorari.** A grant of cert is a decision of the Court that an appellate case raises an important federal or constitutional issue that it is prepared to consider. Law clerks in the chief justice's office prepare a brief summary of each petition for the justices, along with a recommendation on whether or not to grant cert. The clerks, in consultation with the chief justice, prepare a "discuss list" of cases that they are recommending for cert. Under the **rule of four**, petitions are granted cert if at least four justices vote

in favor. There are several reasons why a petition may not command four votes, even if the case involves important constitutional issues: it may involve a particularly controversial issue that the Court would like to avoid, or the Court may not yet have developed a solid majority and wishes to avoid a split decision. Few petitions survive all of these hurdles. Of the 5,000 or so cases that are filed in each session, the Court grants cert for only a little more than 200. For cases denied cert, the decision of the lower court stands.

10 Deciding how freely to grant "cert" is tricky business for the Court. Used too often, it threatens to inundate the Court with cases. Used too sparingly, it leaves in place the decisions of 12 different circuit courts on substantial federal and constitutional questions.

---

## Comprehension Test 17

*Directions: Circle the letter of the best answer.*

**Checking Your Comprehension**

1. This reading focuses on
   a. how justices behave
   b. how the Supreme Court operates under a code of secrecy
   c. how the Supreme Court selects cases
   d. the operations of the Supreme Court

2. The Supreme Court could best be described as
   a. self-regulating and efficient
   b. innovative and adaptable
   c. independent and tradition bound
   d. eccentric and self-interested

3. Little is known about the functioning of the Court because
   a. books like *The Brethren* are inaccurate
   b. the justices maintain secrecy
   c. the press does not consider the Court's operation newsworthy
   d. the justices never meet in public session

4. When cert is granted, the court
   a. reverses a lower court decision
   b. agrees to consider an important federal or constitutional issue
   c. recommends whether or not to consider an important issue
   d. prepares a discuss list

5. An adverse case is one
   a. that has exhausted all appeals
   b. for which a cert has been denied
   c. to which the rule of four does not apply
   d. that involves a real dispute

6. As used in this reading, "norms" (paragraph 3) are
   a. normal procedures
   b. forms of governance
   c. summaries of court decisions
   d. standards of behavior

**Thinking Critically**

7. What would you expect the attitude of the justices to be toward the author of the book, *The Brethren,* which gave "inside" information about the workings of the court?
   a. respect and admiration
   b. disapproval
   c. hate
   d. indifference

8. Which one of the following cases would the Supreme Court most likely consider?
   a. a convicted murderer just about to file an appeal in federal court
   b. a case in which a woman requests that a law be written that prohibits all pregnant women from smoking to prevent possible injury to fetuses
   c. a racial discrimination case that has not yet come to trial
   d. a personal injury case in which the victim has exhausted all appeals

9. The tone of this reading could best be described as
   a. distant
   b. informational
   c. argumentative
   d. critical

10. Which of the following statements can be inferred from the reading?
   a. The Court at times has chosen to avoid controversial issues.
   b. The justices frequently have personality disputes.
   c. The court is unwilling to try cases for which appeals have been exhausted.
   d. The court welcomes theoretical cases that concern possible injury.

**Questions for Discussion**

1. Identify and discuss a current legal issue leading to a hypothetical case in which you believe the court might seriously consider departing from a precedent. On what do you base your hypothetical case?

2. The article states that "the Court sometimes changes definition of standing to make access easier or more difficult." What is the definition of standing? Do you think it is fair for the Court to change this definition seemingly at random? Support your position.

3. Why do you think that granting "cert"—a writ of certiorari—places the Supreme Court in a particularly precarious position?

4. Why do you think the Court will hear cases that are "ripe" as opposed to predicted or hypothetical cases?

| Selection 17: | | | 1029 words |
|---|---|---|---|
| Finishing Time: | _____ | _____ | _____ |
| | HR. | MIN. | SEC. |
| Starting Time: | _____ | _____ | _____ |
| | HR. | MIN. | SEC. |
| Reading Time: | | _____ | _____ |
| | | MIN. | SEC. |
| WPM Score: | | _____ | |
| Comprehension Score: | | _____% | |

**PHYSICS**

# READING SELECTION 18
## MUSICAL SOUNDS

Paul G. Hewitt
From *Conceptual Physics: A New Introduction*

*What is the difference between noise and music? Read this excerpt from a college physics textbook to discover the three characteristics that distinguish music from noise.*

### Noises and Musical Sounds

1    Most of the sounds we hear are noises. The impact of a falling object, the slamming of a door, the roaring of a motorcycle, and most of the sounds from traffic in city streets are noises. Noise corresponds to an irregular vibration of the eardrum produced by the irregular vibration of some nearby object. If we make a diagram to indicate the pressure of the air on the eardrum as it varies with time, the graph corresponding to a noise might look like that shown in Figure 1a. The sound of music has a different character, having more or less sustained tones—or musical "notes." (Musical instruments may make noise as well!) The graph representing a musical sound has a shape that repeats itself over and over again (Figure 1b). Such graphs can be displayed on the screen of an oscilloscope when the electric signal from a microphone is fed into the input terminal of this important instrument.

2    The dividing line between music and noise is not sharp and is subjective. To some contemporary composers, it is nonexistent. Some people consider contemporary music and music from other cultures to be noise. Differentiating these types of music from noise becomes a problem of aesthetics. However, differentiating traditional music—that is, classical music and most types of popular music—from noise presents no problem. A deaf person could distinguish between these with the use of an oscilloscope.

3    Musicians usually speak of a musical tone in terms of three characteristics—the pitch, the loudness, and the quality.

### Pitch

4    The pitch of a sound corresponds to frequency. A shrill high note is produced by rapid vibrations of the sound source, whereas a deep low note is from slow vibrations. We speak of the pitch of a sound in terms of its position in the musical scale. When middle C is struck on a piano, a hammer strikes two or three strings, each of which vibrates 264 times in 1 second. The pitch of middle C corresponds to 264 hertz.

5    Different musical notes are obtained by changing the frequency of the vibrating sound source. This is usually done by altering the size, the tightness, or the mass of the vibrating object. A guitarist or violinist, for example, adjusts the tightness, or tension, of the strings of the instrument when tuning them. Then different notes can be played by altering the length of each string by "stopping" them with the fingers. In wind instruments the length of the vibrating air column is altered to change the pitch of the note produced.

6    High-pitched sounds used in music are most often less than 4000 vibrations per second, but the average human ear can hear sounds up to 20,000 vibrations per second. Some people can hear tones of higher pitch than this, and most dogs can. In general, the upper limit of hearing in people gets lower as they grow older. A high-pitched sound is often inaudible to an older person and yet may be clearly heard by a younger one. So by the time you can really afford that high-fidelity music system, you may not be able to hear the difference.

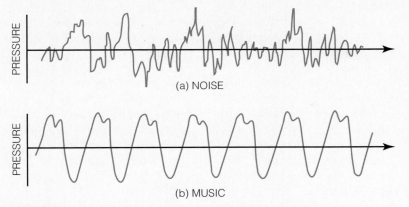

PRESSURE

(a) NOISE

PRESSURE

(b) MUSIC

**FIGURE 1** Graphical representations of noise and music.

## Loudness

7    The intensity of sound depends on pressure variations within the sound wave; it depends on the amplitude (more specifically, like any type of wave, intensity is proportional to the square of the amplitude). Sound intensity is a purely objective and physical attribute of a wave and can be measured by various acoustical instruments (such as the oscilloscope). *Loudness,* on the other hand, is a physiological sensation: it depends on intensity but in a complicated way. For example, if you turn a radio up until it seems about twice as loud as before, you would have to increase the power output, and therefore the intensity, by approximately eight times. Although the pitch of a sound can be judged very accurately, our ears are not very good at judging loudness. The loudest sounds we can tolerate have intensities a *million million* times greater than the faintest sounds. The difference in loudness, however, is much less than this amount.

8    The relative loudness of a sound heard by the ear is measured in *decibels,* a unit named after Alexander Graham Bell an abbreviated db. Some common sounds and their noise levels are compared in Table 1.

## Table 1

| Source of Sound | Noise Level (dB) |
|---|---|
| Jet airplane, 30 meters away | 140 |
| Air raid siren, nearby | 125 |
| Disco music, amplified | 115 |
| Riveter | 95 |
| Busy street traffic | 70 |
| Conversation in home | 65 |
| Quiet radio in home | 40 |
| Whisper | 20 |
| Rustle of leaves | 10 |
| Threshold of hearing | 0 |

9    Decibel ratings are logarithmic, so that 60 decibels represent sound intensity a million times greater than 0 decibels; 80 decibels represent sound 100 times as intense as 60 decibels. Physiological hearing damage begins at exposure to 85 decibels, the degree depending on the length of exposure and frequency characteristics. Damage from loud

sounds can be temporary or permanent as the organs of Corti, the receptor organs in the inner ear, are impaired or destroyed. A single burst of sound can produce vibrations in the organs intense enough to tear them apart. Less intense, but severe, noise can interfere with cellular processes in the organs that cause their eventual breakdown. Unfortunately, the cells of these organs do not regenerate.

10   From the earliest states of human evolution we are subjected to a wide range of light intensities, and our eyes are now well adapted to the light we encounter in today's world. But not so with sound. Hearing loud and sustained sounds is

something new for humans to contend with. Except for occaisional bursts of thunder and the like, early people were not exposed to loud sounds and as a result we did not develop an adaptation to match the noise pollution we experience today. You know that you'll ruin your sense of sight if you stare into a source of light as bright as the sun. Please don't ruin your sense of hearing and blow the fine tuning in your ears by subjecting yourself to loud sounds.

11   Is hearing permanently impaired when attending concerts, discotheques, or functions that feature very loud music?*

------

* *Answer:* Yes, depending on how loud, how long, and how often. Some music groups have emphasized loudness over quality. Tragically, as hearing becomes more and more impaired, members of the group (and their fans) require louder and louder sounds for stimulation. Hearing loss caused by loud sounds is particularly common in the frequency range of 2000 to 5000 hertz, the very range in which speech and music normally occur.

---

## Comprehension Test 18*

### Checking Your Comprehension

1. Explain what a guitarist can do to create different musical notes from a five string guitar.

2. What are the three major characteristics of musical tones?

3. What is the highest pitched sound the average human can hear? As you grow older, what happens to this?

4. What is the difference between the loudness and the intensity of a sound?

### Thinking Critically

1. If humans were to be continually exposed to loud noises over many thousand years, what would probably be the result? Why?

2. What does the author mean when he says that decibel ratings are "logarithmic"?

3. Explain the process by which loud sounds cause hearing damage.

4. What does the author mean when he says that distinguishing between noise and some kinds of music is a "problem of aesthetics"?

------

*Multiple-choice questions are contained in Appendix B (page A18).

## Questions for Discussion

1. What factors other than those described in the selection differentiate music from noise?

2. What sounds are we often exposed to that may damage our hearing?

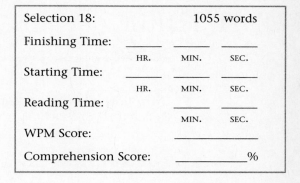

| Selection 18: | | 1055 words | |
|---|---|---|---|
| Finishing Time: | HR. | MIN. | SEC. |
| Starting Time: | HR. | MIN. | SEC. |
| Reading Time: | | MIN. | SEC. |
| WPM Score: | | | |
| Comprehension Score: | | | % |

## Visit the Longman English Pages

For additional readings and exercises, visit the Longman English Skills Web page at:

### http://longman.awl.com/englishpages

For a username and password, please see your instructor.

# Task Performance Assessment
# UNIT THREE

The following task is designed to assess your ability to use and apply the skills taught in this unit.

## THE SETTING

Assume you are taking a course in economics. You have been directed to read a marketing textbook chapter titled *Market Structure, Resource Allocation, and Public Choice.* Your instructor gives tests each month on the assigned chapters. The tests include both multiple-choice and essay questions. Assume that Reading Selection #14, p. 275, is from the assigned chapter. Read this selection completely before beginning any of the following tasks. Reread the selection as often as necesssary.

## THE TASKS

1. Highlight and annotate the reading.
2. Write a one paragraph summary of this reading.
3. Draw a map that shows the relationship of ideas presented in the reading.

# UNIT 4
# Reading Critically

Many college students accept everything they read at face value. They rarely sit back and examine the author's ideas, sources, evidence, or choice of words with a critical eye. In fact, many people still accept the adage "If it's in print, it must be true." Yet, many questionable opinions, beliefs, personal observations, misleading statements, and unwarranted conclusions appear in print every day. To be an alert, informed, and knowledgeable person, you must approach everything you read with an open and questioning mind.

To become an efficient and flexible reader you must think about and react to what you read. To get a writer's full *meaning,* you should go beyond what the author says and consider what he or she intends. Also, you need to evaluate or react critically to what the author says. These two skills—interpreting and evaluating—are the focus of this unit. Chapter 10 deals with interpreting and evaluating literature and the creative language that is essential to it. You will learn about denotative and connotative meanings and how authors use euphemisms and descriptive and figurative language to communicate their ideas. You will learn how to read and analyze short stories and poetry.

In Chapter 11 you will learn that it is necessary to make inferences not only to understand what the author says but also to consider what he or she has suggested. You will also learn to distinguish between fact and opinion, recognize generalizatios, identify tone and author's purpose, and recognize bias.

Chapter 12 is concerned with evaluating persuasive writing. You will learn how to evaluate the source and the authority of an author, to read and evaluate arguments, to identify errors in logic, and to recognize emotional appeals.

# CHAPTER 10
# Language and Literature

IN THIS CHAPTER YOU WILL LEARN:

1. To understand denotative and connotative meanings
2. To recognize euphemisms
3. To read descriptive and figurative language
4. To analyze short stories
5. To analyze poetry

Language is a vehicle of thought and communication—a means by which we shape ideas, thoughts, and feelings and express ideas to others. This chapter discusses how writers use language creatively to express their ideas and shape your thinking. Denotative and connotative meanings, euphemisms, and descriptive and figurative language are devices many writers of both ficton and nonficton use to create meaning. Literature in particular uses language in unique and creative ways. This chapter discusses strategies for reading and analyzing literature and demonstrates ways in which authors of short stories and poetry use language creatively.

## ■ DENOTATIVE AND CONNOTATIVE MEANINGS

If you were asked whether you would rather be the victim of a hoax, a fraud, or a flam, what would you say? If you were to look these words up in a dictionary, you might find that each involves some sort of deception; however, they suggest varying degrees of seriousness. A hoax is often a joke or trick; a flam is a deceptive trick or lie; a fraud often suggests a deception in which someone gives up property or money. Next, suppose you owned a jacket that looked like leather but was not made of real leather. Would you prefer someone to describe your jacket as fake, artificial, or synthetic? Most likely, you would prefer *synthetic*. *Fake* suggests that you are trying to cover up the fact that it is not real leather and *artificial* suggests, in a negative way, that something was made to look like something else. *Synthetic*, however, refers to a product made by a chemical process. You can see that, in addition to their dictionary meanings, words may *suggest* additional meanings.

The meaning of a word as indicated by the dictionary is known as its *denotative* meaning, whereas its *connotative* meaning consists of the additional meanings a word may take on. Let's consider a few more examples to clarify the distinction between these two types of meanings. As an example, think of the word *walk*. Its denotative or primary dictionary meaning is to move forward by placing one foot in front of the other. Here are a few words that also, according to the dictionary, mean to move forward. As you read each word in a sentence, the connotative meaning will become clear to you.

The newlyweds *strolled* down the streets of Paris.
(*Stroll* suggests a leisurely, carefree walk.)

The wealthy businessman *swaggered* into the restaurant and demanded a table.
(*Swagger* suggests walking in a bold, arrogant manner.)

The overweight man *lumbered* along, breathing heavily and occasionally tripping.
(*Lumber* connotes a clumsy, awkward movement.)

From these examples you can see that it is possible to create very different impressions simply by selecting words with certain connotations. Often writers communicate subtle messages or lead you to respond a certain way toward an object, action, or idea by choosing words with positive or negative connotations.

## EXERCISE 10–1

*DIRECTIONS:* For each word listed write another word that has the same denotative meaning but a different connotative meaning.

Example: to drink   *guzzle*

1. to eat _____
2. to talk _____
3. fair _____
4. famous _____
5. group _____
6. to take _____
7. ability _____
8. dog _____
9. fast _____
10. to fall _____

## EXERCISE 10–2

*DIRECTIONS:* For each word listed, write a word that has a similar denotative meaning but a negative connotation. Then write a word that has a positive connotation. Consult a dictionary if necessary.

Example: clean     decontaminate          polish

|  | *Negative* | *Positive* |
|---|---|---|
| 1.  show | _____ | _____ |
| 2.  leave | _____ | _____ |
| 3.  ask | _____ | _____ |
| 4.  task | _____ | _____ |
| 5.  forget | _____ | _____ |
| 6.  look at | _____ | _____ |
| 7.  unable | _____ | _____ |
| 8.  weak | _____ | _____ |
| 9.  car | _____ | _____ |
| 10.  mistake | _____ | _____ |

## EXERCISE 10–3

*DIRECTIONS:* Read each of the following statements, paying particular attention to connotative meanings. In each statement, underline at least one word or phrase with a strong connotative meaning. Decide whether it is positive, negative, or neutral and justify your answer. Then suggest a substitute word with a different connotation that changes the meaning of the statement.

1. Educating the electorate about the nature and actual perils of nuclear weapons is a frightening task.
2. Recently, the anti-gun forces throughout the nation were trumpeting that crimes of violence decreased in cities with strict gun control laws.
3. "What I want to get rid of is the human garbage that willfully perpetrates outrages against the rest of humanity and whom we have come to call terrorists."
4. "Not unlike drugs or alcohol, the television experience allows the participant to blot out the real world and enter into a pleasurable and passive state."

5. "I found Simon Wheeler dozing comfortably by the bar-room stove of the dilapidated tavern in the decaying mining camp of Angel's, and I noticed that he was fat and bald-headed, and had an expression of winning gentleness and simplicity upon his tranquil countenance."

## ■ RECOGNIZING EUPHEMISMS

A euphemism is the substitution of a more pleasant, less negative way of saying something for the straightforward, direct way. For example, *passed away* is a euphemism for the word *died*. *Ladies' room* is a euphemism for *bathroom*. Here are a few others:

| Euphemism | Meaning |
|---|---|
| remains | corpse |
| deploy a missile | set up to fire |
| chemical dependency | drug addiction |
| neutralize | kill |

Can you think of others?

A critical thinker pays close attention to euphemisms because writers can use them to hide unpleasant information. Euphemisms may also lead the reader to misinterpret important issues and events. A good example is the expression *civilian damage*. It refers to the injury or killing of innocent people or damage to property in a warlike setting. The euphemism avoids direct mention of injury or killing and makes the situation seem less destructive and harmful than it is. Similarly, accusing someone of spreading disinformation has less impact than accusing the person of lying.

To grasp the full impact of what a writer is saying, mentally substitute direct language for the euphemism. Also, as you notice a euphemism, circle or mark it. Repeated use of euphemisms may indicate that a writer is attempting to direct your attention away from an issue or shape your thinking in a particular direction.

## EXERCISE 10–4

*DIRECTIONS:* Working with another student, write a list of euphemisms that you have heard or read recently.

# ■ UNDERSTANDING DESCRIPTIVE AND FIGURATIVE LANGUAGE

Textbooks use concrete, objective language; words have very specific and often technical meanings. Seldom is there any question as to intended meaning. The author presents information without personal involvement or reaction. The author's feelings, opinions, and judgments are unknown. Expressive writing, including literature, on the other hand, is often characterized by a more subjective, creative, and imaginative use of language. Words are used to create an emotional impact, evoke a feeling, or establish a mood.

The sections that follow describe two types of subjective language: descriptive and figurative.

## ■ Descriptive Language

Descriptive language uses words that appeal to one or more of your senses. Descriptive words allow you to create a mental or imaginary picture of the object, person, or event being described. Here is a paragraph that contains many descriptive words and phrases. Look for words and phrases that help you to imagine what type of afternoon it was and to suggest that something is mysteriously wrong.

> I went out into the backyard and the usually roundish spots of dappled sunlight underneath the trees were all shaped like feathers, crescent in the same direction, from left to right. Though it was five o'clock on a summer afternoon, the birds were singing good-bye to the day, and their merged song seemed to soak the strange air in an additional strangeness. A kind of silence prevailed. Few cars were moving on the streets of the town. Of my children only the baby dared come into the yard with me. She wore only underpants, and as she stood beneath a tree, bulging her belly toward me in the mood of jolly flirtation she has grown into at the age of two, her bare skin was awash with pale crescents. It crossed my mind that she might be harmed, but I couldn't think how. *Cancer?*
>
> Updike, "Eclipse."

● ● ●

Did you notice the details that suggest something is wrong? Here are a few examples: Although it is only 5 P.M., the birds are saying goodbye to the day; there is a strange silence; only the baby *dared* to walk in the yard (others were afraid); the baby's skin was "awash."

Writers, by their choice of descriptive details, can greatly influence the reader's response to an event, object, or individual. Here are two different descriptions of the same individual. The first is very positive, whereas the second is quite negative.

Jean is an outgoing person who always seems to have a joke or amusing remark on the tip of her tongue. She has a carefree, fun-loving attitude, and she always looks at the good side of life.

Jean is very independent, almost a loner. She has many friends, but they seem to exist as an audience for her constant jokes and off-color remarks. She always seeks a personal advantage in any situation.

You will find that writers choose descriptive details to lend a particular impression or view. The details often seem to "add up" to an overall feeling or image about the subject. The first description of Jean presents her positively (a happy, fun-loving person), and the second describes her negatively (a self-centered person).

## EXERCISE 10–5

*DIRECTIONS:* From the following list of people, select two whom you feel you could describe. For each person, write both a positive statement and a negative statement that accurately describes him or her.

1. Your mother or father
2. A friend
3. Someone who lives in your neighborhood
4. A cousin
5. A brother or sister
6. Your boss
7. An instructor
8. A family friend

### ■ Figurative Language

Figurative language is a way of describing something that makes sense on an imaginative level but not on a literal or factual level. Notice in each of the following sentences that the underlined expression cannot be literally true but that each is understandable and is effective in conveying the author's message.

An overly ambitious employee may find the *door to advancement closed.* (There is no actual door that may close.)

The federal government is *draining* taxpayers of any accumulated wealth. (Nothing is literally being drained or removed from the insides of taxpayers.)

The judge decided to *get to the heart* of the matter.
(Matters do not really have hearts.)

The exam was a *piece of cake*.
(The exam did not contain cake.)

In each of these expressions, one distinct thing is compared with another for some quality that they have in common.

Figurative language is an effective way to describe and limit relationships. By their choice of figurative expressions writers can create either a positive or a negative impression. For instance, this first statement is somewhat negative:

The blush spread across her face like spilled paint.
(Spilled paint is usually thought of as messy and problematic.)

This second statement, however, creates a more positive image.

The blush spread across her face like wine being poured into a glass.
(Wine filling a glass is commonly thought of as a pleasant image.)

As you can see from these examples, figurative language allows the writer a large amount of freedom of expression and judgment as he or she compares one item to another. Because figurative language is not factual, the writer can go beyond a direct, literal presentation of ideas.

Be aware that a writer's impressions and judgments are involved in all figurative expressions. You should therefore regard them as interpretations, as expressions of opinion and judgment rather than as factual information.

Figurative language is used extensively in literature, particularly in poetry, as well as in esays. It is used to communicate ideas and feelings that cannot be expressed as well through literal description. For example, the statement by Jonathan Swift, "She wears her clothes as if they were thrown on by a pitchfork" creates a stronger, more meaningful image than saying "she dresses sloppily."

### *Similies and Metaphors*

Similes make an explicit comparison by using the words "like" or "as." Metaphors directly equate the two objects. Here are several examples of each:

#### SIMILES

1. He says the waves in the ship's wake are like stones rolling away. (Levertov)

2. When she was here, LiBo, she was like cold summer lager. (Williams)

**METAPHORS**

1. I will speak daggers but use none. (Shakespeare, *Hamlet*)

2. Hope is the thing with feathers—
   That perches in the soul—
   And sings the tune without words—
   And never stops—at all—
                        (Dickinson)

## EXERCISE 10–6

*DIRECTIONS:* Explain the meaning of each of the following metaphors or similes.

1. The scarlet of the maples can shake me like the cry of bugles going by. (Carman)
2. Every thread of summer is at last unwoven. (Wallace Stevens)
3. What happens to a dream deferred?
   Does it dry up
   like a raisin in the sun?
   or fester like a sore—
   and then run?
                   (Langston Hughes)
4. An aged man is but a paltry thing,
   a tattered coat upon a stick,. . .
                   (W.B. Yeats)

### Symbolism

Symbols are another type of figurative language. Symbols also make a comparison, but only one term of the comparison is stated. In everyday culture a flag symbolizes patriotism and a four-leaf clover stands for good luck. It suggests more than its literal meaning. The flag is more than a piece of cloth attached to a pole; the clover is more than a green plant. In fact, sometimes more than one meaning is suggested. A writer, then, may dress a character in white to symbolize her innocence and purity, but will not use the words *innocence* and *purity* themselves. It is left to the reader to recognize the symbol and make the comparison. Symbols are often crucial to the writer's theme or essential meaning. For example, Hemingway's short story "A Clean, Well-lighted Place" describes an aging man who visits a cafe. In this story the cafe symbolizes an escape from loneliness, old age, and death. Hemingway's theme is the inevitability and inescapability of death and aging.

Herman Melville's novel, *Moby Dick,* is the story of a white whale named Moby Dick. But the novel is about much more than an aquatic mammal, as defined by the dictionary. The whale takes on numerous meanings. The novel's characters imply that he is the devil. Later, the whale seems to represent the forces of nature or the created universe.

Symbols, then, are usually concrete objects rather than abstract feelings like pity or hate. To recognize symbols, look for objects that are given a particular or unusual emphasis. The object may be mentioned often, or even suggested in the title. The story or poem may open or close with reference to the object. Objects that suggest more than one meaning are possible symbols. Perhaps the best way to identify symbols is to look for objects that lead to the author or poet's theme.

## EXERCISE 10–7

*DIRECTIONS:* Read the following poem by Sylvia Plath and answer the following questions.

### MIRROR

I am silver and exact. I have no preconceptions.
Whatever I see I swallow immediately
Just as it is, unmisted by love or dislike.
I am not cruel, only truthful—
The eye of a little god, four-cornerned.
Most of the time I meditate on the opposite wall.
It is pink, with speckles. I have looked at it so long
I think it is a part of my heart. But it flickers.
Faces and darkness separate us over and over.

Now I am a lake. A woman bends over me,
Searching my reaches for what she really is.
Then she turns to those liars, the candles or the moon.
I see her back, and reflect it faithfully.
She rewards me with tears and an agitation of hands.
I am important to her. She comes and goes.
Each morning it is her face that replaces the darkness.
In me she has drowned a young girl, and in me an old woman
Rises toward her day after day, like a terrible fish.

• • •

1. Explain in what ways the mirror is a personification.
2. Discuss what the mirror symbolizes.
3. Explain the meaning of the metaphor "I am a lake."
4. Explain the meaning of the simile in the last line of the poem.

## ■ READING AND ANALYZING SHORT STORIES

A short story is a brief work of prose fiction that tells a story involving a limited number of people who take part in a series of related events. Its purpose is to convey a message or meaning deeper than the story itself. When reading and analyzing short stories it is essential to pay close attention to basic elements of important features which include:

### ■ Plot

The plot is the basic story line—the sequence of events as they occurred in the work. It also consists of the actions through which the work's meaning is expressed. The plot is a story of conflict and often follows a predictable structure. The plot often begins by setting the scene, introducing the main characters, and providing background information needed to follow the story. Next, a complication or problem often arises. Suspense is built as the problem or conflict unfolds. Near the end of the story, events come to a climax—the point at which the outcome of the conflict will be decided. A conclusion quickly follows as the story ends.

### ■ Setting

The setting is the time, place, and circumstances in which the action occurs. The setting provides a framework in which the actions occur and establishes an atmosphere in which the characters interact.

### ■ Characterization

Characters are the actors in a narrative story. The characters reveal themselves by what they say—the dialogue—and by their actions, appearance, thoughts, and feelings. The narrator, or person who tells the story, may also comment on or reveal information about the characters. The task of the critical reader is to analyze the characters' traits and motives, analyze their personalities, examine character changes, and study their interactions.

## ■ Point of View

The point of view refers to the way the story is presented or from whose perspective or mind the story is told. Often the author of a story is not the narrator. The story may be told from the perspective of one of the characters or by a narrator who is not one of the characters. In analyzing point of view, determine the role and function of the narrator. Is the narrator accurate and knowledgeable, all-knowing, or limited in his or her view? Sometimes the narrator is able to enter the minds of some or all of the characters, knowing their thoughts and understanding their actions and motivations. In some stories a narrator may be naive or innocent, unable to understand the actions or implications of the events in the story.

## ■ Tone

The tone of a story suggests the author's attitude. Like tone of voice, tone in a story suggests feelings. Many ingredients contribute to tone, including the author's choice of details, characters, events, and situations. The tone of a story may be amused, angry, or contemptuous. The author's feelings are not necessarily those of the characters or the narrator. Instead, it is through the characters' actions and the narrator's description of them that we infer tone. The style in which a work is written often suggests the tone. Style is the way a writer writes—especially his or her use of language.

## ■ Theme

The theme of the story is the main point or message the story conveys through all of its elements. Themes are often large, universal ideas dealing with life and death, human values, or existence. To establish the theme, ask yourself "What is the author trying to say about life by telling the story?" Try to explain it in a single sentence. If you are having difficulty stating the theme, try the following suggestions:

1. **Study the title.** Now that you have read the story, does it take on any new meanings?

2. **Analyze the main character.** Does he or she change? If so, how and in reaction to what?

3. **Look for broad general statements** characters or the narrator make about life or the problem(s) they face.

4. **Look for symbols,** figurative expressions, meaningful names (example: Mrs. Goodheart), or objects that hint at bigger ideas.

Now read the short story "The Blackbird" by Victoriano Martinez. Pay particular attention to each of the previously discussed features. The story was first published in 1992.

## THE BLACKBIRD

1    When I was thirteen, except for a box of peaches from Old Man Tito's porch, I never stole anything. Mostly, I would say, this was because of my mother. The thought of anything not hers occupying a space of guilt inside our home, even if just a measly candy bar, had a genuine terror for her. I think she was afraid that this would open her up to rude invasions by police, or housing authorities, or people demanding the return of things she imagined they'd hang their own babies for. People only become dangerous, she'd say, when arguments boil around things they own, or around jelousy, which she said was like a glue that sticks to people.

2    Despite my mother's fear, my friends Albert and Benny Molina and I once lugged a box of peaches off Tito's front porch. I remember the peaches clearly because of Tito's blackbird. He claimed the bird could talk—although he wasn't really a talking bird—and since the bird's cage hung right by the porch window, and we could hear its wings spanking frantically on the wrought-iron bars, we thought surely the bird must have seen us.

3    The next day Tito began roaming the neighborhood telling everyone that his blackbird knew who stole his peaches. He said the bird needed to see the scoundrel's face, however, since birds weren't really good with names. "But he'll squawk, you better believe it, he'll squawk when he sees that thief eye to eye."

4    Tito said this in our kitchen as my mother and sister Rebecca served him coffee and a piece of glazed Mexican bread. "I'll take my bird around the neighborhood until I find out who those *pinche* thieves are. . . oh excuse me, Señora Hernandez," he said, covering his mouth to hide his browning teeth. Then, as if from remorse, he shrugged his shoulders. "And I was planning to give you a bag of peaches, Señora." He meant it, too, because he always gave my mom little presents of fruit, like blush-ripe papayas and mangos, and filbert and brazil nuts from South America.

5    Tito then started reminiscing about how delicious his peaches were, how he had bought them fresh from a farmer in Lodi, how he planned to temper their skins by cooling them in the night air. I could hear him from the living room where I was reading my dad's Archie comic books. My dad didn't like anyone reading his comic books, but I had a deal with my mother that if I stacked them back neatly, without soiling one page, I could read them before he came home from work. I had just slid them down from the top shelf of his closet when Tito appeared at the door, hat in hand, to gossip with my mother.

6    Everyone, except my mother who felt sorry for him and actually liked hearing his wild stories, believed Tito crazy, as mad as his blackbird and almost as dark. My mother liked him because he wasn't a man who twisted words around, or played games of suggestion with her eyes. He had curlicues of raison dark hair that twirled around his battered ears and a grapeknife scar under his left eye which gave that side of his face a wrinkly erosion. My dad said he too thought Tito screwy, but only

because he was Puerto Rican—that was explanation enough for him. Mostly though, people believed Tito crazy because he was a bachelor and didn't have a woman to smooth down the rumples of his clothes and speech. My grandmother said "*solteros*" always lost their marbles. People are like seams in a quilt, she'd say; without others, they're only a thread dangling in the heart of a cloud.

7 Tito lived by himself in a clapboard house bought with money earned from working as a janitor. There was a time when he used to go to Puerto Rico to visit his mother and two sisters. One of his sisters was married to a cigar wrapper at a tobacco factory; the other was too young then to soil herself in the business of men. After his mother died, though, the stray sister married, and both sisters became buried inside family duties and houshold chores. To make matters worse, his sisters' husbands were jealous of him choosing to live in the comfort of the States and for embarrassing them by sprinkling money around to their kids. Tito believed there wasn't much room for any kindness between them, and, over the years, fewer and fewer letters were mailed.

8 When Tito left, I heard my mother and Rebecca joking, saying he was such a crazy man, the craziest man they had ever met. "How could a bird tell him who stole the peaches?" my mother said in Spanish, as if this were a scandal in itself.

9 "It's ridiculous," my sister Rebecca snorted.

10 After she and Rebecca stayed quiet for a while, my mom said, "Maybe Tito isn't so crazy, Becca. After all, a bird can recognize people. They can be *pretty* smart sometimes, no?"

11 "You're right, it isn't *so* crazy," my sister agreed.

12 Mother winked at me from the kitchen. She made a smirk with her lips as though planning to pull Becca's leg all the way to the reservoir and back. Rebecca, kneading dough and mulling over her own ideas, said that even if a bird can recognize a person, how is it going to know what stealing is?

13 My mother flipped over a tortilla on the stove, thought about this for long while, then shifted the iron skillet to another burner. "Why *can't* a bird know what stealing is?" she said. "Don't they know when a cat comes and scavenges their nests? Can't they know what is theirs?"

14 "Sure. . . sure they can!" my sister exploded—a chisel of truth had hit her square on the forhead. Her outburst let the air out of both her doubts, and they predicted Tito's bird would soon recognize the thief and the hands of the police laid upon him. They both laughed like crazy blackbirds themselves.

15 Listening from the living room, I felt my jaws stiffen, a sudden blurring of my eyes. My brain was spinning around inside my head like a stone, grinding against the walls of my skull. Only by squeezing the blood from my fists could I keep it balanced. But the thought of Tito entering through the door with the blackbird perched on his arm, fluttering its wings and squawking accusations at me, tightened the arteries in my neck and, from what seemed like a hub between my temples, the stone unhinged and began to wobble, flashing sparks of alarm all over the room. Quickly, and not too neatly, I put my dad's comic books away and ducked out through a broken slat in the backyard fence, heading for Albert's house.

16    Albert thought we should kill the bird. He was in his front yard, hosing water on his mother's roses. "We got to," he said, "I don't want to go to no Juvy. My uncle says the cops beat you up there because they know you're Mexican and can't do nothing."

17    "Can't we give him back the peaches?"

18    "We can't," he said. "Me and Benny ate mosta 'em. And besides, I threw the rest away!"

19    "You threw the rest away!"

20    "Hey, my mother almos' smelt 'em under the bed! Boy, if she woulda found 'em, I'd be dead, real dead, and you too!"

21    "What do you mean—me too?" I said, indignant but not too surprised that he'd snitch on me.

22    "You know my mother," Albert said. He went to turn off the faucet. "She'd tell your mother in a second, and do you think she wouldn't ask you about 'em? Knowing you, you'd probably squeal on me and Benny."

23    "No, I wouldn't. You're the damn squealer!" I said.

24    Albert didn't say anything, just gazed at the hose he'd rolled over his arm, biting his fingernail. He was a nail-biting fiend, Albert was. At school, he'd chew pencil erasers down to the metal brace. After a while he waved his finger reflectively, "Do you remember what happened to Tony?"

25    A month before, the police had dragged Tony Montez out of his house. They had his legs pulled back and were wrestling to pin his arms so they could handcuff him. Tony was stretching and squirming, begging for somebody to please help him. Nobody did. Everyone was afraid of the police. Even Tony's dad who hugged Tony's mom to quiet her hysterics. She had tried grabbing at one of the officer's arms, but the officer looked at Tony's dad as if to say he better do something about his wife quick, or else. Besides, everyone believed Tony must have done something wrong. Otherwise, why would the police come?

26    "Yeah . . ." I said, frightened at the thought of being dragged out of my own home in the naked glare of family and neighbors. "Do you think they'll do us the same?"

27    "Not if we kill that frickin' bird," Albert said.

28    I figured any way of killing the bird would be messy. I remember my mother once taking a kitchen knife, and after scratching a cross on the dirt, grinding the blade through a chicken's neck. The head scrinched right off. She let the wings flop in her hand, and a few gulps of blood puddled on the ground. Finally she tossed the chicken on the cross. It lay there pumping small, sudden twitches; then it was lifeless. My mom said this was because of the mercy of the cross. There was nothing to it, for her. But the thought of holding a chicken's doomed neck in my hand blazed the back of my own neck with goose pimples.

29    "We could poison it, stupid," Albert said, after seeing my face sour with thoughts of slaughter. "What do you think we're gonna do, chop its head off?" He laughed, but it was a serious laugh. He was thinking hard about the bird now. "We could feed it Clorox or some rat poison. Whatja think? Does your dad have any rat poison?"

30    "No, we don't have any rats," I said. "Only mice." For a crazy second I thought about how we could put a mousetrap loaded with a thimbleful of seed inside the cage and smash the bird to smithereens. That would be too obvious. Tito would know somebody killed his bird and why, and knowing Tito, even if he died twenty years later, his ghost would probably go around searcing for whoever killed his bird. The thought of Tito's dark eyes and eroded cheek roving over me from beyond the grave scared me to death.

31    "What the hell are you thinking, anyway?" Albert broke in. "Every time I look at you, you're like twenty miles away. What the hell's the matter with you?"

32    "I'm just thinking," I said, hissing annoyance. But I couldn't melt the icicles grating inside my blood.

33    "Well, think about that goddamned bird, willya."

34    We thought about it, but here really wasn't any way that we could see. Tito kept the bird locked behind his door, and his porch was visible from almost any window on our block. To make matters worse, Tito had bought a glass doorknop at the supply store down the street and every day, when the afternoon sun angled over his roof ledge, the glass slithered light on almost every maple tree on our street. It attracted curious gazes and sometimes, while walking by it, a shard of light entered our eyes. We were lucky to have stolen Tito's peaches on a night when the moon was empty.

35    Another thought, definitely the most important, was that to enter Tito's porch when he was asleep was one thing, another was to enter his house, asleep or not. Rumors had it that he kept beside his bed a banana machete brought back from Puerto Rico. The thought of him lopping off sugercane stalks and cutting through green coconuts with one swacking blow frightened our imaginations to a frenzy. We went limp over the possible wounds he could rip across our navels, spilling our guts like wet blankets to the floor. No, there was nothing we could do.

36    "When I see that blackbird," Albert said with crazy bravado, "I'm gonna look him strait in the eye."

37    "I'm gonna spit in his eye," I said, stocking up my own courage.

38    Albert stabbed the air with two forked fingers. "I'm gonna poke his eyes, like the Three Stooges."

39    All the same, we went rushing to Bernardo at the first hint of Tito rounding the corner.

40    Bernardo, my older brother, was lying on his bed reading a Spiderman comic book. He elbowed up and listened. He was keen for a scandal almost as much as my mom. He rubbed his chin worriedly for about a minute, then pointed a scolding finger at us for being stupid enough to steal from a neighbor. He never said it was wrong or that we should feel guilty, but that it was stupid—absolutely stupid!— a feat he claimed only we three geniuses were capable of. "I won't put it past Benny," he said. "That thief would steal from his own mother. But you guys!"

41    "Yeah, yeah, it was Benny. He's the one who told us it'd be all right," Albert edged in.

42    "Yeah. . . sure," Bernardo said. He dressed down Albert from the corner of his eye. Then he looked dead at me with deep disappointment. "Well," he said finally,

"the way I see it, you both have got to keep away from Tito—and I mean *away* from him—because he'll find out, you can bet on that, he'll find out."

43   I went away believing that this was the most stupid thing I had ever done. It wasn't like we had stolen gold bars from Fort Knox. My dad's face would probably flush with pride if I'd pulled off something spectacular like that. It'd be a sign that at least one of his sons had ambition. But stealing big from a government didn't mean the same as stealing small from a neighbor. The smudge I'd make on his reputation among his friends would probably stick on him for life.

44   Now my mom. I knew her faith in me would shrivel like a cactus in a winter freeze. How would she explain it to all her *comadres* around the neighborhood who were already jealous of her for having kids who didn't get into as much trouble?

45   For a week then, I stayed away from Tito. Some days I lay paralyzed on my bed, listening for his tap on our door. On Tuesday I bit back the cold and took out the trash early, knowing that on that day he, too, put out the trash. Whenever he came toward me on the street, I ducked behind a corner or turned and greeted people I hardly knew. I felt as if even the people I spoke to during these embarrassing asides knew what I had done, knew that I was hiding to avoid capture. I hated myself for praying that maybe Tito would suffer an injury at work or that one of his sisters would die tragically in Puerto Rico—this, so that his box of peaches could shift further back in his mind.

46   Then one day, as I was putting on my white shirt in front of the mirror, Albert's moist face appeared at my window. He looked happy, anxiously pulling at the collar of his lapel, searching for the right words to spill his excitement. I took the screen off the window and let him climb in.

47   "Manny! Manny!" he said, catching his breath. "I saw the bird! I saw it!" He was raising his arms up and down as though spurring on a cheering audience. "Tito's blackbird. It saw *me*!"

48   "What. . . it *saw* you?"

49   "Yeah, and you know what?" he said, slumping down on my bed like at flattened balloon. "It didn't recognize me. That damned bird is as blind as a bat." All of Albert's energy saved to come and tell me this revelation now seemed exhausted. He groped around tiredly on the bed.

50   "What the hell are you talking about?"

51   "I'm talking about me and Benny going over to Tito's to help him move his refrigerator," he said, catching his breath again. "My dad ordered us to go. We figured there was no way out of it. You know how my dad is, he don't take no excuses."

52   "And you guys went?" I said, grabbing his arm.

53   "I was tired, Manny. I just wanted to get the thing over with. Me and Benny figured, 'What the hell, we'd promise to buy him some more frickin' peaches.'"

54   "Benny too!" I said. I couldn't believe that Benny, being older, would give in to the same fears that were scouring us.

55   "Yeah. . . Benny too. Anyway, when we got there, Tito was sitting on his porch eating a can of pork and beans. The bird was in its cage. And you know what?" he

said, rising up again, "for a minute I thought it recognized us. It started to squawk like we had hatchets in our hands or something. Tito couldn't understand what was going on. He said the bird was blind or almos' blind. . . been that way for a year."

56      Albert lay back, smiling like some damp heavy fog had lifted from his body. He began to finger out a loose thread from the quilt my grandmother had sewn for me the winter before. I stood there not knowing what to think, watching him as he pulled one thread out of its seam and flicked it with his finger.

57      I realized then that I'd been freed. The fear of getting caught and dragged off to Juvenile Hall, where I'd heard of Mexican boys crying and breaking down from the beatings, had been lifted. I remember my heart lurching, then emptying of any feelings in the whole affair.

58      I looked at Albert slouched on the bed, and thought about Tito sitting there on his porch eating out of a can of pork and beans, his spoon clanking against the tin sides. I wondered why he told everybody his bird could see when his bird was blind. Maybe he knew, and just wanted to scare us.

59      Maybe he was just a natural liar. Then it hit me, right there as I was watching Albert pull another thread loose from the quilt, it hit me. The reason why Tito said his bird could talk when he knew it couldn't wasn't because he wanted to scare us but because he wanted people to marvel at his stories, no matter if they believed him crazy. Tito wanted people to recognize him. I knew how he felt, because I was the same. Only I wanted people to approve of me. He was lonely, but I was afraid. And I knew that it was me, and not Tito, who was really the crazy one.

● ● ●

## EXERCISE 10–8

*DIRECTIONS:* Write a paragraph summarizing the plot of "The Blackbird."

## ■ ANALYZING A SHORT STORY: "THE BLACKBIRD"

"The Blackbird" deals with a simple **plot**, the theft of a box of peaches by three young boys from Tito who owns a blackbird. Tito claims the blackbird can talk and will identify the thieves.

The **setting** seems to be the present time somewhere in a small town in Mexico. The major **characters** include Manny, Albert and Benny Molina, Tito, and the blackbird. Secondary characters include Manny's mother, sister, and brother. Martinez reveals the personalities of each character through description and dialogue.

The story is told from the **point of view** of Manny, who tells the story in the first person. Manny, who is both the narrator and a major character in the story, is limited by what he sees and experiences. He is unable to provide insights into the actions or motives of other characters.

The **tone** of the story is friendly and open. The narrator freely shares his experiences with us.

The **theme** of the story focuses on the nature of guilt. The story examines what guilt is, what can be done about it, and what causes it. The blackbird becomes a symbol of guilt because he supposedly, like Manny, knows who stole the peaches. Throughout the story Manny experiences guilt in several different forms. At first, guilt is fear of punishment. Later it becomes fear of being caught. Still later guilt is pictured in remorse over an action and fear of disapproval from family and neighbors. Manny attempts to deal with his guilt in a variety of ways. He considers correcting the wrongdoing by giving back the peaches, but many have already been eaten. Next he contemplates killing the blackbird, thus removing the source of guilt. As the story progresses, Manny in succession tries to talk "big" about it, blame someone else, and hide from it. In the end Manny admits he is crazy—possibly crazy with guilt.

The story also describes the consequences of guilt. There are physical consequences. Mistrust builds among friends, Manny becomes mentally distraught, and he considers desperate, violent actions, such as killing the blackbird. Overall, "The Blackbird" is an examination of guilt, its nature, and its consequences.

## EXERCISE 10–9

*DIRECTIONS:* For the short story "The Blackbird" answer each of the following questions.

1. Identify and explain the meaning of the metaphors and similes contained in paragraphs 14 and 15.
2. Identify three paragraphs in which Martinez uses descriptive language that helps you visualize the person or event. Underline key descriptive words and phrases.
3. What does Martinez reveal about the values of the citizens of this Mexican community (what do they value; what do they fear; what do they dislike)?
4. Most stories end with the guilty confessing or being punished. Are you surprised that Manny and his friends did not confess to their theft? Why do you think Martinez ended the story this way?

## ■ READING AND ANALYZING POETRY

Poetry is a form of literary expression, involving sound and rhythm, in which ideas are presented in a unique format. Poems are written in verse—lines and stanzas rather than paragraphs. Poetry often requires more reading time and greater concentration than other types of writing. In reading prose you can skip a word in a paragraph and your comprehension of the whole paragraph may not suffer. Poetry, however, is very compact and precise. Each word is important and carries a meaning. You have to pay attention to each word—its sound, its meaning, and its meaning when combined with other words. Rhythm is also important in many poems. Here are a few guidelines to help you approach poetry more effectively.

1. **Read the poem once straight through, without any defined purpose.** Be open-minded, experiencing the poem as it is written. If you meet an unknown word or confusing reference, keep reading.

2. **Use punctuation to guide your comprehension.** Although poetry is written in lines, do not expect each line to make sense by itself. Meaning often flows from line to line, eventually forming a sentence. Use the punctuation to guide you, as you do in reading paragraphs. If a line has no punctuation at the end, consider it as a slight pause, with an emphasis on the last word.

3. **Read the poem a second time.** Identify and correct any difficulties, such as an unknown word.

4. **Notice the action.** *Who* is doing *what, when*, and *where?*

5. **Analyze the poem's intent.** Decide what it was written to accomplish. Does it describe a feeling or a person, express a memory, or present an argument?

6. **Determine who is speaking.** Poems often refer to an unidentified "I" or "we." Try to describe the speaker's viewpoint or feelings.

7. **Establish the speaker's tone.** Is he or she serious, challenging, saddened, frustrated? Read aloud; your intonation, your emphasis on certain words, and the rise and fall of your voice may provide clues. You may "hear" a poet's anger, despondency, or elation.

8. **Identify to whom the poem is addressed.** Is it written to a person, to the reader, to an object? Consider the possibility that the poet may be writing to express himself or herself, to work out a problem, or to release emotion.

9. **Reread difficult or confusing sections.** Read them aloud several times. Copying these sections word for word may be helpful. Use context or your dictionary to figure out unfamiliar words.

10. **Check unfamiliar references.** A poet may refer to people, objects, or events outside the poem. These are known as *allusions*. A poet may mention Greek gods or goddesses, historical figures, or biblical characters. Often the allusion is important to the overall meaning of the poem. When you see Oedipus mentioned in a poem, you need to know who he was. (Paperback books on mythology and literary figures are good investments.)

11. **Analyze the language of the poem.** Consider connotative meanings and study figures of speech.

12. **Look for the poet's meaning or the poem's theme.** Paraphrase the poem; express it in your own words and connect it to your own experience. Then put each idea together to discover its overall meaning. Ask yourself: What is the poet trying to tell me? What is his or her message?

Read the poem "Dream Deferred" by Langston Hughes, and apply these guidelines.

## DREAM DEFERRED

What happens to a dream deferred?

Does it dry up
like a raisin in the sun?
Or fester like a sore—
And then run?
Does it stink like rotten meat?
Or crust and sugar over—
like a syrupy sweet?

Maybe it just sags
like a heavy load.

Or does it explode?

● ● ●

One key to understanding the poem is the meaning of the word "deferred." Here it means put off or postponed. Dreams deferred refer to unfulfilled goals, or goals or desires that were postponed. The main action is the poet questioning what happens to a dream that is deferred and offering six alternatives. Notice the connotative meanings of the first four choices: "dry up," "fester," "stink," "crust and sugar over." Each of these suggests some type of decay. A dream, then, may be destroyed. The term *sags* suggests heaviness and inaction. A dream may stultify. Notice, too, the figures of speech such as "dry up like a raisin," "fester like a sore," "stink like rotten meat." These create negative, unpleasant images. The last alternative, "explode," is active: posing a threat and implying danger or violence. The poet's purpose, then, is to explore the negative consequences of unfulfilled goals and to suggest that violent or dangerous outcomes may result.

## EXERCISE 10–10

*DIRECTIONS:* Read each of the following poems and answer the corresponding questions.

### THE SILKEN TENT

She is as in a field of silken tent
At midday when a sunny summer breeze
Has dried the dew and all its ropes relent,
So that in guys[a] it gently sways at ease,   [a]Attachments that steady it.
And its supporting central cedar pole,
That is its pinnacle to heavenward
And signifies the sureness of the soul,
Seems to owe naught to any single cord,
But strictly held by none, is loosely bound
By countless silken ties of love and thought
To everything on earth the compass round,
And only by one's going slightly taut
In the capriciousness[b] of summer air   [b]Changeableness, unpredictableness.
Is of the slightest bondage made aware.

Robert Frost

● ● ●

1. Identify and explain the simile used throughout the poem.

2. What do you know about this woman's personality?

3. What are the ropes (cords)?

4. What is the poem's theme?

### TO HIS COY MISTRESS

Had we but world enough and time,
This coyness[a], lady, were no crime.   [a]Modesty, reluctance.
We would sit down and think which way
To walk, and pass our long love's day.
Thou by the Indian Ganges' side
Should'st rubies find; I by the tide
Of Humber would complain[b]. I would   [b]Sing sad songs.

5

Love you ten years before the Flood,
And you should, if you please, refuse
Till the conversion of the Jews. 10
My vegetable[c] love should grow      [c]Vegetative, flourishing.
Vaster than empires, and more slow.
An hundred years should go to praise
Thine eyes, and on thy forehead gaze,
Two hundred to adore each breast, 15
But thirty thousand to the rest.
An age at least to every part,
And the last age should show your heart.
For, lady, you deserve this state[d],      [d]Pomp, ceremony.
Nor would I love at lower rate. 20
  But at my back I always hear
Time's wingèd chariot hurrying near,
And yonder all before us lie
Deserts of vast eternity.
Thy beauty shall no more be found, 25
Nor in thy marble vault shall sound
My echoing song; then worms shall try
That long preserved virginity,
And your quaint honor turn to dust,
And into ashes all my lust. 30
The grave's a fine and private place,
But none, I think, do there embrace.
  Now therefore, while the youthful hue
Sits on thy skin like morning glew[e]      [e]Glow.
And while thy willing soul transpires 35
At every pore with instant[f] fires,      [f]Eager.
Now let us sport us while we may;
And now, like amorous birds of prey,
Rather at once our time devour
Than languish in his slow-chapped[g] power.      [g]Slow-jawed. 40
Let us roll all our strength and all
Our sweetness up into one ball
And tear our pleasures with rough strife
Thorough[h] the iron gates of life.      [h]Through.
Thus, though we cannot make our sun 45
Stand still, yet we will make him run.

Andrew Marvell

● ● ●

---

To His Coy Mistress. 7. *Humber:* a river that flows by Marvell's town of Hull (on the side of the world opposite from the Ganges). 10. *conversion of the Jews:* an event that, according to St. John the Divine, is to take place just before the end of the world. 35. *transpires:* exudes, as a membrane lets fluid or vapor pass through it.

1. The poem is divided into three parts by the indented lines. Summarize each part.

2. What is the overall purpose of the poem?

3. To what might the phrase "Time's wingèd chariot" refer?

4. Identify and explain several metaphors or similes.

5. This poem was written in 1681 but is still read widely today. Why has it lasted more than 300 years?

---

**Critical Thinking Tip #10**

**Understanding Literary Points of View**

In literature, point of view is the author's relationship to his or her characters and the fictional world he or she has created. Think of it as the position from which the story is told. Point of view is similar to viewpoints discussed in Chapter 10, except that point of view in literature refers to who is telling the story. The four common points of view are:

1. *Omniscient* (all-knowing). In this position the author, known as the narrator (not one of the characters), tells the story. The author has complete knowledge of the character's actions and thoughts and may share them with the reader. The author also may tell the readers what a character thinks.
2. *Limited Omniscient.* The author tells the story but limits his or her knowledge to that of one character. That is, the author understands completely one character but does not understand what motivates others.
3. *First person.* In this position one of the characters tells the story. This character may be an observer or an active participant in the events of the story. The reader must observe and infer what motivates each character.
4. *Objective.* In the objective point of view, the author is the narrator but has no knowledge of the motivations of any of the characters.

It is important to understand and identify point of view: The author may choose a particular point of view to emphasize a particular character who is likely to be important in the plot and who will provide important clues about the theme.

## SUMMARY

**1. What is the difference between a word's denotative meaning and its connotative meaning?**

A word's denotative meaning is its literal or dictionary meaning. Its connotative meaning, however, goes beyond this to include all the other meanings a word may take on. It is through their use of connotative meanings that writers can influence your thoughts on a subject.

**2. What are euphemisms?**

Euphemisms are words or phrases chosen by a writer to avoid the unpleasantness that might be associated with a direct statement of the facts. They are often used to hide the truth when it is negative.

**3. What are the two types of subjective language writers use in expressive writing?**

Writers use *descriptive* and *figurative* language to establish a feeling or mood in their writing. Descriptive words appeal to your senses and help you create mental images as you read. Figurative language involves the use of expressions that make sense on an imaginative level but not on a literal level. These expressions include similes, metaphors, and symbolism.

**4. What are the basic elements of short stories?**

The brief prose fiction work known as the short story contains six basic elements that can aid your interpretation:
- Plot—the series of events as they happen in a story.
- Setting—the time, place, and circumstances in which the story takes place.
- Characterization—the way the writer portrays the characters in the story.
- Point of View—the way the person who tells the story sees the plot, setting, and characters; this person is not usually the writer but one of the characters or someone outside the story.
- Tone—the attitude of the author toward the characters and events in the story.

**5. What should you do to read and analyze poetry more effectively?**

- Theme—the main point or message of the story.

To improve your interpretation of poetry you should:
- Read the poem several times
- Read it the first time just to experience the poem, using its punctuation as a guide to meaning
- Reread it as many times as it takes to identify the action, the poem's intent, the speaker and his or her tone and whom or what the poem speaks to
- Reread confusing parts of the poem, check unfamiliar references, and carefully analyze the language used
- Grasp the theme or meaning behind the poem

## READING SELECTION 19
### WE'RE ALL ROBINSON'S CHILDREN

Sandy Grady
From *USA Today*

*Jackie Robinson was the first black man to play major league baseball. This column from* USA Today *explains the debt we owe to Robinson. Read the column to learn what contributions he made.*

1   Bleacher seats cost 60 cents. Ebbets Feild on that chill, gun-metal-gray day was two-thirds full. The rookie, No. 42, at first base was jittery. So was his wife in the grandstand, sheltering their young son against the cold. The rookie was in a slump. He grounded out, flied out, bounced into a double play. He ran with a pigeon-toed, mincing stride—but Lordy, how he could run. Years later, anyone gifted to have been among the 26,523 witnesses was stuck with one impression: the contrast of the Dodgers' snow-white uniform and the rookie's jet-black skin.

2   Jaded sports writers barely mentioned the rookie in their stories. "Restless as a can of worms," he was described by the *Herald-Tribune's* Red Smith. *The New York Times'* Arthur Daley sniffed, "An uneventful occasion."

3   Sure, uneventful as an earthquake that shook America.

4   It was April 15, 1947, when Jackie Roosevelt Robinson broke the color line in baseball and changed both sports and America forever.

5   I submit that Robinson's debut and the battalions of black atheletes who followed him—

Larry Doby to Arthur Ashe to Michael Jordan—did more to shift the way we think about race than all the preachers, pundits, marchers and politicians.

6 It's not easy to be a racist when you're a white suburbanite standing in line to by $125 Grant Hill sneakers or a $50 seat to cheer for Emmit Smith.

7 That's why Jackie's day matters, the explosion of this slave's grandson from Cairo, Ga., onto the American scene. It's a trip to a mountain top. We look down 50 years and see the trail.

8 And to my mind, Robinson's 50th anniversary comes in the nick of time for baseball, a sport that's lost its memory, its soul and many of its customers.

9 Yes, I know, its hard to wade through the self-congratulatory, feel-good hype: Wheaties boxes with Jackie's picture, ceremonial Coca-Cola bottles, Nike TV ads, gold coins, trading cards. Reminds me of Bill Russell's line about racism: "They'll solve it when somebody figures out how to make money from it."

10 I wonder what Jackie Robinson would think of this anniversary frenzy. He died at age 53, gray, half-blind from diabetes, probably a victim of his stereotype-smashing ordeal.

11 But what if Jackie were alive—he'd be 78 now—to see the World Robinson Made?

12 He'd be proud to see players this summer wearing the insignia "Breaking Barriers." But he'd surely be dismayed that many black players, beyond lip-service platitudes, have no idea who Jackie Robinson was. Or what he endured.

13 Frank Thomas, asked on ESPN if he knew much about Robinson, replied, "Not really. To be honest, I'm more into the new age."

14 Sure, Robinson was a beacon to such older stars as Hank Aaron and Joe Morgan. But sociologist Harry Edwards interviewed 13 of the new breed; 11 didn't know Robinson's story. Only one player, the Red Sox's Mo Vaughan, showed up this winter at the Jackie Robinson Foundation dinner.

15 That's like a young novelist saying, "Uh, Faulkner, what did he ever write?"

16 Too bad Robinson isn't around to tell young, pampered millionaires what his life was like in 1947—bean-balls, flying spikes, racial crud, the N-word and "jungle bunny" and "black b—" that spilled from dugout bigots. Look at Robinson's record, the .300-plus years, stolen bases, six Dodger league titles, and you see pent-up steam exploding.

17 "I look around," Robinson said near his life's end, "and wonder how many now playing could have succeeded under those conditions."

18 Maybe none. Think about American life that April postwar day when Robinson broke the color taboo. No one had heard of Martin Luther King Jr. It would be eight years before Rosa Parks refused to sit in the back of a Montgomery bus. Ten years before Ike sent National Guardsmen to chaperone black kids into a Little Rock school. Jackie was there first cutting through the brush.

19 I can only guess what Robinson would think of the America he left behind. Make no mistake, he was a crusader. Never mind that he worked for Nixon against JFK. He was an NAACP firebrand, a confidant of King and a supporter of Jessie Jackson. He'd surely approve of the burgeoning black middle class. But he'd look at the slums of north Philly, central L.A. and south Bronx, at the drug wars, and at young black males in prison, and wonder if we aren't still stuck in old nightmares.

20 "Jack was impatient," says his widow, Rachel. "He'd look around and see some retrenchment."

21 Perhaps Robinson would have mixed emotions about his sports heritage. True, black athletes dominate: 17% of major-league players, 67% of the NFL, 80% of the NBA. But black managers, coaches, front-office bosses? Scarce. He'd be wide-eyed at salaries. Jackie made $37,500 tops; now the big-league average is $1.1 million. (Albert Belle makes more in a week than Robinson did in a career.) But he'd shake his head at kid's obsession with sports. While SAT's stagnate, two-thirds of young black men believe they can beat 100,000-to-1 odds and make the pros.

22    I doubt if Robinson would be thrilled about the greed and glitter of 1990s pro sports, the yammering over strikes, contracts, salaries and commercials. Jackie and mentor Branch Rickey went through fire for the principle. Will the legacy of Robinson's ordeal turn out to be Dennis Rodman, Deion Sanders and Marge Schott?

23    On Robinson's tombstone is carved his heartfelt quote: "A man's life is not important except in the impact it has on other lives."

24    On that scoreboard, Robinson won big.

25    If the job's unfinished, he still changed a country. As novelist Wallace Stegner once said, "It is madness to amputate the present from the past." That's why April 15, 1947, matters.

26    All black atheletes are Jackie Robinson's heirs. But whatever our skin color, we are all Jackie's children.

## Comprehension Test 19

*Directions: Circle the letter of the best answer.*

### Checking Your Comprehension

1. This article mainly tells about
   a. bigotry in professional sports.
   b. the greed of modern athletes.
   c. Jackie Robinson's life.
   d. Jackie Robinson's legacy.

2. Which sentence best expresses the main idea of this selection?
   a. Jackie Robinson changed sports and our society by breaking baseball's color line.
   b. Jackie Robinson was instrumental in the Dodgers winning six league titles.
   c. Jackie Robinson would not be pleased with pro sports in the 1990s.
   d. Jackie Robinson loved the game of baseball and gave it all he had.

3. When Robinson played his first game of professional baseball, sports writers
   a. wrote whole feature articles on him.
   b. wrote about how many home runs he hit.
   c. wrote about him the same way they wrote about white baseball players.
   d. barely mentioned him in their stories.

4. In his early career other baseball players responded to Jackie Robinson with
   a. friendliness and warmth.
   b. hatred and racial slurs.
   c. respect for his talents.
   d. advice for improving his hitting.

5. Which one of the following prominent figures confided in Jackie Robinson?
   a. Rosa Parks
   b. John F. Kennedy
   c. Malcolm X
   d. Martin Luther King Jr.

6. As used in the reading in paragraph 1, "slump" refers to a(n)
   a. low point.
   b. broken down neighborhood.
   c. time of hard work.
   d. even keel.

### Thinking Critically

7. The author feels that baseball players today
   a. could have done what Robinson did.
   b. are spoiled and coddled.
   c. have every right to their high salaries.
   d. are hardworking and dedicated.

8. The idea of a black man playing major league baseball in 1947 was important because
   a. it had never happened before.
   b. it happened long before the civil rights movement.
   c. everyone in professional baseball liked Robinson.
   d. all the fans cheered for Robinson.

9. The author of this article thinks that if Jackie Robinson were alive today he would
   a. be pleased at how most players stand up for principles.
   b. enjoy the game even more.
   c. be satisfied with the racial progress made since his time.
   d. be disappointed about the way greed has taken over the game.

10. From the article, the reader can conclude that the author's attitude toward Jackie Robinson is one of
    a. scorn and ridicule.
    b. admiration and respect.
    c. pity and sorrow.
    d. disinterest and apathy.

**Questions for Discussion**

1. How might Jackie Robinson's life in the major leagues have been different if he played in the 1980s or 90s?

2. Do you think baseball players took their careers more seriously in the 1940s than they do today? Why?

3. What do you think the author meant when he said that baseball is "a sport that's lost its memory, its soul, and many of its customers"?

4. Would you like to have been Jackie Robinson? Why?

| Selection 19: | | | 965 words |
|---|---|---|---|
| Finishing Time: | _____ | _____ | _____ |
| | HR. | MIN. | SEC. |
| Starting Time: | _____ | _____ | _____ |
| | HR. | MIN. | SEC. |
| Reading Time: | | _____ | _____ |
| | | MIN. | SEC. |
| WPM Score: | | | _____ |
| Comprehension Score: | | | _____% |

LITERATURE

# READING SELECTION 20
# THE USE OF FORCE
## William Carlos Williams
From *The Farmer's Daughter*

*"The Use of Force" was written by William Carlos Williams, an American physician and poet, essayist, and short story writer. Read this short story to discover its theme.*

1    They were new patients to me, all I had was the name, Olson. Please come down as soon as you can, my daughter is very sick.

2    When I arrived I was met by the mother, a big startled looking woman, very clean and apologetic who merely said, Is this the doctor? and let me in. In the back, she added, You must excuse us, doctor, we have her in the kitchen where it is warm. It is very damp here sometimes.

3    The child was fully dressed and sitting on her father's lap near the kitchen table. He tried to get up, but I motioned for him not to bother, took off my overcoat and started to look things over. I could see that they were all very nervous, eyeing me up and down distrustfully.

As often, in such cases, they weren't telling me more than they had to, it was up to me to tell them; that's why they were spending three dollars on me.

4    The child was fairly eating me up with her cold, steady eyes, and no expression to her face whatever. She did not move and seemed, inwardly, quiet; an unusually attractive little thing, and as strong as a heifer in appearance. But her face was flushed, she was breathing rapidly, and I realized that she had a high fever. She had magnificent blonde hair, in profusion. One of those picture children often reproduced in advertising leaflets and the photogravure sections of the Sunday papers.

5    She's had a fever for three days, began the father and we don't know what it comes from. My wife has given her things, you know, like people do, but it don't do no good. And there's been a lot of sickness around. So we tho't you'd better look her over and tell us what is the matter.

6 As doctors often do I took a trial shot at it as a point of departure. Has she had a sore throat?

7 Both parents answer me together. No . . . No, she says her throat don't hurt her.

8 Does your throat hurt you? added the mother to the child. But the little girl's expression didn't change nor did she move her eyes from my face.

9 Have you looked?

10 I tried to, said the mother, but I couldn't see.

11 As it happens we had been having a number of cases of diphtheria in the school to which this child went during that month and we were all, quite apparently, thinking of that, though no one had as yet spoken of the thing.

12 Well, I said, suppose we take a look at the throat first. I smiled in my best professional manner and asking for the child's first name I said, come on, Mathilda, open your mouth and let's take a look at your throat.

13 Nothing doing.

14 Aw, come on, I coaxed, just open your mouth wide and let me take a look. Look, I said opening both hands wide, I haven't anything in my hands. Just open up and let me see.

15 Such a nice man, put in the mother. Look how kind he is to you. Come on, do what he tells you to. He won't hurt you.

16 At that I ground my teeth in disgust. If only they wouldn't use the word "hurt" I might be able to get somewhere. But I did not allow myself to be hurried or disturbed but speaking quietly and slowly I approached the child again.

17 As I moved my chair a little nearer suddenly with one catlike movement both her hands clawed instinctively for my eyes and she almost reached them too. In fact she knocked my glasses flying and they fell, though unbroken, several feet away from me on the kitchen floor.

18 Both the mother and father almost turned themselves inside out in embarrassment and apology. You bad girl, said the mother, taking her and shaking her by one arm. Look what you've done. The nice man . . .

19 For heaven's sake, I broke in. Don't call me a nice man to her. I'm here to look at her throat on the chance that she might have diphtheria and possibly die of it. But that's nothing to her. Look here, I said to the child, we're going to look at your throat. You're old enough to understand what I'm saying. Will you open it now by yourself or shall we have to open it for you?

20 Not a move. Even her expression hadn't changed. Her breaths however were coming faster and faster. Then the battle began. I had to do it. I had to have a throat culture for her own protection. But first I told the parents that it was entirely up to them. I explained the danger but said that I would not insist on a throat examination so long as they would take the responsibility.

21 If you don't do what the doctor says you'll have to go to the hospital, the mother admonished her severely.

22 Oh yeah? I had to smile to myself. After all, I had already fallen in love with the savage brat, the parents were contemptible to me. In the ensuing struggle they grew more and more abject, crushed, exhausted while she surely rose to magnificent heights of insane fury of effort bred of her terror of me.

23 The father tried his best, and he was a big man but the fact that she was his daughter, his shame at her behavior and his dread of hurting her made him release her just at the critical times when I had almost achieved success, till I wanted to kill him. But his dread also that she might have diphtheria made him tell me to go on, go on though he himself was almost fainting, while the mother moved back and forth behind us raising and lowering her hands in an agony of apprehension.

24 Put her in front of you on your lap, I ordered, and hold both her wrists.

25 But as soon as he did the child let out a scream. Don't, you're hurting me. Let go of my hands. Let them go I tell you. Then she shrieked terrifyingly, hysterically. Stop it! Stop it! You're killing me!

26 Do you think she can stand it, doctor! said the mother.

27    You get out, said the husband to his wife. Do you want her to die of diphtheria?

28    Come on now, hold her, I said.

29    Then I grasped the child's head with my left hand and tried to get the wooden tongue depressor between her teeth. She fought, with clenched teeth, desperately! But now I also had grown furious—at a child. I tried to hold myself down but I couldn't. I know how to expose a throat for inspection. And I did my best. When finally I got the wooden spatula behind the last teeth and just the point of it into the mouth cavity, she opened up for an instant but before I could see anything she came down again and gripped the wooden blade between her molars she reduced it to splinters before I could get it out again.

30    Aren't you ashamed, the mother yelled at her. Aren't you ashamed to act like that in front of the doctor?

31    Get me a smooth-handled spoon of some sort, I told the mother. We're going through with this. The child's mouth was already bleeding. Her tongue was cut and she was screaming in wild hysterical shrieks. Perhaps I should have desisted and come back in an hour or more. No doubt it would have been better. But I have seen at least two children lying dead in bed of neglect in such cases, and feeling that I must get a diagnosis now or never I went at it again. But the worst of it was that I too had got beyond reason. I could have torn the child apart in my own fury and enjoyed it. It was a pleasure to attack her. My face was burning with it.

32    The damned little brat must be protected against her own idiocy, one says to one's self at such times. Others must be protected against her. It is a social necessity. And all these things are true. But a blind fury, a feeling of adult shame, bred of a longing for muscular release are the operatives. One goes on to the end.

33    In the final unreasoning assault I overpowered the child's neck and jaws. I forced the heavy silver spoon back of her teeth and down her throat till she gagged. And there it was—both tonsils covered with membrane. She had fought valiantly to keep me from knowing her secret. She had been hiding that sore throat for three days at least and lying to her parents in order to escape just such an outcome as this.

34    Now truly she was furious. She had been on the defensive before but now she attacked. Tried to get off her father's lap and fly at me while tears of defeat blinded her eyes.

## Comprehension Test 20*

### Checking Your Comprehension

1. Summarize the plot and setting.

2. Describe the child's personality. Compare it with the doctor's.

3. From whose point of view is the story told?

4. Describe the tone.

### Thinking Critically

1. What is the significance of the title?

2. What is the theme of the story? What does it say about the use of force?

3. Was the doctor's anger justifiable?

4. Can you think of this story as a struggle between good and evil?

5. Why do you think the author cast the child as physically beautiful?

---

* Multiple-choice questions are contained in Appendix B (page A19).

**Questions for Discussion**

1. Is the use of force sometimes necessary to pre-serve or maintain order?

2. In what situations is force justifiable?

| Selection 20: | | 1475 words |
|---|---|---|
| Finishing Time: | _____ _____ _____ | |
| | HR. MIN. SEC. | |
| Starting Time: | _____ _____ _____ | |
| | HR. MIN. SEC. | |
| Reading Time: | _____ _____ | |
| | MIN. SEC. | |
| WPM Score: | _____ | |
| Comprehension Score: | _____% | |

**Visit the Longman English Pages**

For additional readings and exercises, visit the Longman English Skills Web page at:

**http://longman.awl.com/englishpages**

For a username and password, please see your instructor.

# CHAPTER 11
# Critical Analysis

IN THIS CHAPTER YOU WILL LEARN:

1. To make inferences.
2. To distinguish fact from opinion.
3. To recognize generalizations.
4. To identify tone.
5. To identify an author's purpose.
6. To recognize bias.

Up to this point, we have primarily been concerned with the literal meanings of writing. Each chapter has discussed techniques that enable you to understand what the author says and to retain the literal, factual content. However, you often need to go beyond what authors *say* and be concerned with what they *mean*. Through choice of words, descriptions, facts, arrangement of ideas, and suggestions, an author often means more than he or she says. The purpose of this chapter is to present skills that will enable you to interpret and evaluate what you read. These processes require critical reading and thinking skills—the careful and deliberate evaluation of ideas for the purpose of making a judgment about their worth or value. This chapter presents numerous strategies to help you respond to academic reading assignments that demand critical reading.

Many skills are involved in interpreting what you read. Six of the most useful are discussed in this chapter: making inferences, distinguishing fact from opinion, recognizing generalizations, identifying tones, identifying the author's purpose, and recognizing bias.

## ■ MAKING INFERENCES

Suppose you are 10 minutes late for your psychology class, and you find the classroom empty. After a moment of puzzlement and confusion you might remember that your instructor has been ill and decide that your class has been canceled. Or you might recall that your instructor changed classrooms last week and, therefore, you decide that he or she has done so again. In this situation you used what you did know to make a reasonable guess about what you did not know. This reasoning process is called an *inference*. An inference is a logical connection that you draw between what you observe or know and what you do not know. All of us make numerous inferences in daily living without consciously thinking about them. When you wave at a friend and he or she does not wave back, you assume that he or she didn't see you. When you are driving down the highway and see a police car with its lights flashing behind you, you usually infer that the police officer wants you to pull over and stop.

Although inferences are reasonable guesses made on the basis of available information, they are not always correct. For instance, though you inferred that the friend who did not wave did not see you, it may be that he or she did see you but is angry with you and decided to ignore you. Similarly, the police car with the flashing lights may only want to pass you on the way to an accident ahead. Basically, an inference is the best guess you can make given the available information and circumstances.

If you are a pragmatic or applied learner, you may tend to concentrate on the facts at hand and may overlook their implications. Be sure to question, challenge, and analyze the facts; look for what further ideas the facts, when considered together, suggest.

## EXERCISE 11–1

*DIRECTIONS:* For each of the following items, make an inference about the situation that is described.

1. A woman seated alone at a bar offers to buy a drink for a man sitting several seats away.

2. A dog growls as a teenager walks toward the house.

3. Your seven-year-old brother will not eat his dinner. A package of cookies is missing from the kitchen cupboard.

4. A woman seated alone in a restaurant nervously glances at everyone who enters. Every few minutes she checks her watch.

5. A close friend invites you to go out for pizza and beer on Tuesday. When you meet her at her home on Tuesday, she tells you that you must have confused the days and that she will see you tomorrow evening.

## ■ Making Inferences as You Read

As in many other everyday situations, you make inferences frequently when you are reading. Applied to reading, an inference is a reasonable guess about what the author does *not* say based on what he or she *does* say. You are required to make inferences when an author suggests an idea but does not directly state it. For instance, suppose a writer describes a character as follows:

> In the mirror John Bell noticed that his hair was graying at the temples. As he picked up the morning paper, he realized that he could no longer see well without his glasses. Looking at the hands holding the paper he saw that they were wrinkled.

● ● ●

From the information the author provides, you may infer that the character is realizing that he is aging. However, notice that the author does not mention aging at all. By the facts he or she provides, however, the writer leads you to infer that the character is thinking about aging.

Now, read the following description of an event:

> Their actions, on this sunny afternoon, have been carefully organized and rehearsed. Their work began weeks ago with a leisurely drive through a quiet residential area. While driving, they noticed particular homes that seemed isolated and free of activity. Over the next week, similar drives were taken at different times of day. Finally, a house was chosen and their work began in earnest. Through careful observation and several phone calls, they learned where the occupants worked. They studied the house, noting entrances and windows and anticipating the floor plan. Finally, they were ready to act. Phone calls made that morning confirmed that the occupants were at work.

● ● ●

What is about to happen in this description? From the facts presented, you probably realized that a daytime home burglary was about to occur. Notice, however, that this burglary is not mentioned anywhere in the paragraph. Instead, using the information provided, you made the logical connection between the known and the unknown facts regarding what was about to occur.

## ■ How to Make Inferences

It is difficult to outline specific steps to follow in making inferences. Each inference entirely depends on the situation and the facts provided as well as on your knowledge and experience with the situation. However, here are a few general guidelines for making inferences about what you read.

### Be sure you understand the literal meaning first

Before you can begin any form of interpretation, including inference, you must be sure that you have a clear grasp of the stated facts and ideas. For each paragraph, you should identify the topic, main idea, supporting details, and organizational pattern. Only when you have an understanding of the literal, or factual, content can you go beyond literal meaning and formulate inferences.

### Ask yourself a question

To be sure that you are making necessary inferences to get the fullest meaning from a passage, ask yourself a question such as:

What is the author trying to suggest from the stated information?

or

What do all the facts and ideas point toward or seem to add up to?

or

For what purpose did the author include these facts and details?

In answering any of these questions, you must add together the individual pieces of information to arrive at an inference. Making an inference is somewhat like putting together a complicated picture puzzle, in which you try to make each piece fit with all the rest of the pieces to form something recognizable.

### Use clues provided by the writer

A writer often provides numerous hints that point you toward accurate inferences. For instance, a writer's choice of words often suggests his or her attitude toward a subject. Try to notice descriptive words, emotionally charged words, and words with strong positive or negative connotations. Here is an example of how the choice of words can lead you to an inference:

Grandmother had been an *unusually attractive* young woman, and she carried herself with the *graceful confidence* of a *natural charmer* to her last day.

The underlined phrases "unusually attractive," "graceful confidence," and "natural charmer" suggest that the writer feels positive about her grandmother. However, in the following example, notice how the underlined words and phrases create a negative image of the person.

The *withdrawn* child *eyed* her teacher with a hostile disdain. When directly spoken to, the child responded in a *cold,* but carefully respectful way.

In this sentence the underlined words suggest that the child is unfriendly and that he or she dislikes the teacher.

### Consider the author's purpose

An awareness of the author's purpose for writing is often helpful in making inferences. If an author's purpose is to convince you to purchase a particular product, such as in an advertisement, you already have a clear idea of the types of inferences the writer hopes you will make. For instance, a magazine ad for a stereo system reads:

> If you're in the market for true surround sound, a prematched system is a good way to get it. The components in our system are built for each other by our audio engineers. You can be assured of high performance and sound quality.

• • •

You can guess that the writer's purpose is to encourage you to buy his particular prematched stereo system.

### Verify your inference

Once you have made an inference, check to be sure that it is accurate. Look back at the stated facts to see that you have sufficient evidence to support the inference. Also, be sure that you have not overlooked other equally plausible or more plausible inferences that could be drawn from the same set of facts.

## EXERCISE 11–2

*DIRECTIONS:* Read the following passage and then answer the questions. The answers are not directly stated in the passage; you will have to make inferences in order to answer them.

> One morning I put two poached eggs in front of Charlie, who looked up briefly from his newspaper.
>
> "You've really shaped up, Cassie," he smiled. "A dreadful lady went to the hospital and a very nice Cassie came back. I think you've learned a lesson and, honey, I'm proud of you."
>
> He went to work and I started the dishes, trying to feel thrilled at having shaped up for Charlie. *He sounds as though the hospital performed some sort of exorcism,* I mused, scraping egg off the dish with my fingernail. *Evil is banished, goodness restored. Then why don't I feel transformed?*
>
> The dish slipped out of my hand and smashed into the sink, spraying chips over the counter. I looked down at the mess, then at the cluttered kitchen table, and beyond that to the dust on the television set in the den. I pictured the four unmade beds and the three clothes-strewn bedrooms and the toys in the living room and

last night's newspaper on the floor next to Charlie's reclining chair and I yelled at the cat who was licking milk out of a cereal bowl, "What lesson? What goddamn lesson was I supposed to learn?"

I grabbed my coat and the grocery money and was waiting at the liquor store when it opened.

"You find a place where they give it away for free?" the man behind the counter leered. "We haven't seen you for weeks. Where you been?"

"Nowhere," I answered. "I've been nowhere." He gave me my bottle and I walked out thinking that I'd have to start trading at another store where the creeps weren't so free with their remarks.

Rebeta-Burditt, *The Cracker Factory.*

• • •

1. What problem is Cassie experiencing?

   _____

2. For what purpose was Cassie hospitalized?

   _____

3. How does Cassie feel about household chores?

   _____

4. What is Cassie's husband's attitude toward her problem? Is he part of her problem? If so, how?

   _____

   _____

   _____

## ■ DISTINGUISHING BETWEEN FACT AND OPINION

An essential critical reading skill is the ability to distinguish fact from opinion. Facts are statements that can be verified—that is, proven to be true or false. Opinions are statements that express feelings, attitudes, or beliefs and are neither true nor false. Here are a few examples of each:

### Facts

1. The average American adult spends 25 hours per week on housework.
2. U.S. military spending has increased over the past 10 years.

### Opinions

1. By the year 2020 tobacco will be illegal, just as various other drugs are currently illegal.

2. If John F. Kennedy had lived, the United States would have made even greater advancements against the spread of communism.

Facts, once verified or taken from a reputable source, can be accepted and regarded as reliable information. Opinions, however, are not reliable sources of information and should be questioned and carefully evaluated. Look for evidence that supports the opinion and indicates that it is reasonable.

Some authors are careful to signal the reader when they are presenting an opinion. Watch for words and phrases such as:

| | |
|---|---|
| it is believed | apparently |
| in my view | presumably |
| it is likely that | in my opinion |
| seemingly | this suggests |
| one explanation is | possibly |

In the following excerpt from a social problems textbook, notice how the author carefully distinguishes factual statements from opinion by using qualifying words and phrases (underlined).

The health hazards for working women, moreover, aren't confined to blue-collar industrial or service work. Evidence is accumulating that health-threatening levels of stress are associated with many kinds of clerical work, the biggest source of jobs for American women (Linsenmayer, 1985). According to one study, three features common to much clerical work are particularly correlated with heart disease among women: lack of job mobility, suppressed hostility, and an unsupportive boss. Among women clerical workers with children, these negative job characteristics combine with the "double duty" of household work to produce a much higher susceptibility to stress-related disease (Moore, 1980). As this suggests, what counts in determining women's health (as it does, of course, for men as well) is not simply the fact of working itself, but the quality and quantity of the work and the way it fits with the rest of one's life. In a nutshell, though there is no evidence that achieving rewarding jobs will hurt women's health, there is every evidence that overwork in poor jobs coupled with an unequal division of housework will. All of this helps to explain the frequent finding that single mothers with children tend to have poorer health than men.

Currie and Skolnick, *America's Problems.*

● ● ●

Other authors, however, mix fact and opinion without making clear distinctions. This is particularly true in the case of *informed opinion,* which is the opinion of an expert or authority. Ralph Nader represents expert opinion on consumer rights, for example. Textbook authors, too, often offer informed opinion, as in the following statement from an American government text.

In the early days of voting research, the evidence was clear: voters rarely engaged in policy voting, preferring to rely on party identification or candidate evaluation to make up their minds.

Lineberry and Edwards, *Government in America.*

● ● ●

The author of this statement has reviewed the available evidence and is providing his expert opinion as to what the evidence indicates.

## EXERCISE 11–3

*DIRECTIONS:* Read each of the following statements and decide whether it is fact or opinion. Write "Fact" or "Opinion" in the space provided.

_____ 1. Some evidence indicates that the sexual division of labor in middle-class homes is beginning to change.

_____ 2. An infection is an illness produced by the action of microorganisms in the human body.

_____ 3. When measured by earning power, the American standard of living has increased steadily since the early 1970s.

_____ 4. Work, or the lack of it, is the primary influence in lifestyle.

_____ 5. Increased job opportunities for women and other minorities depends primarily on larger trends in the economy.

_____ 6. Parents now spend less time with their children than they did 30 years ago.

## EXERCISE 11–4

*DIRECTIONS:* Read each of the following passages and underline factual statements in each. Place brackets around clear statements of opinion. In class, discuss the statements about which you are unsure.

### Passage 1

Opponents of day care still call for women to return to home and hearth, but the battle is really over. Now the question is: Will day care continue to be inadequately funded and poorly regulated, or will public policy begin to put into place a system that rightly treats children as our most valuable national resource?

More than 50% of the mothers of young children are in the work force before their child's first birthday. An estimated 9.5 million preschoolers have mothers who work outside the home. Most women, like most men, are working to put food on the table. Many are the sole support of their families. They are economically unable to stay at home, although many would prefer to do so.

Phillips, "Needed: A Policy for Children When Parents Go to Work."

## *Passage 2*

Behold the King's castle—a mansion on a hill, the white-columned portico an image of classical grace, the wrought-iron gate with its undulating musical notes a symbol of his realm. There outside are the faithful: tourists and fans, mothers and fathers, toddlers and teenagers, all patiently waiting to visit the inner sanctum. Cash registers are ringing—$11.95 buys a complete package tour. A ghostly voice floats through the air. It is the King himself singing "Hound Dog" and "Can't Help Falling in Love" and "Crying in the Chapel." Welcome to Graceland—the home and final resting place of Elvis Aaron Presley, once and forever, the King of Rock and Roll.

Miller, "Forever Elvis."

• • •

## EXERCISE 11–5

*DIRECTIONS:* From a chapter in one of your textbooks, identify two statements that represent an author's informed opinion.

## EXERCISE 11–6

*DIRECTIONS:* Visit a Web site or newsgroup or choose a print magazine advertisement or newspaper editorial. Identify statements of opinion and/or informed opinion.

## ■ RECOGNIZING GENERALIZATIONS

A generalization is a statement that is made about a large group or a class of items based on observation of or experience with a part of that group or class. Suppose you interviewed a number of students on campus. You asked each why he or she was attending college, and each indicated that he or she was preparing for a career. From your interview you could make the generalization, "Students attend college to prepare for a career." Of course, you could not be absolutely certain that this statement is true until you asked *every* college student. Here are a few more generalizations. Some may seem very reasonable; you may disagree with others.

1. All college freshmen are confused and disoriented during their first week on campus.

2. Most parents are concerned for the happiness of their children.

3. Psychology instructors are interested in the psychology of learning.

4. College students are more interested in social life than scholarship.

As you evaluate the evidence a writer uses to support his or her ideas, be alert for generalizations that are used as facts. Remember that a generalization is not a fact and represents the writer's judgment only about a particular set of facts. In the following paragraph, generalizations, not facts, are used to support the main idea:

> The wedding is a tradition that most young adults still value. Most engaged couples carefully plan their wedding and regard it as an important occasion in their life. Couples also are very concerned that their ceremony follow rules of etiquette and that everything is done "just so." Most give a great deal of attention to personalizing their ceremony, including their own vows, songs, and symbols.

● ● ●

Notice that the writer does not use concrete, specific information to develop the paragraph. Instead, the author provides generalizations about how young adults feel about their weddings. If the writer is a sociologist who has studied the attitudes toward and customs of marriage, the generalizations may be accurate. However, if the paragraph was written by a parent and based on experience with his or her children and their friends, then you have little reason to accept the generalizations as facts because they are based on limited experience. Both the expertise of the writer and the method by which he or she arrived at the generalizations influence how readily you should accept them.

When reading material contains generalizations, approach the writer's conclusion with a critical, questioning attitude. When a generalization is unsubstantiated by facts, regard it as an opinion. Generalizations presented as facts are dangerous and misleading; they may be completely false.

## EXERCISE 11–7

*DIRECTIONS:* Indicate which of the following statements are generalizations. Then discuss what type(s) of information or documentation would be necessary for you to evaluate their worth or accuracy.

1. Worker productivity in the United States is rapidly declining.
2. Government spending on social programs is detrimental to national economic growth.
3. In 1964 the federal government officially declared a War on Poverty.
4. Male computer scientists earn more than female computer scientists with similar job responsibilities.
5. Illegal aliens residing within the United States are displacing American workers and increasing the unemployment rate.

## EXERCISE 11–8

*Electronic Application*

*DIRECTIONS:* Visit a Web site sponsored by a company that is advertising its product or choose an advertisement from a print magazine. Search and make note of any generalizations made about the product advertised.

## ■ IDENTIFYING TONE

A speaker's tone of voice often reveals his or her attitude and contributes to the overall message. Tone is also evident in writing and also contributes to its meaning. Recognizing an author's tone is often important in interpreting and evaluating a piece of writing because tone often reveals feelings, attitudes, or viewpoints not directly stated by the author. An author's tone is achieved primarily through word choice and stylistic features such as sentence pattern and length.

Tone, then, reveals feelings. Many human emotions can be communicated through tone—disapproval, hate, admiration, disgust, gratitude, forcefulness. Read the following passage, paying particular attention to the feeling it creates.

> Among the worst bores in the Western world are religious converts and reformed drunks. . . . I did give up drinking more than a dozen years ago. This didn't make me feel morally superior to anyone. If asked, I would talk about going dry but, from the first, I was determined to preach no sermons and stand in judgment of no human being who took pleasure in the sauce.
>
> But I must confess that lately my feelings have begun to change. Drinking and drunks now fill me with loathing. Increasingly, I see close friends—human beings of intelligence, wit and style—reduced to slobbering fools by liquor. I've seen other friends ruin their marriages, brutalize their children, destroy their careers. I've also reached the age when I've had to help bury a few people who allowed booze to take them into eternity.
>
> Hamill, "The Wet Drug."

● ● ●

Here the author's disapproval of the use of alcohol is apparent. Through choice of words—slobbering, loathing—as well as choice of detail, he makes the tone obvious.

Tone can also establish a distance or formality between the writer and reader, or can establish a sense of shared communication and draw them together. In the excerpts that follow, notice how in the first passage, a formality or distance is established, and in the second, how a familiarity and friendliness is created.

*Passage 1:*

It's not entirely clear whether party voting differences are caused directly by party affiliation or indirectly by the character of constituencies. Some scholars have found strong independent party effects. Others argue that the tendency of people in the same party to vote together is a reflection of the fact that Democratic lawmakers come from districts and states that are similar to each other and that Republican lawmakers come from ones that are different from those of Democrats. Republicans generally come from higher-income districts than Democrats. Democratic districts, in turn, tend to have more union members and racial minorities in them. The strongest tie, in this line of argument, is between the member of Congress and the constituency and not between the member and the party.

Greenberg and Page, *The Struggle for Democracy.*

*Passage 2:*

Each time I visit my man in prison, I relive the joy of reunion—and the anguish of separation.

We meet at the big glass door at the entrance to the small visitors' hall at Lompoc Federal Correctional Institution. We look at each other silently, then turn and walk into a room jammed with hundreds of molded fiberglass chairs lined up side by side. Finding a place in the crowded hall, we sit down, appalled that we're actually in a prison. Even now, after four months of such clocked, supervised, regulated visits, we still can't get used to the frustrations.

Yet, as John presses me gently to his heart, I feel warm and tender, and tears well up inside me, as they do each weekend. I have seven hours to spend with the man I love—all too brief a time for sharing a lifetime of emotion: love and longing, sympathy and tenderness, resentment and anger.

King, "Love in the Afternoon—In a Crowded Prison Hall."

● ● ●

To identify an author's tone, pay particular attention to descriptive language and connotative meanings (see Chapter 10). Ask yourself: "How does the author feel about his or her subject and how are these feelings revealed?"

# EXERCISE 11–9

*DIRECTIONS:* Describe the tone of each of the following passages.

*Passage 1*

Rude or indifferent waiters and waitresses should be fired. Nothing can ruin a pleasant meal in a restaurant like a snippy waitress or a superior-acting waiter. Part of the cost of any restaurant meal is the service, and it should be at least as good as the food.

*Passage 2*

Welfare makes you feel like you're nothing. Like you're laying back and not doing anything and it's falling in your lap. But you must understand, mothers, too, work. My house is clean. I've been scrubbing since this morning. You could check my clothes, all washed and ironed. I'm home and I'm working. I am a working mother.

A job that a woman in a house is doing is a tedious job—especially if you want to do it right. If you do it slipshod, then it's not so bad. I'm pretty much of a perfectionist. I tell my kids, hang a towel. I don't want it thrown away. That is very hard. It's a constant game of picking up this, picking up that. And putting this away, so the house'll be clean.

Terkel, *Working*.

*Passage 3*

Incidence and Types of Schizophrenia

Schizophrenia was originally thought to be confined to North America and Western Europe. We now understand that the disorder (or varieties of the disorder) can be found around the world at the same rate: about 1 percent of the population (Alder & Gielen, 1994; Bloom et al., 1985). People in developing countries tend to have a more acute (intense, but short-lived) course—and a better outcome—of the disorder than do people in industrialized nations. In the United States, schizophrenia accounts for 75 percent of all mental health expenditures. (Carpenter & Buchanan, 1994). Schizophrenia occurs at the same rate for both sexes, but symptoms are likely to show up earlier in males, and males are more likely to be disabled by the disorder (Grinspoon, 1995).

Currie and Skolnick, *America's Problems*.

● ● ●

# EXERCISE 11–10

*DIRECTIONS:* Choose two of the following end-of-chapter reading selections that appear earlier in the book. Identify the tone of the two that you choose.

1. "We're All Robinson's Children" (Sel. 19, p. 379)
2. "So Few Farmers, So Many Bureaucrats" (Sel. 14, p. 275)
3. "Medical Privacy" (Sel. 11, p. 218)
4. "Why the Sky Is Blue, Sunsets Are Red, and Clouds Are White" (Sel. 6, p. 96)
5. "Hispanic, USA: The Conveyor-Belt Ladies" (Sel. 2, p. 20)

# ■ IDENTIFYING THE AUTHOR'S PURPOSE

Authors write for a variety of purposes: to inform or instruct the reader, to amuse or entertain, to arouse sympathy, to persuade the reader to take a particular action, or to accept a certain point of view. To be an effective reader you must be aware of the author's purpose. Sometimes the writer's purpose will be obvious, as in the following advertisements:

At Hair Design Salons we'll make you look better than you can imagine. Six professional stylists to meet your every need. Stop in for a free consultation today.

Puerto Rican white rum can do anything better than gin or vodka.

The first ad is written to encourage the readers to have their hair styled at Hair Design Salons. The second is intended to encourage readers to use rum instead of gin or vodka in their mixed drinks. In both ads the writer is clearly trying to convince you to buy a certain product. However, in many other types of reading material, even other advertisements, the writer's purpose is not so obvious.

For instance, in an ad for a particular brand of cigarettes, a stylishly dressed woman is pictured holding a cigarette. The caption reads, "You've come a long way, baby." In this case, although you know that all ads are intended to sell a product or service, the ad does not even mention cigarettes. It is left up to you, the reader, to infer that stylish women smoke Virginia Slims.

You will often be able to predict the author's purpose from the title of the article or by your familiarity with the writer. For instance, if you noticed an article titled "My Role in Health Care Systems," written by Hillary Rodham Clinton, you could predict that the author's purpose is to defend her role in proposing a health care system during the Clinton presidency. An article titled "The President Flexes His Muscles but Nobody Is Watching" suggests that the author's purpose is to describe how the president is attempting to exert power but having little success.

## ■ How to Identify the Author's Purpose

To identify the author's purpose when it is not apparent, first determine the subject and thesis of the material and notice how the writer supports the thesis. Then ask the following questions to start thinking critically about the material:

1. **Who is the intended audience?** Try to decide for whom or for what type or group of people the material seems to be written. Often, the

level of language, the choice of words, and the complexity of the ideas, examples, or arguments included suggest the audience the writer has in mind. Once you have identified a potential audience, you can begin to consider what the writer wants to communicate to that audience.

A writer may write for a general interest audience (anyone who is interested in the subject). Most newspapers and periodicals such as *Time* and *Newsweek* appeal to a general interest audience. On the other hand, a writer may have a particular interest group in mind. A writer may write for medical doctors in the *Journal of American Medicine,* or for skiing enthusiasts in *Skiing Today*, or for antique collectors in *The World of Antiques*. Also, a writer may intend his or her writing for an audience with particular political, moral, or religious attitudes. Articles in the *Atlantic Monthly* often appeal to the conservative political viewpoint, whereas *The Catholic Digest* appeals to a particular religious group.

2. **What is the tone?** Determine whether the author is serious or whether he or she is trying to poke fun at the subject. If a writer is ridiculing or making light of a subject, he or she will usually offer clues that alert the reader. The writer may use exaggerations, describe unbelievable situations, or choose language and details that indicate that he or she is not completely serious.

3. **What is the point of view?** Point of view is the perspective from which an article or essay is written. An event, for example, may be described from the point of view of someone in attendance or from that of someone who only has heard or read about it. A controversial issue may be discussed from an objective point of view, examining both sides of the issue, or a subjective one in which one side of the issue is favored. Point of view might be described as the way an author "looks at" or approaches his or her subject. As such, point of view can often suggest the author's purpose in writing.

4. **Does the writer try to prove anything about the subject? If so, what?** Try to determine if the article is written to persuade the reader to accept a certain point of view or to perform a certain action. For instance, a writer may write to convince you that inflation will cause a national disaster, or that abortion is morally wrong, or that the best jobs are available in health-related fields.

To test the use of these questions, read the following passage and apply the critical thinking questions to it.

I moved to Madison, Wisconsin, from Anchorage, Alaska, in 1987 with my husband and our 18-month-old daughter. Education brought us: My husband had been accepted into a Ph.D. program, and I hoped to finish my undergraduate degree once he began working. In May 1992 I did complete my B.A. in English, but not at all in the way I had planned. From September 1988 until December 1990 my daughter and I received Aid to Families with Dependent Children (AFDC).

Like many women, I was thrown into relative poverty as a result of divorce—my marriage broke up during our first year in Wisconsin. I say *relative* because my daughter and I were never in danger of going without food or shelter. But my financial situation as a single parent was alarmingly precarious. Did I have to go on welfare? No—I chose to. Reaching this decision took time and, having worked since I was 15, I was bothered by it a great deal.

Though I knew I needed help to improve my situation, I had internalized many attitudes our society holds concerning work and public assistance. I was keenly aware that many people would deny that I had any right to hold my hand out, ablebodied citizen that I was. Able-bodied, yes; simpleminded, no. When I reached the point of paying 18 percent interest on credit card cash advances to buy food, I knew I was digging myself into a hole I might never get out of. In the beginning, though, I never considered welfare.

Lovern, "Confessions of a Welfare Mom."

● ● ●

The subject of this excerpt is welfare assistance. The essay seems to be written for an audience familiar with the subject. The tone is serious; the author maintains a reasoned, factual, unemotional tone. The point of view is personal; the author is relating events from her life experience. She seems to be suggesting that receiving welfare assistance can be a reasoned decision and one she does not regret.

## EXERCISE 11–11

*DIRECTIONS:* Identify the author's purpose for two of the reading selections listed in Exercise 11–10.

## EXERCISE 11–12

*DIRECTIONS:* Visit a Web site in an area of interest. Browse through the site, evaluate its purpose, and write a brief statement that summarizes its purpose.

## EXERCISE 11–13

*DIRECTIONS:* Read each of the excerpts contained in Exercise 11–9. For each, write a statement describing the author's purpose.

## ■ IDENTIFYING BIAS

Bias refers to an author's partiality, inclination toward a particular viewpoint, or prejudice. A writer is biased if he or she takes one side of a controversial issue and does not recognize opposing viewpoints. Perhaps the best example of bias is in advertising. A magazine advertisement for a new car model, for instance, describes only positive, marketable features—the ad does not recognize the car's limitations or faults. In some material the writer is direct and outright in expressing his or her bias; other times the bias is hidden and left for the reader to discover through careful analysis.

Read the following description of the environmental protection group Greenpeace. The author expresses a favorable attitude toward the organization and a negative one toward whale hunters. Notice, in particular, the *underlined* words and phrases.

Greenpeace is an organization <u>dedicated</u> to the preservation of the sea and its great mammals, notably whales, dolphins, and seals. Its ethic is <u>nonviolent</u> but its aggressiveness in <u>protecting</u> our oceans and the life in them is becoming <u>legendary</u>. In their roving ship, the <u>*Rainbow Warrior,*</u> Greenpeace volunteers have <u>relentlessly hounded</u> the <u>profiteering</u> ships of any nation harming the resources Greenpeace deems to be the property of the world community. Whales, they believe, belong to us all and have a right to exist no matter what the demand for shoe-horns, cosmetics, and machine oil.

Wallace, *Biology: The World of Life.*

● ● ●

To identify bias, apply the following questions:

1. **Analyze connotative meanings.** Do you encounter a large number of positive or negative terms used to describe the subject?

2. **Notice descriptive language.** What impression is created?

3. **Analyze the tone.** The author's tone often provides important clues.

4. **Look for opposing viewpoints.**

## EXERCISE 11–14

*DIRECTIONS:* Read the following passage and underline words and phrases that reveal the author's bias.

Not unlike drugs or alcohol, the television experience allows the participant to blot out the real world and enter into a pleasurable and passive mental state. The worries and anxieties of reality are as effectively deferred by becoming absorbed in a television program as by going on a "trip" induced by drugs or alcohol. And just as alcoholics are only inchoately aware of their addiction, feeling that they control their drinking more than they really do ("I can cut it out any time I want—I just like to have three or four drinks before dinner"), people similarly overestimate their control over television watching. Even as they put off other activities to spend hour after hour watching television, they feel they could easily resume living in a different, less passive style. But somehow or other while the television set is present in their homes, the click doesn't sound. With television pleasures available, those other experiences seem less attractive, more difficult somehow.

Winn, *The Plug-in Drug.*

● ● ●

### Critical Thinking Tip #11

### Slanted Writing

Slanted writing is a technique used to persuade. Slanted writing attempts to push or tip the reader in a particular direction—usually toward a particular belief, attitude, or action. Here are two brief news reports. Notice the slant in each.

**VERSION 1**

The Congressman flapped open his notebook and began his speech in his usual flat tone. He moved mechanically from point to point, dwelling on each longer than necessary.

**VERSION 2**

The Congressman climbed energetically to the podium and began his speech. He moved methodically from point to point, taking care that each point was well understood before moving to the next.

SLANTED WRITING EMPLOYS TWO TECHNIQUES:

1. The use of words that create a favorable or unfavorable impression. In version 1, words such as *flat, flapped,* and *mechanically* create a negative impression. In the second version, words such as *energetically, methodically,* and *well understood* create a favorable impression.
2. Selection of detail. Writers select details that create the desired impression and omit details that do not. In version 1, the writer omitted the detail about how the Congressman climbed to the podium, choosing instead to describe how he opened his notebook. In version 2, the writer omitted the notebook opening but did include the climbing stairs detail.

Slanted writing is dangerous and can be misleading, and it is easy to miss, especially when reading rapidly or when skimming. Keep this question in mind: What has the writer chosen *not* to tell me? When possible try to read more than one source of information, choosing sources or writers likely to have differing viewpoints. Once you suspect writing is slanted, circle favorable or unfavorable words; write questions about omitted information.

## EXERCISE 11–15

*DIRECTIONS:* Choose one of the selections at the end of the chapter and write a one-page paper evaluating the reading. You might:

1. Identify what inferences can be made about the subject
2. Evaluate statements of opinion
3. Identify several generalizations
4. Describe the tone of the article
5. Summarize the author's purpose
6. Discuss the author's bias and describe how it is revealed

## EXERCISE 11–16

*DIRECTIONS:* Visit a Web site or join a newsgroup that concerns a controversial issue. As you browse through the site look for and make brief notes about any bias you detect.

## SUMMARY

**1. What is critical analysis?**

Critical analysis is the interpretation and evaluation of an author's meaning. By applying the tools of critical reading and thinking you can analyze a written work deliberately and carefully and make decisions about its worth and value.

**2. What is involved in making an inference?**

An inference is a reasonable guess made on the basis of available information. To make an inference as you read
- Be sure you understand the literal meaning first.
- Ask questions about the stated information.
- Use clues provided by the writer.
- Consider the writer's purpose.
- Verify your information.

**3. How can facts be distinguished from opinions?**

Facts can be shown to be true or false; they can be verified and regarded as reliable information. Because opinions express attitudes, beliefs, or feelings, they are not reliable and should be carefully questioned and evaluated.

**4. What are generalizations?**

Generalizations are statements made about a large group or class of items based on experience with only a part of the group or class. When generalizations are stated as facts, carefully evaluate them before you accept them as true.

**5. How can you detect a writer's tone?**

The tone of a piece of writing often reveals an author's attitude, feelings, and viewpoints about a subject. Paying attention to the choice of words and the style of writing can reveal a writer's tone.

**6. How can you identify an author's purpose?**

An awareness of the author's purpose—or reason for writing—is important in evaluating a work. To identify an author's purpose you should ask four questions.
- Who is the intended audience?
- What is the tone?
- What is the point of view?
- What is the writer trying to prove about the subject?

**7. How can you detect bias in a piece of writing?**

Bias refers to an author's favoring a particular viewpoint on an issue. To detect bias,
- Analyze connotative meanings.
- Notice descriptive language.
- Analyze the tone.
- Look for opposing viewpoints.

# READING SELECTION 21
## I AM A JAPANESE AMERICAN

Kesaya Noda
*From Making Waves*

*The piece that follows is an excerpt from a longer essay that focuses on the author's experiences as a person of color growing up in the United States. In the full essay, the author confronts stereotypes by reflecting on the many aspects of her identity—racial (Japanese), historical/cultural (Japanese American), gender based (Japanese American woman), and finally, human (for her, a spiritual perspective). The essay describes two experiences of identity : the painful experience of having identity imposed from the outside through stereotypes, and the freeing, empowering experience of defining identity oneself, from within a rich context of culture, family, and community.*

1    Sometimes when I was growing up, my identity seemed to hurtle toward me and paste itself right to my face. I felt that way, encountering the stereotypes of my race perpetuated by non-Japanese people (primarily white) who may or may not have had contact with other Japanese in America. "You don't like cheese, do you?" someone would ask. "I know your people don't like cheese." Sometimes questions came making allusions to history. That was another aspect of the identity. Events that had happened quite apart from the me who stood silent in that moment connected my face with an incomprehensible past. "Your parents were in California? Were they in those camps during the war?" And sometimes there were phrases or nicknames: "Lotus Blossom." I was sometimes addressed or referred to as racially Japanese, sometimes as Japanese American, and sometimes as an Asian woman. Confusions and distortions abounded.

2    How is one to know and define oneself? From the inside—within a context that is self defined, from a grounding in community and a connection with culture and history that are comfortably accepted? Or from the outside—in terms of messages received from the media and people who are often ignorant? Even as an adult I can still see two sides of my face and past. I can see from the inside out, in freedom. And I can see from the outside in, driven by the old voices of childhood and lost in anger and fear.

3    "Weak." I hear the voice from my childhood years. "Passive," I hear. Our parents and grandparents were the ones who were put into those camps.[1] They went without resistance; they offered cooperation as proof of loyalty to America. "Victim," I hear. And, "Silent."

4    Our parents are painted as hard workers who were socially uncomfortable and had difficulty expressing even the smallest opinion. Clean, quiet, motivated, and determined to match the American way; that is us, and that is the story of our time here.

5    "Why did you go into those camps," I raged at my parents, frightened by my own inner silence and timidity. "Why didn't you do anything to resist? Why didn't you name it the injustice it was?" Couldn't our parents even think? Couldn't they? Why were we so passive?

6    I shift my vision and my stance. I am in California. My uncle is in the midst of the sweet potato harvest. He is pressed, trying to get the harvesting crews onto the field as quickly as possible, worried about the flow of equipment and people. His big pickup is pulled off to the side, motor running, door ajar. I see two tractors in the

---

[1] During World War II, many Japanese in the United States were placed in camps.

yard in front of an old shed; the flat bed harvesting platform on which the workers will stand has already been brought over from the other field. It's early morning. The workers stand loosely grouped and at ease, but my uncle looks as harried and tense as a police officer trying to unsnarl a New York City traffic jam. Driving toward the shed, I pull my car off the road to make way for an approaching tractor. The front wheels of the car sink luxuriously into the soft, white sand by the roadside and the car slides to a dreamy halt, tail still on the road. I try to move forward. I try to move back. The front bites contentedly into the sand, the back lifts at a jaunty angle. My uncle sees me and storms down the road, running. He is shouting before he is even near me.

7 "What's the matter with you," he screams. "What the hell are you doing?" In his frenzy, he grabs his hat off his head and slashes it through the air across his knee. He is beside himself. "Don't you know how to drive in sand? What's the matter with you? You've blocked the whole roadway. How am I supposed to get my tractors out of here? Can't you use your head? You've cut off the whole roadway, and we've got to get out of here."

8 I stand on the road before him helplessly thinking, "No, I don't know how to drive in sand. I've never driven in sand."

9 "I'm sorry, uncle," I say, burying a smile beneath a look of sincere apology. I notice my deep amusement and my affection for him with great curiosity. I am usually devastated by anger. Not this time.

10 During the several years that follow I learn about the people and the place, and much more about what has happened in this California village where my parents grew up. The issei, our grandparents, made this settlement in the desert. Their first crops were eaten by rabbits and ravaged by insects. The land was so barren that men walking from house to house sometimes got lost. Women came here too. They bore children in 114 degree heat, then carried the babies with them into the fields to nurse when they reached

the end of each row of grapes or other truck farm crops.

11 I had had no idea what it meant to buy this kind of land and make it grow green. Or how, when the war came, there was no space at all for the subtlety of being who we were—Japanese Americans. Either/or was the way. I hadn't understood that people were literally afraid for their lives then, that their money had been frozen in banks; that there was a five-mile travel limit; that when the early evening curfew came and they were inside their houses, some of them watched helplessly as people they knew went into their barns to steal their belongings. The police were patrolling the road, interested only in violators of curfew. There was no help for them in the face of thievery. I had not been able to imagine before what it must have felt like to be an American—to know absolutely that one is an American—and yet to have almost everyone else deny it. Not only deny it, but challenge that identity with machine guns and troops of white American soldiers. In those circumstances it was difficult to say, "I'm a Japanese American." "American" had to do.

12 But now I can say that I am a Japanese American. It means I have a place here in this country, too. I have a place on the East Coast, where our neighbor is so much a part of our family that my mother never passes her house at night without glancing at the lights to see if she is home and safe; where my parents have hauled hundreds of pounds of rocks from fields and arduously planted Christmas trees and blueberries, lilacs, asparagus, and crab apples; where my father still dreams of angling a stream to a new bed so that he can dig a pond in the field and fill it with water and fish. "The neighbors already came for their Christmas tree?" he asks in December. "Did they like it? Did they like it?"

13 I have a place on the West Coast where my relatives still farm, where I heard the stories of feuds and backbiting, and where I saw that people survived and flourished because fundamentally they trusted and relied upon one another.

A death in the family is not just a death in a family; it is a death in the community. I saw people help each other with money, materials, labor, attention, and time. I saw men gather once a year, without fail, to clean the grounds of a ninety-year-old woman who had helped the

14 community before, during, and after the war. I saw her remembering them with birthday cards sent to each of their children.

I come from a people with a long memory and a distinctive grace. We live our thanks. And we are Americans. Japanese Americans.

---

## Comprehension Test 21

*Directions:   Circle the letter of the best answer.*

### Checking Your Comprehension

1. This reading is primarily about Noda's
   a. racial background
   b. ancestors
   c. racial identity
   d. experiences in America

2. The author's main point is that she
   a. is unsure if she belongs in America
   b. views herself in two ways
   c. feels she has rejected her Japanese heritage
   d. has disappointed her family

3. During her childhood, Noda thought of her grandparents as
   a. weak
   b. important
   c. influential
   d. stupid

4. As described in the reading, death in the Japanese community is regarded as
   a. a private family matter
   b. a religious experience
   c. a completion of the life cycle
   d. a community concern

5. Noda's grandparents willingly went to the camps because they
   a. hated the Germans
   b. knew they would be treated well
   c. did not understand where they were going
   d. wanted to demonstrate their loyalty to America

6. As used in the reading, the word stereotypes (paragraph 1) means
   a. set images
   b. discriminatory acts
   c. insulting comments
   d. racial slurs

### Thinking Critically

7. Which of the following best describes Noda's attitude toward being a Japanese American?
   a. embarrassed
   b. dismayed
   c. angry
   d. proud

8. The author would probably agree with which one of the following statements?
   a. Attitudes are fixed and unchanging.
   b. Ancestors make unfortunate errors in judgment.
   c. Many Americans express stereotyped perceptions of Japanese Americans.
   d. A person's identity is related to his or her ethnic heritage.

9. The author explains her ideas by
   a. analyzing them
   b. recounting events that illustrate them
   c. comparing them with those of her parents
   d. giving reasons

10. The form of this reading suggests it may have been part of
    a. an argumentative essay
    b. a newspaper article
    c. an autobiography
    d. a novel

**Questions for Discussion**

1. Have you ever been stereotyped because of your ethnic background?

2. How is death regarded in your ethnic community? How is this different from the way it is regarded in the Japanese community?

3. What factors other than ethnic origin do you think constitute or define identity?

| Selection 21: | | 1316 words | |
|---|---|---|---|
| Finishing Time: | ____ | ____ | ____ |
| | HR. | MIN. | SEC. |
| Starting Time: | ____ | ____ | ____ |
| | HR. | MIN. | SEC. |
| Reading Time: | | ____ | ____ |
| | | MIN. | SEC. |
| WPM Score: | | _____ | |
| Comprehension Score: | | _____% | |

# READING SELECTION 22
## TIME OUT

Jack L. Mayer
From *The New York Times Magazine*

*Jobs and careers become stressful and frustrating. Read this essay, originally published in* The New York Times Magazine, *to learn why a medical doctor decided to leave his practice in a small town near the Canadian border.*

1 Phillip's mother has had her fourth baby by a third man. The child, my patient, is a boy. I wonder if she'll try again for the girl I know she wants. Twinkies, potato chips and Kool-Aid are still her kids' standard fare. Questions of child abuse haven't been raised in over two years, and the scars on Phillip's neck from the boiling water his mother spilled are not too deforming. All through this pregnancy she smoked a pack a day. She makes me mad.

2 Like so many men, I always thought my work defined me. When I thought about my work, I felt comforted and in touch with exactly who I am. But now, after 10 years as the first pediatrician in this town on the Canadian border, I'm leaving. Despair and human stubbornness have undermined the compassion and dedication of which I was once so proud. Another pediatrician will replace me here after another hard winter.

3 In seventh grade, I decided to become a doctor. Over years of schooling, I constructed an idealized vision of myself bringing quality care to the rural poor, crusading against injustice and inequality. After I entered medical school in 1967, I learned about Vietnam, Woodstock, Chicago and Watts along with biochemistry and pathology. "Medicine is a social science, and politics is nothing more than medicine on a grand scale," wrote Rudolf Virchow, the father of modern pathology. That's why I decided to practice pediatrics in one of the poorest towns in Vermont, a place where you can buy a stately old house on a quiet street for $27,000—hand-turned banisters, elaborate scrollwork on the peaks.

4 When I first came here in 1976 from the Stanford University Medical Center, I had the sum total of pediatric knowledge in my back pocket.

All I had to do, I thought, was lay it out for my eager families and—presto—welcome to the golden age of preventive care, social responsibility, anticipatory guidance and heroic life-saving.

5 Delayed introduction of solid foods to infants' diets was my first crusade. The best pediatric minds in the world had concluded that babies were healthier when solid foods were introduced after 4 months of age, but most of my newborns were eating cereal by two weeks. It was an uphill battle. "My mother told me. . . ." "I've raised three kids and they all started cereal at two weeks. . . ." "How many kids you got, Doc? None?" I have a young son now, but I was childless when the mothers said those things to me.

6 They wouldn't take the contents of my Holy Grail—not about feeding babies, wearing seat belts or treating illness. It was a personal affront. "I'm a pediatrician," I would say, "and I know the right way to feed a baby." "You rubbed Save the Baby on his chest? That won't cure pneumonia." "It's just a cold. He doesn't need penicillin."

7 Poor people's kids are sick a lot, and I was swamped with patients. Malnutrition, child abuse, chronic illness—my patients' lives were so chaotic and desperate that they had precious little interest in anything except a quick cure.

8 Things got worse—budget cuts, Medicaid cuts, worker cuts at the hockey-stick factory. After 38 straight months of "economic recovery," the stock market broke 1,500 and rents to the south, in Burlington, Vermont's largest city, reached $500. Those who couldn't afford it moved north and finally ended up here, with their backs against the border, no place else to go. My waiting room filled with economic refugees. I lost my patient with the new green Saab. She drove 26 miles across the county to see another pediatrician, where her kids could play on slides and tunnels by Creative Playthings without contracting head lice.

9 Weeks grew long and frustrating. The child-abuse team visited my office twice a week instead of twice a month. Children were hungry by the end of each month—their mothers' food stamps

had been cut. One cold day in February, I had two pregnant teenagers within an hour. People who had no phones and no cars walked through the snow to see me.

10 "He won't mind me," Phillip's mother slapped a pack of Winstons onto my desk as if it were my fault and settled her fifth pregnancy into my rocker. "What the hell," she said, "I tried putting him in his room like you said, Dr. Jack, and he just tore the place apart and came out screaming, so I spanked him again."

11 Was nobody listening? Didn't it make any difference that I was here? I hated their wet sneakers in the snow. I hated the constant illness that stalked their children. I hated their abusive discipline, their junk-food diets, empty stares, crumpled Medicaid cards. Stanford University Medical Center seemed so far away.

12 On the ninth anniversary of my practice, I met an old friend at the Botanical Garden in New York, and I told her my secret: "I'm leaving my practice. I hate my patients."

13 My friend, a pediatrician in a South Bronx slum, also a proud veteran of the 1960's, knew my pain. Her diagnosis was precise. "There are so many things wrong," she said, "but it's not their fault."

14 "I know," I said, shaking my head, "I know. But I'm tired of being on the front lines, tired of treating what should be prevented. My patients are worse off now than they were 10 years ago. I guess it's easier to leave hating them."

15 "It's O.K. to leave. You don't need a rationalization." She touched my arm. "Don't give up the dream unless you really want to."

16 I don't want to. But I need time to reflect, to revitalize. I think Phillip's mother and I share an important anger. We have been doing the best we can against terrible odds. Her kids have been denied health and equal opportunity from conception, and I feel like a man defeated.

17 I'm leaving this town to work part-time in Middlebury, Vt., a middle-class college town where I can hear jazz and string quartets and see foreign films. Leaving the Canadian border is a

tactical retreat, R and R. I don't have the answers anymore. My carefully nurtured image of myself as Dr. Schweitzer is inadequate, and I humbly confront the real man who is tired and frustrat-

ed. Although my ideals are very much alive, my feelings cannot be suppressed. I hope the anger that has built up for 10 years can be channeled as a force to redefine myself as a healer.

## Comprehension Test 22*

### Checking Your Comprehension

1. What did Mayer find most discouraging about his medical practice?

2. Describe Phillip's mother.

3. Describe the economic situation of the town in which Mayer practiced.

4. What is Mayer's attitude toward Phillip's mother?

### Thinking Critically

1. What is the author's purpose for writing? Does he attempt to educate? To change behavior? To gain sympathy?

2. What is the significance of the patient in the green Saab? What does she symbolize?

3. Why is Phillip's mother not referred to by her own name?

4. Why did Phillip's mother refuse to accept Mayer's advice?

### Questions For Discussion

1. Did Mayer hold an idealized view of the medical profession before he began his practice? If so, what were its effects?

2. Will Mayer ever return to a full-time practice in the same or a similar town?

3. Was Mayer a victim of burnout? Will he recover? What other professions or occupations face similar discouragement?

| Selection 22: | | 1063 words | |
| --- | --- | --- | --- |
| Finishing Time: | HR. | MIN. | SEC. |
| Starting Time: | HR. | MIN. | SEC. |
| Reading Time: | | MIN. | SEC. |
| WPM Score: | | | |
| Comprehension Score: | | | % |

## Visit the Longman English Pages

For additional readings and exercises, visit the Longman English Skills Web page at:

**http://longman.awl.com/englishpages**

For a username and password, please see your instructor.

---

* Multiple-choice questions are contained in Appendix B (page A21).

# CHAPTER 12
# Evaluating Arguments and Persuasive Writing

IN THIS CHAPTER YOU WILL LEARN:

1. To evaluate source and authority.
2. To understand and evaluate arguments.
3. To identify reasoning errors.

A criminal justice professor opens a class discussion on the issue of gun control by distributing the following statement:

> People kill people, but handguns make it easier. When other weapons (knives, for instance) are used, the consequences are not so often deadly. Strangling or stabbing someone takes a different degree of energy and intent than pulling a trigger. Registration will not interfere with hunting and other rifle sports but will simply exercise control over who can carry handguns. Ordinary people do not carry handguns. If a burglar has a gun in his hand, it is quite insane for you to shoot it out with him, as if you were in a quick draw contest in the Wild West. Half of all the guns used in crimes are stolen; 70% of the stolen guns are handguns. In other words, the supply of handguns used by criminals already comes to a great extent from the households these guns were supposed to protect.
>
> Smith, "Fifty Million Handguns."

● ● ●

She then asks the class to analyze and respond to the statement. An impulsive student responded immediately, saying "The writer favors gun control, but I disagree with him." The instructor seemed dissatisfied with this response, suggesting she wanted more detailed and carefully reasoned responses.

How would you analyze the statement? If you agreed with the writer's position, how would you defend it? If you disagreed, how would you dispute it?

To analyze the statement, you must study the writer's line of reasoning and thought process. You must also evaluate how he presents his ideas, and evaluate their worth. This chapter focuses on techniques to evaluate persuasive writing. Specifically, you will learn to evaluate source and authority, recognize the structure of and evaluate arguments, identify reasoning errors, and evaluate nonlogical appeals.

# ■ EVALUATING SOURCE AND AUTHORITY

Two very important considerations in evaluating any written material are the source in which it was printed and the authority, or qualifications, of the author.

## ■ Considering the Source

Your reaction to and evaluation of printed or electronic material should take into account its source. Obviously, a reader cannot check or verify each fact that a writer provides, but you must assess whether or not the writer has carefully researched and accurately reported the subject. Although many writers are careful and accurate, some are not. Often the source of a piece of writing can indicate how accurate, detailed, and well documented the article is. For example, in which of the following sources would you expect to find the most accurate, up-to-date information on the gas mileage of various cars?

- An advertisement in *Time*

- A research report in *Car and Driver*

- An article in *Reader's Digest* on buying an economical car

The report in *Car and Driver* would be the most likely source for information that is detailed and up-to-date, because it is a magazine devoted to the subject of cars and their performance. *Reader's Digest*, on the other hand, publishes selected articles and condensed writing from other periodicals and may not provide such timely information on a subject. A paid advertisement in *Time*, a weekly news magazine, most likely would not provide completely objective information.

Let's consider another example. Suppose you are in the library trying to find information on sleepwalking for a term paper. You locate the following sources, each of which contains an article on sleepwalking. Which would you expect to be the most factual, detailed, and scientific?

- An encyclopedia entry on sleepwalking

- An article titled "Strange Things Happen While You Are Sleeping," in *Woman's Day*

- An article titled "An Examination of Research on Sleepwalking" in the *Psychological Review*

Again you can see that from the source alone you can make predictions about the content and approach used. You would expect the encyclopedia entry to provide only a general overview of the topic. You might expect the article in *Woman's Day* to discuss various abnormalities that occur during sleep; sleepwalking might be only one of the topics discussed. Also, you might expect the article to relate several unusual or extreme cases of sleepwalking, rather than to present a factual analysis of the topic. The article in *Psychological Review*, a journal that reports research in psychology, would be the one that contains a factual, authoritative discussion of sleepwalking.

In evaluating a source you might ask the following questions:

1. **What reputation does the source have?**

2. **What is the audience for whom the source is intended?**

3. **Are documentation or references provided?**

## ■ Considering the Authority of the Author

To evaluate printed or electronic material, the competency of the author also must be considered. If the author lacks expertise in or experience with the subject, the material he or she produces may not meet an acceptable level of scholarship and accuracy.

Depending on the type of material you are using, you have several means of checking the qualifications of an author. In textbooks, the author's credentials may be described in one of two places. The author's college or university affiliation, and possibly his or her title, may appear on the title page beneath the author's name. Second, in the preface of the book, the author may indicate or summarize his or her qualifications for writing the text. In nonfiction books and general market paperbacks, a synopsis of the author's credentials and experiences may be included on the book jacket or the back cover. However, in other types of material, little effort is made to identify the author or his or her qualifications. In newspapers, magazines, and reference books, the reader is given little or no information about the writer. You are forced to rely on the judgment of the editors or publishers to assess an author's authority.

## EXERCISE 12–1

*DIRECTIONS:* Predict and discuss how useful and appropriate each of the following sources will be for the situation described.

1. Using an article from *Working Women* on family aggression for a term paper for your sociology class.

2. Quoting an article in *The New York Times* on recent events in China for a speech titled "Innovation and Change in China."
3. Reading an article titled "Bilingual Education in the Twenty-first Century" printed in the *Educational Research Quarterly* for a paper arguing for increased federal aid for bilingual education.
4. Using an article in *TV Guide* on television's coverage of crime and violence for a term paper on the effects of television on society.
5. Using information from a book written by former First Lady Nancy Reagan in a class discussion on use and abuse of presidential power.

## ■ READING ARGUMENTS

Argument is a common mode of presenting and evaluating information. It is also used to establish and evaluate positions on controversial issues. In a philosophy course you might read arguments on individual rights, the rights of the majority, or the existence of God. For a literature class you may read a piece of literary criticism that argues for or against the value of a particular work, debates its significance, or rejects an interpretation.

An argument generally refers to a piece of writing that makes an assertion and provides supporting evidence to support that assertion. Two types of arguments are common—inductive and deductive. An inductive argument reaches a general conclusion from observed specifics. For example, by observing the performance of a large number of athletes, you could conclude that athletes possess physical stamina.

A deductive argument, on the other hand, begins with a general conclusion and moves to specifics. For example, from the general conclusion that "Athletes possess physical stamina," you can reason that because Anthony is an athlete, he must possess physical stamina.

Both types of arguments begin with statements that are assumed to be correct. Basically, both follow a general pattern of "If that is so, then this is so. . . ." At times, an argument may be more complex, involving several steps—"If that is so, and this happens, then this should be done." Here are a few examples of arguments:

1. Many students have part-time jobs that require them to work late afternoons and evenings during the week. These students are unable to use the library during the week. Therefore, library hours should be extended to weekends.

2. Because parents have the right to determine their children's sexual attitudes, sex education should take place in the home, not at school.

3. No one should be forced to inhale unpleasant or harmful substances. That's why the ban on cigarette smoking in public places was put into effect in our state. Why shouldn't there be a law to prevent people from wearing strong colognes or perfumes, especially in restaurants, since sense of smell is important to taste?

When reading arguments, use the following steps:

1. **Identify the assertion—what is being argued for.** Determine what position, idea, or action the writer is trying to convince you to accept. Often, a concise statement of this key point appears early in the argument or in the introduction of a formal essay. This point is often restated.

2. **Read the entire article or essay.** Underline important parts of the argument.

3. **Watch for conclusions.** Words and phrases like "since," "thus," "therefore," "accordingly," "it can be concluded," "it is clear that," and "it follows that" are signals that a conclusion is about to be given.

4. **Notice the types of evidence the author provides.**

5. **Identify the specific action or position the writer is arguing for.**

6. **Reread the argument and examine its content and structure.** What is stated? What is implied or suggested? What assertions are made?

7. **Write a brief outline of the argument and list its key points.** Pragmatic learners may find this step especially helpful.

8. **Discuss the argument with a friend or classmate.** Especially if you are a social or auditory learner, you may "hear" yourself summarizing the assertion or evaluating the evidence supplied.

Now, read the following brief article and apply the previous steps.

#### EQUALITY ISN'T SAMENESS

Soldiers guilty of misconduct must be punished, but let's not sacrifice common sense and our national defense on the altar of feminism and political correctness.

It's unconscionable that military supervisors would take advantage of female subordinates. These officers have violated a special trust. But the Army's scandal raises a very serious question: Does placing men and women in forced intimate settings for extended periods promote or detract from military effectiveness?

Desert Storm commander Gen. Norman Schwarzkopf testified to Congress, "Decisions on what roles women should play in war must be based on military standards, not women's rights."

On the modern battlefield, every soldier is a potential combatant, and all should have equal opportunity to survive. Women don't. That doesn't mean women and men aren't equal. They are, but equality is not sameness. Women are not equally equipped to survive in the violent and physically difficult environment of combat because they have 50% less upper body strength and 70% of a man's aerobic fitness.

The Clinton adminstration removed many exemptions for women in the military. Congress helped by rescinding laws that precluded their combat service. All without considering the findings of the 1992 President's Commission of the Assignment of Women in the Armed Forces.

Integrating the sexes has become a difficult challenge for commanders. Merely raising the women-in-the-military issue is to jeopardize one's career.

Commanders have the nearly impossible task of fighting the enemy while minimizing the impact of sexual tensions, which creates readiness problems, such as increased fraternization, sex-based rivalries and many unwanted pregnancies. Readiness also suffers because many pregnant soldiers can no longer perform their mission and often must be replaced on short notice with less experienced personnel.

The goal of the military is to protect and defend the United States, but social experiments are weakening the armed forces. Those who engage in sexual improprieties must be prosecuted, but the status of women in the armed services must be reviewed in light of reality instead of some mystical feminist agenda. We have a duty to support those who volunteer to serve us.

Maginnis, "Equality Isn't Sameness."

● ● ●

This article is arguing for reconsidering the place of women in the armed forces. The author makes a four-part argument, offering four reasons why we should rethink women's military roles. The argument can be outlined as follows.

REASONS:

1. Women are not equally equipped to survive in combat.

2. Commanders face the added task of controlling sexual tensions and at the same time fighting the enemy.

3. Military readiness suffers because of pregnancies.

4. The armed forces are being weakened by "social experiments" such as placing women in combat roles.

CONCLUSION:

Therefore the current role of women in the military should be reconsidered.

## EXERCISE 12–2

*DIRECTIONS:* Read the following argument and answer the questions that follow.

"The life of each man should be sacred to each other man," the ancients tell us. They unflinchingly executed murderers. They realized it is not enough to proclaim the sacredness and inviolability of human life. It must be secured as well, by threatening with the loss of their own life those who violate what has been proclaimed as inviolable—the right of innocents to live. Else the inviolability of human life is neither credibly proclaimed nor actually protected. No society can profess that the lives of its members are secure if those who did not allow innocent others to continue living are themselves allowed to continue living—at the expense of the community. To punish a murderer by incarcerating him as one does a pickpocket cannot but cheapen human life. Murder differs in quality from other crimes and deserves, therefore, a punishment that differs in quality from other punishments. There is a discontinuity. It should be underlined, not blurred.

Van Den Haag, "Capital Punishment."

● ● ●

1. What is the author's position on the death penalty?
2. Summarize the argument.

## ■ EVALUATING ARGUMENTS

Once you have understood the article by identifying what is asserted and how it is asserted, the next step is to evaluate the soundness, correctness, and worth of the argument. Specifically, you must evaluate evidence, both type and relevancy, definition of terms, cause-effect relationships, value systems, and recognition of counterarguments.

### ■ Types of Evidence

The validity of an inductive argument rests, in part, on the soundness and correctness of the evidence provided to draw the conclusion. The validity of a deductive argument, on the other hand, rests on the accuracy and correctness of the premises on which the argument is based. Evaluating each type of argument involves assessing the accuracy and correctness of statements on which the argument is based. Writers often provide evidence to substantiate their observations or premises. As a critical reader, your task is to assess whether or not the evidence is sufficient to support the claim. Here are a few types of evidence often used:

#### *Personal Experience*

Writers often substantiate their ideas through experience and observation. Although a writer's personal account of a situation may provide an interesting perspective on an issue, personal experience should not be accepted as proof. The observer may be biased or may have exaggerated or incorrectly perceived a situation.

### Examples

Examples are descriptions of particular situations that are used to illustrate or explain a principle, concept, or idea. To explain what aggressive behavior is, your psychology instructor may offer several examples: fighting, punching, and kicking. Examples should *not* be used by themselves to prove the concept or idea they illustrate, as is done in the following sample:

> The American judicial system treats those who are called for jury duty unfairly. It is clear from my sister's experience that the system has little regard for the needs of those called as jurors. My sister was required to report for jury duty the week she was on vacation. She spent the entire week in a crowded, stuffy room waiting to be called to sit on a jury and never was called.

● ● ●

### Statistics

Many people are impressed by statistics—the reporting of figures, percentages, averages, and so forth—and assume they are irrefutable proof. Actually, statistics can be misused, misinterpreted, or used selectively to give other than the most objective, accurate picture of a situation. Suppose you read that magazine X has increased its readership by 50 percent while magazine Y made only a 10 percent increase. From this statistic some readers might assume that magazine X has a wider readership than magazine Y. However, if provided with complete information, you can see that this is not true. The missing, but crucial, statistic is the total readership of each magazine before the increase. If magazine X had a readership of 20,000, and increased it by 50 percent, its readership would total 30,000. However, if magazine Y's readership was already 50,000, a 10 percent increase (bringing the new total to 55,000) would still give it the larger readership despite the fact that it made the smaller increase. Approach statistical evidence with a critical, questioning attitude. (See Critical Reading Tip #6, p. 215)

### Comparisons and Analogies

Comparisons or analogies (extended comparisons) serve as illustrations and are often used in argument. Their reliability depends on how closely the comparison corresponds or how similar it is to the situation to which it is being compared. For example, Martin Luther King Jr., in his famous letter from the Birmingham jail, compared nonviolent protesters to a robbed man. To evaluate this comparison you would need to consider how the two are similar and how they are different.

## EXERCISE 12–3

*DIRECTIONS:* For the article "Equality Isn't Sameness" on p. 417, evaluate whether the author uses adequate evidence to support his claim.

### ■ Relevancy and Sufficiency of Evidence

Once you have identified the evidence used to support an argument, the next step is to decide if there is enough of the right kind of evidence to lead you to accept the writer's claim. This is always a matter of judgment; there are no easy rules to follow. You must determine whether the evidence provided directly supports the statement, and whether sufficient evidence has been provided.

Suppose you are reading an article in your campus newspaper that states that Freshman Composition 101 should not be required of all students at your college. As evidence, the writer provides the following:

> Composition does not prepare us for the job market. Besides, the reading assignments have no relevancy to modern times.

This argument provides neither adequate nor sufficient evidence. The writer does nothing to substantiate his claims of irrelevancy of the course to the job market or modern times. For the argument to be regarded seriously, the writer needs to provide facts, statistics, expert opinion, or other forms of documentation.

## EXERCISE 12–4

*DIRECTIONS:* Read the following argument and pay particular attention to the type(s) of evidence used. Then answer the questions that follow.

It is predictable. At Halloween, thousands of children trick-or-treat in Indian costumes. At Thanksgiving, thousands of children parade in school pageants wearing plastic headdresses and pseudo-buckskin clothing. Thousands of card shops stock Thanksgiving greeting cards with images of cartoon animals wearing feathered headbands. Thousands of teachers and librarians trim bulletin boards with Anglo-featured, feathered Indian boys and girls. Thousands of gift shops load their shelves with Indian figurines and jewelry.

Fall and winter are also the seasons when hundreds of thousands of sports fans root for professional, college and public school teams with names that summon up Indians—"Braves," "Redskins," "Chiefs." (In New York State, one out of eight junior and senior high school teams call themselves "Indians," "Tomahawks" and the like.) War-whooping team mascots are imprinted on school uniforms, postcards, notebooks, tote bags and car floor mats.

All of this seems innocuous; why make a fuss about it? Because these trappings and holiday symbols offend tens of thousands of other Americans—the Native American people. Because these invented images prevent millions of us from understanding the authentic Indian America, both long ago and today. Because this image-making prevents Indians from being a relevant part of the nation's social fabric.

Hirschfelder, "It's Time to Stop Playing Indians."

● ● ●

1. What type(s) of evidence is used?
2. Is the evidence convincing?
3. Is there sufficient evidence?
4. What other types of evidence could have been used to strengthen the argument?

## ■ Definition of Terms

A clear and effective argument carefully defines key terms and uses them consistently. For example, an essay arguing for or against animal rights should state what is meant by the term, describe or define those rights, and use that definition through the entire argument.

The following two paragraphs are taken from two different argumentative essays on pornography. Notice how in the first paragraph the author carefully defines what he means by pornography before proceeding with his argument, while in the second the term is not clearly defined.

### *Paragraph 1—Careful Definition*

There is unquestionably more pornography available today than 15 years ago. However, is it legitimate to assume that more is worse? Pornography is speech, words, and pictures about sexuality. No one would consider an increase in the level of speech about religion or politics to be a completely negative development. What makes speech about sexuality different?

Lynn, "Pornography's Many Different Forms: Not All Bad."

### *Paragraph 2—Vague Definition*

If we are not talking about writing laws, defining pornography doesn't pose as serious a problem. We do have different tastes. Maybe some of mine come from my middle-class background (my mother wouldn't think so!). I don't like bodies presented without heads, particularly female bodies. The motive may sometimes be the protection of the individual, but the impression is decapitation, and I also happen to be someone who is attracted to people's faces. This is a matter of taste.

Rule, "Pornography Is a Social Disease."

● ● ●

## ■ Cause-Effect Relationships

Arguments are often built around the assumption of a cause-effect relationship. For example, an argument supporting gun control legislation may claim that ready availability of guns contributes to an increased number of shootings. This argument implies that availability of guns causes increased use. If the writer provides no evidence that this cause-effect relationship exists, you should question the accuracy of the statement. (See Critical Reading Tip #5,p 174.)

## ■ Implied or Stated Value System

An argument often implies or rests on a value system (a structure of what the writer feels is right, wrong, worthwhile, and important). However, everyone possesses a personal value system, and although our culture promotes many major points of agreement (murder is wrong, human life is worthwhile, and so forth), it also allows points of departure. One person may think that telling lies is always wrong; another person may say it depends on the circumstance. Some people have a value system based on religious beliefs; others may not share those beliefs.

In evaluating an argument, look for value judgments and then decide if the judgments are consistent with and acceptable to your personal value system. Here are a few examples of value judgment statements:

1. Abortion is wrong.

2. Financial aid for college should be available to everyone regardless of income.

3. Capital punishment violates human rights.

## ■ Recognition of Counterarguments

An effective argument often includes a refutation of counterarguments—a line of reasoning that can be used to deny or refute what the writer is arguing for. For example, if a writer is arguing against gun control, he or she may recognize the counterargument that availability of guns causes shootings and refute it by saying "Guns don't kill people, people kill people."

Notice how in the excerpt from an essay advocating capital punishment, the author recognizes the counterargument that everyone has a right to live and argues against it.

> Abolitionists [of the death penalty] insist that we all have an imprescriptible right to live to our natural term: if the innocent victim had a right to live, so does the murderer. That takes egalitarianism too far for my taste. The crime sets victim and murderer apart; if the victim died, the murderer does not deserve to live. If innocents are

to be secure in their lives murderers cannot be. The thought that murderers are to be given as much right to live as their victims oppresses me. So does the thought that a Stalin, Hitler, an Idi Amin should have as much right to live as their victims did.

Van Den Haag, "Capital Punishment."

● ● ●

### ■ Identifying Assumptions

Many writers begin an argument assuming that a particular set of facts or principles is true. Then they develop their argument based on that assumption. Of course, if the assumption is not correct or if it cannot be proven, the arguments that depend on that assumption may be incorrect. For instance, the following passage begins with an assumption (*underlined*) that the writer makes no attempt to prove or justify. Rather, he uses it as a starting point to develop his ideas on the function of cities.

Given that the older central cities have lost their capacity to serve as effective staging areas for newcomers, the question inevitably poses itself: What is the function of these cities? Permit me to suggest that it has become essentially that of a sandbox.

A sandbox is a place where adults park their children in order to converse, play, or work with a minimum of interference. The adults, having found a distraction for the children, can get on with the serious things of life. There is some reward for the children in all this. The sandbox is given to them as their turf. . . .

Palen, *City Scenes*.

● ● ●

The author offers no reasons or evidence in support of the opening statement: it is assumed to be true. This assumption is the base on which the author builds his argument that the city is a sandbox.

As you read arguments, always begin by examining the author's initial assumptions. Decide whether you agree or disagree with them as a check to see whether the author provides any evidence that his or her assumptions are accurate. Once you have identified an assumption, consider this question: If the assumption were untrue, how would it affect the argument?

## EXERCISE 12–5

*DIRECTIONS:* Read the following argument by Luis Rodriguez and answer the questions that follow.

### REKINDLING THE WARRIOR

Over the past year and a half, I have spoken to thousands of young people at schools, jails, bookstores, colleges, and community centers about the experiences addressed in my book *Always Running: La Vida Loca, Gang Days in L.A.*

What stays with me is the vitality and clarity of the young people I met, many of them labeled "at risk." They saw in my experiences and my book both a reflection of their lives and the possibility of transcendence, of change, which otherwise appears elusive. In those faces I saw the most viable social energy for rebuilding the country and realigning its resources. They are the future, but this society has no clear pathway to take them there.

For one thing, today's youth are under intense scrutiny and attack. Schools, for the most part, fail to engage their creativity and intellect. As a result, young people find their own means of expression—music being the most obvious example, but also the formation of gangs.

Despite conventional thinking, gangs are not anarchies. They can be highly structured, with codes of honor and discipline. For many members, the gang serves as family, as the only place where they can find fellowship, respect, a place to belong. You often hear the word love among gang members. Sometimes the gang is the only place where they can find it.

Gabriel Rivera, director of the Transitional Intervention Experience of Bend, Oregon, and a former East Los Angeles gang member, came up with a concept he calls "character in motion" to describe the essence, not the form, of gang participation.

"[Character in motion] is marked by the advertent or inadvertent beginnings of physical, psychological, and spiritual struggle that happens for every young person," writes Rivera. "[It] is what happens when a young person responds to the inevitable inner call to embrace 'the journey,' and chooses to honor that journey above all else with a courage that relies upon connecting with one's 'warrior energy.'"

The warrior needs to be nurtured, directed, and guided—not smothered, crushed, or corralled. This energy needs to be taken to its next highest level of development, where one matures into self-control, self-study, and self-actualization. Most anti-gang measures have nothing to do with any of this. A serious effort would address the burning issue of adolescent rage. It would address a basic need for food, shelter, and clothing, but also needs for expressive creativity and community.

Sociopathic behavior exists within the framework of a sociopathic society. Under these circumstances, gangs are not a problem; they are a solution, particularly for communities lacking economic, social, and political options.

Two examples: Two years ago, I did a poetry reading in a part of eastern Ohio that was once alive with coal mines and industry but now has 50 to 70 percent unemployment in some areas. Many of the young people are selling drugs to survive. In this sense, they could be from the South Bronx or the Pine Ridge Reservation. They are, however, "white." They are listening to their own music ("Wherever kids find obstacles, I find music," an independent record producer recently told *Rolling Stone* magazine), and establishing ganglike structures to survive.

Soon after the 1992 Los Angeles rebellion, members of the Crips and the Bloods, two of the city's most notorious gangs, circulated a plan. They included proposals to repair the schools and streets and get rid of drugs and violence. At the end of the plan, they wrote: "Give us the hammers and the nails, and we will rebuild the city."

It was a demand to take responsibility, which rose from the inner purpose of Crip and Blood warrior consciousness, and a demand for the authority to carry out the plan. Unfortunately, no one took them up on it.

These young people face great barriers to educational advancement, economic stability, and social mobility—but little or none to criminal activity or violence (as everyone knows, prison is no deterrence; for some youth it is a rite of passage).

Power is the issue here. Without autonomy to make decisions that affect their lives, these young people can only attempt to approximate it, too often with disastrous results.

You want to stop the body count? Empower the youth.

● ● ●

1. Summarize the author's position on gangs.
2. What assumptions does Rodriguez make?
3. What type(s) of evidence is offered?
4. Do you feel the evidence is adequate and convincing?
5. What values does the author hold?
6. Does the author refute counterarguments? If so, describe how he does this.

## ■ ERRORS IN LOGICAL REASONING

Errors in reasoning, often called logical fallacies, are common in arguments. These errors invalidate the argument or render it flawed. Several common errors in logic are described below:

### ■ Circular Reasoning

Also known as begging the question, this error involves using part of the conclusion as evidence to support it. Here are a few examples:

Cruel medical experimentation on defenseless animals is inhumane.

Female soldiers should not be placed in battle situations because combat is a man's job.

In circular reasoning, because no evidence is given to support the claim, there is no reason to accept the conclusion.

### ■ Hasty Generalization

This fallacy means that the conclusion has been derived from insufficient evidence. Here is one example: You taste three tangerines and each is sour, so you conclude that all tangerines are sour. Here is another: By observing one performance of a musical group, you conclude that the group is unfit to perform.

## ■ Non Sequitur ("It Does Not Follow")

The false establishment of cause-effect is known as a non sequitur. To say, for example, that "Because my instructor is young, I'm sure she'll be a good teacher" is a non sequitur because youth does not cause good teaching. Here is another example: "Sam Goodwin is the best choice for state senator because he understands the people." Understanding the people will not necessarily make someone an effective state senator.

## ■ False Cause

The false cause fallacy is the incorrect assumption that two events that follow each other in time are causally related. Suppose you walked under a ladder and then tripped on an uneven sidewalk. If you said you tripped because you walked under the ladder, you would be assuming false cause.

## ■ Either-Or Fallacy

This fallacy assumes that an issue is only two sided, or that there are only two choices or alternatives for a particular situation. In other words, there is no middle ground. Consider the issue of censorship of violence on television. An either-or fallacy is to assume that violence on TV must either be allowed or banned. This fallacy does not recognize other alternatives such as limiting access through viewing hours, restricting the showing of certain types of violence, and so forth.

# EXERCISE 12–6

*DIRECTIONS:* Identify the logical fallacy in each of the following statements:

1. All Native American students in my accounting class earned A grades, so Native Americans must excel with numerical tasks.
2. If you are not in favor of nuclear arms control, then you're against protecting our future.
3. My sister cannot compose business letters or memos because she has writer's block.
4. A well-known senator, noting a decline in the crime rate in the four largest cities in his state, quickly announced that his new "get-tough on criminals" publicity campaign was successful and took credit for the decline.
5. I always order cheesecake for dessert because I am allergic to chocolate.

## EXERCISE 12–7

*DIRECTIONS:* The following two essays were written in response to the question "should animals be used in research?" Read each essay and answer the questions that follow.

### DIALOGUE
### ARGUMENT #1: SHOULD ANIMALS BE USED IN RESEARCH?

The use of animals in research has become an extremely emotional as well as legal issue. Very strict federal regulations on the care, maintenance, and use of animals in research now exist. But even though research using animals is closely monitored to identify and eliminate any potential source of pain or abuse of experimental animals, activists still object to the use of animal species, particularly the vertebrates, for research.

Those who oppose the use of animals have become caught up in the developments of the "high tech" world and frequently propose the use of simulators and computer modeling to replace biological research with live animals. Unfortunately, simulators and computer modeling cannot generate valid biological data on their own. Scientific data obtained from experiments using live animals must first provide base data before modelers can extrapolate results under similar conditions.

Simulators and computer modeling do have their place in teaching and research, but they will not and cannot replace the use of animals in many kinds of critical medical research. For example, consider modern surgical procedures in human organ repair and transplanting. The techniques in use today were developed and perfected through the use of laboratory animals. Would you want a delicate operation to be performed by a physician trained only on simulators?

Laboratory animal research is fundamental to medical progress in many other areas as well. Vaccines for devastating human diseases like polio and smallpox and equally serious animal diseases like rabies, feline leukemia, and distemper were all developed through the use of research animals.

The discovery, development, and refinement of drugs that could arrest, control, or eliminate such human diseases as AIDS, cancer, and heart disease all require the use of laboratory animals whose physiological mechanisms are similar to humans.

I have only noted above a few of the many examples where animals have been used in human and veterinary medical research. It's also important to note that studies in behavior, ecology, physiology, and genetics all require the use of animals, in some capacity, to produce valid and meaningful knowledge about life on this planet.

Donald W. Tuff

### ARGUMENT #2: SHOULD ANIMALS BE USED IN RESEARCH?

I cannot accept the argument that research on animals is necessary to discover "cures" for humans. Many diseases and medications react very differently in animals than they do in humans. Aspirin, for example, is toxic to cats, and there are few diseases directly transmittable from cats to humans.

I particularly abhor the "research" conducted for cosmetic purposes. The Draise test—where substances are introduced into the eyes of rabbits and then examined to see if ulcers, lesions or other observable reactions take place—is archaic and inefficient. Other alternatives exist that are more accurate and do not cause unnecessary suffering to our fellow creatures.

Household products such as the LD–50 test are also tested needlessly on animals. This test is routinely used in substances like bleach. Animals, in many cases puppies, are force-fed these toxic chemicals to determine the dosage at which exactly 50 percent of them die. These tests are not necessary and do not give very useful information.

Many top medical schools no longer use animals for teaching purposes, but have their medical students practice on models, computer simulations, and then observe techniques on human patients. A medical doctor is expected to honor and revere life, and this approach emphasizes that idea.

If medical students are deliberately taught that animal life is not important, then the next step to devaluing human life is made that much easier. Anatomy and biology classes do not need to use cats for all their students, either. A video of a dissection that is shown to the entire class or a model or computer simulation would be just as effective.

If an experiment using animals is deemed absolutely necessary, then that claim should be fully documented and all previous research should be examined thoroughly to avoid needless replication. In addition, the facility should not be exempt from cruelty laws and should be open to inspection by animal rights advocates not affiliated with the research institution.

Humans have a duty to take care of the earth and to respect all life, for if we poison the earth and annihilate other life on the planet, we are poisoning and annihilating ourselves. We were put on this earth to take care of our earth and the creatures upon it.

Angela Molina

● ● ●

## ARGUMENT #1

1. Summarize Tuff's position on the use of laboratory animals.
2. Outline the main points of his argument.
3. What types of evidence does he offer?
4. Evaluate the adequacy and sufficiency of the evidence provided.
5. Does the author recognize or refute counterarguments?

## ARGUMENT #2

1. Summarize Molina's position.
2. Outline the main points of her argument.
3. What types of evidence does she offer?
4. Evaluate the adequacy and sufficiency of the evidence provided.
5. Does the author recognize or refute counterarguments?

**Critical Thinking Tip #12**

**Evaluating Emotional Appeals**

Emotional appeals attempt to involve or excite readers by appealing to their emotions, thereby controlling the reader's attitude toward the subject. Several types of emotional appeals are described here.

1. **Emotionally Charged or Biased Language** By using words that create an emotional response, writers establish positive or negative feelings. For example, an advertisement for a new line of fragrances promises to "indulge," "refresh," "nourish," and "pamper" the user. An ad for an automobile uses phrases such as "limousine comfort," "European styling," and "animal sleekness" to interest and excite readers.

2. **Testimonials** A testimonial involves using the opinion or action of a well-known or famous person. We have all seen athletes endorsing underwear or movie stars selling shampoo. This type of appeal works on the notion that people admire celebrities and strive to be like them, respect their opinions, and are willing to accept their viewpoints.

3. **Association** An emotional appeal also is made by associating a product, idea, or position with others that are already accepted or highly regarded. Patriotism is already valued, so to call a product "All American" in an advertisement is an appeal to the emotions. A car being named a Cougar to remind you of a fast, sleek animal, a cigarette ad picturing a scenic waterfall, or a speaker standing in front of an American flag are other examples of association.

4. **Appeal to "Common Folk"** Some people distrust those who are well educated, wealthy, highly artistic, or in other ways distinctly different from the average person. An emotional appeal to this group is made by selling a product or idea by indicating that it is originated from, held by, or bought by ordinary citizens. A commercial may advertise a product by showing its use in an average household. A politician may describe her background and education to suggest that she is like everyone else; a salesperson may dress in styles similar to his clients.

5. **"Join the Crowd" Appeal** The appeal to do, believe, or buy what everyone else is doing, believing, or buying is known as crowd appeal. Commercials that proclaim their product as the "Number one best selling car in America" are appealing to this motive. Essays that cite opinion polls on a controversial issue in support of a position—"sixty-eight percent Americans favor capital punishment"—are also using this appeal.

**BOTH ARGUMENTS**

1. Which argument do you feel is stronger? Why?
2. Compare the types of evidence each uses.

## EXERCISE 12–8

*DIRECTIONS:* From among the reading assignments you have completed this semester, list one that involved persuasive or argumentative writing. Review this piece of writing and then complete the following:

1. Summarize what is being argued for.
2. List the key points of the argument.
3. Indicate what type of evidence the writer uses.
4. Determine if the evidence is adequate and sufficient to support the author's point.
5. Identify any counterarguments the author recognizes or refutes.

## EXERCISE 12–9

*DIRECTIONS:* Visit a newsgroup that focuses on a controversial issue and either observe or participate in the discussion. What persuasive techniques or emotional appeals (See Critical Thinking Tip #12) did you observe?

## SUMMARY

**1. What is involved in evaluating arguments and persuasive writing?**

Persuasive and argumentative writing urges the reader to take action or accept a particular point of view. To evaluate this type of writing readers must learn to evaluate source and authority, recognize the structure of arguments and identify logical fallacies in arguments.

**2. Why should you consider the source of the material and the author's authority when reading this type of writing?**

Evaluating both the source in which material was printed and the competency of its author are essential in evaluating any argument or piece of persuasive writing. Where a piece of writing came from can be an indication of the type of information that will be presented as well as its accuracy and value. The author's qualifications and level of expertise with the subject provide a further indication of the reliability of this information.

**3. How can you read arguments more effectively?**

Since both inductive and deductive arguments make assertions and give evidence to support them, when reading them it is important to
- identify what is being argued for.
- read very closely and carefully.
- watch for conclusions.
- be alert to the types of evidence given.
- reread to examine both content and structure.
- underline or outline the key parts.

**4. How should you evaluate an argument?**

Critical readers evaluate the soundness, correctness, and worth of an argument. To do so,
- determine the type of evidence used.
- decide if there is enough and the right kind of evidence.
- notice if key terms are defined and used properly.
- be alert to value judgments, assumptions, or cause-effect connections.
- look for counterarguments and whether they are adequately refuted.

**5. What are the common errors in logical reasoning?**

Five common logical fallacies that can weaken or destroy an argument are:
- circular reasoning
- hasty generalization
- non sequitur
- false cause
- either-or fallacy

## READING SELECTION 23
### FROM A VEGETARIAN: LOOKING AT HUNTING FROM BOTH SIDES NOW

Timothy Denesha
From *The Buffalo News*

*This editorial, originally published in* The Buffalo News, *explores the issue of sports hunting. Read the essay to answer the following questions:*

*1. What was Denesha's original position on sports hunting?*

*2. How has his position changed?*

1    Deer hunting season opened Nov. 18, and as the gunfire resumes in our woodlands and fields so will the perennial sniping between hunters and animal rights supporters. I always feel caught in the cross-fire on this matter, because I have been a vegetarian and animal rights advocate for over 25 years, but I also have friends I respect who are hunters. I've learned the issue is not as black-and-white as I once believed.

2    Growing up with many beloved pets and no hunters in my life, I assumed these people were bloodthirsty animal haters. When, in my 20s, I read the great humanitarian Albert Schweitzer's writings on reverence for life, I became a vegetarian and even more contemptuous of hunters.

3    But I had to revise my opinion after seeing the classic 1981 African film, "The Gods Must Be Crazy." The hero, a good-hearted bushman slays a small gazelle, then tenderly strokes her, apologizing for taking her life. He explains his family is hungry and thanks her for providing food. I was stunned: a hunter practicing reverence for life! Later, I learned that Native American tradition has the same compassionate awareness about life lost so another life may be sustained.

4    My position softened further several years ago when Alex Pacheco, a leading animals-rights activist, spoke here. Detailing inhumane practices at meat-packing plants and factory farms,

he said the most important thing anyone could do to lessen animal suffering was to stop eating meat. I decided to work toward being vegan (eating no animal products) and reluctantly admitted that hunters were not the animal kingdom's worst enemies. However, I still disliked them.

5    What really changed my perspective was getting to know some hunters personally, through my job at a Red Cross blood-donation center. Some of my co-workers and a number of our donors are civic-minded people who donate blood (which most people don't) but also shed animal blood with their guns and arrows. Confronting this paradox brought me some realizations.

6    First, hunters are like any group that differs from me: lacking personal experience of them made it easier to demonize them. They aren't monsters. I don't know if any of them apologizes to or thanks his kill as the hungry bushman did, but I do know they aren't cruel, sadistic or bloodthirsty—quite the opposite, as I later discovered.

7    Second, these people aren't just amusing themselves by ending a life; they are acquiring food. This death that sustains another life has a meaning that, for example, fox hunting does not. To the animal, this distinction may mean little. But it is significant when considering a person's intentions.

8    Also, I was informed that hunters don't "like to kill." They enjoy the outdoors, the comraderie and the various skills involved. (One of these skills, the "clean kill," is prized precisely because it minimizes suffering). Like vegetable gardeners, they enjoy providing food [for] themselves and their families with their own hands. Like those who fish, they enjoy a process of food

acquisition that involves an animal's death, but not because it does. Again, this may seem a small point (especially to the prey), but I feel it is meaningful from the standpoint of the hunter's humanity.

9   In addition, I've come to see a certain integrity in hunters as meat-eaters who "do their own dirty work." Packaged cold-cuts and fast-food burgers mask the fact of lives bled out on the killing floor. Hunters never forget this, for they accept personal responsibility for it.

10   Furthermore, were I an animal that had to die to feed a human, I'd rather it happen one-on-one, at the hands of that person in the woods that were my home, than amidst the impersonal mass-production machinery of a meat factory. Either way is death, but one way had more dignity, less fear and less suffering.

11   There are bad hunters who trespass, shoot domestic animals, hunt intoxicated or disregard that cardinal rule of hunting's unwritten code of ethics: wounded prey must not be allowed to suffer. Last Thanksgiving morning in Chestnut Ridge Park, I found a fresh trail of deer tracks in the snow, heavily splashed with blood. It was horrible.

12   One of my hunter co-workers was also upset when I told him about it, and had this story . He himself was able to hunt only one day last season and sighted a small, wounded doe. As a student on a tight budget with a family, he hunts for food and would have preferred to ignore the doe's plight and meet his license limit with a large buck. Instead, he devoted a long, difficult day to trailing her until he was close enough to end her suffering. This was an act of mercy and even self-sacrifice, not the action of a heartless person insensitive to animals. It we reverence for life. He claims many hunters would do and have done the same.

13   And I realized that compassion has many faces, some of the truest the most unexpected.

## Comprehension Test 23

*Directions: Circle the letter of the best answer.*

**Checking Your Comprehension**

1. This reading is primarily concerned with
   a. the barbarism of hunting.
   b. the reverence hunters have for human life.
   c. the defensibility of hunting.
   d. why people become vegetarians.

2. The main point in this reading is
   a. it is unethical to hunt.
   b. animals suffer as a result of hunting.
   c. hunters have as much integrity and compassion as nonhunters.
   d. most hunters are only interested in killing helpless creatures for sport.

3. It is clear from the article that the author is *not*
   a. a vegetarian.
   b. a health care worker.
   c. a hunter.
   d. an animal rights advocate.

4. According to the article, hunters
   a. have little respect for animal life.
   b. don't eat processed meat.
   c. hunt only to acquire food.
   d. don't enjoy killing.

5. Initially, what made the author begin to change his mind about hunters?
   a. a speech by Alex Pacheco.
   b. the African film "The Gods Must Be Crazy."
   c. the Red Cross blood donation center.
   d. the writings of Albert Schweitzer.

6. According to the reading, hunters hunt for all of the following reasons, *except*
   a. to acquire food.
   b. for the comaraderie.
   c. for the joy of killing.
   d. to enjoy the outdoors.

**Thinking Critically**

7. As used in the first paragraph, a synonym for "sniping" is
   a. shooting.
   b. cutting.
   c. killing.
   d. arguing.

8. Which of the following statements best describes the author's attitude about hunting?
   a. Hunters are aggressive and blood thirsty.
   b. Hunters often take animals' lives with respect and compassion.
   c. Hunting should not be allowed under any circumstances.
   d. Hunting is just a sport like any other sport.

9. From this reading, we can infer that deer hunters' licenses allow them to
   a. kill as many deer as they choose.
   b. hunt on any property where deer can be found.
   c. hunt only one day per season.
   d. kill only a limited number of deer.

10. Which of the following is an example of a deer hunter abiding by hunting's unwritten code of ethics?
   a. He hunts with a bow and arrow instead of a rifle.
   b. He kills a deer that is already wounded.
   c. He brings a wounded deer to the vet for treatment.
   d. He kills only to supply his family with food.

**Questions for Discussion**

1. Do you think hunting is moral or immoral? Justify your position.

2. Discuss the ways in which hunters prevent animals from suffering.

3. What lessons can be learned from the author's statement that "Hunters are like any group that differs from me: lacking personal experience of them made it easier to demonize them"?

4. When the author refers to hunting he states that "compassion has many faces." What does he mean? Give an example to support your point.

| Selection 23: | | 822 words |
|---|---|---|
| Finishing Time: | | |
| | HR.     MIN. | SEC. |
| Starting Time: | | |
| | HR.     MIN. | SEC. |
| Reading Time: | | |
| | MIN. | SEC. |
| WPM Score: | | |
| Comprehension Score: | | % |

SOCIOLOGY

# READING 24
## OUT OF TIME

Alan Weisman and Sandy Tolan
From *Societies: A Multicultural Reader*

*Taken from a collection of multicultural readings that accompany a sociology textbook, this essay focuses on the destruction of lands and cultures of primitive societies.*

*Read it to discover what effects such destruction has had and may have in the future.*

1    An old Indian stands in the rain in northern Argentina, amid the charred ruins of his village. His name is Pa'i Antonio Moreira. Over his thin sweater two strings of black beads crisscross his chest like bandoliers, signifying that he is a ñanderú, a shaman[1] of his people. They are among the last few Guaraní Indians in this country, part of a cultural group that once inhabited a forest stretching from Argentina to the Amazon. Now only remnants of that forest and its creatures and people are left.

2    The night before, government men in forest-service uniforms torched the community's village. The 1,500-acre tract of semitropical woodland where they lived is only a few miles from Iguazú Falls, the biggest waterfall in South America. Once sacred to the Guaraní, Iguazú is now overwhelmed by tourists. Moreira's village was burned to make way for yet another hotel. The next Indian village to the south is also gone, swallowed by the waters of a new reservoir. The villages beyond that are no longer surrounded by black laurel and ceiba trees, which sheltered the deer and tapir the Guaraní once hunted, but by silent forests of Monterey pine, imported from California and planted by a nearby paper company for its superior fiber content.

3    The old shaman's kinsmen huddle around a fire, while the embers of their homes hiss and sizzle in the rain. The people descend from a stubborn band of Guaraní who refused to be evangelized when Jesuits arrived here 400 years ago. Moreira tells us that these ills curse the Guaraní's world because white men ignore the true way of God. Only the Indian, he says, remembers how God intended the world to be.

4    Then why, we ask, has God allowed the white man to triumph, and the Indian to suffer?

5    He gazes at us from beneath heavy-lidded eyes filled with loss and compassion. "The white man hasn't triumphed," he says softly. "When the Indians vanish, the rest will follow."

6    Throughout the Americas, great changes fueled by visions of progress have swept away the habitats of countless plants and animals. But entire human cultures are also becoming endangered. During the past two years, we traveled to 15 countries, from the United States to Chile, to document this swift, often irreversible destruction.

7    Nations with growing, impoverished populations strike a Faustian[2] bargain with the developed world: to create jobs and electricity for industry, they borrow hundreds of millions of dollars from foreign banks. They build huge dams that flood their richest lands and displace thousands of rural poor. To repay the massive debt, they invite foreign companies to mine their timber, gold, oil, and coal, or convert their farmlands to produce luxury crops for consumers in North America, Europe and Japan. To

---

[1] Spiritual leader.

[2] Faust is a legendary figure who sold his soul to the devil in return for power and knowledge.

ease pressures on overcrowded lands, they allow poor settlers to slash and burn their way into virgin forests, where they clash with the indigenous people already living there—including some of the last uncontacted tribes in the hemisphere.

8    For centuries the Yuguí Indians of the Bolivian Amazon roamed naked through jungles so remote they thought no one else existed. Their word for *world* translates simply as *leaves.*

9    "When we first saw the white people, we thought they were the spirits of our dead ancestors," recalled Ataiba, the last of the Yuguí chiefs. He recalled how his people had begun to encounter strange things in the jungle—fresh fish hung from trees, sacks of sugar, cooking pots, machetes—all laid beside new trails. One day, at the end of one of these gift trails, Ataiba saw light-skinned people watching him. After many months, the pale strangers, evangelicals from the Florida-based New Tribes Mission, convinced Ataiba that they could offer safe haven from the growing violence of confrontations with loggers and settlers. One morning late in 1989, Ataiba led his people out of the forest forever, to become permanent wards of the mission village.

10    Often, on the heels of the missionaries, come the forces of development. In Ecuador during the early 1970s, the government contracted with Texaco to build an oil industry in the Ecuadorian Amazon and help bring the country into the global economy. Until then, many natives there had never even heard of a nation called Ecuador, let alone petroleum.

11    "We didn't know the sound of a motor," explained Toribe, a young Cofán leader. The Cofán, who live along Ecuador's Tío Aguarico, were still hunting peccaries and monkeys with blowguns. "We couldn't figure out what animal could be making those noises." The sounds were Texaco's helicopters. Soon settlers streamed down the oil-company roads, changing life irrevocably for the Cofán.

12    "With the petroleum companies came epidemics," recalled Toribe. "We didn't know flu,

measles, and these other illnesses. Many fled from here. Those that stayed were finished. It was all contaminated. There were fifteen thousand of us on this side of the Río Aguarico. Now we are only four hundred."

13    Oil from Ecuador, hardwoods from Bolivia, and from Honduras to Costa Rica to Brazil, beef cattle raised for export where forests once stood; we had stumbled onto another kind of gift trail, this one leading back to the United States. The savanna surrounding Bogotá, Colombia, with some of the finest soil in Latin America, produces not food but bargain-priced roses, chrysanthemums, and carnations to sell on street corners and in supermarkets in the United States and beyond. In Honduras, mangrove forests lining the Gulf of Fonseca's estuaries are threatened by modern mariculture. Huge shrimp farms resist local fishermen's access to the crabs, mollusks, and small fish they have netted for generations.

14    In Brazil, the biggest dam in the Amazon, Tucurui, has displaced thousands of people and created such mosquito infestations that thousands more are leaving. Tucurui was built to power aluminum smelters owned by U.S., European, and Japanese companies. The ore comes from the Amazon's largest mine, which strips away hundreds of acres of jungle each year to provide foil and cans.

15    On South America's second-biggest river, the Parana, we watched men building the longest dam in the world: Yacyreta, along the Argentina-Paraguay border. More than $1 billion in World Bank and Inter-American Development Bank loans was allegedly diverted from the dam project to finance things like Argentina's Falklands war. Now there's not enough money to relocate the 40,000 people whose cities and farms will be flooded. As much as $30 million was spent, however, on an elevator to carry fish like dorado, a prized local species, upstream to spawn. Unfortunately, the elevator, built by North American dam contractors, was designed for salmon, which go upstream, spawn, and die.

Dorado need to return. And there's no down elevator.

16 Our travels did reveal a few signs of hope: a land-recovery program run by villagers in southern Honduras, a proposal to put Kuna Indians in charge of protecting the watershed of Panama's Bayano Dam. But these projects are exceptions. Alone, they are not enough to half the momentous effects of uncontrolled development. Sustainable development must be contoured to local needs rather than imposed from afar by economic forces.

17 When we reached the Strait of Magellan, residents of southern Chile showed us great inland sounds that soon will be dammed to power yet more aluminum smelters—this time Australian.

On Tierra del Fuego, they took us to ancient hardwood rainforests, scheduled to be turned into fax paper by Canadian and Japanese companies.

18 Finally, we stood with Professor Bedrich Magas of Chile's Magellan University at the tip of the Americas, looking out toward the growing polar ozone hole. Magas reminded us that the National Aeronautics and Space Administration had recently discovered destructive chlorine over the northern United States—just like that which was found over Antarctica only a few years earlier. It was a disturbing reminder of the warning of the Guaraní shaman: what we do to the lives and lands of others may ultimately determine the fate of our own.

## Comprehension Test 24*

### Checking Your Comprehension

1. Why is Iguazú no longer sacred to the Guaraní?

2. Why were the black laurel and ceiba trees in the Indian villages of Argentina replaced by Monterey pine?

3. Explain why the Yuguí Indians of the Bolivian Amazon referred to "world" as "leaves."

4. Why were many people from the Cofán in Ecuador forced to leave after the petroleum companies came?

### Thinking Critically

1. What did the authors mean when they said that impoverished populations struck a "Faustian bargain with the developed world . . ."?

2. Why did Ataiba, a Yuguí chief, lead his people from the forest to the mission village? Was this decision in the best interest of his people? Why or why not?

3. How has life for the Cofán in Ecuador "irrevocably changed"? Was it changed for better or for worse?

4. What do you think Moreira meant by saying "when the Indians vanish, the rest will follow"?

---

* Multiple-choice questions are contained in Appendix B (page A6).

**Questions for Discussion**

1. How are human cultures becoming an "endangered species"?

2. What are the moral implications of poor nations borrowing huge sums of money from foreign banks to build dams that displace native poor people?

3. According to the passage, Indian villages in Argentina are being systematically destroyed by the government, *without* the permission of the inhabitants, to make way for commercial developments. What does this say about the financial and cultural interests of the government in South America?

| Selection 24: | | 1330 words |
|---|---|---|
| Finishing Time: | | |
| | HR.    MIN.    SEC. | |
| Starting Time: | | |
| | HR.    MIN.    SEC. | |
| Reading Time: | | |
| | MIN.    SEC. | |
| WPM Score: | | |
| Comprehension Score: | | _____% |

---

**Visit the Longman English Pages**

For additional readings and exercises, visit the Longman English Skills Web page at:

**http://longman.awl.com/englishpages**

For a username and password, please see your instructor.

# Task Performance Assessment
# UNIT FOUR

The following task is designed to assess your ability to use and apply the skills taught in this unit.

## THE SETTING

Assume you are taking an English class and you have been given the assignment of writing a paper analyzing an argument. Your instructor has given you two articles on gun control and expects you to read both articles and then choose one to write about. You are expected to analyze the article and explain the strengths and weaknesses of the arguments. As you read the articles, you are evaluating each argument. In particular, you are looking to see how each author defends his or her position.

## THE TASKS

The two attached readings discuss gun control. Be sure to read them carefully and completely before beginning any of the tasks listed. You may reread the pieces as often as necessary. Feel free to highlight or write marginal notes.

### READING A

Guns don't kill people, people kill people. Gun laws do not deter criminals. (A 1976 University of Wisconsin study of gun laws concluded that "gun control laws have no individual or collective effect in reducing the rate of violent crime.") A mandatory sentence for carrying an unlicensed gun, says Kates, would punish the "ordinary decent citizens in high-crime areas who carry guns illegally because police protection is inadequate and they don't have the special influence necessary to get a 'carry' permit." There are fifty million handguns out there in the United States already; unless you were to use a giant magnet, there is no way to retrieve them. The majority of people do not want guns banned. A ban on handguns would be like Prohibition—widely disregarded, unenforceable, and corrosive to the nation's sense of moral order. Federal registration is the beginning of federal tyranny; we might someday need to use those guns against the government.

Smith, "Fifty Million Handguns."

**READING B**

People kill people, but handguns make it easier. When other weapons (knives, for instance) are used, the consequences are not so often deadly. Strangling or stabbing someone takes a different degree of energy and intent than pulling a trigger. Registration will not interfere with hunting and other rifle sports but will simply exercise control over who can carry handguns. Ordinary people do not carry handguns. If a burglar has a gun in his hand, it is quite insane for you to shoot it out with him, as if you were in a quick draw contest in the Wild West. Half of all the guns used in crimes are stolen; 70% of the stolen guns are handguns. In other words, the supply of handguns used by criminals already comes to a great extent from the households these guns were supposed to protect.

Smith, "Fifty Million Handguns."

1. In preparing to write your paper, identify each author's stand on gun control and examine his or her reasons for taking that position. Pay particular attention to how each author supports his or her position. Begin by preparing a summary sheet for each reading. Do this by supplying the missing information in the summary sheet below.

**READING A**

Position on Gun Control:

_____

_____

_____

Supporting Information:

a.

b.

c.

**READING B**

Position on Gun Control:

_____

_____

_____

Supporting Information:

a.



b.



c.



2. Write a one-page paper in which you evaluate the position taken by either Author A or Author B. State the author's position, examine the evidence, and explain the strengths and weaknesses of the argument. Be sure to evaluate fact versus opinion and give examples. Discuss the author's use of generalizations, again giving examples. Evaluate the relevance and sufficiency of evidence and indicate what further information is necessary.

# UNIT 5

# How to Increase Your Reading Rate and Flexibility

Before beginning this section it is essential that you agree with the following statement: Not everything in print is equally important, and depending on your purpose, some material is not worth reading at all. In many situations reading material is important only if it contains information you need to learn or that you are interested in learning. Of course at times you may read for entertainment or enjoyment, in which case you are not concerned with importance. An efficient reader should be able to locate portions of material that fulfill his or her purpose and skip those portions that do not. For example, you may decide to read a newspaper movie review to get a general impression of the film. In that case, it is not necessary to read detailed descriptions of particular scenes or of actors' performances. Or, you may read a magazine article to find a specific piece of information. In that case, most of the article is unimportant, and reading it would be an inefficient use of your time.

The purpose of this section is to present several very useful techniques that will allow you to read selectively—reading what is important and skipping what does not suit your immediate purpose. Chapter 13 discusses a technique called skimming, or locating only the most important ideas in any type of material. It also discusses scanning, the technique of rapidly locating particular types of information. Chapter 14 describes several techniques for reading faster.

# CHAPTER 13
# Skimming and Scanning

IN THIS CHAPTER YOU WILL LEARN:

1. To skim to get an overview of an article.
2. To scan to locate specific information quickly.

Most students are accustomed to reading everything completely. In fact, in most academic reading, full, complete reading *is* necessary. However, there are times when complete comprehension is not needed. In those situations, skimming and scanning are alternate reading strategies that may save you time.

## ■ SKIMMING

Suppose that you are browsing through magazines in the library, and just before it is time to leave for your next class, you find a two- or three-page article that you are interested in reading. You cannot check out the magazine, and you do not have time to read it before class. You know that you will not take the time to come back later to find the magazine and read the article. What do you do?

One alternative is to forget about the article and go to class. A second alternative is to *skim* the article, reading some parts and skipping others, to find the most important ideas. You would read the parts of the article that are most likely to provide the main ideas and skip those that contain less important facts and details. *Skimming* means reading selectively to get a general idea of what an article is about.

This chapter discusses the purposes and types of skimming, presents a step-by-step procedure for skimming, and shows how to adopt the technique to various types of reading material.

### ■ Purposes for Skimming

It is not always necessary to read everything completely. In fact, in some circumstances thorough reading may be an inefficient use of your time. Let's take a moment to consider a few examples of material for which skimming would be the most effective technique to use:

**445**

1. **A section of a text chapter that reviews the metric system.** If you have already learned and used the metric system, you can afford to skip over much of the material.

2. **A section of a reference book that you are using to complete a research paper.** If you have already collected most of your basic information, you might skim through additional references, looking only for new information not discussed in sources used previously.

3. **A newspaper report of a current political event.** If you are reading the article only to learn the basic information, skimming is appropriate. You can skip sections of the article that give details.

4. **A movie review.** If you are reading the review to decide whether you want to see the movie, you are probably looking for the writer's overall reaction to the movie: Was it exciting? Was it boring? Was it humorous? You can skip in-depth descriptions of characters, particular scenes, and particular actors' or actresses' performances.

Now try to think of some other situations or types of material that might be appropriate for you to skim. List them in the spaces provided.

1. _____

2. _____

3. _____

You can see that skimming is appropriate when complete information is *not* required. Use skimming when you need only the most important ideas or the "gist" of the article. Your *purpose* for reading is crucial in determining when it is appropriate to skim.

## ■ How to Skim

In skimming, your overall purpose should be to read only those parts of an article or selection that contain the most important information. Skip what is not important. The type of material you are reading will, in part, determine how you should adapt your reading techniques.

To acquaint you with the process of skimming, a basic, step-by-step procedure is presented and applied to a sample article. Then adaptations of this general technique to specific types of reading materials are discussed.

As a general guide, read the following items:

**The title.** The title often announces the subject and provides clues about the author's approach or attitude toward the subject.

**The subtitle or introductory byline.** Some types of material include a statement underneath the title that further explains the title or is written to catch the reader's interest.

**The introductory paragraph.** The introductory paragraph often provides important background information and introduces the subject. It may also provide a brief overview of how the subject is treated.

**The headings.** A heading announces the topic that will be discussed in the paragraphs that follow. When read successively, the headings form an outline or list of topics covered.

**The first sentence of each paragraph.** Most paragraphs are built around a topic sentence, which states the main idea of the paragraph. The most common position for the main idea is in the first sentence of the paragraph. If you read a first sentence that clearly *is not* the topic sentence, you might jump to the end of the paragraph and read the last sentence. (See Chapter 4 for a more detailed discussion of main ideas and topic sentences.)

**Key words.** Quickly glance through the remainder of the paragraph. Try to pick out key words that answer who, what, when, where, or how much about the main idea of the paragraph. Try to notice names, numbers, dates, places, and capitalized or italicized words and phrases. Also notice any numbered sequences. This quick glance will add to your overall impression of the paragraph and will confirm that you have identified the main idea of the paragraph.

**The title or legend of any maps, graphs, charts, or diagrams.** The title or legend will state concisely what the typographical aid depicts and suggest what important event, idea, or relationship it is intended to emphasize.

**The last paragraph.** The last paragraph often provides a conclusion or summary for the article. It might state concisely the main points of the article or suggest new directions for considering the topic. If it is lengthy, read only the last few lines.

Now that you are familiar with the procedure for skimming, you are probably wondering how fast to skim, how much to skip, and what level of comprehension to expect. Your reading rate should generally be 800 wpm or above for skimming, or about three or four times as fast as you normally read.

As a general rule of thumb, you should skip more than you read. Although the amount to skip varies according to the type of material, a safe estimate might be that you should skip about 70 to 80 percent of the material. Because you are skipping large portions of the material, your comprehension will be limited. An acceptable level of comprehension for skimming is often 50 percent, although it may vary according to your purpose.

To give you a better idea of what the technique of skimming is like, the following article has been *highlighted* to indicate the portions of the article that you might read when skimming. Of course, this is not the only correct way to skim this article. Depending on their purposes for reading, readers could identify different parts of the article as important. Also, readers might select different key words and phrases while glancing through each paragraph.

## FUNCTIONS OF THE FAMILY

We can see from the functionalist perspective that the family in virtually all societies serves the same basic functions. Although the importance of each function varies from one society to another, the family provides for sexual regulation, reproduction, socialization, economic cooperation, and emotional security.

### SEXUAL REGULATION

No society advocates total sexual freedom. Although societies have very different sexual norms, all impose some control on who may have sex with whom. Even societies that encourage premarital and extramarital sex restrict and channel these activities so that they reinforce the social order. The Trobrianders of the South Pacific, for example, use premarital sex to determine whether a girl is fertile and to prepare adolescents for marriage. Traditional Eskimo society condones extramarital sex, but under conditions that do not disrupt family stability: as a gesture of hospitality, husbands offer their wives to overnight guests.

Traditionally, Western sexual norms have been relatively restrictive, demanding that people engage in sex only with their spouses. Tying sex to marriage seems to serve several functions. First, it helps minimize sexual competition, thereby contributing to social stability. Second, it gives young people an incentive to marry. Even today, most young adults eventually feel dissatisfied with unstable, temporary sexual liaisons and find a regular, secure sexual relationship in marriage an attractive prospect. Even most of the divorced, who usually find their postmarital sex lives very pleasurable, eventually remarry because they are more interested in sex with commitment, as available in marriage. Finally, encouraging people to marry and confining sexual intercourse to those who are married tends to ensure that children will be well cared for.

### REPRODUCTION

In order to survive, a society must produce children to replace the adults and elderly who die, and practically all societies depend on the family to produce these new members. In some traditional societies, such as the Baganda of Uganda, children are considered so important that a marriage must be dissolved if the wife turns out

to be barren. In many industrialized nations like the United States, families with children are rewarded with tax exemptions, and sexual acts that cannot produce pregnancy, such as homosexuality and anal intercourse, are condemned as perversions.

## SOCIALIZATION

To replace its dead members, a society needs not just biological reproduction but also sociological reproduction. It needs, in other words, to transmit its values to the new generation, to socialize them. [. . .] the family is the most important agent of socialization. Because parents are likely to be deeply interested in their own children, they are generally more effective socializing agents than other adults.

## ECONOMIC COOPERATION

Besides socialization, children also need physical care—food, clothing, and shelter. Fulfilling these needs is the core of the family's economic function, and it can facilitate effective socialization. Generally, however, the family's economic role goes beyond care for children and embraces the whole family. Family members *cooperate* as an economic unit. Each person's fate rises and falls with that of the family as a whole.

## EMOTIONAL SECURITY

Finally, the family is the center of emotional life. [. . .] the relationships we form in our families as children may shape our personalities and create hard-to-break patterns for all our relationships. Throughout life, the family is the most important source of primary relationships, the most likely place for us to turn to when we need comfort or reassurance.

## VARIATIONS

At various times and places, some of these functions have been more important than others. In some societies in the past, the family was the center of educational, religious, political, economic, and recreational activities. Children received all their education from their parents. Religious practices were an integral part of family life. The head of the family assumed authority for allocating chores and settling disputes. The whole family pitched in to work on their farm or to make tools and other products in their home. Leisure activities were typically a family affair, with members entertaining one another [. . .]

Although business, schools, churches, and government have taken over a large share of many of the family's functions, these impersonal organizations cannot provide intimate emotional support. This function still falls almost entirely on the family. A large extended family provides diffuse emotional security, in which the married couple expects companionship not only from each other but also from many other relatives. In the nuclear family, relations between husband and wife become more intense and exclusive. Their emotional importance is accentuated in societies such as the United States, which emphasizes individualism and privacy.

Often, we view the world outside as a mass of strangers. We feel lonely, isolated, and alienated from that world, and see the family as a refuge. The emotional satisfactions of the family have become its main bond, its main reason for being.

Thio, *Sociology: A Brief Introduction.*

• • •

## EXERCISE 13–1

*DIRECTIONS:* After you have skimmed the article on the family, answer the following questions. For each item, indicate whether the statement is true or false by marking T or F in the space provided.

_____ 1.   The family serves similar functions in different societies.

_____ 2.   Compared with others, Western sexual norms are liberal.

_____ 3.   A family cooperates to provide for its members' physical needs.

_____ 4.   The central function of a family is socialization.

_____ 5.   All functions of the family are equally important.

## EXERCISE 13–2

*DIRECTIONS:* Skim the following article by Susan Gilbert from *Science Digest* on noise pollution. Your purpose for reading is to learn about the causes, effects, and control of noise pollution. Answer the questions following the article when you have finished skimming.

### NOISE POLLUTION
#### THE VOLUME CONTINUES TO RISE, YET THE RESEARCH MONEY DWINDLES

Loud noise is the most pervasive kind of pollution. Scientific studies have shown that it not only harms the ears, it alters moods, reduces learning ability and may increase blood pressure. It doesn't take the earsplitting clatter of a jackhammer for a city dweller to experience, daily, enough noise to cause permanent hearing loss. The screeching of traffic, the din in a crowded restaurant, the roar of airplanes overhead—even music from blaring radios—are enough to exceed the maximum noise the federal government permits in workplaces for an eight-hour day.

The Environmental Protection Agency, once committed to reducing the insidious problem of noise, has been stifled in its attempts to do anything. Its $14-million program to curb noise pollution was eliminated four years ago. Some government agencies, however, have been successful. The Federal Aviation Administration has forced airplanes to cut noise levels by half within two miles of taking off and landing at major airports. New York City adopted the nation's first antinoise code in 1972 and imposes $25 fines for violations, although a majority of cab drivers still lean more on their horns than on their brakes. Chicago, San Francisco and a host of other cities have taken similar measures. In fact, it was such legislation that rallied the forces opposed to the Chicago Cubs playing night baseball at Wrigley Field.

## HAZARDOUS HEADPHONES

Many of the most damaging noises, however, are within the power of all of us to control, simply by using a little common sense. Consider the use of stereo headphones—devices that mask uncomfortable noise with entertaining sound. A study by otolaryngologist Phillip Lee, of the University Hospital in Iowa City, disclosed that teenagers who used stereo headphones for three hours suffered temporary hearing loss. These devices proved to be exceptionally damaging when played at 100 decibels or more, the intensity of a chain saw. "People should not turn them up above a normal, conversational level," says Lee.

While stunning and sudden explosions can cause deafness by rupturing an eardrum, hearing can be at least partially restored by surgery. Not so with sustained environmental noises; the damage they cause is often irreversible. As sounds enter the inner ear, they wave hair cells back and forth, causing them to release a chemical transmitter to the nerve fibers that carry auditory messages to the brain. This is how we hear. But too much noise can exhaust—even kill—some hair cells. The effect may be a slight temporary hearing loss or a ringing in the ears.

"A few missing hair cells won't damage hearing permanently," says neurobiologist Barbara Bohne, of the Washington University School of Medicine in St. Louis. "But a few lost each weekend will gradually lead to noticeable hearing problems. Once this happens, it's too late to do anything." But some precautions can be taken. Earplugs and muffs, which reduce noise by as much as 25 decibels, can make the difference between hazardous and safe exposure. And, adds Bohne, "If you have to cut wood with a chain saw, do it for an hour one Saturday and another hour the following week, rather than for two hours at once." Separating periods of intense noise with at least a day of relative quiet can allow stunned hair cells time to recover.

Noise certainly makes us angry, but does it increase our blood pressure? Studies have been contradictory. Otolaryngologist Ernest Peterson, of the University of Miami, found that noise makes monkeys' blood pressure rise. But in a letter published in *The Lancet* last fall, a Swedish doctor reported no such effect on shipyard workers after studying them for eight years.

Noise's impact on the brain has been measured with more certainty. Children in schools located on loud streets score well below their socioeconomic counterparts in quiet schools, according to the California Department of Health Services.

Two British psychologists, reporting last year in the *Journal of the Acoustical Society of America*, found that suburban traffic of about 46 decibels (comparable to the hum of a refrigerator) impairs sleep. When the amount of noise entering subjects' bedrooms was reduced by five decibels (to the level of soft speech), their brains showed an increase in low-frequency, high-amplitude delta waves—a sign of deep sleep.

Audiologist John Mills, of the Medical College of South Carolina, believes that the brain is "the most significant area in need of further study." He reports that in several animal experiments, 65 decibels of sound sustained for 24 hours (the same level as that produced by an air conditioner) were found somehow to damage the brain stem. This, says Mills, is reason enough to investigate whether the same damage occurs in humans. "When does injury to the brain begin?" he asks. "Is it independent of injury to the ear? These are the things we must learn."

● ● ●

1. How does noise pollution affect humans?

   _____

2. Give several examples of noise pollution.

   _____

3. Has the Environmental Protection Agency been successful in controlling noise pollution?

   _____

4. What questions remain unanswered about the effects of noise pollution?

   _____

## ■ Using Skimming Effectively

Now that you are familiar with the steps involved in skimming, you may realize that it is very similar to a technique you learned earlier in this book—prereading. Actually, prereading may be considered as one form of skimming. Generally, there are three types of skimming:

1. **Preview skimming:** to become generally familiar with the organization and content of material *before* reading it. This is the type of skimming that is equivalent to prereading. (See Chapter 2.)

2. **Overview skimming:** to get an *overview* of the content and organization without reading the material completely. Often referred to as skim-reading, this form of skimming is used when you do not intend to return to reading the material for another more thorough reading and when skimming alone meets your needs.

3. **Review skimming:** to go back over material you have already read to *review* the main points. Your purpose is to become reacquainted with the basic content and organization of the material. (Chapter 8 discusses review in detail.)

### Limitations of Skimming

Because skimming involves skipping large portions of the material, you should not expect to retain the less important facts and details. As mentioned previously, you can expect a comprehension level of about 50 percent when skimming. Use skimming *only* when your purpose for reading allows you to read for general concepts rather than specific information.

### Alternating Skimming and Reading

Many effective readers alternate between skimming and more careful reading. In a given article, for example, you may skim several sections until you come to a section that is of particular interest or that fulfills your purpose for reading. At that point, you may read completely rather than skim, and then continue skimming later sections. At other times, it may be necessary to read completely when you feel confused or when you encounter difficult or unfamiliar ideas.

### Skimming Electronic Sources

Skimming electronic sources is easily done by scrolling through the document by using the down arrow or the page down key. Soon you'll develop a rhythm that allows you to quickly glance at each screen before moving on to the next.

When you skim an electronic source you do not have the benefit of the full text in front of you at one time. By paging through a print source, you can pick up initial clues about length, organization, placement of graphics, and relative importance of ideas. To obtain these initial clues, consider scrolling through the entire document very quickly, noticing only major headings, graphics, and length. Then skim the document using the suggestions given.

## ■ Skimming Various Types of Material

Effective skimming hinges on the reader's ability to recognize the organization and structure of the material and to locate the main ideas of the selection. The procedure for skimming outlined in the earlier section, "How to Skim," is a general guide that must be adapted to the material. Table 13.1 on page 454 lists suggestions for skimming textbooks, reference sources, newspaper and magazine articles, and nonfiction books.

**Table 13.1** Adapting Your Skimming Strategy

| Type of Material | Focus on |
|---|---|
| Textbook chapters | 1. Chapter objectives and introductions<br>2. Headings and typographical aids<br>3. Graphic and visual aids<br>4. Review and discussion questions |
| Reference sources | 1. Date<br>2. Organization of the source<br>3. Topical index |
| Newspaper articles | 1. Title<br>2. Opening paragraphs<br>3. First sentences of remaining paragraphs |
| Magazine articles | 1. Title/subtitle/byline<br>2. Opening paragraphs<br>3. Photograph/captions<br>4. Headings/first sentences<br>5. Last several paragraphs |
| Nonfiction books | 1. Front and back cover of book jacket<br>2. Author's credentials<br>3. Table of contents<br>4. Preface<br>5. First and last chapters |

## EXERCISE 13–3

*DIRECTIONS:* Suppose you are taking a course in environmental studies; the following article by William Booth has been assigned by your instructor. It is one of 15 recommended newspaper articles to be read for the purpose of discussing recent scientific developments. As an overview, skim the article. As you skim, underline key statements. Then answer the questions that follow.

### NEVER-ENDING QUEST FOR ABSOLUTE ZERO
#### IT'S A PLACE OF BEAUTY, MYSTERY

WASHINGTON—Until recently, the coldest spot in the universe has been the empty void of deep space. But space is balmy compared to the ultra-frigid temperatures being pursued by laboratories in New York and Florida, where dueling refrigerators are approaching the ultimate in cold: a state called absolute zero.

For scientists who pursue record cold temperatures, absolute zero is a place of beauty and mystery. In this super-cold clime, strange and new phenomena begin to unfold: Conductors become superconducting (losing all resistance to the flow of electricity); fluids become superfluid (losing all viscosity), and all matter attempts to reach a state of perfect order.

"We have theories. We have laws. But we really don't know what will happen until we cool things down," said Robert Richardson of Cornell University. "Low-temperature physics is largely the physics of the unknown."

Near the ultimate limits of cold, the research refrigerators that fill entire buildings are so sensitive that even stray radio waves, or earthquakes on the other side of the world, can create vibrations that jiggle the supercold atoms, which—like rubbing two sticks together—will send temperatures in the experiment soaring.

Absolute zero is 459.67 degrees below zero Fahrenheit. Scientists measure such extremes not in degrees, but in a scale that uses units called kelvins, or K, which are named for William Thomson Kelvin, the 19th century British physicist who proposed the scale. Absolute zero is 0 K.

Until scientists learned to manipulate cold in their laboratories, the lowest known temperature in the universe was 3 K, occurring in the void of space between the stars. Early in this century, scientists managed to liquefy helium gas by subjecting it to repeated cycles of cooling in special refrigerators. Once liquefied, helium stays colder than 4 K and can be stored in the laboratory equivalent of a thermos bottle. Several years later, in 1911, scientists found that certain materials suddenly become superconductors at these low temperatures.

In the past few years, laboratories in Britain, Japan and Finland—using ever more sophisticated refrigerators and better insulators—have reached temperatures of a few millionths of a kelvin. In special settings, individual atomic nuclei have been cooled to a few billionths of a kelvin. Scientists at new laboratories funded by the National Science Foundation at Cornell University and the University of Florida are now trying to match, and perhaps exceed, these record lows. They hope to learn how matter organizes itself without the disturbing effects of heat and why materials become superconducting or superfluid. Researchers are trying to cool down silicon, helium and thin films of metals such as silver and platinum.

In all materials, solids as well as gases and liquids, atoms are constantly in motion, vibrating and colliding with each other, creating thermal energy. The wilder the motion, the greater the heat.

"Before the laws of quantum mechanics were revealed, absolute zero was thought of as the temperature when all motion would come to a stop," when atoms, and their subatomic components such as electrons and protons, would stop their frenetic vibrations and collisions, "and would collapse as if into a black hole," said Dwight Adams, a low-temperature physicist at the University of Florida at Gainesville.

This is now known to be untrue. At absolute zero, atoms would still vibrate. Electrons would still swirl in a cloud around the nucleus. Indeed, helium would even remain in a liquid state at absolute zero, unless it was placed under enough pressure to force it into a solid.

But the atomic order at 0 K would be perfect. In a solid, each atom, though quietly wiggling, would occupy a precise location in the material. In a liquid or gas, even though the atoms may move from spot to spot, they would move in unison. They would all be in perfect order, or in what physicists call the same quantum state.

To reach this state, all thermal energy must be extracted from the system. Atomic motion must be slowed to a crawl. To get to this cold, scientists must first employ a special "dilution refrigerator," basically an elaborate version of an ordinary kitchen fridge, but with a lot more pumps, valves, heat exchangers, condensers and tubes, which are filled with liquid helium instead of Freon.

Liquid helium, already under 4 K, can cool materials down to a few thousandths of a kelvin. But to go further requires superconducting magnets. These magnets are immersed in the liquid helium and surround a rod of copper. The low temperatures and the high magnetic field cause all the nuclei in the copper atoms to align like tiny compass needles that all point in the same direction. The researchers then reduce the magnetic field, which causes the copper nuclei to resume their random orientations. This return to random order absorbs the last rays of heat from the environment.

But these temperatures are the most tenuous of states. The enemy is stray heat from outside. The researchers at Cornell and Florida have constructed whole rooms and buildings to shield their refrigerators from heat, which sneaks in as radio waves, or from cosmic background radiation, or from anything that causes vibration: trucks on the freeway, distant earthquakes, slamming doors. Each creates minute vibrations that jar the supercold atoms and cause them to bump, raising temperatures.

Yet no matter what the scientists do, they will never quite achieve absolute zero. The closer they get, the larger the relative effect of the slightest amount of heat that gets in. "We can get close, very close, but it will always be beyond us." said Richardson of Cornell. And that, he said, is part of its allure.

● ● ●

1. What is absolute zero?

_____

2. Explain the title. That is, explain why the quest will be never-ending.

_____

3. How have scientists attempted to reach absolute zero?

_____

4. Why are scientists interested in absolute zero?

_____

## EXERCISE 13–4

*DIRECTIONS:* Assume you are a member of a collegiate sports team, and you notice the following article by Andrea Dorfman in a magazine you are browsing through between classes. Read the first two paragraphs completely to learn what is meant by "flow state"; skim the remainder of the article and look for techniques that might improve your athletic performance. (You may stop and read completely any sections that are of particular interest.) Then answer the questions that follow.

## RACING THE BRAIN
## DO "FLOW STATES" PROVIDE THE WINNING EDGE?

When the checkered flag drops at the start of the Indy 500 on May 26, drivers will push their fine-tuned machines to 220 miles an hour—over a football field a second. The winner of this endurance test will be determined in part by skill and strategy, but mental attitude also counts. Some maintain that the key is an experience called a "flow state."

Despite its name, a flow state has nothing to do with engineering. It's a race-car driver so in tune with his machine that split-second decisions become automatic. "It's when you know what you have to go after, and that's all that matters," says Mario Andretti. "Anything else is a distraction." To driver Benny Parsons, "Everything is under control. The world is at your fingertips, and you're revolving it any way you want to."

Researchers are exploring scientific explanations for this phenomenon. The brain has two hemispheres, each with its own responsibilities. The left half is involved in analytical or tactical reasoning, while the right side is intuitive and deals with spatial tasks. Electroencephalogram (EEG) studies of Olympic marksmen and archers have shown that their actions are reflected in the brain. While the athletes are thinking of loading their rifle or positioning their arrow, the left side of the brain is active. As they focus, aim and fire, the right hemisphere takes over.

Although these results could be explained by the shift from an analytical to a spatial task, the right brain does become dominant during exercise. "Coaches always say, 'Concentrate, concentrate, concentrate,'" says Ohio University exercise physiologist Fritz Hagerman, who helped conduct a study of NASCAR drivers' fitness. "But the last thing you want to do is let the mind interfere, at least on a conscious level. A sports psychologist once said to me that once you learn how to do something, you should have your head cut off."

Exercise researcher Brad Hatfield, who did the Olympic athlete studies with Daniel Landers, of Arizona State University, Tempe, is now investigating whether "runner's high" is a type of flow state. In his laboratory at the University of Maryland, Hatfield is looking for shifts in brain-wave activity in the EEGs of highly conditioned runners before and after they spend 45 minutes on a treadmill. (EEG recordings are too sensitive to be made while the subject is moving.) Using an opiate-blocking drug called naloxone, Hatfield may also test whether endorphins, the body's endogenous opiates, help to induce runner's high.

### UNCONSCIOUS ACTIVITY

The possibility that flow states involve seemingly unconscious actions is reinforced by Benjamin Libet's work, reported in a 1983 issue of *Brain.* A neurophysiologist at the University of California, San Francisco, Libet found that the brain is active nearly one-half second before a person becomes aware of a weak electrical pulse on his skin. Libet speculates that this unconscious activity involves the supplementary motor area on the midline of the cerebral cortex.

Time distortion is another aspect of flow states frequently cited by athletes: Complex maneuvers that occupy milliseconds feel like they're done in slow motion. "The monitoring of time is primarily a left-hemisphere activity," Hatfield says. "We know from EEG recordings that left-hemisphere activity becomes reduced, so it's not surprising that its time-monitoring capabilities are inhibited."

If flow states can be documented scientifically, could athletes be trained to achieve them—and thus improve their performance? Both Landers and Hatfield believe that flow states are a learned response, perhaps available only to highly skilled athletes. Timothy Gallwey's theories of Inner Tennis and Inner Skiing propose that learning to make what he calls the reasoning "Self 1" stand aside so that the intuitive "Self 2" can operate unencumbered would produce better performance.

Richard Suinn, who heads the Colorado State University psychology department, developed visual motor behavior rehearsal (VMBR), which trains an athlete first to relax discrete muscle groups and then to "image"—in detail—his upcoming performance. "You might be a tennis player preparing for a match at Wimbledon," Suinn explains. "If you know your opponent's style and strengths, you might practice one aspect of the game, like return of serve. Or you might be a cross-country runner who needs to familiarize himself with a course by visualizing the whole thing."

A study of New York City college basketball players found that VMBR increased their free-throw accuracy far more than relaxation or imagery alone. "People say there are different types of motor learning," Suinn notes. "Imaging may have to do with a transfer of what you have in left-brain learning into right-brain storage. Flow, then, approximates a state in which information is stored so well in the right brain that you don't have to use the left to trigger it to become active." But, he cautions, content is crucial: Imaging the wrong behavior can make the correct one harder to learn.

Training techniques will be more effective when scientists determine how to induce a flow state. "We know it exists, but we don't know why," Suinn says. "If we did, we'd see records fall within minutes of each other. We're not anywhere near this. We're just scratching the surface of speculation."

1. What is a "flow state"?

   _____

2. Name several sports or activities for which flow states are discussed in the article.

   _____

3. What is VMBR?

   _____

4. How will athletic training change if the projected flow state research proves fruitful?

   _____

Electronic Application

## EXERCISE 13–5

*DIRECTIONS:* Locate an article on a topic of interest on the Internet. Skim it and then answer the questions that follow.

1. What is the main point of the article?
2. How did the author support or explain this point?
3. How is skimming an internet source different than skimming a print source?

Academic Application

## EXERCISE 13–6

*DIRECTIONS:* Select a chapter from one of your textbooks, skim-read the first five pages of it, and answer the following questions.

1. What general subject is discussed in the chapter?

   _____

2. How is the chapter organized?

   _____

3. Write a brief list of ideas or topics that are discussed in the pages you skimmed.

   _____

   _____

   _____

## EXERCISE 13–7

*DIRECTIONS:* Choose one of the reading selections at the end of the chapter. Skim-read the selection and answer the questions that follow the selection. Do not be concerned if you are unable to answer all the questions correctly; you should expect your rate to be higher but your comprehension lower than on most other readings you have completed up to this point.

## ■ SCANNING

Have you ever searched through a crowd of people for a particular person or looked through a rack of clothing for an item of a particular size, color, or price? Have you ever used a telephone directory to find someone's phone number or address? Have you checked a bus schedule or located a particular book on a library shelf? If so, you used a technique called *scanning*. Scanning is searching for a specific piece of information; your only purpose is to locate that information. In fact, when you scan you are not at all interested in anything else on the page; you have no reason to notice or remember any other information.

Although scanning is a commonly used skill, many people do not know how to scan effectively. Have you ever become frustrated when trying to locate the ad for a particular movie on the entertainment page of a newspaper or when trying to find out at which theater a particular movie is playing? Have you ever had to read a particular article completely to find a particular section or fact? These frustrations probably occurred because you were not scanning in the most effective, systematic manner. That is precisely the focus of this section of the chapter—systematic scanning. Its purpose is to provide you with an organized procedure that will enable you to scan more effectively and efficiently.

## ■ How to Scan

Many people do not scan as efficiently as possible because they randomly search through material, hoping to stumble on the information they are seeking. Scanning in this way is time consuming and frustrating, and it often forces the reader to "give up" and read the entire selection. The key to effective scanning is a systematic approach, described in the following steps:

### 1. Check the Organization

Before you begin to scan, check to see how the article or material is organized.

For *graphics*, check the title of the item you are scanning and other labels, keys, and legends. They state what the graphics are intended to describe and tell you how it is presented.

For *prose selections*, notice the overall structure of the article so that you will be able to predict where in the article you can expect to find your information.

For *electronic* sources, scroll through the entire document to discover its overall organization.

### 2. Form Specific Questions

Fix in your mind what you are looking for by forming specific questions about the topic. For example, when scanning for information about abortions in New York State, ask questions such as these:

- How many abortions were performed in a certain year?
- What rules and limitations restrict abortions?
- Where are most abortions performed?

**Table 13.2** Clues for Scanning

| Type of Information Needed | Clues | Example |
|---|---|---|
| Statistics, amounts, quantities | Numbers (words or digits): words expressing quantities | 1,389,000 gallons of oil . . . |
| Dates, times | Digits, clue words: before, after, during, . . . | After 1986, . . . |
| Definitions | Boldface or italicized print; clue words: is referred to as, can be defined as, means, is termed; pairs of commas enclosing parenthetical information, dashes, parentheses | The playbill (poster) reviewed . . . |
| Reasons/causes | Clue words: because, consequently, for that reason, as a result; enumeration; one cause . . . , a second cause . . . | Consequently, air flows upward . . . |
| Names, places | Capitalized nouns; pairs of parenthetical commas | The famous general, George C. Marshall, . . . |
| Locations, positions | Capitalized nouns, clue words: besides, next to, adjacent, below . . . | In Venezuela . . . |
| Characteristics | Items listed in a series separated by commas; synonyms; features, variables, qualities | Platinum is a steel-gray, malleable, ductile chemical element . . . |
| Process (How does . . . ) | Clue words: first, then, next . . . ; enumeration: 1) . . . , 2) . . . , 3) . . . | First, blood is circulated . . . |

### 3. Anticipate Word Clues

Anticipate clues that may help you locate the answer more rapidly. For example, if you were trying to locate the population of New York City in an article on the populations of cities, you might expect the answer to appear in digits such as 2,304,710, or in words such as "two million" or "three million." If you were looking for the name of a political figure in a newspaper article, you should expect to find two words, both capitalized. Table 13.2 lists additional clues for finding various types of information. Try to fix the image of your clue words or phrases in your mind as accurately as possible before you begin to scan.

### 4. Identify Likely Answer Locations

Try to identify likely places where the information you are looking for might appear. You might be able to identify a column or section that contains the needed information. You might be able to eliminate certain sections, or you might be able to predict that the information will appear in a certain portion of the article.

### 5. Use a Systematic Pattern

Scanning should be organized and systematic. Do not randomly skip around, searching for clues. Instead, rhythmically sweep your eyes through the material. The pattern or approach you use will depend on the material. For material printed in narrow six- or seven-word columns, such as newspaper articles, you might move your eyes straight down the middle, catching the phrases on each half of the line. For wider lines of print, a zigzag or Z pattern might be more effective. Using this pattern you would move your eyes back and forth, catching several lines in each movement. When you do come to the information you are looking for, clue words may seem to "pop out" at you.

### 6. Confirm Your Answer

Once you think you have located your information, check to be sure you are correct. Read the sentence that contains the answer to confirm that it is the information you need. Often, headings and key words seem to indicate that you have found your answer when in fact you have located related information, opposite information, or information for another year, country, or similar situation.

Now let us try out this procedure. Assume that you are writing a paper on different types of school environments and you need to find out on what school program the "open classroom" setting was based. You have located a reference book on educational programs that contains the following section. Use each of the steps previously listed to find the answer to your question.

#### TYPES OF SCHOOL SETTINGS

There are all kinds of schools—large or small, rural or urban, public or private, rich or poor, and so forth. While it is impossible to discuss each of the numerous ways in which schools differ from each other, we can consider some of the more important dimensions and the effects they have on the development of children.

One of the dimensions that has reached attention is school size. In a well-known study, Barker and Gump focused on schools with student populations ranging between 35 and 2,200. While a wider variety of extracurricular activities was available in larger schools, there was greater participation in such activities in the smaller schools, producing stronger school identification. Perhaps as a result, dropout rates were lower in smaller schools than they were in larger ones.

Probably of greater importance is the type of curriculum or classroom structure children encounter. Until the period between 1960 and 1970 most children could be expected to be taught within a *traditional classroom* setting. This is still the most common arrangement and the one with which the majority of us are most familiar. It generally consists of children seated in rows in a rectangular classroom all listening to a teacher lecture or all working on the same task. Most of the tasks focus on developing the basic skills of reading, writing, and mathematical computation.

During the last two decades a new approach, often referred to as the *open classroom* setting, was adopted in some American schools. It was based on the British Infant School programs, but its philosophy was quite different. Greater attention was given to individuality and an emphasis on active involvement, or "learning by doing." The atmosphere in an open classroom contrasts sharply with that in a traditional setting. For example, children will be observed working individually or in groups at different tasks. Some may be in a corner reading by themselves, two or three others may be cooperating on a science project, while others may be receiving instruction from the teacher on how to operate a computer.

Gander and Gardiner, *Child and Adolescent Development.*

● ● ●

First, in assessing the organization of the material, you see that it is divided into four paragraphs, but that no additional headings are provided. Next, fixing in your mind what you are looking for is an easy task because this hypothetical situation is already well defined. Then, in anticipating the form of the answer, you suspect that the name of a program would be capitalized and that it may use words such as *school, system,* or *education.* Also, because you are looking for the program on which the "open classroom" setting is based, you might also use *open classroom* and *based* as possible clue words. In choosing the likely location for the answer, you should identify the fourth paragraph because it contains the phrase *open classroom* in italics. Then, in scanning that paragraph, a Z pattern would be one effective approach and would help you locate the clue word *based* and the word *school,* capitalized. Finally, suspecting that the answer to your question is the British Infant School program, you would read the context to be sure you have identified the correct information. Although the process seems complicated when explained step-by-step, it is actually a very rapid procedure for locating particular facts and ideas.

## ■ Scanning Columnar Materials

Columnar material includes all sorts of information presented in lists, tables, columns, schedules, or charts. Examples of columnar material include dictionaries, plane schedules, TV listings, the *Readers' Guide to Periodical Literature,* and lists of course offerings.

1. **Check to determine the overall organization and then see if it is divided in any particular way.** Notice whether column titles, headings, or any other clues are provided about the material's organization. For instance, you would note that a TV program schedule is organized by day of the week but that it is also arranged by time. In scanning a zip code directory you would see that it is arranged alphabetically but that there is a separate alphabetical list for each state.

2. **Scan for a specific word, phrase, name, date, or place name.** For example, in checking the meaning of a term in *Taber's Cyclopedic Medical Dictionary,* you are looking for a specific word. Or, in looking up a metric equivalent in the glossary of your physics textbook, your purpose is quite specific.

3. **Use the arrow scanning pattern; it is a straight-down-the-column pattern.**

4. **Focus on the first letter of each line until you reach the letter that begins the word you are looking for.** Then focus on the first two letters until you reach the two-letter combination you are searching for. Successively widen your focus until you are looking for whole words.

## EXERCISE 13–8

*DIRECTIONS:* Scan the table shown in Figure 13.1 to answer each of the following questions:

1. How is this table organized?
2. What are the highest and lowest ranking occupations?
3. How does the job of child care worker rank?
4. How does the job of mail carrier rank?
5. What four occupations have the same rank?

## EXERCISE 13–9

*DIRECTIONS:* Suppose you are doing a research paper on plant reproduction and you are using as a reference a book titled *Plants: Basic Concepts in Botany* by Watson Laetsch. Using the portion of the book's index shown in Figure 13.2 on page 456, scan to locate the answer to each of the following questions.

1. On what page(s) would you find information on the reproduction of ferns?

## How Americans Rank Occupations

Occupation is probably the most important source of prestige. All kinds of Americans tend to give the same prestige rating to an occupation. The ranking of various occupations has largely remained the same for the last 45 years. How do people evaluate the occupations? The following table suggests that generally they give higher ratings to those jobs that require more education and offer higher incomes.

| Occupation | Score | Occupation | Score | Occupation | Score |
|---|---|---|---|---|---|
| Physician | 82 | Journalist | 60 | Child care worker | 36 |
| Lawyer | 75 | Dietician | 56 | Hairdresser | 36 |
| College professor | 74 | Statistician | 56 | Baker | 35 |
| Architect | 73 | Radio/TV announcer | 55 | Upholsterer | 35 |
| Chemist | 73 | Librarian | 54 | Bulldozer operator | 34 |
| Physicist | 73 | Police officer | 54 | Meter reader | 34 |
| Aerospace engineer | 72 | Aircraft mechanic | 53 | Bus driver | 32 |
| Dentist | 72 | Firefighter | 53 | Hotel clerk | 32 |
| Geologist | 70 | Dental hygienist | 52 | Auto body repairman | 31 |
| Clergy | 69 | Social worker | 52 | Apparel salesperson | 30 |
| Psychologist | 69 | Draftsman | 51 | Truck driver | 30 |
| Pharmacist | 68 | Electrician | 51 | Cashier | 29 |
| Optometrist | 67 | Computer operator | 50 | Elevator operator | 28 |
| Registered nurse | 66 | Funeral director | 49 | Garbage collector | 28 |
| Secondary-school teacher | 66 | Real estate agent | 49 | Taxi driver | 28 |
| Accountant | 65 | Machinist | 47 | Waiter/waitress | 28 |
| Air traffic controller | 65 | Mail carrier | 47 | Bellhop | 27 |
| Athlete | 65 | Secretary | 46 | Freight handler | 27 |
| Electrical engineer | 64 | Insurance agent | 45 | Bartender | 25 |
| Elementary-school teacher | 64 | Photographer | 45 | Farm laborer | 23 |
| Mechanical engineer | 64 | Bank teller | 43 | Household servant | 23 |
| Economist | 63 | Welder | 42 | Midwife | 23 |
| Industrial engineer | 62 | Farmer | 40 | Door-to-door salesperson | 22 |
| Veterinarian | 62 | Telephone operator | 40 | Janitor | 22 |
| Airline pilot | 61 | Carpenter | 39 | Car washer | 19 |
| Computer specialist | 61 | TV repairman | 38 | Newspaper vendor | 19 |
| Office manager | 60 | Security guard | 37 | Shoe shiner | 9 |

*Source: General Social Survey Cumulative File.* 1972–1992, Ann Arbor, Mich.: Inter-University Consortium for Political and Social Research. 1992.

**FIGURE 13.1** Columnar material.

**FIGURE 13.2** Reference book index.

2.  On what pages are plants' reproductive organs classified?

    _____

3.  Under what other headings should you check for further information on plant reproduction?

    _____

4.  Does this reference contain information on how potato tubers reproduce? On what page?

    _____

## EXERCISE 13–10

*DIRECTIONS:* Scan the excerpt from the *Readers' Guide to Periodical Literature* shown in Figure 13.3 on page 468 to locate rapidly the answer to each question listed.

1.  Locate the title of an article written by Dan Rather.

    _____

2.  Under what heading should you look to find information about the rating of airline pilots?

    _____

3.  In what periodical did an article appear that discussed rape and pornography?

    _____

4.  What is the source and date of an article written by Nestor Ratesh?

    _____

5.  What periodical contains an article about rap music in California?

    _____

### ■ Scanning Prose Materials

Prose materials are more difficult to scan than columnar material. Their organization is less apparent, and the information is not as concisely or obviously stated. And, unless the headings are numerous and very concise, you may have to scan large amounts of material with fewer locational clues. For prose materials you must rely heavily on identifying clue words and predicting the form of your answer. It is useful to think of scanning prose materials as a floating process in which your eyes drift quickly through a passage searching for clue words and phrases. Your eyes should move across sentences and entire paragraphs, noticing only clue words that indicate that you may be close to locating the answer.

**RAP MUSIC**—Moral and religious aspects—*cont.*
The Dogg is unleashed [interview with Snoop Doggy Dogg] C. J. Farley. il por *Time* v142 p78 D 13 '93
Let's stop crying wolf on censorship. J. Alter. il *Newsweek* v122 p67 N 29 '93
Restricted access [Musicland's labeling of rap albums] D. E. Thigpen. il *Rolling Stone* p13 S 16 '93
Shootin' up the charts [gangsta rappers] R. Lacayo. il *Time* vl42 p81–2 N 15 '93
    **Study and teaching**
Fear of a hip hop syllabus [required listening for rap college courses] il *Rolling Stone* p56+ S 30 '93
    **California**
Is Oaktown in the house? [hip hop in Oakland, Calif.] Touré. il *Rolling Stone* p121 N 25 '93
**RAPAZZINI, JON**
    *about*
"Socially, it's very prestigious . . . ." N. Rotenier. il pors *Forbes* v152 p118+ D 6 '93
**RAPAZZINI, ZONDRA**
    *about*
"Socially, it's very prestigious . . . ." N. Rotenier. il pors *Forbes* v152 p118+ D 6 '93
**RAPAZZINI WINERY**
"Socially, it's very prestigious . . . ." N. Roteiner, il pors *Forbes* v 152 p118+ D 6 '93
**RAPE**
    *See also*
    Acquaintance rape
    Campus rape
    Child molesting
    Date rape
    Marital rape
    Statutory rape
The case for fighting off a rapist. S. Brink. il *U.S. News & World Report* v115 p74 D 20 '93
Cultural assault: what feminists are doing to rape ought to be a crime. M. D. Bonilla. il *Policy Review* no66 p22–9 Fall '93
Rapper sheets [T. Shakur faces charges of sexual assault] B. Hewitt. il pors *People Weekly* v40 p89–90 D 6 '93
Turning rape into pornography: postmodern genocide [rape of Bosnian women; cover story] C. A. MacKinnon. il *Ms.* v4 p24–30 Jl/Ag '93
**RAPIDS, RUNNING OF** *See* Running rapids
**RAPPAPORT, MARK**
    *about*
Rock Hudson's home movies [videotape] Reviews *Premiere* il v6 p43–5 Jl '93. J. Hoberman
**RAPPING, ELAYNE, 1938–**
Who needs the Hollywood Left? il *The Progressive* v57 p34–6 S '93
**RAPPING (MUSIC)** *See* Rap music
**RAPPLEYE, CHARLES**
A star reporter's fall from grace. il pors *Columbia Journalism Review* v32 p41–5 Jl/Ag '93
**RAPTORS** *See* Birds of prey
**RARE ANIMALS**
    *See also*
    Endangered species—Animals
**RARE BIRDS**
    *See also*
    Eagles
    Endangered species—Birds
    Honeycreepers
    Woodpeckers
**RARE BOOKS**
    *See also*
    Manuscripts
New books, big bucks: today's bestseller could become tomorrow's valuable first edition. P. Sherrid. il *U.S. News & World Report* v115 p78–9 D 6 '93
A string of firsts. D. Darlin. il *Forbes* v152 p160–1 O 11 '93
**RARE FISH**
    *See also*
    Endangered species—Fish
**RARE INSECTS**
    *See also*
    Endangered species—Insects
**RARE PLANTS**
    *See also*
    Hawaii Plant Conservation Center
**RARE SPECIES** *See* Endangered species
**RASCHE, JEFFREY A.**
All I need to know about marketing I learned fishing for trout. *The Writer* v106 p9–10 O '93

**RASOLT, MARK**
    *about*
Obituary
    *Physics Today* v46 p133–4 O '93. T. Kaplan and M. Mostoller
**RASSEMBLEMENT POUR LA RÉPUBLIQUE**
Balladur riding the waves. J. Valls-Russell. il por *The New Leader* v76 p8–10 S 6–20 '93
**RATEAU, ARMAND-ALBERT, 1882–1938**
    *about*
Natural talent. C. Petkanas. il por *House & Garden* v165 p84–9+ Jl '93
**RATEGAN, CATHIE**
He said, she said: good talk with good friends. il *Current Health 2* v20 p4–6 S '93
**RATES, ELECTRIC UTILITY** *See* Electric utilities—Rates
**RATES, INTEREST** *See* Interest (Economics)
**RATESH, NESTOR, 1933–**
Romania: slamming on the brakes. *Current History* v92 p390–5 N '93
**RATHER, DAN**
Call it courage [address, September 29, 1993] *Vital Speeches of the Day* v60 p78–81 N 15 '93
    *about*
Over to you, Dan. J. Katz. il pors *Rolling Stone* p44–5+ O 14 '93
**RATHJE, WILLIAM L.**
Less fat? Aw, baloney. il *Garbage* v5 p22–3 S/O '93
**RATINER, STEVEN**
Thinking of Sam. il *Reader's Digest* v143 p120–2 Ag '93
**RATING OF AIR PILOTS** *See* Air pilots—Rating
**RATING OF BONDS** *See* Bonds—Rating
**RATING OF COLLEGE TEACHERS** *See* College teachers—Rating
**RATING OF COLLEGES AND UNIVERSITIES** *See* Colleges and universities—Evaluation
**RATING OF EMPLOYEES** *See* Employees—Rating
**RATING OF EXECUTIVES** *See* Executives—Rating
**RATING OF MOTION PICTURES** *See* Motion pictures—Ratings
**RATING OF TELEVISION PROGRAMS** *See* Television broadcasting—Ratings
**RATIONAL DRUG DESIGN**
Brain by design. R. M. Restak. il *The Sciences* v33 p27–33 S/O '93
**RATIONING, MEDICAL CARE** *See* Medical care rationing
**RATNER, MICHAEL**
Stop repatriation. *The Nation* v257 p624 N 22 '93
**RATS, WOOD (FOSSIL)** *See* Wood rats, Fossil
**RATTLES, TOY** *See* Toys
**RATTLESNAKES**
Rattlesnakes: perfect predators? K. McCafferty. il *Field & Stream* v98 p38 N '93
**RATZINGER, JOSEPH, CARDINAL**
    *about*
Keeper of the straight and narrow. R. N. Ostling. il pors *Time* v142 p58–60 D 6 '93
Sacramental choreography. P. Rosenthal. *America* v169 p14 D 11 '93
**RAUCH, BILL**
    *about*
A community carol [drama] Reviews
*Time* il v142 p68 D 20 '93. W. A. Henry
**RAUF, MAHMOUD ABDUL** *See* Abdul-Rauf, Mahmoud
**RAVAGE, BARBARA**
Staying alive: your choices matter [cover story] il *Current Health 2* v20 p 7–13 S '93
**RAVE CULTURE**
Rave on! D. Bradburn. il *Dance Magazine* v67 p YD5 Jl '93
**RAVEN-SYMONE**
    *about*
Raven-Symone joins Mark Curry as a star of 'Hangin' with Mr. Cooper' [cover story] il pors *Jet* v85 p58–60 N 8 '93
**RAVENS**
    **Food and feeding**
A birdbrain nevermore [ravens] B. Heinrich. il *Natural History* v102 p50–7 O '93
**RAVES** *See* Rave culture
**RAVICHANDRAN, K. G., AND OTHERS**
Crystal structure of hemoprotein domain of P450BM–3, a prototype for microsomal P450's. bibl f il *Science* v261 p731–6 Ag 6 '93
**RAVICHANDRAN, KODIMANGALAM S., AND OTHERS**
Interaction of Sch with the $\zeta$ chain of the T cell receptor upon T cell activation. bibl f il *Science* v262 p902–5 N 5 '93

**FIGURE 13.3** *Readers' Guide to Periodical Literature.*

## EXERCISE 13–11

*DIRECTIONS:* Scan each of the following prose selections to locate the answer to the question indicated. Write your answer in the space provided.

1. From what part of the pepper plant is black pepper made?

   _Black pepper is made from the dried ground fruit on pepper plants_

   Pepper, which has nothing whatever to do with the bell and chili pepper of the family Solanaceae, is one of the oldest and most treasured spices. It is universally incorporated in flavoring, pickling, and preserving food. New trade routes to the "Indies" were sought eagerly in the fifteenth century mostly because of the desire for pepper. Black pepper and white pepper are both obtained from Piper nigrum, of the family Piperaceae. The pepper plant is a high-climbing perennial vine that holds on with **adventitious roots,** which grow from leaves or stems. Black pepper is made from the dried ground fruit of the pepper plant; white pepper comes from the dried ground seeds.

   Laetsch, *Plants: Basic Concepts in Botany.*

   • • •

2. What two countries produce most of the world's supply of cloves?

   _Zanzibar and Indonesia are now the world's greatest producers of cloves_

   The first time that cloves were used as a spice or perfume was recorded in China in the third century B.C., and cloves are still among the most important of commercial spices because of their many uses. As a powder, they flavor sweet and savory dishes and are used in pickling and in making sauces and ketchup. Dried cloves are the desiccated, unexpanded flower buds of the evergreen Eugenia aromatica in the family Myrtaceae (myrtle), which also gives us allspice and the fruit guava. The Moluccas are the original home, but Zanzibar and Indonesia are now the world's greatest producers of cloves, growing 90 percent of the whole crop.

   Laetsch, *Plants: Basic Concepts in Botany.*

   • • •

3. What object do penguins use to identify the sex of another penguin?

   _Song & behavior_

   At the same time as proclaiming their species, individual birds must also declare their sex to one another. Ducks do so with their head patterns for only the drakes develop them. In many species, however—among them, sea birds and birds of prey—the male and female look the same throughout the year. Their sexual identity therefore has to be conveyed by their song and behavior. The male penguin has a particularly charming way of discovering what he wants to know about his uniformly suited companions. He picks up a pebble in his bill, waddles over to a bird standing alone and solemnly lays it before it. If he gets an outraged peck and the squaring up for a fight, he knows he has made a dreadful mistake—this is another male. If his offering is met with total indifference, then he has found a female who is not yet ready to breed or is already paired. He picks up his spurned gift and moves on. But if the stranger receives the pebble with a deep bow then he has discovered his true mate. He bows back and the two stretch up their necks and trumpet a celebratory nuptial chorus.

Attenborough, *Life on Earth.*

● ● ●

4. What organizations use group therapy to help individuals cope with their problems?

*AA, weightwatcher*

One of the most recent innovations in psychotherapy is group therapy. This method is based on the belief that an individual may feel freer to reveal himself when interacting with others who are also troubled. The idea is to create a community feeling in which the individual discovers that he has many experiences and feelings in common with other people. Group therapy is designed to counteract the feeling of alienation, of being "different," or totally alone. A number of techniques, including physical contact and psychodrama, are employed to facilitate interaction. Many groups like Alcoholics Anonymous, Synanon, Gamblers Anonymous, and Weight Watchers now use a modified form of group therapy with considerable success in helping individuals with specific behavioral problems. Lately family therapy also has been tried in an effort to treat the disturbed individual in the environment that possibly contributed to his disturbed behavior.

Perry and Perry, *Face to Face: The Individual and Social Problems.*

● ● ●

5. What factors are controlled to slow the ripening of bananas?

*Ship Before ripe   low tempeture + controlled humidity balance to gases*

Would you have guessed that the foremost commercial fruit is the banana? It is much more than the breakfast or dessert item that so many fruits are, since it is a staple in many countries. When eaten raw, the mature fruits are sweet and delicious, but the unripe fruits and, more commonly, the related plantain can be cooked to provide a starchy food nutritionally similar to the potato.

The banana, which has several species in the genus Musa, is a perennial with a short underground **rhizome** (a rootstalk) that produces both roots and shoots. All edible bananas derive from only two species in the genus Musa, both native to Southeast Asia, from which they have spread widely. The banana is cultivated in plantations and in gardens. A plant is started using **suckers**, shoots arising from the rootstalk. Seven to nine months later the plant will flower, but another few months are needed for the fruit to mature. The flowers grow in compact groups on a large stalk, and in many types the fruit contains no seeds. The fruit itself is white and pulpy, with a tissue of large cells filled with starch and protected by a thick skin. During the ripening much of the starch is converted to sugar.

Banana fruits for export are usually harvested before they are fully ripe and shipped at low temperatures, with carefully controlled humidity and balance between oxygen and carbon dioxide, to slow the ripening. Once at the destination, the fruits are allowed to ripen. Bananas continue to ripen even after you buy them.

Laetsch, *Plants: Basic Concepts in Botany.*

● ● ●

6. How do birds that fly at night know where they are going?

_Stars_

But how do the birds manage to find their way? There seems to be no single answer: they use many methods. Some we are beginning to understand; some mystify us; and there may be some that depend on abilities we have not yet suspected. Many birds certainly follow major geographical features. Summer migrants from Africa fly along the North African coast, converging on the Strait of Gibralter and cross there, where they can see Europe ahead of them. Then they follow valleys, flying over recognized passes through the Alps or the Pyrenees and so arrive at their summer homes. Others take an eastern route by way of the Bosphorus.

But all birds cannot use such straightforward methods. The Arctic tern, for example, has to fly at least 3000 kilometres across the Antarctic Ocean with no land to guide it. We know that some birds, flying at night, navigate by the stars for on cloudy nights they tend to get lost and if they are released in a planetarium where the constellations have been rotated so that they no longer match the position of the stars in the heavens, the birds will follow the visible and artificial ones.

Day-flying birds may use the sun. If they are to do so, they must be able to compensate for the shift of the sun across the sky each day and that means that they must have a precise sense of time. Still others appear to be able to use the earth's magnetic field as a guide. So it seems that many migrating birds must carry in their brains a clock, a compass and the memory of a map. Certainly, a human navigator would need all three if he were to match the journeys that a swallow can make within a few weeks of its hatching.

Attenborough, *Life on Earth.*

● ● ●

7. What is one likely cause of depression?

This form of anxiety is usually classified with the neuroses, but is so widespread that it deserves separate coverage. The characteristic symptoms of depression are sadness, anxiety, insomnia, withdrawal from everyday life and relationships with others, a reduced ability to function and work, and generally agitated behavior. The intensity of depression varies widely: some experience only a mild sense of sadness and others are drawn into suicidal despair. In cases in which despair becomes so profound as to distort reality, the individual is said to be psychotic.

Depression is probably the most common form of mental disorder. Many people will see a physician on the pretext of a physical ailment when in reality they simply feel depressed. Not all sources of depression are clear, but one likely cause is emotional upheaval, whether as the result of losing a close friend or family member, losing one's position in the community, or losing a valued job and status. In our society, many people who are past retirement age experience depression. Presumably, their depression stems from their diminished status in society and the less-than-reverent attitude of the younger generation toward them.

The most significant danger of depression is the possibility of suicide. Suicide will be discussed later in the chapter, but it is important to note that suicide in cases of severe depression is likely to be attempted either at the beginning of the condition or when a cure seems to be successful. It is important, then, that depressed patients be kept under constant observation, even when they seem to be much better.

Perry and Perry, *Face to Face: The Individual and Social Problems.*

● ● ●

8. How were prostitutes regarded during Victorian times?

_____

A definition of prostitution is probably totally unnecessary. We all know that it is the exchange of sex for money or other objects of value. Curiously, prostitution has existed in almost all societies from the earliest times, although societal attitudes toward those who engaged in it have varied greatly. In some societies, and in some historical eras, prostitutes served religious functions: the act was part of ritual, or perceived as a sacrifice to the gods. At other times and in other societies they provided intellectual, as well as sexual stimulation, while wives functioned chiefly to provide heirs and keep the family alive. Often prostitutes were the only well-educated women in a time when women were generally kept in a state of vast ignorance.

For the past several centuries in the societies of Western civilization, however, prostitutes have held less exalted positions. In Victorian times, although they were widely patronized, they were despised by most people as sinful, fallen women who engaged in activities that no self-respecting woman would even think about. Today, although our norms are much more liberal with regard to marital, premarital, and extramarital sex, prostitutes are still considered disreputable and promiscuous because they use sex to make a living without even the pretense of affection or feeling. We should perhaps mention in passing that prostitution is not strictly a feminine trade. There are also male homosexual prostitutes. Although they share some of the characteristics of their female counterparts, they are best discussed in the context of the homosexual subculture.

Perry and Perry, *Face to Face: The Individual and Social Problem.*

● ● ●

## EXERCISE 13–12

*DIRECTIONS:* Make a list of your academic reading tasks for the past week. Indicate which of these tasks involved overview or review skimming and which involved scanning.

### Critical Thinking Tip #13

### Anticipating Your Reading Assignments

Skimming can help you to make predictions about the content and organization of your reading assignments. By preview skimming you can anticipate what an assignment will contain and how it will be presented. Knowing this will enable you to make decisions about how to approach the material and which reasoning and thinking strategies will be needed to learn the material.

To improve your ability to anticipate your reading tasks, keep the following questions in mind when you preview skim:

1. What is the difficulty level of the material?
2. How is it organized?
3. What is the overall subject and how is it approached?
4. What type of material is it (practical, theoretical, historical background, case study)?
5. Are there logical breaking points where you might divide the assignment into portions, perhaps leaving a portion for later study?
6. At what points might you stop and review?
7. What connections are there between this assignment and class lectures?

## SUMMARY

**1. What is skimming?**

Skimming is a selective reading technique used to obtain important ideas. It is used when complete detailed information is <u>not</u> required.

**2. What steps should you follow to skim effectively?**

Skimming involves reading only those parts of articles or selections containing key ideas, such as
- the title and subtitle
- headings
- the introductory paragraph
- the first sentence of other paragraphs
- key words
- graphic elements
- the last paragraph

**3. What are the three types of skimming?**

There are three general types of skimming depending upon your purpose:
- Preview—for becoming familiar with the material before reading it thoroughly

- Overview—for getting just the main ideas when you won't read the material completely
- Review—for refreshing your memory about material you have already read

**4. What is scanning?**

Scanning is a process of rapidly locating information in printed material. It differs from skimming in that scanning involves looking only for a specific piece of information—a word, fact or statistic—and ignoring the rest of the material.

**5. What steps are involved in the process of scanning?**

Effective scanning involves the following steps:
- checking the organization
- forming specific questions
- anticipating clue words
- identifying likely answer locations
- using a systematic pattern
- confirming your answer

**BUSINESS**

## READING SELECTION 25
### BARRIERS TO EFFECTIVE LISTENING

Norman B. Sigband and Arthur Bell
From *Communication for Business and Management*

*Listening is an important part of the communication process. Read this excerpt from a business communication textbook and answer the following questions.*

*1. What factors interfere with effective listening?*
*2. What can you do to improve your listening skills?*

1    Perhaps the most important barrier to effective listening results from the fact that most of us talk at about 125 to 150 words per minute, while we can listen to and comprehend some 600 to 800 words per minute. Quite obviously if the sender talks at 125 words and the receiver listens at 600, the latter is left with a good deal of time to think about matters other than the message; and he or she does: illness, bills, cars, the baseball game score, what's for dinner tonight, and so on. This is the **internal competition** for attention.

2    However, there is also the **external competition** to effective listening. These are the distractions caused by clattering typewriters, ringing telephones, noisy production lines, heated arguments, intriguing smells, captivating sights, and dozens of other factors we all encounter in a busy, complex society.

3     **Time,** or more accurately, the lack of it, also contributes to inefficient listening. Effective listening requires that we give others a block of time so they may express their ideas as well as their feelings. Some individuals require more time than others to do this. If we are—or appear to be—impatient, they will either not express themselves fully or will require more time than usual. And yet the listener possesses a limited amount of time also. In addition, there are some individuals who will monopolize *all* of your listening time. If you begin to listen to such a person at noon, you could still be listening at 3:00 P.M.

4     You must turn off a person like this as tactfully as possible. However, there are others with whom you work or live that you should give time to so that you may listen with undivided attention. Remember, if *you* don't listen to *them*, they will always find someone who *will*.

5     If employees feel their supervisor won't listen to them, they will find other employees or the union representative who will; if young people feel their parents won't or don't listen to them, they may find friends, gang members, or people whose influence might be detrimental. And if customers feel a supplier really isn't listening, they will find a competitor to the supplier who will. There is no such thing as a vacuum in communication.

6     **Conditioning** is still another factor that contributes to poor listening. Many of us have conditioned ourselves not to listen to messages that do not agree with our philosophy or that irritate, upset, or anger us. TV and radio play a role in this conditioning. If the program we see or hear doesn't entertain or intrigue us, we have been conditioned to reach over and simply change channels or stations. And we carry this habit of changing the channel to tune a message out into our daily listening activities.

7     **Evaluating** what we hear may constitute still another barrier. So often we listen and almost immediately evaluate and reject the idea before it is completely voiced. Or we listen and then detour mentally while the individual is still talking. Of course, it is not possible not to evaluate, but one should continue to listen after evaluating. The problem is that most of us tune out as soon as we hear an idea or point of view that does not agree with ours.

8     **Emotions,** if colored or at a high level, may also get in the way of effective listening. Surely if you hear ideas that are counter to yours, or if you are involved in a confrontation or are emotionally upset because of fear, anger, or happiness, effective listening becomes very difficult.

9     **Lack of training** on how to listen is still another barrier. Most of us have received much instruction on how to write more concisely and clearly, read more efficiently and rapidly, and speak more forcefully and effectively. But few of us have ever received any instruction on how to listen. Perhaps this flaw in our educational system stems from the belief on the part of many educators that if one hears, one is listening. The fact remains that more effective listening can be taught. Fortunately, increasing numbers of schools today are teaching pupils how to listen more effectively, and there are even programs available in many universities.

10     Our **failure to concentrate** is another barrier to effective listening. That may be due to the fact that many of us have not been taught how to listen, or to the fact that we don't work at listening. . . .

## Listening for Facts

11     If you are a student, you have probably experienced missing an important class. If you are a manager, you have occasionally missed a meeting. The problem is playing "catch up." As a result, you approach Mitchell and ask about Monday's class and what you've missed.

12     If Mitchell can tell you little more than it was "an interesting class and I really thought the financial analysis of the case was OK," he probably is not very efficient in his attentive listening for facts. If you continue to press him, he may go

on to say, "It was a great case," or, "It emphasized financial aspects of a major corporation." Then you surely know that he doesn't listen very well (or attentively) for facts.

13 On the other hand, you may find Jan's response to the same question on the same class quite different. "Yes," says Jan, "it was a very interesting class. First, Professor Maxwell set the stage by indicating we would look at three aspects of high interest rates and the problem of getting residential mortgages: the trend in home sales, the cost of mortgage money, and the tax benefits secured by the residential purchaser."

14 Jan may then go on to list the specific subpoints under the three items noted and even give you Professor Maxwell's summary statement.

15 What is the difference between Mitchell's ability to listen for facts and Jan's ability? To some extent, Mitchell has not used his class time very well and will surely spend much more time reviewing for his final exam than Jan will. And the real pity is that his store of knowledge doesn't grow as quickly or as efficiently as Jan's.

16 Jan listens and retains facts; Mitchell does not. How do you listen? Like Jan or like Mitchell?

## How to Improve Your Ability to Listen for Facts[1]

17 **Catalog Key Words** In almost every discussion or presentation, several key ideas are presented. Each of these ideas can be retained if a key word is remembered that can be associated with each of the key ideas. In the discussion above, Jan probably remembered "home sales," "cost of money," and "tax benefits." Because she remembered these key words, she was able to discuss intelligently the concepts presented during the class.

18 **Resist Distractions** A dozen distractions take place while you listen. Whether you are in a group listening to a speaker or having a conversation with one other person, distractions are present. There are the external ones such as heat and humidity, noise and smell, bickering, illumination, and competing activities. Internally there is our own tendency to daydream, evaluate, and think of other important matters as well as our emotions, values, and the speakers' personality.

19 But we must resist these distractions and focus on the key concepts and words. No one maintains that such concentration is easy. It requires effort, but the task is made easier if we assume a posture of attentiveness and mentally force ourselves to pay attention to the task at hand. Many people find that taking notes during the presentation assists them in resisting distractions. If our friend Jan took notes during the class in question, she possibly wrote and underlined the key words, "home sales," "cost of money," and "tax benefits."

20 **Review Key Ideas** In the course of Professor Maxwell's lecture, both Mitchell and Jan had a good deal of free time. Professor Maxwell spoke at an average pace of about 140 words per minute. Both Mitchell and Jan comprehend approximately 650–700 words per minute. Mitchell used the "extra time" to think about last night's dinner with Betty and the fact that Chablis might have been a better wine to order than Blanc de Blanc. Jan, on the other hand, used her "extra time" to review the evidence Professor Maxwell cited in relation to home sales, cost of money, and tax benefits. Learning is a constant search for key ideas. As Keith Davis stated in his book, *Human Behavior at Work*, "Hearing is with the ears, but listening is with the mind."[2]

21 **Be Open and Flexible** The old saw, "Don't bother me with the facts, my mind is made up," may be humorous, but it is also true for many people. Their biases are so strong that they may

---

[1] See also R. G. Nichols, "Listening Is a 10-Part Skill," *Nation's Business*, July 1957, and Norman B. Sigband, "Listen to What You Can't Hear," *Nation's Business*, June 1969.

[2] K. Davis, Human Behavior at Work. Prentice-Hall, 1977, p. 9.

prefer not to listen. Or perhaps their instant assessment of the speaker's clothes, ethnic background, hair style, accent, or beard is enough for them to fix their opinions.

22 Obviously this attitude is an injustice not only to the speaker but most certainly to the listener as well. It is true that Mitchell had a very unhappy experience in a real estate transaction last year. But is that any reason for him not to listen to Professor Maxwell today?

23 Listen to whatever is being directed to you. Be flexible and receptive. No one suggests that you must accept the idea and concepts presented by others. However, you should listen to them.

## Comprehension Test 25

*Directions:* *Circle the letter of the best answer.*

### Checking Your Comprehension

1. The reading focuses on
   a. reasons for ineffective listening and how to overcome them
   b. causes of ineffective listening
   c. external and internal listening barriers
   d. techniques for becoming a more effective listener

2. Internal competition refers to
   a. a vacuum in communication
   b. environmental distractions
   c. mental distractions
   d. dealing with competing messages

3. If a listener appears impatient, the speaker may
   a. require more time than usual to express himself or herself
   b. respond to external distractions
   c. become emotional
   d. find someone else to talk to

4. The author cautions against
   a. spending too much time listening to emotional messages
   b. revealing emotions during speech
   c. conditioning ourselves not to evaluate
   d. not listening to those with whom we must work or live

5. According to the article, if you have difficulty resisting distractions during a class lecture, you should
   a. ask questions to keep your mind focused
   b. take notes on the lecture
   c. make a list of distractions
   d. listen with a purpose

6. Which of the following best defines the word "saw" as used in paragraph 21?
   a. cutting tool
   b. saying
   c. sharp remark
   d. figurative expression

### Thinking Critically

7. The author includes Jan and Mitchell as examples primarily to
   a. make the article more interesting
   b. discuss internal competition
   c. describe listening flexibility
   d. emphasize the differences between effective and ineffective listeners

8. A student has strong feelings on the issue of abortion and had recently been involved in local antiabortion demonstrations. Her sociology instructor conducted a class discussion on the abortion issue. The student did not hear her instructor ask each student to write a paragraph summarizing the prochoice position.
   The reason she did not hear the assignment may be best explained by
   a. conditioning
   b. evaluation
   c. internal competition
   d. time

9. The statement "Hearing is with the ears, but listening is with the mind" was quoted in the article to
   a. suggest a strategy for overcoming distractions
   b. distinguish types of listening
   c. emphasize that listening is thinking
   d. define the terms

10. The selection uses which of the following methods of organization?
    a. comparison-contrast
    b. cause-effect
    c. enumeration
    d. time order

**Questions for Discussion**

1. Describe a situation or example in which conditioning functions as a barrier.

2. Which of the barriers to effective listening do you experience when listening to classroom lectures? How have you overcome them?

3. Are there other types of listening, other than listening for facts? If so, describe them.

4. What features of this excerpt made it easy or difficult to read?

| Selection 25: | 1544 words |
|---|---|
| Finishing Time: | _____ _____ _____ |
| | HR. MIN. SEC. |
| Starting Time: | _____ _____ _____ |
| | HR. MIN. SEC. |
| Reading Time: | _____ _____ |
| | MIN. SEC. |
| WPM Score: | _____ |
| Comprehension Score: | _____% |

INTERPERSONAL COMMUNICATION

# READING SELECTION 26
## STRESS MANAGEMENT: PERSONALLY ADJUSTING TO STRESS
Richard L. Weaver
From *Understanding Interpersonal Communication*

*Why do we suffer stress? How can we cope with stress? This reading, taken from an interpersonal communication textbook, addresses these questions. Read the excerpt to find some helpful suggestions to cope with stress.*

1   *Stress is a state of imbalance between demands made on us from outside sources and our capabilities to meet those demands.* Often, it precedes and occurs concurrently with conflict. Stress, as you have seen, can be brought on by physical events, other people's behavior, social situations, our own behavior, feelings, thoughts, or anything that results in heightened bodily awareness. In many cases, when you experience pain, anger, fear, or depression, these emotions are a response to a stressful situation like conflict.

2   Sometimes, in highly stressful conflict situations, we must cope with the stress before we cope with the conflict. Relieving some of the intensity of the immediate emotional response will allow us to become more logical and tolerant in resolving the conflict. In this brief section, some of the ways we have for controlling our physical reactions and our thoughts will be explained.

3    People respond differently to conflict just as they respond differently to stress. Some people handle both better than others do. Individual differences are not as important as learning how to manage the stress we feel. The goal in stress management is self-control, particularly in the face of stressful events.

4    Stress reactions involve two major elements: (1) heightened physical arousal as revealed in an increased heart rate, sweaty palms, rapid breathing, and muscular tension, and (2) anxious thoughts, such as thinking you are helpless or wanting to run away. Since your behavior and your emotions are controlled by the way you think, you must acquire skills to change those thoughts.

5    Controlling physical symptoms of stress requires relaxation. Sit in a comfortable position in a quiet place where there are no distractions. Close your eyes and pay no attention to the outside world. Concentrate only on your breathing. Slowly inhale and exhale. Now, with each exhaled breath say "relax" gently and passively. Make it a relaxing experience. If you use this method to help you in conflict situations over a period of time, the word "relax" will become associated with a sense of physical calm; saying it in a stressful situation will help induce a sense of peace.

6    Another way to induce relaxation is through tension release. The theory here is that if you tense a set of muscles and then relax them, they will be more relaxed than before you tensed them. Practice each muscle group separately. The ultimate goal, however, is to relax all muscle groups simultaneously to achieve total body relaxation. For each muscle group, in turn, tense the muscles and hold them tense for five seconds, then relax them. Repeat this tension-release sequence three times for each group of muscles. Next, tense all muscles together for five seconds, then release them. Now, take a low, deep breath and say "relax" softly and gently to yourself as you breathe out. Repeat this whole sequence three times.

7    You do not need to wait for special times to practice relaxing. If, during the course of your daily activities, you notice a tense muscle group, you can help relax this group by saying "relax" inwardly. Monitor your bodily tension. In some cases you can prepare yourself for stressful situations through relaxation *before* they occur. Practice will help you call up the relaxation response whenever needed.

8    For other ways to relax, do not overlook regular exercise. Aerobic or yoga-type exercise can be helpful. Personal fitness programs can be tied to these inner messages to "relax" for a complete relaxation response.

9    Controlling your thoughts is the second major element in stress management. Managing stress successfully requires flexibility in thinking. That is, you must consider alternative views. Your current view is causing the stress! You must also keep from attaching exaggerated importance to events. Everything seems life-threatening in a moment of panic; things dim in importance when viewed in retrospect.

10    Try to view conflict from a problem-solving approach: "Now, here is a new problem. How am I going to solve this one?" (A specific problem-solving approach will be discussed in the next section.) Too often, we become stressed because we take things personally. When an adverse event occurs we see it as a personal affront or as a threat to our ego. For example, when Christy told Paul she could not go to the concert with him, he felt she was letting him know she disliked him. This was a blow to Paul because he had never been turned down—rejected—before. Rather than dwell on that, however, he called Heather, she accepted his invitation, and he achieved his desired outcome—a date for the concert.

11    One effective strategy for stress management consists of talking to ourselves. We become our own manager, and we guide our thoughts, feelings, and behavior in order to cope. Phillip Le Gras suggests that we view the stress experience as a series of phases. Here, he presents the phases and some examples of coping statements:

1. *Preparing for a stressor.* [Stressors are events that result in behavioral outcomes called stress reactions.] What do I have to do? I can develop a plan to handle it. I have to think about this and not panic. Don't be negative. Think logically. Be rational. Don't worry. Maybe the tension I'm feeling is just eagerness to confront the situation.

2. *Confronting and handling a stressor.* I can do it. Stay relevant. I can psych myself up to handle this, I can meet the challenge. This tension is a cue to use my stress-management skills. Relax. I'm in control. Take a slow breath.

3. *Coping with the feeling of being overwhelmed.* I must concentrate on what I have to do right now. I can't eliminate my fear completely, but I can try to keep it under control. When the fear is overwhelming, I'll just pause for a minute.

4. *Reinforcing self-statements.* Well done. I did it! It worked. I wasn't successful this time, but I'm getting better. It almost worked. Next time I can do it. When I control my thoughts I control my fear.

12     The purpose of such coping behavior is to become aware of and monitor our anxiety. In this way, we can help eliminate such self-defeating, negative statements as "I'm going to fail," or "I can't do this." Statements such as these are cues that we need to substitute positive, coping self-statements.

13     If the self-statements do not work, or if the stress reaction is exceptionally intense, then we may need to employ other techniques. Sometimes we can distract ourselves by focusing on something outside the stressful experience—a pleasant memory, a sexual fantasy—or by doing mental arithmetic. Another technique is imaging. By manipulating mental images we can reinterpret, ignore, or change the context of the experience. For example, we can put the experience of unrequited love into a soap-opera fantasy or the experience of pain into a medieval torture by the rack. The point here is that love and pain are strongly subjective and personal, and when they are causing us severe stress we can reconstruct the situation mentally to ease the stress. In both these cases the technique of imaging helps to make our response more objective—to take it *outside* ourselves. The more alternatives we have to aid us in stress reduction, the more likely we are to deal with it effectively.

## Comprehension Test 26*

### Checking Your Comprehension

1. Define the term *stress*.

2. How are stress reactions characterized?

3. How can physical stress symptoms be controlled?

4. How can thoughts be controlled to manage stress?

5. List the four phases in coping with the stress experience as suggested by Le Gras.

6. Explain the technique of imaging.

### Thinking Critically

1. What evidence does the author provide about the effectiveness of the stress management techniques he describes? Does the evidence or lack of it alter your opinion of the techniques?

2. What is the author's purpose in writing?

3. Identify the stress control technique(s) used in the following situation: A student receives an "F" grade on a term paper in psychology. She says to a friend, "Oh well, it is just another grade among many!"

---

* Multiple-choice questions are contained in Appendix B (page A24).

**Questions For Discussion**

1. What are some of the major causes of stress for college students?

2. How useful do you think the relaxation response is or might be?

3. In what situations, other than those suggested by the author, might imaging be useful?

| Selection 26: | | 1186 words |
|---|---|---|

Finishing Time: _____  _____  _____
                  HR.     MIN.     SEC.

Starting Time: _____  _____  _____
                  HR.     MIN.     SEC.

Reading Time: _____  _____
                  MIN.     SEC.

WPM Score: _____

Comprehension Score: _____%

**Visit the Longman English Pages**

For additional readings and exercises, visit the Longman English Skills Web page at:

**http://longman.awl.com/englishpages**

For a username and password, please see your instructor.

# CHAPTER 14
# Techniques for Reading Faster

IN THIS CHAPTER YOU WILL LEARN:

1. To control your eye-movement patterns.
2. To increase and vary your reading rate.

One of the first steps in becoming a more efficient and flexible reader is learning to vary your reading rate. Many adults read everything in the same way: at the same rate with the same level of comprehension. This chapter discusses several methods for increasing and varying your reading rate.

The chapter first describes the physical aspects of reading. Then, a technique for grouping words into meaning clusters is presented as a means of improving both rate and comprehension. Finally, five other methods for increasing your reading rate are discussed—key word reading, cue words, rapid reading drills, pacing, and rereading.

## ■ EYE-MOVEMENT PATTERNS

Reading is primarily a thinking process. However, it has physical aspects: your eyes recognize words and transmit them in the form of signals to the brain. These physical aspects of reading are far less important than the cognitive processes. Still, the following brief overview of the physical aspects will help you recognize habits that interfere with rate and comprehension.

### ■ What Happens When You Read

Your eyes are highly specialized and complicated instruments. They have the capacity to recognize words rapidly and to transmit them in the form of signals to the brain. Mental processes become involved as your brain attaches meaning to the signals it receives. As these two processes occur, you comprehend what you are reading. To explain what occurs as your eyes move across a line of print, let us look at some physical features of the eye-movement process.

### Left-to-Right Progression

Your eyes are already well trained to move in a left-to-right pattern across the page. The speed of this progression, however, is variable and can be significantly increased with practice and training.

### Fixation

As your eyes move across a line of print, they move and stop, move and stop. When your eyes are in motion, they do not see anything. When your eyes stop, or focus, this is called a *fixation.* As your eyes move across a line of print, they make a number of stops, or fixations, and the number of fixations you make per line is directly related to your reading efficiency.

### Eye Span

As your eyes stop, or fixate, while progressing from left to right across the line, they see a certain number of words or letters. The amount you see during each fixation is called your *eye span.* Some readers see only a part of a word in each fixation; others are able to see a whole word in one fixation. Still others may see several words in each fixation.

You may find that your eye span varies greatly according to the type of material you are reading. For example, if you are reading a children's book to a child, you may be able to see several words at a time. On the other hand, when you read a chemistry textbook, you may need to focus on single words. Occasionally, when identifying an unfamiliar word, you may look at one part of a word and then another part.

### Return Sweep

When your eyes reach the end of a line of print, they return to the beginning of the next line. This return motion is called the *return sweep.* Although your eyes are already trained to return automatically, the speed with which they make this return is variable.

### Regression

Your eyes normally progress in a left-to-right direction, seeing each word in the order it was written. Occasionally, your eyes will move backward, or *regress,* to a word already read instead of moving to the next word. This word may be on the same line or on a previous line. In the following line, each fixation is numbered consecutively to show a sample reader's regression pattern.

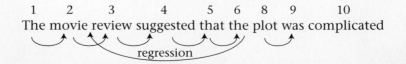

Notice that this reader moved from left to right through the sixth fixation. Then, instead of progressing to the next word, the reader regressed to the word "review" before proceeding with the sentence.

Regression is often unnecessary and slows you down. In fact, regressing may scramble the sentence order. As a result, you may have difficulty comprehending what you are reading.

## ■ Observing Eye-Movement Patterns

Most of the processes described so far can be readily observed by watching another person read. To get a better understanding of eye movement patterns, choose another person to work with and try the following experiments. Be sure to sit so that the other person is facing you, and select sample pages from a book or text neither of you has already read.

### Experiment 1: Observing Eye Movement

Ask the other person to hold up the book so that you can see his or her eyes as he or she reads. Then direct the person to start reading a paragraph. As he or she reads, notice how the eyes move and stop, move and stop. Also notice the return sweep to the beginning of the next line.

### Experiment 2: Counting Fixations

As the person reads, count the number of eye stops or fixations made on each line. By counting the average number of words on the line and dividing it by the average number of fixations per line, you will be able to compute the person's eye span.

### Experiment 3: Regression

When observing the other person reading, ask him or her to deliberately regress to a word on a previous line. Notice the eye movement that occurs. Then have the person continue reading, and notice if he or she unknowingly makes any regressions.

Now allow the other person to try each of these three experiments while you read.

Now that you are familiar with the eye-movement process, you can begin to develop habits and eye-movement patterns that will increase your efficiency.

## ■ Reducing Regressions

Although even very good readers occasionally regress, you will find that frequent regression interferes with your comprehension and slows you down. Various mechanical devices can reduce regression, but you can easily get the same results by using one or more of the following techniques:

1. Be conscious of your tendency to regress, and force yourself to move your eyes only from left to right. Do not regress in the middle of a sentence. Instead, if the meaning of a sentence is unclear after you have finished reading it, reread the entire sentence.

2. Use a 5" × 8" index card to prevent regression to previous lines. As you read, slide the index card down the page so that it covers what you have already read. This technique will help you eliminate regressions because when you look back to a previous line it will be covered up. Eventually, if you look back often enough and find the line is not visible, you will stop looking back.

3. Use a pen, pencil, or finger to guide your eyes in a left-to-right direction across each line as you read. Move the object or your finger at the speed at which you normally read. You will find that the forward motion of your finger or the pen will force you to continue reading toward the right and will discourage you from regressing.

## ■ Vocalization and Excessive Subvocalization

Some ineffective readers actually vocalize or sound out each word on a page by moving their lips and pronouncing each word. Others "hear" each word mentally as they read silently. This process is known as *subvocalization.* Research indicates that while subvocalization may be necessary and, at times, may enhance comprehension, it should not occur continuously as one reads. Mentally hearing each word may help clarify a confusing passage, but when done continuously, subvocalization usually limits the reader to word-by-word reading. Some students vocalize or subvocalize as a habit even though it is not necessary.

If you find that you vocalize or subvocalize frequently, practice pushing yourself to read so rapidly that it is impossible. Also, if you discover that you move your lips as you read, place your hand or fingers near your lips as you read. You will feel your lips moving and can work to eliminate the habit.

## ■ READING IN MEANING CLUSTERS

When you read a paragraph do you read one word and then another word OR do you jump from one group of words to another group of words? Most adult readers concentrate on a single word at a time, as illustrated in the first half of the preceding sentence. Although most are capable of grouping words together, they have not developed the skill of doing so. Word-by-word reading is time consuming and, in many cases, actually detracts from understanding the meaning of a sentence.

To understand how slow word-by-word reading can be, read the following paragraph. It is written so that you will have to read it from *right to left,* forcing you to read each word separately.

spirits neutral of combination a is Vodka
bring to added is water The .water and
neutral Since .proof final its to vodka
,neutral equally much pretty are spirits
but subtle for makes that water the is it
.differences appreciable

Clustering is the technique of grouping words together. You recall that your eyes move and stop, move and stop, as they proceed across a line of print. Clustering involves widening your eye span so that you see several words in one fixation.

## ■ How to Cluster Read

Essentially, clustering involves widening your eye span or point of concentration to encompass two or three words. To cluster most effectively, however, you should try to group words together that naturally fit or go together. In both written and spoken language, words fall into natural groupings. Our language contains many words that carry little meaning alone but, when combined with others, express a thought or idea. For example, the words *in* and *the* have meaning mainly when combined with other words: for example, "in the house." The word grouping "in the house" is a meaningful cluster and could be read as a unit. When you group words together in meaning units, you will find that it is easier to understand what you read. To illustrate this point, read both versions of the following sample paragraph. One version divides the paragraph into meaningful clusters; the other does not. Decide which version is easier to read.

### Version 1

(Public libraries) (provide access) (to a world) (of information.) (But they also) (contribute to the) (preservation of) (our valuable forests.) (Each library) (saves a forest) (of trees) (by making) (individual purchase) (of books and periodicals) (unnecessary.)

### Version 2

(Public libraries provide) (access to a) (world of) (information. But they) (also contribute to the) (preservation of our) (valuable forests. Each) (library saves a) (forest of) (trees by) (making individual) (purchase of books) (and periodicals unnecessary.)

● ● ●

You probably decided that the first version is easier to read because the words that belong together are grouped together.

Cluster reading can have a dramatic effect on your reading efficiency. By grouping words together into meaningful clusters, you make sentences easier to understand. Also, by widening your eye span, and thereby reducing the number of fixations per line, you are reducing the time it takes to read a line and are increasing your reading rate.

## ■ Learning to Cluster Read

For most students, learning to read in clusters requires considerable practice. It is not a skill that you can develop after a few trial reading sessions. Instead, you may find that it takes several weeks of continued practice to develop the habit. To develop the skill, try to read as many things as possible in clusters. Begin by reading easy material, such as newspaper and magazine articles, in phrases. Later, as you feel more confident about the skill, progress to more difficult types of material.

As you begin cluster reading, you may find that you frequently lapse back into word-by-word reading. This is a natural happening since as your attention focuses on the content of the material rather than the technique of reading. Once you realize that you have lapsed into word-by-word reading, just switch back to cluster reading and continue reading. As you become more skilled with phrase reading, you will find that fewer lapses will occur.

## EXERCISE 14–1

*DIRECTIONS:* Read the following passages that have been divided into clusters. They are designed to give you an idea of how it feels to cluster read. As you read, you should feel your eyes moving from cluster to cluster in a rhythmical motion.

1.  When you   cluster read   it should feel   like this.
    Your eye should   move and stop,   move and stop.
    Each time   your eye stops   or fixates   it should see
    a meaningful phrase.   Cluster reading   will improve
    your comprehension   and help you   read faster.

2.  As a   used car shopper,   your first task is
    to decide   what kind   of car   is going   to fill

your needs. Then shop around until you
have a good feel for the market value of that car.
This way you'll know a bargain when you see one.
You can also check the National Automobile Dealers
Association Used Car Guide and the Kelly Blue Book
for prices of used cars. They'll give you prices
to work with, *but they're only guides.*
Condition and mileage will adjust the price up
or down.

3. Anytime you're told that you need surgery
   and it's not an emergency, it's a good idea
   to get a second opinion from a qualified specialist
   in the appropriate field. To find this specialist,
   ask your primary care physician for a recommendation,
   or call the nearest teaching hospital or an accredited
   hospital for a recommendation. You can also consult
   the *Directory of Medical Specialists.*

4. Actually, the common cold is not as simple
   as it seems. It can be caused by any
   of 200 different viruses, and it can bring misery
   eight ways: sore throat, sneezing, runny nose,
   watery eyes, aches and pains, mild fever,
   nasal congestion, and coughing. Thus
   the thinking behind "combination" products: they
   supposedly contain a little something for the
   different symptoms. One pill or capsule,
   the advertisers say, handles the whole malady.
   A little like one-stop shopping.

5. Psychological principles can be applied by everyone.
   You can learn to use scientific psychology
   to help solve your own problems. There are
   a number of important advantages of do-it-yourself
   psychology. One factor is manpower. For most people
   the major problem a few generations ago
   was physical survival: now it is psychological survival.
   We seem to be tense, alienated, confused.
   Suicide, addiction, violence, apathy, neurosis—
   are all problems of the modern world.
   Psychological problems are accelerating
   and there are not enough professional psychologists

to go around.   Non-psychologists *must*   practice psychology
if psychology   is to be applied   to our problems.

## EXERCISE 14–2

*DIRECTIONS:* The following material has already been clustered. Practice reading each cluster with only one eye fixation. Move your eyes down each column, making only one fixation per line.

1.  There is                  opportunity to
    no better way             try out
    to test                   the fishing boat
    fishing boats             under the most
    than under                adverse weather
    actual fishing            conditions and
    conditions.               the most rapid
    Actual conditions         and unexpected
    provide the               passenger movements.

2.  The purpose of            life insurance
    life insurance            by simply
    is to prevent             asking yourself
    financial difficulty      if your death
    for someone else          would put someone
    in the event              else in a tough
    of your death.            financial position.
    With that in mind,        If the answer
    you can determine         is yes,
    if you need               you need insurance.

3.  The job interview         will be impressed
    is your best chance       if you can
    to sell yourself,         ask intelligent questions
    so it pays                about their company,
    to be well-prepared.      questions that show
    First, rehearse           you've done
    in your mind              your homework.
    the qualifications        Your local librarian
    that would make           can direct you
    you an asset              to a number
    to the organization.      of reference books
    Second, learn             that "profile"
    something about it.       business organizations.
    Most employers

4. The most important
   tool you have
   in job-hunting
   is your resume.
   It's your calling card,
   and it should reflect
   what it is
   about you
   that makes
   you eminently employable.
   To put
   the resume
   in proper perspective,
   think about
   your potential employer.
   He or she
   is busy,
   harassed, has a pile
   of resumes
   on the desk,
   and has only
   an hour
   and a half
   to read them.
   All of them.
   Then he hits
   four pages
   that follow you
   from being
   high school valedictorian
   to shooting
   the rapids of
   the Congo.
   Chances are
   he'll shoot your resume—
   rapidly—
   into the wastebasket.
   Many employers
   spend only
   15 to 30 seconds
   on each resume.

5. The best exercise
   is the endurance type—
   cardiovascular activities
   that make you
   breathe deeply,
   elevate your pulse,
   and make you sweat.
   Dr. Kenneth Cooper,
   expert on fitness,
   lists the following
   as the best activities
   for physical fitness:
   running, swimming,
   cycling, walking or striding,
   stationary running,
   handball, basketball, squash.
   *Any* activity that elevates
   the heart rate
   is beneficial.
   The exercise should be
   vigorous enough
   to produce
   a temporary feeling
   of fatigue.
   At this level
   of intensity,
   it strengthens the heart
   and other muscles
   and increases circulation.
   Strenuous activity
   should be scheduled
   at least two
   to three times
   a week
   for at least
   a half hour each time.

## EXERCISE 14–3

*DIRECTIONS:* Choose one of the reading selections at the end of this chapter. Read the first five paragraphs and, as you read, divide each sentence into meaningful clusters. Separate each cluster by using a slash mark (/) as has been done in the following example.

Studying economics/is difficult/because it requires/careful attention/to facts and figures.

Then, reread the five paragraphs, trying to see each cluster rather than each single word.

## ■ KEY WORD READING

Read each of the following versions of a paragraph.

### Version 1

KEY WORD READING NEW TECHNIQUE. FASTER THAN CAREFUL READING. DECREASE FACTUAL COMPREHENSION. WORTH LOSS, DEPENDING PURPOSE TYPE MATERIAL. (18 words)

### Version 2

Key word reading is a new technique. Although it is faster than most of the careful reading techniques, the reader must expect a decrease in factual comprehension skill. In some situations, it is worth the loss, depending on the reader's purpose and the type of material being read. (48 words)

● ● ●

Were you able to understand the passage conveyed in Version 1? If so, then you are already on your way to mastering the technique of key word reading. You have already read in a manner similar to key word reading. Compare the number of words in each version. Notice what is deleted in the first version that is included in the second. Did you gain much additional information about key word reading from the complete version that you had not acquired in the first?

## ■ What Is Key Word Reading?

From our example, you can see that key word reading involves skipping nonessential words and reading only those words and phrases that carry the primary or core meaning of each sentence.

To further understand key word meaning, read the following paragraph in which the key words have been underlined. Read the paragraph two ways. First, read only the underlined key words in the paragraph. Can you understand the message the paragraph is conveying? Second, read the entire passage. How much additional information did you acquire?

America's <u>only nonelected president, Gerald Ford,</u> became chief executive at a time when the <u>nation</u> desperately <u>craved</u> an <u>end</u> to <u>distrust</u> and <u>uncertainty. Ford</u> seemed the <u>right man</u> to <u>initiate</u> the <u>healing process.</u> A stolid <u>legislator</u> who had served in the <u>House</u> for <u>many years without</u> great <u>distinction,</u> he was an <u>open,</u> <u>decent,</u> and <u>generous</u> person, and <u>most Americans</u> seemed to <u>like him.</u>

Unger, *These United States: The Question of Our Past.*

● ● ●

By reading only the key words, you were probably able to understand the basic message of the paragraph. Then, when you read the complete paragraph, you only learned a few additional details about Ford.

In developing skill in key word reading, it sometimes helps to think of the process as similar to that of reading a telegram, a headline in a newspaper, or a news caption that is run across the bottom of a television screen while a program is in progress.

Telegram: ARRIVING TUESDAY 6 P.M. AMERICAN FLIGHT 321. LAGUARDIA.

TV News Caption: AIRLINE HIJACKING LOS ANGELES. 52 HOSTAGES. FOUR HIJACKERS. IDENTITY AND PURPOSE UNKNOWN.

Both of these messages contain only the words that carry the basic meaning. Most frequently, these meaning-carrying words are nouns, action verbs, and important descriptive adjectives and adverbs. They are the words that tell the "who, what, when, and where" and frequently include names, dates, places, numbers, capitalized words, and italicized words.

## ■ When to Use Key Word Reading

You will find that key word reading is a valuable and efficient technique for some reading situations. You should expect your comprehension to be 70 percent or lower, usually in the 50–70 percent range. But, as a tradeoff for lower comprehension, you can expect an increase in rate. You actually gain more than you lose because, although you read less than half the material, normally you can expect to get more than 50 percent of the message. You might expect to achieve reading rates of between 600 and 700 words per minute when using key word reading.

Key word reading cannot be used on all types of material. In many situations a comprehension level below 80 percent is not acceptable. Especially when reading textbooks or highly technical material, your goal should be to understand everything, and key word reading is obviously not appropriate. However, in many other situations, a level of comprehension in the 60–70 percent range is adequate. In these situations, key word reading will suit your purposes and enable you to cover the material at a high reading rate.

Here are a few situations in which key word reading might be an appropriate technique:

- When you are reading magazine movie reviews to decide if you want to see the movie

- When you are reading encyclopedia entries to determine if this encyclopedia contains any information you do not already have

- When you are reading newspaper articles to find the key ideas and primary details in a recent local event

- When using reference books to gain a general idea of an author's approach and treatment of an event, idea, concept, or theory

- When reading correspondence to determine the writer's purpose and the level and nature of response required

## ■ Aids to Key Word Reading

The ability to key word read draws on many comprehension skills and reading techniques. Your knowledge of sentence structure, specifically your awareness of punctuation and your ability to identify key parts of a sentence, will enable you to key word read. You will also be using your knowledge and familiarity with the structure of the English language, which you have acquired naturally throughout your lifetime, to help you locate key words. Although you may not be aware of them, you have learned many rules and patterns of the structure of English.

### *Using Sentence Structure*

Sentences contain core parts that tell you what the sentence is about (the subject), what action occurred (the predicate), and who or what received the action (the object). These parts carry the basic meaning of the sentence. To illustrate this, look at the following paragraph in which all but these key parts have been deleted. As you read through it, you will notice that you get the basic meaning of each sentence and the paragraph as a whole.

And so, by 1968 or 1969, the country found itself caught in a giant whirlpool of anger and change. Nothing from the past, apparently, was sacred any longer. Patriotism was in bad repute: students burned their draft cards and desecrated the American flag. Chastity had become a thing of the past: college students lived in open "sin," and skirts had crawled two-thirds the way up the female thigh. Civility in public life had almost disappeared: every group was demanding "liberation" and would take to the streets, occupy public buildings, attack the police, riot, or even throw bombs to get it. Worst of all, the family was disintegrating: despite parental protest, children dressed the way they wanted, smoked "pot," and abandoned promising careers and futures to become political activists. Wives demanded that husbands share household chores so they could take jobs or go back to school.

● ● ●

Now read the complete paragraph. Notice that it fills you in on the details you missed when you read only key words, but also notice that you did not miss any of the key ideas.

And so, by 1968 or 1969, the country found itself caught in a giant whirlpool of anger and change. Nothing from the past, apparently, was sacred any longer. Patriotism was in bad repute: students burned their draft cards and desecrated the American flag. Chastity had become a thing of the past: college students lived in open "sin," and skirts had crawled two-thirds the way up the female thigh. Civility in public life had almost disappeared: every group was demanding "liberation" and would take to the streets, occupy public buildings, attack the police, riot, or even throw bombs to get it. Worst of all, the family was disintegrating: despite parental protest, children dressed the way they wanted, smoked "pot," and abandoned promising careers and futures to become political activists. Wives demanded that husbands share household chores so they could take jobs or go back to school.

Unger, *These United States: The Question of Our Past.*

● ● ●

As you begin to read key words, concentrate on looking for the key parts of each sentence. Looking for sentence key parts is essentially a process of searching for the basic meaning of a sentence.

## EXERCISE 14–4

*DIRECTIONS:* In each of the following sentences, draw a line through the words that do not carry the essential meaning of the sentence. Only key words should remain. After completing each sentence, check (by rereading only the words that remain) to see if the basic meaning of the sentence has been conveyed.

Example: Work ~~should be~~ arranged so ~~there are~~ specific stopping points ~~where you can~~ feel something ~~had been~~ accomplished.

1. In some large businesses, employees are practically strangers to each other and often do not discuss problems or ideas.
2. Criminal law as we know it today is a product of centuries of change.
3. From the standpoint of criminal law, a criminal is an individual who is legally capable of conduct that violates the law and who can be shown to have actually and intentionally engaged in that conduct.
4. By the time Congress assembled on December 4, 1865, the Republican majority—Radicals as well as most moderates—were seething with anger at the Johnson government.
5. During the 1960s the United States attained a level of material well-being beyond anything dreamed of in the past.

### Using Punctuation

Punctuation can serve as an aid in locating key words. Punctuation may signal what is to follow, separate nonessential parts of a sentence from the main sentence, or indicate the relationships of various parts of a sentence to one another.

The use of a colon or semicolon indicates that important information is to follow. When you see a colon, you may anticipate a list of items. Often, you can expect to find a separate but closely related idea when a semicolon is used. In both cases you are alerted to look for key words ahead.

Commas, depending on their use, provide several types of clues for the location of key words. When used to separate an introductory phrase from the main sentence, the comma tells you to pay more attention to the main sentence as you look for key words.

When used to separate items in a series, the comma indicates that all items are important and should be read as key words. When a comma is accompanied by a conjunction and is used to join two complete thoughts, expect to find key words on both sides of the comma. The parenthetical use of the comma tells you that the information enclosed within the commas is nonessential to the basic meaning of the sentence and may be skipped when you read key words.

### Using Typographical Aids

Most printed material contains typographical features that will help you locate key words and phrases. Typographical aids include boldface print, colored print, italics, capitalization, underlining, enumeration, or lists of information. Most typographical aids emphasize important information; others help the reader organize the information. Italics, underlining, and boldface print are all used to make important information more noticeable.

### Using Grammatical Structure

Your knowledge of grammar can also help you read key words effectively. You have learned that certain words modify or explain others. You know that adjectives explain or describe nouns and that adverbs give further information about verbs. Adjectives and adverbs that modify the key parts of the sentence, then, are also important in key word reading.

For example, in the following sentence you see that the adjectives and adverbs (single underlining) make the meaning of the key parts (double underlining) more complete.

The psychology instructor hastily summarized his lecture.

You also know that many words in the English language work very much like glue—they stick other, more important, words together. If classified by parts of speech, these "glue words" are usually prepositions, conjunctions, or pronouns.

In the following sentence, all the glue words have been deleted.

. . . summary, it seems safe . . . say . . . society, . . . whole, believes . . . individuals can control their destiny.

Can you still understand the sentence? Most likely you can guess the words that were deleted. Try it. Now, compare the words you supplied with the complete sentence.

In summary, it seems safe to say that society, on the whole, believes that individuals can control their destiny.

You probably guessed some words exactly, and for others you supplied a synonym. In either case, you supplied a word that fit into the meaning of the sentence.

You will find that as you read key words, you mentally fill in the glue words that tie the sentences together. This mental ability to supply missing information is based on a psychological principle called *closure*.

In key word reading, then, you are reading a stripped-down version of each sentence. You might also think of it as viewing a skeleton or forming a word outline of a paragraph or passage.

## EXERCISE 14–5

*DIRECTIONS:* Assume you are working on a research paper on the psychological effects of color. You located the following article by Kelly Costigan in *Science Digest,* and you want to see if it presents any new information on the psychology of color that you do not already have. Read the article using the key word reading technique. To help you get started, the first few lines have been shaded so that the key words are emphasized. After reading the article, answer the questions that follow.

## HOW COLOR GOES TO YOUR HEAD
### ORANGE MAKES YOU HUNGRY; BEIGE MAKES YOU NEAT AND EFFICIENT

Can simply looking at a color affect your behavior or alter your mood? Although some researchers are skeptical, others suggest that color may have a profound influence on human behavior and physiology.

A recent report in the *International Journal of Biosocial Research* revealed that after a change in the color and lighting scheme at a school in Wetaskiwin, Canada, the IQ scores of some students jumped and absenteeism and disciplinary problems decreased. The study, conducted by visual-arts professor Harry Wohlfarth of the University of Alberta, involved substituting yellow and blue for orange, white, beige and brown and replacing fluorescent lights with full-spectrum ones.

Clinical psychologist Alexander Schauss, director of the American Institute for Biosocial Research in Tacoma, Washington, spearheaded the now widespread use of bubblegum-pink rooms to calm delinquents and criminals in correctional facilities across the country. In 1979, Schauss evaluated the effect on subjects as they looked at this pink shade on a piece of cardboard. He reported later in the Bulletin of the Psychonomic Society that the color relaxed the subjects so much that they did not perform simple strength tests as well as they did when viewing other hues. A U.S. Navy brig in Seattle took notice of Schauss's work and permitted him to test his calming-color hypothesis on its inmates. Now hundreds of institutions place individuals in pink rooms when tempers flare.

"We used to have to give them drugs, even use handcuffs," says Paul Boccumini, director of clinical services at California's San Bernardino County Probation Department. "But this works."

Schauss and Wohlfarth are not certain how color can have an impact on biology or behavior. But Schauss conjectures that response to color is determined in the brain's reticular formation, a relay station for millions of the body's nerve impulses. And there have been studies indicating that when subjects look at warm hues, such as red, orange or yellow, their blood pressure rises, brain-wave activity increases, respiration is faster and perspiration greater. In the late 1970s, a UCLA study showed that blue had the opposite effect. Given these data, researchers speculate that the perception of color by the eye ultimately spurs the release of important biochemicals in the body.

The human eye is sensitive to millions of colors. Each is a distinctive wavelength of light that strikes color-sensitive cones on the back of the eye in a unique way. These cells then fire, sending nerve signals to the brain. Wohlfarth and others contend that the release of hormones or neurotransmitters may be triggered during this process, and they in turn influence moods and activities such as heart rate and breathing.

**COLORED LIGHT AIDS HEALTH**

There is also some evidence that colored light affects health. Baths of light emitting a high concentration of blue wavelengths are now used in many hospitals to cure infants of neonatal jaundice. The light penetrates the skin and breaks down the chemical bilirubin, which causes the condition.

Psychologists and commercial color consultants are already prescribing the use of a variety of hues to elicit certain behaviors. Gradations of blue are used on the walls of a Canadian dental clinic to ease patients' fears; rooms painted in peach, yellow and blue are said to relax residents at Aid for the Retarded in Stanford, Connecticut; and orange, which stimulates the appetite, adorns the walls of fast-food chains. Even machinery is painted light blue or beige instead of battleship gray to inspire neatness and efficiency in workers at a gas-turbine plant in the northeastern United States.

But the idea that color is a legitimate tool for modifying behavior is still being debated. "We need to speak from hard data," says Norman Rosenthal, a psychiatrist at the National Institute for Mental Health. "And how do you get by the cultural bias that might be built into a response, that red is stimulating and blue is connected to depression?"

• • •

1. The article mentions numerous effects of color. List as many as you can recall.

   _____

2. Summarize one theory that explains how color affects behavior.

   _____

3. What references or sources does the article provide for further research?

   _____

# EXERCISE 14–6

*DIRECTIONS:* Select a magazine or newspaper article or two or three pages from a nonfiction paperback you are reading. Before beginning to read, underline the key words in the first paragraph and in five to six sentences randomly selected from the remainder of the passage. Use key word reading on the article and record your results in the space provided. (See chapter 1 for information on how to estimate number of words and your words-per-minute score.)

Source of Material: _____

Finishing Time: _____

Starting Time: _____

Reading Time: _____

Estimated Total Number of Words: _____

WPM: _____

## ■ USING CUE WORDS

You have already learned that not all materials need to be read in the same way or at the same speed. The same principle also applies to reading a single piece of material. Not every sentence, paragraph, or section within a work must be read in the same way. When reading an essay or textbook chapter, for instance, your speed may vary, depending on the content and its relative importance. Fortunately, many materials contain cue words and phrases that indicate when to speed up, when to maintain your pace, and when to slow down. These words and phrases often function as transitions, connecting and leading from one idea to another. These transitions also cue the reader as to what is to follow and indicate its relative importance.

For example, readers often find it necessary to slow down when a new or different idea is presented. One word that signals a change in thought is *however,* as in the following statement.

> Selecting a career to match your interests, skills, and abilities is critically important. *However,* few students are able to find a perfect match. Instead, most students must settle for. . .

● ● ●

In this statement the author is switching from discussing a perfect match to other alternatives.

A decrease in reading speed may also be necessary when the author is presenting key points, emphasizing important information, or concluding or summarizing. Cue words and phrases for these conditions are listed in Table 14.1 on page 500. A reader can afford to speed up when the material is repetitious, familiar, or unimportant to his or her given purpose. Maintaining the same speed is appropriate when the author is continuing with the same line of thought or presenting information of equal importance. Speed-up and maintain-speed cue words are also shown in Table 14.1.

**Table 14.1** Reading Rate Cues

*Speed-Up Cues*

| | |
|---|---|
| Repetitious information | Again, in other words, that is |
| Examples | To illustrate, for example, suppose, for instance, such as |

*Slow-Down Cues*

| | |
|---|---|
| Change in thought | However, nevertheless, instead of, despite |
| Summary | In summary, for these reasons, to sum up, in brief |
| Conclusion | In conclusion, thus, therefore |
| Emphasis (above all, indeed) | Most important, it is essential |

*Maintain-Speed Cues*

| | |
|---|---|
| Continuation | Likewise, similarly, also, furthermore, and added to, in addition |
| Enumeration (listing) | First, second . . . , next, then, 1) . . . , 2) . . . |

Academic Application

## EXERCISE 14–7

*DIRECTIONS:* Choose a section of a chapter from one of your textbooks and circle the reading rate cues contained in it. Determine if each cue is a speed-up, slow-down or maintain-speed cue.

## ■ RAPID READING DRILLS

Many students read more slowly than is necessary. In fact, some students read so slowly that it interferes with their comprehension. A gap sometimes occurs between rate of intake of information and speed of thought. If information is taken in too slowly, the mind has time to drift or wander, resulting in loss of concentration or weak comprehension.

One effective way to build reading rate is to practice reading various materials at an uncomfortably high rate. Do not be too concerned if at first your comprehension is incomplete. Your first goal is to gain speed—to cover material faster than ever before. Then, as you become more skilled at faster reading, you will find that your comprehension will improve.

You might think of this strategy as similar to stretching a rubber band. A new rubber band is very tight and narrow in length. However, as it is stretched, it loosens and becomes longer and more flexible. A similar change occurs with reading rate: it loosens, stretches, and becomes more flexible.

The following rapid reading drills are intended to stretch your reading rate. Complete each drill as rapidly as possible.

## EXERCISE 14–8

*DIRECTIONS:* For each item, match and underline a word in column B that means the same as the word in column A. Sweep your eye rapidly across each line. Do not reread if you are unable to find a match; go to the next item. Stop reading as soon as you've found a match for each item. Try to reduce your time on successive sets.

### Set I

Begin timing.

| Column A | Column B | | | | |
|---|---|---|---|---|---|
| secure | secret | output | luckiness | improve | possess |
| imprint | bearable | engrave | treaty | flutter | improper |
| fabricate | extra | eyeless | make | facade | tremor |
| disturb | question | review | tremble | interrupt | dilute |
| blush | redden | submit | treasure | social | dim |
| backing | shaken | support | register | grate | obstacle |
| desert | observer | goodness | quarter | typical | abandon |
| authentic | twisting | resign | genuine | stimulate | reasonable |
| dateless | ageless | serving | qualm | permit | perjury |
| cunning | perish | clever | rejoice | grateful | graphic |

Time: _____ seconds

### Set II

Begin timing.

| Column A | Column B | | | | |
|---|---|---|---|---|---|
| author | query | tread | writer | grave | miracle |
| defect | ministry | grapple | misbehavior | murky | flaw |
| posterior | back | haven | facade | frontal | haul |
| sentiment | shadow | extort | feeling | mirage | extreme |

| equivalent | cheeky | decompose | opposite | equal | declare |
| decrease | historical | flog | bombard | cheat | diminish |
| defer | reign | together | dual | token | delay |
| extract | remove | quarter | hoard | snap | tipple |
| squeal | tread | object | yelp | pester | soar |
| hint | profane | sensual | suggest | taint | uprising |

Time: _____ seconds

## Set III

Begin timing.

| Column A | | | Column B | | |
|---|---|---|---|---|---|
| derelict | quantity | integrity | nutrient | sentenced | abandoned |
| extravagant | posture | popular | urban | wasteful | sensible |
| postpone | resist | wager | delay | intact | perceive |
| rehearsal | treat | practice | ordering | wayward | original |
| stipend | portion | payment | sect | penchant | organic |
| tangible | touchable | intellectual | nurture | upright | secrete |
| objectivity | ageless | fairness | wariness | tattered | tasteful |
| subsequent | obedient | subside | treasure | later | pervert |
| resemblance | reserve | positive | likeness | tipster | weakness |
| potent | powerful | quarrel | rejection | intelligent | willing |

Time: _____ seconds

# EXERCISE 14–9

*DIRECTIONS:* Read as rapidly as possible each of the following passages from *Discovering Mass Communication* by Samuel L. Becker. Time yourself, circle the speed closest to yours, and answer the questions that follow each passage. Try to increase your words per minute (wpm) score on successive passages. Do not hesitate to take risks: read faster than you think you are able to.

### Passage A

#### EXPOSURE TO TELEVISION

A television receiver in the average American household is on for about seven hours a day. Almost every year that figure increases. Just twenty years ago the average time was only five and one-half hours. The viewing of network television, though, is not increasing. In fact, it is dropping. Cable and videotapes are attracting the attention of a larger and larger percentage of the audience each year. Those inroads into the network and station audience are not yet tremendous, but they are sufficient to cause concern by network and station executives.

The reason people in the industry label the evening hours "prime time" is evident if you examine data on the percentage of households using television at each hour of the day. About 10 percent of homes have a television set on between 7:30 and 8:00 in the morning. That percentage rises very slowly during the day until about 4:00 or 4:30 P.M., when somewhat over 30 percent have sets on. At that point, viewing begins to rise sharply and steadily to its peak, which comes between 8:00 and 10:00 P.M. On a winter evening, from 8:00 to 10:00 P.M., a television set is on in more than 60 percent of American households. Somewhat fewer are on during summer evenings.

• • •

Words: 210
Timing:

| Seconds | WPM |
| --- | --- |
| 20 | 630 |
| 30 | 420 |
| 40 | 315 |
| 50 | 252 |
| 60 | 210 |
| 70 | 180 |

## ■ Questions:

1. Television watching is (increasing, decreasing). Circle one.

2. Television viewing is highest during the _____ season.

### *Passage B*

#### IMPLICATIONS FOR THE MEDIA OF SEX ROLE SHIFTS

The combination of sexual revolution and economic need is bringing a far larger percentage of adult American women into the work force and out of the home. This, combined with the increased numbers of males at home, may force [radio and television] broadcasters to rethink totally their daytime programming. By the twenty-first century, female homemakers may no longer dominate the daytime radio, television, and cable audience.

The fact that rapidly increasing numbers of adult women are moving into the work force will probably also affect the readership of books and magazines. Traditionally, women have been the major consumers of light fiction, both in book and magazine form. In good part this has been because they had more leisure time. As they enter the work force, however, and still retain many household duties in most cases, whether married or not, their time for reading fiction will be sharply reduced. Publishers may need to strive harder for older readers to maintain their circulation.

As more women enter the work force, a breakdown is occurring in the sharp division between male and female roles in the home. Men increasingly are sharing in the homemaking tasks, from cooking, caring for children, and cleaning to shopping for household necessities. This change in life-styles will affect mass communication in two ways. It will mean that men have less time to devote undivided attention to the media during prime time and on weekends. Perhaps more important, it will mean that all advertising presently designed to appeal largely to housewives will need to be redesigned to appeal equally to househusbands.

● ● ●

Words: 262
Timing:

| Seconds | WPM |
| --- | --- |
| 20 | 786 |
| 30 | 524 |
| 40 | 393 |
| 50 | 314 |
| 60 | 262 |
| 70 | 224 |
| 80 | 196 |

### ■ Questions:

Indicate whether the statement is true or false by marking "T" or "F" in the space provided.

1. In the future men may have less time to watch TV. _____

2. Advertising is likely to remain the same in the future as it is now. _____

### *Passage C*

Much graffiti is simply a safe form of exhibitionism. You can feel bold writing dirty words on the walls of a toilet, for example, without risking the criticism you might receive on saying the words aloud in public. A somewhat different form of exhibitionism is the desire to see your name etched forever on a tree in a public park or on a schoolroom desk. Although they obviously communicate something, these kinds of graffiti hardly qualify as mass communication in any meaningful sense.

Some graffiti, on the other hand, are as much mass communication as the billboards along the highways and as the local newspaper. The scrawled sign on a wall, "Divest now" or "U.S. out of everywhere!" speaks to the concerns of many people today. There is a great range of such messages, from "Gay Rights" to "Beat Illinois." Graffiti obviously are giving voice to the thoughts of many people and reinforcing them; just as obviously, since much graffiti is anti-establishment, such messages are also designed to discomfort those who disagree.

Some societies have tried to institutionalize graffiti, providing special walls where people can write their messages for all to see. The People's Republic of China has had such walls, for example. And some colleges provided similar space for graffiti during the late 1960s and early 1970s when anti-Vietnam feeling was at its height. The colleges hoped that students would use these specially constructed walls instead of painting their antiwar and other messages on buildings and sidewalks where they were costly to remove. Not surprisingly, the ploy did not work. Much of the pleasure from the creation of graffiti clearly comes from putting the messages in forbidden places.

● ● ●

Words: 279
Timing:

| Seconds | WPM |
|---------|-----|
| 20 | 837 |
| 30 | 558 |
| 40 | 418 |
| 50 | 335 |
| 60 | 279 |
| 70 | 239 |
| 80 | 209 |

## ■ Questions:

1. List one function of graffiti.

2. Are special graffiti walls effective in controlling graffiti?

### Passage D

#### THE ROLE OF TELEVISION IN OUR LIVES

Some comparisons may help you appreciate the large role the video medium plays in the lives of most Americans. In this country, more families have a television set than have a refrigerator, vacuum cleaner, telephone, or even indoor plumbing. About 98 percent of households have at least one receiver and over 55 percent have two or more—and these figures continue to rise. The average child between the ages of two and eleven watches over three and one-half hours of television a day and sees an estimated 20,000 commercials a year. Evidence indicates that Ronald McDonald, the clown who advertises McDonald's hamburgers on television, is the second best recognized figure by children in the United States, second only to Santa Claus. When some researchers asked children between the ages of four and six, "Which do you like better, TV or Daddy?" 44 percent of the youngsters said they preferred television[. . . .]

A news story about an attempted robbery in Cedar Rapids, Iowa, suggests that Americans not only watch a great deal of television, they attend to it closely. According to the news report, a man with a pistol entered a bar in Cedar Rapids one morning when the woman tending bar and her three customers were watching the CBS News. When the gunman warned them not to move, the bartender told him, "Nobody is getting robbed while I'm watching the news." Failing to get anyone's attention—even after cocking his pistol twice—the robber complained that he wasn't being taken seriously and left to get some help. When police caught him later and brought him back to the bar, they discovered one of the customers could not even identify the robber because he had never taken his eyes off the television set during the attempted holdup.

● ● ●

Words: 249
Timing:

| Seconds | WPM |
| --- | --- |
| 20 | 474 |
| 30 | 498 |
| 40 | 374 |
| 50 | 298 |
| 60 | 249 |
| 70 | 213 |
| 80 | 187 |

■ **Questions:**

1. What was the outcome of the robbery described in the second paragraph?

2. What is the main point of the passage?

### *Passage E*

**MODELING THEORY**

**Modeling theory** is a very sophisticated refinement of the old-fashioned idea that much of what we know and do we learned by example. That is, it suggests that we learn to behave the way we do in good part by watching and imitating models. Children watch their parents and friends and others and they try out some of the things they see them do. If a behavior they copy is reinforced in some way, they are more likely to retain that behavior more or less permanently. Children, and even adults, find models to imitate not only from among the people they know, but also from the true and fictional characters they see, hear, and read about in the mass media.

Through exposure to these various kinds of models, little boys learn how boys are supposed to behave and little girls learn how girls are supposed to behave. Somewhat older boys and girls learn from models how to dress, what to do in different kinds of situations, and what adult roles they may play and how to play them: student, lover, parent, working man or woman, and consumer.

Thus, a theory of modeling explains the ways the media help socialize children into the society in which they live. Many children see the same models on television, but because the models they have at home and elsewhere differ and because their imitation of models is reinforced in different ways, those media models affect them differently.

● ● ●

Words: 245
Timing:

| Seconds | WPM |
| --- | --- |
| 20 | 735 |
| 30 | 490 |
| 40 | 368 |
| 50 | 294 |
| 60 | 245 |
| 70 | 210 |
| 80 | 184 |

■ **Questions:**

Indicate whether the statement is true or false by marking "T" or "F" in the space provided.

1. Modeling theory explains how we learn by example. _____

2. Children learn how to behave and dress from models. _____

■ **PACING TECHNIQUES**

An established method of improving reading rate is called *pacing.* Pacing involves forcing yourself to read slightly faster than you normally would and trying to keep up with a preestablished pace. To better understand the concept of pacing, imagine that you are in a crowd of people and suddenly everyone starts walking forward quickly. You are forced along at the pace at which the crowd is moving, regardless of how fast you want to move. Similarly, in reading you can read more rapidly if you are "forced along" by some external means. Pacing is a way of forcing yourself to read faster than your normal speed while maintaining your level of comprehension.

## ■ Pacing Methods

There are numerous ways to pace yourself for speed increase. Among the most common are:

1. **Use an index card.** Slide a 3" × 5" card down the page, moving it so that it covers up lines as you read them. This technique will force you along and keep you moving rapidly. Move the card down the page at a fixed pace. How fast you move the card will, of course, depend on the size of the print, the length of the line, and so on, and will then vary for each new piece of material you read. At first you will need to experiment to find an appropriate pace. Try to move at a pace that is slightly uncomfortable and that you are not sure you can maintain.

2. **Use your hand or index finger, or a pen or pencil.** Use your hand or index finger, or a pen or pencil, in the same manner as the index card. Using your hand does not completely obstruct your view of the page and allows you to pick up clues from the layout of the page (to see that a paragraph is ending, that a graphic example is to follow, and so forth).

3. **Use a timer or alarm clock.** Start by measuring what portion of a page you can read in a minute. Then set a goal for yourself: Determine how many pages you will attempt to read in a given period of time. Set your goal slightly above what you measured as your current rate. For example, suppose in a particular book you can read half a page in a minute. You might set as your goal reading five pages in nine minutes (forcing yourself to read a little more than a half page per minute). The next day, try to read five pages in eight or eight and a half minutes. Use an alarm clock or timer to let you know when you have used up your time.

As you begin to use one of these pacing methods, here are several suggestions to keep in mind:

1. **Keep a record of your time, the amount you read, and your words per minute.** A quick way to estimate your speed is given in the Appendix at the end of the book.

2. **Be sure to maintain an adequate level of comprehension.** To test your comprehension, try to summarize what you read. If you are

unable to remember enough ideas to summarize what you read, you have probably read too fast.

3. **Push yourself gradually, across several weeks of practice.**

4. **Try to keep your practice material similar from day to day.** Consistently use newspapers, magazine articles, or the same paperback book for practice.

## ■ Why Pacing Works

Pacing is built on the principle that rate gain occurs in slow, incremental steps. Essentially, pacing provides a framework and a means to accomplish these incremental gains. Pacing is effective partly because it establishes a goal to be met, a speed to attain. It is psychologically motivating to work toward a goal, and when you attain a goal it is rewarding and encourages you to keep on working. It also provides a way for you to keep moving, without "getting lost in the print," so to speak. At times it is easy to become so involved with what you are reading that you become unaware of your speed and automatically shift to a slow but comfortable speed. Pacing forces you to keep moving at a given rate unless you deliberately decide to slow down. Pacing also improves your concentration by forcing you to pay closer attention to the text.

# EXERCISE 14–10

*DIRECTIONS:* Select an article from a periodical or use material that you have been assigned to read for one of your courses. Using one of the pacing techniques described in this section, try to increase your current reading speed by approximately 50 wpm. Record your results in the space provided. (See Chapter 1 for information on how to estimate the number of words and your WPM score.)

Material Used: _____

Estimated Level of Comprehension: _____

Finishing Time: _____

Starting Time: _____

Reading Time: _____

WPM: _____

**Critical Thinking Tip #14**

**Recognizing Judgments**

It is easy to miss nuances and shades of meaning when reading rapidly. Be sure to read articles and essays carefully and critically before you accept the information presented. One important critical reading skill is recognizing judgments.

Judgments are reasoned decisions based on evidence. They are decisions about the value or worth of an object, event, person, or idea. Here are a few examples:

Professor Lopez is the best lecturer on campus.

Ronald Reagan was the most politically aware president in the twentieth century.

Sam's serves the tastiest pizza in town.

Writers may make judgments based on factual information and use some standard or set of criteria to make them. As a critical reader, be sure to question the criteria used. For example, what criteria were used to decide that Professor Lopez was the *best* lecturer? Is she the most interesting, the best organized, or the most understandable? Similarly, what criteria were used to judge political awareness or tastiness?

Judgments often involve personal opinion. It is therefore possible that two authors may make two different judgments about the same topic. (Another writer may state that Professor Hargrave is the best lecturer.)

As a critical thinker, study the standards used to make a judgment before accepting it or agreeing with it. If none are provided, treat the judgment as merely a personal opinion. If standards are provided, evaluate them.

- Are they reasonable?
- Are they comprehensive?
- Does the author justify them?

## ■ REREADING FOR RATE INCREASE

Rereading is an effective method that builds your reading rate. This technique is similar to pacing in that it involves building your rate gradually by using small increments.

To reread for speed increase, use the following steps:

1. Select an article or passage and read it as you normally would for careful or leisure reading.

2. Time yourself and compute your speed in words per minute after you finish reading.

3. Take a break (five minutes or so). Then reread the same selection. Push yourself to read faster than you read the first time.

4. Time yourself and compute your speed once again. You should be able to reread the selection at a faster rate than you read it initially.

5. Read a new selection, pushing yourself to read almost as fast as you reread the first selection.

You are probably wondering how rereading helps you read new, unfamiliar material faster. Rereading serves as a preparation for reading the new material faster. Rereading establishes the mechanical process of more rapid eye movements and gives you preliminary practice, or a "trial run," with reading at a higher reading rate. It helps you learn things about reading faster while keeping your comprehension in balance. Because you already have a basic understanding of the selection from your first reading, you are free to focus and concentrate on improving your rate.

How fast you will be able to reread depends on the type of selection and the difficulty of its organization as well as your purpose for reading it. Of course, your rereading speed will be faster than your original speed because you are familiar with both the organization and content of the material. You know what to expect and can go back quite rapidly over ideas that are already familiar.

The last step of the process—the transfer of your increased speed to new, unfamiliar material—is the most important. Be sure to select material that is of the same difficulty, or perhaps a little easier, than the first piece of material you used. As in pacing, you should not try to make dramatic rate increases in any one practice session. Increases should be gradual.

## EXERCISE 14–11

*DIRECTIONS:* For one of the selections at the end of this chapter, apply the technique of key word reading. For the other, use the cluster reading technique. When you have completed both selections, compare your performance by reviewing your rate and comprehension scores. What can you conclude about the relative effectiveness of the two techniques?

## SUMMARY

**1. What are five aspects of eye movement that can directly affect your reading rate?**

Reading rate is directly affected by the following physical aspects of eye movements:
- speed of left-to-right progression
- number of fixations or "eye stops"
- size of eye span or amount of print seen in each fixation
- speed of return sweep from the end of one line to the start of the next
- number of regressions or backward eye movements

**2. What two reading habits, when taken to excess, can decrease your reading efficiency?**

Unnecessary regressions and vocalization/subvocalization can reduce your reading efficiency. Frequent regressions can increase your reading time and interfere with your comprehension. Likewise, your speed and comprehension are decreased by vocalizing (saying every word) and subvocalizing (mentally hearing every word) because they limit you to word-by-word reading.

**3. What techniques can you use to read faster?**

There are five techniques, which with practice, can help you to read faster.
- Cluster reading—widening your eye span to read words in meaningful groupings.
- Key word reading—reading only important words and skipping nonessential words.
- Using cue words—using transitional words to know how to adjust your rate.
- Pacing—forcing yourself to read slightly faster than normal.
- Rereading for rate increases—rereading previously read material at a higher speed and then attempting to read new material at the same speed.

# READING SELECTION 27
## FLIRTATION—THE SIGNALS OF ATTRACTION DECIPHERED

Maggie Paley
From *Vogue*

*This article, reprinted from* Vogue *magazine, explores the courtship ritual known as flirting. Read this article to discover the elements of flirting and how behaviorists study it.*

1   The art of flirtation is going out of style. I began to think about this the first time I heard Timothy Perper, Ph.D., discuss his work. We were both at his older sister's apartment for dinner. Perper, then a biologist at Rutgers University, with an interest in animal behavior, announced, by way of filling his sister in on his recent activities, that he'd been taking students with him to observe human flirtation at New Jersey singles bars. He'd discovered, he said, that most often women were the ones who chose the men. He hoped to get a grant to study the phenomenon further.

2   "You're going to get a grant to go to bars to prove that women choose men?" said Perper's belligerent sister. "You don't need a grant. Why don't you just ask me? Of course, women do the choosing. Any woman could tell you that."

3   At the time, Perper was thirty-nine and recently separated from his wife. His new line of research struck me as a peculiarly modern solution—in the self-help spirit—to the plight of the single scientist. In the old days, if a man wanted to watch people engage in "the first stages of becoming intimate," as Perper put it, he wouldn't have told anybody. In the old days, I could not have been lured into a singles bar, even to watch a behavioral scientist. Yet this was what, with some enthusiasm, I ended up doing a number of times recently.

4   It was a transition period in the history of the war between the sexes. Those women who'd been brought up to think you batted your eyes, smiled at a man, and then he made all your troubles disappear were beginning to see the flaws in this point of view. There were rumors that men were changing, and that some of them wanted equal relationships with women. These so-called "new men," instead of trying to amuse you, liked to talk about their feelings and health habits ("Can I make you a hamburger?" "I say the faster an animal moves the less fat is on it. I won't eat anything slower than a chicken.") You paid your own way with them, and you were direct instead of demure.

5   To be direct and seductive at the same time took a discouraging amount of energy. I found it hard to flirt at all under these conditions. Everyone was so confused about the things that should be most natural—how to assert themselves, enjoy themselves, be themselves. What *was* correct flirtation behavior? I got tired of trying to decide. I phoned Perper.

6   By ignoring his sister's advice at that dinner four years ago, Perper had become an authority on flirtation behavior and was beginning his third year of research in singles bars supported by a grant from the Harry Frank Guggenheim Foundation.

7   He had now ventured far beyond his sister's area of expertise. As a biologist, he told me, he'd learned to watch people flirt in much the same way he'd once watched rats engage in "copulatory behavior." Using this method, he'd discovered that all human flirtation, like mate selection among rats, took place in the form of body movement. What others called "chemistry," or "sexual attraction," he referred to as "body-movement compatibility." In his opinion, everyone worried

too much about good opening lines and clever conversation with strangers, when what they were really doing when they met was the human equivalent of sniffing each other out. Since no one could control such a process, he wished people would just relax and enjoy it.

8   We sat at a table at the Greenwich Village singles bar, One University Place. "I think there are a lot of unhappy people around," he said, "who don't really know how to make contact. And I would have put myself in that category, before I learned to read signals."

9   Most of the people who didn't know how to make contact, he told me, were men, and he thought it was a matter of training: men were so *ignorant* about behavior that a man could easily be in the middle of a flirtation without even knowing it. Women almost always knew when they were flirting, and it was in this sense that they could be said to be the ones doing the choosing. He had confirmed his observations with interviews; most men didn't notice cues and signals, and they didn't understand what women meant with their languorous looks and graceful gestures, though women assumed they did. A man didn't have to be good-looking or smart to be successful with women under these circumstances, according to Perper; he just had to pay attention to what they were doing.

10   Flirting, which I liked to think of as light, graceful, and easy, Perper had broken down into a sequence with four parts. Every flirtation he'd watched so far, he said, went through "approach" (the couple acknowledge each other's presence and begin talking); "swivel" (they turn gradually to face each other); "synchronization" (their movements begin to match); and "touch." Perper said "synchronization" was the most important step and made people feel, when they reached it, that they had "good vibes" together. I asked him to take me with him to watch this mating dance that I, a lifelong flirt, presumably had many times performed, smiling, nodding, and batting my eyes, in a semiconscious state.

11   Most of the men and women at the bars Perper showed me appeared to be suffering from a failure of imagination. They were there, but pretending not to be. The men were just lolling around by themselves, drinking beer and watching television. The women, who traveled in pairs, or in packs of three or more, seemed to have dressed up and gone out to have a good gossip with each other. It was as if the courage it took to enter a bar, seeking the company of strangers, had exhausted their supply of enthusiasm for the opposite sex. The men looked frightened and the women exasperated, and no one seemed capable of entering into a flirtation sequence.

12   I spent five nights with Perper, looking for a pickup to watch, and listening to his complaints about men—a welcome change from listening to my women friends' complaints about men. Perper spoke of men affectionately, as a high-school football coach might speak of a promising team that was always dropping the ball. During flirtation, he said, this happened particularly at what he called "escalation points," the moments when one partner, usually the woman, would act to move things forward—by turning to begin a "swivel," for example, or by putting a hand on the table where it could easily be touched. If the other partner, usually the man, didn't respond, the result would be "de-escalation." Perper hated to see a man de-escalate by accident.

13   With some agitation he would point out, say, a woman in a red dress, whom he'd refer to as "Red Dress." Red Dress would be sitting on a bar stool, facing "Check Suit" with adoration in her milk-chocolate eyes while Check Suit stood pivoting nervously back and forth. "That dumb jerk!" Perper would whisper to me. "If he doesn't turn towards her, she'll give up. You'd think he'd figure out that someone who's looking at him that way must like him."

14   Sometimes, Perper said, it was hard to stop himself from rushing to the aid of a floundering couple. "Once again now," he could imagine himself telling the man, "this time when she does that, take her hand." Check Suit looked to

me like a man wracked [*sic*] by ambivalence—which was what most men and women seemed to feel for each other most of the time. Perper said he thought what women did when they flirted was absolutely beautiful, and he felt sorry for the men who couldn't see it.

15 Now, there are male flirts who know perfectly well what women do when they flirt. I can assure you; men who know how to laugh and bat their eyes in return. But few of any sex can have studied, with the absorption Perper has, the entire arsenal of the human gestures of flirtation. These are sure signs that the person using them is flirting—what else could he be doing?—and once Perper was comfortable in a bar, he liked to mimic them. Some of the gestures he showed me were as obvious as the "eye avert"—when a man who's been looking a woman up and down then casts his eyes sideways (Perper mimed looking demure); or "brushing"—when a woman brushes against a man as if by accident ("It's never by accident," Perper said, brushing my left leg). Other gestures were disturbingly indirect, and apparently unconscious. Flirting people, he pointed out, spend a great deal of time preening and caressing themselves: stroking the neck, massaging an arm or leg. Touching the hair is a giveaway. Perper explained this phenomenon as "displacement"—you do to yourself what you'd like to do to the other person.

16 In a bar, Perper was a man in an invisible lab coat. His eyebrows seemed perpetually raised above steel-rimmed spectacles and pale eyes that focused on the middle distance; his high-bridged, beaked nose probed the air as if searching for a decent smell. He wore calculatedly nondescript clothes: the technique he practiced, "participant observation," required that he blend in with his environment. He ordered his drinks according to what bar he was in, and for the sake of appearances, he told me, he always worked as a "mixed-sex couple," and flirted with his partner. At regular intervals, when we were out together, he would lovingly touch my arm; I'd remind myself this was for the benefit of the people watching

us. No one was watching us, but it wasn't my business to disturb his equilibrium.

17 I did worry about the fact that there was nothing happening for us to watch. Then, on our fifth night, I saw synchronization. We were at a back table at The Mad Hatter of Second Avenue in Manhattan, a singles bar as cozy as home, with sawdust floors and mad hats hung from the ceiling beams. Perper had brought one of his regular partners with him, a bouncy anthropology graduate student named Marilyn Frasier.

18 Perper and Frasier were like hunters watching for lions. First they would scan the bar, where twelve men were lined up looking at the Yankee game and two women in jeans were talking to each other near the jukebox. Then they'd turn to the dining room which was crowded with young couples on dates, all of whom, according to Perper, were struggling through the flirtation sequence. Then, for a break, Perper and Frasier would flirt with each other. In the middle of my dinner, they located some action.

19 The couple at the table directly in front of us were engaging, Perper said heatedly, in "synchronization of drink-stirring behavior." This meant they'd stirred their drinks at the same time, and it didn't impress me. I continued to work on my filet of sole when Perper and Frasier gossiped about the couple.

20 "They're clasping their hands in unison."

21 "They're taking a drink. It's hard to see who's leading there."

22 "When you're really attracted to someone, you just seem to come towards each other at the same time, don't you?"

23 I thought something must actually be happening at that table. When I looked, a fluttering movement of the woman's right hand caught my attention. Almost at the same moment, the man made the same gesture with his right hand. Then the heel of his right hand went thoughtfully to his chin, and the heel of her right hand went to her chin, too. Next, he pulled his right earlobe. She pulled her right earlobe. Their gestures were light and graceful.

She clasped both hands under her lower lip, and so did he. Both of them sipped from their drinks, causing Perper and Frasier to chortle. The lifting of glasses was apparently a well-known chorus in the ongoing dance of hands at the table. I felt like a voyeur.

24 No such reverence for privacy inhibited the gleeful Perper. "I'm waiting for the first touch," he said confidentially. "They have to get the ketchup out of the way, and then the drinks, so they can touch by accident."

25 To contemplate manifestations of the unconscious in people I'd never met was an unsettling experience. I thought the sheer amount of energy being concentrated on this couple would cause them to turn around and glare back at us. I looked away from them to find that Perper was in sync with Frasier. The two of them smiled, forearms on the table, right hands grasping left elbows. They didn't know what they were doing. "Sometimes I think this is more fun than sex," Frasier said.

26 That night none of us was to reach a climax. The unfortunate couple couldn't negotiate their next escalation point. When Perper said it was time for them to touch, they didn't. The woman caressed her glass (a "touch invitation"), and the man mistook the signal and lifted his glass to drink ("de-escalation"). The woman dropped her hands to her lap, giving up, and after that they gestured to each other in nervous jabs. They had lost the beat. "Dummy," Perper said in a small pained voice as if he were the one who'd been de-escalated. "She made overtures, he did not respond, and he should have. It has an unhappy ending."

27 "Don't jump to conclusions," Frasier told him, "just relax." But the couple ate their dinner, paid their check, and left without ever synchronizing their body movements again.

28 By this time, the men at the bar were three-deep, watching the Yankee game. Two women in jeans sat on the jukebox. "The more I think about that, the more I think his inability to respond was absolutely classic," Perper said to Frasier.

29 "He got more and more uncomfortable," Frasier agreed. A man at the bar asked the two women to get off the jukebox. They stood by his side while he made his selections, but he didn't talk to them. He wore a T-shirt with a drawing of a molecule on it and the name of the male sex hormone, "testosterone."

30 Perper is writing a book about his findings. He says he thinks everyone should be "comfortable with their biology," and I hope he helps people to take it easy when they flirt. As for me, now that I've seen synchronization I can hardly gesture across a dinner table without checking to see what my partner is doing. I'm not sure all humans were meant to have their consciousness raised.

## Comprehension Test 27

*Directions:  Circle the letter of the best answer.*

### Checking Your Comprehension

1. The main idea of this article could be stated as follows:
   a. Men generally prefer women to de-escalate during the flirtation process.
   b. Flirtation is composed of several distinct steps of which most people are not conscious.
   c. In all flirtation situations it is the woman who begins the conversation.
   d. Most people are highly skilled in the flirtation process and practice it at bars.

2. The so-called "new men" would not prefer to
   a. have an equal relationship with a woman
   b. have women be direct with them

c. tell women about their feelings

d. discuss their health habits with women

3. During the scene that took place at The Mad Hatter of Second Avenue, the couple being observed had to move the ketchup and the drinks before moving on in the flirtation process because
   a. these items were a barrier to his de-escalation
   b. she felt intimidated by having a barrier between them
   c. these items were a barrier to touching accidentally
   d. the author could not observe them with these obstructions

4. Men often found themselves in the middle of a flirtation without even knowing it because
   a. women were ignorant of this type of behavior
   b. men were ignorant of this type of behavior
   c. women had better opening lines and caught the men off guard
   d. men did not usually go to bars to flirt

5. The four parts of flirtation behavior are
   a. approach, swivel, synchronization, touch
   b. approach, synchronization, swivel, touch
   c. approach, touch, swivel, synchronization
   d. approach, swivel, touch, synchronization

6. As it is used here, the word mimic (paragraph 15) means to
   a. insult
   b. disturb
   c. imitate
   d. influence

**Thinking Critically**

7. In the case of the couple being observed at The Mad Hatter, the flirtation was ended due to the fault of the
   a. observers
   b. bartender
   c. woman
   d. man

8. Perper ignored his sister's advice because he
   a. needed to prove it scientifically
   b. believed she was wrong
   c. thought it would be fun to go to bars himself
   d. needed to spend the grant money

9. Judging by the author's experience in singles bars, you can conclude that
   a. there are a great many examples of flirtation to be viewed there
   b. not as much flirtation goes on there as many people think
   c. men are really experts at flirtation
   d. women are very clumsy and inept flirters

10. When the author refers to Perper as "a man in an invisible lab coat," she means that
    a. his coat really was invisible
    b. he wore a coat of clear plastic
    c. he was being a scientist but nobody knew it
    d. his clothes were nondescript

**Questions for Discussion**

1. Does the four-part flirtation sequence accurately describe what you personally have observed? Why?

2. Why do you think men are unable to respond to flirting as well as women?

3. In what situations, other than flirtation, do you think synchronization might occur?

| Selection 27: | | 2528 words | |
|---|---|---|---|
| Finishing Time: | _____ | _____ | _____ |
| | HR. | MIN. | SEC. |
| Starting Time: | _____ | _____ | _____ |
| | HR. | MIN. | SEC. |
| Reading Time: | | _____ | _____ |
| | | MIN. | SEC. |
| WPM Score: | | _____ | |
| Comprehension Score: | | _____ | % |

MASS
COMMUNICATION

## READING SELECTION 28
## THE FUNCTIONS AND EFFECTS OF MUSIC
Samuel L. Becker
From *Discovering Mass Communication*

*This excerpt from a mass communication textbook explores the uses of music. Read the excerpt to answer these questions.*

*1. What are the political uses of music?*
*2. What other functions of music does the excerpt discuss?*

1     You are well aware of the fact that books, newspapers, magazines, motion pictures, radio, and television have been used for persuasive purposes: to sell beer and soap, ideas and political candidates; to bring about social change or to quell a revolution. Few of us think about music or recordings being used for these purposes, but they are and have been for a long time.

2     Every war has had its songs that whipped up patriotic fervor or, in the case of the Vietnam War, that encouraged protest against it. Some titles of records popular in this country during World War II suggest the extent of the mobilization of the recording industry for the war effort: "Remember Pearl Harbor," "Have to Slap That Dirty Little Jap," "There's a Star Spangled Banner Waving Somewhere," "Any Bonds Today," and "'Round and 'Round Hitler's Grave."

3     The anti-Vietnam protests of the sixties and early seventies brought forth quite another kind of song. One was "Big Muddy," about a group of soldiers blindly following their commanding officer into a river where many were drowned. Those who sang and heard the song knew that the "Big Muddy" referred to Vietnam and the commander to President Lyndon Johnson, and their anti-war passions were intensified. "Where Have All the Flowers Gone," "The Times, They are A-Changin'," and "Give Peace a Chance" were other popular songs whose recordings were widely played and used to build resistance to the war.

4     Music is used not only to add persuasive bits of information for the messages in our heads about war. Persuasive music plays an important role in peacetime also. "We Shall Overcome" was a tremendously important force in the civil rights movement, just as the folk songs of Joan Baez, Pete Seeger, and Woody Guthrie have been important to the peace movement. In recent times, music has been used to raise money as well as consciousness for various causes. The Live Aid, Farm Aid, Band Aid, and U.S.A. for Africa concerts and recording sessions raised funds for such causes as famine relief in Africa and destitute American farmers.

5     Somewhat further back in this country's history, the radical left adopted many old Negro spirituals to communicate its message effectively. "We Shall Not Be Moved," for example, was adopted as the official song of the radical Southern Tenant Farmers Union in the 1930s. In the 1930s also, "Gimme That Old Time Religion" was transformed into "Gimme That New Communist Spirit." That sort of adaptation of songs—giving them new lyrics—has been a favorite tactic of many groups who want to use music for persuasive purposes. The idea is to take a song that people like or that has particular meaning or emotional association for them and use it with new words, hoping that some of the liking, meaning, or emotional associations will transfer to the new ideas being communicated. And it often works.

## Threats of Censorship

6    Such political uses of music have never caused much controversy in this country. There has been some pressure at times to keep certain anti-war songs or songs associated with the radical left off the air, but this pressure has been neither strong nor persistent. Far more pressure and controversy has been aroused by the lyrics of some of the popular songs of the last twenty or thirty years. Many critics have charged that certain rock-and-roll songs encourage sexual promiscuity and the use of drugs. Rightly or wrongly, the dress and antics of some of the rock music stars, both on and off the stage, reinforce these beliefs. As a result, a number of community and national groups have applied pressure on stations to keep these songs and performers off the air. These charges also stimulated investigations by the Federal Communications Commission, the regulatory agency charged with overseeing broadcast practices. The FCC has taken the position, unpopular with many broadcasters, that the station licensee has the same public service responsibility in selecting and rejecting music to be played on the station as it has in selecting and rejecting any other content of the station. The FCC position is that the station should exercise the same supervision of what is sung on the station as of what is said. In a general sense, this is a reasonable position and the only one the FCC could take, given present law. A problem arises with the interpretation of this injunction, however. Does it mean a station should permit no language or ideas in a song that it would not permit on the news or in a sports program? Or does it mean the station should recognize that different forms of communication or entertainment, or programs designed for different kinds of audiences, should have different standards concerning language and ideas? This issue is still far from settled.

7    Having been largely unsuccessful in keeping sexually suggestive songs or songs that seem to be promoting drug use off the air, some parents' groups in recent years have been attempting to force companies to label their recordings in the same way film companies now label motion pictures. The assumption is that such labels will provide parents with information they need to control the kinds of music to which their young children are exposed. One of the major pressure groups involved in this attempt is the Parents Music Resource Center based in Washington, D.C. The leaders in this group include the wives of some powerful congressmen and other government officials, so it is taken seriously by leaders in the music industry. The concern of many people in the music business, though, is that the labeling being advocated could be just a first step toward other forms of control or censorship.

## The Impact of Recordings on Our Perceptions

8    Whatever the direct effects of musical recordings on our attitudes and behaviors, they are certainly an ever-present and important part of our communication environment, and they contribute to the realities in our heads. No one who listened to popular music during the '80s could escape the perception that drugs were a major factor in the lives of many people. Popular music of the early '70s contributed to the belief that most people opposed the war in Vietnam. These messages, sneaking into consciousness from the background music around us, formed an important part of our communication mosaics, just as the messages in today's music form an important part of our present communication mosaics.

## The Role of Music in Identification and Rebellion

9    Popular music has two other major functions or effects. It provides each generation of young people a common and cherished experience. Years later, the sound of that music can bring strangers together and stimulate memories of that

earlier era. Vivid evidence of the meaningfulness of such experiences can be seen by watching the tourists who are attracted to Graceland, Elvis Presley's former home and now the site of his grave in Memphis. A common sight there is the middle-aged married couple bringing their children to see and, they hope, to feel some of the special magic Presley created for them during their courtship and early married years.

10    Another major function popular music serves is the provision of a relatively harmless source of rebellion for the young. Each generation of young has its own music, almost invariably unappreciated by parents, just as parents' favorite music was unappreciated by their parents. This music is important in part because older people do not like it, and in part because demonstrating one's love of it is part of the ritual of affiliation with peers.

11    One author has suggested that popular music also serves a "rite of passage" function for young girls. The teenage singing idols may serve as non-threatening substitutes for actual boys until boys' maturation catches up with that of girls and some semblance of easy boy-girl relationships can be established.

## Comprehension Test 28*

### Checking Your Comprehension

1. How was music used during World War II? During the Vietnam War?

2. Describe peacetime uses of music.

3. To what do critics object in current rock-and-roll songs?

4. List the major effects and functions of music.

### Thinking Critically

1. Identify the basic issues in the FCC regulatory position.

2. What problems do you foresee in the development of record labeling plans?

3. How does music function as a form of rebellion?

4. What types of evidence does the author use to support his contentions?

---

*Multiple-choice questions are contained in Appendix B (page A29).

**Questions for Discussion**

1. Adaptation of popular or favorite songs is a persuasive tactic. Where is this technique used today? Cite several examples. (Hint: Advertising commercials)

2. If music shapes our perceptions and attitudes, should we be forced to listen to music in public places such as restaurants and shopping malls?

3. Does music have other effects that are not included in this article?

Selection 28:                    1291 words

Finishing Time:    _____  _____  _____
                     HR.      MIN.     SEC.

Starting Time:    _____  _____  _____
                     HR.      MIN.     SEC.

Reading Time:              _____  _____
                            MIN.     SEC.

WPM Score:        _____

Comprehension Score:    _____%

**Visit the Longman English Pages**

For additional readings and exercises, visit the Longman English Skills Web page at:

**http://longman.awl.com/englishpages**

For a username and password, please see your instructor.

# Task Performance Assessment: UNIT FIVE

The following task is designed to assess your ability to use and apply the skills taught in this unit.

## THE SETTING

This semester you are working as a tutor for psychology in the Academic Skills Center. One of the students you are tutoring complains that he must spend too much time reading his assignments. On questioning him further, you learn that he reads all information the same way: He uses the same technique on everything and reads all materials slowly. When you tell him that you vary your technique and speed to suit what you are reading and why you are reading it, he asks you if you can help him change his approach.

After consulting with your supervisor, you ask the student to bring samples of the reading he must do. The student brings the following:

1. His psychology textbook, on which his instructor bases multiple choice exams.
2. A sample of the additional readings that are on reserve in the library. The instructor requires students to be familiar with important ideas in each reading in preparation for a class discussion.
3. A research article from the *Journal of Psychology* that describes an experiment conducted to measure aggressive tendencies of young children. The instructor has asked students to read it critically and write a summary of the article.

## YOUR TASK

Make a list of strategies and advice you would give the student that would help him read *each* of the materials effectively and efficiently. Be specific. Suggest the level of comprehension he needs and suggest reading techniques that would help him read at an appropriate speed. Also, suggest what the student should do before, during, and after reading, if anything, to help him achieve his purpose for reading. Describe each technique or strategy that you suggest. You may include any technique you have learned so far (you need not limit yourself to techniques taught in Unit Five).

# APPENDIX A
# Learning Style Questionnaire

*DIRECTIONS: Each item presents two choices. Select the alternative that best describes you. In cases in which neither choice suits you, select the one that is closest to your preference. Write the letter of your choice in the blank to the left of each item.*

**Part One**

_____ 1. I would prefer to follow a set of
   a. oral directions.
   b. written directions.

_____ 2. I would prefer to
   a. attend a lecture given by a famous psychologist.
   b. read an article written by the psychologist.

_____ 3. When I am introduced to someone, it is easier for me to remember the person's
   a. name
   b. face

_____ 4. I find it easier to learn new information by using
   a. language (words).
   b. images (pictures).

_____ 5. I prefer classes in which the instructor
   a. lectures and answers questions.
   b. uses films and videos.

_____ 6. To follow the current events, I prefer to
   a. listen to the news on the radio.
   b. read the newspaper.

_____ 7. To learn how to operate a fax machine, I would prefer to
   a. listen to a friend's explanation.
   b. watch a demonstration.

**Part Two**

_____ 8. I prefer to
   a. work with facts and details.
   b. construct theories and ideas.

_____ 9. I would prefer a job involving
   a. following specific instructions.
   b. reading, writing, and analyzing.

_____ 10. I prefer to
   a. solve math problems using a formula.
   b. discover why the formula works.

_____ 11. I would prefer to write a term paper explaining
   a. how a process works.
   b. a theory.

_____ 12. I prefer tasks that require me to
   a. follow careful, detailed instructions.
   b. use reasoning and critical analysis.

_____ 13. For a criminal justice course, I would prefer to
   a. discover how and when a law can be used.
   b. learn how and why it became law.

_____ 14. To learn more about the operation of a high speed computer printer, I
   would prefer to
   a. work with several types of printers.
   b. understand the principles on which they operate.

**Part Three**

_____ 15. To solve a math problem, I would prefer to
   a. draw or visualize the problem.
   b. study a sample problem and use it as a model.

_____ 16. To best remember something, I
   a. create a mental picture.
   b. write it down.

_____ 17. Assembling a bicycle from a diagram would be
   a. easy.
   b. challenging.

_____ 18. I prefer classes in which I
   a. handle equipment or work with models.
   b. participate in a class discussion.

_____ 19. To understand and remember how a machine works, I would
   a. draw a diagram.
   b. write notes.

_____ 20. I enjoy
   a. drawing or working with my hands.
   b. speaking, writing, and listening.

_____ 21. If I were trying to locate an office on an unfamiliar campus, I would prefer
   a. a map.
   b. written directions.

**Part Four**

_____ 22. For a grade in biology lab, I would prefer to
   a. work with a lab partner.
   b. work alone.

_____ 23. When faced with a difficult personal problem I prefer to
   a. discuss it with others.
   b. resolve it myself.

_____ 24. Many instructors could improve their classes by
   a. including more discussion and group activities.
   b. allowing students to work on their own more frequently.

_____ 25. When listening to a lecture by a speaker, I respond more to the
   a. person presenting the idea.
   b. ideas themselves.

_____ 26. When on a team project, I prefer to
   a. work with several team members.
   b. divide the tasks and complete those assigned to me.

_____ 27. I prefer to shop and do errands
   a. with friends.
   b. by myself.

_____ 28. A job in a busy office is
   a. more appealing than working alone.
   b. less appealing than working alone.

**Part Five**

_____ 29. To make decisions I rely on
   a. my experiences and gut feelings.
   b. facts and objective data.

_____ 30. To complete a task, I
   a. can use whatever is available to get the job done.
   b. must have everything I need at hand.

_____ 31. I prefer to express my ideas and feelings through
   a. music, song, or poetry.
   b. direct, concise language.

_____ 32. I prefer instructors who
   a. allow students to be guided by their own interests.
   b. make their own expectations clear and explicit.

_____ 33. I tend to
  a. challenge and question what I hear and read.
  b. accept what I hear and read.

_____ 34. I prefer
  a. essay exams.
  b. objective exams.

_____ 35. In completing an assignment, I prefer to
  a. figure out my own approach.
  b. be told exactly what to do.

To score your questionnaire, record the total number of *a*'s you select-ed and the total number of *b*'s for each part of the questionnaire. Record your totals in the scoring grid provided.

## ■ SCORING GRID

| PARTS | TOTAL # OF CHOICE **a** | TOTAL # OF CHOICE **b** |
|---|---|---|
| Part One | _____ | _____ |
| | Auditory | Visual |
| Part Two | _____ | _____ |
| | Applied | Conceptual |
| Part Three | _____ | _____ |
| | Spatial | Verbal |
| Part Four | _____ | _____ |
| | Social | Independent |
| Part Five | _____ | _____ |
| | Creative | Pragmatic |

Now, circle your higher score for each part of the questionnaire. The word below the score you circled indicated a strength of your learning style. The next section explains how to interpret your scores.

## ■ INTERPRETING YOUR SCORES

Each of the five parts of the questionnaire identifies one aspect of your learning style. These five aspects are explained here.

## ■ Part One: Auditory or Visual Learners

This score indicates whether you learn more effectively by listening (auditory) or by seeing (visual). If you have a higher score on auditory than visual, you tend to be an auditory learner. That is, you tend to learn more easily by hearing than by reading. A higher score on visual suggests strengths with visual modes of learning—reading, studying pictures, reading diagrams, and so forth.

## ■ Part Two: Applied or Conceptual Learners

This score describes the types of learning tasks and learning situations you prefer and find easiest to handle. If you are an applied learner, you prefer tasks that involve real objects and situations. Practical, real-life examples are ideal for you. If you are a conceptual learner, you prefer to work with language and ideas; you do not need practical applications for understanding.

## ■ Part Three: Spatial or Nonspatial Learners

This score reveals your ability to work with spatial relationships. Spatial learners are able to visualize or mentally see how things work or how they are positioned in space. Their strengths may include drawing, assembling, or repairing things. Nonspatial learners lack skills in positioning things in space. Instead they rely on verbal or language skills.

## ■ Part Four: Social or Independent Learners

This score reveals whether you like to work alone or with others. If you are a social learner, you prefer to work with others—both classmates and instructors—closely and directly. You tend to be people-oriented and enjoy personal interaction. If you are an independent learner, you prefer to work alone and study alone. You tend to be self-directed or self-motivated and often goal oriented.

## ■ Part Five: Creative or Pragmatic Learners

This score describes the approach you prefer to take toward learning tasks. Creative learners are imaginative and innovative. They prefer to learn through discovery or experimentation. They are comfortable taking risks and following hunches. Pragmatic learners are practical, logical, and systematic. They seek order and are comfortable following rules.

If you disagree with any part of the Learning Style Questionnaire, go with your own instincts rather than questionnaire results. The questionnaire is just a quick assessment; trust your knowledge of yourself in areas of dispute.

# APPENDIX B

# Multiple-Choice Questions for Even-Numbered Reading Selections

## Reading Selection 2 "Hispanic, U.S.A.: The Conveyor-Belt Ladies"

*DIRECTIONS:* *Circle the letter of the best answer.*

**Checking Your Comprehension**

1. The reading is primarily about
   a. the poor working conditions of all migrant workers
   b. the relationship the author developed with the other worker
   c. male-female relationships
   d. wife abuse

2. This reading is organized using which of the following patterns of thought?
   a. cause-effect
   b. definition
   c. time sequence
   d. comparison-contrast

3. The author received special treatment from the women workers during her last summer because
   a. they felt inferior to her
   b. they knew it would be her last summer
   c. they were protecting her from harassment by male supervisors
   d. they respected the level of education she had achieved

4. Why did the author continue to work in the tomato sheds even though she disliked the work?
   a. The job presented and opportunity to learn about Hispanic culture from other women.
   b. Her mother insisted that she work there.
   c. It was the highest paying job she could get.
   d. Working in the sheds was the only job she could get.

5. What technique did the male supervisors use to try to stop the women from talking as they worked?
   a. docking the women's pay

   b. ridiculing them
   c. reducing their work hours
   d. changing their work stations

6. Which of the following best describes the meaning of the word *stigmatize* as used in paragraph 10?
   a. criticize
   b. label in a negative way
   c. embarrass
   d. strongly influence

**Thinking Critically**

7. The author compares working on the conveyor belt to belonging to the cast of a play to emphasize the job's
   a. routine nature
   b. lack of importance
   c. focus on human relationships
   d. unrealistic quality

8. The women workers' attitude toward their station in life was one of
   a. contentment
   b. denial
   c. anger
   d. acceptance

9. The author's attitude toward the women workers
   a. remained the same throughout her work experience
   b. changed from one of disdain to one of respect
   c. is not revealed in the reading
   d. became a point of contention between the author and the workers

10. It is reasonable to conclude from the article that the author
   a. grew to like her coworkers simply because she felt sorry for them
   b. maintained a cool, distant relationship with her coworkers
   c. came to respect the women who worked on the conveyor belt for their strength of spirit, especially during hardship
   d. always felt superior to her coworkers

## Reading Selection 4 "Just Walk On By: A Black Man Ponders His Power To Alter Public Space"

*DIRECTIONS: Circle the letter of the best answer.*

**Checking Your Comprehension**

1. Which of the following statements best describes the reading?
   a. Is an essay about why white women fear black men.
   b. It is a descriptions of racial tensions in large cities.

    c. It is an argument for greater racial equality.

    d. It is a personal account of a black man's experiences and feelings about the way he is perceived in public places.

2. The author may have been unaware of public reactions to him before age 22 because
   a. he was a member of a gang
   b. he lived in a small town in Pennsylvania
   c. he wasn't noticeable among criminals and street gangs
   d. he was shy and withdrawn

3. The "mugging literature" the author cites is
   a. other authors who have written about fear of black males
   b. crime statistics about muggers
   c. essays that describe muggers and their intentions
   d. literature describing the role of black men in society

4. The author regards the attitude that men must be powerful and valiant as
   a. a personal expression
   b. nonsense
   c. having historical justification
   d. legitimate

5. The "hunch posture" as described by the author, is a(n)
   a. protective, defensive posture
   b. disrespectful gesture
   c. aggressive movement
   d. signal that assistance is needed

6. Which of the following best defines the word *alienation* as used in paragraph 6?
   a. problems
   b. feeling of separation or aversion
   c. anger or fear
   d. repulsiveness

### Thinking Critically

7. The author's primary purpose in writing the article is to
   a. persuade people to alter their public behavior toward blacks
   b. describe his feelings about reactions to him in public space
   c. familiarize the reader with problems of large cities
   d. argue that public space should not be altered

8. The author whistles Vivaldi to
   a. announce his presence
   b. suggest that he is unlike typical muggers
   c. indicate his level of musical expertise
   d. announce that he is unafraid

9. Which of the following best describes the author's attitude about women's fear of black men?
   a. The author thinks their fear is unfounded.
   b. The author regards their fear as exaggerated, as a hallucination.
   c. The author finds their fear understandable but still has difficulty when it is applied to him.
   d. The author is angry and feels he is not understood.

10. To communicate his ideas, the author relies most heavily on
    a. logical reasoning
    b. statistics and "mugging literature"
    c. personal experience
    d. fact

## Reading Selection 6 "Why the Sky Is Blue, Sunsets Are Red, and Clouds Are White"

*DIRECTIONS:   Circle the letter of the best answer.*

### Checking Your Comprehension

1. This reading is primarily about
   a. light
   b. atoms
   c. sound
   d. vibrations

2. The main point of the reading is that
   a. ultraviolet light is absorbed by ozone gas
   b. a certain frequency of sound causes a similar frequency of sound to vibrate
   c. the way in which light responds under various conditions affects several natural phenomena
   d. the color blue scatters with greater frequency than any other color

3. The blue of the sky varies in color because of
   a. water vapor
   b. intensity of sunlight
   c. low-level haze
   d. high-frequency light

4. The author uses the ringing of bells to
   a. demonstrate how sound scatters
   b. explain how light scatters
   c. explain what particles look like
   d. show how frequencies change

5. Astronauts do not see the blueness of the sky because
   a. the speed with which they are moving distorts the color
   b. the earth's surface is bright

    c.  the blue light doesn't scatter easily

    d.  the angle of reflection interferes

6.  The word *progresses* (paragraph 7) as used in the reading means
    a.  increases suddenly
    b.  moves forward
    c.  shows improvement
    d.  becomes brighter

**Thinking Critically**

7.  Which of the following has the lowest frequency?
    a.  blue light
    b.  yellow light
    c.  red light
    d.  white light

8.  If molecules in the sky scattered low-frequency light instead of high-frequency light, how would sunsets appear?
    a.  red
    b.  blue
    c.  green
    d.  yellow

9.  Based on information in the reading, which of the following actions do you think the author would support?
    a.  policies restricting research in outer space
    b.  laws restricting seeding clouds to control weather
    c.  laws limiting automobile pollution
    d.  further research on the effects of color

10. Distant mountains appear bluish because
    a.  the atmosphere between us and the mountains is blue
    b.  light is reflected from the mountains
    c.  it frequently rains on the mountain tops
    d.  sunlight on the mountains is absorbed

## Reading Selection 8 "The Future of Zoos"

*DIRECTIONS:    Circle the letter of the best answer.*

**Checking Your Comprehension**

1.  The major topic of this reading concerns
    a.  what happens in zoos
    b.  preserving wildlife
    c.  the treatment of zoo animals
    d.  the effects of deforestation

2. The main idea of this selection is that
   a. zoos should work to ensure biodiversity
   b. zoos should house more species of animals
   c. many species of animals have become extinct
   d. money is an important factor in animal preservation

3. Four to six thousand animal species a year are being killed off because of
   a. poaching
   b. deforestation
   c. pollution
   d. disease

4. According to this article, the group that is most qualified to manage and preserve a high level of biodiversity in wildlife population is
   a. zoo professionals
   b. the National Wildlife Foundation
   c. the United Nations
   d. conservation groups

5. The population of large wading birds in Florida's Everglades National Park was nearly wiped out by 1989 due to
   a. continued hunting on the preserve
   b. the sale of park land for home building
   c. activities on land bordering the preserve
   d. the large number of tourists visiting the park

6. The word *stake* in paragraph 2 means
   a. investment
   b. charge
   c. authority
   d. claim

## Thinking Critically

7. The author's purpose in writing this selection is to
   a. entertain
   b. complain
   c. protest
   d. educate

8. The author supports her position by
   a. presenting theories
   b. providing opinions
   c. stating facts
   d. illustrating ideas

9. Bill Conway, of the Bronx Zoo, says, "All kinds of conservation activities ultimately come down to buying time." What would he consider the best way of "buying time?"
   a. purchasing land in order to save a species from being wiped out by poachers

b. extending the life of a particular species by caring for those animals that are still alive

c. investing in a rain forest so that more animals can mate, thereby increasing the population of many species

d. finding the time to become an active advocate for animal conservation issues

10. This selection supports the conclusion that in order for zoos to survive into the twenty-first century they must change their
    a. obsolete architecture
    b. fund raising methods
    c. staff training
    d. central goals

## Reading Selection 10 "How Students Get Lost in Cyberspace"

*DIRECTIONS:    Circle the letter of the best answer.*

**Checking Your Comprehension**

1. According to the reading, the World Wide Web is useful for
   a. scholars
   b. professors
   c. students at universities
   d. the average citizen

2. The Internet is least useful for
   a. focusing information to make a point
   b. finding information related to a topic
   c. determining the reliability of sources
   d. overcoming the limitations of your college library

3. At what point did Adam Pasick find the information that he needed?
   a. when he first searched the Internet
   b. when he was guided by a reference librarian
   c. when he asked his professor for help
   d. when he decided to use paper journals not on the Internet

4. From the point of view of a professor, the problem with doing research on the World Wide Web is
   a. that there is so much information available students don't research an issue thoroughly
   b. students often plagiarize information from the Internet
   c. students can't tell the reliable Internet information from the unreliable
   d. students will become unaccustomed to using paper sources in the library when they need to

5. Students can expect to find the least valuable information for research papers at a home page set up by
   a. an academic publication

    b. an educational institution or foundation

    c. an agency of the federal government

    d. an individual interested in a particular issue

6. In paragraph 6, the author states that the cost for information is "borne by universities." In this context, "borne" means

    a. created by

    b. paid by

    c. determined by

    d. increased by

**Thinking Critically**

7. When beginning a research project, you should first

    a. select the most efficient search engine

    b. browse the Web for useful information

    c. go directly to a home page

    d. seek the assistance of a reference librarian

8. The problem with online subscriptions is that they are

    a. wasteful since they are available in paper also

    b. not reliable sources of information

    c. too difficult to locate on the Web

    d. too expensive for many colleges

9. One form of assistance that the Web will probably never provide in the future is

    a. a wide variety of search engines

    b. screening for the reliability of information

    c. a wide range of scholarly journals

    d. a time-efficient method to search for information

10. The best reason for including both Internet and paper sources in a major research paper is to

    a. lend it the variety it needs

    b. save time doing the research

    c. produce a more thorough paper

    d. add interest to it

## Reading Selection 12 "Changing the Pattern of Gendered Discussion: Lessons from Science Classrooms"

*DIRECTIONS:   Circle the letter of the best answer.*

**Checking Your Comprehension**

1. Which one of the following does *not* account for why boys achieve more than girls in high school science classes?

    a. Boys tend to dominate group discussions more than girls.

    b. Boys generally score higher on intelligence tests than girls.

    c.  Teachers themselves unknowingly promote gender bias in their classrooms.

    d.  Boys and girls promote gender bias through their communication styles.

2.  When studying the language patterns of males and females in discussion groups, the author quickly discovered that

    a.  males were more likely to volunteer to be a "shill" during discussions

    b.  females were more likely to argue with males than with other females

    c.  males were more inclined to listen and probe than to discuss and argue

    d.  males and females had similar language styles in group discussions

3.  In group discussions, when females posed questions rather than engaging in direct argumentation, boys thought girls

    a.  were just being polite according to social conventions

    b.  were attempting to get them to think more globally or critically about a topic

    c.  didn't know as much as they did about the basic facts and concepts of science

    d.  were concealing their knowledge to keep from being perceived as competitive

4.  Females who voiced their opinions during refutational discussions later reported feeling

    a.  their opinions had been dismissed by the boys

    b.  that the boys thought less of them

    c.  like they had been "showing off" how much they knew

    d.  that the boys respected them more for asserting themselves

5.  What did the study conducted by the authors illustrate about boys in group discussion?

    a.  They argue as directly as girls do.

    b.  The really do know more about the technical aspects of science than girls.

    c.  They are less confident about their arguments than they seem to be.

    d.  They enjoy the process of arguing more than girls do.

6.  The term *refutation* used throughout the reading refers to

    a.  engaging in a formal, in-depth debate

    b.  disproving another's point of view

    c.  presenting an argument based upon logical premises

    d.  initiating a claim in an argument

### Thinking Critically

7.  If the author had not conducted same-sex lab groups during the second year of the study, it is likely that the girls would have

    a.  refused to sit back and allow the boys to take control

    b.  realized how the boys were dominating discussions

    c.  argued as much as the boys because of their increasing discomfort

    d.  continued to feel uncomfortable in the small and large group discussions

8.  In what way do the authors believe that separating boys from girls in small refutational group discussions will be beneficial?

    a.  It will help boys to become better listeners and less domineering.

    b. It will assist both girls and boys in being less distracted by the opposite sex.

    c. It will help girls not to lose confidence when they get an answer incorrect.

    d. It will encourage girls to debate scientific concepts on fair ground.

9. From the author's viewpoint, which one of the following should teachers do to help both boys and girls?

    a. Arrange entire classrooms to include discussion and other activities by gender.

    b. Encourage girls to be less emotional and boys to be less logical while discussing scientific concepts.

    c. Use questioning as a device for argumentation, thereby encouraging listening as a good argumentative quality.

    d. Consistently interrupt boys who excitedly debate their views in order to give girls an opportunity to do the same.

10. When the authors stated that teachers should provide "an intellectually safe environment" they meant that teachers should

    a. encourage girls to debate only with other girls and boys only with other boys so no one will feel left out

    b. provide additional readings in which both boys and girls can maintain an equal interest

    c. be positive to girls' responses by calling on girls, restating their responses, and praising them for their comments and questions

    d. not allow debate of important concepts when conducting classroom instruction

## Reading Selection 14 "So Few Farmers, So Many Bureaucrats"

*DIRECTIONS:*   *Circle the letter of the best answer.*

### Checking Your Comprehension

1. This reading is primarily about

    a. farm productivity

    b. supply and demand

    c. the relationship between farming and bureaucracy

    d. farm subsidies

2. The main point of this reading is that

    a. farm productivity is increasing

    b. farm subsidies do more harm than good

    c. lobbyists and well-to-do farmers produce a vicious circle

    d. large numbers of bureaucrats are kept in place

3. One reason that farming is becoming a business is

    a. farm workers are becoming more productive

    b. there is a greater demand for agricultural products

c. government subsidy encourages treating farming as a business

d. the bureaucratic structure encourages business developments

4. Subsidies (payments) to farmers by the government have
   a. reduced the cost of agricultural products
   b. allowed farmers to plant less
   c. maintained farm prices
   d. increased pressure on farmers

5. Which of the following in not a member of the iron triangle?
   a. members of Congress
   b. consumers
   c. Department of Agriculture bureaucrats
   d. agribusiness farmers

6. The term *paradoxes* (paragraph 1) means
   a. contradictions
   b. problems
   c. outcomes
   d. expectations

**Thinking Critically**

7. The author's attitude toward bureaucrats can best be described as
   a. supportive
   b. indifferent
   c. sympathetic
   d. critical

8. Which of the following is the most plausible explanation for the dramatic increase in worker productivity over the past 60 years?
   a. two-career families
   b. bureaucratic support
   c. improved technology
   d. the availability of subsidies

9. The iron triangle may have been given its name from its
   a. importance
   b. influence
   c. function
   d. strength

10. Which of the following actions would the author most strongly support?
    a. a reduction in federal subsidies to well-to-do farmers
    b. creation of a federal commission to study the problem of agribusiness
    c. an increase in Department of Agriculture staff
    d. an increase in the number of farm lobbyists

# Reading Selection 16 "The Domestic Sphere of Culture"

*DIRECTIONS:  Circle the letter of the best answer.*

## Checking Your Comprehension

1. This reading is primarily about
   a. domestic habits of various cultures
   b. how native tribes differ
   c. reasons for cultural differences
   d. how living arrangements in other cultures developed

2. The author's main point is that
   a. living arrangements elsewhere differ from those in the United States
   b. the Masai and Zumbaqua peasants have a primitive lifestyle
   c. modern industrial societies have more advanced educational systems than others
   d. domestic arrangements vary by culture, but many separate their children for various purposes

3. An Ashanti man is most likely to eat dinner with
   a. his children
   b. his wives
   c. other males
   d. his sisters

4. Zumbaquan peasant married couples prepare their own food
   a. as soon as they are married
   b. after the birth of their first child
   c. after the birth of additional children
   d. after their parents die

5. During adolescence Nyakyusa boys
   a. live completely apart from their parents
   b. live with their parents
   c. visit their parents only during the daylight
   d. prepare their own food

6. The word *sphere* as used in paragraph 1 means
   a. a defined problem
   b. an area of concern or influence
   c. a circular shape
   d. a changing pattern

## Thinking Critically

7. The domestic sphere includes all the following activities *except*
   a. making breakfast
   b. ironing

   c. holding a job

   d. caring for a pet

8. Which of the following most completely separates young adults from the domestic scene?

   a. college life

   b. military barracks

   c. housing developments

   d. church activities

9. In some cultures, married men spend a good deal of time in special men's houses. In western culture, which of the following is most similar to a men's house?

   a. a college fraternity

   b. a football team

   c. a favorite restaurant

   d. a health club

10. The writer recognizes that

   a. men and women are treated differently

   b. tribal customs reflect lack of sophistication

   c. men deserve to be treated to special living arrangements

   d. men and women should share domestic duties

## Reading Selection 18 "Musical Sounds"

*DIRECTIONS:   Circle the letter of the best answer.*

### Checking Your Comprehension

1. The three most important parts of musical sounds are

   a. pitch, amplitude, and harmonics

   b. pitch, aleatorations, and quality

   c. loudness, tone, and pitch

   d. pitch, quality, and loudness

2. Chance or randomly produced music

   a. may seem like noise to some listeners

   b. is characterized by regular patterns

   c. is restricted to traditional forms

   d. is limited by the various sounds instruments can produce

3. Most forms of classical and pop music can be distinguished from noise

   a. only with great difficulty

   b. more easily by the composers than by listeners

   c. with relative ease

   d. using the oscilloscope

4. The oscilloscope records

   a. levels of noise

   b. levels of pitch

   c. vibrations

    d. irregularities in sound

5. A decibel measures
   a. quality of sound
   b. variation in pitch
   c. frequency
   d. relative loudness

6. When the author says decibel ratings are "logarithmic" (paragraph 9) he means that
   a. decibels equal intensity
   b. decibels increase faster than intensity
   c. intensity increases faster than decibels
   d. decibels are unrelated to intensity

**Thinking Critically**

7. If humans are continually exposed to loud noises over the next several thousand years, you might expect that they would
   a. continue to be highly sensitive to loudness
   b. become tone deaf
   c. react more sensitively to sound than to light
   d. develop the ability to adapt to loud noises

8. You can expect that the pitch of the sound of a bicycle wheel rotating
   a. increases as you pedal faster
   b. depends on your direction
   c. remains unchanged
   d. varies with the size of the wheel

9. If you worked in an industrial plant and experienced hearing loss in one ear caused by a loud explosion, you can expect
   a. the loss to be permanent
   b. to regain your hearing suddenly after several months
   c. to regain your hearing gradually
   d. to develop greater capacity in your other ear

10. Primarily, the author explains musical sound by
   a. comparing it to light and vision
   b. explaining its characteristics
   c. analyzing individual responses to sound
   d. giving examples from particular musical pieces

## Reading Selection 20 "The Use of Force"

*DIRECTIONS:   Circle the letter of the best answer.*

**Checking Your Comprehension**

1. Which of the following statements best describes the plot of the story?
   a. A rebellious child is subdued by force.
   b. A child is diagnosed as having diphtheria.

  c. A sick child and her parents meet a country doctor.
  d. A sick child violently refuses an examination by a doctor, and it must be done by force.

2. Which of the following statements best describes the setting of the story?
  a. the home of well-established residents of the countryside
  b. a simple home of well-meaning parents
  c. the bedroom of an angry sick child
  d. the home of a wealthy family

3. The story is told from the point of view of
  a. the parents
  b. the child
  c. an all-knowing narrator
  d. the doctor

4. The doctor regarded the mother's comments to the child as
  a. helpful
  b. interfering
  c. resentful
  d. encouraging

5. The parents' attitude toward their child's behavior could best be described as
  a. embarrassed
  b. loving
  c. protective
  d. disapproving

6. Which of the following statements best defines the word *abject* as used in paragraph 21?
  a. lacking self-respect
  b. angry
  c. hateful
  d. fearful

**Thinking Critically**

7. Which of the following statements best expresses the theme of the story?
  a. The use of force is never justifiable.
  b. The use of force always creates resistance and injury.
  c. The use of force may be necessary to protect others, but it is reprehensible and ugly.
  d. The use of force is demeaning and unnatural.

8. Which of the following statements from the story provides the strongest clue about the story's theme?
  a. "Others must be protected against her. It is a social necessity."
  b. "Her tongue was cut and she was screaming in wild hysterical shrieks."
  c. "Look how kind he is to you."
  d. "Stop it! Stop it! You're killing me!"

9. Which of the following sets of words most strongly and clearly reveals the doctor's attitude toward their final struggle as he looks back on it?
   a. unreasoned assault, adult shame
   b. furious, defeat
   c. valiant, desisted, neglect
   d. hysterical, pleasure, burned

10. The child is described "as strong as a heifer in appearance." This statement is an example of
    a. connotative language
    b. descriptive language
    c. denotative language
    d. figurative language

## Reading Selection 22 "Time Out"

DIRECTIONS:   *Circle the letter of the best answer.*

### Checking Your Comprehension

1. The main point of the article is:
   a. The doctor had learned to hate the rural poor.
   b. The doctor has lost his ideals and become a realist.
   c. The doctor is facing burnout.
   d. The doctor wants to work in an environment where patients need his advice.

2. It is possible that Philip's mother is guilty of
   a. abandonment
   b. child neglect
   c. welfare abuse
   d. child abuse

3. One of the primary reasons that the doctor was discouraged by his patients is
   a. they are unable to pay for care
   b. they do not follow his advice
   c. they have too many children
   d. they do not respect him

4. The doctor states that through his education he developed
   a. a realistic understanding of people
   b. an idealized picture of a doctor crusading against injustice
   c. useless social attitudes about poverty
   d. useful skills for dealing with the rural poor

5. When the doctor left medical school and began his practice, he thought his patients would
   a. resist preventive medicine
   b. resent his youth and status
   c. welcome his advice
   d. regard him as foreign

6. The best meaning for the word *suppressed* as used in paragraph 15 is
   a. put down by force
   b. released
   c. abolished by authority
   d. concealed

**Thinking Critically**

7. The attitude of the doctor's friends toward him was one of
   a. understanding
   b. reproach
   c. disdain
   d. disappointment

8. The reading uses which of the following methods of organization?
   a. time order
   b. cause-effect
   c. enumeration
   d. problem solving

9. Which of the following information included in the reading most directly supports the doctor's view that his patients are worse off than they were 10 years ago?
   a. The patient with the green Saab found a new doctor.
   b. Layoffs occurred at the local factory.
   c. Mothers feed their children solid foods too soon.
   d. The stock market broke 1,500.

10. The author's purpose in writing is to
    a. gain sympathy
    b. argue for more aid for the poor
    c. express his feelings and frustrations
    d. justify his decision to move to Middlebury

## Reading Selection 24 "Out of Time"

*DIRECTIONS:   Circle the letter of the best answer.*

**Checking Your Comprehension**

1. This reading primarily concerns
   a. technology and innovation
   b. tribesmen and leaders
   c. cultures and environments
   d. a writer's experiences

2. The main point of this reading is that
   a. native lands and civilizations are being destroyed and endangered
   b. Indian tribes are losing their leadership
   c. technology has improved the quality of life of native tribes
   d. native tribes seek and desire change

3. When the Yuguí Indians first saw white people, they thought they were
   a. warriors who wanted to fight
   b. missionaries trying to help
   c. spirits of dead ancestors
   d. Indians from a lighter skinned tribe

4. The elevator that carried the dorado upstream was environmentally harmful because
   a. it replaced valuable forests
   b. the fish did not use it
   c. there was no downstream elevator
   d. its operation used valuable natural resources

5. The Cofán tribe thought the sounds of helicopters were
   a. wild animals
   b. spirits
   c. ancestors
   d. gifts

6. As used in the reading, the term *peccaries* (paragraph 11) refers to
   a. a flower species
   b. unknown tribes
   c. insects
   d. a type of animal

**Thinking Critically**

7. The author supports his points about the destruction of native cultures and environments by
   a. describing statistical trends
   b. making comparisons
   c. recounting his travel experiences
   d. quoting experts

8. Based on information given in the reading, you can conclude that the author regards missionaries as
   a. helpful in locating remote tribes
   b. initiating the destruction of a culture
   c. the end result of global economics
   d. necessary for the survival of religion

9. The attitude of Moreira, the Guaraní shaman, toward the destruction of his village was
   a. resignation
   b. anger
   c. disbelief
   d. sadness

10. The shaman's warning, "What we do to the lives and lands of others may ultimately determine the fate of our own" means
    a. fate is culturally determined and not within our control

b. in a global environment, all events and changes are interrelated

c. ozone holes are a threat to the entire civilization

d. each culture should preserve its artifacts and traditions

## Reading Selection 26 "Stress Management: Personally Adjusting to Stress"

DIRECTIONS:    Circle the letter of the best answer.

**Checking Your Comprehension**

1. The main point of this reading is that
   a. stress is an imbalance of internal and external demands
   b. controlling physical reactions and thoughts are effective means of managing stress
   c. relaxation is the key to successful stress management
   d. stress management requires a problem-solving approach

2. Controlling your thoughts always involves
   a. considering the situation from alternative viewpoints
   b. visualizing yourself managing the stressful situation successfully
   c. relaxation techniques to eliminate physical symptoms
   d. a sense of being overwhelmed by the situation

3. In the tension release method of relaxation, you should tense all your muscles together
   a. after tensing each muscle group separately
   b. before tensing each muscle group separately
   c. while thinking relaxing thoughts
   d. only if you feel tension in each group

4. Human response to stress is
   a. universal
   b. variable according to sex
   c. unchanging
   d. individual

5. Talking to ourselves is an effective means of managing stress because
   a. it takes our minds off the conflict
   b. it releases tension
   c. it is a means of directing out thoughts and feelings
   d. it facilitates imaging

6. Which of the following best defines the meaning of the word *reconstruct* as used in paragraph 13?
   a. refer back to
   b. re-create
   c. reestablish
   d. focus

**Thinking Critically**

7. The author's primary purpose in writing the selection is to
   a. explain the relationship between stress and conflict
   b. instruct the reader in how to control stress
   c. describe relaxation techniques
   d. persuade the reader to reduce stress through successful management

8. A basketball player who, before an important game, visualizes himself making every jump shot in the game instead of missing each as he did in the last game is using the technique of
   a. relaxation
   b. tension reduction
   c. self-talk
   d. imaging

9. Which of the following statements included in the reading most directly supports the writer's view that stress is controllable?
   a. Things dim in importance when viewed in retrospect.
   b. Stress is an imbalance between outside demands and our capabilities to meet those demands.
   c. People respond differently to conflict, just as they respond differently to stress.
   d. Because your behavior and your emotions are controlled by the way you think, you must acquire skills to change those thoughts.

10. A student who, before taking her final exam in biology, says to herself: "I am just as smart as everybody else in this class, and I've worked harder than most, so I should get an A or B on this," is
    a. confronting and handling the stress
    b. coping with the feeling of becoming overwhelmed
    c. using imaging
    d. reconstructing the situation

## Reading Selection 28 "The Functions and Effects of Music"

*DIRECTIONS:   Circle the letter of the best answer.*

**Checking Your Comprehension**

1. The main point of the article is that music
   a. has political, attitudinal, and social effects
   b. is primarily a political tool
   c. is subject to censorship, as are other forms of communication
   d. distinguishes generations from one another

2. The technique of giving an old familiar song new lyrics is intended to
   a. transfer feelings or associations from old to new

    b.  bring back fond memories

    c.  create new folk heroes

    d.  reestablish familiar environments

3.  From the information presented in this reading, you can infer that the recording industry
    a.  prefers to remain politically neutral
    b.  was forced by the public to release patriotic songs
    c.  has remained antiwar throughout the past 50 years
    d.  has taken a political stand in past wars

4.  According to the reading, music has played an important role in the
    a.  political campaigns of national leaders
    b.  civil rights movement
    c.  legalization of abortion debate
    d.  socialist propaganda

5.  The Federal Communications Commission's position on censorship of music states that it is
    a.  the artist's responsibility
    b.  the station's responsibility
    c.  the disc jockey's and program director's responsibility
    d.  the listener's or parent's responsibility

6.  Which of the following best defines the word *mosaics* as used in paragraph 8?
    a.  artistic models
    b.  bits of information and perceptions
    c.  skills
    d.  beliefs

### Thinking Critically

7.  The author's primary purpose in writing is to
    a.  discuss the functions of music in our society
    b.  argue that music has been used by age groups as a form of identification and rebellion
    c.  urge censorship of controversial lyrics
    d.  describe music as a political tool

8.  Which of the following conclusions can be most clearly drawn from this article?
    a.  Music will continue to be a form of social and political expression.
    b.  The Federal Communications Commission will soon change its position on censorship.
    c.  Music will cease to distinguish one generation from another.
    d.  Elvis Presley will diminish in popularity with successive generations.

9.  From the last paragraph of the reading, it is reasonable to infer that
    a.  singing idols are important in the establishment of boy-girl relationships
    b.  boys' emotional maturation is equal to that of girls of the same age

c. boys prefer not to become involved with girls
d. girls mature more rapidly than boys during early teenage years

10. The opening paragraph of the reading suggests that the functions of music are
a. unique
b. diverse
c. of questionable value
d. extraordinary

# APPENDIX C
# Words-Per-Minute Conversion Chart

Reading Selection

| Reading | 1 | 2 | 3 | 4 | 5 | 6 | 7 | 8 | 9 | 10 | 11 | 12 | 13 | 14 |
|---------|---|---|---|---|---|---|---|---|---|----|----|----|----|----|
| Time (minutes) | | | | | | | | | | | | | | |
| 1:00 | 959 | 1320 | 1514 | 1645 | 794 | 944 | 853 | * | 1171 | 1219 | 753 | * | 999 | 952 |
| 1:15 | 767 | 1056 | 1211 | 1316 | 635 | 755 | 682 | | 937 | 975 | 602 | | 799 | 762 |
| 1:30 | 639 | 880 | 1009 | 1097 | 529 | 629 | 569 | | 781 | 813 | 502 | | 666 | 635 |
| 1:45 | 548 | 754 | 865 | 940 | 454 | 539 | 487 | | 669 | 697 | 430 | | 571 | 544 |
| 2:00 | 479 | 660 | 757 | 822 | 397 | 472 | 427 | | 586 | 610 | 377 | | 499 | 476 |
| 2:15 | 426 | 587 | 673 | 731 | 353 | 419 | 379 | | 520 | 542 | 335 | | 444 | 423 |
| 2:30 | 384 | 528 | 606 | 658 | 318 | 378 | 341 | | 468 | 488 | 301 | | 400 | 381 |
| 2:45 | 349 | 480 | 550 | 598 | 289 | 343 | 310 | | 426 | 443 | 274 | | 363 | 346 |
| 3:00 | 319 | 440 | 505 | 548 | 265 | 315 | 284 | | 390 | 406 | 251 | | 333 | 317 |
| 3:15 | 295 | 406 | 466 | 506 | 244 | 290 | 262 | | 360 | 375 | 232 | | 307 | 293 |
| 3:30 | 274 | 377 | 433 | 470 | 227 | 270 | 244 | | 335 | 348 | 215 | | 285 | 272 |
| 3:45 | 256 | 352 | 404 | 439 | 212 | 252 | 227 | | 312 | 325 | 201 | | 266 | 254 |
| 4:00 | 240 | 330 | 378 | 411 | 199 | 236 | 213 | | 293 | 305 | 188 | | 250 | 238 |
| 4:15 | 226 | 311 | 356 | 387 | 187 | 222 | 201 | | 276 | 287 | 177 | | 235 | 224 |
| 4:30 | 213 | 293 | 336 | 366 | 176 | 210 | 190 | | 260 | 271 | 167 | | 222 | 211 |
| 4:45 | 202 | 278 | 319 | 346 | 167 | 199 | 180 | | 247 | 257 | 156 | | 210 | 200 |
| 5:00 | 192 | 264 | 303 | 329 | 159 | 189 | 171 | | 234 | 244 | 151 | | 200 | 190 |
| 5:15 | 183 | 251 | 288 | 313 | 151 | 180 | 162 | | 223 | 232 | 143 | | 190 | 181 |
| 5:30 | 174 | 240 | 275 | 299 | 144 | 172 | 155 | | 213 | 222 | 137 | | 182 | 173 |
| 5:45 | 167 | 230 | 263 | 286 | 138 | 164 | 148 | | 204 | 212 | 131 | | 174 | 166 |
| 6:00 | 160 | 220 | 252 | 274 | 132 | 158 | 142 | | 195 | 203 | 126 | | 166 | 159 |
| 6:15 | 153 | 211 | 242 | 263 | 127 | 151 | 136 | | 187 | 195 | 120 | | 160 | 152 |
| 6:30 | 148 | 203 | 233 | 252 | 122 | 145 | 131 | | 180 | 188 | 116 | | 154 | 146 |
| 6:45 | 142 | 195 | 224 | 243 | 118 | 140 | 126 | | 173 | 181 | 112 | | 148 | 141 |
| 7:00 | 137 | 189 | 216 | 235 | 113 | 135 | 122 | | 167 | 174 | 108 | | 143 | 136 |
| 7:15 | 132 | 182 | 209 | 226 | 110 | 130 | 118 | | 162 | 168 | 104 | | 138 | 131 |
| 7:30 | 128 | 176 | 202 | 219 | 106 | 126 | 114 | | 156 | 163 | 100 | | 133 | 127 |
| 7:45 | 123 | 170 | 195 | 212 | 102 | 122 | 110 | | 151 | 157 | - | | 129 | 123 |
| 8:00 | 120 | 165 | 189 | 205 | - | 118 | 107 | | 146 | 152 | - | | 125 | 119 |
| 8:15 | 116 | 160 | 183 | 199 | - | 114 | 103 | | 142 | 148 | - | | 121 | 115 |
| 8:30 | 113 | 156 | 178 | 193 | - | 111 | 100 | | 138 | 143 | - | | 117 | 112 |
| 8:45 | 110 | 151 | 173 | 188 | - | 108 | | | 134 | 139 | - | | 114 | 109 |
| 9:00 | 107 | 147 | 168 | 183 | - | 105 | - | | 130 | 135 | - | | 111 | 106 |
| 9:15 | 104 | 143 | 164 | 177 | - | 102 | - | | 127 | 131 | - | | 108 | 103 |
| 9:30 | 101 | 139 | 159 | 173 | - | 99 | - | | 123 | 128 | - | | 105 | 100 |
| 9:45 | 98 | 136 | 155 | 168 | - | 97 | - | | 120 | 125 | - | | 102 | 98 |
| 10:00 | 96 | 132 | 151 | 165 | - | 94 | - | | 117 | 122 | - | | 100 | 95 |

*Due to the extreme length of these readings, word-per-minute conversions are not provided.

## Reading Selection

| Reading | 15 | 16 | 17 | 18 | 19 | 20 | 21 | 22 | 23 | 24 | 25 | 26 | 27 | 28 |
|---|---|---|---|---|---|---|---|---|---|---|---|---|---|---|
| Time (minutes) | | | | | | | | | | | | | | |
| 1:00 | 635 | 790 | 1029 | 1055 | 965 | 1475 | 1316 | 1063 | 822 | 1330 | 1544 | 1221 | 2528 | 1291 |
| 1:15 | 508 | 632 | 823 | 844 | 772 | 1180 | 1053 | 850 | 658 | 1064 | 1235 | 977 | 2022 | 1032 |
| 1:30 | 423 | 528 | 686 | 703 | 643 | 983 | 877 | 709 | 548 | 887 | 1029 | 814 | 1685 | 861 |
| 1:45 | 363 | 451 | 588 | 603 | 551 | 842 | 752 | 607 | 470 | 760 | 882 | 698 | 1445 | 737 |
| 2:00 | 318 | 395 | 516 | 528 | 483 | 737 | 658 | 531 | 411 | 665 | 772 | 611 | 1264 | 645 |
| 2:15 | 282 | 351 | 457 | 469 | 429 | 656 | 585 | 472 | 365 | 591 | 686 | 543 | 1124 | 574 |
| 2:30 | 254 | 316 | 411 | 422 | 386 | 590 | 526 | 425 | 329 | 532 | 618 | 488 | 1011 | 516 |
| 2:45 | 231 | 287 | 374 | 384 | 351 | 536 | 478 | 386 | 299 | 484 | 561 | 444 | 919 | 469 |
| 3:00 | 212 | 263 | 343 | 352 | 322 | 492 | 439 | 354 | 274 | 443 | 515 | 407 | 843 | 430 |
| 3:15 | 195 | 243 | 317 | 325 | 297 | 453 | 405 | 327 | 253 | 409 | 475 | 376 | 778 | 397 |
| 3:30 | 181 | 226 | 294 | 301 | 276 | 421 | 376 | 303 | 235 | 380 | 441 | 349 | 722 | 369 |
| 3:45 | 169 | 211 | 274 | 281 | 257 | 393 | 351 | 283 | 219 | 355 | 411 | 326 | 674 | 344 |
| 4:00 | 159 | 197 | 257 | 264 | 241 | 369 | 329 | 266 | 206 | 332 | 386 | 305 | 632 | 322 |
| 4:15 | 149 | 186 | 262 | 248 | 227 | 347 | 310 | 250 | 193 | 313 | 363 | 287 | 595 | 304 |
| 4:30 | 141 | 175 | 229 | 234 | 214 | 328 | 292 | 236 | 183 | 295 | 343 | 271 | 562 | 287 |
| 4:45 | 134 | 166 | 217 | 222 | 203 | 310 | 277 | 223 | 173 | 280 | 325 | 257 | 532 | 272 |
| 5:00 | 127 | 158 | 206 | 211 | 193 | 295 | 263 | 213 | 164 | 266 | 309 | 244 | 506 | 258 |
| 5:15 | 121 | 150 | 196 | 201 | 184 | 280 | 251 | 202 | 157 | 253 | 294 | 232 | 482 | 246 |
| 5:30 | 115 | 144 | 187 | 192 | 175 | 268 | 239 | 193 | 149 | 242 | 280 | 222 | 460 | 235 |
| 5:45 | 110 | 137 | 179 | 183 | 168 | 256 | 229 | 185 | 143 | 231 | 268 | 212 | 440 | 225 |
| 6:00 | 106 | 132 | 171 | 176 | 161 | 245 | 219 | 177 | 137 | 222 | 257 | 203 | 421 | 215 |
| 6:15 | 102 | 126 | 165 | 169 | 154 | 236 | 211 | 170 | 132 | 213 | 247 | 195 | 404 | 206 |
| 6:30 | - | 121 | 158 | 162 | 148 | 226 | 202 | 163 | 126 | 205 | 237 | 188 | 389 | 199 |
| 6:45 | - | 117 | 152 | 156 | 143 | 218 | 195 | 157 | 122 | 197 | 228 | 181 | 374 | 191 |
| 7:00 | - | 113 | 147 | 151 | 138 | 210 | 188 | 151 | 117 | 190 | 220 | 174 | 361 | 184 |
| 7:15 | - | 109 | 142 | 146 | 133 | 203 | 181 | 146 | 113 | 183 | 212 | 168 | 349 | 178 |
| 7:30 | - | 105 | 137 | 141 | 129 | 197 | 175 | 141 | 110 | 177 | 206 | 163 | 337 | 172 |
| 7:45 | - | 102 | 132 | 136 | 124 | 190 | 170 | 137 | 106 | 172 | 199 | 158 | 326 | 166 |
| 8:00 | - | 99 | 129 | 132 | 121 | 184 | 164 | 132 | 103 | 166 | 193 | 153 | 316 | 161 |
| 8:15 | - | 96 | 125 | 128 | 117 | 179 | 159 | 128 | - | 161 | 187 | 148 | 306 | 155 |
| 8:30 | - | 93 | 121 | 124 | 114 | 173 | 155 | 125 | - | 156 | 181 | 144 | 297 | 152 |
| 8:45 | - | 90 | 118 | 121 | 110 | 168 | 150 | 121 | - | 152 | 176 | 140 | 289 | 147 |
| 9:00 | - | 88 | 114 | 117 | 107 | 164 | 146 | 118 | - | 148 | 172 | 136 | 281 | 143 |
| 9:15 | - | 85 | 111 | 114 | 104 | 159 | 142 | 114 | - | 144 | 166 | 132 | 273 | 140 |
| 9:30 | - | 83 | 108 | 111 | 102 | 155 | 138 | 111 | - | 140 | 162 | 129 | 266 | 136 |
| 9:45 | - | 81 | 105 | 108 | - | 151 | 135 | 109 | - | 136 | 158 | 125 | 259 | 132 |
| 10:00 | - | 79 | 103 | 106 | - | 147 | 132 | 106 | - | 133 | 154 | 122 | 253 | 129 |

## APPENDIX D

## Reading Progress Graph

DIRECTIONS:  For each reading selection you complete, record the date and selection number. Then place a dot in the appropriate column to indicate the words-per-minute score and the comprehension score you achieved. Connect the consecutive dots to form a line graph.

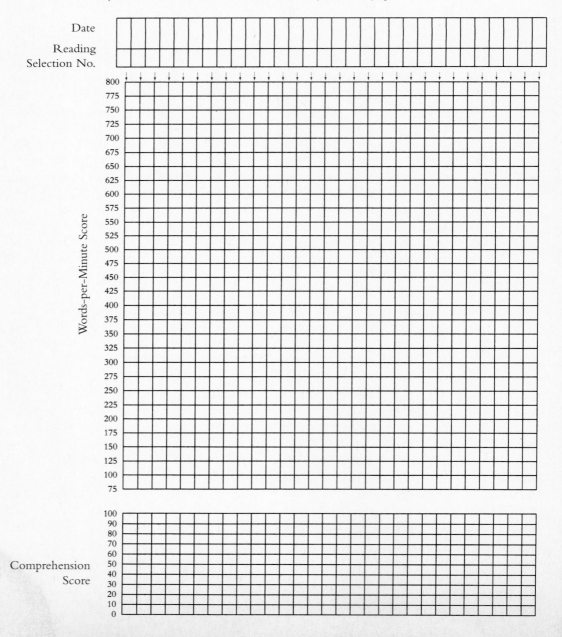

# Credits

*Chapter 1*

p. 17:   James E. Challenger, "How to Brag About Yourself to Win and Hold a New Job," 1997. Reprinted by permission of Herbert Rozoff Public Relations, Inc. for James E. Challenger.

p. 17:   © John & Guy (tc)/The Picture Cube.

p. 20:   From "Hispanic USA: The Conveyer Belt Ladies" by Rose Del Castillo Guilbault as appeared in *The San Francisco Chronicle*, April 15, 1990. Reprinted by permission of the author.

*Chapter 2*

p. 28:   From Carl E. Rischer and Thomas A. Easton, *Focus on Human Biology*, 2nd ed. New York: HarperCollins, 1995, p. 141.

p. 29:   From John C. Merrill, John Lee, and Edward J. Friedlander, *Modern Mass Media*, 2nd ed. New York: HarperCollins, 1994, p. 139.

p. 37:   Richard Weaver II, *Understanding Interpersonal Communications*, 5th ed. Copyright © 1990 by Scott, Foresman and Company. Reprinted by permission.

p. 50:   From James Geiwitz, *Psychology: Looking at Ourselves*, 2nd ed. Boston: Little, Brown, p. 276. Copyright © 1980 by James Geiwitz. Reprinted by permission of Little, Brown and Company.

p. 50:   Paul Lohnes and W. W. Cooley, *Introduction to Statistical Procedures*. New York: Wiley, 1968, p. 11.

p. 55:   From Josh R. Gerow, *Essentials of Psychology: Concepts and Applications*. Copyright © 1993 by HarperCollins Publishers.

p. 56:   © Michael Grecco/Stock Boston.

p. 60:   Brent Staples, "Just Walk On By: A Black Man Ponders His Power to Alter Public Space." *MS*. September 1986. Reprinted by permission of the author.

*Chapter 3*

p. 93:   From Brian M. Fagan, *World Prehistory: A Brief Introduction*. Copyright 1979 by Brian M. Fagan. Reprinted by permission of Little, Brown and Company.

p. 96:   Paul G. Hewitt, "Why the Sky is Blue" from *Conceptual Physics*, 7th ed. Copyright © 1993 by Paul G. Hewitt. Reprinted by permission of HarperCollins Publishers, Inc.

*Chapter 4*

p. 104:   Robert W. Kolb, *Investments*. Glenview, IL: Scott, Foresman, 1986, p. 59. Reprinted with permission.

p. 104: From Paul G. Hewitt, *Conceptual Physics,* 7th ed. Copyright © 1993 by Paul G. Hewitt. Reprinted by permission of HarperCollins Publishers, Inc.

p. 105: From Roger Chisholm and Marilu McCarty, *Principles of Economics.* Glenview, IL: Scott, Foresman, 1978, pp. 91–92. Copyright © 1978 by Scott, Foresman. Reprinted by permission.

p. 105: From Joseph A. DeVito, *Messages: Building Interpersonal Communication Skills,* 3rd ed., p. 302. Copyright © 1996 by HarperCollins College Publishers. Reprinted by permission of Addison-Wesley Educational Publishers, Inc.

p. 106: From Robert A. Wallace, *Biology: The World of Life,* 7th ed., p. 82. Copyright © 1997 by Addison-Wesley Educational Publishers, Inc. Reprinted by permission.

p. 106: From Robert J. Ferl, Robert A. Wallace, and Gerald P. Sanders, *Biology: The Realm of Life,* 3rd ed., p. 790. Copyright © 1996 by HarperCollins College Publishers. Reprinted by permission of Addison-Wesley Educational Publishers, Inc.

p. 107: From Alex Thio, *Sociology,* 4th ed., p. 347. Copyright © 1996 by HarperCollins College Publishers. Reprinted by permission of Addison-Wesley Educational Publishers, Inc.

p. 107: From Watson Laetsch, *Plants: Basic Concepts in Botany.* Boston: Little, Brown, 1979, p. 146. Copyright © 1979 by Little, Brown and Company, Inc. Reprinted by permission.

p. 108: From Richard H. Buskirk, *Principles of Marketing: The Management View,* Third Edition. Copyright © 1970 by Holt, Rinehart, and Winston. Reprinted by permission of the publisher.

p. 108: Mary J. Gander and Harry W. Gardiner, *Child and Adolescent Development.* Boston: Little, Brown, 1981, pp. 7–8. Copyright © 1981 by Mary J. Gander and Harry W. Gardiner. Reprinted by permission of Little, Brown and Company.

p. 108: From Louis Berman and J. C. Evans, *Exploring the Cosmos,* 2nd ed. Boston: Little, Brown, 1980, p. 247. Copyright © 1980 by Louis Berman and J. C. Evans. Reprinted by permission of Little, Brown and Company.

p. 109: Bowman O. Davis, Noel Holtz, and Judith C. Davis, *Conceptual Human Physiology,* Columbus, OH: Charles. E. Merrill, 1985, pp. 201–202.

p. 110: From S. L. Washburn and Ruth Moore, *Ape into Human: A Study of Human Evolution,* 2nd ed. Boston: Little, Brown, 1980, pp. 169–170. Copyright © 1980 by S. L. Washburn and Ruth Moore. Reprinted by permission of Little, Brown and Company.

p. 111: Hewitt, p. 524.

p. 112: Bernard Campbell, *Humankind Emerging,* 3rd ed. Boston: Little, Brown, 1979, p. 93.

p. 112: Thio, *Sociology,* 4th ed., pp. 170–171.

p. 113: Wallace, p. 49.

p. 113: From George C. Edwards III, Martin P. Wattenberg, and Robert L. Lineberry, *Government in America: People, Politics, and Policy,* 7th ed., p. 107. Copyright © 1996 by HarperCollins College Publishers. Reprinted by permission of Addison-Wesley Educational Publishers, Inc.

p. 114: DeVito, *Messages: Building Interpersonal Communication Skills,* 3rd ed., p. 360.

p. 114: DeVito, *Messages: Building Interpersonal Communication Skills,* 3rd ed., p. 338.

p. 115: Edwards III, Wattenberg, and Lineberry, p. 134.

p. 115: Wallace, p. 24.

p. 116: From James Benjamin and Raymie E. McKerrow, *Business and Professional Communication: Concepts and Practices,* p. 146. Copyright © 1994 by HarperCollins College Publishers. Reprinted by permission of Addison-Wesley Educational Publishers, Inc.

p. 116: Thio, *Sociology,* 4th ed., p. 290.

p. 117: Benjamin and McKerrow, p. 84.

p. 117: Wallace, pp. 567–569.

p. 118: From David H. Knox, *Exploring Marriage and the Family.* Copyright © 1979 by Scott, Foresman and Company. Reprinted by permission of Addison-Wesley Educational Publishers.

p. 118: Berman and Evans, p. 438.

p. 119: Buskirk, p. 138.

p. 119: Knox, pp. 13–14.

p. 119: Knox, p. 37.

p. 120: Gander and Gardiner, p. 48.

p. 120: From Joseph B. Aceves and H. Gill King, *Introduction to Anthropology.* Copyright © 1979 by McGraw-Hill. Reprinted by permission of the The McGraw-Hill Companies.

p. 121: DeVito, *Messages: Building Interpersonal Communication Skills,* 3rd ed., p. 29.

p. 122: Benjamin and McKerrow, p. 175.

p. 122: DeVito, *Messages: Building Interpersonal Communication Skills,* 3rd ed., p. 153.

p. 123: Wallace, p. 52

p. 123: Thio, *Sociology,* 4th ed., p. 245.

p. 124: Aceves and King, pp. 18–19.

p. 124: From Edward J. Fox and Edward W. Wheatley, *Modern Marketing.* Glenview, IL: Scott, Foresman, pp. 18–19. Copyright © 1980 Scott, Foresman. Reprinted by permission.

p. 124: Henrietta Flack, *Introduction to Nutrition.* 2nd ed. New York: Macmillan, 1971, p. 418.

p. 124: Frans Gerritsen, *Theory and Practice of Color.* New York: Van Nostrand, 1975, p. 9.

p. 125: From Alan Monroe and Douglass Ehninger, *Principles and Types of Speech,* 6th ed. Glenview, IL: Scott, Foresman. Copyright © 1967 Scott, Foresman. Reprinted by permission.

p. 127: Geiwitz, pp. 543–544.

p. 128: John Perry and Erna Perry. *Face to Face: The Individual and Social Problems.* Boston: Little, Brown and Company, pp. 130–131.

p. 130: From Gary Wasserman, *The Basics of American Politics,* 3rd ed. Boston: Little, Brown. Copyright © 1982 by Gary Wasserman. Reprinted by permission of Little, Brown and Company.

p. 131:    Thio, *Sociology,* 4th ed., p. 54.

p. 131:    From Josh R. Gerow, *Psychology: An Introduction,* 5th ed., p. 530. Copyright © 1997 by Addison-Wesley Educational Publishers, Inc. Reprinted by permission.

p. 131:    Chester R. Longwell and Richard F. Flint, *Introduction to Physical Geology,* 2nd ed. New York: Wiley, 1962, p. 402.

p. 132:    Brian M. Fagan, *World Prehistory: A Brief Introduction.* Boston: Little, Brown, 1979, p. 14. Copyright © 1979 Brian M. Fagan. Reprinted by permission of Little, Brown and Company.

p. 133:    From William E. Thompson and Joseph V. Hickey, *Society in Focus: An Introduction to Sociology,* p. 489. Copyright © 1994 by William E. Thompson and Joseph V. Hickey. Reprinted by permission of HarperCollins College Publishers, Inc.

p. 134:    From Leonard Broom and Philip Selznick, *Sociology,* 3rd ed. New York: Harper & Row, 1963, p. 455.

p. 134:    James B. Hall and Elizabeth C. Hall (eds.), *The Realm of Fiction.* New York: McGraw-Hill, 1977, p. 192.

p. 136:    From Bruce E. Gronbeck, Kathleen German, Douglas Ehninger, and Alan H. Monroe, *Principles of Speech Communication,* 12th Brief Edition, pp. 57–58. Copyright © 1995 by HarperCollins College Publishers. Reprinted by permission of Addison-Wesley Educational Publishers.

p. 139:    From Mary J. Gander and Harry W. Gardiner, *Child and Adolescent Development.* Copyright 1981 by Mary J. Gander and Harry W. Gardiner. Reprinted by permission of Little, Brown and Company.

p. 142:    Reprinted with the permission of Scribner, a Division of Simon & Schuster from *The Modern Ark, The Story of Zoos: Past, Present, and Future* by Vicki Croke. Copyright © 1997 by Vicki Croke.


*Chapter 5*

p. 151:    Bryan Pfaffenberger, *Personal Computer Applications: A Strategy for the Information Society.* Boston: Little, Brown, 1987, p. 65.

p. 151:    Dorothy Cohen, *Advertising.* Glenview, IL: Scott, Foresman, 1988, pp. ii–iii. Reprinted by permission.

p. 153:    Wasserman, pp. 150–151.

p. 154:    Rischer and Easton, p. 40.

p. 155:    From Terry G. Jordan, Mona Domosh, and Lester Rowntree, *The Human Mosaic: A Thematic Introduction to Cultural Georgraphy,* 6th ed. Copyright © 1994 by HarperCollins, pp. 897–899. Reprinted by permission.

p. 157:    From Robert A. Wallace, *Biology: The World of Life,* 6th ed. Copyright © 1992 by HarperCollins Publishers. Reprinted by permission.

p. 158:    From Michael C. Mix, Paul and Keith I. King, *Biology: The Network of Life.* New York: HarperCollins, 1992, p. 50. Reprinted by permission of publisher.

p. 160:    Laetsch, p. 393.

p. 162: From J. Ross Eshleman and B. G. Cashion, *Sociology: An Introduction,* 2nd ed., p. 98. Copyright © 1985 by J. Ross Eshleman and B. G. Cashion. Reprinted by permission of Little, Brown and Company.

p. 163: From Curtis O. Byer and Louis W. Shainberg, *Living Well: Health in Your Hands,* 2nd ed., p. 306. Copyright © 1995 by HarperCollins College Publishers. Reprinted by permission of Addison-Wesley Educational Publishers, Inc.

p. 165: From Henry L. Roediger III et al., *Psychology,* 2nd ed., p. 184. Copyright © 1984 by Henry L. Roediger III, J. Philippe Rushton, Elizabeth D. Capaladi, and Scott D. Paris. Reprinted by permission of Little, Brown and Company.

p. 166: Laetsch, p. 152.

p. 168: Gerow, pp. 87–89.

p. 169: Eshleman and Cashion, p. 165.

p. 170: Eshleman and Cashion, p. 366.

p. 172: Laetsch, p. 11.

p. 173: Wasserman, p. 197.

p. 173: Wasserman, p. 198.

p. 173: Burton Wright and John P. Weiss, *Social Problems.* Boston: Little, Brown, 1980, p. 31.

p. 174 Wright and Weiss, p. 64.

p. 176 Julius Fast, "Eye Language." Reprinted by permission from *Family Health* Magazine, September 1978. All rights reserved.

p. 180: Steven R. Knowlton, "How Students Get Lost in Cyberspace," from *Education Life,* November 2, 1997. Copyright © 1997 by the New York Times Company. Reprinted by permission.p. 180:

p. 181: © Andy Manis/NYT Pictures

*Chapter 6*

p. 186: Andrea Martin, "Citizenship or Slavery" in *Utne Reader,* May–June 1996, pp. 14, 16. Reprinted with permission from Utne Reader and Andrea Martin.

p. 190: From Mortimer B. Zuckerman, "Attention Must be Paid," *U.S. News & World Report,* August 18/August 25, p. 92. Copyright, August 18–August 25, 1997, U.S. News & World Report. Reprinted by permission.

p. 194: Richard Selzer, *Mortal Lessons.* New York: Simon and Schuster, 1976, pp. 45–46.

p. 194: Lucinda Franks, "The Story of James B," from *The New York Times* Magazine, October 20, 1985. Copyright © 1985 by The New York Times Company. Reprinted by permission.

p. 198: From *Nobody Ever Died of Old Age* by Sharon R. Curtin. Copyright © 1972 by Sharon R. Curtin. By permission of Little, Brown and Company.

p. 199: Brenda Peterson, "Seagull Song" from *Nature and Other Mothers: Personal Stories and the Body of Earth,* pp. 174–177. Published by Ballantine Books. Copyright © 1992, 1995 by Brenda Peterson. Reprinted by permission of the author.

p. 202: Andrea Martin, "Why Get Married" in *Utne Reader,* January February 1996, pp. 17,18. Reprinted with permission from Utne Reader and Andrea Martin.

p. 203: © Sue Kyllonen

p. 207: "Lawsuits Seek Heart Monitoring for Users of Withdrawn Diet Drugs" by Beth Powell. Copyright © 1997 by The Associated Press. Reprinted by permission of The Associated Press.

p. 209: From Richard Folkers, "Everyday Mysteries: Why Do Dogs Bark?" in *U.S. News & World Report,* August 18/August 25, pp. 86–87. Copyright, August 18–August 25, 1997, U.S. News & World Report. Reprinted by permission.

p. 218: Anne Reilly Dowd, from "Medical Privacy" in "Protect Your Privacy." Reprinted by permission from the August 1997 issue of *Money* by special permission; Copyright © 1997, Time Inc.

p. 221: From Guzetti, Barbara J. and Williams, Wayne O., "Changing the Pattern of Gendered Discussion: Lessons from Science Classrooms." (1996, September) Journal of Adolescent & Adult Literacy, 40 (1), 38–47. Copyright © 1996 by the International Reading Association. All rights reserved. Reprinted by permission of the International Reading Association and Barbara J. Guzetti.

*Chapter 7*

p. 236: Thio, *Sociology,* 4th ed., p. 397.

p. 237: Thio, *Sociology,* 4th ed., p. 363.

p. 238: From Nora Newcombe, *Child Development: Change Over Time,* 8th ed., p. 400. Copyright © 1996 by HarperCollins College Publishers. Reprinted by permission of Addison-Wesley Educational Publishers, Inc.

p. 240: From Gerard J. Tortora, *Introduction to the Human Body: The Essentials of Anatomy and Physiology,* 3rd ed. Copyright © 1994 by Biological Sciences Textbooks, Inc. and A & P textbooks, Inc. Reprinted by permission of Addison-Wesley Educational Publishers, Inc.

p. 242L: © J.T. Gwynne.

p. 242R: © Glen Allison/Tony Stone Images.

p. 243: © Mark Peters/Sipa Press.

p. 245: From Richard Appelbaum and William J. Chambliss, *Sociology,* p. 287. Copyright © 1995 by HarperCollins College Publishers. Reprinted by permission of Addison-Wesley Educational Publishers, Inc.

p. 246: Thio, p. 60.

p. 247: From Thomas C. Kinnear, Kenneth L. Bernhardt, and Kathleen A. Krentler, *Principles of Marketing,* 4th ed., p. 593. Copyright © 1995 by

HarperCollins College Publishers. Reprinted by permission of Addison-Wesley Educational Publishers, Inc.

p. 248:  From James William Coleman and Donald R. Cressy, *Social Problems,* 6th ed., p. 429. Copyright © 1996 by HarperCollins College Publishers. Reprinted by permission of Addison-Wesley Educational Publishers, Inc.

p. 249:  From Maxine Baca Zinn and D. Stanley Eitzen, *Diversity in Families,* 4th ed. Copyright © 1996 by HarperCollins College Publishers. Reprinted by permission of Addison-Wesley Educational Publishers, Inc.

p. 250:  From Donald C. Mosley, Paul H. Pietri, and Leon C. Megginson, *Management: Leadership in Action,* 5th ed., p. 562. Copyright © 1996 by HarperCollins College Publishers. Reprinted by permission of Addison-Wesley Educational Publishers, Inc.

p. 251:  Edwards III, Wattenberg, and Lineberry, p. 369.

p. 253:  From Edward S. Greenberg and Benjamin Page, *The Struggle for Democracy, Brief Version,* p. 88. Copyright © 1996 by HarperCollins College Publishers. Reprinted by permission of Addison-Wesley Educational Publishers, Inc.

p. 253:  Mix, Farber, and King, p. 752.

p. 255:  Jordan, Domosh, and Rowntree, p. 408.

p. 256:  Mosley, Pietri, and Megginson, p. 258.

p. 257:  Mosley, Pietri, and Megginson, p. 540.

p. 258:  Coleman and Cressy, p. 423.

p. 259:  S. Gross © 1993 from The New Yorker Collection. All Rights Reserved.

p. 265:  From Nike home page (Internet Site) http://www.nike.com, 12/2/97. Reprinted with permission of Nike, Inc.

p. 266:  From Saint Mary's College web site "Sociology," http://yesod.stmarys ca.edu/study/soc/#crime. February, 1998. Reprinted by permission of Saint Mary's College of California, Moraga, CA.

p. 271:  From Carl E. Rischer and Thomas A. Easton, *Focus on Human Biology,* 2nd ed. Copyright © 1995 by HarperCollins College Publishers. Reprinted by permission.

p. 275:  From Roger LeRoy Miller, *Economics Today,* 8th ed. Copyright © 1994 by HarperCollins College Publishers. Reprinted by permission.

## *Chapter 8*

p. 281:  Hugh D. Barlow, *Introduction to Criminology,* 2nd ed. Boston: Little, Brown, 1984, p. 336. Copyright © 1984 by Hugh D. Barlow. Reprinted by permission of Little, Brown and Company.

p. 289:  From J. Ross Eshleman, Barbara G. Cashion, and Laurence A. Basirico, *Sociology: An Introduction,* 4th ed., p. 118. Copyright © 1993 by HarperCollins College Publishers. Reprinted by permission of Addison-Wesley Educational Publishers, Inc.

p. 291:  From Joseph A. DeVito, *Human Communication: The Basic Course,* 7th ed., pp. 108–110. Copyright © 1997 by Addison-Wesley Educational Publishers, Inc. Reprinted by permission.

p. 299:    Kenneth Budinshki, *Engineering Materials: Properties and Selection.* Reston, VA: Reston Publishing Co., 1979, p. 15.

p. 300:    Herbert E. Ellinger, *Auto-Mechanics,* 2nd ed. Englewood Cliffs, NJ: Prentice-Hall, 1977, p. 183.

p. 300:    Robert C. Nickerson, *Fundamentals of Structured COBOL.* Boston: Little, Brown, 1984, p. 271.

p. 303:    Barbara London Upton and John Upton, *Photography.* Glenview, IL: Scott, Foresman, 1989, p. 156. Reprinted by permission.

p. 305:    Paul G. Hewitt, "Color" from *Conceptual Physics,* 7th ed. Copyright © 1993 by Paul G. Hewitt. Reprinted by permission of HarperCollins Publishers, Inc.

p. 311:    Edwards III, Wattenberg, and Lineberry, pp. 184–185.

p. 314:    From Marvin Harris, *Cultural Anthropology,* 3rd ed. Copyright © 1991 by HarperCollins Publishers, Inc. Reprinted by permission.


*Chapter 9*

p. 319:    John Dorfman et al., *Well-Being: An Introduction to Health.* Glenview, IL: Scott, Foresman, 1980, p. 278. Reprinted by permission.

p. 320:    Dorfman et al., pp. 172–173.

p. 322:    Sydney B. Newell, *Chemistry.* Boston: Little, Brown, 1980, pp. 457–458.

p. 326:    B. W. Spradley, *Community Health Nursing,* 2nd ed. Boston: Little, Brown, 1985, p. 31.

p. 327:    Fox and Wheatley, p. 49.

p. 327:    Wallace Stevens, "Anecdote of the Jar" from *The Collected Poems of Wallace Stevens.* Copyright © 1923 and renewed 1951 by Wallace Stevens. Reprinted by permission of Alfred A. Knopf, Inc.

p. 330:    From Jean-Paul Sartre, *Existentialism. The Norton Reader,* 7th ed. Edited by Arthur M. Eastman et al. New York: W. W. Norton, 1988, p. 1196. From *Existentialism,* Philosophical Library Publishers. Reprinted by permission of Philosophical Library Publishers.

p. 330:    From William E. Thompson and Joseph V. Hickey, *Society in Focus: An Introduction to Sociology,* 2nd ed., pp. 352–353. Copyright © 1996 by William E. Thompson and Joseph V. Hickey. Reprinted by permission of Addison-Wesley Educational Publishers, Inc.

p. 333:    Dorfman et al., pp. 208–209.

p. 334:    Brian Fagan *In the Beginning: An Introduction to Archaeology,* 5th ed. Boston: Little, Brown, 1985, pp. 13–14.

p. 339:    Joyce Carey, "Art and Education." From *On the Function of the Novelist.* New York: New York Times, 1949. Reprinted by permission of Andrew Lownie, Literary Agent on behalf of the estate of Joyce Carey.

p. 340:    James Thurber, "A Dog's Eye View of Man" from *Thurber's Dogs.* Published by Simon & Schuster. Copyright © 1955 by James Thurber. Copyright © 1983 by Helen Thurber and Rosemary A. Thurber. Reprinted by permission of Rosemary A. Thurber.

p. 341:    Josh R. Gerow, *Essentials of Psychology: Concepts and Applications.* New York: HarperCollins, 1993, p. 468.

p. 344:  From Edward S. Greenberg and Benjamin I. Page, *The Struggle for Democracy.* Copyright © 1993 by HarperCollins Publishers. Reprinted by permission.

p. 345:  J. Floyd Yewell/Collection of the Supreme Court of the United States.

p. 348:  Paul G. Hewitt, "Musical Sounds" from *Conceptual Physics,* 7th ed. Copyright © 1993 by Paul G. Hewitt. Reprinted by permission of HarperCollins Publishers, Inc.

### Chapter 10

p. 359:  John Updike, "Eclipse," *Assorted Prose.* New York: Alfred A. Knopf, 1963.

p. 363:  "Mirror" from *Crossing the Water* by Sylvia Plath. Copyright © 1963 by Ted Hughes. Originally appeared in *The New Yorker.* Reprinted by permission of HarperCollins Publishers, Inc. and Olwyn Hughes.

p. 366:  Victor Martinez, "The Blackbird," pp. 157–165, from *Mirrors Beneath the earth: Short Fiction by Chicano Writers,* edited by Ray Gonzalez. Copyright © 1992 by Victor Martinez. Reprinted by permission of the author, Victor Martinez.

p. 374:  Langston Hughes, "Dream Deferred" from *The Panther and the Lash.* Copyright © 1994 by the Estate of Langston Hughes. Reprinted by permission of Alfred A. Knopf, Inc.

p. 375:  "The Silken Tent" from *The Poetry of Robert Frost,* edited by Edward Connery Lathem. Copyright © 1942 by Robert Frost, © 1970 by Lesley Frost Ballantine, © 1969 by Henry Holt and Company, Inc., © 1997 by Edward Connery Lathem. Reprinted by permission of Henry Holt and Company, Inc.

p. 375:  Andrew Marvell, *To His Coy Mistress.*

p. 379:  Sandy Grady, "We're All Robinson's Children" in *USA Today,* April 3, 1997. Reprinted by permission of Sandy Grady.

p. 381:  © Archive Photos.

p. 383:  William Carlos Williams, from *Doctor Stories.* Copyright © 1938 by William Carlos Williams. Reprinted by permission of New Directions Publishing Corporation.

### Chapter 11

p. 391:  Rebeta-Burditt, *The Cracker Factory.* New York: Macmillan, 1977, pp. 3, 5.

p. 393:  Elliott Currie, and Jerome H. Skolnick, *America's Problems.* 2nd ed. Glenview, IL: Scott, Foresman, 1988, pp. 300–301. Reprinted by permission.

p. 394:  Robert A. Lineberry and George C. Edwards, *Government in America,* 4th ed. Glenview, IL: Scott, Foresman, 1989, p. 309.

p. 394:  From Maxine Phillips, "Needed: A Policy for Children When Parents Go to Work." Appeared in the *Los Angeles Times,* December 6, 1987. Reprinted by permission of Maxine Phillips, Dissent Magazine.

p. 395:  From Jim Miller, "Forever Elvis." *Newsweek,* August 3, 1987. Copyright © 1987, Newsweek, Inc. All rights reseved. Reprinted by permission.

p. 397:  Pete Hamill, "The Wet Drug," *San Jose Mercury News,* March 24, 1983.

p. 398: From Edward S. Greenberg and Benjamin I. Page, *The Struggle for Democracy.* New York: HarperCollins, 1993.

p. 398: Sarah King, "Lover in the Afternoon—In a Crowded Prison Hall," *Los Angeles Times,* November 5, 1976.

p. 399: Studs Terkel, *Working: People Talk About What They Do All Day and How They Feel About What They Do.* New York: Random House, 1972.

p. 399: Currie and Skolnick, p. 217.

p. 401: Beth Lovern, "Confessions of a Welfare Mom." *Utne Reader,* July/August, 1994, pp. 81–82. Reprinted by permission of the author.

p. 403: Wallace, p. 518.

p. 404: Marie Winn, *The Plug-In Drug.* New York: Viking, 1981.

p. 407: Keyasa E. Noda, "Growing Up Asian in America," from *Making Waves* by Asian Women United. Reprinted by permission of the author.

p. 410: Jack L. Mayer, "About Men: Time Out," from *The New York Times* Magazine, October 19, 1986. Copyright © 1986 by The New York Times Company. Reprinted by permission.

*Chapter 12*

p. 413: Adam Smith, "Fifty Million Handguns." *Esquire,* 1981.

p. 417: Robert L. Maginnis, "Equality isn't Sameness" in *USA Today,* November 20, 1996. Reprinted by permission of Robert L. Maginnis.

p. 419: From "Capital Punishment" by Ernest Van Den Haag as appeared in *National Review,* May 31, 1978. Copyright © by National Review, Inc., 150 East 35th Street, New York, NY 10016. Reprinted by permission.

p. 422: From Arlene B. Hirschfelder, "It is Time to Stop Playing Indians." *Los Angeles Times,* November 25, 1987. Reprinted by permission of the author.

p. 422: Barry W. Lynn, "Pornography's Many Forms: Not All Bad." *Los Angeles Times,* May 23, 1985.

p. 422: Jane Rule, "Pornography Is a Social Disease." *The Body Politic,* Jan/Feb 1984.

p. 423: Van Den Haag, pp. 88–89.

p. 424: John J. Palen, *City Scenes,* 2nd ed. Boston: Little, Brown, 1981, p. 14.

p. 424: Luis J. Rodriguez, "Rekindling the Warrior." *Utne Reader,* July/August 1984. Reprinted by permission of the author.

p. 433: Timothy Denesha, "From a Vegetarian: Looking at Hunting from Both Sides Now." Copyright © 1996 by Timothy Denesha. Reprinted by permission.

p. 436: Alan Weisman and Sandy Tolan, "Out of Time." Reprinted from *Audubon,* the magazine of the National Audubon Society, November/December, 1992, pp. 68–80.

*Chapter 13*

p. 448: From Alex Thio, *Sociology: A Brief Introduction,* 2nd ed. Copyright © 1994 HarperCollins College Publishers. Reprinted by permission.

p. 450: Susan Gilbert, "Noise Pollution," *Science Digest,* March 1985. Copyright © 1985 by the Hearst Corporation. Reprinted by permission of Science Digest.

p. 452: Gander and Gardiner, pp. 7–8.

p. 454: William Booth, "Never-Ending Quest for Absolute Zero." Copyright © 1990 The Washington Post. Reprinted by permission.

p. 457: Andrea Dorfman, "Racing the Brain," *Science Digest,* June 1985. Reprinted by permission of *Science Digest,* copyright 1985 by the Hearst Corporation.

p. 465: Thio, *Sociology: A Brief Introduction,* 2nd ed., p. 141.

p. 466: Laetsch, p. 507.

p. 468: From *Reader's Guide to Periodical Literature,* February 1994, Volume 93, Number 16. Reprinted by permission of H. W. Wilson Co.

p. 469: Laetsch, p. 152.

p. 469: Laetsch, p. 153.

p. 469: From David Attenborough, *Life on Earth.* Boston: Little, Brown, 1979, p. 188. Copyright © 1979 by David Attenborough Productions Ltd. Reprinted by permission of Little, Brown and Company and William Collins Sons & Company Ltd.

p. 470: Perry and Perry, p. 192.

p. 470: Laetsch, pp. 143–144.

p. 471: Attenborough, pp. 184–185.

p. 471: Perry and Perry, p. 408.

p. 472: Perry and Perry, p. 456.

p. 474: Norman B. Sigband and Arthur Bell. *Communication for Business and Management.* 5th ed. Glenview, IL: Scott, Foresman and Company, 1989: 417–421. Reprinted by permission.

p. 478: From Richard L. Weaver II, *Understanding Interpersonal Communication,* 7th ed., pp. 397–400. Copyright © 1996 by HarperCollins College Publishers. Reprinted by permission of Addison-Wesley Educational Publishers, Inc.

*Chapter 14*

p. 487: From Richard George, *The New Consumer Survival Kit.* Boston: Little, Brown, 1978, p. 69. Copyright © 1978 by the Maryland Center for Public Broadcasting. By permission of Little, Brown and Company.

p. 488: George, p. 97.

p. 488: George, p. 103.

p. 488: Morris K. Holland and Gerald Tarlow, *Using Psychology,* 2nd ed. Boston: Little Brown, 1980, pp. 8–9.

p. 489: George, p. 219.

p. 489: George, p. 214.

p. 489: George, p. 213.

p. 490: George, p. 138.

p. 492:   From Irwin Unger, *These United States: The Question of Our Past,* 2nd ed. Vol. II. Boston: Little, Brown, 1982, p. 871. Copyright © 1982 by Irwin Unger. Reprinted by permission of Little, Brown and Company.

p. 494:   Irwin Unger, *These United States: The Question of Our Past,* Vol. 2. Boston: Little, Brown, 1978, p. 897.

p. 495:   Barlow, p. 12.

p. 495:   Barlow, p. 16.

p. 495:   Unger, 1982, p. 421.

p. 495:   Unger, 1982, p. 848.

p. 497:   Kelly Costigan, "How Color Goes to Your Head," *Science Digest,* December 1984. Reprinted by permission of the author.

p. 502:   Samuel L. Becker, *Discovering Mass Communication,* Glenview, IL: Scott, Foresman, 1987, p. 306. Reprinted by permission.

p. 503:   Becker, p. 330.

p. 504:   Becker, p. 377.

p. 505:   Becker, p. 307.

p. 506:   Becker, p. 459.

p. 513:   Maggie Paley, "Flirtation—The Signals of Attraction—Deciphered." *Vogue,* February 1982. Copyright 1982 by The Conde Nast Publications, Inc. Reprinted by permission.

p. 520:   From Samuel L. Becker, *Discovering Mass Communication,* 2nd ed. Glenview, IL: Scott, Foresman, 1987. Reprinted by permission.

# Index